THE LOST WORLD OF DEMILLE

HOLLYWOOD LEGENDS SERIES
CARL ROLLYSON, GENERAL EDITOR

DeMille seated in his home office with the Crown of Thorns from his epic film *The King of Kings* (1927). Estate of John Kobal

The Lost World of DeMille

JOHN KOBAL

INTRODUCTION BY ROBERT DANCE

UNIVERSITY PRESS OF MISSISSIPPI • JACKSON

The University Press of Mississippi is the scholarly publishing agency of
the Mississippi Institutions of Higher Learning: Alcorn State University,
Delta State University, Jackson State University, Mississippi State University,
Mississippi University for Women, Mississippi Valley State University,
University of Mississippi, and University of Southern Mississippi.

www.upress.state.ms.us

Designed by Peter D. Halverson

The University Press of Mississippi is a member of the Association of University Presses.

First printing 2019

∞

Library of Congress Cataloging-in-Publication Data

Names: Kobal, John, author. | Dance, Robert, 1955– author.
Title: The lost world of DeMille / John Kobal, Introduction by Robert Dance.
Other titles: Hollywood legends series.
Description: Jackson : University Press of Mississippi, [2019] | Series: Hollywood legends series |
"First printing 2019."
Identifiers: LCCN 2019017231 (print) | LCCN 2019022110 (ebook) | ISBN 9781496825230
(cloth : alk. paper)
Subjects: LCSH: DeMille, Cecil B. (Cecil Blount), 1881–1959. | Motion picture producers and
directors—United States—Biography.
Classification: LCC PN1998.3.D39 K63 2019 (print) | LCC PN1998.3.D39 (ebook) | DDC
791.4302/33092 [B]—dc23
LC record available at https://lccn.loc.gov/2019017231
LC ebook record available at https://lccn.loc.gov/2019022110

British Library Cataloging-in-Publication Data available

CONTENTS

INTRODUCTION

THE LOST WORLD OF DEMILLE TRACES THE COMPLETE TRAJECTORY OF THE great director's life and career but it is not quite a formal biography. John Kobal was interested in all aspects of early Hollywood history, the producers, stars, and directors as well as all the other folks critical to films being made. Found in this book are the voices of secretaries, writers, art directors, his producing and directing friends and foes. John's book is like a long brilliant lecture with a strong central focus but never worrying much about veering off course a bit to make an interesting point or aside.

John finished this book shortly before his death in 1991. With a contract signed, he expected it to be published by Knopf, which had brought out his two most important books, *The Art of the Great Hollywood Photographers* (1980) and *People Will Talk* (1985). Twenty-five years later, with the text still in manuscript, John's sister Monika on behalf of his estate reclaimed the book. John had originally written a two volume work numbering 1100 pages. When the University Press of Mississippi expressed interest in publishing the manuscript, they requested that the text be substantially shortened and edited. Graham Coster in London took on the structural edit and put the DeMille book largely in the shape you see it here.

John was the first scholar to have unfettered access to DeMille's house at 2000 DeMille Drive, where his papers, collections, and memorabilia were left essentially in place as they were when the filmmaker died in 1959. John describes roaming from room to room, up in the attic, and down in the basement, everywhere finding treasures. And he incorporates into his story many of the telegrams, letters, memos, and files he found and which the DeMille estate allowed him to publish.

But John's book languished. Many other authors took on DeMille as a subject, and as the decades passed it seemed unlikely that this book would find an audience. Why bring out *The Lost World of DeMille* now? John Kobal was a unique film historian. His training was not in the classroom but watching movies and collecting photographs and magazines. Soon he was collecting people as well, and what he liked best were the great stars of old Hollywood. John never met DeMille but he met, interviewed, and wrote about many of the folks who played a part in the DeMille story. Gloria Swanson was one of John's subjects and anyone familiar with Hollywood history or who has watched *Sunset Blvd.* knows that DeMille and Swanson are two names indelibly linked in Hollywood history. John has a story to tell that depends on the personalities surrounding DeMille rather than simply recounting an historical narrative. He was an enthusiast who loved almost everything there was to love about Hollywood and the movies. As chronicler of the era, John's observations are keen and enrich our understanding of DeMille the man and filmmaker.

Readers will notice that this book does not contain endnotes or bibliography. Although there were notations for many endnotes they were never completed in John's manuscript. Similarly, no record of John's bibliography survives. In most cases, quotations have been identified as to author and often to a specific source. Occasionally John references books in his text, and it is evident that he depended on DeWitt Bodeen's *The Films of Cecil B. DeMille* (1969) as an anchor especially to the early obscure films. John wrote this book before the proliferation of DVDs brought many rarely seen old films back into circulation. He undoubtedly relied on films released in the VCR format, but most of his understanding of DeMille's work behind the camera came from watching the movies projected in 16mm or, when fortunate in a theater sitting, under the beam of light created by 35mm, when the format was still commonplace.

The journey from writing to publication has been a long one. Monika Kobal never lost faith that her brother's final book should be the capstone to a long list of important film studies reaching back to his early biographies *Greta Garbo* (with Raymond Durgnat, 1965) and *Marlene Dietrich* (1968) and continuing with *Rita Hayworth: The Time, the Place and the Woman* (1979) and, perhaps most significantly, *The Art of the Great Hollywood Portrait Photographers* (1980). Craig Gill, editor at the University Press of Mississippi, saw the potential in a still rough manuscript and watched over the project as *The Lost World of DeMille* took shape. Twenty-eight years later, we are privileged at last to offer John Kobal on Cecil B. DeMille.

ROBERT DANCE

THE LOST WORLD OF DEMILLE

CHAPTER ONE

CECIL B. DEMILLE HAD BEEN DEAD ALMOST TWENTY YEARS WHEN I FIRST
went to his house. Except for the daily visits of his old secretary and a cleaner, this house on the hill was empty: a fortress to memory. After the habits of
a long life, with time the atmosphere in the house had begun to settle. Still,
DeMille's spirit lingered as long as there was a housekeeper to dust the furniture and a secretary to remember to place a fresh red rose in the vase on his
desk every day as during his life.

His presence was still palpable to me. The sound of countless conversations
and studied debates had receded into the old wood and the thick leather. The
projection booth, built into the wall of the entrance hall and discreetly hidden behind velvet draperies, reminded guests that they were in the home of
a filmmaker. Before his grandchildren sold the house, people visiting Hollywood approached it with awe. It was charged with echoes of the man whose
films they felt they knew without having had to see them.

When DeMille came to write about his house in his autobiography, he did
so with the voice of a man long accustomed to people making way at his approach. The photograph he chose for the jacket of his autobiography showed
a man who might have been posing for a statue of invincibility. This imposing
elder statesman of movies, master of grand hokum, now invited those who
read on a conducted tour of his domain: "The house next door was later
occupied by Charlie Chaplin. Later still, I was able to buy it and connect the
two houses by a covered walk, using the Chaplin house for my offices and
library and its upper story as a guest house for the relatives and friends we
have often loved to have with us, but who overflowed our own fairly modest
dwelling space. When the narrow winding roads in Laughlin Park were given
names, some of them were called after people who lived on them . . . our
street was named DeMille Drive."

2010 DeMille Drive—or "the old Chaplin house," as it's still known—is
linked to the family residence by walls of ivy-bordered French doors. De-
Mille had bought it from Chaplin in 1926, after the success of his first film,
The Squaw Man, shortly after Chaplin had taken over the running of his
own, motion picture studio. DeMille commissioned architect Julia Morgan

DeMille's house in the Laughlin Park neighborhood of the Los Feliz section, Los Angeles, 1940. Photo: Acme. Courtesy John Kobal Foundation

to design the conservatory. One side of the long window-lined passage overlooks Los Angeles; the other looks in on the garden joining the two houses. A scene for *King of Kings*, in which the little girl gets Christ to mend her broken doll, was shot here.

The large cream-colored stucco house, fringed by tended vines and set among lovely gardens, sat imperiously on the highest point of Laughlin Park, a hilly enclave in the heart of old Hollywood. From the back it looked down on Motor Avenue and Griffith Park. From the front, the road winds to the iron gated entrance that leads out into Hollywood.

Once regarded as an outstanding horticultural arboretum, Laughlin Park had been the brainchild of two turn-of-the-century property speculators. The pepper trees soon gave way to progress, and seventy years of development later, the sprawling chaos of Hollywood jams against it. When Homer Laughlin and Wilber Cummings started building the DeMille house, the Mediterranean motif was all the rage. A 1915 prospectus described the subdivision as a "residential paradise on a noble eminence, a replica of Italy's finest landscape gardening lined to the city by a perfect auto-road." Previously the three-mile route to the city and to his office at the Lasky studio was a rocky road covered with sagebrush. Originally intended to contain forty "exclusive" villas, the development ended up with sixty: some with shake roofs, others with asphalt-and-rock roofs, or slate roofs; W. C. Fields's hot pink palazzo a stone's throw from DeMille's, is topped by tile.

In 1988, having been offered unsuccessfully to the Motion Picture Academy Historical Society and other institutions, the house was finally sold for $2,000,000. The rooms were refurbished and given names. Now there is a Cleopatra Room, with pictures of Claudette Colbert on the wall, and costumes from the film. Another old guest bedroom is the Delilah Room, with one of the costumes Hedy Lamarr wore in that film dressing a dummy.

Once inside the gates, the estate, with its poinsettias and tree-lined drive, seems remote from the teeming world. Gardeners tend the lawns. Servants clean and sweep the driveways and the pools. The arched porch leads into the house through a heavy oak door with a large pane of frosted glass. Heavy burgundy drapes shield the interior. The illusion of an earlier privileged age is further evoked by the swish of lazily rotating garden sprinklers on quiet manicure lawns.

The impression one is left with is of botanical villas by the sea, redesigned for the pretentious inhabitants of a Henry James novel. Pools (DeMille had one of the first) are sheltered by artful landscaping. Unlike the airy Italian villas that inspired them, DeMille's villas were a somber sight, with heavy paneling and Victorian drapes. But the gloomy aspect changes at night, when the city of the angels lights up and a carpet of stars spreads out below the windows looking across the city, as if the starry heavens had come to rest in the Los Angeles basin. This was the setting for the headquarters of the DeMille empire.

When he wasn't in the midst of producing, or was away at his ranch, or sailing his yacht, DeMille would be up at the house viewing the latest films from around the world, always on the lookout for new faces, talents, and ideas. DeMille and his guests would have a free and open exchange of opinions, as it had been for him when his father would read his scripts aloud to his family, and invite their comments.

When I saw the big living room where the family lived and entertained, it was shrouded in curtains, lace tablecloths, and white shawls over a Steinway grand piano. The room had the orderly and polished look of an age when families gave large parties attended by guests in formal attire. This room, now strangely listless, with its columned mantel, Kerman rug, and curtains drawn to prevent the sunlight from fading the upholstered furniture, had a sunken feeling about it. "Constance kept that home," recalled her niece, who spent much of her formative childhood years there. "It was incredible, this great big house. And filled with flowers. Cecil went off to work, and then the family went about its business. After dinner, they were gathered in the great living room with a fireplace; on the other wall was a copy of a Rubens, which was always claimed to be an original. I doubt it, is all I can say! On

the other wall was a painting as big as this entire window section here. . . .
Velasquez. A portrait of a proud young Infanta of Spain. Also a copy but a
very good picture."

Even before his wife joined him in California, after twelve years of marriage, their domestic life had settled into a routine. She rose early; he worked
late. Separate bedrooms ensured that they wouldn't disturb each other until
they met in the evening.

However, DeMille was more comfortable elsewhere: aboard the *Seaward*,
his 106-foot schooner, or at Paradise, his thousand-acre ranch in the Sierra
Madre Mountains. DeMille's rustic cabin on the ranch conjured up a set out
of an Edgar Rice Burroughs or Rider Haggard adventure story.

At Paradise, away from all business ties and pressures, he could hunt. Unlike friends like director John Huston or producer Darryl Zanuck, who killed
for sport, DeMille only shot what he could eat. At Paradise, he could also
forget his cares in the company of like-minded male companions and wom-
en, such as actress Julia Faye, who knew how to make him laugh. On special
occasions, the younger members of his family, his daughters and nieces and
their boyfriends, would also be invited up for weekend parties. But this was
DeMille's preserve. Here he raised chickens, turkeys, and his famous peacocks.
Being a practical fellow even in his retreat, he sold the eggs, gave turkeys as
Thanksgiving and Christmas presents to his staff and friends, and hoarded the
feathers from his peacocks for the day he would need them for props or costumes. He was a hoarder, and he had the space to indulge this passion.

Paradise, of course, had other claims in the rumor market. Guests returned with tales of extravagant parties. Though no one who went there ever
confirmed it, stories circulated of orgies. These were largely apocryphal, but
people like to believe them. Costumer Gilbert Adrian, who worked for DeMille for five years in the twenties and was sometimes sent to New York to buy
gifts for the guests at Paradise, provided a firsthand account of a Christmas
party: "On Christmas Eve, a dinner, twelve or fifteen persons sat down to an
Arabian Nights table. The men wore vermilion Russian blouses and evening
trousers especially made for the night and given to them upon their arrival
at the ranch. The women wore very formal evening gowns. The table was
set with exquisite china and crystal, pheasants in full feather, caviar in three
foot wells of ice with electric lights hidden inside, foods flown from distant
parts of the world, and a finale of great birds of ice glowing with lights in a
suddenly darkened room. After dinner a table was wheeled in upon which
lay the Christmas gifts, not wrapped, but draped or placed upon the wagon.
Fur scarves, perfumed jewels, gold embroidered shoes from India, cufflinks,
and watches. A pair of great black satin dice a foot high was brought in. Each
lady was to roll the dice. The highest number could choose a present from
the table, after which the men could throw the dice and choose . . . Mitchell
Leisen, C. B.'s art director, spent weeks preparing surprises to delight him
[and his guests]. I had never seen such opulence except in the movies."

A view of the long, window-lined corridor connecting DeMille's two houses: his principal residence, purchased in 1920, and the former Charlie Chaplin house, which he later added to his property (circa 1940). Courtesy John Kobal Foundation

Most guests, whether actors, employees, or friends, when invited to De-Mille's house were entertained in the office wing. Screenings and social functions connected with the work of the studio were held there. DeMille's massive workplace, a Gothic revival oak kneehole desk, was set in the window-lined recess of this arched and raftered room. Presiding over the room DeMille held meetings with his staff and discussed scripts with his writers.

His baronial office at the Lasky studio was even more ornate, before shifts in tastes demanded a more modern interior. The original Lasky studio office in the twenties included shrewdly hidden spotlights which left DeMille in shadow while his guests sat in full glare.

Lining the walls, resting on the floors, or half-hidden in corners behind couches and chairs of his office and the other rooms around his house were statues and other reminders of his films. There were flags and banners, fifteenth-century war hammers, huge battle swords, exquisite rapiers, shackles and spears, Spanish lantakas, Indonesian cannons, Persian battleaxes, as well as swords and guns, ancient and modern, from around the world. This created the effect of an ancient armory and bears witness to DeMille's love of the curious and the beautiful.

As De Maupassant wrote, "the surest way to ever know the very kernel of a man's work is to study not what he writes or says but the surroundings he has built for his habitat as an artist." And so to DeMille's office we turn to find his scripts and the mountain of artwork for his films, that previously were stored at his ranch.

On DeMille's desk sat the camera he used when he made *The Squaw Man*. To the right stood a lectern, on which rested the DeMille family Bible. Gustav Dore's dramatic black and white drawings of scenes from the Old Testament in this Bible were to exert a powerful and long-lasting influence on his imagination. When DeMille came to recreate similar moments for his films, such as the crucifixion scene in *King of Kings*, he worked from Dore's drawings. Just as many of the early filmmakers would one day influence the work of those who came after them, so had these pioneers been first influenced by their contact with the popular literature and art of their youth. Indeed, DeMille's Egypt owed a great deal to David Robert's famous nineteenth-century drawings and prints.

After his death, DeMille's collection was guarded by Florence Cole, a woman straight out of central casting for "the woman bound to service," who for most of her life looked middle-aged. She was soft-spoken, straight-backed, loyal, and single. She had never had any other cause but DeMille. Cole began working for DeMille as a twenty-nine-year-old part-time secretary in 1929. Working from his office at the studio, she stayed with DeMille until his death in 1959. Afterward his daughter brought Cole from the studio to the house to run the estate, working from behind the desk of Gladys Rosson, who had worked as a secretary for DeMille until her death in 1953. Cole enjoyed telling how she had originally been sent to DeMille by a "Girl Friday" service to work "for a week," but had never been asked to leave. Florence Cole was eighty-one and still working for the DeMille estate when she died.

In her way, Cole was typical of the many women in DeMille's life: the women who raised him, spoiled him, flirted with him, and worked for him. Cole is an example of the many women who remained affectionate and loyal though he was often thoughtless, arrogant, and bombastic.

On my first visit to the DeMille mansion to research this book, Florence Cole led me to a room on the second floor lined with filing cabinets on two sides and rows and rows of photographic albums on a third. As producer, director, and a major Paramount shareholder, DeMille had received a bound set of photographic stills documenting the course of production of every movie. Additionally, there were hundreds of fine photographic prints in various sizes, some engraved, some hand-tinted, many signed, all carefully maintained in map-sized leather cases, stacked four deep against the walls.

Other rooms and closets turned up similar treasures. One of the guest bedrooms housed suits and dresses and old clothes stored in garment bags. Suddenly a glint from the back caught my eye. Inside a long black plastic clothing bag was the famous peacock robe Edith Head had designed for Hedy Lamarr in *Samson and Delilah*. It seemed as though thousands of peacock feathers were stitched onto many yards of precious aquamarine cloth.

Memories of the DeMille spectacle flooded back, of Lamarr's beauty, of Delilah's wickedness, of the bacchanalia Victor Young composed to intermingle with the cries of the blood-seeking crowd as Delilah left her seat beside the Saran. Wearing the spectacular peacock robe, Lamarr walked down into the arena where the blind Samson was being tormented by jawbone-wielding dwarfs, pretending to mock him, but really wanting to help, to make amends, to die for him. The peacock robe! The thousands of feathers DeMille personally collected from the peacocks he raised at his ranch and saved for the day when he could dazzle his public with some "real" Philistine splendor. Here the robe hung forgotten, on an ordinary cloth-covered hanger, behind a lot of everyday suits.

Down below, Florence Cole went about her day. The footsteps overhead told her all she needed to know: where I was and what I likely would find. At 5 o'clock, she stood at the base of the stairs, keys in hand ready to lock up. "Well, you've certainly been here a long time," she said.

"There has to be an exhibition," I told her, "and I must do it." Once I had Miss Cole's approval, I knew DeMille's daughter Cecilia would agree to it as well.

After DeMille's death, Cecilia weeded out pictures, books, and papers, apparently looking for items from his rumored collection of pornography, which she feared would end up in the wrong hands. In truth he did own nude art studies taken by 1920s photographers such as Edward Bower Hesser, Karl Struss, and William Mortenson, but they were tame and elegant, and studies such as these were reproduced at the time in serious photographic journals. Nevertheless, many were stored hidden among Constance deMille's table linens. Agnes claims to have seen DeMille's "erotic" photos hidden between the pages of books in his library, but from her description of these nudes, they are likely identical to those I found. But one has to remember that at that time photos of naked women (especially when tucked away between the pages of books) would have been considered shocking.

Bookshelves lined the recesses; large, richly leather-bound art books were piled on top of carved tables. DeMille, his niece says, "bought up whole libraries," and many were books containing prints. There were old treasure chests, including one made in Spain and with a heavy padlock dating from 1510. A seventeenth-century Nuremberg iron strongbox standing in an alcove in the conservatory between a pair of Renaissance-style wrought-iron six-light torchiere had first seen the arc-lights in a flashback for his 1919 production *Don't Change your Husband*. Hollywood's moguls like MGM's Louis B. Mayer furnished their homes with antiques originally bought for their studio's prop departments, picked up for a song in Europe between the two wars.

DeMille was passionate about books and, as soon as he could afford to, began to collect them, often giving them as gifts. What his collection lacked in Tolstoy and Dreiser it made up for in size, with over 6,000 volumes divided among three houses and his yacht. According to Ella Adams, his mother-in-law, who moved to Hollywood and became the head of his research library, DeMille's collection, "contains one of the world's most comprehensive private collections of books on biblical history. Some of his Bibles are of fabulous size and worth. For example, the two-foot square volume printed for Thomas Macklin by Thomas Beasley in 1800, the Dutch edition of 1729, and the profusely illustrated one printed in 1690 by Samuel Roycroft for Richard Blome in London. On the ground floor there are bound volumes of letters received from important personages about the DeMille pictures, many volumes such as Adolph Rosenberg's *The Design and Development of Costume* and Racinet's *Le Costume Historique*, as well as illustrated works on art, architecture, jewelry and iron work . . . For his bookplate he has a design showing a phoenix rising from the chaotic mists of matter." The most striking of all the Bibles in the house was a reproduction by someone at the studio, of the famed Gutenberg Bible. Made for *Joan the Woman* (1916), DeMille's film about the heroic French saint Joan of Arc, nothing less would do but this book, even though the Gutenberg Bible wasn't printed until twenty years after the saint's death.

DeMille's shelves bulged with Bibles of every description, as well as with Korans and Torahs, many bound in fine leathers, embossed with gold, and usually sumptuously illustrated. Long before the end of his life, DeMille ceased to be interested in organized religion, but as this collection suggests, he never abandoned belief in God, perhaps the only being he considered more powerful than himself.

Of course, the books and stills dispersed throughout the house were only the beginning. Several filing cabinets were given over to scripts for every one of the seventy films he produced or directed. He also saved suggestions for films, unsolicited scripts, threats of lawsuits, and aborted film projects. It was his custom to establish claims to a property simply to prevent another studio from getting it. This trove of proposals showed the range of ideas he toyed with: films about Benedict Arnold, Omar Khayyam, biblical themes like David and Goliath or the story of Esther, and even one titled *Queen of Queens*, based upon the life of the Virgin Mary. Additionally, there was a project about Mexico's history, Russian projects including a story by the actor Ivan Lebedeff, a film about the Hudson Bay, and an adaptation of Anatole France's *Thais* to star Hedy Lamarr and Burt Lancaster. Alongside sat records of all salaries paid, down to the least bit player in every film. Here is where I discovered that the sacrificial nude in *The Sign of the Cross*, whose picture in a book in London first got me interested in the DeMille collection, was marked down for one day's work at $25.

I stumbled on to the attic by accident. While squashed between the cleaner's pots and brushes and the filing cabinets, I closed one door to make room and found behind it, a very narrow door. Up its dusty steps led me into a huge exposed space, illuminated by a large skylight. It was crammed everywhere with crates and boxes filled with books and records, wax disks and old photos, chandeliers and candelabra, yards of fabrics, and padlocked theatrical touring trucks.

It became apparent that much of what might be termed "private and confidential" had not been stored with his lawyer Neil McCarthy. What excitement when I came across a box which I could only conclude had been overlooked. This included papers containing DeMille's opinions about his partners, his fellow members at the Screen Directors Guild, and other sensitive topics. There was an undistinguished and otherwise unmarked black container tied with string were papers dealing with events that occurred during DeMille's three years at MGM. A quick look showed me further private information. There were secret memos from private detective agencies, hired by DeMille to spy on the unions. Here was evidence that gangsters had been infiltrating the unions, and through them the studios. Phrases leapt out at me from the pages: "should be handled very confidentially for if it leaks out it would be disastrous" and "great care will have to be used in this work as they [members of the Central Labor Council] have openly given notice that any informer caught will be taken for a ride. Three men who talked too much were killed in Chicago."

Here was an important personal collection, a goldmine for a researcher on DeMille. And after the attic and the wardrobes, the cellar contained more treasures. Florence Cole pointed to the door leading to the cellar and asked only that things be put back the way I found them. And she warned me about the dirt.

Poking out from every shelf, from every corner, was the work of four decades by an army of studio draftsmen. At the center of the room stood a massive round oak table almost buried under stacks of early 5 x 7-inch photographic production stills. Here was the great American diva Geraldine Farrar in her armor as Joan of Arc, sitting on a deck chair in the open fields, having lunch with handsome co-star Wallace Reid. Reid was shown wearing little dark glasses to soothe his eyes after the strain of working beneath the early klieg lights. Seated at their feet in the grass in a formal black bank-er's suit was Sam Goldwyn. In another photo, writer Jeanie Macpherson is caught sharing a joke with the man she adored. Actress Julia Faye, dressed to go for a ride in a plane, strikes a pose in leather jacket and smart goggles. Un-retouched snapshots lay about in the thousands. Some depicted stars, others people who would become famous, and many who never did, but they all looked like a family, basking in the California sunshine and blessed by natural exuberance. And DeMille appeared in many.

The stills from the files were guarded in crackling brown wrapping pa-per. One great find was precious blue prints, beautifully made and mount-ed by photographer Edward S. Curtis (who had originally caught DeMille's eye with his series depicting American Indians and their vanishing way of life). Curtis shot stills for DeMille's productions of *Adam's Rib* and *The Ten Commandments*.

There were photographs by the pioneering New York photographer Karl Struss, who came from the east to work in the movies and who began his dis-tinguished Hollywood career as a later Oscar-winning cameraman by taking photographs on DeMille's *Male and Female*. There were sets of hand "printed 'art'" studies by the flamboyant California pictorialist William Mortenson. Famous for his nudes and elaborately staged, re-touched, hand-colored al-legorical subjects in the style of the old masters, Mortenson worked on *King of Kings*.

There were many portraits of DeMille covering his entire career. His rep-utation for photographing the world's leaders made the celebrated Cana-dian photographer Youssef Karsh the natural choice for taking the official portraits of Charlton Heston as Moses and Yul Brynner as Ramses II in *The Ten Commandments*. Karsh's portrait of DeMille was used on the cover of the filmmaker's autobiography.

The thousands of photographs took up only a fraction of the enormous room, the largest space having been given over to the artwork. DeMille em-ployed leading illustrators to realize his dramatic ideas. Delilah as depicted by Henry Clive was a busty full-length redheaded nude, while Dan Groes-beck's drawings of a half-naked Delilah cutting virile Samson's hair helped to convince Paramount's executives of the box-office appeal of the old Bible story. For DeMille, Groesbeck's work brought Charles Kingsley's "muscular Christianity" to life and DeMille was inspired by Groesbeck's drawings when casting his film.

He also admired and kept works by Fortunino Matania, the Neapolitan painter who had worked as an illustrator in England. His work included the glass paintings for the Albert Hall sequence in Hitchcock's 1935 version of *The Man Who Knew Too Much* before he joined DeMille on *The Ten Commandments*. Another DeMille favorite in his later years was Arnold Friberg, a noted Mor-mon painter of historical and religious subjects. DeMille used Friberg's paint-ings for the promotional tour for his films, as he had done with Groesbeck and other such works in the past. And finally, Norman Rockwell painted Hedy Lamarr and Victor Mature, the stars of *Samson and Delilah*.

For *Cleopatra*, seventy-six sketches, set designs by Boris Leven and Roland Anderson; vivid storyboards with twenty different sketches on a board; costume sketches by Shannon Rogers; the Bucklands, the Groesbecks, the Fribergs. He took home and stored away drawings by costume designers such as Natasha Rambova, Travis Banton, Ralph Jester, and Edith Head, all detailed and full of expression. Four decades of work. More than eight thousand pages of 4 x 5-inch continuity sketches. Large scale oil and tempera paintings. I was kept busy for days going through this trove.

Holding one of Anton Grot's masterful pen-and-ink drawings in my hands made it possible to understand DeMille's excitement when he made a film. Who can forget the impact of his surrealistic sets on the Warner Brothers musicals of the '30s? Others who worked for DeMille included the architect turned designer Mitchell Leisen, who eventually went on to direct super-smart, visually lustrous comedies; and the equally brilliant Adrian Adolph Greenberg, who became known for his costumes the world over simply as Adrian, a young man who had come to DeMille having briefly worked for Rambova and Rudolph Valentino.

I found work by the influential French designer Paul Iribe, who had first met DeMille in 1919 and worked for him, as designer as well as assistant director, on films like *Manslaughter*, *The Ten Commandments*, and *King of Kings*. From Broadway came Norman Bel Geddes, who did sets for *Feet of Clay* (1924). William Cameron Menzies, known for his work on *Gone with the Wind*, designed the "candy ball" sequence for *Golden Bed* (1925).

DeMille's basement was a time capsule, recording not only the planning that went into his films but the contributions of all the men and women who work behind the scenes. The wall along the steps down was hung with weapons. A massive broadsword in its leather scabbard had belonged to a soldier in *The Crusades*. King Richard's crown and his elaborately tooled two-hander, crafted in the old ways by the armorer employed by New York's Metropolitan Museum, rested on a velvet cushion upstairs. The armaments of an entire infantry were stored in the basement: dented medieval crossbows, rusted American flintlocks, Eskimo harpoons, discolored knives and enough bows and arrows to have ensured the survival of more than the last of the Mohicans. There was a sheathed bowie knife, which could have been the one Gary Cooper used to slice his venison when he wasn't cutting Jean Arthur's thongs in *The Plainsman*. I hit my head on a bola, three balls attached to long cords joined at the upper end, normally used by Patagonian natives for catching the rhea (or South American ostrich) and small cattle. In a dark recess under the stairs a cask had split wide open, spilling axes, swords, lace-heads, spearheads, arrows, and bows in profusion.

There was a wooden trough filled with maps, rolled-up posters, floppy citations. A glass case held magazines: twenty copies of *Life* magazine's issue on the *Ten Commandments*, fifty copies of a special number of *Knowledge* devoted to DeMille. Two sturdy metal bookshelves faced each other; four rows on either side were taken up with scrapbooks, each over a foot tall and fatter than the Los Angeles telephone directory. Reviews and press cuttings about his Oscar-winning circus epic, *The Greatest Show on Earth* (1952), filled ten volumes. For the same film, a broadly grinning Betty Hutton swinging fearlessly from her trapeze graced magazine covers from India, Egypt, Israel, France, and Poland—proof that Paramount's press department had done its work well.

The glass-fronted cabinets turned out to be packed with rare trade annuals interspersed with a recipe for chicken gumbo from Mary Pickford, and those now-collectable ten-cent illustrated novelizations of films. Scattered throughout were histories of Los Angeles and California, and early histories of the movies from England, France and Germany. Autographed books filled the shelves written by many of DeMille's friends, peers, and actors, along with his brother William's modest reminiscences about starting up, *Hollywood Saga*.

I found DeMille's films stored in a specially constructed fireproof vault. Not just the features, but rare footage taken on the sets, with stars and family, gala premieres, and home movies taken from his earliest days in Hollywood.

Shelves and cabinets held treasures. Room after room revealed surprises. DeMille's house saw the fulfillment of a fantasy that originated in his childhood, spawned by popular Victorian novelists like Charles Kingsley and Sir Walter Scott. For me, amazement gave way to weariness. I began to wish for less, but I couldn't leave until I had seen it all. It seemed endless, fascinating, and mammoth—much like the man himself.

C⁻

CHAPTER TWO

WITHOUT JESSE LASKY, HIS CLOSEST FRIEND AND PRODUCING PARTNER, DeMille might never have become involved in films. And, according to Lasky, without DeMille's enthusiasm, he probably would have eventually lost interest. After all, in the teens movies were not respectable. They might have been increasing in popularity, but theater's own hard-won respectability was only too recently acquired for its leaders to tarnish their gains by associating with this vulgar upstart. In the fall of 1913, despite the limited success of several five-reel epics from Europe, American theater managers, playwrights, and actors largely avoided the movie industry.

Soon events conspired to change these attitudes. In 1913, no theatrical name stood higher than that of the French tragedienne Sarah Bernhardt. The famed actress decided to recreate on film one of her greatest stage roles, the title character in *Queen Elizabeth*. Few in the trade believed that a big enough audience would sit through a movie that was longer than two reels to make it economically viable. Bernhardt's four-reeler proved successful and demonstrated that respectable people were willing to pay theater prices for the right sort of cinema attraction. This new source of income was given social respectability by the divine Sarah's willingness to step from the sanctity of the proscenium arch on to the screen.

Lasky's first step was to introduce two of his strong-willed friends. Neither DeMille nor Samuel Goldwyn had hitherto shown much interest in one another. Lasky, with his gentle smile and little round glasses perched on the bridge of his nose gave the appearance of a friendly friar. His conciliatory nature would bind together these two rough characters.

Although similar in ambition, the backgrounds and attitudes of DeMille and Goldwyn were radically different. Goldwyn, unlike his future partners, had been raised and fed on the sort of poverty they only knew from books. Grinding with ambition, he rose from poverty as one who learned to find nourishment in rejection. Despite this hardship, or perhaps because of it, Goldwyn never bothered to master the English language. Friends and colleagues came to accept his characteristically cantankerous behavior and seeming ignorance as merely amusing corollaries to his linguistic

At Adolph Zukor's eightieth birthday party in 1953, DeMille greets his former partners: Zukor, the longtime Paramount chief (second from right), Samuel Goldwyn (at left), and Jesse Lasky (right). The man in the center has not been identified. Courtesy John Kobal Foundation

shortcomings. Not as blatantly vulgar as Harry Cohn, or as stupid as Jack Warner, Goldwyn got away with this behavior because he spoke English so badly it made people laugh, though never to his face.[1] DeMille might have been Lasky's choice as business partner, but Goldwyn wasn't going to entrust him immediately with directing their first film together. None of the three knew how to make a picture. While Lasky was persuading DeMille to joining the partnership, Goldwyn approached D. W. Griffith, whose films had played a role in establishing the medium as an art to be taken seriously. Griffith listened to Goldwyn and suggested a minimum $250,000 investment would be required to launch the company. This was a polite but firm rejection. A year later, when the young Lasky Company was in a solid financial position, Goldwyn lured some of Griffith's stars away from the proud man.

1. Sam Goldwyn changed his name from Samuel Goldfish when he teamed up with brothers Edwin and Archibald Selwyn in 1916. I met Sam Goldwyn on the lawn of his palatial Holly-wood home. He was playing croquet the way he spoke English, with some of the surviving members of the British establishment in Hollywood, among them David Niven, George Sanders, and Louis Jourdan. The Frenchman had been accepted as an honorary Brit because he was good at the game and put up with Sam's cheating. This was not regarded as a sign of old age according to Sanders, he'd been cheating all his life. Like the others, George put up with it because Goldwyn's was the only decent croquet lawn in town.

With Griffith no longer a possibility in the partnership, the team of Lasky, Goldwyn, and DeMille was set. The three agreed that regardless of the low quality of most films, and how confident DeMille was in his own gifts as a director, he could not be allowed to direct the company's all-important first film on his own.

DeMille prepared for his new role as nascent director by seeing as many films as possible. He became a familiar figure on the old Edison Studio lot, so much so that they thought he was after a job. One day he found a wooden box on which he stood to peer through a window at a film being made. For three hours he stood on that box—there wasn't much to watch because studio work at that time was almost laughably simple. Then he went back to his partners and said: "Well, I know all about it now . . . If those men can make pictures, we will be knighted."

His confidence boosted that of Lasky and Goldwyn. What they now needed was money. With a studio a producer could make a two-reeler at a cost of a little under $1,000. But the newly formed team were starting from scratch. Additionally, they wanted to launch the new enterprise with a film that would make a big splash. In 1913, a five-reeler would cost close to $5,000, and as much would be needed for advertising and promotion. They figured at least $30,000 would be required. Among them they could only raise two-thirds of this amount—all coming from Lasky and Goldwyn, as DeMille did not have the funds to contribute. He hoped to make up his share by borrowing from his brother, but, as DeMille loved to recall, "Bill said he thought he had better keep his money to pay my fare home from the west when, as he confidently expected, the company folded up." In the end, Lasky and Goldwyn each put up $7,500.

As the nominal head of the deMille family, brother William had other objections to fronting money for the film business. The proud deMille name was, he wrote in his memoirs, "honorably known in the theatre for two generations, and now he was going to drag it in the dust of a vulgar, unworthy scheme of coaxing nickels away from poor little children. I suggested that if he really desired to become a cheap mountebank there was open to him the time-honored field of the travelling Punch and Judy show," William concluded, "and I'll try to save enough to pay your fare back." "Years later," he wrote, "I used the money I'd kept for him to pay my own fare back."

What they needed was a property to film. What was cheaper to film than a Western? It's all outdoors—some sagebrush, some desert, some outpost, some extras on horseback. One day when Lasky and DeMille were lunching at the Lamb's Club in New York, fate struck. As they were leaving, they ran into actor Dustin Farnum, whom DeMille knew slightly. He had been the star a decade earlier of one of Broadway's biggest hit, *The Virginian*: "How would you like to star in a major motion picture for us?" DeMille asked Dustin. He had the audacity that comes with having nothing to lose. Farnum was intrigued. DeMille's knew such a project would be expensive, but getting the right project and star was necessary if the fledging company was to be successful.

It so happened that playwright Edwin Milton Royle was at another table. Royle was the author of the *The Squaw Man*, which in its original dramatic form had been touring since 1905. It had also been turned into a novel that DeMille had read. Farnum had starred in a traveling production. If DeMille and Lasky could convince Royle to sell them the rights to his play, Farnum would be their star.

Lasky went straight to work. He approached the author who named a price—$15,000, which was everything they had. Lasky rushed off to phone Goldwyn: "We're in business!" On the strength of Farnum's name, they were able to borrow another $11,500.

On November 23, 1913, the Jesse L. Lasky Feature Play Co. was incorporated with a capital stock of $50,000. DeMille would be the Director General, which meant he would organize the production end of the business; Goldwyn would serve as treasurer; and Lasky, whose name was a standard for quality in the theater, became president.

In addition to being required to purchase fifty shares of stock, a $5,000 investment, DeMille was also obligated, as "General Producing Director and play/scenario writer/manager" to "procure to said corporation the right to use for motion pictures the plays and scenarios on which the same are founded which are controlled by the so-called deMille Play Agency, by which term is meant the play brokerage business conducted by Mrs. H. C. deMille and her associates . . . and also the plays and scenarios owned and controlled by the legal representatives of the late Henry C. deMille." This meant not only plays written by DeMille, but also those by his father Henry, his brother William, and those written by his mother's other clients. The penniless neophyte was also required to work "without salary or other compensation of any nature whatsoever until such time as the Board of Directors of the said corporation shall, . . . give to (C. B.) a regular salary . . . which . . . shall be reasonable in amount." Initially, this "reasonable' amount was to be $100 a week.

After Royle's fee, they were left with the $11,500 they borrowed from the bank to make the film, but they had not considered Farnum's compensation. He wanted $5,000 cash. "When I first adopted the movies—or they me," Farnum reflected later, "I was vigorously denounced by my contemporaries. I still have a number of letters written me by prominent actors and actresses calling my 'abandonment' of the legitimate 'disgraceful' and a 'prostitution of the art' as well as other disagreeable things. Now, the same people are writing me, asking me how to get into the business."

In an attempt to convince him to defer his salary, Goldwyn offered Farnum a 25 percent stake in the company. In less than a decade that stake would be worth several million dollars. But Farnum was an actor, not a gambler, and when it became obvious that the film would not be made in New York, but in distant Flagstaff, Arizona, thousands of miles away, "where a man could get bitten by a rattler," he decided to take his money upfront. "Opportunity knocked on my door," he later recalled, "and I wasn't in." Farnum's salary left them with a mere $6,500, and Lasky offered the $5,000 worth of shares to his wife's uncle Abe Lehr, 'the glove king.'

Now they looked around for an experienced film director, someone to work with DeMille and teach him the craft of filmmaking. Their first choice was a man who had directed Farnum in his only previous film appearance, thirty-six-year-old William "Silent Bill" Haddock.

"Silent Bill" had been directing movies at many of the early film companies, and, in 1907, had directed the first American talking picture that utilized synchronized records. Four years later, he directed one of the earliest features, *The Clansman*, which he shot in color. D. W. Griffith saw it and was inspired to make what became his celebrated version of the same property, *The Birth of a Nation*.

"They offered me $300 a week and stock in the company," recalled Haddock. "I took some bad advice and turned it down. I was told that they only had $25,000, that they would make one picture, close it up, and I would be held responsible for their failure. Everybody said, 'You've got a good reputation Bill, don't lose it.'" Instead of becoming a millionaire, Haddock went on to direct W. C. Fields.

Next they turned to Oscar Apfel, only a year or two older than DeMille, but already a veteran movie director, grinding out one- and two-reelers like sausages. He loved what he did and didn't object to teaching DeMille about directing as long as he was paid his salary. With him came cinematographer Alfred Gandolfi, who claimed to have invented the lens shade and to be the first to shoot double-exposures in motion pictures.

Armed with the Pathé camera they had bought on the sidewalks of New York for $350, DeMille and his newly acquired team left New York for Arizona on or about December 13 on the Southern Pacific train via New Orleans. In 1913, California had not yet become the center of motion picture production. DeMille's decision to film in Arizona was in part because of the climate, but was also motivated by a desire to avoid the Film Trust, which controlled distribution in New York and most of the Eastern seaboard. Although *The Squaw Man* was set in Wyoming, it was considered neither warm nor sunny enough for winter filming. It was Lasky who first suggested Arizona, having remembered seeing Indians hanging around the train depot at Flagstaff when he had toured there with *Hermann the Great*. With no better idea, they decided on Arizona. Lasky stayed in New York, presumably minding the business.

While aboard the train, cast and crew sat around playing poker and enjoying their beer as well as the passing desert scenery when the wind wasn't creating dust storms. DeMille and Apfel spent those traveling days writing a screen adaptation of Royle's play. Apfel, who knew about screen composition and the camera angles, showed DeMille how they would take advantage of the spectacular landscape. Instead of lengthy captions to describe the hero's divided state of mind Apfel developed photographic effects such as split screen and edited inserts. By the time their train chugged across the last miles of Arizona desert, they had produced some twenty pages of penciled script.

But when they reached the little outpost in Flagstaff, there was no sign of the promised Indians, and, instead of necessary sunshine, according to DeMille, they found "a snow storm was raging . . . Before us stretched a wretched wilderness, some sorry wagons and the pump, that inevitable complement of all American countryside. I have never seen so horribly ugly a place! We continued on to Los Angeles as a last resort."

In later years, DeMille revised the muddied legend, which had attained mystical status and had for so long served Lasky and others when they wrote about DeMille's revelation on the road to Hollywood. Only Flagstaff now remained, as DeMille recalled to his bemused ghost writer, "It was a beautiful day. Somehow the story has got about that it was raining. It was not. I suspect that, years later, some press agent may have felt that it made a better story to picture the four of us standing on the station platform drenched and discouraged. We should have been a sorry lot if a little rain had discouraged us. What actually happened was that we made a far more disastrous discovery . . . with one accord, we saw and knew that for our purposes Arizona, beautiful, healthy, sunny Arizona, was all wrong."

Rain or shine notwithstanding, DeMille made the sort of spontaneous decision that was typical of this period in his life. It was one made quickly, if not lightly, since the onward journey would eat up more of their tightly budgeted investment, but ambition, not creation, was north of DeMille's compass, from which he might occasionally depart but always return. They would stay on the train and continue right on to the end of the line.

CHAPTER THREE

ON A SUNNY FRIDAY, DECEMBER 18, 1913, 800 MILES AND ANOTHER DAY
and half later, after zipping thorough desert sands at forty miles per hour, De-
Mille's little party reached the end of the line, Los Angeles. After which there
was no way to go on except to learn Japanese and proceed by ship.

Beneath a blue and sunny sky, the city was the home of approximately 300,000 residents, ranchers, citrus fruit growers, and small businessmen,
with Mexican, Indian, and Asian laborers making up the rest. Orange groves
were everywhere and, on warm nights, the air was heavy with their scent.
Snow-capped mountains were seemingly close enough to touch.

The population of Los Angeles had more than tripled since DeMille's first
visit twelve years earlier, but other than that the city did not seem to have
changed much. Hollywood, eight miles northwest of the business district of
Los Angeles (and as late as 1909 having a population of only 4,000 people),
only became a part of greater Los Angeles in 1910 when, in return for water
supplied by the city, practically for free, the sleepy orange grove incorporated
as an independent municipality. The white-washed adobe houses had given
way almost entirely to stone and brick business blocks and wooden houses,
but even so, the streets, shaded by luxuriant palm and pepper trees seemed
exotic to the new arrivals from Manhattan.

Not all the early pioneers were so enamored of the place. Cameraman
Billy Bitzer, one of the early arrivals, mused, "in Hollywood there was this
vast space to cover to get even a glass of beer. I had to keep my workshop
bungalow well stocked with the stuff or go without. . . . To me, at this stage,
California left much to be desired—the land where the flowers had no perfume and the women no virtue." But, to Lillian Gish, "the city smelled like
a vast orange grove, and the abundance of roses offered a cheery welcome."

With a successful showman's instinct for making the right first impression, DeMille booked into the luxurious Alexandria Hotel on the corner of
Fourth and Spring streets in downtown Los Angeles, the hotel of choice for
sophisticated travelers. Popular with cattle barons, it would soon become
the hub of motion picture dealmaking, and the rug in the lobby would be
dubbed the "million-dollar carpet" in honor of the many film deals that were

consummated within its view. DeMille knew no one in Los Angeles, but fortunately, contrary to popular legend which credited him with having been Hollywood's first filmmaker, other film folk had gotten there before him. Word of the "rich" newcomers quickly got around. Among their first visitors were "two enterprising gentlemen named L. L. Burns and Harry Revier. They owned, they told me, a little laboratory about ten miles out. They would like to develop our film. . . . In and around the building that housed their laboratory there was space that could be rented for a studio. There was a stage equipped with diffusers, and room to build another one if we wanted it. . . . If I have sometimes been mistakenly called the father of the Hollywood film industry, Burns and Revier deserve to be called its obstetricians."

Revier owned a number of movie theaters throughout the southwest, and had worked for both American Gaumont and Universal before joining forces with Burns, the founder of Western Costume Company and co-owner of a rental studio and film laboratory in the heart of Hollywood. According to DeMille, "There is a photograph which hangs on my wall . . . of a little barn in an orange grove on a street called Vine in a place called Hollywood. There, in a little painted canvas set on a homemade stage, Dustin Farnum is playing a scene in *The Squaw Man* while our one painter, our one carpenter, and a handful of other people look on. Incidentally, the actors dressed in the horse stalls! Half was studio and half was barn, because the owner of the property kept half . . . and when he washed his buggy, the water ran under the partition to the drain that was under my desk, and I had to put my feet in the waste paper basket to keep them dry!"

To DeMille's happy surprise, as he told newspaper columnist and later DeMille employee Art Arthur, he discovered that a previous occupant had already pulled down some of the horse stalls and constructed a kind of little platform, which extended for some yards outside and was protected from the sun by a large awning.

Meanwhile, back in New York, Goldwyn was proceeding with selling distribution rights to the film he and Lasky thought was being shot in Arizona. Imagine their surprise when they received this cable from DeMille: "Flagstaff no good for our purpose. Have proceeded to California. Want authority to rent barn in place called Hollywood for $75 a month. Regards to Sam. Cecil."

This was Goldwyn's and Lasky's first encounter with the hidden costs of filmmaking, not to mention their partner's unilateral switch from their mutually agreed plans. Lasky recalled that "Sam hit the ceiling. I insisted that Cecil must know what he was doing, although I really didn't feel too sure of it . . . We argued for hours."

Soon they would discover many more hidden costs in the picture business and many more flare-ups ensued, as Goldwyn struggled to adjust to the fact that art, unlike selling gloves, is not a positive science. A cautious confirmation came from both of them: "Authorize you to rent barn but on month to month basis. Don't make any long-term commitment."

Samuel Goldwyn, along with DeMille and Jesse Lasky, was a partner in the Lasky Picture Play Company. Goldwyn was the first to leave after the merger with Paramount Pictures. Photo: Ruth Harriet Louise, 1932. Courtesy John Kobal Foundation

On December 22 (a mere nine days after arriving), DeMille signed a sublease for the Burns & Revier studio: four months at $250 per month (not the meager $75 Jesse remembered), with a three-year renewal option. Burns and Revier agreed to enlarge the existing open-air stage to 40x70 feet and build a second stage which the Lasky Company could use when it was not otherwise occupied. But Goldwyn was not the only one who knew how to haggle. Burns and Revier offered to develop their negatives and make one print at the rate of one-and-a-half cents a foot: DeMille got them down to ¾ cents a foot.

According to Scott Berg, who wrote a biography of Goldwyn, the initial budget for *The Squaw Man* quickly ran up to $47,000, "more than twice the company's assets." Goldwyn's solution was simplicity itself: he and publicity director Harry Reichenbach[2] trumpeted that the Lasky Company was going to produce a yearly slate of similar five-reel marvels, all of which could be purchased in advance.

Communication between New York and Hollywood was made even more difficult by the primitive state of the transcontinental telephone line. Connections were expensive, of poor quality, and often took a whole day to set up, by which time everybody in Hollywood, not to mention their rivals on both coasts, knew about the call and could listen in. "Some rare morsel of conversation would be retold as a juicy bit of gossip for the neighbors," remembered Billy Bitzer, "or even at times told to the scandal sheets, which were becoming more bold and popular. . . . Mr. Griffith cautioned us to comport ourselves extra carefully, for this was a small town, more dangerous than the city." It was simpler to send telegrams and night letters, and easier to forget to mention in a telegram every little detail that cropped up.

Besides necessary items like buying a truck in which to ferry their crew about, and finding cheaper and more permanent accommodations, DeMille chatted up the local smart set, convincing Los Angeles society to offer their homes, their lawns, and their wives for use in his film. DeMille shrewdly got a distinguished society matron, Mrs. A. W. Filson, to portray Lady Diana's mother. All she had to do was walk across a lawn, a small step for her, but a big step in making the despised movies respectable. Whenever the early filmmakers saw a spot or building that looked like what they needed, they just hopped out of their trucks, set up their cameras, trampled the lawns, and started shooting.

Because *The Squaw Man* opens in the luxury of Edwardian England, the scenes showing the cast at the Derby had to be bought from a stock footage service and intercut with shots of Dustin Farnum, Winifred Kingston, Monroe Salisbury, and extras dressed in Sunday finery, standing about in a decidedly modest grandstand. The New York harbor scenes were shot in San Pedro, and the Western saloon was built beside the rail tracks in that vast desert that was once the San Fernando Valley. The shots set in New York, including one of Times Square at night (reduced to a freeze frame in existing prints), were probably shot before they left New York. Fortunately, the bulk of their locations were available for free in California.

---

2. Reichenbach was the man who, prior to joining the Lasky Company, had made *September Morn* the most famous painting of the day by hiring a crowd of kids to stand around a reproduction of the nude in a Fifth Avenue art gallery window and then phoning the New York Society for Suppression of Vice and telling them that the picture was corrupting youth. As a result of the furor that followed, the picture was exhibited on a nationwide tour and made a fortune for its promoters.

DeMille: "We had one painter, one property man, one grip. We did not have an electrician because there were no electricians at the time (films then were shot outdoors by natural sunlight on sets built in the open air, and cameras were hand-cranked) . . . Oscar Apfel . . . really did most of the direction for which I got the credit."

The shrewdness of the decision to quit Flagstaff for Los Angeles became more evident every day. For early movie pioneers, Los Angeles was a boom town, rich in real cowboys and Indians, broken-down actors stranded by bankrupt theatrical companies, and in human labor of both sexes, unorganized but willing to turn their hands to any task that paid two or three dollars a day. Extras were plentiful, and thrifty producers sometimes obtained big mobs by merely providing a barbecue lunch.

"There were no unions, no casting organizations," remembered Allan Dwan, another pioneer who had been out in Los Angeles since 1909, "none of the order and regimentation one has today. People gathered at the gates of the studios to see if they could get work. If one set of gates were not available or open, they'd rush off to the next set of gates of a studio nearby." This was a profession in which flexibility was all-important. A woman hired as DeMille's secretary might find herself being used in the background of a scene, or found to have a natural bent for scriptwriting, or could serve as a film editor. As money was tightly budgeted, the extras were expected to do everything: act, nail, saw, even paint!

DeMille's actors were a cosmopolitan lot. Dick L'Estrange (Grouchy), was a German who had been on the stage for a decade; Dick LaReno (Big Bill) was English and had been on stage and screen twice as long; Joseph Singleton (the drunken Tabywana, father of the Indian girl) was Australian. Billy Elmer (the villainous Cash Hawkins) was a boxer turned movie extra; Baby DeRue (little Hal, the Squaw Man's son) was actually a girl named Carmen. Monroe Salisbury (the deceitful Lord Henry) was the genuine article, a New York stage actor who had appeared alongside some of the biggest names.

Besides Farnum, the only other player brought from New York was his lively blonde leading lady, Winifred Kingston, who played Lady Diana, the archetypal English rose. She had previously co-starred with Farnum in *Soldiers of Fortune* (released after the success in *The Squaw Man*) and was to appear in several more films with him, during the course of which they fell in love and married. "She was a fine enough trouper," DeMille recalled. "She didn't ask what performer last used the dressing room."

Recently it has become fashionable for stars like Raquel Welch and Cher to speak of their Indian blood, and play Indian women on the screen. But long before this rise in social consciousness, a Native American actress called Red Wing was cast by DeMille to play the squaw, Nat-U-Rich, completing the play's eternal triangle. In DeMille's films, the Indians received greater recognition and individuality than they typically got in movies. In John Ford's celebrated cavalry Westerns, the Indians were savages and played by unknowns. In DeMille movies, the American Indian was the noble savage, and their chiefs were played by Shakespearian-trained actors like Boris Karloff and Walter Hampden. Contrary to the story that she had been discovered on a reservation in California, Red Wing was a professional actress with considerable film experience, including *The Mended Lute* in 1909, directed by D. W. Griffith. While she never had another role as significant as Nat-U-Rich, Red Wing continued to work, and in the 1920s toured the country lecturing to educate the public about Native Americans.

Among others whose names and salaries DeMille had neatly recorded in his small red leather-bound notebook were Hal Roach, a former driver from Seattle who would go on to become a legend in his own right as a producer of slapstick comedies.

DeMille's first employee as the company's secretary/bookkeeper was Stella Stray. DeMille hired her at $15 a week, which New York considered too much. Since she refused to take a pay cut, she quit and threatened to take her precious typewriter with her. She was rehired on the spot.

DeMille recalled: "Stella was delightful. She had worked for one of those companies around Hollywood that was making Westerns. They went broke and . . . owed her about $300. So they gave her 20 cow-ponies and 2 mules. There was a tribe of Indians that had been used but they didn't owe them very much, so they gave them a typewriter . . . And suddenly she discovered that ponies eat. And she made a quick swap with the Indians. She gave them the ponies and took the typewriter!"

Rodeo champ Art Accord walked up to DeMille in the lobby of the old Alexandra Hotel dressed in cowboy clothes, high-heeled boots, silver spurs, chaps, ten-gallon hat, and cartridge belt and said, "I've heard you're one of the rich men who have come out from the east to make films or something?" DeMille said he was from the East but not rich. "Rich enough to pay me five dollars a day for rope-spinning?" He showed DeMille and the astonished hotel guests some pretty good rope tricks, which got him a job. Largely forgotten today, Art Accord was one of the most popular early cowboy stars until sound ruined his career. He ended his days as a miner in Mexico, and died in 1931, apparently having committed suicide.

The first official act of filming was not a shot but a still. On Monday, December 29, DeMille lined his historic team up outside the barn for a photograph of the entire company.

Once filming was underway, DeMille discovered a host of unforeseen problems. There was the difficulty with the film itself. It was highly flammable stock that could be ignited by a careless match, destroying weeks of work. "I didn't know film would burn like that," reflected DeMille. "Puff! It was gone. All our investment up in smoke. . . . I gave Al Gandolfi a really extravagant order. We'd shoot two negatives for every scene in the picture. I'd leave one at the barn and take one home with me every night. Then, if the barn or my home burned, we would be protected by the negative." Sure enough, a deliberate act of sabotage soon proved the value of his foresight: "Our film was processed in the dark little laboratory next to the barn. One morning, when I went in there, before my eyes had grown accustomed to the dim light, my feet scuffled over something that made a rustling sound . . . It was our film—it was THE SQUAW MAN—unwound, thrown in a heap on the floor, scraped, pitted, disfigured, as if someone had put it on the floor . . . and dragged it between heel and floor. It was completely ruined." Stella Stray remembered how often some of the people DeMille had to hire—carpenters and plumbers, printers and developers—might turn out to be spies or saboteurs, planted by rival film companies.

In addition, before he hired people to screen his mail, there were many crank letters warning DeMille to clear out of town. He didn't take these threats seriously, but more for show than fear exchanged the little gun he had brought with him from New York for a bigger one worn conspicuously in a holster. Sure enough, "while I was riding home from the studio, on horseback, a shot rang out." A few days later, he was shot at again.

One didn't waste valuable time tracking down bad shots or laying blame. DeMille simply worked harder and faster than the opposition. He even slept in a bunk at the studio. He knew that if anything went wrong, Lasky's money and hopes, and all of their ambitions, would go down the drain. Nevertheless, before his eyes the miracle began and DeMille recalled, "It was a new feeling, a new experience, and I was enamored of the way Mr. Apfel went about focusing his camera, getting his actors and actresses within range of the lens and the way in which our cameraman followed every move, studied the sun, tried to dodge a cloud, edged his camera into a more advantageous position."

By the end of shooting, DeMille would know as much as his co-director and be confident enough to make a film on his own. "Every picture broke boundaries," recalled his niece distinguished choreographer Agnes deMille. "Every day brought new things, new discoveries, a new way of cutting, a new way of handling the camera, a new way of lighting. And they'd be excited by it."

So sure was DeMille of his future that in January, with *The Squaw Man* only half completed, and its success unknown, he brought his wife and child west from wintry New York. He was at the station to welcome them in an open touring car he had rented for the occasion, the back seat extravagantly filled with violets at five cents a bunch (back when five cents bought a bowl of soup and ten cents bought a meal).

Looking to cut costs, DeMille had taken a room on Lexington Avenue, which he shared with the tame grey prairie wolf he had bought for a scene in the film. Now he took rooms for his family in a boarding house. As it was, local prejudice was so strong they almost didn't get the rooms. Boarding houses around town often posted a sign: "Rooms to Let. No movies need apply." "I knew what discrimination was," Agnes, who came out the following year, would still remember seventy years later, "because I was a 'movie' you see." Previous encounters with movie people taught landladies to be careful as movie folks were well known for running off without paying rent when they went bust. DeMille's wife, Constance, prevailed over a suspicious landlady. Radiating respectability, integrity, and trust, she convinced the landlady that the DeMilles weren't the sort to skedaddle in the night.

Shooting *The Squaw Man* took eighteen days, three working weeks, to complete. Not counting the $20,000 paid upfront to author and star, the six-reel feature came in on budget, at $15,450.25. After having seen a complete assembly of the film, an excited DeMille cabled Goldwyn on January 22: "Just completed our eighty-seventh consecutive hour of assembling and cutting. Without sleep. Farnum leaves with film 1 o'clock today arrives New York Penn station 5 thirty Sunday evening. . . . How about one thousand dollars. Bills to meet so get the other thousand to me at earliest convenience. Jesse's coming. Great . . . C. B."

Lasky's arrival represented good news. During the weeks of preparation and shooting, he had become encouraged by DeMille's glowing reports. But he was brought down to earth with a jolt when he discovered their glamorous studio wasn't quite what it had been cracked up to be. "I arrived at the old Santa Fe Depot in Los Angeles, called a taxi, and told the driver I wanted to go to Hollywood, He gave me a puzzled look but said, 'Get in, boss—we'll find it.' He set his course out of the city over dirt roads, past endless orchards and an occasional farmhouse. . . . The taxi driver suggested that I make enquiries inside the [Hollywood] Hotel about the Lasky studio. 'I'm sorry,' said the clerk, 'I've never heard of the it.' 'Perhaps I should have told you that the Director General of the company is Cecil B. DeMille,' I stated impressively. 'Never heard of him, the clerk said.'" Lasky was as overjoyed as his friend at their reunion, but it didn't blind him to some other purchases that hadn't been accounted for. Among other things, DeMille had rented a two-ton Ford truck. It was standing in front of the stage, with "'Jesse L. Lasky Feature Play Company' emblazoned prominently on its side. When he [DeMille] saw me coming, he ran out, grabbed my hand, summoned the company, made a speech of welcome, pushed me against the truck, and signaled the photographer. He knew I would automatically smile for a snapshot, and I think he wanted to send Sam photographic evidence of what would appear to be my happy endorsement of his extravagance in renting the truck."

Last-minute delays prevented Farnum from leaving for New York with the film: one was the editing. Two, the rain. And three, getting the prints made. Pressures for delivery were mounting on both coasts. A practical Goldwyn sent DeMille a night letter on the eve of January 23: "Give us by return wire some idea how much money you will require to start *Brewster's Millions* [the next film on their schedule], as until *Squaw Man* is released, we have very low funds and cannot proceed except very carefully. Of vital importance should know your opinion on *Squaw Man*. When can we expect first print?

Sam G." Besides fire, ambush, espionage, and theft, California had another disagreeable surprise. The all-important weather wasn't all sunshine. "Ohhh, that rain!" exclaimed Stella Stray. "We had to perforate our own stock, and it rained, and the roof leaked . . . day after day, and it was either the printing machine or the perforating machine that we had to hold an umbrella over! . . . We had to develop the negative one night and let that dry, and then print it and let the print dry, and then put it together and run it. It could be three or four days, sometimes."

But now a situation arose that would test the mettle of all three partners. The culprit wasn't a hired saboteur, but DeMille himself. He had a problem. It was the need for a decent Eastman perforator to cut sprocket holes as DeMille didn't have enough perforated stock on which to print the first positive copy for his screening. Bargain hunting during pre-production, he had bought a secondhand perforator from a bankrupt English production company. As he wanted to screen the film for the cast and crew in Los Angeles, DeMille would have to perforate the film himself. New to the business, DeMille didn't know that there were two different types of perforators. And the difference was only an extra hole for every sixty-four! This slight discrepancy, easy to rectify if only someone had spotted it at the time, spread panic and visions of ruin. And all, as DeMille would later claim, because of his "English bargain" and his "Dutch thrift." DeMille cabled Goldwyn on January 24,

Can't arrange perforation unless you can force Eastman to give you positive to match first negative; Sam rush perforating machine with twin dials as per night letter and fifty thousand feet unperforated positive . . . Can send first print five days after receiving perforator. Or sixty-five positive. Answer.

DeMille and Lasky decided to make a special occasion of the first official screening. About fifty people attended, including the cast and crew, their family and friends, and DeMille's six-year-old daughter, Cecilia. It began innocuously. The titles flashed up on their makeshift screen, with Farnum's name in big letters followed by, "*THE SQUAW MAN*, A Jesse L. Lasky Production." Faces flashed on the screen: Dustin Farnum, handsome in black tie and tails, smiling, and Winifred, looking as lovely on film as she did in person, and both ennobled by being projected on the screen. Suddenly the familiar became magical. The "English" gardens shot in Mrs. Filson's estate looked authentic. Locals brought in as dress extras—women in long dresses and men in regimental uniforms and black tie and tails—walked across gracious lawns, bowing to each other like stately aristocrats.

At the beginning, all was fine. Soon a fine line began creeping into view on the top of the screen. Slowly, but inevitably, Farnum's feet unmistakably appeared over his head. DeMille's first thought it was the fault of the projectionist. The projectionist, probably acutely embarrassed himself, made a quick adjustment of the film and brought the picture back to the center of the screen. DeMille gave Lasky a reassuring shrug, and the film continued.

But the same thing happened again. The tell-tale line, then the picture cut in two, bottom above top. No matter how hard the projectionist tried to adjust the picture, every few minutes the same thing happened. The image was sparklingly clear, but as before, it wouldn't stay put on the screen.

Lasky didn't have to know much about the technical side of things to realize that there was no way they could sell a film that had to be constantly readjusted in the projector. Without a salable movie, the partners saw their futures fade into the blank white on the wall. "We're ruined," Lasky gasped. They sent the audience home. Farnum may have secretly heaved a sigh of relief that he had insisted on money upfront. Lasky: "We brooded and discussed the situation until three or four o'clock in the morning. We had used up all our capital, spent all Sam could collect as advances from states'-rights men, and there remained unpaid bills. And all we had to show for it was a film that wouldn't project . . . We didn't dare tell Sam what happened, fearful he would blow a fuse." By dawn, and no closer to a solution, DeMille was at his wit's end. Lasky was in despair. Afraid to report to Goldwyn with the news, Lasky simply fled. DeMille knew instinctively that there must be a simple solution. He repeatedly checked over everything: the film in the camera, the film in the projector, the film on the Moviola. Because he couldn't figure out the problem, DeMille naturally feared that it had to do with the negative and thus would recur on every positive print struck from it. Goldwyn, waiting in New York, would want to know how the screening had gone and why the promised print still wasn't on its way. "Something terribly wrong with print. Please advise. Regards, Cecil." DeMille even wondered if sabotage could not be ruled out as the cause of their dilemma. In fact, a lot of the people working on the film, like Mamie Wagner, continued to believe for years that it had been sabotage, since DeMille either forgot or did not choose to enlighten them later as to the real cause of the problem.

Goldwyn had even less technical know-how than Lasky, but he remembered Sigmund Lubin, head of the Lubin Film Laboratory in Philadelphia. Lubin had only recently joined the fearsome Trust, whose avowed aim it was to wipe out upstarts like the Lasky Company. The mess Goldwyn and his partners were in couldn't be more advantageous to the Trust had they arranged it themselves. Like DeMille, Goldwyn had swallowed too much humble pie in his youth to want another slice. Still, Old Man Lubin knew more about film than anyone else in the business. We'll never know what it cost Goldwyn to persuade the wily Lubin to help out. In the end, Lubin told him to send the film to him in Philadelphia, and he'd see what he could do. DeMille boarded the first train to Philadelphia.

Throughout the seemingly interminable train ride with its forty-nine stops between Los Angeles and Chicago, DeMille traveled with the cans of film packed into specially bought saddlebags to ensure that nothing else happened. To insure plenty of space, Constance reserved him a compartment for two—for security and also for additional space so he could continue to edit the second negative to match the first.

DeMille: "I rigged up a cutting apparatus so that I could lay it across the seat opposite me in the compartment and, . . . as the train roared eastward, I worked as I had never worked before. I cut the negative and spliced it together, poring over the tiny pictures until my head was reeling . . . The train pulled into Philadelphia and I was still at work, though dead on my feet. I had not slept for 48 hours; but the film was practically edited."

Considering you could hardly read a book on a train in those days, this was a Herculean feat. D. W. Griffith was alleged to have cut a film by eye, but not a feature-length film and *not* on a moving train. But, this feat begs another question: why?—when DeMille could simply have brought the negative he and Mamie Wagner had spent eighty-seven sleepless hours cutting? And since he didn't as yet know what caused the error, wouldn't he have been afraid he was running the risk of repeating it? Which was apparently what he did. He perforated the second negative with his "English bargain."

At Lubin's offices, poor Lasky's nerve failed him again: he waited outside. DeMille went in with Lubin. He remembered later how "Pop" took a strip of the film, held it up to the light, looked at it, turned it round, studied it some more, called in one of his technicians, and handed him the film. Fifteen minutes later, the technician returned: "Nothing wrong with the negative, it's just the sprocket holes. You punched the wrong ones."

Lubin simply cut off the sprocket holes from the negative and applied fine, unperforated strips on either side onto which were punched correctly spaced sprocket holes. It was long, slow work and the new print wasn't perfect, but the panic was over. The problem that had almost wrecked them was solved. They were back in the picture business.

The prints back in Los Angeles were all faulty and had to be scrapped. They needed new prints and more time. According to DeMille the release date was Sunday, February 15. Goldwyn arranged the press show for three days hence. They had three weeks to raise more money to make the prints customers had already ordered and paid for. Harry Reichenbach recalled frantic efforts to try and raise an extra three thousand dollars: "For three thousand dollars Lasky was willing to part with a very large interest in his company. I thought that theatrical producers would be the most logical and most susceptible prospects for this investment. . . . Across the hall from us was the office of Harry Frazee, then in the heyday of his theatrical triumphs. His reaction to my proposition was blunt and typical. 'I'll have nothing to do with those nuts,' he said. I finally persuaded one, Harry Cohn who is today an officer of Columbia Pictures, to throw in three thousand on a chance. Four months later he sold out his interest for $55,000 with a sigh of relief and doubtless congratulated himself on his shrewdness and foresight."

The credibility of Reichenbach, the undisputed king of sensational hoaxes, might be questionable, but he seems to be the only one to write about the final great hurdle *The Squaw Man* had to overcome.

Goldwyn fretted on the business side. At that time, picture producers did not have direct outlets to the public. They sold territorial rights to central distributors in different states. Lasky had to guarantee the delivery of his film on a certain day, the failure of which entailed a forfeit and nullification of the contract. . . . "I stayed up all night in the Jersey freight yards waiting for the case of prints to arrive. It was a February blizzard, the telegraph wires were blown down, the tracks buried in three feet of snow and above all, it was the Erie. . . . A second day and night I waited under the sheds of the freight yards for the sign of the train, and every hour of delay brought us nearer to the time when it seemed that the Erie had decided to wait till Summer, a speck of moving ice became visible through black clouds of smoke.

"The Erie puffed and snorted in a winner against the elements. It was only seventy-two hours late. Twenty dollars slipped unseen between me and somebody and immediately the seal of the mail truck was broken and the box of prints lifted out. I made the delivery to the Loew theatre on Broadway where all the buyers were assembled just as they were ready to claim the forfeit and call up their lawyers."

At last they were ready. Goldwyn organized the screening at the prestigious Longacre Theatre insuring that *The Squaw Man* was thought of as just another movie—even if the primitive screen was a large coarse piece of muslin, and the projector had "sprocket holes constantly obtruding themselves, reinforced by a crackling condenser." This problem stemmed from the hastily corrected negative that Lubin had provided. "Pop" had saved their bacon, but the film was decidedly streaky.

On Tuesday morning, everyone they knew in New York was there. DeMille's mother sat surrounded by friends and clients. His brother William, the Lasky clan, Blanche Goldwyn, Arthur Friends's friends, Dustin Farnum's colleagues, as well as early rising members of New York society, and, of course, the all-important buyers and exhibitors. Among the audience was Anne Bauchens, a bright young blonde who would join William deMille when he went to Hollywood as his secretary and subsequently would become DeMille's film editor for the rest of his and her life. At the back, behind the last row of seats, in their dinner suits and winged collars, stiffly holding on the brass railing with a white knuckled grip, were Lasky, Goldwyn, and DeMille.

If the casting had been slapdash, the acting was uniformly good. Whether in black tie or leather chaps, everyone emoted. Even if the movies would soon retire this style of acting and replace it with the close-up, there was no need here to apologize for a theatrical style. In 1913, the revolutionary Russian actress Alla Nazimova may have been the sensation of sophisticated New York in plays by Strindberg and Ibsen, but the rest of Broadway and the bulk of the theater-going public were still swept away by heroes who declaimed and heroines who fainted. They reveled in blood and thunder.

Today it is difficult to assess how good Farnum was in his historic role portraying the lead character Jim. The audience saw Farnum, in dusty chaps, astride a real horse, herding cattle into a pen for branding, just like a real cowboy. These were the sort of authentic visual details with which DeMille and Oscar Apfel expanded the original stage-bound play for the screen.

Because of Jim's (Farnum) ignorance of local sensibilities (and his "English" sense of fair play), he intervenes when he sees Nat-U-Rich, the daughter of a drunken Indian, being molested by the "hissable" Cash Hawkins. As a result, Jim is ambushed, blinded, and left to die in a cave full of poisonous gas, before being rescued and nursed back to health by Nat-U-Rich. Without captions or close-ups, Jim's loneliness and other needs are communicated by glances at the ceiling.

The reason for the title was about to become apparent. Back then in movies it was taken for granted that when a man and a woman were left alone together the result was inevitable. Either marriage or dishonor would follow. A scene showing a man and a woman alone in a cabin is followed by another in which the Indian woman is seen busily sewing tiny moccasins. Jim forces the judge at gunpoint to perform the wedding ceremony. The American West may have been wild and lawless, but when it came to racial prejudice, it was deeply conventional. Marrying Nat-U-Rich Jim has done the unpardonable. Henceforth is looked down on as "the squaw man."

Cash Hawkins plots his revenge, but while trying to carry it out is shot by Nat-U-Rich. Re-enter the widow Diana, still ignorant of Jim's married state, to bring Jim home. The dilemma of these three "good people" is solved when Nat-U-Rich, knowing her arrest is imminent, stoically commits suicide. As her sobered-up father proudly says, "Her man had loved her, he loves her no more. He took her son from her, and gave him to the woman he had loved before. She was my daughter. She knew what to do."

Fifty years after DeMille's first version of *The Squaw Man*, Hollywood had produced only a handful of films about the Indians' plight. But with this film, DeMille showed Indians in a sympathetic, revisionist light. For a director who has come down over the years as an old bigot, DeMille could rightly be proud of the film for that if for nothing else.

Did the film have what it took to succeed? At a time when every cough was thought a rejection and every rustling piece of paper a thunderclap, when it was over there was prolonged applause. Folks who hadn't been used to films much longer than a thirty minutes enjoyed the sort of drama they were accustomed to seeing on stage. Today the film is surprisingly watchable. Though primitive, it stands up. Even though the screening had been interrupted by half a dozen breaks in the film, words like "art" were tossed about. Distributors who hadn't yet bought rights to the film for their territories now approached Goldwyn to make deals. Among them was another future film tycoon, Louis B. Mayer.

It was after that screening that Lasky and Goldwyn got to know Adolph Zukor, the dynamic, barely five-foot-two Hungarian-born film tycoon, whose presentation of *Queen Elizabeth* had first inspired them to get into this business. "I was flattered to find among the congratulatory wires one from the president of Famous Players." According to Lasky, "Zukor was small in stature, but I began to think of him as a titan when he expounded astute theories about the future of the motion-picture business . . . His vision and quiet dignity still infused me as I walked with Sam to the offices we had taken on Fifth Avenue opposite the Public Library.

"'That man is an inspirational force!' I said. 'I want to keep in close contact with him.'" Sam agreed, "and we never failed to have lunch with Zukor whenever I came to New York."

Out of this initial contact grew a friendship and a powerful new partnership which was soon to supplant others, and in the process wrench earlier ties apart.

As DeMille's train sped west back to California, Goldwyn was optimistically busy picking up more distribution deals, and selling rights to *Brewster's Millions*, their next planned film. Two weeks after screening *The Squaw Man* Goldwyn had sold it to thirty-one of the forty-eight state territories. A week later, only Iowa, Kansas, Missouri, and Nebraska were still unsold. Before returning to the coast, a euphoric DeMille had crowed to the *New York Dramatic Mirror* about the superiority of movies over theater: "Imagine, the horizon is your stage limit and the sky your gridiron. No height limit, no close fitting exits, no conserving of stage space, just the whole world open to you as a stage; 1,000 people in a scene do not crowd your accommodations . . . I felt inspired, I felt that I could do things which the confines of a theater would not permit."

CHAPTER FOUR

CECIL B. DEMILLE ARRIVED IN CALIFORNIA ON NOVEMBER 13, 1913. THE number thirteen didn't worry him; he often said that his father's name, like his own, had thirteen letters. His father, Henry Churchill deMille, was born and raised as an Episcopalian in the small town of Washington, North Carolina. He was an ardent Christian whose original calling had been to the ministry. On his father's side, DeMille and his brother could lay claim to a distinguished Franco/Dutch ancestry: during the persecution of the Huguenots, one branch of the family went into Holland and crossed the last "l" which made the name "deMilt." Another branch used the letter "y." "My own branch of the family came directly to North Carolina," DeMille, a passionate genealogist, explained to fellow family historian Kathleen deMilly, "exploring up the Pamlico River and settling in a town called Washington, where they remained until my own father, Henry C. deMille, migrated to New York."

Henry was of average height, thin, and wiry. In his photographs, he looks like an ascetic Victorian schoolmaster, somewhat on the plain side with a thick nose and high forehead, but his looks belied his passion. There was a clue in a fine sensitive mouth, and especially in his bright, searching blue eyes. Henry was drawn to the theater, which wasn't really so different from the rural churches where ranting preachers hailed the Lord and pounded their pulpits, though to the devout churchgoers of those landlocked congregations, what was godlike in church was the devil's work outside its four walls.

Henry's mother, a devout churchgoer, was so upset when her son spoke of becoming an actor that for a long time he didn't dare go against her tearful wishes, and attempted to channel his creative longings towards a career in the Church. But they could not be held in check forever. One fateful day, the fourteen-year-old Henry went to visit his grandfather in Brooklyn. Across the East River lay New York, a city that possessed a sinful allure. Wide-eyed in Babylon, the devoted son saw and was drawn to the theater. Before his parents could get him home, he fell ill, stayed on to recover, and, with his grandfather's help, persuaded his parents that he should remain to finish his studies for the ministry in New York, which was a bit like going to hell for firewood.

35

To a dreamy boy with a love of drama, New York was, by the second half of the nineteenth century, already a Nineveh and Xanadu rolled into one. It was a city of chaotic streets, teeming millions, scandalous poverty, rowdy drunks, packed theaters, gaslight streets, horses, carriages, and cable cars—a city every bit as intoxicating then as it is a hundred years later. Henry was a sincere young man, an early convert to the Rev. Charles Kingsley's call for "muscular Christianity," a belief that he was to pass on to his sons, but he was also part of a dynamic new age, and he had no difficulty in convincing himself that the theater would allow him to carry the gospel to a far larger audience. If he still needed to persuade his parents, there was the example of several esteemed academic religious men already running theaters, foremost among them the highly respected Episcopalian, the Rev. Dr. George S. Mallory, who had taken over the Madison Square Theater.

Before settling on theater, Henry switched from religion to teaching at the Lockwood Academy for girls in Brooklyn, and it was at Lockwood, in 1872, that at nineteen years old, scholarly, and bespectacled, he met Matilda Beatrice Samuel, Tillie to her friends, nine months older than him, and astute enough to see the ambition he thought was hidden behind his glasses.

Unlike Henry, Beatrice was an immigrant and hailed from Liverpool, England, the country an awestruck American like Henry considered the cradle of drama. Beatrice Samuel was an extrovert. She wasn't beautiful but had dash. Small, straight-backed, with the large and sparkling eyes that her younger son would inherit, she was a young woman with great presence and boundless energy. She was also Jewish.

Soon they shared a daily two-mile walk to and from school. He confided to her his mother's horror at the idea of his wanting to be an actor. And the thought that he had fallen for a Jewish girl would hardly calm his mother's southern Episcopalian heart. If anything, all her fears about the dangers of the great Yankee metropolis had been realized. But Beatrice Samuel was by nature adventurous and flexible, and she gave the shy, bespectacled country boy confidence. They talked of their shared passions for theater, art, and literature. Henry probably also shared with Beatrice his love of nature, which he had sacrificed for life in the city.

Their courtship lasted four years. After meeting his family and perceiving the importance of religion in their life, Beatrice began to take part in their family prayer meetings, and before their marriage she converted and became an Episcopalian. They were wed on the morning of July 1, 1876, at St. Luke's Church in Brooklyn.

Beatrice Samuel sacrificed much when she married Henry deMille. Her conversion profoundly shook her Orthodox parents. They did not attend the wedding. Still, for their eighteen years together, she was his shield and armor. From Henry's diaries, this barely legible entry reveals the physical depth of the passion which existed between them: "Friday, March 27th in evening thinking of my wife. It seemed as though our spirits came especially together that night. Is there not a spirits' voice that speaks in spite of the body? I certainly felt the sweet influence of her spirit that night. I have never had a greater proof of the sympathy of soul with soul."

Encouraged by his wife, between continuing with his religious studies and earning a living through his teaching, Henry continued to write and produce plays for amateurs. Their first son, William Churchill deMille, was born in Washington, North Carolina, on July 25, 1878. Cecil Blount DeMille was born on August 12, 1881. Like his brother, DeMille was also supposed to see the first light of day in the Old South but, typically, was born ahead of time in a boarding house in Ashfield, Massachusetts, where Henry, to get his pregnant wife away from New York's steaming summer heat, had come to work as a private tutor.

With a wife and two children to support it was difficult at first for Henry to give up his modest but secure teaching post. But the decision, long delayed, became reality in 1882. Henry had gone to audition one of his plays for the Madison Square Theatre.

In the first half of the nineteenth century, many American theaters were little more than vast barns, in part because of a strong prejudice against the theater. By the time Henry joined the profession, hundreds of theaters had sprung up in New York alone. Popular plays were showing the effects of the streams of immigrants flooding into the United States. Germans, Irish, and Russians all had theaters of their own. American managers like Augustine Daly had begun to go to Europe to buy up plays in great quantities, which they then adapted for the American market. With works by contemporary British and Irish playwrights like Tom Taylor (*Our American Cousin*) and Dion Boucicault (*The Shaughraun*), American audiences developed a taste for subjects involving everyday life.

By the time Henry entered the profession, a new breed of producers, enterprising Jewish immigrants like the three Frohman brothers—initially hired to do the dirty work as road managers and advance men for the shows—were seeing an opportunity for advancement in the New World. With so much new blood and ideas pouring into the country, prejudice was rampant. For Henry, being married to a Jewish woman meant that he forfeited a certain social mobility, such as membership in some clubs. Working in the theater, the deMilles would be accepted without prejudice.

Although Henry's play wasn't accepted, he was hired as a play reader at $1,500 a year, with an extra thousand if a play he discovered was produced and ran for more than six months. The job soon taught him to refine and polish his own skills, and it brought him and Beatrice into contact with the Frohmans: Daniel, who managed the Madison Theater, and his brothers, Charles and Gustave, who looked after the theater's touring companies. Through the Frohmans, and while trying to get one of his own plays produced, Henry met the man who would help establish his fame and fortune.

David Belasco—later to become known as "the Bishop of Broadway" because of his custom of wearing his shirt collars back to front—was a short, dark, dynamic twenty-four-year-old ball of motion. He had been in the theater most of his life, first as a child actor, appearing in Charles Kean's *Richard III*, and later he worked as secretary to Dion Boucicault. Gustave Frohman hired Belasco to be stage manager at the Madison Square. When Frohman finally decided to produce one of Henry's plays, he assigned Belasco to direct. This first venture lasted six nights, the first flop in the Madison's history. The Frohmans left the Madison to run the new Lyceum Theater and took Belasco with them. Henry stayed, and augmented his small salary by acting in shows on the road.

Life on the road was hard. Trains were unheated, missed connections were the rule, and few towns had restaurants. Theaters away from the big cities were dingy affairs, their walls blackened by tobacco spit; rats ran through the orchestra pits and ate bits of grease paint left in the dressing rooms. When Henry and Beatrice toured, often bringing the baby along, they lived in constant fear that rats might get into the toddler's crib while they were on stage. Living accommodations on the road were not much better. A powerful religious prejudice and suspicion about theater folk meant the young couple and their baby would often end up spending their nights in barns or on railroad station platforms. Things were still almost as bad when DeMille, married and acting with his wife, toured in 1905.

Henry and Bea decided to take a small summer house at Echo Lake, New Jersey, a town within commuting distance of New York, so that their sons could grow up in the healthier atmosphere of the countryside. Bea's father had not forgotten his daughter in his will and had left her a small legacy. They rented a pre-revolutionary war house with pegged wooden floors, a bit run down, but at $50 a year, it was an incredible bargain, and a relief from crowded, unsanitary tenement life.

This was DeMille's first home. The backyard opened onto a neighbor's barnyard. Everything that mooed and crowed and chirped on a farm or in the woods and the lake nearby became the boys' companions, but after the noise of the city it was quiet enough for Henry to work and recover from the strain of keeping a roof over their heads. The house was big enough for serious-minded eight-year-old William to study, and for five-year-old Cecil, a rambunctious, inquisitive, and imaginative child, to play. With his golden locks hanging in the fashionable Lord Fauntleroy curls, the high-spirited youngster was already a handful—demanding, restless, always up to something, and inclined to fall asleep at unfortunate moments. At Echo Lake, he could run and play, explore at length, and switch his attention from tenement cockroaches to more sensible pets, like a dog of his own. His oft-cited lack of fear and great rapport with animals derived from his parents' concern to provide their children with an outdoor life.

DeMille's childhood years were idyllic. He grew up with the sounds of nature and the smells of the changing seasons. The country provided animals, insects, the murmurs of streams, and the rustle of leaves—sounds a child takes for granted, but remembered at the end of his days. Back in their apartment in New York, there were the clanging of fire bells, the cries of the newsboys calling out the latest headlines, the barking of dogs, the voices of a hundred nations, the rattle of horses, and wagons in the teeming streets. Much of DeMille's early film work was set in this world and had the smell of near documentary realism about it.

When Henry was able to afford it, he bought his sons a horse to ride to school. On Jack, a strawberry roan, DeMille became a passionate and expert horseman. His love of horses was inherited by his daughter and grandchildren, who devoted their lives to racing and breeding horses instead of following him into the movies. DeMille's early love of nature would bloom into Paradise, his secluded estate set deep in a valley among the San Bernardino Mountains, which he maintained like a wildlife preserve. Though DeMille was a sportsman, he rarely hunted. On his ranch, rattlers slept beneath the steps, pumas, deer, and wolves roamed freely.

When Henry's contract with the Madison, struggling to keep its doors open after the Frohmans left, was up, he confided in his diary, "I had to get along by borrowing and other such doglike means of living," He and Beatrice went back on the road. For acting and managing a company, Henry earned $80 a week, and for her acting role, Beatrice received $50. Debts were mounting. But, even at his lowest point, Henry never doubted his decision when he chose the theater. And, spurred by Beatrice, he continued to write.

In the fall of 1886, Daniel Frohman produced Henry's new play, *The Main Line*, a story about the railroads, and assigned Belasco to direct. Again, the play failed. When Frohman wanted to close, Belasco and Henry stormed into his office and convinced him to give it a second chance while they reworked it. With their changes, including adding a spectacular train crash, *The Main Line* became successful enough at the Lyceum for it to be sent out on the road.

With *The Wife*, their third collaboration and first as co-authors, Henry and Belasco hit pay dirt. Charles Frohman's eyewitness account of their working methods foreshadows DeMille's style of collaboration on the scripts for his films: "For hours at a time during these pangs of creation, Belasco would occupy the stage of the theater, alone, but impersonating the entire company, while deMille would sit at a table in the front row, write a few lines of dialogue, then Belasco would act out each part, altering the lines to meet his most exacting tests as stage manager. 'Now Henry,' I have heard him specify, 'Give me a speech that begins here' pacing slowly across the stage, 'and takes me over here. Then I turn suddenly like this and see the woman I love.'"

The Wife ran for 239 performances. From its success, Henry was finally able to pay off his debts, and to rent a larger apartment in New York for his family, as well as another for his mother, two younger sisters, and brother John. Father also found time to take Cecil, nearly eight, to the museum where the boy became fascinated by the Egyptian gallery with its mummies, strange statues, and bright paintings. He became a regular visitor, and it wasn't long before the little boy with the thousand questions knew the guard by name. But his mischievous nature put an end to those solo excursions when one day his curiosity got the better of him and he climbed into an open mummy case. When he sat up, a woman walked in and fainted dead away.

Belasco had become a regular figure in the deMilles' life at Echo Lake. Cecil and William grew up with grownups who spoke about actors, actresses, plays, the theater in New York, plans for the future profits and losses, other people's failures, and their successes. Belasco would do most of the talking, mostly about himself and what he was doing, with the deMilles listening, entranced. Another of DeMille's strongest childhood memories was the time the sharpshooter Annie Oakley spent a week at a house nearby. While De-Mille was setting up her practice marks, she told him stories of Buffalo Bill's Wild West Show, and of the kings and queens she met when touring Europe.

In the peace of Echo Lake, Henry and Belasco would write, his mother would transcribe what they had written, and then, in the late afternoon, the day's work would be read out loud, with the boys invited to listen and to comment. Having rousted about all day, young DeMille sometimes fell asleep. But later, when he had a fine house and came home at the end of a long day of making movies, he kept up this practice with his own family. He never lost the memory of the child he had been, and because of it, he never lost his respect for a child's imagination.

DeMille was a student of human nature. Unlike the self-contained, scholarly William, he was always being told by his mother to hush, not to bother father when he is at work, to keep out of the way. The way his family remembered him, Cece (his brother's nickname for him) was always rushing into the house with a new discovery, being frowned at, and sent out again. Until he went to school, he had no one his own age to play with. He was curious about everything. He wasn't deprived of affection, just the attention he craved.

The boys began to entertain themselves by putting on plays themselves, either on their own or with the neighborhood children. Among these playmates were Anna and Margaret George, the beautiful young daughters of Henry George, the celebrated economist and land reformer, and author of *Progress and Poverty*, whose humanitarian and religious arguments naturally had a strong attraction for Henry. Anna George would later become William's wife and the mother of Agnes.

In four years, Belasco and deMille produced some of the most successful plays of the period: *The Wife, Lord Chumley, The Charity Ball*, and in 1890, *Men and Women*, whose on-stage kissing, references to adultery and divorce created a sensation. Though most of the money from these successes seemed to go to the producers and to Belasco (a growing if unresolved source of discontent), the deMilles were financially sound.

The successful partnership foundered in 1889, when a prominent actress and notorious society divorcee, Mrs. Leslie Carter, became involved both personally and professionally with Belasco. Whereas Belasco was a born showman who realized that stars brought people to the theater, the small-town preacher still lurking beneath his skin made Henry, still a practicing lay reader at his local church, disapprove of the alliance and he ended his association with Belasco. Henry would write several more plays on his own, but he died without ever again achieving his earlier success.

With the birth of a third child, Agnes, in April 1891, Henry bought a plot of land sixty miles from New York, out at Pompton Lake, New Jersey. Seventy-six acres of his own, surrounded by the green Ramapo Mountains, he intended to build a house large enough for his growing family. DeMille would never forget the afternoon when his sister died, on February 12, 1895, two months short of her fourth birthday. His mother took her sons to the coffin and "made each of us boys put our hand over the dead child's heart and pledge that we would never treat any woman other than we would have wanted Agnes treated, if she had lived." To the end of his life DeMille carried a picture of his sister in a locket on his watch chain.

By the end of their first year in their new home, Henry had paid off the mortgage. He commuted regularly to New York to see plays, to meet with friends at the Lambs Club, and take part in rehearsals. Life was going well. Then, at 4:12 a.m. on February 10, 1893, he was dead at the age of fifty-six. According to his granddaughter, the cause was typhoid, from eating a bad oyster. According to DeMille, it was the fumes from a sewer being repaired outside where he was staying in New York. Either way, typhoid was fatal.

DeMille: "The effect on his family was traumatic. 'He sent for me,' recalled DeMille later, and he saw the family one at a time, and he asked me a question. And I couldn't answer because I was choked and I couldn't answer—I did not know that he was dying.

"I didn't know how sick he was even. I was a little boy, but something prevented me talking because my throat was tight as you are when you are about to cry—so I couldn't answer and he waited for a few minutes and he said, 'Well, run along and play.' I've never forgotten that, and I never could get it from my mind that he couldn't understand that I wanted to—I'm sure that he didn't—but he couldn't understand at the time what I wanted to tell him—I wanted to express my love and affection for him but I couldn't. I couldn't see. I was nine or ten at the time."

As he lay dying, Henry's attitude to the theater underwent a change. Recalling his many disappointments in the profession, he told his wife, "Make the boys butchers or grocers or candlestick makers or anything, but keep them away from the stage." Whenever he was reminded of this, DeMille claimed that his father had made that request with a touch of humor.

DeMille was eleven when his comfortable secure world was shattered. With the purchase of the house, most of the family's savings were gone, so his mother had to fall back on her wits and her teacher's training to support the family. DeMille's life changed in other ways as well. At a time when a father figure is considered to be most important to an adolescent boy, over-night DeMille's home had gone from being dominated by the sound and presence of men—his father, Belasco, William, and John—to a place overrun with schoolgirls and women. Two months after his father's death, his mother turned their recently completed house into the Henry C. deMille Memorial School for Girls. With Beatrice's eye for the fineness of things (an eye De-Mille inherited), the girls in her school wore crisp uniforms and the tables were set with linen, fine glassware, china, and silver. Nor did she stint on the quality of the food: "the art of dining properly is essential to a young lady's training." But keeping the school going with such standards was hard. Finan-cial struggle ensued, and soon it was clear that the school was costing more to operate than it was earning.

Beatrice's husband's last request had as little hope of succeeding with her sons as the admonitions of Henry's mother's had had on their father. For a time, William tried to follow his father's wishes. He left to study engineering at Columbia University, but switched to a course in playwriting in his senior year. By the age of twenty-five, he had written his first Broadway hit, *Strong-heart*. Prior he had earned his living teaching stage direction and manage-ment in schools of dramatic art around New York.

Throughout his long and distinguished life as writer, director, and teacher, William's tolerant, noncompetitive, and witty personality endeared him to men as well as women in a way that DeMille, whose ego was concentrated on his own ambition, failed to do. William would follow his brother to Holly-wood, but while DeMille made "movies," William made "films," and conse-quently never achieved the same financial or popular success. He ended his career, like his uncle, as a highly respected university professor. A man who knew both brothers, the stage designer Norman Bel Geddes (father of actress Barbara), drew this picture of William: "William deMille had almost none of the rough strength and drive of his younger brother. He was probably more sure of himself than Cecil, but made no effort to prove it, or himself, to anyone. He had a pleasant sense of humor, but never appeared happy. He was quite uninterested in making an impression upon anybody. Certainly, throughout his Hollywood career, he was never able to emerge from un-der the shadow cast by Cecil. Maybe it was simply a lack of ambition. If so, William's daughter, Agnes, who went on to become a talented and famous choreographer, took after her uncle more than her father."

Agnes's opinion of the relationship between her father and his younger brother was that, "William was a much more thoughtful, educated and liter-ate man, and he thought a lot of what Cecil did was pompous and over-bear-ing, although he tactfully never said so. There was a great estrangement be-tween the brothers later in life. They had been extremely close as young men and as boys, helping one another in everything. It was very sad, but as Cecil's own daughter, Cecilia, said to me once: 'Father has no friends, hundreds of admirers, but not friends, not one in the world.'" To be fair the same could be said of any a man who rose to great heights and found himself on top, alone.

After four years spent mostly in the company of women, his mother decided that DeMille, now a strapping fifteen-year-old, had to be sent away to school. She enrolled him in the Pennsylvania Military College. Beatrice thought that DeMille, though he could fight and ride, needed more preparation for manhood. DeMille was beginning to notice girls, and this may also have influenced his mother's decision. Among the charges in her keeping, DeMille recalled, "there was one girl in particular. How I remember her delicate grace, her wealth of lovely hair, her fair young face, her slender hands, her poetry of movement as she walked. I planned very carefully the proper setting for laying at her feet my smitten heart. It was to be at sunset. I hitched up mother's horse and buggy and slowly drove the precious object of my affection through the green bordered Jersey lanes to a spot where we could sit and watch the slow darkening of the gold-red western sky."

The sudden change in DeMille's circumstances was drastic. From an environment dominated by women, he was now packed off to live miles away with nothing but boys, all of whom were strangers. It would be three months before he would be allowed back home. The boy used to affection was thrown into a military environment devoid of feminine charm. DeMille was a survivor. Military school didn't ruin his life, but might have provoked his lifelong need to be surround by the comfort of women. It made it possible for him to divide himself between several women rather than just one.

To get to his new school meant a train to Newark, changing there for Philadelphia, and on to Chester. Because finances were tight, DeMille planned to make the ninety-mile trip by bicycle. The day before his departure, he learned that he wasn't going to make the journey alone; his mother planned to accompany him. With a few belongings strapped to his bike, and more on hers, mother and son set out at dawn, traveling through the New Jersey and Pennsylvania countryside, stopping in a field for the lunch she had prepared, taking joy in the sights and in each other's company. Before they reached the school, Beatrice got off her bike, dusted herself off, and transformed herself once again into a proper headmistress. It didn't do to let her son lose face before his new classmates before he'd even begun. Creating the right image isn't all vanity; it can be done out of love.

He never completed his four-year term, but the Pennsylvania Military College achieved the desired result. Though the physical training was rigorous and the discipline stern, the school's academic standards were high. DeMille enrolled in a course in the arts, at the successful completion of which he would have earned a bachelor of arts degree. He wasn't a natural joiner, but he made friends, charmed the daughters of his teachers, and came to accept the unvarying routine regulations. Cards and dice were forbidden. Drinking meant instant expulsion. It was all very strange, of course. Most of the other boys were used to the shouting and marching and the uniforms that had to be clean and perfect—cleanliness hadn't been one of DeMille's concerns growing up in the country surrounded by women who took care of such matters. Now, his obsession with detail and order, his need for control, his self-discipline, and keen interest in physical fitness, already begun under his father's strictures from Charles Kingsley, didn't make him a soldier but did encourage his natural flair for leadership. He would always be noted for his military style of direction, and it marked a further distinction between him and his Hollywood peers.

Letters to his adored aunt Bette, starting soon after he arrived at the College in September 1896, illustrate the last stage in the forming of his character.

> February 21, 1897: Now I have some very sad news to tell you on Friday I walked my first guard (and I hope my last) for dropping gun [at] drill, the gun slipped [sic] from my hand while we were at rest, and I made a grab for it, hit it on the lower band and knocked [it] so far out of line that it hit our royal first sergeant on the toe, hence an hours guard, the penalty. Really its two hours but being my first guard it was cut 50 per cent.

DeMille's high spirits hadn't been curbed. In his days, it was considered adventurous to climb into the dome and write one's name and cadet number. Carved into the wood with many others is Cecil, cadet #214. Even then, possessed of the excellent physique he was to maintain for life, DeMille was something of a dandy.

> January 27, 1898: You know that ring I wore while I was home, by some chance (I don't know why) I wore it to Chester with me, and it looked so plain with the stone out, that I have had a very pretty little Opal set in it. Do you think I was foolish? I did it with the money Grandma S. gave me. (Secret.)

Indeed, the college sharpened his natural high spirits and lust for adventure. In 1898, at the time that the Spanish-American War broke out, DeMille had the honor of a full-dress review by President McKinley on a visit to Philadelphia. There he stood with his fellow classmates, long gray lines of uniformed cadets, their boots and swords and buttons shining in the sun. The impressionable young blade, full of romantic notions, thrilled to the growing patriotism of the American nation. Later that day, DeMille walked through downtown Philadelphia with a friend, and he tasted the admiration that a uniform got him. He loved being acknowledged, and the way that young women stood aside to let him pass in the street, the way it made him feel like a man. It appealed to his sense of drama. Four months shy of seventeen, he was so carried away by the president's call for volunteers to liberate the

Cubans and avenge the *Maine* that he was down at the recruiting station in Chester bright and early. But his plan was discovered in time and brother William had to leave his studies at Columbia to head him off.

DeMille wouldn't have made a good recruit. He wasn't cut out to be one of many, unless he was their leader. He never graduated from military school, but he would take to drama school a head crammed full of precision, art, literature, religion, and a strong sense of honor and military discipline.

Later in his life, he was honored with a doctorate when he attended the school's 110th anniversary in May 1931. "You would think that a college like P.M.C. with its military training would be the last place in the world to train for the theater," he said in his acceptance speech. "But it is a fact that the training helped me a lot in the theatrical business. In the first place, the military end of it taught me to handle men. Take for instance my motion picture *The Ten Commandments*, where some ten thousand men were used. The position of director in this situation is like that of a general—he must know how to handle men, and without the fundamentals I learned at P.M.C., I would have been unable to successfully produce this picture."

Two months after he left the academy, and to make sure he wouldn't run off on any other foolhardy adventure, DeMille's mother helped him enroll at the American Academy of Dramatic Arts. He lived at Pamlico to save money, rising at dawn to catch the 7:15 commuter train to New York for daily classes, returning each evening except when he stayed overnight in William's rooms near Columbia.

It may never have crossed DeMille's mind that, being the second son, he automatically got the short end of the deal. With their mother's skimping and saving, there was enough money only to send William to live in New York and attend his father's alma mater, Columbia. DeMille's admission to the academy was possible only because his fees had been waived in memory of his father, who had not only named the academy but taught there for seven years without taking a salary. This situation placed DeMille and his brother in different relationships with their mother. Agnes says that because William wouldn't stand for his mother's interference and bossing, it eventually led to an increasing estrangement between them. "She quarreled with my father, and apparently it was about money. Father said she had grown up with the idea that every dollar bill had her name personally printed on it and not anybody else's. And it belonged to her. And that every dollar that the boys earned really was hers. And she let them keep it by sufferance. Now that was my father, and my father was stingy. Cecil wasn't. He took care of Beatrice out in California; he took all of her expenses."

Beatrice's letters to DeMille in Hollywood are full of querulous complaints about William. DeMille, who had brought her out to live in Hollywood, just laughed and tolerated her meddling. He was used to it in a way that William never learned to be. Although DeMille was odd man out during his father's lifetime, in the wake of Henry's death, and Williams's subsequent departure to study in Germany, DeMille became the center of his mother's attention. He soon developed the ego problem peculiar to boys brought up alone by their mothers: he became overly assertive and intolerant of masculine challenge. It was a trait noted by many of the men who were to work closely with him in future years.

Certainly for much of his first thirty-some years, DeMille was to be very much at his mother's beck and call, and for many of those early years depended upon her for work and professional advancement. Her conversion had changed nothing in her essential nature. Beatrice was in many ways the archetypal Jewish mother, protective, intrusive, and overbearing. And DeMille, whether consciously or not, owed his mother's rich Jewish heritage far more than he ever conceded. His weakness for the ornate stemmed from his intoxicating childhood memories. Like other strong personalities who made movies their career, he would convert those memories into arresting cinematic images.

But what had begun for Beatrice as a painful and audacious gesture born out of love became in time a reason for DeMille to reject her heritage, which might prove embarrassing for a man eager to pass himself off as a true blue American patrician. As an inevitable result of her conversion, Beatrice came to adopt, along with her husband's religion, its inherent prejudice against her own people. Raised in this milieu, her younger son automatically followed his mother's lead.

Near the end of his life, DeMille belatedly tried to acknowledge his dual heritage in his work by filming *The Ten Commandments*: in many ways that last thundering epic was an act of contrition, a hope that, like a modern Moses, he would leave a living legacy behind. Instead, like the pharaohs of Egypt, all that his exhausting labors left was a monumental, lifeless pyramid, an airless mausoleum. A great price to pay for having denied the Samuel in his soul.

When it came time to write the story of his life, he praised his mother's valor and accomplishments but he didn't have too much else to say about her. Almost certainly the minor feuding and sallies that took place between them, mostly regarding money and her idea of the role she was to play in his life, had somewhat soured that relationship as well. In contrast, it is clear that his father remained his hero to the end of his own life.

But there were many other traits that did carry over from his mother. DeMille inherited her conviction that love was stronger than all of man's restrictions. Like his Delilah in *The Ten Commandments*, Beatrice was a remarkable woman. When she wanted something, she went after it. It was a trait common in new immigrants to America, and this drive was one of the most valuable gifts she brought to her husband and passed to her sons.

Now DeMille was eighteen, traveling by train to New York, jumping blindly again into space, smiling, self-confident, with the same love of adventure and the same firm belief that, whatever the obstacles, he would overcome them—though a betting man might still have put his money on William.

He was nineteen when he performed in his class graduation play. In the audience was Charles Frohman. Along with three other of his classmates, DeMille was engaged for a small part. He made his official debut on February 21, in *Hearts are Trumps*.

With both her sons safely on their own, Bea decided to put her instinct for telling a hit from a flop to work. She closed the girls' school, sold the house, rented an office in New York, and went into business selling her husband's old plays as well as William's. Eventually she added other clients, like Clyde Fitch, Avery Hopwood, and Mary Roberts Rinehart. At last she could support herself in the business she loved, while continuing to keep an eye out for her sons.

CHAPTER FIVE

NEW YORK CITY WAS IN ITS HEYDAY. WEALTHY FROM SPECULATION IN RAIL-road, land, and the stock market, the nouveau had become the riche. Ten percent of the nation had all the money and spent it lavishly to show off their new status, while the other ninety percent toiled and lived in near-poverty. The term "conspicuous consumption" was coined to describe the extravagant lifestyles of these East Coast nabobs—whose extravagant lifestyle so impressed the young DeMille that he ended up recreating it in his films.

It was to this new world that DeMille came. He lived on forty-five cents a day, in a tiny two-dollar-a-week room which he shared with a fellow actor, where "the Sixth Avenue Elevated ran over the foot of our bed." There wasn't much left over, after money spent on food and travel, for courting.

When DeMille did find a girl (and his first "real" girlfriend would become his wife), the ultimate in Sunday treats was a round trip to Staten Island on the ferryboat, a nickel each. Ice cream sodas and boat charges were another nickel. But DeMille, who regularly walked a hundred city blocks to save a nickel, wouldn't have dated a girl if he couldn't have shown off a bit. Luckily, because of his family, theater tickets were free. And so sure was he of himself that, not twenty and quite probably still a virgin, he felt sufficiently confident to take on the responsibility of a wife. Whether his choice when he met her was governed by true love, ambition, or simply his physical needs, he doesn't say. But when DeMille met the right girl he proposed.

In the late fall of 1900, he was on the road in Washington with *Hearts Art Trumps* when a new actress joined the cast. Constance Adams, eight years older than her future husband, was the first of five children born to Judge Frederick Adams of East Orange, New Jersey. Tall and confident, she carried herself with the assurance that comes from being a judge's daughter, and her evident beauty was crowned with rich thick brown braids of hair becomingly swept up in the fashionable Gibson Girl style. Constance had gone on the "wicked" stage in defiance of her conservative family. DeMille recalled his first impressions of her: "I was playing the part of a young barrister, I was very bad. She had a smaller part. I'm not sure which of us was worse. But the quiet girl who had a tiny part in one scene appealed to me more than any of them. I did not appear in her 'big moment,' so every night I would pull on a big coat over my stage clothes, dash to the back of the auditiorium and watch the girl with the beautiful face. . . . Somehow, we never became friends until a rather strange incident brought us into closer touch with one another. I can truthfully say that a custard pie brought me a wife. One night, after spending a free afternoon in Newark, New Jersey, I made tracks for the Boston train. Just as I reached the station, an overwelming desire for custard pie came upon me. Contentedly, I turned around and surveyed the restaurant. There, beautifully alone, was the girl I had admired. . . .

"I asked her where she was staying in Boston. It was a very old boarding-house with lavender-colored window panes. At No. 9 Beacon Street. Lavender-colored window panes! That was a touch which appealed to me.

"'But where do you stay, Mr. DeMille?'

"'D'you know,' I replied, 'this is really a most amazing coincidence. I stay at 9 Beacon Street, too.' I determined to get a room in that boarding house by stealth. Next day I changed my address."

In type and temperament, Constance was a lot like DeMille's father, but, similar to his mother, she listened. Her amused but not ironical eyes worked on him like the torch of a lamplighter who touches into flame, one by one, a long row of gas jets. DeMille talked and talked. He talked of the theater, of his family and his dreams, of the passion absorbed from books, of his plans, and of the noble sacrifice of future years as yet unknown. If Constance entertained doubts about the difference in their ages, DeMille's self-possession made them seem unimportant. He remembered, "The old century was running out. We sat together on the steps of the brownstone lodging house with the lavender window panes. It was December 31, 1900. Completely oblivious to the cold, we were both excited about the New Year, because it meant a New Century as well. The bells and hooters began to sound over the still houses. The girl who stood with me at the window laughed. 'Where do you suppose we'll be at the beginning of the next century?' she asked.

"'I can't tell you the place,' I replied, 'but I know one thing—we'll be together.' [And so] we celebrated the beginning of a new year and a new century by becoming engaged."

Judge Adams wasn't about to hand his daughter over to this ambitious and youthful talker. He didn't want an actor, particularly an out-of-work actor, for a son-in-law. It took time for him to come around. By the end of 1901, DeMille finally gained Judge Adams's consent to the marriage and, almost two years after they met and four days after celebrating his twenty-first birthday, DeMille and Constance were married August 16, 1902, by an Episcopal minister, at the Adams home in East Orange, with William as best man. DeMille's mother was the only member of the Samuels family to be invited.

The newlyweds honeymoon had to be tucked into a tour booked by Charles Frohman and led by DeMille's father's distinguished old friend, actor E. H. Sothern. Its schedule would take the company halfway across America to California. Long before moving to Hollywood, this job brought the DeMilles to Los Angeles, where they were playing at the Mason Theater.

Their salaries were meager—DeMille earned $20 a week and Constance even less—and some nights DeMille left Constance alone while he went off to gamble. On one occasion, he was told that his wife thought she heard prowlers. He sent back a message to hold on and use their pug to protect her because he was in the middle of a win that would pay their rent. Married to such a cavalier, she certainly needed her sense of humor.

Those strenuous and poorly paid theatrical tours were nothing if not educational for a man with ambition. He later explained how he learned what he knew about directing crowds: "Travelling with E. H. Sothern was like going back to school, the best school a future director could attend. What I learned from him . . . can still be seen in any of my pictures, I think. . . . Sothern gave every single extra an appropriate, distinct, individual line to say. The audience could not hear the lines, but they saw and heard a crowd of real people talking and acting like real people."

Life on the road, twenty years after his parents had trudged it, hadn't changed much. Actors still provided their own costumes, were not paid for rehearsals, which were usually called after a late performance or on Sundays, and actors often found themselves broke and stranded in strange towns when a manager absconded with the receipts. Some of the DeMilles' adventures eventually found their way into his films. One spectacular train crash later filmed was rememebred after a one-night stand at Parkersburg, West Virginia. "Mrs. deMille was sitting in the chair beside me. . . . She had been admiring the wild flowers all along the banks. It was spring and the wild flowers were very beautiful. And while she was sitting there looking out the window . . . there was a little Jewish travelling man, who was just giving his mileage book to the conductor, and the conductor started to check the mileage off. There was a little old lady across the way, sitting who I don't think had ever been on a train before, sitting very primly and the train stopped. . . . And this thing came on us from the back—crash! An engine plowed right through the car, just crumpled it right up—right to where we were sitting. The conductor went head over heels down the aisle. And this man jumped up and said, 'Hey, come back with my mileage.' . . . And one of those three bottles of fire extinguishers . . . came down and hit me on top of the head and broke. This awful stuff came down. My first line was, 'I've got the damndest taste in my mouth. Mrs. deMille said, 'Oh, now we can pick some wild flowers.' The little woman who was sitting in front and had never been on a train apparently thought that was the way trains always stopped . . .

"I tried to . . . reproduce that wreck in the *The Road to Yesterday*. It came off fairly well. It wasn't quite as good as the original."

Together the young couple crossed the land, from Florida to Alaska. Because of all that touring, DeMille got to know his country and his future audience. He would boast that he could name "the other" hotel in every town in the United States. Constance would tell her sister-in-law of the problems they had with hotel clerks because of DeMille's pets. These included two little squirrels with loose bowels, which he kept in a basket cage and who went everywhere with them. When they were stranded without funds to get home, DeMille turned other means of employment. "Did you know that I dug more ditches than anyone else west of the Mississippi?" he asked his niece once.

The strain of travel also took its toll on their health. Once, when they were touring Canada in the winter, "we could not afford to stay in hotels with heated rooms. . . . our rooms were as icy as the street in Montreal where I froze an ear because I stood looking too long and too longingly at a fur collar in a show window."

With his mother's encouragment and with father and brother as successful examples, DeMille decided to try his hand as a playwright. He and his brother collaborated on *The Genius*, *The Royal Mounted*, and *After Five*. William was doing DeMille a great favor, though his self-confidence was not helped when William's failures were usually the plays they wrote together. William also helped out with loans.

Being close to people at the top stoked DeMille's hunger for fame, and also his impatience with excuses for failure. He abhorred alibis. "Maybe that stems in part from the explanations the theater managers on the road had for sparse attendance at some of our efforts. There was always a reason, which never had anything to do with bad acting on our part or bad showmanship on the manager's. . . . If it had only been some other night, if we had only come to town on Saturday instead of Wednesday, why, Madison Square Garden could have held the multitudes that would have been turned out to see us. In five towns out of six, we were told that Saturday night was the night we should have come. . . . I reminded one theater manager of that on a Saturday night when we played to a half-empty house. 'Well, you know, Mr. DeMille,' he said, 'on Saturday night everybody in this town goes to the barbershop to get shaved. That's why they weren't here.'"

DeMille wasn't a star, but he was good, and he was good-looking. In the first of a discreet series of articles written in the late twenties by one of his earliest leading ladies, she remembered him, "at almost 5'11", weighing in at 173 pounds, with an excellent physique exuding vitality, his head of thick dark wavy hair, his piercing blue eyes and soft voice, and a flawless diction, DeMille made a striking figure on a stage with a commanding if flamboyant presence." He must have loved this description since he was five foot eight— barely. Other than his premature baldness, which both he and William inherited from their father, DeMille might easily have had a long and successful career as a leading man. And though he gave up the stage, he certainly never ceased to be an "actor."

In the fall of 1907, David Belasco made a dramatic reappearance in De-Mille's family's life. He was rich and famous throughout the land, the first

American producer whose name alone attracted audiences, and by 1908, had even built his own theater. After having spent seventeen years guiding her to fame and fortune, Belasco had split up with the tempestuous Mrs. Leslie Carter, who slipped away to get married. Her stormy arrival in his life caused Belasco's break with the DeMille family, and her equally stormy departure heralded his return.

Belasco was preparing to produce William's semi-biographical Civil War play, *The Warrens of Virginia*, somewhat based on DeMille's grandfather's capture by the enemy during the Civil War, and there was a part for DeMille. Playing a small part was a fourteen-year-old Canadian actress named Gladys Smith, who had been on the stage since age five. Gladys asked DeMille what he thought of Mary as a name. He replied that Gladys by any other name would smell just as sweet. But Belasco approved of the change, and Mary it was. The Pickford surname she took from her Northern-Irish grandmother's maiden name.

For DeMille, this reunion with Belasco was "the beginning of one of the richest and most beneficial associations of my career. . . . What I learned from Belasco can be seen in any of my pictures." During weeks of unpaid rehearsals and the four weeks out of town, DeMille had the opportunity to watch his idol in action, to see, to study, to learn, and to never forget how the wizard of Broadway achieved his effects. Mary Pickford recalled one startling incident: "The set was a stately dining room of one of the old Virginia mansions, authentic in every detail, from the rugs and antiques down to the crystal and silver molasses container. Suddenly his voice boomed out: 'Hold everything!' Mr. Belasco climbed up on the stage and elaborately stalked the molasses jar. Everyone froze. Mr. Belasco adjusted his glasses and leafed through the manuscript in his hand. Then he reached for a spoon and tasted the contents of the molasses jar. In evident disgust he flung down the spoon, and with the roar of a lion called for the property man.

"'Taste that!' commanded Mr. Belasco.

"'What is it?' bellowed the maestro.

"'Maple syrup, sir.'

"'And if you please, what does the manuscript call for?'

"'Molasses, sir.'

"'And you dare waste my time and the time of the ladies and gentlemen of my company with maple syrup?'

"With that he dashed the jar into a thousand pieces on the floor, and began to jump up and down on the sticky mess, thereby driving it deeper and deeper into the beautiful Oriental rug. When at length his fury was spent, he orderd the property man to clean up the stage and gave one last shout: 'Never, never presume to take such liberties with me again!' Mr. Belasco suddenly made a sticky beeline for the box where I was seated. . . . looked at me with twinkling eyes and asked: "Betty, tell me, what did you think of my performance?"

"'This is a great secret between you and me,' he said in mock confidence. 'I find it absolutely necessary to break something at least once before an opening night in order to keep the cast on their toes.' . . . To me David Belasco was like the King of England, Julius Caesar, and Napoleon all rolled into one."

Belasco's infinite attention to detail was always directed toward the single objective, the success of the play. "Some thought of him as the greatest figure in the American theater, towering over two generations," DeMille reflected. "To others, he seemed almost a charlatan, an admittedly magical showman, but one who contributed next to nothing to dramatic art." DeMille's description of Belasco could well apply to himself.

Warrens opened in November 1907, and ran for almost a year before going on tour without DeMille, who didn't want to leave his pregnant wife on her own. But there was another reason for remaining behind. DeMille apparently learned more than stagecraft from his idol. A young, beautiful, and ambitious actress had entered his life.

Twenty years later, Mary Evelyn Martin wrote about it. It wasn't her real name. Her real name, Mary Doyle, only surfaced when she published her autobiography. When Mary met DeMille, he was his own advance man and press agent, in fact, the entire staff of Cecil B. DeMille Productions, Inc., and she was still Ruth Rogers, her stage name. Ruth Rogers: "When I was his leading lady—not merely one of his leading ladies, but all the leading lady he had—my salary was seventy-five dollars a week when I got it; and I didn't get it. When he wanted me to sign that seventy-five-dollar a week contract, he took me to dinner. The check was two dollars, and he borrowed that from me."

His charm must have been formidable because other lunches and dinners followed, presumably unknown to his wife. They'd pause on the sidewalk in front of the Plaza Hotel, with DeMille telling her that they too would soon be a part of the glistening row of silk-hatted men and jeweled, fur-wrapped women. As DeMille played Belasco to her Mrs. Carter, he poured his heart out to his youthful protegé. He told her of his early theatrical ambition and of the time when he had wanted to be an opera singer (he had made his professional singing debut with a short-lived summer opera company in St. Louis), and that he had thought his life was over when his voice gave out. Since his failure in operetta, he had played on Broadway in a long-running hit written by his brother. With such a well-known name, and dazzled by his friendship with the great Belasco, Mary was hardly likely to doubt the glowing future DeMille assured her would be hers. Meanwhile, as a further sign of his serious intent, and until he could put on his own play, he got Mary a few acting jobs. It wasn't his fault that these plays never amounted to much. Meanwhile, he kept looking for the money to put on the play he wrote with the great role for her which would make them both famous.

At last DeMille raised enough to finance an out-of-town production of *Baxter's Partner*, written the year his daughter was born, with money that came mostly from the actors in the company he put together (quite a bit of which, wrote Mary, was hers), "and in it was a wronged wife, and had a chance to suffer—oh, to suffer like anything! And Cecil himself explained to the awed and big-eyed young woman who was just aching not only to suffer but to dare all with and for him, how very poor he was, and how completely he had staked his all upon the sucucess of this play; and so it was that that seventy-five dollar a week contract was signed—at my expense."

Even Constance, the wronged wife, reading these genteel reminiscences, might naturally infer more than Mary could say that the relationshiip between Mary and DeMille had gone beyond that of the Model and the Genius.

After six years of marriage, though their financial prospects hadn't improved dramatically, the DeMilles decided to have a child. Constance was thirty-six, and her pregnancy proved difficult. Their only child, Cecilia, was born on October 5, 1908. "Grandfather helped deliver her [with a doctor] as he could not afford a hospital or nurse," wrote Cecilia's own daughter, Citzie. "Yes, Grandmother almost died. . . . I believe, because of it, she closed the bedroom door."

It can be inferred that from then on sexual relations virtually ceased between DeMille and Constance. He may have looked elsewhere although, except for Mary's pointed reminiscences, there is no proof of any infidelity on his part. But their granddaughter was convinced that even if he did play around: "C. B. was in *love* with Constance. She was *the* great love in his life. I know for a fact that after mother was born, he pleaded with her to be his wife, his confidante, his mistress, he did not want her to leave his bed—she did. . . . What was C. B. to do, young, virile, handsome—well you know the rest. But you can't understand events in history unless you understand the times in which they occurred. Back then, expecially in Europe, mistresses were not that uncommon, and it did not take away from the wife's standing in society [important to grandmother]. I always felt she viewed the other women with relief and felt very much above them. But C. B. and Constance never stopped loving each other. . . . Nobody has ever understood Constance's place in C. B.'s life—how important she was to him." Which may well have been true, but this would not have soothed the pain the first time Constance caught him with another woman.

Throughout the years, DeMille would come to test the bonds of Constance's love to near breaking. She developed a private philosophy to deal with his extramarital flings. Constance forged a marriage that made them pillars of society. Katherine, the second of her three adopted children, recalled her mother as the sort of woman for whom men would doff their hats, extinguish their cigars, and rise when she entered a room. Her niece and her granddaughter both spoke of her quiet but formidable sense of humor. Though she kept her private feelings to herself, women liked to confide in her. Combined with her unhurried speech, delicacy, and the other marks of good breeding, these were qualities reminiscent of the father DeMille had loved and lost.

Baxter's Partner closed out of town, and with it Mary's (Ruth Rogers) experience of working with DeMille. Broke but wiser, Mary got a job modeling and vanished from DeMille's life.

David Belasco, meanwhile, had hired DeMille to write a play adapted from a short story on the subject of reincarnation, a theme that fascinated DeMille. Titled *The Return of Peter Grimm*, it was his only successful play. DeMille's play propounded the comforting notion that life after death is merely a continuation of this earthly existence, with its unpleasant aspects removed. But Belasco took the author's credit for himself. "The program described it as a play by David Belasco," recalled DeMille. "There was a note in very fine print giving credit to Mr. C. B. DeMille for the idea. I was hurt when I read that. It was evident from the first night that *The Return of Peter Grimm* would be a greater success than any play I had been associated with up to then. It would have meant much to have joint authors' credit." Such a state of affairs was certainly not unknown in the theatrical world, or later in Hollywood, in which the last writer to work on a script in production was often the first name to appear on the film's credit. Belasco didn't do anything that hadn't been done before. It was just that DeMille wished his idol hadn't done it to him.

DeMille may have tried not to sound bitter, but while the play was still out of town, he gave an interview. Belasco, who read it, demanded retraction of a statement crediting the young DeMille as "part-author." DeMille, prodded by his mother, who had never forgotten what Belasco had done to her husband, threatened to sue, but the case never went to court. Ultimately, the authorship of *The Return of Peter Grimm* remained with Belasco, in the playbill, in the books, and in the public's mind.

More important to DeMille in the long run were the things he absorbed watching Belasco at work, from his style to his ornate cathedral-like office (which DeMille would recreate in Hollywood) to the way he handled actors, and especially his showmanship, which made his name a household word and his plays a sell-out. *The Return of Peter Grimm* notwithstanding, nothing could mar DeMille's admiration of the man or make him deny what Belasco meant to his career in films.

His mother's business was thriving and she needed an office manager. By 1910, Mrs. H. C. deMille, author's representative, had become the deMille Play Company, with offices in the Astor Theater Building in the heart of New York's theatrical land. DeMille was hired to keep her books straight. It was while working for his mother that fate introduced him to the man who would become his best friend, and the collaborator with whom he would make his fortune.

CHAPTER SIX

DEMILLE: "GOLDWYN WAS A GLOVER. LASKY WAS A DISAPPOINTED GOLD-seeker from Alaska, who became a musician when he returned south. Carl Laemmle was an assistant in a clothing store. Adolph Zukor was a furrier. And B. P. Schulberg was a reporter. But I was brought up to regard the entertainment of the public as a family profession."

Jesse Lasky was a California boy who had been a newspaper reporter in San Francisco, followed the Gold Rush to Alaska, and played the cornet, a childhood passion, from Alaska to Hawaii, where he became the first white man in the Royal Hawaiian Band. He later teamed up with his cornet-playing sister as *The Musical Laskys*, a popular if small-time vaudeville act. Realizing that performing would not make his fortune, Lasky started to promote other acts, staging and dressing them with a flair that made audiences and theater circuits take notice.

By 1911, some success led Lasky to stake his future on a big idea. At great expense he brought the celebrated Follies *Bergère* to New York. But his timing was off. The troupe arrived in a summer heatwave and the theater had no air-conditioning—not a problem for the naked ladies of the Follies—but audiences melted away along with Lasky's savings. He was famous, but broke.

Lasky saw the prospect for one-act comic operas. He came up with the story of a girl found by Indians who is raised by a priest, falls in love with a railroad surveyor, and discovers that her mission stands in the way of progress. Jesse's title was *California*. But he was a producer not a writer. "I went to Mrs. H. C. deMille, a play broker of high repute in the Hudson Theater building, where I had recently had my own offices." He wanted William, who had previously written a one-act play for him back in 1909. William, Mrs. deMille told Mr. Lasky, was unavailable, but she had another son up her sleeve: "Cecil has a better comedy touch." Jesse wasn't too sure: when they had passed in the corridor, "Cecil . . . looked at me in a way that made me uncomfortable or ignored me in a way that made me more uncomfortable. The chilly feeling was mutual, and we passed each other without speaking for a year."

Nonetheless, Mrs. deMille insisted he tell her son about his idea for the operetta. "When I finished, he leaned forward and exclaimed, 'Say, I like that!' The minute he said, 'I like that,' I liked him. And I've never stopped."

It was the beginning of a lifelong friendship, and for DeMille, aside for romantic entanglements, his most significant surviving even the strains of working in business together. Lasky always appreciated DeMille, and his understanding of his friend so well enabled him to overlook those traits others found unbearable. DeMille's tremendous ego never posed a threat to Lasky, and his enthusiasm and charm always delighted Lasky and spurred him along.

They were a good balance for each other's strengths and weaknesses. DeMille was impetuous, Lasky considered. Lasky was nervous, filled with last-minute doubts and hesitations, and lacked the hard edge that sustains great success. DeMille made up for Lasky's failings. On the other hand, Lasky was a man of innate taste and culture, and of humor. Moreover, both shared a passion for hard work and the big outdoors. DeMille recalled, "I think that part of Jesse's genius for friendship lay in his spirit of adventure. I always found that one of his most appealing traits. . . . We had sort of watchword that we applied to everything from the plot to our next operetta to a swim in the cold waters of some lake in Maine: Jesse or I would propose something by saying, 'Let's do thus and so,' and the other would instantly respond, 'Let's.'"

Their first collaboration was the prophetically titled *California* (1912) co-authored and directed by DeMille. The production was an early example of DeMille's indebtedness to his Belasco training. Instead of a jar of molasses, "we had on the stage a real orange tree, from which the characters picked oranges and peeled and ate them—an expensive piece of business for the two-a-day!" DeMille asked for one hundred dollars upfront and $25 a week royalty, and the partnership began.

California was a success, and other shows followed. Some, like *In the Barracks*, had big names in the lead, like the dashing Fritz Sturmfels, but it wasn't all smooth sailing. Vaudeville theaters had begun showing movies, usually as a way to clear the house between performances. DeMille claimed never to have seen a film until Jesse came up with the idea of going into that fledgling business. After two years writing vaudeville skits and one-act operettas they had not made enough money or achieved sufficient recognition to satisfy DeMille. Even the composer received more money than he did.

DeMille once again found himself at a crossroads. For a moment he contemplated joining in the Mexican revolution supporting the "just cause" of the long-suffering peasants under Pancho Villa and Emilio Zapata fighting to cleanse their land of feudal injustice. Forty years later, DeMille would invest more than a year of his time and almost half a million dollars in pre-production work on a film on the subject. But, in 1913, what kept DeMille from actually joining the revolution was Lasky, who, not wishing to lose his friend, came up with an exciting get-rich-quick scheme that would keep him at home.

The initial idea had been brought to Lasky by his brother-in-law Sam Goldwyn, a successful glove salesman from Warsaw, whose ambition had enabled him to overcome anything and anyone who stood in the way of getting to the top. Goldwyn had met Blanche, Lasky's adored sister, through Lasky's wife, Bessie, who was looking for ways to get her sister-in-law out of the house so she could start her own family. In 1910, Goldwyn married her despite her brother's misgivings. "It wasn't much of a love match," according to her nephew, Bill Lasky. "Sam married my aunt because he wanted to get into show business, and he figured the best way he could do that was through my father."

But Bessie hadn't reckoned on Lasky's overwhelming filial concern for his sister, and instead of losing a sister-in-law, she found she had gained Goldwyn, who moved in with them. Despite a daughter, their only child together, the marriage didn't survive.

One of his wife's friends was Arthur S. Friend, a young New York lawyer with a prophetic sense of the future of pictures, who got Goldwyn interested. He had previously approached Lasky because of his distinguished position in the world of theater—as Friend saw it, a man who understood the mind of the vaudeville audience would understand the mind of the future film audience. But Jesse's disastrous losses with his Follies *Bergère* had made him cautious. The following year, however, with the Democrats in power and business bad for gloves, Goldwyn was in the mood for new ideas. Unlike DeMille, he had been to the movies, and seen the crowds flocking to the two-reel Westerns like *Bronco Billy*. Naturally he needed an experienced front man, and having one in the rooms next to his, he turned to his brother-in-law. Finally, Lasky capitulated, and agreed to lend his name to the movie venture on condition, in writing, that he shouldn't be bothered further on the subject. Then he learned that his writing partner was planning to go to Mexico. To keep his brother-in-law quiet, Lasky had gotten involved in a new venture. Now, to keep his best friend from leaving town, he talked him into joining it.

"I laughed out loud," DeMille recalled. "After a few moments, Lasky began to grin, too. At that time the idea of sinking money in films was considered about as sane as the financing of a perpetual motion machine." But then DeMille put out his hand, grabbed Lasky's, and said, "Let's!"

CHAPTER SEVEN

WITH *THE SQUAW MAN* FINISHED, DEMILLE BEGAN HIS FIRST SOLO EFFORT, *The Virginian*.

From the moment the book was published in 1902, Owen Wister's quiet-spoken and courteous young Southern cowpuncher known by all as the Virginian (though the story is set in Wyoming) caught the imagination of boys everywhere. Set in the contemporary west, Wister's novel's popularity coincided with America's change from a rural to increasingly industrialized society. Moreover, the story appealed to the many European immigrants who had left hopelessness for new opportunities. A year after the publication of *The Virginian*, nickelodeon audiences thrilled to *The Great Train Robbery* (1903), the first movie to tell a story, one of hold-ups and casual violence.

As recently as the first decade of this century, folks on the range didn't have to go to the movies to see a "Western" hold-up. A decade later, when films were made in barns, the last great cattle drives were being photographed for posterity. Cowboys went into pictures straight from ranges, exchanging rough nights in the open for $5 a day as extras in pictures pretending to be themselves. American filmmakers created new myths out of the men who shot it out over cards and women. From Europe to Asia, audiences enjoyed action-packed American Westerns. Amidst vast, rough but romantic landscapes, men and women struggled heroically to carve out a share in the land and to adhere to a moral code as clear as the warning shadow cast by a rustler swinging from a branch of the hanging tree.

By 1914, there was hardly a soul in America who hadn't read *The Virginian* or seen one of the constantly touring stage versions. The story was so familiar that the silent film almost didn't require narration: everyone would have understood the cheerful Dustin Farnum loud and clear when he eyed his foe, nailed him with his glance, and dared him to do his worst.

Begun two months after completing *The Squaw Man*, *The Virginian* was directed by DeMille without Apfel to guide him. Its success heralded the birth of an important filmmaker. DeMille's flair for the medium, which soon would bring his name to a level equal to that of Griffith, is apparent.

DeMille's comedy scenes, arising out of the action, proceed at a spanking pace, while the intimate moments have charm, qualities not normally associated with his late work. Instinctively he seemed to know how to insert bits of business that might have been lost or left out of a stage production. For example, when the Virginian is attracted to the young teacher and knowing no other way to get to know her, he becomes a student in her class. With Farnum (a bit mature for the role) as the only other adult in a one-room school full of children, DeMille could easily have turned this scene into Sennett-style slapstick. But something else was needed. Ordered to stand by the blackboard for misbehaving, the Virginian uses the opportunity provided by chalk and board to write, "I love you," while the teacher's back is turned.

Conventions of the genre established in *The Virginian* would influence Westerns in years to come. The Virginian must choose between Molly, who has fallen in love with him but who won't marry a man with blood on his hands, and the time-honored code of the West, which dictates that he must kill his pal. Almost forty years later, this same dilemma confronted the sheriff in *High Noon*.

With *The Virginian*, DeMille began one of his key creative collaborations with cinematographer Alvin Wyckoff, with whom he worked for nearly a decade. DeMille would sum up the importance the cameraman played in a lecture he gave in the 1920s: "Once the scenario is written the cameraman becomes the director's interpreter . . . The director composes and draws the picture, but it is the cameraman who paints the drawing. . . . Matters of lighting come largely under the jurisdiction of the cameraman. . . . Your cameraman paints broad strokes with 'sun arcs' of over a million candlepower; delicate effects are sketched in by incandescent lamps; the direction of every light is arranged so that an effect very nearly stereoscopic is achieved. In handling large sets and masses of people the director does his grouping in connection with the scheme of lighting, working his people through planes of brightness and of shadow until the effect of a great painting is attained."

Smart directors, once they found such a collaborator, tended to stick close, as in celebrated partnerships such as Frank Capra and Joseph Walker, Eric Rohmer and Nestor Almendros, or Ingmar Bergman and Sven Nykvist. DeMille had found such a man in Wyckoff, and they must have gotten on well because they worked together on forty-four films. DeMille wanted ideas, and Wyckoff usually came up with them. On their first film, he introduced coated lenses that enabled shooting directly into the sun without showing reflections. And he developed a special technique that seemed to depict a darkened room lit only by a single match.

Dramatic lighting effects quickly became popular features of a DeMille movie. Audiences applauded these special effects. When DeMille would get an idea for a freeze frame or a soft fade, or the subtle drama created by shadows flickering over a woman's face, Wyckoff found a way to realize it photographically. In those early years, Wyckoff was as important to DeMille as Billy Bitzer was to D. W. Griffith.

In the most famous scene in the book, the drama turns to tragedy as the Virginian, sworn to uphold law and order, discovers that his pal Steve is one of the band of cattle rustlers and that the rope awaits him. All the Virginian can do is to keep his friend company until dawn.

DeMille shot the scene simply, overlaying the young man's sad vigil with scenes from happier times. Instead of long subtitles, which would have been difficult to read, for the lynching DeMille showed only the rope being placed around the outlaws' neck, their horses being whipped out from under them, and then a cut to swinging shadows on the morning ground. In a subsequent scene, two children are shown playacting this dramatic moment. Such innovations were a huge artistic advance over earlier Westerns.

Reviews singled out these two scenes for their technical and artistic innovation. Although the technology of the time dictated that the night be shot in daylight, DeMille created a moonlight effect by washing the film stock with a blue stain. He later repeated this for a more romantic effect at the climax of the film. Beneath another moonlit sky, Molly and the Virginian kissed by the hand-tinted glow of a campfire.

The Virginian had cost $17,022.08, but it returned almost seven times that amount. It was not released until five months after its completion.

That summer a new company had been formed to provide programs to cinemas showing films produced by independents producers. The brainchild of W. W. Hodkinson, who had spearheaded the expansion of the Edison Trust to the West Coast, it covered all forty-eight states. No longer would men like Goldwyn have to sell their films to exhibitors state-by-state, territory-by-territory, and cinema-by-cinema. Hodkinson named his company Paramount Pictures. He had passed the Paramount apartments on his way to a meeting, and the image of a snow-capped mountain top was born out of a doodle he made on a blotter. By summer, this swaggering concern had contracted to distribute 104 pictures a year. Adolph Zukor's Famous Players was responsible for fifty-two. Lasky contributed thirty. While negotiations ensued, the Lasky group thought it best to delay the release of *The Virginian* in order to benefit from the larger market. The effect on the Lasky Company's fortunes was that after a mere six months the goal of "one picture a month" had to be tripled. This put a great deal of pressure on the filmmakers.

Brewster's Millions was released one month after *The Squaw Man*. As their second big film, its success was critical. It is the story of a man's frantic efforts to spend $100,000 in a month in order to inherit a million dollars. No matter how hard he tries to unload the money, he could only make more. When Adolph Zukor saw the movie, he congratulated the partners. Before the year was out, the Lasky Company merged with Zukor's Famous Players. By the end of World War I, Famous Players-Lasky had become the world's leading producer and distributor of movies.

DeMille was one of the few directors to act in partnership with his producers. In the first few years, he not only wrote the scenarios for his films he directed but, with the assistance of Lasky, oversaw all day-to-day activities, from okaying budgets to casting. He was responsible for finding costume designers, seamstresses, fashion costumes, set designers and carpenters, cameramen, and reliable printers and processors. There was a growing need for electricians and grips. DeMille took a hand in everything to do with running the rapidly expanding studio, including hiring and firing the people who cleaned the barn. Six months after he first arrived in California, he was lucky if he managed to catch five hours of sleep a night. Out of necessity, he slipped into wearing the outfit that would become his trademark: sporty broad-beamed caps, worn back to front when working, leather puttees neatly wrapped around his legs, riding breeches, and, detesting neckties and collars, open-neck flannel shirts. Given the nature of the terrain in the San Fernando Valley, all sagebrush and sand, scorpions, centipedes, and rattlers, this outfit functioned as a suit of armor. Anything else would have been shredded from the waist down. Long after, even inside the comfort and safety of a studio, DeMille continued to wear variations on this uniform with all the gravity and flamboyance of the actor he once was. It had become a matter of pride.

While DeMille was hard at work making films, Sam Goldwyn was studying the cost sheets and constantly harassing him to find the best possible people at the lowest possible prices and to bring in films ever quicker. Friction was everywhere. One of Goldwyn's biographers, Groucho Marx's son Arthur Marx, tells of the time Arthur Friend had asked Goldwyn why he fought all the time, *even* with the people who agreed with him. Goldwyn confessed, "I have to keep in practice." It was almost in to be out with Goldwyn. Early casualties included his wife Blanche, his brother-in-law Lasky, his business partner Adolph Zukor, their star Mary Pickford, producer Edgar Selwyn, and lawyer Arthur Friend. One typically silly dispute was over an ad that mysteriously appeared in the *Motion Picture World* for *Brewster's Millions*—with no mention of Goldwyn, then still using his earlier name, Goldfish. Weeks later a second ad appeared, proclaiming, in bolder and larger type than the rest,

Samuel Goldfish
Head of Jesse L. Lasky Feature Picture Company.

When an irate Lasky confronted him, Goldwyn, in all innocence, told him, "I don't know who wrote it, Jesse, but it's true. I am the head of the company. I have it in writing that you are to keep your hands out."

Still, Lasky was good at his job. As the financial brains of the Lasky Company, he built their fortunes, found investors and new markets and increased outlets, often for films only just announced. By the end of May, only six months after they had struggled to raise $15,000, their capital stock had increased to half a million dollars.

On June 6, DeMille began production on *The Call of the North*, having signed for the rights to Stewart Edward White's enormously popular play. This saga of the frozen north came to be regarded by some as one of America's greatest films. Ultimately *The Call of the North* cost $16,540.52, and, though still sold state-by-state, made $52,284.48.

So keen was the Lasky Company to get the rights that White was able to negotiate an extraordinary deal. Among other things it specified that the supporting players "must be as near the robust type inhabiting the Canadian north-west as it is possible to procure; that Lasky agree to send the entire company to Moose Factory, Canada, during the severest part of the Canadian winter for reasons of authenticity; that in the event of the weather not being severe enough at Moose Factory, Mr. White would be able to select a location as far as Meridian Fifty North; and that the real Tiger Tribe Indians appear."

Little of this proved practicable. Eighteen actual Tiger Tribe Indians were engaged and, after special permission from the Canadian government, came to Los Angeles, and canoes were borrowed from a museum in Montreal. But the film could not be shot in Canada, and certainly not in the dead of winter. With the release of *The Virginian* delayed, Lasky needed a big attraction quickly, and it was far quicker and cheaper to shoot above Big Bear Lake, California. Despite his contractual commitment to the author, DeMille had strict instructions to shoot the film in high summer.

A flotilla of trucks followed the unit crammed with salt, which was to serve as a substitute for snow. Instead of raging blizzards, the film was shot in ferocious 100-degree temperatures. DeMille asked White, who had come along to do some fishing and was listed as technical advisor, if he wouldn't like to sacrifice authenticity for comfort by taking off some of his heavy clothes. The manly White declined. Appearing as an extra rowing a canoe, the makeup ran down his face under the hot sun. DeMille remembered that "he suffered grimly for his pains."

The Call of the North marked the start of DeMille's close friendship with old-time actor Theodore Roberts, who played the feudal head of the isolated trading post. Already in his early fifties, Roberts would become a regular character actor for Paramount and for DeMille, playing bankers, aging roués, Wall Street swindlers, and Moses.

The production of *The Call of the North* was a testing experience for all, as the cast and crew canoed across Big Bear Lake, shoved through thick forests, and climbed rocky mountain slopes. The snow, whether real or salt, tested the patience as well as the resources of cameraman, Alvin Wyckoff. On the lake, he shot low to include as much water as possible. The clear western sky was fiercely stark, beautiful, and chilling.

The action scenes were problematic, too. Pitched hand-to-hand combat was usually shot from a distance because of the impossibility of getting the actors, director, and cinematographer on the same small hilltop together. A blow on the chin seen from a long way off might be real to the actor who received it, but not as apparent to the audience. Still, the fact that it was a real blow gave DeMille's film the sort of punch he cherished.

Conveying the passage of time also proved a challenge, and was often indicated only by the opening of a door into one room and the closing of another. "Later" was continuously flashed on the screen to convey a few hours, days, weeks, or years. The longer transitions were sometimes indicated by beards on formerly clean-shaven men.

In retrospect, DeMille might be forgiven these hiccups in the narrative flow since White's novel was a bald-faced transposition of Shakespeare's *Othello* to the French–Canadian wilderness, with the insertion of Indian lore and a boy's guide to camping. (White's insistence on the film observing the strictest accuracy was a tendency often observed among writers who took their best ideas from other people's works.)

In the film, Galen Albert (Theodore Roberts), the Factor, finds Elodie (Winifred Kingston), his Desdemona, entering his life when she and her father find him near death in the woods and nurse him back to health. The infatuated Elodie steals away with him while her father, who is opposed to the match, is asleep. Here, as so often, the noisy flight that wakes no one is made possible because of that particular kind of deafness common only to characters in silent films. DeMille would learn to avoid this, but either Galen or Elodie were too callous to care or the continuity girl wasn't doing her job, for they also run off into the cold leaving the door wide open.

A man called Rand (Horace B. Carpenter) is the Iago, one of Elodie's rejected suitors, and instead of Shakespeare's "handkerchief," we get an innocent note Elodie had written to her father signed, "with my dearest love," which Rand keeps instead of delivering and leaves where the Factor can find it, leaving him maddened with jealousy.

The Call of the North packs a great deal of plot into 4,786 feet of film, which left little room for subtlety or inventiveness to relieve the eye. DeMille needed a writer to help him shape stories like this one to the screen, and meanwhile did what White had done: disguised the weaknesses in the plot with a lot of peripheral accuracy. "I will challenge anyone to find an incorrect detail," he wrote Goldwyn: "The only point in this picture which I believe might be opened to criticism is, that the piece of plug tobacco used in the second reel is wrapped in a piece of paper, and paper was a rare article on Dog River; but Steward Edward White . . . informs me that it is not at all impossible or improbable that some special treasure might have reached Dog River wrapped in a piece of paper." His precaution had been right. The *Variety* critic praised the film for its unusual degree of realism. "White's New York publisher saw the film at the Strand Theater, the biggest place in New York, which was full at an afternoon performance. There must have been 1500 people in the building, and it was hotter than the hinges. . . . There was one place where the girl comes to the door and her figure is outlined in the light, which brought down the house with spontaneous applause."

Movies were still in such a primitive stage that pleasure was to be found in little things!

Meanwhile, two other films had been completed and released. The studio was now averaging a film per month. In the first, another Western, *Where the Trail Divides*, in a scene of a white woman slung over the back of an Indian's pony, DeMille added the painterly enhancement of her long, loose hair trailing down the rump of the horse, a sort of equestrian Lady of Shalott. Such was the difficulty of finding a woman with enough hair willing to be slumped across a horse that he persuaded Constance to make one of her rare film appearances.

The other film was *The Man on the Box*, a movie about making movies, sometimes erroneously credited to DeMille, Apfel, and Buckland. DeMille and Apfel acted in it, since it was a story revolving around the two directors at work that could be pieced together in a few days.

Meanwhile, Constance was busy as well as a senior partner in his business with a role of increasing importance. Most of the companies DeMille formed carried her signature. Constance, like one of Henry James's liberated prototypes and perhaps also because of her theatrical background, behaved in many ways much like a European wife. She was ready to overlook her husband's extramarital adventures provided that he didn't threaten her position as wife and mother, and in return expected to be involved in his business affairs. (She wasn't so European as to have her own affairs on the side; for that she was too much the American.) In a 1925 affidavit, when DeMille's taxes were being given close scrutiny by the Internal Revenue Service, his lawyer referred to Constance as, "a very capable executive [who has] . . . A very thorough and up-to-date knowledge of the motion picture business . . . I consider her counsel and advice as valuable as that of anyone in the business, not alone because of her knowledge of the business, but because of her *ability* to think clearly—She has always advised with and consulted in every step taken by Mr. DeMille and in every step taken by the companies."

For *What's His Name*, finished in ten days, DeMille cast his daughter (no budding Shirley Temple) as the little girl who reunites her parents at her sickbed. The scenario had been adapted from the novel by George Barr Mc-Cucheon. He repeated the device employed in *The Call of the North* of having his cast step out from life-sized photographs of themselves. Starting with this film, DeMille is credited on screen with his last name beginning with a capital "D."

DeMille did a lot with this ridiculous story of a pretty girl married to a like-able soda-jerk who jumps at the chance of a week's work in a touring musical, then meets a millionaire in New York, and becomes a star. The backstage scenes are wonderful: small dressing rooms crowded with bloomer-clad girls; sets being shifted; people knocking into each other; the dance director drilling the girls in their routines; and the number performed before a packed house, and in the approaching Christmas mood, American audiences, blissfully out of touch with the gathering world crisis, still believed that a small child and a kiss were worth more than fame and a million dollars in the bank.

Cecilia did all that her father required of her except to show a flair for acting. At one point, he stopped the action to try to get her to stop looking into the camera. That evening, she asked her mother why her daddy was so different when he wasn't at home. As Cecilia grew up, she made it clear that the DeMille family's theatrical tradition was not going to be perpetuated by his own kith.

There was now a growing family to support, for that September, shortly before DeMille started on *The Rose of the Rancho*, Constance had adopted a boy named John. He was from a Los Angeles orphanage and the son of a man called Ralph Gonzales. Even with his early successes, DeMille's expenses still exceeded his income. After *The Squaw Man* was released DeMille, Lasky and Goldwyn had always paid themselves equally—at first $250 a week, then $500, and later $1,000. The Lasky office in New York dealt with DeMille's bills by deducting money owed the company directly out of his salary. Now, with *What's His Name* completed, DeMille decided to take charge of his own finances.

Lasky to DeMille (August 11, 1914): "I have just taken up the matter of your retaining your full salary and although for the time being, we will have our hands full in financing the business at this end, principally on account of no income from Europe, and payments being slow in the summer months, our folks were quite willing to grant your request. You will therefore draw $200 commencing this week, ending Saturday, Aug. 15th. We will continue to pay Mrs. H. C. $50 per week which will be charged to your present account. It seems that some of your creditors are beginning to bother Mr. Friend, so I wish you would let us know if, after three or four weeks, you could not allow us, say $30 per week, out of the $200 which you will be drawing as Mr. Friend thinks he probably can make some arrangement to pay them small sums until the debts are settled."

"Mrs. H. C" was his mother. DeMille's other creditors were lawyers, playwrights, furniture storage proprietors, etc. The "no income from Europe," to which Lasky referred, was due to the European conflict begun six weeks earlier. Lasky was expressing a far-sighted fear. The sale of their pictures abroad was not yet a major source of Hollywood's income. "Europe really had the jump on us," Jesse would recall. "These countries might have seized a far greater portion of the world trade, had not the war stopped their movie activities just when they were getting well under way. . . . By the end of the war we were so far ahead technically and had such a grip on foreign audiences that our gross revenues put us in an impregnable, commanding position."

DeMille had his raise by the time he began filming *The Man from Home* in August, based on the play by Booth Tarkington and Harry L. Wilson. To keep up the schedule, he completed it in eleven days.

The story of naïve American heirs and heiresses bamboozled by cynical Europeans was a story popularized by writers such as Henry James and effectively satirized after the war by directors such as Erich von Stroheim in films like *Blind Husbands*. It was a topic to which DeMille would return the next year with romantic "Ruritanian" stories, including *The Captive*. The story's locations ranged from Siberia to Sorrento, and scenery to match was all to be found in California. DeMille shot the Riviera scenes on lavish estates belonging to the welcoming members of San Francisco society. The view of the Mediterranean was matched from the top of the cliffs overlooking the stunning Carmel coastline. With DeMille in the lead, thousands of filmmakers churned out ersatz views of the world shot entirely in California: the little wooden bridges spanning the canals in Venice, California, were used for scenes set in Japan; the Pacific Palisades passed for every wonderful view from the Bay of Nagasaki to the Bay of Naples. The competition among directors for picturesque bits of scenery made the cruising automobile a prime necessity. By 1916, Los Angeles had more private cars per capita than any other city in the United States.

One reviewer thought *The Man from Home* the best he had seen from the Lasky Company. "It is a veritable triumph of screen dramatization," wrote the *Moving Picture World*. "As a medium of dramatic expression, the film has no metes and bounds." Everyone was entranced by the same thing. This movie, instead of talking its way through titles, moved through pictures. DeMille's next film would launch the company's prestigious Belasco acquisitions with *Rose of the Rancho*, one of the popular hits of the day. After that, it seemed nothing could stop him. No longer would DeMille have to rely on the public's enthusiastic willingness to overlook his plots; they became intricate and astonishingly subtle and mature. Along with increasing proficiency came increased self-confidence. A dozen times during the course of a scene, DeMille would stop the camera and illustrate what he wanted by acting the part himself. He was all over the place, missing nothing, and seemed to draw the work out of his cast by the sheer force of his personality.

After the day's filming, he worked into the night going over the processed film. There would be no more problems with sprocket holes. With Lasky, Wyckoff, and one of his exhausted secretaries, he would sit in the darkened corner of the barn where the film made its first appearance on a screen. As soon as a scene was in the can, it was sent to the developing room. And when the negative was dry enough, it was up on the screen and scrutinized for defects. So many things could have gone wrong between camera and darkroom—maybe the actors were out of focus, or Wyckoff had got it wrong. But more often the condition of the film itself presented a reason for rejecting it. There might be pinholes or tiny electric flashes generated inside the camera, known and cursed under the name of "static." Blisters often appeared on the emulsion side, and there were those queer perpendicular scratches called rainstorms. All of these were a constant worry since a damaged negative could mean costly reshoots. Having checked for technical errors, DeMille proceeded to edit the film. Having finished the day's editing, he might work on future scenarios. He slept when he dropped, but was ready to roar at the crack of dawn. Before DeMille had others to do this part of his work he was out location hunting, rising with the dew still wet and the sand still cold. He celebrated his thirty-third birthday on the set of *The Man from Home*.

That first full year, Apfel and DeMille both turned out six more features. In December, he began work on his eighth, *The Warrens of Virginia*. Seven successful releases, at least six of which were subsequently remade, some as many as three or four times, was a remarkable achievement for the first year's work of a man who had never made a film before.

The partners of the Lasky Company had guessed right instituting a policy of producing longer features and setting higher standards. Distributors were clamoring for more. But even with films being shot in two weeks, demand was outstripping the supply. And even after Lasky teamed with Zukor, those first two years were a constant race to keep ahead. Much of the other studios' quality may have been inferior, but the public was hungry and uncritical. The failure to supply enough films would be the eventual downfall of Bosworth and other small companies. From his New York office in the Longacre Theatre overlooking West Forty-eighth Street, Goldwyn kept an eagle eye on the competition. With the zeal of a convert, he watched the rapid strides of a business barely out of its infancy. And all the time he kept after DeMille to produce more, for less, and quicker.

Yes, there were growing pains. But it was rewarding for DeMille to find that the films he made quadrupled their investment, and more even if the success of their policy meant that Vitagraph, Biograph, Bison, Edison, Seligh, Lubin, and Universal were also going to have to keep up with them. With so much competition, prices began to skyrocket. Lasky was on a constant lookout for big properties, with name writers to adapt them. They had access to the stories Mrs. deMille controlled, but they also needed properties with a pre-sold market value. Now he was about to achieve a coup, a deal with Belasco for, "a block of ten choice plays for $100,000 against 50 percent of the film profits. This was one of the first percentage deals in the business. We were naïvely assuming that any play would make a good movie. . . . Nine of them made very successful pictures. . . .

"Cecil naturally had first call on the plays we bought and the stars we signed. He picked the juiciest plums from the Belasco buy for himself, and unwittingly got hold of the one lemon in the lot. *The Darling of the Gods* had starred Blanche Bates and brought acclaim to George Arlisss. Dealing with the conflict between the new and old regimes in the Japanese feudal period, it was a masterpiece on the stage.

"Anticipating that we would make a movie to eclipse anything seen before, Cecil imported shipments of Japanese costumes, samurai swords, and art treasures from Japan. Then we began to realize that nineteenth-century Japanese customs were too unfamiliar and the story too complicated to be understandable on the silent screen, and there were insurmountable make-up problems. . . . So we never filmed the best play of all, and the huge stock of Japanese relics and curios was a memorial to a lost cause. For years afterwards Cecil's office looked like a Shinto shrine."

Even with the Belasco plays, which others had also been chasing, and four of which were directed by DeMille in 1914, they needed more material. With superhuman effort, they had turned out twenty-one films that first year, and were committed to another thirty for the second.

To all who knew him at this time, DeMille was a man transformed. These were the times of learning how to make movies and figuring out what the public wanted to see. In the beginning a creative director only had his own personality to go on. To paraphrase Ralph Richardson on his own craft, "to be a great director one has to build on all the qualities that make one stand out, no matter what these might be, for these are your true self." To some, such as historian Kevin Brownlow, this meant that to keep pace with himself DeMille would have to exaggerate more and more. But what he lost in detail he made up in scale.

Working on locations, which required great physical strength, stamina, and ingenuity because of the unpredictable conditions, freed DeMille from his theatrical restraints. Unlike later generations of directors who revived the West, DeMille knew it firsthand. The Western palate was used for its scenic splendor and for the freedom of action it made possible. DeMille's Westerns were vehicles for big men of action and physical robustness like himself.

Halfway into his first year, he had found his destiny behind the camera. From there on, his achievement would be to put things on the screen that had never been photographed before, and force others to follow in his wake. His scripts and sets were full of action. Fearless himself, he made sure to surround himself with likeminded people.

DeMille's ego kept pace with his accomplishments. He loved the cartoons that began to appear showing him in Napoleonic poses, his hair turned into a laurel wreath, his hand raised to command the multitude. Not given to false modesty, DeMille told interviewers that nobody in the studio could possibly understand as much about movies and the public as himself. His great work was just beginning. He had truly arrived.

CHAPTER EIGHT

THE LASKY COMPANY WAS GROWING AT THE SAME INCREDIBLE SPEED AS the film industry, its power increasing as fast as that of the Trust was crumbling. In making a movie, photography was one of the producers' largest expenses. The pressure to compete provoked technical innovations and dramatic inspirations, from Griffith's effective use of close-ups to Reichenbach's recycling of old plots. The potential was unlimited, the future unimaginable. Do something new, and do it first, was DeMille's motto, though it drove some of his colleagues almost to the point of insanity.

The continual pressure of time, money, and the need to make each new stunt better than the last one, revealed unexpected talents among the Lasky crew. Secretaries were pressed into service as editors or script girls, often with great success; real cowboys were roped in as extras, became stuntmen, and eventually found new careers as actors. The pace was never allowed to flag, but each problem solved only revealed a dozen more.

With each film, the company's payroll doubled. With DeMille's films, it trebled—but, then, so did profits. His films soon made their costs back ten times, and then a hundredfold. But in that first year they couldn't make money fast enough because every dollar was needed for expansion. Thus Goldwyn treated each new West Coast expenditure that he hadn't personally OK'd as justification for another outburst.

For much of those first few years, Lasky had his hands full controlling the excitable personalities of his passionate partners, each believing their efforts misunderstood or not properly appreciated by the other. None of their rows were irreparable, but without Lasky's intervention, they could have been. At first, conscious that he hadn't put up his share of the money, DeMille deferred to Goldwyn's admonitions. But changes were measured in weeks. A blast from Goldwyn in January was barely tolerated by DeMille in September, with twelve profitable films behind him. There came a time when, after one of DeMille's sarcastic ripostes, an unusually subdued Goldwyn told Lasky, "DeMille is always sore at this office." But he had to admit that, although "he kicks more than all the other directors we got . . . he also delivers the goods." Manners came with profits.

The New York office's failure to assure DeMille of his screen credit soon became a bone of contention with Goldwyn. DeMille's early insistence on getting his name above the title and credit on all the company's releases was to pay off handsomely in the years ahead. This kept his reputation intact even in later years when his career was in a trough. But if he hadn't insisted, Goldwyn, who just thought of profit, might not have remembered to give it to him.

Suddenly other companies were competing for established plays and players. The lesser-known plays DeMille had brought with him could come in handy to fill out growing schedules, but they needed the big projects to sell the rest. And so the deal with Belasco couldn't have come at a better time.

Working with Oscar Apfel, DeMille acquired the fundamentals of direction. But his sense of visual drama had come from Belasco, and he developed and expanded it for the screen. For *The Warrens of Virginia*, he told Art Arthur, he recreated Belasco's staging for the little battle where, "the hero has gotten into the Southern home under false pretenses as a Northern officer who has been in love with the girl. While this love scene is going on, the supply train is being ambushed . . . I just borrowed from Belasco and played the scene exactly as he had played it, because it was one of the tensest scenes I've ever seen on the stage."

DeMille also brought his experience as a writer. Writing for movies was principally distinguished by chaos and crudity. "If it moves, shoot it," was an old western expression that applied equally to rattlers, rustlers, and films. One of DeMille's innovations was to give the actors dialogue to speak. One has only to see a typical film produced by Vitagraph or Selig or any of the other Trust companies to see the difference. If the performances in some of DeMille's early films seem over the top and crude by modern standards, they are restrained and realistic in contrast to those of most others. "I use dialogue exactly as if I were staging a play," DeMille told a New York interviewer. "The dialogue is written in my manuscripts by the author, and even the choice of words, pronunciation and enunciation are insisted upon, to get 'just right' time and facial expressions."

Of course, he would exaggerate the importance of such details when talking to the press, to make his movie work sound as serious and respectable as working for the stage. While he certainly drew on the use of dialogue to make his close-shots more dramatic, his action scenes were specifically sculpted for films. DeMille went from dramatizing plays for the screen to putting the integrity of dramatic construction into his original film scripts. Actors, writers, and directors before him had made the move from stage to film, but DeMille not only grasped the difference between the two mediums—what was appropriate for the stage was suggestion, while realism was what movie audiences expected—he also knew how to put it into practice.

Being a partner made it easier for DeMille to get away with innovations, but Goldwyn badgered him at every turn, especially when it involved newfangled visual effects like the candlelit scenes in *The Warrens of Virginia*. Goldwyn worried that exhibitors might offer only half the fee when they were shown only half of Blanche Sweet's face, and repeated his foolish fear to DeMille. DeMille cabled Goldwyn that it was incredible he hadn't been able to see that what he had given him was "Rembrandt lighting," and instead of fretting, DeMille suggested, for such art Goldwyn should charge the exhibitors double. Which he did.

DeMille, his imagination fired by something he had read as a child or some picture he had in mind, might work forty men and women as they had never worked before, using up miles of costly film, to build to a carefully thought-out stunt, only to find when he got to it that the stunt was a physical impossibility. The Lasky Company paid the bills, but the telegrams from Goldwyn in New York were all the incentive DeMille needed not to make the same mistake twice. He eventually learned to make sure of his stunts first, to write action that wasn't beyond the capabilities of his actors and animals, and to shoot only what was needed for the scene.

If there was one rule everybody working for DeMille had to learn, it was that in his movies a man or woman has to be willing to do almost everything, and do it well! Thus, while he was up in the hills or out in the desert shooting the day's scene, what could be more natural than for him to ask Stella to start assembling the previous day's footage for his return. When the only film they had to think about had been *The Squaw Man*, their cutter had been a young woman, Marie (Mamie) Wagner, who was the presiding and sole genius of the projecting and assembly rooms. But now with two, three, and four films simultaneously in the works, there were thousands of feet of film to be gone through. Even with DeMille and Apfel editing their own work, and Mamie editing the remaining films, there was soon a pressing need for more editors. Critics often failed to mention a film's director, but they were quick to point out sloppy editing jobs. DeMille's responsibility was to maintain high standards and, seeing how ably Stella had proved herself as a secretary, he switched her to editing on the theory that a good secretary's persnickety attention to detail was just what was required to cut out the flannel and keep the narrative.

If the cameraman is the director's eyes, his set designer gives him the material to focus his camera on. Of enormous importance to DeMille's growing reputation was the arrival of Wilfred Buckland. A longtime friend of the DeMille family, Buckland was well established on Broadway, but he was almost fifty, and felt his career was in a bit of a rut. DeMille heard from Beatrice that Buckland might be willing to consider a move, and he arrived early in June to serve as Lasky's artistic director, at a starting salary of $75 per week for the first three months—he had other offers with more money—because "I was seeking an opportunity to picturize in a more 'painter-like' manner, applying to motion pictures the same rules which govern the highest art of painting."

Buckland's formative contribution to set design for movies was acknowledged by Cedric Gibbons, the celebrated MGM art director: "He was the first man of recognized ability in his field to forsake the theater for the motion pictures, and to him are attributed the first consistent and well-designed motion picture sets. He brought to the screen a knowledge of mood and a dramatic quality which until then was totally lacking." Buckland left the Lasky studio in 1921 to join Douglas Fairbanks's company, where he created the legendary sets for *Robin Hood*, but by then he had set up the Lasky art department and established the style and look for which Lasky films, and especially DeMille's, had become known, and DeMille had begun to work with other designers Buckland had brought in, like the Frenchman Paul Iribe.[3] Prior to Buckland, the men who designed sets for movies weren't acknowledged in the credits. As late as 1916, though it was known that Griffith had brought the Italian creator of the spectacular Tower of Lights at the San Francisco World's Fair to Hollywood to build the unforgettable Babylonian set for *Intolerance*, it was assumed by the public and by his fellow filmmakers to be Griffith's creation.

When Buckland arrived, the Lasky film stage was an unroofed platform, two feet high, adjoining the barn. It had a telephone pole at one end that was rigged with a boom, with sail attached. This was moved around, as the sun moved, to diffuse its hot rays and glare. At first, the interior sets he designed and built were generally one-wall affairs, but they were dressed with *real* furniture. No longer was furniture painted on the walls.

Like DeMille and Lasky, Buckland was inspired by a challenge. He ignored established cost-saving conventions by introducing artificial light, obtaining two Klieg lights (powerful open-arc floodlights) to control dramatic effects whether inside or out, and did so without the tyranny of the sun. Although these Kliegs were so strong their glare nearly blinded the actors, they soon became standard equipment throughout the film industry. Actors suffered, resting between takes with slices of cucumber or potato over their smarting eyes. Movie sets moved inside, out of the sun, which, only a year earlier, had been a major reason for moving to California.

Buckland's first film was *Rose of the Rancho*, a play he had previously designed for the stage. "With Wyckoff," says Kevin Brownlow, "Buckland created a complete set by lighting alone." According to a fellow art director, Leo Kuter, "the sets had been laid out to accord with the fact that the camera was stationary in a long shot position. White lines were painted on the stage floor, to show the 'camera angle,' and no actor moved outside those lines unless specifically directed to do so. Several of these sets could be laid out on one 'stage.' [But] the dramatic values of this new 'art' became evident with the release of the films beginning with *Rose of the Rancho*, and the race toward greater realism and higher artistic achievement was on."

3.Buckland died, aged eighty, of self-inflicted gunshot wounds July 18, 1946.

As photography improved, Buckland recognized that the settings for films would have to become more realistic and less theatrical, even as the lighting became more artificial. Sets for DeMille's films grew from one wall to include many rooms. Interiors were combined with exteriors so that all the action could be filmed on the studio stage, avoiding whenever possible location expenses. From now on, sets for films would be planned in terms of art, architecture, and lighting. DeMille had no doubt about Buckland's importance to his movies. "If anyone is ever inclined to catalogue contributions I have made to motion pictures," he said, "I hope that my having brought Wilfred Buckland to Hollywood will be put near the head of the list."

The company also needed someone of high caliber to write and adapt scripts, and develop the script department. Sets and lights were fine, but no story, no movie. The obvious choice was apparent to all three partners: DeMille's established and distinguished older brother. William had been so skeptical about movies that he had refused DeMille's loan to invest in them. But after the success of *The Squaw Man*, William found himself going to movies with increasing regularity, amazed and intrigued at DeMille's progress as well as by the Lasky Company's rapid growth. And now, nine months after setting out on this fool scheme, his brother was offering him a job! William hesitated, but with Goldwyn, Lasky, and his own mother all encouraging him, he accepted,

Sept. 17, 1914.

Dear C.—
    . . . I suppose Sam and Jesse have written you that they have arranged for me to join your forces. I am coming, prepared to jump right in and if I fit stay a year or two. I will discuss plans, etc. when I see you. In any case I will not bring the family until I am sure that there is a place there that I can fill with credit to myself and the company . . .
    Billy

His decision wasn't as definite as it sounded—he had agreed only to work on scenarios taken from the plays he had written, giving him an exit if he didn't like life in Hollywood.

The journey west on the Atchison, Topeka, and the Santa Fe opened William's eyes to the beauty of his country. The closer he got to Hollywood, the brighter the sun seemed, the bluer the sky, and the keener his emotions. His feelings about that trip were still fresh twenty-five years later: "Suddenly I was in California. . . . Few of us can jump from mediocrity to perfection within an hour and not feel a trifle dizzy. The sun was so beautifully bright that I risked my eyesight every time I tried to look out over the warm sands. And the sands were warm: about 135 degrees in the shade, if you could find any shade. But what of it? I thought of the first men who had blazed this trail, and sat back in my soaking garments to enjoy the next three hundred miles of God's country. The desert was really stunning and exciting, and even though I felt the heat at first, I was much helped by a kind Californian who pointed out cooling patches of snow on mountain-tops not more than thirty miles away. . . . As I descended from the car and took my first step upon the soil of Los Angeles, I felt like saying: 'Balboa, we are here.'"

His sister-in-law, a lovely tanned native after only eight months, met him. DeMille was at work shooting *Rose of the Rancho* in the San Fernando Valley, some twenty miles north, and Connie whisked him to the several hundred acres of wilderness that would shortly become the Lasky ranch but, for the time being, was still being leased for their location shots.

Upon their arrival, the noise was deafening. Ironically, the production of silent films was far from silent. A three-piece orchestra was resting for the moment, but soon the piano and violins would start up again creating the mood for the actors. And, always, the sound of people shouting instructions in all directions, carpenters banging sets together, live guns going off, cowboys spitting and cursing, and, of course, silent movie directors before microphones were never without a megaphone. The size of this cone-shaped organ depended upon the scene being shot. A really big one was used to carry the voice for a long shot, a small one for directing close-ups. Since they were currently shooting a big dramatic outdoor scene, the megaphone took one man to lift and hold to DeMille's mouth while he yelled his orders.

Rose of the Rancho was a tale set in "Old California" shortly after the formerly Spanish territory had become part of the United States. It was a time when many Spanish landlords became victims of the ruthless "jumpers" who seized their rancheros and registered the lands as their own. In the scene DeMille was directing when William came on the set, the villainous "jumper" Esra Kincaid and his band of rowdies were about to break into an old hacienda on the side of a hill.

But William knew none of this. He only knew that there, in the midst of sand and sagebrush, was his brother transformed, looking as if he had every right to be pleased with himself. DeMille had less hair than when William had last seen him, but he was tanned by the sun and finely muscled by work. He was dressed in corduroy pants and puttees, a flannel shirt open at the neck, dark sunglasses to shield his eyes, and a slouch hat pulled well down to protect his bald head. His clothes were wet with sweat, and his firmly jawed face, thick neck, and bare bulging arms were burned a dark red brown and caked with dust. He wore a gun at his waist, a megaphone with his name stenciled across it was by his side, and his shirtsleeves were unconventionally rolled up to free his arms for giving orders. Could this bronzed dynamo out of the pages of the penny dreadful be his "little" brother?

DeMille was in the center of a circle of tired dirty, rough-looking cowboys when he spotted William. "Bill! How's mother! You couldn't have come at a better time. Here, put on one of those cowboy rigs and get on a horse—you're one of the attacking gringos in this scene. The boys will show you what to do." DeMille knew that in movies numbers count. He had a flair for making few seem like many, and publicity could boast of a cast of thousands.

A bemused William was handed a gun, given a pony, and with a cowboy on either side to make sure he didn't fall off or get lost, he joined the group. None of the others knew much more than William about the details of the scene, or whether they were villains or heroes. Their job was to ride and shoot for a day's work at $5 per man.

"Aim high if you can't shoot straight," one of the cowboys told William. It seems the gun he'd been given was loaded. While they normally used blanks with black powder, which would show impressive white puffs when the gun went off, one still didn't want them exploding in one's face.

Suddenly he heard DeMille's voice again, booming through his megaphone from the back of a battered old Model T Ford, Wyckoff holding on to his camera to catch it all as they bumped along the desert sands: "Now then you men up there. Ready—action—go!" William had never before heard the three words that move the movie, but the men around him knew what they meant.

Later that day, William found himself sharing a ditch with another extra from which they shot live bullets at a closed door. Frank Hopkins, a crack shot, explained the need for real bullets. They made the splinters fly, and naturally, should anyone miss their target, they made an even deeper impression in the people rushing out from behind. "Don't you worry none," an amused Frank told the city slicker. "These fellows know what they're doing."

William was swept along in the excitement. Although he couldn't see much, he could hear DeMille giving instructions. Based on what he was telling the actors to do, it was to be the worst scene of rape and carnage since the Romans violated the Sabine women: "Dick, listen, you break in. You're looking for something to steal when you see her. Move closer to her. . . . Like a bull. . . . Come on, put some feeling into it. What kind of man are you! Here is this girl, she's young, she's helpless, she's beautiful. There's nobody to stop you." Now DeMille was coaching the actress: "Get as far away from him as you can, back against the wall, over by the table, by the crucifix. That's right. He's your savior . . . That's right, that look, perfect . . . Now Dick's got you. Fight him. Try to ward him off. Fight him! *Fight!* Give it all the strength you've got. Hit out. Hard . . . But it's hopeless. You're growing weak."

William didn't remember this scene from Belasco's play. In his ditch, he wondered just what he was needed for in this circus. After all, he was a playwright, a man who wrote dialogue for actors to speak. He soon found that a different kind of writing was needed for film. "You can open things out in movies the way we never could on the stage," DeMille would tell him later when they had time to talk and catch up. "I never allow my actors to read the script. It only confuses them, and they get their ideas mixed with mine. I outline each scene as we come to it, explain the business, give them their lines, and rehearse the action. The first thing every one of them has to learn is to do exactly what they are told." And that, of course, was why DeMille was cut out to be a director.

DeMille worked the same way as other silent directors, including John Ford, Henry Hathaway, and Henry King, and continued to do so long after sound came in and dialogue took over. Younger generations saw their behavior as tyrannical and old-fashioned especially towards actors used to subtle emotions. But the movies these men made endured.[4] Over the next few weeks, William learned the difference between working in the theater and in film. He learned when to provide real dialogue for the actors, and how to write scenes that conveyed what audiences needed to know through the juxtaposition of action with expression and lighting. While his brother believed in the spoken word, this was only when all else failed, and the more confident DeMille became, the more he wanted to do the "real" talking through the camera.

When William had been sitting in a darkened theater back in New York, the films, good or bad, moved across the screen, incident following incident, to tell the story in much the same way as in the theater. But watching them being made was a different experience entirely. Scenes were photographed with an eye to background or location, and with no regard for sequence. The complete plan seemed to exist only in his brother's head. He told people what to do and they did it.

It had been another lively day. DeMille, mindful of his enlarged payroll and anxious to complete the outdoor scenes before the sun set, drove his company at top speed. He seemed always to want more. The extras were herded here and there like sheep. Two cameras clicked constantly to insure at least one produced viable film. While DeMille rehearsed and directed one scene, his assistant busied himself preparing the next set-up.

Finally, it was too dark to continue. When William joined him, DeMille was swearing softly. As he checked off the list of scenes completed that day, he determined it was shorter than it should have been. And this was from a director who worked fast, usually figuring on getting in twenty or twenty-five runs a day.

Back at the barn, William was invited to look at rushes. Luckily there were no mistakes, and the sky had come out a treat. The exteriors were splashed with sunlight, heightening the contrast with the violence. While the film was running, DeMille and Alvin Wyckoff were making comments on the action. A young girl was sitting behind, furiously writing down all that was said.

---

4. Young director Elia Kazan had a conversation on the subject with John Ford when both were working for Zanuck. Kazan wanted to know how the revered old master staged a scene. Ford told the New York greenhorn: "From the set. Get out on location early in the morning, before anyone else is there. Walk around the set and see what you've got. . . . Don't look at the fucking script. That will confuse you. You know the story. Tell it in pictures. Forget the words."

"What else?" the fearless Kazan asked.

"The actors," Ford said. "Don't let them act. Direct it like you were making a silent."

From now on all William heard was movies, movies—movies. That's all the talk there was, even from Buckland. That's all anyone was interested in, talking movies. Editing, lighting, great locations, or ideas for new bits of terrific business. As William saw it, DeMille prepared for each new feature as a general might prepare for the decisive battle of a campaign.

After that first day, William familiarized himself with the studio, looking for a corner where he could set up his desk and typewriter. He visited with the actors on other sets. He'd known a number of them in New York, like Robert Edeson, who'd made his name in *Strongheart*, and was now acting in *Where the Trail Divides*, directed by another old friend, James Neill, and chubby, cheerful Jane Darwell, who played Bessie Barriscale's mother in *Rose of the Rancho* and another mother in *The Only Son*. Things were a bit less frenzied on those sets. Jane's claim to fame would come in 1940 when she won her Oscar for playing Ma Joad in *The Grapes of Wrath*, after a career playing mothers. More actors William knew were pouring in from New York all the time. The dams of prejudice had been pierced, and a flood of Broadway's more established talents was on its way. Before the week was out William was hooked by what he saw and what his bronzed brother told him. Thoughts of New York were fast receding. "It's action that people want," DeMille told William. "A few years ago they faked that Western stuff and got away with it, but nowadays audiences are too well educated and too smart. They've been brought up on the real thing and they won't stand for the bunk. Every company out here has got real riders and ropers. In this business we leave nothing to the imagination." As DeMille wrote Goldwyn when preparing his autobiography, "Sure, actors may get injured from time to time, and they may be incapacitated for two or three days afterwards, but the wonderful effect on the screen acts as balm for his wounds." William probably thought this attitude a bit cavalier, if not downright callous, but DeMille had an answer for everything. More important, his enthusiasm, and what movies had done for him personally, was a convincing testimonial for working in them.

Soon William was busy adapting Cameo Kirby as a vehicle for Dustin Farnum with Apfel to direct. Now that he had agreed to take over the script department he was kept busy. Besides plays for the studios of other directors, he adapted *Warrens of Virginia* and *The Wild Goose Chase* for his brother. Soon William had so much work on his hands that a half-dozen writers were working for him. He was overworked but not unsung: his name appeared prominently in the publicity for the films.

It wasn't long before William turned his talents to directing. Although he had a long career in films he never really grasped, as his brother had, what made a film a hit: how it could be artistic *and* make money. After all, it wasn't so long ago that he'd heard that little Gladys Smith (who became Mary Pickford) was going to act in movies, and wrote Belasco asking him to find the girl a job to save her from this awful fate. William was still a man of words in a world of vision. When words *serve* the image, you have film as art; when the image serves the word, you have a play or a documentary. William was so outraged by the filmed result of his script for *The Goose Girl* that he would not allow his name on the picture as he was certain it would flop. It became one of the most successful films of 1916.

Ultimately, William would become an admired though never commercially successful film director. His films brought respectability rather than cash to the till. Then, like so many others, his career faded with the advent of sound—ironic, considering he had begun as a playwright. But this was his last lesson in filmmaking. Words date; images don't; and stars not at all.

Having decided to stay in California, he returned to New York to collect his wife and daughters and to recruit other writers. One, Hector Turnbull, later headed up the studio's scenario department in New York. Meanwhile, DeMille's secretaries' mettle was being severely tested. He not only dictated his scenarios, but countless long letters as well. Dealing with Bea's importunate stream of requests, complaints, instructions, and her continual need for money was a full-time job in itself. So too was maintaining the press clippings about Lasky Company productions. In addition, DeMille had begun investing in property and new businesses.

After struggling for almost a year, William finally convinced DeMille to approve hiring his New York secretary, Anne Bauchens. DeMille whittled her salary from $45 to $40 a month, but she was one of the best investments DeMille ever made, going on to become a noted film editor. On *We can't Have Everything,* his thirty-first film, he shared the credit with Bauchens, and from then on she edited all his films. Over the years, when DeMille wandered from studio to studio, Bauchens followed him wherever he worked, including up to Paradise or aboard his floating office on the *Seaward*. So essential was she that every contract he signed included a clause stipulating her as his editor. Like many of the single women DeMille worked with, she was loyal and devoted, but unlike the others in his closely knit team, she was never physically involved with him.

Now the one thing DeMille still needed was a collaborator to work directly with him. Cecil B. DeMille was an "auteur" long before that term gained currency, and what he sought was an arrangement like the one Belasco had with Henry deMille. DeMille hadn't forgotten how Belasco would arrive at all hours of the day or night, flushed with some new idea, and how his father, roused from sleep, would listen to his dynamic partner and then turn Belasco's stream of consciousness into a play. DeMille saw himself as the Belasco of motion pictures.

DeMille's ideal partner would have to be someone who combined his father's nature with the total devotion of his mother, who would be all the things he was not and could not be: patient, tolerant, flexible. A person capable of working as hard as he did, with some ideas to complement his own, and yet somehow willing to devote these talents to his service. But no man

DeMille is shown with two of his most important colleagues, Jeannie Macpherson, who wrote many of his screenplays, and Vernon Keays, who served often as his assistant director. Courtesy John Kobal Foundation

would be that. It would have to be someone who believed in him, like a wife, a dutiful lover, or a doting mother. Where was this paragon?

Even as William arrived in California, the very soul DeMille needed was already out there, waiting in the wings, currently doing a day's work as an actress on the *Rose of the Rancho*. Her name was Jeanie Macpherson, a good Scot girl, and she would give her life in DeMille's service.

DeMille had already met her once. At least she claimed to have seen him since he didn't remember the occasion. He'd been preoccupied scouting locations. She had been acting in and directing a little film called *Tarantula* at the time, and had already spent two days at her preciously guarded location in the desert when suddenly this man on a horse appeared "poaching" on her preserve. Those early filmmakers were a suspicious lot, but before Macpherson could challenge the intruder he'd gone. She sent him a note to warn him off and in her abrupt style signing it J. Macpherson, giving no clue to her gender. His curt response was to tell this Macpherson person to mind his own business. In the meantime, she'd found out more about him and, with her film finished, saw him as a possible source of employment. Macpherson did not play the simple ingénue. Instead, her style might have even been described as assertive. She first bearded DeMille in the barn. Her entry was like a little tornado. With a nose that turned up, and hair that curled up, and a disposition that turned up too, she informed the preoccupied DeMille that she was the Macpherson of the note. Furthermore, she told him, she was a damn good actress and that he could avail himself of her services. DeMille barely glanced at her. After a humiliatingly long pause, she stormed out.

Later she had sent a note telling him what a "rude" person he was. He may still have been chuckling when she returned to his office demanding an apology. Again, DeMille gave nothing away, although by now he must have been intrigued. Macpherson returned a third time and now he offered her a day's work. But when offered a mere $10 after she had earned $200 a week as star, writer, and director of her own films, she stormed back into his office and threw the $10 at him. By this time, DeMille was hooked. Perhaps the reason he had held out so long was that her challenge was emotional as well as professional.

Macpherson had started as an actress. She had toured in Edgar Selwyn's production of William deMille's *Strongheart*. She began her film career under the direction of D. W. Griffith, the man whose films had first impressed her. When Griffith took his company out west in 1911, she went along. In California, this time for Universal, which she joined in 1912, one day her director found himself without a story. Macpherson had had an idea for a film during the long train ride. She was asked to put it into scenario form, and (for the same fee) to act in it. Sometime later, they let her do her story again and this time direct it as well. Soon she had her own unit for which she wrote, starred, and directed. "I figured that to accomplish this I must work twice as many hours and twice as hard as the average person," she later wrote. "I have. While other authors gave themselves long vacations to woo inspiration, I sat and worked at my desk."

Constant moving between fly-by-night projects serving as a marvelous apprenticeship, she recalled, "I played the leading feminine role in Jack London's *Sea Wolf* (1913). I was in a boat with Henry King (who was still an actor then) which was being lowered from a schooner when the rope broke and we were tossed into the Pacific. . . . Henry could swim a little, I not at all. . . . I had hit the water 'flat,' as the saying is, and had so completely lost my wind that I wasn't able to think very clearly, but I did know one thing, the thing that every well-trained 'movie' remembers on all occasions—the camera. I signaled to the cameraman on the ship to keep turning the crank. He caught it all. It was just the sort of scene we needed!"

It was with the advent of feature-length films that Macpherson realized that "with your looks you're not cut out to be a star," and decided to concentrate on being a writer. Thus, the Lasky Company, with its four- and six-reel features, was a natural target. But DeMille was looking to recruit established writers from New York, not two-reel writers from Los Angeles.

Initially he offered her $25 a week to take dictation. (By 1925, she and June Mathis would be the two highest-paid screenwriters in the world, earning $150,000 a year). Talking about her working relationship with DeMille, Macpherson said, "I shall always be grateful for his assistance. He is a hard task master and he demands that a thing shall be perfect. He used to scold me and show me where my scenarios were wrong, and we would work them out together." During the day, Macpherson was still acting, but come evening, she was writing and tossing ideas back and forth. In her spare time, DeMille used her experience to scout locations for his next project. "[I] never thought of Jeanie as a writer, but as an exceptional collaborator for an exceptional man," said Beulah Marie Dix, a New York playwright who worked with her on the adaptation for *The Road to Yesterday*. "Cecil, with his past experience in writing and acting and his unsurpassed showmanship, knew not only what he required in every story he directed, but in every scene. Jeanie had a genius for putting this on paper."

Soon it was clear to everyone that they shared more than just a passion for astrology and hard work, but from the start Macpherson knew their relationship could never be formalized. With film fans expert at reading between the lines, Macpherson had no choice but to present an image of herself as a hard-nosed career woman. Yet from the time she began to work with DeMille, writing almost exclusively for him until she died, Macpherson was as loyal as a wife, as loving as a mistress, and ultimately as selfless as a slave. As the experience of her fellow Scot, another victim of loving the wrong man, the doomed Lady Macbeth, might have told her, love is funny that way.

Jeanie Macpherson was one of a small band of pioneering women writers and directors in the film industry whose significant role in the history of Hollywood has been overlooked. However, if she has been given even less credit than June Mathis or Anita Loos, it is in part because she chose to devote her best years to working for a man whose own ambition would cast a shadow so large as to obliterate all others. None of her work prior to joining the Lasky Company survives. Everything she is known for now was done for DeMille. Professionally they were a perfect match. Like her boss, Macpherson had been willing to put her hands and talents to anything that would get her ahead. Only later did the balance shift. By hitching her wagon to a star she lost her own identity. And, in the end, with her head buried in work, she failed to see that the man she loved was finding an outlet for his physical needs in the arms of yet another woman. It became another fact she had to accept about this man, if she wanted to hold him she would have to share him.

CHAPTER NINE

THE ROSE OF THE RANCHO WAS FINISHED. THE WELL-CHOSEN LOCATIONS, the careful photography, and the exquisite tinting, all received praise. "It was a dream, to sit in my theater last night," wrote Belasco, for whom this play had special meaning, to DeMille, "and see my production . . . unfold in all its beautiful color and with all its dramatic action. You have caught the very shadows of the land of my childhood."

But there were shortcomings, like the poor quality of the prints being made by the Lubin Company. "In the moonlight the faces came out almost black, and in others dark blue," DeMille's mother wrote to him. Moreover, characters came up to one another completely unnoticed until they stood right in front of them. DeMille cut away from his star, Bessie Barriscale, in one scene only to return to her twenty minutes of running time and two screen days later, still wearing the same clothes and sitting in the same spot. Just eight days after *The Rose of the Rancho* was in the can, on November 7, DeMille completed *Girl of the Golden West*, and "its production history might have been shorter still if the guardian angels had not been alert around Mount Palomar," mused DeMille, referring to a near-fatal incident. "We were on location shooting mountain scenes one day and using a big, high-wheeled Oldsmobile to get from place to place in a hurry, over the extremely crude mountain roads of San Diego County. Careering down one of them, with mountains on one side and a thousand-foot drop on the other one of the wheels. . . . went off by itself. . . . Everyone in the car expected that that awful moment would be crystallized into eternity; but something stopped us on the edge of the road."

The risks he took, and made his team share, seemed justified by the results he was getting. "Great pains seem to have been taken to secure the proper location for the exteriors," wrote the *Motion Picture News*, "and the mountain views are marvels of clear, perfect photography. In fact it is only fair to state that the entire five reels, from the opening sequence to the beautiful sunrise effect at the finale, are wonderful examples of what can be done by competent cameramen and directors." The story of a girl (which inspired the Puccini opera) raised in a gambling saloon, who stakes her freedom on a game of cards to give the man she loves time to escape, looked and felt authentic in every way.

With Buckland's presence as a spur, DeMille's demand for authenticity intensified and he inaugurated Hollywood's first research department and library. "I developed the habit of sending one of our secretaries, Bessie Mc-Gaffey (her husband was one of the studios location managers. He was the one who found that San Francisco could double for New York!) to the public library to bring me books on costume, architecture, gunnery, or whatever subject I was dealing with in planning a picture. Now, public libraries are most admirable institutions, but they have one irritating custom. They want their books back. When, as often happened, Bessie found it necessary to remind me of that, I would tell her: 'Well then, buy a copy of the book and next time we'll have it when we need it.' Bessie's office soon became crowded with books, and her time crowded with consulting them in answer to my questions."

DeMille's increasing obsession with historical accuracy would lead to some pretty obscure details, such as zippers on a Roman matron's cocktail dress. The joke was that he was actually right. A popular bit of doggerel went as follows,

> Cecil B. DeMille
> Much against his will,
> Was persuaded to keep Moses,
> Out of the War of the Roses

At the time of films like *Girl of the Golden West*, Hollywood had not yet come to recognize the power that wardrobe could exert on audiences. Accuracy, and a close fit, was what the studios wanted. The stars sought the right clothes from any source they could find. "The Indian dress I wear in *Girl of the Golden West*," recalled Anita King, "was loaned me by an old Indian woman at Keane's Camp, in the San Josito mountains where the film was made. I had a dress, but when this old Indian woman saw me, she said it was not quite right for the tribe I was supposed to represent, and she brought from among her treasures the one in which I appear."

If a star went shopping for a fashionable modern outfit she would, of course, be wearing what any other smart young woman might be wearing, and think nothing of it. A decade later, Joan Crawford naïvely went outside the studio to shop for "real clothes," not realizing that the dresses in the stores were inspired by costumes in her films. She ended up in a flood of tears when the director stormed at her for wearing "Joan Crawford" shoulder pads. It became clear, with so many films in production, that an in-house wardrobe department was necessary.

By the end of 1914, Lasky occupied three city blocks in Hollywood—a wonderful ranch including 20,000 acres of land with every imaginable variety of scenery—as well as offices in New York. "Elegance is the quality of Lasky land," reported *Photoplay*.

But the company's most valuable property was their Director General. *Girl of the Golden West* had been made for $15,109.69 and recouped $102,224.46. It was Lasky's first film to pass the magic $100,000 mark. The man who only a year before had wondered what his future might hold was now a huge success. Incredible deadlines were being met. Speed seemed to sharpen his mettle. DeMille joked about his growing reputation as a martinet: "I am about to produce *The Warrens of Virginia*, and expect to kill a lot of perfectly good actors and good horses. Why don't you come down and see the fun?"

DeMille began *The Warrens of Virginia*, the third and last of his Belasco features, in December 1914, a year after he began his first film. It was a family affair: his brother had written the story loosely based on their Southern grandfather's capture by the enemy during the Civil War. Every care was lavished and it cost twice as much and took four times longer to shoot than his previous films.

The Warrens of Virginia was of interest because here DeMille began casting star personalities who had been "made" by the movies instead of hiring stage actors to recreate their original roles. Lasky's signing of Blanche Sweet came hard on the heels of Adolph Zukor's new contract with Mary Pickford, which had made her the highest-paid performer in movies. Despite DeMille's privately expressed doubts about Sweet's ability to play the feminine lead in *The Warrens of Virginia*, on the ground that she was not "stage-trained," the camera proved otherwise. The camera, DeMille, would learn, made stars on its own.

Signing the golden-haired Sweet was an auspicious event. The popular, five-foot-four, nineteen-year-old had been happy working with D. W. Griffith, and in the fall of 1914 had been a sensation as *Judith of Bethulia*. But Griffith didn't pay his actors well, and Sweet felt that she deserved at least $250 per week as she was making about sixteen films a year for Biograph. To her surprise and chagrin, Griffith, who had described her as "the greatest natural actress in film land," refused not only to meet her price, but also advised her to go and make more elsewhere. It was an Olympian slap for his golden protégé, though his proud attitude in time to come would lead to his own slip from the world he ruled. There was no shortage of bidders. "Probably one of the reasons Goldwyn signed me was that the stage names they had brought out weren't drawing at the box office the way the movie people were," Sweet recalled sixty-five years later. "They came to my house and offered me a wonderful financial deal. They wanted to pioneer with me as their first fully established screen star.

"Cecil and I didn't get along together well at first," she went on—perhaps she sensed the stage-trained Cecil's reservations about her. "Years later he told me, 'You looked at me so strangely every time I told you anything to do, as if you were puzzled.' I confessed apologetically . . . that if I seemed sullen and uncooperative it was really because I was afraid of him. He smiled and said, 'You know, Blanche, you're the only actress I was ever afraid of.'"

Around this time DeMille realized he needed a new secretary. Gladys Rosson joined him, on December 13, 1914, and would remain in that post until the end of her life. She soon became the power behind his throne. From the outset, no aspect of DeMille's life, professional or personal, was hidden from her. She handled not only his affairs but those of his mistresses as well. Of all the women in his life, she was the one he could not have done without.

Rosson came from a large family of brothers and sisters, many of whom also worked in movies. Arthur, the eldest, became one of DeMille's best-known assistant directors, and featured in tales of the portable phone out on some far-off desert location ringing furiously into the night while Arthur knowing it was C. B. back in the studio, ready to give an order let it ring.

Small, prim, and proper, Rosson wore her hair in a net, and her eyes were hidden behind little steel-framed glasses. Her lips were firm, the gaze from her brown eyes clear and shrewd, her hair too short to make much difference when she let it down—but she was a paragon of devotion and application. No man gave her a second look. Women like Gladys Rosson seemed complete in themselves. But she possessed the qualities DeMille found far more attractive: loyalty and hard work. DeMille always preferred women with character.

DeMille: "As I look back to 1914, the fact that *The Squaw Man* eventually grossed $244,800 means much less, very much less, than the two $1 bills I found on my desk when I arrived at the barn one morning in that year. Standing by the desk, where she had just put the $2, looking very grim, with her lips set in a thin line of determination, was a girl I had hired some weeks before, just out of high school, to help with the secretarial work. Gladys had written a note about the $2, reminding me that two weeks previously she had asked me for a $2 raise in her weekly salary. I had refused or postponed it. I remembered that. She proceeded to inform me that she had then gone with the same request to Jesse Lasky, who had expansively granted it. Gladys was in triumph until she went home and told the story to her mother. Mrs. Rosson was less impressed than Gladys with her daughter's cleverness. 'The first thing tomorrow morning you'll take the $2 and give them to Mr. DeMille and tell him what you did!' And there was Gladys, doing her duty, with much more the air of a stoic martyr than a repentant criminal . . . From that day, she remained with me for thirty-nine years as secretary, and as closest, most trustworthy, most patient and unselfish, most fiercely loyal of friends, until she died."

DeMille told the following anecdote: "One evening, when she was dining with me and I fell asleep exhausted at the dinner table, [she] calmly sat all night with her hand under my chin, so that I might sleep undisturbed by a ducking in the soup plate." Until he died he felt her loss.

Rosson couldn't have arrived at a more opportune moment. Expansion was everywhere. Telegrams like these from Lasky to Goldwyn provide a firsthand picture of the hectic activity in the first month of 1915.

JANUARY 2, 1915: Try to get Frank Reicher now with Francis Starr. Would make splendid director. Regarding Santley, we all including Blanche (Sweet), think it a mistake not to take him. His name is really good. He is strong favored among girls and women and will make excellent picture star. Have decided not to use Woodruff. Farnum still stalling for time. Can't get him to close.

JANUARY 3, 1915: Kaufman wants Eddinger. Shall I let him go? Our fourth play not settled and Eddinger in an emergency would be excellent for LADY'S GARTER." GENTLEMAN OF LEISURE best release for March 1 as we will need Thursday release for April, Eddinger in LADY'S GARTER might be good.

Having announced the signing of Blanche Sweet, they were having second thoughts about spending a lot of money on a major launch of her debut in their Civil War picture. D. W. Griffith's *The Birth of a Nation* premiered on February 8 in Los Angeles, under its original title *The Clansman*, accompanied by the Los Angeles Philharmonic to play the score specially arranged by composer Joseph Carl Breil. Along with the rest of elite Hollywood, DeMille and Lasky were in attendance. They knew immediately that Griffith's film would steal their thunder. From the moment it began, it was evident American cinema had entered a new era and could be considered a political, moral, and social force. In the age of the 10 cent movie, *The Birth of a Nation* would show at one Broadway house to capacity business, at $2 a ticket, for 804 consecutive performances.

The Warrens of Virginia opened across America a week later and two weeks before *The Birth of a Nation*'s sensational New York opening on March 3. The battle scenes in *Warrens* were praised as being "worthy of being termed educational." *Variety* compared it to newsreel footage of the war between Turkey and the Baltic states.

DeMille learned another thing that Griffith knew already: the director should choose carefully the musical score to accompany a new film. "When *The Warrens of Virginia* played Talley's Theatre down here . . . occasionally you cut to the battle and then cut back to the love scene. Well, Tally with the music, with his orchestra, wouldn't make those cuts—he was interested in the battle music at the time, and the battle played right on through the love scene and everything else without being diminished or distanced or anything else. And the result was that it ruined the love scenes completely. . . . I remonstrated with him and he said, 'Well, Mr. DeMille, they come here to hear my orchestra. They don't come here to see your picture.' So that was the last picture I played at Tally's."

Next was the *Unafraid*, Ruritanian tosh starring the beautiful, somber star Jolivet as a spoilt American on the Riviera caught up in an operetta without music. Even a car hurtling out of control down Mulholland Drive wouldn't be going fast enough to keep up with the plot. When it opened on April 1, the *New York Dramatic Mirror* saluted DeMille as "a film architect. . . . That he built so well is quite a film feather in his cap, for some of his materials were of the king to try the mettle of the best picture constructor."

The Captive returned to a Middle Eastern milieu, with Blanche Sweet's heroine given a Turkish captive (British-born House Peters, for whom Lasky had great hopes) to work on her farm in place of her dead brother. The shift from hatred to love was subtly charted across three reels. Whatever the true inspiration for the powerful love scenes, the writing and direction must have made more than one member of the Lasky Company who knew about De-Mille and Macpherson (also appearing as Milka) feel that they were watching a "film a clef." Sweet, twenty and in full blossom, was the beneficiary of all this directorial sublimation with a ravishing series of close-ups. DeMille discovered making *The Captive* that he had a real flair for creating sexual tension. The growing eroticism in his films contributes a sharp, underlying taste of tragedy.

It was during this production that, after an increasing number of near misses, DeMille had the first fatality on one of his sets. It was another reason Sweet never warmed to DeMille. "We all wanted realism, but he would go too far. *Captive* was a war story . . . and C. B. had them put real ammunition in their guns. In the course of the hammering and pushing against each other, one soldier's gun went off and blew the brains out of the man behind."

DeMille: "The reason that I had live cartridges was that I wanted to fire a volley through the door, and see the door blown first by the bullets, and then they reversed the guns and hammered through it. We rehearsed with empty guns, of course, and then we got ready to shoot and had them load the guns. Then something happened . . . so I had to rehearse them again. I ordered them to unload their guns, to fire, and everybody did it but one man. And then I had them reverse their arms to hammer at the door. Well, they reversed their arms and hammered, and there was a shot. I was looking right at the man—I got some of his brains on my coat. This funny expression came into his face. There was a little bullet hole here, in the front, and the whole back of his head was blown out. We stopped shooting and everything and I went inside the house, and here was a big, tall, funny-looking fellow, his head in his hands, sobbing and sobbing and sobbing. This fellow said, 'My God, I didn't unload my gun, I didn't, I didn't.' This fellow had a wife and two kids. So, I said, 'Pull yourself together and get out of here and join with the men. One thing: leave Hollywood after the inquest, and never come back. That's your price.' We had the inquest. Nobody knew who killed him. Nobody knew whose gun had been loaded. The coroner's jury brought in a verdict of accidental death. The dead man's widow was kept on the studio's payroll for many years." William remembered the dead man's name: it was big, good-natured Bob Fleming, the cowboy who had shown him the ropes.

The Captive was DeMille's first film to credit Jeanie Macpherson as writer. How serious their relationship had become is evident from an incident in February. Six months after they had first met, and during one of the hottest times of the year in Los Angeles, Sweet, who'd been Macpherson's friend back at Biograph, found her unconscious behind a barn on the set. Macpherson never revealed the cause of her illness but told a journalist while she was working on *The King of Kings*, "it is very terrible thing to see a strong man cry . . . It was when I was lying very ill in a hospital. Everyone thought I was going to die, but myself. I was vaguely conscious that Cecil was sitting beside my bed, crying. I heard him say, and it seemed to come from a million miles away: 'I can't do anything to save my little pal.' That's the way he is about his 'pals.' Friendship means more to him than love to most men."

The Wild Goose Chase, with a script by William, started filming eleven days after *The Captive*, was completed, and was finished twenty days later. DeMille claimed it only took seven days to shoot. It marked the film debut of one of the Broadway's brightest young talents, the comedienne Ina Claire. Movies were never to be this champagne-bubbly actress's real métier, but her performance in a few films leaves one with a most delicious rush. Years later, when DeMille met her at a party, "She had completely forgotten that there ever had been a film called *The Wild Goose Chase*. So has everyone else."

The Arab, a romantic desert saga filled with exotic characters filmed in Palm Desert, was completed on April 21. Lasky's wife Bessie brings a lyrical painter's eye to her description of Hollywood and DeMille at the time: "The wives were very important in those days as we were always notified when a set was ready and dressed with people. We rode to the studio in their one and only rented car to be given seats of honor. These were generally placed in such a position that we could see the handsome, picturesque young director in puttees, boots and cap. He acted out the scenes for the people and put on the best show himself. Sometimes we sat cheerfully in the blazing sun on a ladder, all day. Just to see a few extras ride into a desert scene to make a few gestures. Of course we had to read what they called the 'script' and spent evenings before the fire trying to choose the most fitting title. All the wives competed for titles . . . Then there were long discussions which lasted into the early morning hours. We sat on crude wooden benches with a temporary light, planning and working and it was so exciting we could hardly wait for the next telephone call to be on the lot for a still greater experience: a town in Baghdad where Edgar Selwyn would ride before us on a white horse as a Sheik."

William deMille also recalled shooting *The Arab* in Palm Springs: "This was in the days when Palm Springs had not yet been adopted by the movie colony as a resort. The town was only a cluster of weather-beaten dwellings, served by a typical, Western country store; a desert settlement in an Indian reservation. If you walked a few hundred yards from the little oasis of the village, you were in the trackless waste of the desert itself, with all its mysterious sense of loneliness, its mirages, its deceiving distances and its cruel grandeur . . . There was no ice within fifty miles. If you wanted a drink of water you took it warm and noticed that it was strongly 'on the alkaline side.'"

In the meantime, Goldwyn continued to bombard DeMille with the sort of constructive criticism that only ignited his short fuse, "I saw *The Arab* at the Strand, and noticed that Captain Ford while directing some soldiers who were supposed to be Arabians, looked at his wrist watch. I never knew that Arabian soldiers wore wrist watches." DeMille's own fondest memory of *The Arab* was the acting debut, as an American tourist, of one of America's foremost humorists, Irvin S. Cobb, a writer in the Mark Twain mold, whose stories would later be filmed by John Ford.

With *Chimmie Fadden*, DeMille reluctantly turned to the unfamiliar field of comedy. Chimmie, the baby-faced Bowery tough, played by baby-faced Ziegfeld comic Victor Moore. Chimmie lived with his thievin' family in one of New York City's lower East Side tenements. Despite DeMille's reservations, the reviews praised it for being achingly funny without resorting to slapstick, and a sequel followed four months later.

During the filming of *Chimmie Fadden*, DeMille learned that Lasky and Goldwyn had achieved the impossible. By offering the moon, a carriage to take her there, and the guarantee that the films were to be directed by DeMille, they had lured Geraldine Farrar, the golden-throated idol, to appear in movies in Hollywood. But before he could begin working with Farrar, he had one other film to direct, *Kindling*.

Kindling was a film of greater significance than any that had gone before. It remains a strong attack on American double standards, one law for the rich and another for the poor. Afraid to tell her husband that she is pregnant, and desperate to give her unborn child a chance, Maggie Schultz (Charlotte Walker) takes a job as a seamstress with her wealthy landlady at an appalling wage, becoming an accomplice to theft when a crook gives her a jeweled brooch as her share of the loot. A detective, hot on her trail, cornered the desperate Maggie, who cried out, "I lied, I fought, I stole to keep my baby from being born in this hell-hole of yours. And now he's going to be born in jail!"

By then, DeMille has shown us the poor, straggling along gaslit streets, foraging in bins and gutters for cigarette stubs, or reusable junk; glazed-looking children, aged eight or nine, sitting on beer barrels outside bars, keeping an eye out for the law and being given beer out of a bucket. He was thirty-four and he cared passionately about the plight of the poor. Directors like Griffith and Ince were tackling social injustice too, and these sorts of films found large audiences. The depiction of harsh life in the city is typically more familiar to us today from post-World War I Russian or German films than films of prewar America. *Kindling* was an example of cinema neo-realism long before that word was coined.

Hollywood was becoming respectable. "I never thought," DeMille reminisced, "that one day there would be an imposing bank where we had once shot movies on an open-air stage in the midst of orange and lemon trees. I was even in doubt then if there'd be a bank in Hollywood. We used to cash our checks in those days at Hall's Grocery Store on Hollywood Boulevard."

Soon he would be part-owner of a bank.

CHAPTER TEN

SHE WAS AMERICA'S MOST ADORED SONGBIRD AND GRAND OPERA'S grandest diva. Geraldine Farrar was thirty-three and already a legend at home and abroad when she came to Hollywood to play *Carmen*, and conquered highbrow and lowbrow alike with her glamor and personality. With her the prestige attached to grand opera descended on the patrons of the lowly nickelodeon, and American cinema took a giant leap forward in its march toward respectability and higher admission prices. Farrar wasn't the first opera star to appear in movies, but she was the first one whose appearance in movies mattered.[5]

At nineteen, the tall, sporty American girl had taken staid Germany and its old Kaiser by storm after her debut at Berlin's Royal Opera House. Not everyone thought it was because of her voice. Farrar was a wasp-waisted, high-busted, white-skinned, raven-haired young beauty. Puccini was also one of her suitors, as were Antonio Scotti and Arturo Toscanini. Within a year, she was the rage of Europe. Marconi, inventor of the wireless, told everyone that "she has the biggest brain of any woman I have ever met." At twenty-four, with Europe conquered, she returned to America in triumph to become the queen of the Metropolitan Opera in New York.

Only Enrico Caruso (Don Jose to her Carmen) matched her at the box office. Farrar's Victrola records sold in the millions. Her royalties reached a record $130,000 in a single year and her spending kept pace. "Well, everybody knows that once Geraldine wore an expensive and marvelously well-cut gown," said Lou Tellegen, the Dutch actor accounted one of the handsomest men in the world, who later became her husband. "No one ever saw her in it a second time. One day she told me she had a bill from Bendel's and asked me if I could add it up for her. I nearly dropped dead. It was over a hundred thousand dollars!"

The long and short of it was that in terms of glamor and prestige, Farrar was to opera what her friend Sarah Bernhardt was to the theater. Only in the

---

5. As early as 1914, the San Francisco opera singer Beatrice Licninia appeared in films produced by her husband.

92

movies was Mary Pickford, America's sweetheart, her equal in popularity. "Geraldine Farrar," reflected DeMille, "without benefit of radio, television or films, had achieved a height of acclaim which I do not believe has been equaled in my lifetime."

Unbeknownst to the Lasky Company, Farrar had been having problems with her vocal cords and been advised by her doctors to take a rest from singing, so she sent her agent to strike a lucrative bargain. Lasky offered her an unprecedented deal: "For every minute of daylight she is in Southern California, whether she is at the studio or not, I will pay her two dollars and royalty, and a share of all the profits." This queenly sum, excluding other royal perks, amounted to $35,000, for eight weeks or $4,500 a week—this at a time when Lasky and Goldwyn were haggling with Blanche Sweet over paying her $300 a week. "In addition to the largest salary we had ever paid for a star," noted DeMille, "her contract included provision of a private railway car for her journeys between the coasts, a two-story house in Hollywood staffed with butler, cook and maid, a limousine and chauffeur, a private bungalow at the studio equipped with a grand piano as well as other amenities, an augmented orchestra on the set for mood music, worthy of the reigning queen of the opera, living expenses for the star and her entourage, billing as Miss Geraldine Farrar, and, Jesse added, 'our best director.'"

When Farrar arrived in Los Angeles, stars' salaries were still ridiculously low in relation to their popularity. The average salary for a leading man was from $100 to $400 a week; female stars were getting from $200 to $500. Vitagraph's Clara Kimball Young, second in national popularity to Mary Pickford, was only taking home $500 a week. But the stars were quick to learn their value. Charlie Chaplin was getting $1,200 a week, fifty-two weeks a year, and behind-the-scenes bidding for Mary Pickford was getting so frenzied that Adolph Zukor upped her salary to $104,000 a year, regardless of whether she worked or not! A year after *Carmen*, salaries rose to even greater heights. Pickford and Chaplin were asking and getting close to $1 million per year, while admission to their films averaged ten cents a person. In the summer of 1915, Farrar's salary was the talk of the industry and nobody doubted she was worth every penny.

So it was that the diva and her entourage—including her parents, two maids, secretary, a manservant, a chef, a chauffeur, and her hairdresser—set out for Hollywood. There had been a last-minute hitch when the hairdresser didn't want to leave his wife and their three children alone for eight weeks, so she invited them all along.

When Farrar detrained at the old Santa Fe depot she found a red carpet sprinkled with flowers, a crowd of cowboys, and a large chorus of school children threw flowers and sang a greeting. The mayor of Los Angeles stepped forward to lead her to the magnificent Hispano-Suiza which awaited her. Farrar was the first star to receive what was afterwards known as the "full treatment." Goldwyn too had come out to join his partners in greeting her.

The next night, there was a grand dinner at the Hollywood Hotel. "The men wore white ties," remembered Bessie Lasky, "and the ladies long sweeping gowns dusting the old floors of the creaking Hollywood Hotel. The decoration consisted of awkward bowls of poppies, wisteria and roses. The wives stood in line with their husbands, introducing everyone to the guest of honor and her family. Miss Farrar looked ravishing dressed in a white brocaded satin evening gown trimmed in black Chantilly lace. The party became a gala affair. The Cecil B. DeMilles, Dustin Farnums, William deMilles, Douglas Fairbanks, Bucklands, all the early pioneers with their families enjoying a happy reunion; in those days we were just a large family. Later we persuaded Miss Farrar to sing one of her arias from *La Boheme*, and her gracious presence, standing beside the rented piano, transformed the lobby into a tiny scene such as at the opera."

By Monday, radiant and recovered, Farrar was ready for work. And she made an equally grand impression on the cast and crew. According to Bessie Lasky, "One day, shortly after she arrived, I sent to the studio to pick up some mail. To my astonishment I heard the glorious finale of *Madame Butterfly* coming from her bungalow. And best of all, the most amazing sight came into view. All the studio had heard her singing and had tiptoed to her quarters, sitting on the ground, perhaps seventy-five in all,—Indians, bootblacks, extras from her picture, cowboys, writers, electricians, grips, secretaries all sitting in silent wonderment, listening to this glorious voice. Many of them had never heard an opera sung before. Can you imagine their expressions, and their heart throbs as they heard the farewell scene from *Madame Butterfly* tenderly and sadly sung? Needless to say, she became the idol of the lot."

The three films Farrar made with Lasky that year were *Maria Rosa*, *Carmen*, and *Temptation*, the last of which was a contemporary drama to show off her continental wardrobe. Although *Carmen* was meant to be first, DeMille decided to start with *Maria Rosa* so that Farrar could get some filmmaking experience.

Wallace Reid would be her leading man in all but one of her first six films, and after *Maria Rosa*, she would have no other. His height made her seem more fragile, his boyishness made her more alluring. His glances made her more attractive. DeMille had spotted him in *The Birth of a Nation*, and he went on to become one of the studio's most potent attractions and one of America's most beloved stars. He died at thirty-two, addicted to morphine after a serious injury in a train crash on the way to a shooting location.

DeMille's caution with Farrar had proved largely unnecessary. The diva loved the camera. The only problem discovered during the early rushes, was her eyes. They were such a light grey that under the harshness of early lights, a close-up gave her "the sightless orbs of a Greek statue." Wyckoff solved the problem by hanging up a cloth of black velvet and getting Farrar to gaze steadily at to enlarge her pupils. *Maria Rosa*, made for a little under $19,000 returned $102,767.81, $24,303.96 of which were foreign sales. As

America was still politically neutral, Lasky was able successfully to sell the film abroad as Farrar still had a lot of fans among the Prussian elite and the German in the street.

Even as *Maria Rosa* was being shot, costumes were being gathered and sets built for *Carmen*. Buckland was busy creating the ramparts of Seville, Pastia's place, the cigarette factory, and the Plaza del Toros. DeMille wanted to capture the realism of Merimee's great novel. For the celebrated bullring, although they only needed to show it from the outside, Buckland, with five tons of plaster of Paris, created an exact replica of the entrance.

The same passion for accuracy was evident in the costumes. For Farrar's Carmen, off-the-peg mantillas wouldn't do. As yet, the studio had no professional to organize and run its wardrobe department, so actresses and wives of employees would go shopping and search for appropriate costumes. Fortunately, there was a large Spanish community in Los Angeles. Old trunks and wardrobes were rifled for clothes to give to the extras, festooned for the bullfight, to achieve an authentic "worn" look. The soldier's uniforms were new but none were spotless, and the critics noted and appreciated such concern.

What Farrar didn't know was that due to a copyright problem she would not be singing music from the opera. Even if the "golden voice" with the light-grey eyes turned out to be as wooden as the slats before the camera, Bizet's libretto, and the "Habanera" in particular would stir audiences. If as DeMille told his brother, "[if] they only know the 'Toreador's Song,'" audiences will be enthralled. But they couldn't use the opera libretto. No Bizet story, no Bizet music! The Bizet story, Carmen's spirit, and her powerful sexuality all would have to be conveyed by pantomime. Cleverly, they came up with a touch original to the film, one full of enough visual excitement to set mood and Carmen's character, the fight between Carmen and the envious Frasquita, played by Jeanie Macpherson.

Carmen began filming three days after *Maria Rosa* was completed. DeMille confirmed that the position of the camera had been determined before Farrar got off the train—DeMille had learned since *The Squaw Man* to make his decisions before, not during shooting. He had barely two months in which to shoot, and wasted not a minute. Could movies reach the artistic heights of opera? Music filled the set. Farrar could be heard singing from her trailer. DeMille had reworked the script to begin with a bang. The story is no sooner under way before it explodes into the first great "catfight." Farrar: "My biggest fighting moment was not the traditional third act, where the two women [Carmen and Micaela] claim the bewildered Don Jose, but a vigorous quarrel in the tobacco factory where the amiable Jeanie [*sic*] Macpherson, Mr. DeMille's right-hand scenarist and an actress of no mean ability, loaned herself to my assault in a battle that made screen history." The ensuing no-holds-barred nail-tearing brawl was compared favorably to the bruising battle between two men in *The Spoilers*, which had ended in broken ribs. There were no such casualties here and the scene was shot in one take.

The melee is broken up by the arrival of the Spanish militia, led by Don Jose (Reid), a simple fellow who is shocked to discover such behavior among the gentle sex. What follows is well known. Even without the benefit of Bizet's "Habanera" to stir the pulse, the love scenes have an obvious combustibility. Carmen ruffles Don Jose's shirt, she teases his hair, she wiggles and wriggles in his embrace like a snake shedding its skin.

At the film's climax, Carmen, having abandoned Jose for the bullfighter Escamillo, is seated in the front row of the crowded arena. Before the first bull is released she is told Jose is outside. Jose pleads with her to leave with him. She shrugs, "My love is mine. To give or to deny." All she wants is to see the main event, which only serves to inflame Jose's desperate ardor. He catches hold of her long thick hair (a nice touch), and yanks her to her knees. Although it means her own destruction, Carmen defiantly continues to mock him. His whining self-pity disgusts her. Almost unconsciously his knife now slides into her body. There is no mistaking the sexual implications as he twists the blade. In 1915, the public had rarely seen such passion shown on the screen in such realistic and adult terms. But Carmen's truly existential disdain for the pedestrian existence Jose offers still packs a punch today.

All the advance publicity for *Carmen* taught those pioneers another costly lesson. By the time the film opened, it was no longer the only version in release. Not only was an earlier version—based on the opera—reissued, but wily William Fox's newly formed company, built and financed by the success of his sensational overnight star, Theda Bara, American film's first full-fledged sex symbol, rushed into production a new version of *Carmen* starring Bara. Although generally considered inferior (though its young director Raoul Walsh would also go on to become one of Hollywood's finest), Bara's version inevitably stole some of DeMille's thunder and a share of the market. Goldwyn couldn't sell it for as much as they all expected, and their *Carmen* didn't make much more than *Maria Rose* or *Temptation*.

Even so, the press and public were still enthusiastic, though the real reason for its appeal was neatly summed up as "an orgy of flesh." Flesh might still be taboo, but here there was a lot of it.

Books, opera, and now theater were by and large safe from censorship, since the working classes weren't likely to afford them. But movies attracted a far wider audience. Thus, wives, mothers, and sisters of upstanding pillars of communities formed committees. These self-ordained judges were on the watch for any departure from the norm, and the norm in a rapidly expanding world could be anything, depending on which state one was in and which part of the Bible they thumped in righteous anger. DeMille fought back against any suggestion of censorship, "In a very real sense we are defending morality when we fight censorship, when we refuse to yield to the ridiculous demands of pressure groups, and I am not saying that all of their demands are ridiculous. But some of them certainly are."

But you could no more censor Farrar's passion than wipe the smile off the Mona Lisa. She held Jose with her eyes and even harder with her arms, crushing her loosely bound breasts against him. The flamboyant upstart Bara was one thing, but "the great Farrar" was quite another, and even Arkansas and Minnesota hesitated to excise such moments from a performance acclaimed by Kaisers, kings, and New York's 500 as one of the great interpretations of the day. For most of the film, she was in the chemise bodice of an Andalusian female, her muscular but lovely arms playing like swords, naked to her shoulders, before the camera's enraptured gaze, and there was nothing they could do about it.

Farrar was to take some of her realistic DeMille touches back to the Met, but her new interpretation created more than even she bargained for. After Farrar, now a movie star, slapped Enrico Caruso in the face, he told the management to get themselves another Don Jose. "Where does she think she is?" the tenor grunted, licking his wounds in the wings. "Hollywood?"

After a fourteen-day break from his cast (allowing time to concoct a script), DeMille was back to work with *Temptation*. For this contemporary drama, Farrar played a promising singer who almost sacrifices her virtue to help a struggling young composer. In a single film, she had the chance to wear some of her celebrated wardrobe, resist seduction, cope with murder (the death of the importuning impresario caused by his jealous mistress), and sing "Home! Sweet Home!" Neither the star nor her director thought highly of the film, Farrar opining that it was "a story that has since served anybody who can lay claim to a vocal chirp—how the little home-town girl makes good in grand opera, upon merit and virtue."

There's an old theater saying that when an actress doesn't like her script there's usually something wrong with her appearance. DeMille confided his own doubts on the matter to Lasky: "Farrar is terribly disappointed at her appearance in modern clothes. She has intimated, now that thirty-nine scenes have been taken, that maybe we ought to change the scenario and do TOSCA; but I have succeeded in convincing her that she was very beautiful. There is a great deal in what she says. So far, she seems a little flat in modern stuff."

Neither Farrar nor DeMille came up with the sort of invention she would bring to her last great operatic role as Leoncavello's Zaza. As that French cocotte, in the midst of an aria, she perfumed her underwear. Movie censors had nothing like that to worry about in *Temptation*. The murder, in dimly lit interiors, was a prelude to the branding scene he was to create for *The Cheat*.

Ironically, because of its contemporary setting, *Temptation* was perceived to be more risqué than either of Farrar's previous films. Goldwyn worried that the suggestiveness of some scenes might not pass all the states' censors without cuts, and suggested that DeMille change a few titles as well as cutting the

DeMille's partner Jesse Lasky (right) is shown shipboard on a return from Europe with Adolph Zukor's brother-in-law and Paramount executive Albert Kaufman. Photo: International Newsreel. Courtesy John Kobal Foundation

scene where the mistress stabs her lover "considerably," rather than have the censors do it.

Her work completed, Farrar was preparing to return east, and she gave a farewell party for her hundreds of new friends, the likes of which the good folks of Hollywood had never known. It began at 8 p.m. and lasted till 11 the next morning. It was during this party that Farrar's friendship with Lou Tellegen turned serious. They were married in February, and soon her highly emotional husband's demands would become a burden on Lasky, and his-off stage advice to his wife a thorn in DeMille's side.

The strain was beginning to show on Lasky. Traveling back and forth between New York and the coast, between vaudeville and film, between Lasky and Famous Players, it was no wonder. "I started out to write a personal letter and not a business one," would go a typical missive to the old friend he used to go camping in Maine with, "but as you see—I have become a machine-and there isn't anything else in my life except business." In turn, Goldwyn unburdened himself to DeMille about his own "domestic troubles": "I have taken it in the best possible manner, and I also feel that this entire affair has made a better man of me as my viewpoint of things in general are absolutely different to what they have been up to date."

It was rare to find Goldwyn in such a sensitive mood. According to one of his biographers, A. Scott Berg, Goldwyn realized that he didn't love his wife and that she didn't love him. Despite sufficient warning from relatives and friends, Blanche married Goldwyn as an escape from show business. Goldwyn had wanted affection. Neither made the other, nor their child, happy. Goldwyn had thrown himself even more feverishly into his work and pursued other women. Of course, the last person he could turn for understanding in this situation was to his brother-in-law, Lasky, who was devoted to his sister. But in his correspondence with DeMille the usually bullheaded dynamo sounds more like a lonely man calling out to friends. In their two years as partners, they had polished a lot of rough edges off one another, and reached a good understanding that would last over the years.

Meanwhile, Beatrice was sorting out her affairs in New York in preparation for joining her sons in California. Although DeMille helped his mother, he never gave her exactly what she asked for. She would ask for $100, and he would send her $75. He described it as a game they played. The game was not always to her liking and created bad feelings. When things weren't going her way, Beatrice knew just what to say and how to say it to make her children feel like ingrates. Now DeMille was expecting her to come live with him, but (not for the first time) she changed her mind. When his mother finally did arrive, DeMille supported her, and provided her with a house of her own.

After finishing the sequel to *Chimmie Fadden*, DeMille had gone straight into *The Cheat*, and during its last week of production he began working on *The Golden Chance*, shooting one by day and the other by night. From his very first film, DeMille would become progressively more attracted to challenging themes for his films, introducing them in an offhand but realistic manner.

The Cheat is the story of Edith Hart played by Fannie Ward, a pampered wife who gets into financial hot water when she spends charity funds on clothes and, finding her husband's own finances are in a mess, goes to the rich "Oriental" importer Hishituru Tori, played by Sessue Hayakawa, for the money, and in return agrees to sleep with him. When she attempts to renege on the bargain by repaying Tori in cash he brands her with his mark, and in rage and terror she shoots him. Her husband takes the blame and is about to be convicted when his wife confesses. After the court sees the livid mark of the branding on her shoulders, she is exonerated.

When he made *The Cheat*, DeMille treated a subject that exploded sexual stereotypes: relationships between a white woman with a non-white lover was not tolerated on the screen—and the mere suggestion of "white slavery" could lead to violent protests. Released in 1915, *The Cheat* was a direct challenge to the double standard by which what was right for a man was not accepted for a woman. DeMille further stacked the odds in favor of his villain by casting the part with a sinuously attractive actor who made the women in the audience have second thoughts about a fate worse than death at his hands.

These days, silent films are rarely screened. Prints are too poor. Too many allowances have to be made for the primitive conventions of storytelling. Their reputations rest in books. But *The Cheat*, like *Carmen*, was so remarkable, such a success, that it is one of a handful of early silent films which remained a landmark. Unlike *Carmen*, which rested on Farrar's shoulders, the credit for *The Cheat*'s sensational success was DeMille's. His flair was creating sexual tension, already revealed in *The Captive* and *Carmen*, and adding the unashamedly erotic. In the scene where Hayakawa (playing Tori) brands Fannie Ward, in his shadowy lit and richly decorated study, as she lies like a discarded puppet on the floor, DeMille cuts to show only what is beautiful and necessary: the fine embroidery of his housecoat; the fringe of fur on her dress; his precise, controlled demeanor, like a ceremonial sword made flesh. Ward's hair, in clustered curls swept up for the dinner party she was dressed to attend, has been loosened in the struggle and hangs down her back and shoulders.

This scene remains effective today. As the critic Simon Harcourt-Smith wrote in 1951, "Here for the first time was displayed a restraint in direction and acting which was to give the cinema a completely new style, an ideal of sophistication, which it has never renounced."

For some, *The Cheat* remains DeMille's most admired work. What it had that his other films of that period lacked was sex. *Carmen*, of course, was all sex but it was set in another time, in another country, and concerned the antics of two people with whom most American audiences had little in common. *The Cheat* felt and looked as if it had been taken from the tabloids. European audiences especially admired DeMille's superb *mise-en-scene* of this adult subject. In DeMille's films, women stepped out of the past to become the moral equal of men. Simpering was not permitted. A Griffith charmer would not have survived long in DeMille's world. *The Cheat* was one of those films with which American movies came of age.

With his role as the high-powered financier, Sessue Hayakawa became not only the first Asian film star but also one of the first male sex symbols of the silent screen. It would be five years before Valentino rode forth as *The Sheik*. Years later, by which time he had gone on to have a distinguished career, Hayakawa still proudly recalled the role: "Forbidding as he appears to be at times—and to some people all the time—Mr. DeMille was a patient and understanding man whose job fascinated him, and whose grasp of its essentials and imaginative use of them was phenomenal. . . . Actually, he did not direct me. Now and again he made suggestions, but for the most part he left me alone to go my way according to my own understanding of the role. 'All right, Sessue, you do it the way you feel,' he would say. And when the cameraman began to shoot the scene Mr. DeMille would lapse into silence."

DeMille had actually been making a second film at the time he was shooting *The Cheat*. When that film was only two-thirds completed, troubles between another Lasky director and the leading lady on *The Golden Chance* blew up, and with the studio going full throttle to meet its deadlines, the Director General had no choice but to take over. He directed Fannie Ward, Sessue Hayakawa, and the cast of *The Cheat* from nine o'clock in the morning straight through until five in the afternoon, recalled Hayakawa, "then, after a short nap in his office, and dinner on his desk, he directed the cast of *The Golden Chance* from eight in the evening till two the following morning. The strain was terrific, particularly when the leading ladies of both pictures became difficult to work with." As Fannie Ward was giving off dramatic fireworks on the soundstage next door, Goodrich, the star of *The Golden Chance*, developed a drinking problem. DeMille remembered that he "escorted her to the door and said goodbye to her." She was replaced by Cleo Ridgely.

The action in *The Golden Chance* was divided between grim New York tenements and Park Avenue mansions. Reduced to living in slum-like conditions, a young wife from a good family is employed as a seamstress and, because of her beauty, is asked by her rich employer to join a dinner, after a guest drops out, to help to entice a millionaire into closing an important business deal with her husband. Inevitably, the young man played by Wallace Reid falls for this Cinderella. It was clear from the costumes and sets that DeMille in his struggling years had known something of this world. The shoot-out in the one-room cold-water flat is well staged. The heroine's sad plight is convincingly presented.

He didn't begin *The Trail of the Lonesome Pine* until four days after Christmas. There is none of the glamor of *The Cheat* or *The Golden Chance* in the rustic world of the Tollifers, mountain folk who live barely a notch above the animals and exist by their own code of law among the tall, uncombed pines, making their living by selling illicitly distilled hooch. When the government has passed a law against this, Jack Halle (the brawny Thomas Meighan) is the district revenue officer sent to break up their business. The Tollifers tie up Jack and throw him into the empty cowshed until they can move their still. A daughter, June (Charlotte Walker), brings him a blanket; their hands brush up against each other. The sequence of budding emotions is conveyed by great timing, editing, and a superb use of close-ups.

The scenes leading up to the climax are as good as any DeMille ever filmed. Events are conveyed with an almost complete absence of titles. The few needed are powerful in their brevity. *Carmen* was exciting, *The Cheat* was shocking, but these scenes in *The Trail of the Lonesome Pine* have a startling sense of realism. Having been shot, a nearly lifeless Jack is carried into the cabin. June is horrified to see the man she helped almost dead from loss of blood. Her anguish is so intense that her father is taken aback. The young girl is learning a lesson that is tearing her apart. She has to choose between her people and the man she loves. Finally, his danger overcomes any last residue of family loyalty. He has to have a doctor. "You can't let him die," she pleads. Giving up a last residue of family loyalty. The camera depicts these emotions as DeMille cuts from face to face. June moves to Jack's cot, holding a shard

After a career in the Follies, Mae Murray made her third film, *The Dream Girl*, for DeMille in 1916. She is shown here with early movie heavy Charles West. Courtesy John Kobal Foundation

of glass as if it were a magic crystal. This is the moment DeMille chooses for the tightest close-up yet as she brings the shard closer, and closer still, until it almost touches his lips. Then there are only two profiles, with his reflection between. There is a slight fogging.

"He's still breathing!"

The scene in the crowded room lasted almost ten minutes. DeMille would often be accused in later years of not handling intimate scenes well, but these three films, made in a six-month period, show that he could have gone on to become one of the great romantics of the screen, on a par with King Vidor, Frank Borzage, and even Josef von Sternberg. He believed in one commandment above all, that the love between a man and a woman is the purest and most powerful emotion in the world.

The Heart of Nora Flynn was next, but like *The Golden Chance*, it was no more than a summer diversion, starring the gorgeous, raven-haired Marie Doro. Doro would subsequently marry her co-star, Elliot Dexter, who went on to a long career as one of DeMille's favorite leading men. Three weeks later, DeMille was busy with *The Dream Girl*, made to repair the damage done to another recent Lasky acquisition, the petite Ziegfeld dancer Mae Murray when she was still a brunette and before she acquired the description "the girl with the bee-stung lips."

According to Murray, Adolph Zukor had written to her suggesting that she was motion picture material when he saw her in a Follies skit impersonating Mary Pickford. Within weeks, she was Hollywood bound, looking forward to the promised "Farrar treatment"—red car, red carpet, red roses. Unfortunately, her first film was not a happy experience. When she saw some film stills, Murray was so unhappy by her appearance that she tore them up. Her next film was no better, so her third *The Dream Girl* would have DeMille directing. She portrayed a waif named Meg, whose only refuge from a brutal father was to hide in a barrel. "DeMille was a martinet on the set, lashing everyone toward the perfectionism he strove for. . . . He himself jumped up to do a drunk scene, staggering about breaking chairs, smashing bottles the way he wanted . . . it, while Mae cowered in the barrel with one side missing for the camera to peer in."

Under California sun and with the seemingly endless open spaces, motion pictures were becoming a big business. DeMille, Lasky, Goldwyn, and Zukor were flourishing at the moment the world in Europe was starting to crumble. Still, America remained neutral. Even after entering the war in 1917, Hollywood continued to grow and to profit. When the war was over, the European film industry would find it had been conquered by Hollywood.

CHAPTER ELEVEN

IN THE FIRST YEAR OF "THE WAR TO END ALL WARS," THE FEAR OF THE UN-sentimental Hollywood producers, mostly immigrants, recent refugees scrambling with survivor's skill up the gold-plated industrial ladder, was what effect the European conflict was going to have on increasingly import-ant foreign revenues.

It didn't take long for them to understand that the longer the war went on and the worse things got "over there," the better for business. Having replaced the Seligs, Lubins, Kleines, and Edisons, the next generation—men of little charm from varied yet similarly impoverished backgrounds, tougher, sharper, cannier, led by the Zukors, Laemmles, Foxes, and Goldwyns, with Mayers, Cohns, and Warners soon to follow—were making movies not be-cause of any inborn flair for the medium, but because it offered riches greater than selling meat, or gloves, or furs. DeMille had little in common with these men other than ambition. Yet he worked and associated with them success-fully. Outwardly they were peers, because the world saw all movie moguls as cut from the same cloth. But if, in the privacy of his own home, DeMille denied any form of kinship with them, it wasn't to be wondered at.

The moguls learned from the collapse of Edison and his Trust: Trust-No-One. They were out of their corners before anyone else heard the bell. "Stars" made the American industry unique, technicians perfected the means to improve the screen. But their masters were men without morals. Photo-graphs of them in their tight-fitting jackets and stiff snap-down collars show faces radiating a lust for power like steam from hot tar. Opportunists all, they quickly learned to change their shirts more often and discovered how easily the right appearance could fool the many. Washed, shaved, and pomaded but otherwise unchanged, these pioneers in the film trade were ready to fight for their right to cheat one another off for a bigger share of the pie.

Before the war, German, Danish, British, and French film companies had been superior in quality and output to the Americans. Feeding the war ma-chine had crippled Europe's film industry and destroyed its preeminence not only in the world markets but in their own as well. By 1916, hardly any films except newsreels were being produced by European filmmakers. Before the war, American movies (except for Westerns, all bang-bang and gallop) had made little dent overseas. Now there was an enormous captive audience hungry for entertainment and grateful for anything that smacked of escapism.

"Into this vacuum," wrote Will Irwin, an early biographer of Adolph Zukor, "poured the flood of American films. Mary Pickford's sunny curls, Mae Marsh's girlish innocence, and Theda Bara's sinister allure sweetened the war for millions of young and impressionable soldiers." No matter how badly contrived their plots, Americans films were full of hope.

William deMille, writing in 1939, noted the mood in Hollywood back in 1915, "war films were not popular in America." Tuned to this sentiment, Thomas H. Ince produced his pacifist epic *Civilization*, in which Christ took the war-mongering king (who looked a lot like the German Kaiser) on a tour of shelled homes, battlefields, graveyards, and grieving widows, to bring home the tragedy his aggression created. *Civilization* was such an enormous success that it was said to have helped President Wilson win his re-election on a peace platform.

But once America launched itself into the war effort, the virulence of Hollywood's propaganda was unrelenting. The metaphorical "rape of muddy Europe" was shorn of its metaphor, and reduced to the highly inflammatory rape of women and the slaughter of "innocent" children. The American government became so embarrassed by these films that it requested Hollywood to tone down the roll call of atrocities. There was a genuine fear that scenes of leering Huns bayoneting mothers and babies would make it even harder to achieve a just peace.

Meanwhile, the Kaiser's old sweetheart Geraldine Farrar was about to start work on her next film. Lasky hadn't decided on a story, but it needed to be suitably grand to capitalize on her previous screen successes. Expecting to make another three films in quick succession, Farrar didn't learn until she arrived in California that her work would be limited to one, and that it would take all summer to make.

At this time, two topics were the talk of Hollywood: the war, of course, and the awesome movie set that had sprouted above Hollywood at the end of the previous year. It was colossal, unavoidable, and towered over the skyline. Even from the outside, it was clear that this was the lost city of the hanging walls, mighty Babylon itself, one of the seven wonders of the ancient world—rebuilt with plaster and wood in the heart of Hollywood.

D. W. Griffith was making an epic, *Intolerance*, his answer to *Cabiria* and *Quo Vadis*. To guard against shifty fly-by-night companies hoping to shoot his exteriors and working them into their plots, his set was closed and carefully guarded. No one, not even those working with him, was sure what Hollywood's acknowledged genius was planning. DeMille knew a grand spectacle was in the making.

With thoughts of war and Griffith's epic dominating his mind, DeMille decided that Farrar's project would be a story based on the life of Joan of Arc.

Work began on June 19, 1916, and finished on October 7. A year earlier, De-Mille had turned out four films in the same time and at the same expense—a little over $300,000. By any sort of calculation, *Joan the Woman* was the most expensive Lasky production to date. Ince had his *Civilization*, Griffith his *Intolerance*. Now the Lasky Company was going to finance DeMille's *Joan the Woman*. Cautious Goldwyn came to the set and was impressed. Zukor and the always supportive Lasky came too, wondering at what their money had wrought.

The Lasky ranch was converted into a fourteenth-century French village, complete with castles and turrets and all the trimmings. Although the press was kept away until almost the end of shooting, nearly everyone connected with the company came down to look. The settings and the props looked authentic, but everyone knew the script had to have wide appeal with a story that audiences would be anxious to see.

The one problem no one recognized at the time was that Farrar was physically unsuited to the role of Joan, who was a slip of a girl, and Farrar wasn't, but this did not become clear until it was too late to do anything about it. Not that anybody ever said that Farrar, a matron with all the world behind her, was wrong to play a maid with all the world against her. As the cost of the film rose to the point where profits would be hard to insure, the studio figured the film's prestige would carry the day.

DeMille's version of the martyr was based on an idea of Jeanie Macpherson's. It was titled *Joan the Woman* "because Jeanie," DeMille said, "wished to emphasize the humanity of Joan of Arc rather than project the conventional, and so frequently false, image of a saint."

Despite the hardships of filming battle scenes on horseback (she was deathly afraid of horses), Geraldine Farrar never got over the joy of making the film, "I was practically helpless in my high saddle, being lifted on and off by two men especially designated for this service. Encumbered not only by my armor and huge sword, I carried aloft a heavy banner that floated out for a good three yards on a stiff breeze. Yet when the bugles shrilled for our charge and maneuvers, I couldn't help thrill, and forgot my fears, my inexpert horsemanship everything, in fact save that I was actually the Maid bent on her holy errand."

Photoplay's reporter wrote about the film with unusual reverence: "The day the scenes where the French captured the upper parapet of La Tourelle were taken, Mr. DeMille offered a bonus to several of the men if they would fall off this parapet and make the forty-foot drop into the moat below. Forty feet is quite a drop for a man in armor and the men, fearful of being injured, jumped, instead of falling. It was tried several times, and still the men could not get up the courage to fall. Finally Mr. DeMille remarked quietly to 'Our Jerry' (Farrar)—'I guess the men are afraid to do it. We will have to cut out that scene.' 'Our Jerry' replied, 'Yes, I am afraid so, but it would be very effective.' That night, Mr. DeMille received a note signed by 25 of the extra men to the effect that if he would make the scene over, they would guarantee to fall and not to jump from the top of the wall, and unless it was done to the entire satisfaction of both Miss Farrar and himself, they wanted no money for it. Next day the scene was retaken and the wall rained struggling men. Several were slightly injured by having other steel-clad companions clash down upon them, but the doctor was always there and, outside of a few cuts and bruises, nothing serious befell them. In fact, both armies seemed to glory in their wounds. For the next day they had the pleasure of being asked by 'Our Jerry' if they were all right." This account fails to convey the real danger to life and limb these men risked during days before the advent of professional stuntmen. Heroic extras fell to the ground and put their faith in heaven.

Seventy years later, the results DeMille achieved on the screen are as exacting as any battles filmed subsequently, charged with documentary realism that makes them as impressive as newsreel films of the fighting in the trenches. A trick shot that accidentally showed the camera tracks besides the horse's hooves makes the film seem more real: proof that there were real people there risking their lives. This was the moment when DeMille's love for the spectacular took possession of him. The artist had found his genre. It's apparent in the dust swirling around the actors and horses, clinging to faces and costumes; the relish for embroidery; the dramatic lighting. DeMille got his taste for recreating important moments from history. He frames, reducing the screen to a narrow strip; he circles a face or a weapon of war; he enlarges. A man pulls an arrow from his mouth. Spears, swords, and arrows enter men with incredible realism. Figures, clearly human, tumble down thirty-foot walls and can be seen bouncing off the ground. Although critics eventually mocked DeMille's style, few other directors ever made as great an impact. *Joan the Woman* was his launch as a director of epics.

Still impressive for its scale and realism is the sight of Joan leading her men into battle, a magnificent gathering of thousands of Lasky staffers and Los Angelenos filling the screen. No one knew or thought about how to fake it. Often what one saw was no more than naked courage. While the film is silent, one can almost hear the din of yells, swords, and lances clashing on helmets and breast plates, and of horses screaming. There's an injured horse expiring on the ground with men falling over him as they charge to the walls. There certainly couldn't have been opportunities for retakes. It was now or never.

These sword-waving, lance-pointing soldiers, charging up and leaping over heavily spiked defenses, were not actors. They were extras earning their $5 a day, whipped by their director into a holy rapture. They believed that this movie was special, that it would live forever. No fear in these men's eyes that each "unforgettable" achievement would be quickly obliterated by a new stream of screen miracles. *Joan the Woman* was being made when Hollywood was in its age of "firsts." Without going to fight in France, they could nonetheless all experience what it must be like to be part of an assault.

Farrar stands out in her heavy armor, up to her waist in the moat, now just missed by a downpour of boiling oil (in reality, water that had been heated up by standing all day in the hot California sun). Having broken through the line of battle, calling her men to follow, Joan is struck in the shoulder by an English arrow. The English captain (Wallace Reid), about to finish the job, recognizes her as the girl who had befriended him when she was still a maid: Scene 90. First time Eric sees Joan in the shed. He starts by trying to rape her, but is seduced by the fearless look in her eyes and the soft radiance, which begins to glow behind her head. Eric is so moved that he is willing to leave her alone and even protect her from his fellow soldiers.

Now, he sees her again. To make sure we remember, DeMille gives us a great, tight, enormous two-shot. Now it is Eric who saves her from death. History bends to the will of drama. The battle goes on for another two reels, or twenty minutes. With victory comes the first intermission: End of First Epoch. The audience, familiar with newsreels from the front, must have been shattered. It was like the real thing.

Part two of Griffith's *Intolerance* opened with a full-blown orgy of celebration: nearly nude dancing girls, huge roasts on spits. DeMille launched his second half with a somewhat more uplifting Christian spectacle: the crowning of the king in the cathedral at Rheims and Joan's reward. Both films used enormous, tumultuous crowds that would be prohibitively expensive to film today. At one point, the screen is a sea of flags, spears, and banners, filled with people pressing out of windows to catch sight of Joan's triumphal entrance into the liberated city. Claire West made her reputation with DeMille with her costumes for this film. She remained head of his wardrobe department for the next seven years. Her first engagement to design costumes for the screen was for *Intolerance*, whose Babylonian scenes brought her to the attention of DeMille. Given the short time West had to prepare for the start of shooting, what a remarkable bunch they must have been to get 43,000 items of costume together in time.

Wilfred Buckland's superb art direction, conjuring medieval France out of sagebrush and thistle, is also hardly conceivable as the product of a few short weeks even if, admittedly, set design and preparation continued almost through the end of production. DeMille himself was up at dawn, writing and preparing, discussing and planning, filming from 10 a.m. to 7 p.m. as long as the light held, and then going over the latest pages of the script till 1 a.m.

Especially notable are the large sets shot from several angles to heighten the mood, as trumpets blow and courtiers jostle for a better view of the heroine. For Joan's entry, DeMille cut from a brightly lit and crowded room to darkness, with only the white-clad Joan walking along an ethereally shining rose-strewn carpet toward her king. Not even the nudging cutaways to evilly smiling clerics spoil the effect.

Work on *Joan the Woman* stretched every inch and ounce of studio manpower. For the big battle scenes, as many as twelve assistant directors were needed, stationed at cameras around the field, each equipped with a standard telephone set which enabled DeMille to control and direct the action from his post at the central camera stand. This strategy was leaked to the press because it was considered so revolutionary.

Those years at the military academy now came in handy. One can imagine those California cowboy extras once herding cattle in chaps, now dressed in heavy armor, scratching their heads under their hot helmets during a break in fighting, wondering as they waited to go charging across the 1,200-acre ranch in the boiling August sun, what the hell it was all about? This much is evident from reading one of DeMille's copies of the script.

The transparent, parchment-like rice paper script is covered with the notes of DeMille and Jeanie Macpherson. Sometimes there appears the third hand of his editor, Anne Bauchens. They show DeMille's attention to detail—he even had opinions on the exact shade of a handkerchief—and his search for new techniques. He noted the importance of using certain colors by tinting the flames of Joan's immolation. Thus, *Joan the Woman* became one of the first films to use a new color process, developed in an experimental photographic department established under Wyckoff. Working in this department was Max Handschiegl, a noted St. Louis engraver, who adapted the principles of his trade to motion pictures. "I had seen lithographs made," explained DeMille subsequently, "and I didn't see why they couldn't do that in color . . . by making a plate out of the picture itself, so it would move . . . So we invented a way. Where they have, say, yellow, blue and red film . . . and you print three times . . . We had a yellow film with the yellow just on the part where the candle flame is and the green just on the leaves, or whatever. That had to be done by hand in the printing after we had photographed it. It was magnified so that you could paint it and then reduced . . . That's the beginning of color, long before Technicolor." Even if the technical mysteries of color film aren't resolved by DeMille's explanation, and although some form of the Handschiegl process had been used in earlier films, these were three color sequences whose effect, even now, evokes the wonder audiences must have felt at the time.

DeMille often took his inspiration from a particular artist or painting (in *Intolerance*, which was released a month earlier, Griffith included in one of his titles the explanation that a scene showing Christ was after a painting by Tissot):

SCENE 21—Country road near Joan's house. (LONG SHOT) Joan is driving sheep toward camera—back lighting on her head if possible. (NOTE: this scene should suggest a "Millet.")

SCENE 508—Finally a great platter with a whole swan on it (like the Russian painting of the *Wedding Feast*) is brought on . . . This whole scene should be played in the brightest possible light.

SCENE 529—And at the end of the room still sits Charles. (NOTE: His attitude should suggest a picture of Maxfield Parrish's).

Careful attention was paid to the time of day at which filming took place:

> SCENE 190—Exterior Gate: Beaudricourt's Castle—(Instructions to the cameraman—Take this scene, if possible, at sunset, as we can get stunning effect of horsemen riding off into sunset.)
> SCENE 239—The Blessing of the Standard before Joan leads her men into the battle to reconquer the city of Orleans—Exterior: CAMP: CLOSE-UP: SUNSET (NOTE: This scene should be taken very late so the last rays of the sun can glorify Joan in streaming cross-light.)

DeMille included instructions on costumes and props:

> SCENE 42—Int. Shabby Court of Charles (in contrast to the splendor of Burgundy). . . . The Page's coat is faded, though once elegant, and in one of his hose is a good sized hole that has been darned—over his back is slung a lute.
> SCENE 388—There must be dark banner draped back of Saint so that we may play the two faces against dark background.

Contrary to conventional wisdom, which holds that DeMille did little by way of directing his crowds of actors and extras, his notes contain explicit instructions:

> SCENE 357—crowd must be smiling and joyous and full of "pep."
> SCENE 366—crowd go crazy!
>   Calm and cool as a cucumber!
> SCENE 373—Page quickly (but not *too* quickly) shows signs of poison.

And always, there are instructions that reveal his fetish for authenticity:

> SCENE 20—the D'Arc's living room. Sunset. (FULL SHOT) Six little partridges are hung in a row on a spit across the fireplace—(Mrs. D'Arc) is basting them.

> In ashes of fire are baking a row of potatoes—(NOTE: This supper should be real in every point.)

> SCENE 376—baskets full *of real* flowers
> SCENE 377—King now mounts steps of altar to waiting Archbishop (or Archbishop comes to foot of altar to King). (NOTE: ask priest which way is right.)
> SCENE 421—(Note: Look up what kind brushes or paraphernalia was used for "illuminating.") A young monk is working on a Bible.

Reading my notes written in the dark while first seeing *Joan* on the big old screen in DeMille's home, the full first impact returns. Images filled the wall above the massive fireplace. Let someone ask what made DeMille famous. I'd point to these scenes and say, there is the reason and there is the answer.

Acting styles, of course, have changed greatly since then. Theodore Roberts as Cauchon and Tully Marshall as the Mad Monk, who between them conspire in Joan's downfall and burning, were strutting their stuff in conventional villainous style. It was the first (but it wouldn't be the last) time that DeMille would lay the blame for many of the world's problems on the shoulders of organized religions and their leaders. It was hardly surprising that such scenes would provoke censorship problems. When Joan has been captured, the monk rushes into the Bishop's study saying, presumably, "Guess what, we've got her," to which the bishop, eyes raised sanctimoniously to heaven, replies, "Go thou, and pray for her soul." As he gloats the window blows open and a lamp flame sets on fire the dress on a statue of the Virgin. The statue flickers and burns as Cauchon's eyes grow large. Catholics were agitated, and when objections poured in, DeMille got his first taste of the power of organized religion on the box office. He never really stopped being provocative but became subtler.

Live music played a major part in raising emotions and carrying his audience across the lengthy titles needed to set the narrative. This script is full of specific references to musical instruments of the era like a lute, which were intended to be not just seen, but heard in the special score William Fuerst composed. DeMille wasn't the first silent director to have a special score composed for his films. Italian and French filmmakers had used them as far back as 1906, and Thomas Ince's *Civilization* had an original score by Victor Schertziner, who would go on to write many popular hits for movies. Although "music" is a part of *Joan the Woman,* in the opinion of Agnes deMille, "Cecil's knowledge of music was very slight. His taste, nonexistent. His scores were ragtag accumulations of show tunes assembled with no great skill and no historic reasons. For instance, in *Joan the Woman*, the English battle song was 'Britons Never Shall be Slaves,' eighteenth-century and off the mark by 450 years. The real battle songs of Joan of Arc's time were terrific, with iron in them and stark, full of valor, but they were unknown to most people and certainly to Cecil. I don't think it wise to talk about his music."

Accordingly, the "Marseillaise," a constantly recurring theme, was anachronistic (it wasn't written until the French Revolution), but DeMille wanted music Americans would instantly recognize as French. DeMille interest was rousing emotions rather than historical accuracy. If history couldn't provide him with what he needed for the great picture, then he would take what he needed from an available source.

For the scene depicting Joan burning at the stake, DeMille went all out. No one wanted to miss it. All the DeMilles were present for the filming. Agnes remembered: "During the burning, Cecil stood at the stake for hours,

trying out smoke. We were very proud of his courage, which was always no-
ticeable on these occasions. He never asked an actor to do what he would not
do himself. Farrar stood until she was obliterated by the smoke and flame,
although everyone said it would do her voice no good at all. But when they
burned the dummy and its hair caught and flaked off in a single shower of fiery cinders, she turned sick and had to go to her dressing room and lie down.
I stayed throughout, transfixed. I was impressed by the horrible heat given
off by the burning pyre."

Farrar was more modest. She had suffered through partridges, pigs, and
horses, and didn't mind the prison rats running over her, for they were really
"charming little white mice," disguised and following trails of sugar.

Farrar: "My clothing, skin and hair were treated with a fluid to make
scorching impossible. I had cotton, saturated with ammonia, placed in my
nostrils and mouth. . . . The flames were truly terrifying, and the experience was not without some danger. For the final immolation, in the long
shots a figure of wood was used cleverly arranged with shrouded, drooping
shoulders, and the face well forward, covered with disarranged locks. For the
'close-ups,' I was placed in the middle of tanks filled with oil; their ignition
and spectacular flames, together with the clouds of rolling smoke, gave a
perfect illusion in the 'cut-backs.'"

As DeMille readied *Joan the Woman*, the talk in Hollywood was about Griffith's *Intolerance*, soon to be unveiled in New York. Its fate was bound to affect
Joan the Woman in a way that *Civilization*, a modern-dress story, wouldn't. A
triumph would open the gates for historical spectacles which *Joan the Woman*
could sweep through. Failure would consolidate all the naysayers who had
held out against its cost and its length.

From Lasky to DeMille (September 6, 1916):

> Griffith picture *Intolerance* opened last night. It is being severely crit-
> icized on all sides and opinion everywhere is that it doesn't compare
> with *Birth of a Nation*. The lack of consecutive story is the picture's worst
> fault. In fact it proved a disappointment as far as the first night audience
> was concerned. However that part of the production which deals with
> the fall of Babylon is wonderful and in my opinion the picture will be
> a general success. . . . Mr. Zukor and I are convinced that we have a
> wonderful chance with the Farrar picture. You will be coming into New
> York with it at just the right moment, and if you have a story you will
> be giving the public just what they are clamoring for.

DeMille had one month of filming left.

Farrar, despite her great enthusiasm, was now running into overtime, and
she expected to be paid another $10,000 for it. Her attitude threw a canker
into the idyllic working relationship with DeMille. "She seems to have lost
a little something of the great spark of genius that animated her last year,"

DeMille wrote Lasky: "also, she has gotten pretty plump." Nevertheless, filming was completed happily in October. It was scheduled to premiere in New York on January 7, 1917, which gave four months to see how audiences reacted to *Intolerance*.

On his way to New York with the heavily guarded film, DeMille stopped off in Chicago, where Farrar was singing, and screened the film for her and her husband. Louella Parsons reported, "Miss Farrar cried and Mr. Tellegen shuddered with horror when Joan was burned at the stake."

Joan the Woman's most serious weakness, DeMille later came to realize, was not Farrar but the prologue and epilogue, a narrative device he would use with greater success in the future. He had allowed himself to be talked into framing the story with contemporary scenes set in the trenches, in which Eric Trent, a young officer, turns out to be the reincarnation of the fifteenth-century English soldier responsible for Joan's downfall. Now Eric II must atone for Eric I by saving France in World War I (France and England were now on the same side, but never mind), and, to give Eric courage, Joan returns to inspire him. Not only was the audience asked to accept the high-flown concept of reincarnation, but all this convoluted plotting took place before they got to Joan's story. It also made an already long film longer—it ran over ten reels. As late as May, distributors and States Rights buyers asked for cuts that would bring it down to less than two hours.

But ultimately the problem came down to DeMille's forthright blaming of the Catholic clergy for their part in the capture, trial, and burning of Joan. Then, as now, movies had to appeal to all shade of opinion, and there were enough Catholics in the US for their feelings to make a significant difference at the box office. Lose the Catholics, and the Evangelicals might not be far behind. Joan was burnt by the English while the Church was about to make the brave girl a saint: that was what people were taught in schools, and they were not ready to blame their clergy.

When it came down to profit he could be positively ruthless, though it must have hurt him. DeMille's reaction, once he saw that his view had lost, was "to let the State Rights buyer, himself, make these eliminations, inasmuch as the different parts of the country would probably prefer to see different scenes cut out. That is, in the strong Catholic communities, those scenes relating to the Catholic Church might best be spared; while in the Protestant portions of the country, it might be desirable to retain such scenes." If the masses wanted to trim Joan's burning (after all the effort it had cost him and her), let them. If the Catholics couldn't stomach the truth about their clergy, chop all that subtle lighting and leering and conspiring. Some of the footage that was cut from *Joan the Woman* eventually ended up in Sarah Bernhardt's film *Mothers of France*. With the war in Europe still on everyone's mind, scenes of Wallace Reid, wearing his smart uniform in the trenches, stayed in.

Although *Joan the Woman* eventually made back its cost (more than a quarter of it from foreign sales), it took a long time, and was considered an unsatisfactory return for such a huge investment. Moreover, just one film was made during the course of the summer instead of three. As an untested epic running over two hours and necessitating special promotion and distribution campaigns, it completely tied up Lasky's sales force and publicity department.

Back in June, while DeMille was launching one kind of movie history, his partners were making another. While the Lasky productions were selling and the demand for more was ever-increasing, the still small company was working to the limit of its financial and physical capacities. A fourteen-hour day would only be"'work as usual." Even though Goldwyn, Lasky, and Adolph Zukor ate lunch together at Delmonico's in New York at least once a week, the long but friendly competition between Lasky and Famous Players was a rivalry that was beginning to make Goldwyn's life absolutely miserable.

DeMille met Zukor the previous September under dramatic circumstances. Zukor's Famous Players Studio was going up in flames. He was standing on Twenty-sixth Street in New York, recalled DeMille, "silhouetted in the light of the flames eating up his first studio. And in all the turmoil and excitement he stood there calmly watching it, watching his investment and his hopes go up in smoke. I had not met him before, but I went over to commiserate with him. His only reply was 'We'll build a better one.' And with his eyes always on the future, he did build a better one."

The two companies found themselves constantly bidding for the same properties and stars. This problem was resolved by doing a deal with the man they hoped would be their d'Artagnan, but who proved instead to be their Richelieu. They decided to merge the two companies, leading to the creation of the most powerful film studio in Hollywood, Paramount Pictures—and make them millionaires.

Lasky to DeMille (June 24): "Have seen negotiations for merger Famous with us and have Zukor's consent to fifty-fifty basis which we feel makes attractive proposition. All of us including yourself will be officers and directors and will have five-year contracts with new corporation to be called Famous Players Lasky Corporation. Control of producing end will vest in us so there will be no change in your position or plans for special releases but feel certain merger will make everybody's stock more valuable and probably market will be created. This deal just between Famous and us, no banker, no brokers or other leeches."

Lasky approved, the merger went through, and, according to the ubiquitous Harry Reichenbach, "The toss of a coin decided whether the name of the combination should be 'Famous Players-Lasky' or 'Lasky-Famous Players.'" The coin landed on "Famous Players-Lasky."

As the partners prospered, others, whose contribution had played a significant part in the success of the little company, felt disgruntled. One of the first to show his discontent was William deMille. DeMille's brother had grown increasingly impatient, and tired of wrangling with the studio's directors over

their treatment of his scripts. He was fed up with still being head of the scenario department. His brain, he said, had begun to feel like a melting pot
"into which all the stories in the world had been poured. Recipes as written
in a cookbook may be perfect, but in the last analysis, much depends upon
the cook." He decided he would "rather be a mother than a midwife." De-
Mille, though sorry to lose his ally in the scenario department, supported
William.

And then there was Wilfred Buckland, head of the art department, two
years on and still grossly underpaid. Buckland had enough of unfulfilled
promises. DeMille was in New York preparing for the launch of *Joan the Woman* when Buckland's letter reached him. In it, the art director made clear his
bitter frustration on discovering that although he "may be the head of a vital
creative department, this gives him no real say as to how his work will end
up in the finished product." Whether Buckland's plea for "artistic control for
his work" was the first on record or not (he did receive screen credit, which
was more than Griffith would have given him), it has rung out from every
film department ever since: "Why, if you hire me for my unique and special
talents, don't you allow me to exercise them?"

Buckland's letter posed a special dilemma for DeMille. The older man was
a friend. DeMille had been responsible for Buckland giving up his career on
Broadway and moving to Hollywood. Once Buckland had been DeMille's
mentor, now he was working for his former teacher.

Dear Cecil, (Nov. 30th, 1916)

The company must realize my value has increased as the value of their
stock has. In this connection I understand there has been some vague-
ness on the part of the Company as to what "scope" I wanted . . . It is
impossible to get results which will advance firm's interests and my
own unless given more scope, and a voice in formulating new projects. [D. W.] Griffith agrees with me that time has come when Picture
Industry will suffer unless new methods I advocate are adopted. I am
perfectly willing to remain Art Director and design the settings—but I
ask a voice in the way my sets are "shot," and the figure grouped, which is
indispensable to the best results.

Peace was preserved. Lasky needed Buckland, but it was clear that this was
no longer a family business. Nothing made this clearer than the boardroom
row that took place in New York. Zukor had been made president; Lasky was
vice president and Goldwyn chairman of the board of directors. But peace
between Goldwyn and his new partners would be short-lived. Zukor, as De-
Mille and later Lasky were to find out, was a hard fighter, and Goldwyn was
notoriously hardheaded. Once they began to work together their mutual
dislike quickly surfaced. DeMille, 3,000 miles away, was protected from the

boardroom battles by the din of the French charge on the walls of Orleans. He was probably the most fairly positioned and least biased of the group to evaluate what had happened.

In the beginning, the transition had gone smoothly enough. Zukor even entrusted the very delicate matter of negotiating Pickford's contract to Goldwyn. This proved to be a major mistake. It was the first time Pickford had dealt with Goldwyn, and it marked the beginning of a lifelong antipathy. From the outset, Pickford, the undisputed queen of Famous Players, was not well disposed towards the merger, blaming much of what happened on the new partners. "Where there had been an intimate little family group, threshing out its problems in a warm, personal spirit of team work, there was now a higher machine, cold, critical, automatic, and impersonal. Thanks to the interference from the new parent group I made two pictures, the memory of which I have tried sedulously to wipe from my mind." This was a reference to her two films with DeMille. "Famous Players had promised me a sizeable sum before the merger if I would delay signing my next contract. I went to see Mr. Zukor to remind him of our agreement. In the discussion that ensued I saw Mr. Zukor put his hand under the desk and, I supposed, press a button. An office boy instantly appeared, stating that Mr. Samuel Goldfish wished to see Miss Pickford in his private office. Annoyed as I was by this unexpected interference, I went. 'What's all this nonsense?' Mr. Goldfish flung at me. 'It's not nonsense at all, Mr. Goldfish,' I said. 'I made an agreement with Mr. Zukor that I scarcely think concerns you. I was put under contract by Famous Players. Mr. Zukor and I will decide it, if you don't mind . . .' 'Now you listen to me,' he broke in. 'And the next time,' I went on, paying no attention, 'please don't send the office boy for me. If you wish to see me, come yourself. Good afternoon.'"

Writing in 1955, knowing Goldwyn would read it, Pickford did not pull her punches: "Mutual antipathy started then that is still very much alive today. . . . I am told that Mr. Goldwyn looked out of his office window one day and observed me in the street. 'My God,' he is said to have exclaimed. '$10,000 a week and she is walking to the set yet. She should be running!'"

Goldwyn had picked the wrong adversary. Like so many of the moguls who thought they could make a star, he often failed to spot what the public really wanted. Louis B. Mayer thought Garbo's feet were too big. Carl Laemmle Jr. thought Bette Davis had all the sex appeal of a Slim Summerville. Zanuck never realized Monroe's appeal. More than anything, it was the animosity between Goldwyn and Mary Pickford which led to his break with the company. Goldwyn was a bull, and every room he entered was a potential china shop. Just after Lasky's return from a vacation, Goldwyn burst into his office: "Jesse," he burst out, "don't let Zukor butt into this picture. He's okay as an executive but we've always made better movies than Famous Players, so see that you keep the production reins in your hands!" He failed to see that Lasky wasn't alone, but was conferring with Pickford about the script of *Less than the Dust*. (She called it *Cheaper than the Dirt*.) Pickford, who owed everything to Zukor, ran straight to him and reported what Goldwyn had said.

Three months after the formation of Famous Players-Lasky, the conflict reached its head. Zukor informed Lasky that either Goldwyn must leave the company or he would. "He left it for Jesse to decide," recalled DeMille. "It is a sign of Jesse's strength and balance that he kept his own counsel until he had made his decision. He did not write to me about the matter until the middle of September." Eventually a vote was taken and Goldwyn was out. Lasky to DeMille (September 15): "Sam resigned yesterday, and I am particularly glad that we did not have to call upon you to cast a vote. . . . As a matter of fact, every director in the organization (six Lasky and six Famous Players) except you, whom we tried to keep out of the controversy, was determined to support Zukor."

But being a good loser was never one of Goldwyn's strong points. According to his early biographer Arthur Marx, "Informed of the decision, he ranted, threatened, and even cried some. And when that failed to touch the hearts of his partners, he demanded a recount of the vote. . . . After Sam cleared out his desk at 485 5th Avenue, he didn't speak to Jesse for another forty years, which is a long time to hold a grudge against someone, even a brother-in-law."

Lasky had spared DeMille the gory details. What he explained to DeMille was that he had been doing what he thought was right for the company. But he had begun in the business with Goldwyn, not Adolph Zukor. It was Goldwyn who had talked Lasky into the venture in the first place, and there was a bond between them. Of course, had they never met Zukor they might still have had one quarrel too many. Zukor may well have been a better businessman, but his loyalty to Lasky and DeMille, as they would both find out, was strictly business.

Goldwyn and Pickford never became friends, although as partners in United Artists they both had a seat in the boardroom. He was never friendly with Zukor, but it was Lasky he couldn't forgive, not until 1958.

Shortly before Lasky's death, the old triumvirate came together again. Life and Hollywood had dealt harshly with Lasky. More than either Goldwyn or DeMille, he had always tried to do what was right, but good intentions left him broke. He produced for Fox; he teamed up with Mary Pickford; he produced for Jack Warner and later for Louis B. Mayer. But his credits were taken away and his profits were minimal. Then the IRS came after him. He needed money desperately. DeMille took it upon himself to talk with Lasky's friends, asking if they would help. He called Goldwyn, "There was silence at the other end of the wire for few seconds, then Sam said, 'Let me think about it, Cecil. I'll call you tomorrow.'" The next day Sam telephoned. "I'll do it,' he said. "Early in January, 1958, I brought Jesse and Sam together, the first time in more than forty years that they had met as friends."

And so, three years to the month from the time DeMille, Lasky, and Gold-wyn decided to go into the movie business together, the first partner went off on his own. They had all risen high: from $200 a week their salaries had leapt to $2,500 a week. Goldwyn's share of the Paramount stock was worth $900,000. He went off and started his own company.

CHAPTER TWELVE

BY THE END OF 1916, IT WAS CLEAR THAT THE DESIRE FOR PEACE WHICH had re-elected Woodrow Wilson in November had been a last-ditch effort, and public opinion was now reconciled to intervention on the side of the Allies. Until America was officially in the conflict, Hollywood films were still being distributed and screened in Germany and other enemy countries. As late as January 1917, the studios were still hedging their bets, making films with war backgrounds but "un-specified" heroes and ambivalent villains. Such films could easily be doctored with new subtitles to give names and places to enemy faces. *Civilization*, the film whose "message of peace" had done so much to sustain pacifism, was re-cut, re-titled and re-released as a pro-war film.

At this crucial point, Hollywood studios took their cue not from the nation's moral outlook, but from how Americans spent their money. To look to Hollywood for any sort of moral lead was like electing a munitions manufacturer as president and being surprised when he declared war. A film company's line of battle was drawn up within sight of a bank.

When early filmmakers were independent and not answerable to the boardrooms, they had the freedom to express individual beliefs. But as production companies grew in power and strength, caution which came late soon evolved into a collective reluctance to take risks.

On the second of April, only four days before his inauguration, the peace-seeking Wilson went before Congress to ask for the long-awaited declaration of war. While the first shipload of Yanks wouldn't be sailing until June, and the US drums wouldn't begin their rum-tum-tumming anywhere except in their barracks until the following spring, Hollywood suffered no such delays. With Germany now official the enemy (and its territories no longer a market for American films), Hollywood began operating as a propaganda machine. Never before had there been such a villain as the Kaiser, the Beast of Berlin, the man who kept Chaplin and Pickford from the Germans. Lasky went to war.

There were other problems to resolve. Even with Goldwyn out, the situation with Mary Pickford remained unresolved. Her last two pictures had been colossal flops. Moreover, Zukor and his board feared that her latest, *Poor Little Rich Girl*, not yet released—a film she had made with complete freedom over choice of script, cast, and director—would be an even bigger disaster. Zukor and Lasky's concern for the future of their "golden goose" infected everyone, and shook the usually unflappable Mary, whose emotional stability and judgment were further undermined by her turbulent home life. As Pickford's star rose and her Irish husband, actor Owen Moore's career stalled, he turned to drink and became increasingly jealous of his wife; he even beat her, and at one point tried to kill her.

Both Pickford's mother and Zukor thought it would be best for her to get away from New York and out to California. The move proved to be permanent. It brought Pickford and DeMille together again, ten years after they had first acted together in *The Warrens of Virginia*. Since then both had become giants, used to wielding great influence on their sets. But DeMille thought Pickford had too much of the sort of power that only he, the Director General, should have. He told as much to Zukor, who loved Pickford like a daughter and passed on the message. DeMille was then informed that Pickford would expect to have a say in every decision. When DeMille objected again, Zukor instructed Pickford to back down. "In the deepest misery I wrote a most abject note of humility to Cecil DeMille. 'I have no desire to interfere in the choice of stories,' read the telegram, 'in the casting of the different actors, including myself, and in the final editing. I am placing myself unreservedly in your most capable hands. Obediently yours, Mary Pickford.' The weeks that followed were one grim ordeal of wretched home life and anxiety about my career. Owen's constant bickering, and the fact that I had not heard from DeMille, left my whole future, personal and professional, hanging in the balance."

Although DeMille didn't want to brook interference from a star, he was as eager to give her a box-office hit.

DeMille to Lasky (January 18, 1917): "After giving all my thought to Pickford matter, I am convinced that it would be grave mistake for me to do a light subject with her, and your letter has doubly convinced me of this. Pickford needs some big smashing subject to lift her from the present mediocrity in which we find her. Such subject is also necessary if she is to benefit by my direction. . . . I can promise a Pickford picture that will do for her what *The Cheat* did for Ward. I do not mean to make the picture anti-German in any way."

Lasky cautioned DeMille to remember the foreign market (January 19): "Particular care has to be exercised in choice of Pickford plays account of large sale in foreign countries other than England particularly including Germany and Austria where Pickford was and is very popular. . . . There is unanimous feeling that we ought not at this time produce any picture that has anything to do with European conflict or its aftermath. . . . Pickford's first two pictures were foreign and exhibitors are all clamoring for American material." Lasky's concern over offending the overseas market is indicative of industry sentiment at this time.

Eager to make his war film, DeMille promised that "this story is an arraignment against 'Prussianism' or German Militarism—never an invective against the German people—but against their National Military 'System,' a system which victimizes its own citizens more thoroughly than the enemy; retards the progress of civilization by 500 years by an open retreat to 'barbarism'—and dwarfs the national viewpoint by 'hammering' the dangerous slogan that 'Might makes Right'!"

Meanwhile, the Pickford caravan—consisting of Mary's mother, her sister Lottie, her baby Gwynne, and brother Jack—left New York in January 1917 to take up residence in California. Mary had a commitment of two pictures with DeMille, the first of which was *Romance of the Redwoods*. This was a vigilante Western which allowed Mary to play herself, spunky, determined, inventive, and golden, in a role that would otherwise have suited Blanche Sweet, Anita King, and half a dozen other actresses, all of whom lacked the box-office appeal to justify such a large production.

DeMille was familiar with the genre. He loved the rugged landscape and admired the people who had only recently hewed their lives out of it. As the girl who travels west to claim her deceased uncle's fortune, Pickford was full of her own natural pioneer spirit. She was photographed gloriously against giant redwoods and snow-capped mountains, looking even more diminutive and helpless by contrast, but showing her mettle in furious rides and comic tumbles. For six-and-a-half fast-paced reels, she labored to save her lover from the vigilantes' rope. She gave audiences just what they wanted.

While directing *Romance of the Redwoods* and overseeing pre-production on Pickford's next film, *The Little American*, DeMille was also planning upcoming projects for Geraldine Farrar. Lasky to DeMille (March 10): "It was strongly urged that you produce two pictures with Farrar six thousand feet each costing about seventy-five thousand dollars each including her salary instead of one long expensive picture as planned."

By the time work began on the Farrar vehicle *The Woman God Forgot*, Lasky's cautionary advice was forgotten. The film went $40,000 over budget, although DeMille brought in Farrar's second film, *The Devil Stone*, for $7,000 under.

Meanwhile, Griffith, having departed the ailing Triangle Film Corporation, joined the Paramount fold.

Lasky to DeMille (March 13): "Griffith is about to sign . . . for one year to do six pictures of six reels each without stars. Since *Intolerance* he is convinced there is no money in big pictures and will not do a big picture for at least another year. However, Griffith has absolutely no bearing on your doing a big picture. *Joan the Woman* is doing absolutely no business in New Jersey and indications are that state rights men will have difficulty in exhibiting *Joan the Woman* at high prices. We would probably not be able to profitably dispose of another long picture with Farrar as the star. On the other hand two six-reel pictures would cause a sensation booked through Artcraft and we would be assured of handsome profits with much smaller investment. This our only motive in suggesting change in plans. You should know that I personally would not stand for an alliance with Griffith interfering with any of your plans."

Redwoods finished shooting on March 23, and DeMille was ready to start shooting his war film on April 13. *The Little American*, like *Redwoods*, had been tailored specially for Pickford by her former colleague Jeanie Macpherson. The prop department had their work cut out for them. Everything had to be accurate, from the uniforms of French and German soldiers, to banners and streamers and cannons. The research department flooded DeMille with information.

• Saddles on horses must have dark rug wrapped in front of saddle, and wrapped cloak in back of saddle. . . .
• We need long French bread for peasants to give soldiers.
• Autos and ambulances must have military and civil numbers on front back and sides.
• French and German airplanes have distinctive markings visible from a great distance. Wounded men should have tags attached to the top button of their tunics. They will keep their overcoats and helmets.
• Wounded men do not always tumble right over. In nine cases out of ten they grope around for some time and then quietly drag themselves to a sheltered place. Every man wears an identification disk. Every officer wears a wristwatch. Every officer should be equipped with cigarettes. Especially should smoke them during the artillery attacks.
• Streets are cobbled in France.

And so on. The story itself might be hokum, but the cobbling would be first-rate.

Wilfred Buckland was building the complicated hydraulic sets needed to sink a ship. *The Little American*'s highlight would be DeMille's recreation of the torpedoing of an undefended ocean liner. The ship was based on the *Lusitania* torpedoed and sunk by a German submarine while crossing from New York to London. The *Lusitania* became the *Veritania*, a British luxury liner returning with a shipload of passengers from America.

The customary farewell party took place the night before the ship was to dock in Liverpool. Cheerful, unworried revelers, exquisitely tinted in amber, are depicted in the ballroom unaware that in the blue-black darkness outside a German U-boat has been tracking the ship. The submarine commander gives the order to fire. For a moment, the passengers stand stunned. Nothing moves. Then the ship lists. Panic erupts with the first rush of water. Men trying to assist women find themselves sliding into the rising water. Agnes deMille, who watched the shooting of this scene, recalled, "the slowly tilting floor, which was cantilevered up in an extraordinary engineering operation. The set had been built in the Lasky's swimming pool, which was filled with water, and the water actually rose around the actors' bodies." DeMille's mastery is seen in the deployment of the crowds, the cutting for dramatic emphasis, and the selection of the party decorations, from streamers, confetti, funny hats, and whistles bobbing mockingly on the water. Innocent objects are turned into dangerous debris, like ladies' scarves, babies' bottles, and decks of cards. Chairs and furniture, dislodged by the force of the water, float about banging into people and wedging them against the walls. Clothes are torn off, hairdos collapse. Pickford, thinking of others, finds herself awash up to her neck in confetti and party favors. Men and women scramble desperately for a place in the lifeboats. Others are shown sliding down the ship's side into the water, spotted struggling and dying in the black sea. Searchlights play across the chaotic scene. Pickford, without a lifebelt, is swimming desperately. The last shot is of her on a raft, cradling an orphaned child and wrapping the infant in her hair to keep it warm. To remind the public of the inspiration for this disaster, only the last six letters—"itania"—of the *Veritania*'s name are shown before it is swallowed up in the darkness.

DeMille's first blood-and-guts contribution to the war effort followed an already familiar pattern: Pickford, having been rescued from the ship, is a "neutral" American girl working on war relief in Belgium; she is captured by the Germans and held as a spy. Macpherson's plot worked in every propaganda cliché: violation of Belgian neutrality; the sinking of the passenger liner; the Prussian desire for world conquest; atrocities against "helpless" women and "innocent" children; and (very important given the number of Germans in America) the conflicting loyalties of German Americans. To this end, the plot features a German American antihero who returns to the fatherland to study and became a Prussian army officer. But he is redeemed by Mary's love of his childhood sweetheart and helps her to escape, before he dies in the French/German crossfire.

The significant differences between *The Little American* and other propaganda films of the period were DeMille's wizardry at telling a story and Pickford's embodiment of American innocence. When the brutal Prussian colonel threatened her with rape and death it was an affront to Americans. *Poor Little Rich Girl* was acclaimed as Pickford's greatest success to date. Free of her husband, and of any doubt about her creative judgment, Pickford became her old self and never gave up creative control again.

Pickford was a star long before DeMille directed her and, like Blanche Sweet, and to some degree Geraldine Farrar, was not happy working with him. DeMille played down their differences in his autobiography, and although almost all his stars bent over backwards to give him his due, Pickford wrote as she thought. In an interview a few years after DeMille's death, she was even more direct: "I am glad I had the opportunity of working with him, but at the time it was like being in an iron cage, and I decided I would not appear again under his direction." DeMille was ultimately happier working with the stars he created.

There were growing problems at the studio over working conditions among senior members. Wilfred Buckland noted an early sign of the discontent in the ranks that eventually led to unionization. "Regarding the unsatisfactory progress of construction work you complained of today," he reported. "I find on investigation what I consider a serious condition pervading the entire mechanical department. . . . The general discontent seems principally due to dissatisfaction with the amount of 'over-time' the men are called on to do, as under the new wage arrangement they find that despite the hourly increase, they work longer for less money than formerly." Something could have been done to avoid the costly and bitter infighting, but it was always "tomorrow" until years went by and it was too late.

DeMille was involved in aiding the war cause. The studio's walls were papered with recruitment ads, news about bond drives, and instructions for the Field Artillery of California. DeMille, thirty-six and with a family to support, was excused from the draft, but he used his powerful position to set a good example—and he, of course, was made a captain. "The Governor appointed us the 51st California Home Guard, and after everyone finished work all day, they would go out on Vine Street at night. . . . You saw stars and property men and grips and writers and directors all carrying a gun shoulder to shoulder. This barn suddenly turned into a bristling barracks. Some of the men that went from this barn didn't come back."

Under the command of Captain DeMille, with "Mr. William" (as his staff fondly liked to call him) claiming he did all the dog work in the "laborious, generally thankless and friendless position of top sergeant," the Lasky studio was put on a war footing. "All women of the studio put on nurse's garb," recalled William, "and attended instructional meetings where they rolled bandages and made surgical dressings. At home they knit socks and sweaters, and deprived themselves, their children and their husbands of sugar. On the day war was declared our studio organized itself into a military company. . . . Several of us had military training and officered the company, which drilled three nights a week for the whole period of the war. . . . It was very democratic: officers by day were privates at night, and it was quite refreshing to hear an assistant property boy barking orders at his director while teaching him the manual of arms . . . Every other Sunday the whole outfit piled into studio cars and went out to the ranch for field drill and machine-gun practice. There we made heroic efforts to learn how to use the various expensive and extremely dangerous implements of war we had acquired."

CHAPTER THIRTEEN

GERALDINE FARRAR WAS DUE IN LOS ANGELES FOR HER SUMMER BREAK from opera to make two pictures for DeMille. In the first, she would play Tecza, Moctezuma's daughter in Jeanie Macpherson's *The Woman God Forgot*, a highly theatrical script involving Cortez, Moctezuma, and the Aztecs, a people "civilized enough to use finger bowls—barbarous enough to offer human sacrifice." It was filmed in part among the lofty grandeur and mighty yellow cliffs of Yellowstone Park. In the second, she portrayed Mercia Manot, a Breton fisher-maid who finds a rare gem which proves to be cursed, in *The Devil Stone*.

Although a handsome woman in her mid-thirties, she was not the best choice to play a young Aztec virgin. Although DeMille's tale of the Aztecs didn't have elaborate sets such as he used in *Joan the Woman*, it still managed to look splendid. For *Joan the Woman*, DeMille had drawn on original sources for his recreation of fifteenth-century France. He brought the same passion for accuracy in his film about the Aztecs. He attempted to get the exotic richness correct down to the last feather or golden trinket. Jaguar skins by the ton and the plumage of exotic birds were used throughout. Fowl and beast were sacrificed to create the film's barbaric splendor. Although DeMille loved animals, and had given up hunting for personal pleasure, conservation did not interfere where his films were concerned.

Throughout his career, DeMille would be accused for being too exacting with sets and properties and of having objects made at great expense which would only flash by on the screen. In this respect, he was similar to contemporary directors such as Kurosawa and Spielberg. With DeMille, there was always the danger that this excess might overwhelm the story, putting form before content. DeMille had learned from Belasco that sets and costumes are important audience pleasers and can also influence the actors' performances. If the jewelry they wear is real, if the feathers and the furs of the costumes are authentic, if the plan of a palace and the design of the interiors are done properly, even the lowliest extra will move about with more authority. De-Mille took the adage "clothes make the man" very seriously.

He sent Macpherson and the Russian émigré dancer Theodore Kosloff, a newcomer who was to play the savage prince intended for the hand of the princess, off to Tenochtitlan, once the capital of the Aztec's rulers but now mostly buried under Mexico City. Ornately designed as the film was, apparently it was nothing compared to the real thing, as Kosloff reported in a letter to Gladys Rosson written some twenty-five years later when he went back in 1942 to research another project with a Mexican background: "If I only knew. . . . before so much about the Tlaloc civilization and the history of the Aztecs, I would have given to C. B. different details in the research for the picture. . . . Now I remember how C. B. thought the scenes of the swimming pool, the different birds and especially our costumes, props, sets and furnishings were all too exaggerated. But if he had exaggerated seventy-five per cent more, it would have been historically and perfectly correct."

Kosloff was a colorful and popular addition to DeMille's team. He may have exaggerated his background in Russia and Agnes wrote that he "had only been a minor member of the Moscow Ballet Company, not the Imperial Ballet at St. Petersburg. He then joined the Diaghileff Ballet Company as a very minor soloist, never a leading dancer. But, he possessed a remembering eye and could reproduce Michael Fokine's ballets and call them his own in a land where no one knew the originals. He was an appallingly bad choreographer."

But this sinewy, long-legged Tartar's leap from the steppes of Russia led to the steps of a Hollywood pyramid with a grand jeté. Over the next decade, he would play a shifty assortment of characters for DeMille: musical impresarios who made stars pay for their own wardrobe; Italian butlers who lifted the silver; Mexican spivs who sold blonde women down the river; kings in exile who stole other men's wives; the cuckold Marquis de San Pilar in *The Golden Bed*, etc.

Together with one of his mistresses, Winifred Hudnut, who took the name Natasha Rambova, Kosloff helped design the costumes for the film. When it came to creating the costumes of the 250 nobles, and the garments of Moctezuma, his daughter and her immediate court, it was estimated that at least 400 pounds of cleaned and dyed plumage would be required for all the cloaks, headdresses, vests, and even the curtains, rugs, and screens. The huge workroom in the wardrobe department was filled with women stitching and sewing. Two eight-hour shifts of forty people each did nothing but paste and work out the feathered designs.

Even today *The Woman God Forgot* stands up magnificently. The film opens with a sacrifice in the temple in which the priest is plunging an obsidian knife into victim's chest in order to rip out the still pumping heart. DeMille cuts away to a huge gong on top of the pyramid before revulsion can take over, as his way of grabbing his audience through their guts, and what follows is as lyrical as the preceding scene was stark. The camera slowly opens up on a large white bloom, perhaps a water lily, held lovingly to Geraldine

Farrar's smiling lips, from which the frame opens out until the screen is filled with a Rousseau-like paradise around a lake-sized pool. Exotic birds stalk through the rich and varied flora, swans glide on the lake, and smiling girls break through the surface all bare limbs and glistening little teeth. We're in the retreat of Tecza, Moctezuma's daughter. It's only the pristine condition of the temple which signals to the alert viewer that these are specially built sets and not the real thing. As always, there was a subtext to DeMille's narrative. Like *The Squaw Man* and *The Cheat*, this film is a tale of sexual relations across forbidden barriers.

As Farrar and company laugh and joke, one would like to linger. This is where a slow tracking shot would have come in handy. But DeMille rarely followed anyone across a set. Why pan when you can cut? This seemed to be his moviemaking philosophy. Camera movement seemed wasteful to a director always under pressure in these early years to cut unnecessary costs. It wasn't that he couldn't move the camera; he just rarely saw the necessity. His camera observed it, took it all in, but it didn't participate. Instead, he created the sensation of swift movement by fading in and out, and in a scene's climax, DeMille used dynamic cutting. Quick cutting allowed DeMille to move plots forward. He trusted audience reactions to carry off the effect he wanted. A burst of amazement can wipe out a lot of weak continuity. Moviegoers blissfully allow incongruities as long as the sets or the effects are worth it.

The *Woman God Forgot* was a great deal more than a vehicle for Farrar. DeMille's authority dominated this movie in the way that Farrar had dominated *Carmen*. The half-naked, feather-clad Indians scowl like actors but move like a pride of lions. The great set pieces draw on the rich imagery and colors of Mexican art. The battle scenes outdid *Joan the Woman*, with hundreds of fighting extras spilling over the steep-inclining walls of the pyramid, rolling and sliding pell-mell down the steps to the stone floors a hundred feet below. The doctors, nurses, and ambulances waiting for them below made good copy. DeMille at work shooting one of his big scenes, once the occasion for family outings, now became a spectacle in themselves to which he regularly invited a host of dignitaries.

Among the fresh faces in the cast was Julia Faye, who was to become the third important woman in DeMille's private life. They were introduced by actor Wallace Reid. She had formerly been a Sennett bathing beauty and pie catcher. DeMille looked for his future stars and leading ladies among the ranks of Sennett's smash-and-splash academy. Faye remembered her year with Sennett as invaluable, "but it almost killed me. I did stunt after stunt and finally landed in bed with a nervous breakdown, but with a sense of motion picture tempo and technique, which has stood by me to this day. For Sennett I cascaded out of a wrecked apartment house in a bathtub, was caught up in a real flood among oil wells and derricks when a huge tank broke too soon, received 100 custard pies alternately on right and left eyes, and was picked out of the ocean by a clam-dredging machine. That last stunt was too much."

Actress Julia Faye had a long-standing professional and personal relationship with DeMille. She appeared in his 1917 film *The Woman God Forgot* and in two dozen more through *The Ten Commandments* (1956). Estate of John Kobal

Faye's first encounter with DeMille while working on a film with Wallace Reid, was inauspicious: "It was just after lunch while I was sitting on the set with a group of girls that a tall, broad-shouldered man wearing a slouch hat, green riding breeches, puttees and shirt open at the throat, walked by. His shoulders were bent slightly forward, his head held down and this gave the effect that his head was at least a foot in front of his body. He walked with long, heavy strides, looking neither the right nor left. As he passed I asked one of the girls who he was and she answered: 'Why, don't you know? That's Mr. DeMille, the Director General of the company.'

"At that moment, having walked a few steps, Mr. DeMille wheeled about and came over to the group of girls. Looking at me, he said, 'Is your name Jean Johnson?'

"'No, Mr. DeMille. My name is Julia Faye,' I answered.

"'Oh,' was all he said, and went on."

But DeMille was apparently intrigued enough to invite Julia to his office for a chat, where she revealed her ambition to be a writer: "He told me to bring him an idea that he would like to see what I could do. . . . Every line of that conversation is indelibly written in my memory. I shall never forget the thrill of it! It started a friendship that has lasted over thirty years."

Over the next few weeks, Julia, often in scanty costume, encountered DeMille rehearsals and felt sure she had caught his eye. The swimming pool built for the Aztec production provided an unexpected relief in the hot weather, and the means of catching his eye again.

DeMille invited her to dine with him alone at the studio one evening, but to tell her mother she was working. Faye told him she couldn't do that, because if she told her mother she was working late, her mother would appear on the set with sandwiches. DeMille then told her to tell her mother whatever story was necessary. And thus began a happy time of lies for them both: DeMille's to his wife; Julia's to her mother.

DeMille continued to encourage her writing and agreed to find her a part in his next picture, while advising her that she would never be a star, "because you haven't the right kind of personality. You're the 'cute' type. In the theater we called them 'soubrette.' Also your face is too round, your nose is too long and I want you to write. . . . I have one writer now, Miss Macpherson, but it is impossible for her to keep up with me. I need another young woman with a good dramatic mind whom I can train in my way of writing to alternate with her.'"

Did DeMille really think this would work with Macpherson? They had now worked together almost inseparably for three years. She was Scottish, proud, and explosive. To keep Julia Faye on hand, and Jeanie Macpherson's fierce temper at bay, required great tactical skill. As Julia was new in his life, and in the midst of work pressures, he dropped his caution. Soon the affair with Faye was the wink of the studio. Her laughter and increasing ease in his presence raised many an eyebrow. There are reasons to suppose that the rumor of an affair reached his wife. It certainly didn't have far to go.

At that time, a group of women from the Lasky studio—including actress Anita King; Anne Bacuhens; DeMille's sister-in-law, Anna deMille; Lois Webber, one of the few important women directors; and Mrs. A. Gilbert of the Los Angeles' City Mothers Bureau—founded the Hollywood Studio Club. Membership was open to any girl connected with a motion picture studio in any capacity. More importantly, young women could stay there inexpensively, and along with board and lodging could be chaperoned properly. The influx of impressionable young women was becoming a serious problem in the streets of the city. Fatherless, brotherless, husbandless, an endless stream without jobs or homes, and all of them hoping to achieve success in the photodrama, many young women arrived in Los Angeles in such destitute circumstances that there were grave possibilities of moral deterioration should they fail to find employment.

Something had to be done. First, the good Lasky ladies launched a little club of drama study in a basement room of the Hollywood public library. Later, they rented a colonial mansion on Carlos Avenue. Anne Bauchens was voted the club's first president. "It is run by girls, for girls," she told the press. Guest speakers like Geraldine Farrar were invited. Bauchens served tea, listened to newcomers, and gave advice. Civic-minded Constance deMille was an organizer of the Hollywood Studio Club, and rumors of his affair with Faye may have reached her there. When and how Constance found out isn't certain, but fact that rumors reached her at all was an indication of the seriousness of this relationship in her husband's life.

Before DeMille's affair with Faye there had been others starting even before they left New York. Since the DeMilles set up home in Laughlin Park, there was talk of his having had a fling with the actress Ann Little who would play Nat-U-Rich in his 1918 remake of *The Squaw Man*.

Julia Faye was colorful and flamboyant. She laughed out loud. She made people talk and she was ambitious. Constance took this affair to heart in a way she hadn't with Macpherson. She had been able to accept Macpherson's role in her husband's life on an intellectual level as his collaborator. No such rationalization was possible with Faye. This relationship was largely physical. She had brought home to Constance the degree to which her husband needed the sexual satisfaction she denied him. Faye's presence touched Constance's pride.

Under stress, Constance confided in her highly moral sister-in-law, Anna deMille, a woman who couldn't imagine any man of their acquaintance cheating on his wife, not to mention such a wife putting up with such a husband. For a time, Constance seriously contemplated giving DeMille his freedom, but common sense prevailed. It wasn't in Constance's nature to confront her husband. "I don't think for one moment he wanted to leave Constance and marry Julia," Agnes reflected years later: "Julia was a pleasing idiot and just two steps above a chorus girl. . . . She certainly was not in Constance's class." Possibly, but DeMille wouldn't have been the first nobleman to marry a chorus girl while his head was turned.

After some considerable self-searching, Constance came to understand the terms of her marriage. From that time on, except for specific occasions, such as when the whole family trooped down to watch DeMille shooting one of his spectacular scenes, or when she accompanied her husband to a premiere or to New York, Constance stayed away from the studio. And she never went to Paradise.

There is reason to suppose that DeMille and Constance made a pact to maintain the status quo of their marriage. After all, they loved each other. She understood him, and indeed she would condone his behavior provided it was not all thrown in her face. In return, she would help DeMille deflate any future rumors before they had a chance to embarrass either of them. She might invite the woman in question home for tea, thus acknowledging her as a friend and showing friends that there was nothing to the gossip. She even spoke to Faye when their path crossed on her husband's set.

And so Constance colluded in her husband's infidelities. Both of them had shared too much: sixteen years of marriage, the early years of touring and dingy hotel rooms, the child they had nearly lost. A sensible wife overlooks certain things. She was happy to be his wife, the queen of his house, the mother of his family, a partner in his career, and a person whose opinions he sought and valued. She was always number one. The other women, to her way of thinking, were colleagues, friends, and concubines. As she told her sister-in-law: "Cecil will do what he has to do, but there is nobody alive who will be Mrs. Cecil DeMille while I live."

But she never invited laughing Julia Faye, and her husband never asked her to. Faye took her position philosophically: "She may be the lady of the house, but I'm the mistress of Paradise."

In a way, this affair was much harder on Macpherson. She had only her work, and him. DeMille, with typical male arrogance and obsessed with his work, may have thought his affair with Faye could be kept a secret. But on a studio lot, and with women of Faye's vibrant personality and Macpherson's Scotch temper, he would have been fooling only himself.

Of course, when the affair with Faye was in its first flush, few there would have sympathized with Macpherson. Some of the women on the lot might have been trying to catch the Director General's eye. The common consensus was likely that Macpherson had no one to blame but herself once she discovered him doing to her what she had done to his wife. What she couldn't confide in others she put in her next script for DeMille's *Old Wives for New*. A classic confrontation in which one mistress (played by Faye) storms into the apartment of a rival, catches her in the arms of her lover, and after beating her up turns her gun on the man who did her wrong. There is also the surprise encounter of wife and mistress in *Don't Change Your Husband*, with the mistress played, of course, by Julia Faye.

But when Faye also wanted to muscle her way into his behind-the-camerawork, Macpherson drew the line. DeMille's scenarios were her territory. Suddenly Faye found that when she wanted to see DeMille about her ideas for stories, Gladys Rosson was always telling her he was busy. In the evenings, he would show her his head of Buddha, teach her how to use a

Japanese shield, and describe the way ancient Hawaiians used an old point-ed knife to tell fortunes in the sand, but he wouldn't talk about her scripts. Faye didn't write much more, and she didn't write anything for DeMille. Macpherson won this round.

Confronted day after day with her rival, and unable to prevent DeMille from using Faye as an actress, Macpherson worked her resentment out in the parts she wrote for Faye: drug addicts, homewreckers, and flighty mistresses. Hardly one of them had a second name.

DeMille probably found their fights amusing. Macpherson was his right hand for his creative work. Theirs was a romance of shared dreams and am-bitions. And Faye could make him laugh and help him relax without becom-ing as demanding as Macpherson. Perhaps Macpherson, with her bossy kind of love, was making him feel uneasy, since he knew he wasn't going to leave his wife for her. Love without hope can turn into a rucksack loaded with stones. The best way to get rid of the guilt is to start another affair. Faye was his clown princess. She would never allow him to take himself too seriously in her presence. She was perky, funny, game for anything, took rebuffs with a shrug, and never showed if she was jealous. Her happy-go-lucky temper-ament was perfect for a man like DeMille, who was burdened with heavy responsibilities and much inclined to take himself too seriously.

There was another, perhaps even more striking reason for DeMille's in-fatuation with her: Julia resembled a young version of his mother. They had the same birdlike nose, pointed chin, strong brow, and lively personality. Maintaining his marriage, his muse, and his mistress in perfect harmony was a hat trick that came with a price.

Had Constance insisted on a divorce, he might have remarried and had more children of his own. Instead of a divorce, DeMille and Constance adopt-ed three children, but none of these ever meant as much to him as his own blood. "Cecil treated his children in proportion to their genetic propinquity," wrote Richard, the second of his two adopted sons. "He confided only in Cecilia and left her and her children 95% of his estate." Except for the trusts that were set up for John, Richard and Katherine, the rest of the estate—fur-nishings, books, houses, horses, land, businesses—all went to Cecilia.

DeMille began to change. His career would become all. He turned his en-ergies to building up his own unit, a studio within a studio, and surrounded himself with men and women whose first loyalty was to him. He had power, but he had yet to learn that a man must fashion his freedom himself. As Wagner's Wotan discovered after his clash with his wife, all he could father with money was devoted slaves. DeMille could trust Buckland to deliver; the same with his cameraman, and with William. Along with Macpherson, they allowed DeMille's imagination incredible freedom. But once the last links in this chain were gone, his films would lose some of their surprise and excite-ment. They became more polished, and were certainly technically flawless, but the heart only occasionally quickened its beat.

DeMille cast Faye in most of his films for more than forty years. When he introduced her to Lasky, she recalled, "Mr. Lasky looked me over and said I had pretty legs." So whenever close-ups of stars' legs or feet were needed in Paramount films, Julia became the "legs of the Lasky lot." She was also looked after by DeMille. There was a period in the thirties when they parted. She got married and became Mrs. Walter Anthony Merrill. When they later divorced, she came back and worked for him again. In her last years, DeMille's daughter helped Faye out with loans and purchases of gifts and shares her father had made to her. In a way, like Lord Nelson leaving Lady Hamilton to the nation in his will, Faye was part of DeMille's bequest to his family.

There were other clouds on DeMille's set. *The Devil's Son* was the last time he worked with Farrar. They broke up for a classic reason: a wife who is successful and a husband who is not. Jesse Lasky, as a favor to his star, had given the ambitious Lou Tellegen a film to direct over DeMille's objections, but the picture he made was not satisfactory. Farrar sided with her husband and did not renew a further engagement with Lasky. "In this instance," as she later reflected, "wifely loyalty prevailed over professional discretion." When she returned to Hollywood, it was under the Goldwyn banner.

Could it have been coincidence that the upheaval in DeMille's home life was followed, in his next film, by his only introspective, intensely analytical, and only downbeat work, one that would gain him the sort of praise he was never to receive again? *Old Wives for New*, started two months after the completion of *Whispering Chorus*, encouraged the right to divorce when a wife failed to keep up with her husband.

CHAPTER FOURTEEN

DEMILLE MADE NO FILMS FOR THREE MONTHS AFTER FARRAR LEFT THE studio. The Lasky Home Guard occupied him with drilling and marching on Saturday nights. In an economy drive dictated from on high, the New York office resolved a policy of shorter and cheaper films. He must have read these letters and telegrams with some rise in temper.

Lasky to DeMille (December 7, 1917): "My dear Cecil, in an attempt to economize all along the line, I called a meeting here one evening last week and invited all of our directors making Artcraft-Paramount and Select Pictures. It was unanimously resolved that all Artcraft Pictures would be limited in length to 5000 feet and all Paramount and Select Pictures would be limited in length to 4500 feet. Exhibitors are constantly complaining because our pictures are too long. In the smallest theaters, it is necessary to play a comedy, a weekly news reel and a feature, and the combined footage of the entertainment has grown so long that the theaters are forced to either rush through their shows or they are not able to give enough performances each night and still dismiss their audience at an early hour. Therefore, Exhibitors, large and small are clamoring for shorter pictures then we have been giving them. Now, from our viewpoint as producers, if the above footage rule is properly enforced, I figure we will save between $200,000 and $300,000 per year on positive stock alone." Since, in theory, cheaply made films cut to a prescribed length were just as profitable as the longer and more expensive ones, office-bound executives tried to curb tendencies to artistic self-expression. From the outset, economy and art were in conflict.

Meanwhile, Famous Player-Lasky's shares were rising on the stock market, and DeMille looked after his own. He bought shares for his mother, and for Julia Faye—a further indication of the hold she had on his affections. Whenever the opportunity arose to make some money, he seems to have included the women in his life as well. Jeanie Macpherson also had shares.

There were also some underhanded dealings, as in the continuing matter of Mary Pickford's future position with the company. Rumors were that she had received lucrative offers from other companies.

Pickford continued to get her own way as her unrivaled popularity at the box office made any opposition to her demands futile. Not only did her films make a profit, but distributors eager to get them were happy to take the rest of the package. The time would soon come when Pickford's demands would get too big even for Paramount and off she would go to form her own studio. For the moment she was kept satisfied but it made DeMille think it was time to find new stars.

DeMille originally believed that good writing and good direction could make successful films even without big stars. Later, he persuaded his partners that he could find promising young actors, still comparatively unknown, cheap to hire but enthusiastic. By putting them in the right parts in the right stories, and with careful direction, they would become noticed. The public would do the rest and the company would have new stars at little cost. In the end, they let Pickford go. DeMille started on his new program of "all-star" pictures, which was another way of saying pictures without any stars. If there was to be temperament on his set, it was to be his and his alone. If the star of a DeMille picture grew too popular it might enhance box office. If it threatened the authority of the director, then they would be let go—as Griffith had let Blanche Sweet find increased fame on her own. For DeMille, it was the era of the director, not the star.

DeMille became involved with a new passion, aviation, to the point that it threatened his film career. His interest took off soon after America's entry into the war. Although DeMille was not subject to the draft, he nonetheless wanted to join, as his lawyer Neil McCarthy recalled: "He wanted to do so as a flyer." In a speech he gave in 1956 to the prestigious and exclusive Wings Club, whose members were pilots, DeMille recalled his first stirrings, "There was no civil air patrol when I learned to fly thirty-eight years ago. We were in the First World War then. . . . I was feeling rather frustrated at having been born at just the wrong time to serve my country, when someone told me that the army needed pilots so badly that they would even take an old man of 36 if he knew how to fly. I decided that this was my chance to enlist. I flew first in 1917 from a rented field near Venice, which is now called Clover Field. In fact, there is a charming young lady whom you have met here tonight [Julia] as a little girl accompanied me on my second solo flight. But then after we were up a thick fog came in. . . . After a while I realized I had to come down, and I began groping though the fog. And we came out right over the roller-coaster on Venice Field. I executed a maneuver that has seldom been executed in air; it was the quickest pull-up that I think anybody ever made to avoid taking a ride on the roller coaster ourselves. The young lady looked round at me delightedly clapping her hands and nodding, 'Wonderful!' 'Wonderful!' She thought I was giving her an aerial roller coaster ride. This lady did not realize that she was very close to her last thrill."

His brother seems to have been less impressed. "For weeks C. B.'s conversation had been full of 'nose-dives,' 'tail-spins' and 'Immelmann loops,' and I had observed him at odd moments manipulating an imaginary stick in an imaginary plane, bringing it out of an imaginary fall to an imaginary safe landing. Just to watch him gave me imaginary heart failure." DeMille would complete his flying course and be on his way to Fort Sill, Oklahoma, to enlist when the Armistice was declared.

His fascination with flying led to the formation of the Mercury Aviation Company, according to his lawyer Neil McCarthy, the first commercial aviation transport company in the United States. "At that time at Venice, California, there was a man named Al Wilson, later a stunt flyer in pictures. Al Wilson had an old Curtiss 'Jenny.' I went to Venice, looked at the plane and talked to Wilson and made one of the most profound statements of my life. I said, 'Well, take me up in it and if it flies all right, we will buy it.' That was the first time I had ever been in a plane. . . .

"After a few months, we acquired deMille Field No. 1, that's what is now the corner of Melrose and Fairfax Avenues. . . . I told [McCarthy] to try and get another plane. We would go into the business of taking people on short rides. Five and ten minutes. We found our second plane in Canada, then we needed a third and fourth, so on. One day a businessman had to reach Bakersfield in a hurry. Al took him up. They had to come down in a bean field because there was no other place to land. But the man made his appointment on time. Thus was born the Mercury Aviation Company. Soon we were able to announce scheduled flights between San Diego—San Francisco via Bakersfield and Fresno. With the two stops for refueling, it took nearly eight hours to fly to San Francisco . . . I believe that the Mercury Aviation Company was the first commercial airline in the US to carry passengers on scheduled flights between cities."

The Mercury Aviation Company was ahead of its time. Exciting tales of aerial heroism in the skies over Europe notwithstanding, flying was still the domain of daredevils. Although the company's operations were expanding, it was never able to make a profit. When it was dissolved, McCarthy recalled that DeMille insisted on paying back investors and took the entire loss himself. He never yielded in his insistence that commercial aviation transport would be the means of travel in the future, and that it would become as safe as any. It was his proud boast that in all 25,000 flights made by Mercury Aviation Company not a single accident had occurred. Another reason why he gave up on this project was that DeMille realized that to make it successful he would have had to choose it over the movies. Show business won out.

DeMille sold out to the Rogers Airport on September 15, 1921. The fleet of Junkers planes were later sold to the Mexican government and captured by the Zapata revolutionists. He never lost his enthusiasm for flying. For years, he kept a Spad (a biplane fighter) for his own use. When he had given up flying altogether, he kept it "shorn of its wings" in his garage, where occasionally he would run his fingers lovingly over the old machine. Years later, DeMille was asked to design the uniforms for the cadets of the newly founded Air Force Academy in Colorado. When the cadets first saw slides of their new uniforms, it is recorded, they did more than applaud, they cheered.

Back on the ground he now embarked on the most curious film he would ever make. *Whispering Chorus*, begun in December, was an art film, the sort one would come to expect from European directors, mostly to be seen at festivals and art houses. As hard-edged as *The Cheat* but devoid of glamor, it was as realistic as *Kindling*, but without its sentimental touches and upbeat ending. Instead, looking for new ways to stretch himself, DeMille made what may well have been Hollywood's first "Freudian" film. Here was drama with a vengeance, a grimly realistic contemporary subject that made few concessions to public sympathies. There was little to distract the audience from the relentless realism of the tale.

Having robbed his employer, John Trumble (Raymond Hatton) flees to escape arrest, abandoning his wife and responsibilities. While on the run, he stumbles across a corpse and decides to takes the dead man's identity for his own. From boarding houses to alleyways to brothels, at last he is caught and ends up on death row for "his own murder." Julia Faye played a dope addict in a Chinese opium den—a role Jeanie Macpherson may have written deliberately for her—but it was also her best part to date. She had gone from playing an Aztec maid to being featured in a showy dramatic role in DeMille's most personal and ambitious work.

The "whispering chorus" represents the small voices and thoughts of the "average mind"—Trumble's mother, wife, the men and women along the road, and, most of all, himself. To depict this psychology, DeMille makes vivid use of double, triple, quadruple, and multiple simultaneous exposures. DeMille had used this device on and off since *The Virginian*, where he used double exposures to introduce the cast and their characters, but never to such dramatic purpose before. "For the final appearance of all the faces," explained DeMille, "the representatives of the thoughts struggling in his troubled mind—now gathered together in the condemned man's cell, we faded in and out, around his figure on the screen. To achieve this there had to be as many exposures as there were faces, accomplished with all the carefulness and precision which such treatment of film demanded." Every inch of the condemned man's cell is filled with grinning, crying, leering, chattering heads. John Trumble's conscience is killing him.

DeMille is dramatic but not sentimental. It smacked of Brechtian alienation before Brecht, and its style informs the audience that the director is being "serious." Casting ratty-faced Raymond Hatton as the antihero—a grizzled regular in hundreds of cowboy films whose last screen credit in 1967 was another realistic death-row drama, *In Cold Blood*—was DeMille's boldest move. *Whispering Chorus* was the sort of work in which a young director makes his reputation, and an established director risks his. The critics were full of praise, calling it "one of the most bizarre, fanciful and powerful photodramas of the year" (*Motion Picture Magazine*).

The film was cast for the roles and not for stars, and the actors came from Paramount's contract pool. At a length of 6,555 feet (1,500 feet longer than the recent head office ordinance), it cost $12,000 more than the studio wished to spend on such productions and filming took seven weeks. DeMille's artistic indulgence was not cheap. But it was not the box-office failure he later cited as the reason for not doing more such pictures: it grossed a handsome $242,109.27 around the globe.

DeMille wasn't given to heavy introspection but, for those who knew the man, he did expose his private life in his professional work, but never again on such a scale. He knew that with *Whispering Chorus* he had proven something vital to himself; the film was important for his artistic evolution. It showed off every skill he had learned as a director. It was melodramatic, but it was hard and unrelenting. It was fascinating, but not a film to recommend to friends as a good night out. Art, as he realized from experience, draws high praise but small crowds.

In Hollywood, art is considered to be an indulgence, while directing is first and foremost a craft. In one of his rare public reflections, John Ford told a French journalist, "Directors who want to make only artistic films get a chance to do so about once every ten years. If the film is a commercial success, they get another chance, but otherwise they are through. . . . The secret . . . is to turn out films that please the public, but that also reveal the personality of the director. That isn't easy." Ford might have been talking about *Whispering Chorus*.

With that experience out of his system, DeMille moved on, and brought a great deal of what it had taught him to *Old Wives for New*, which began shooting a month later. It cost $6,000 less than *Whispering Chorus*, but earned $40,000 more. This film was also ahead of its time, but for popular reasons. Women wore shorter skirts, shorter hair, and wanted to be at one with men. Characters in *Old Wives for New* took events in stride, and didn't die over a broken heart. According to DeMille biographers Gabe Essoe and Raymond Lee, "DeMille catered to the postwar trend toward higher living, heavier drinking and looser morals. Dwelling on both the desirability and foibles of the rich, he opened up a whole new world for the films, a world that middle-class audiences, won to the movies by the newsreels and luxurious theaters then springing up, very much wanted to see. . . . It was DeMille's insight the strait-laced Puritanism of prewar days was weakening and needed only to be given lip-service to be placated." True in general, this theory was a bit far-fetched when it came to *Old Wives for New*, which was begun in May 1918, six months before the Armistice was declared. DeMille may not have known that this film would be the start of something new in his career. There were aspects of *Old Wives for New* that anticipated the sort of films he would launch after the war. *Old Wives for New* had been Lasky's idea, not DeMille's: "What the public demands today is modern stuff with plenty of clothes, rich sets, and action. Nothing prior to the Civil War should be filmed."

In fact, Lasky thought his friend was in danger of too much variety and not enough originality. As he continued in his letter to DeMille, "I am strongly of the opinion that you should get away from the spectacle stuff for one or two pictures and try to do modern stories of great human interest."

Based on a bestselling novel, *Old Wives for New* was the story of a man who married in haste. The book, which had been praised as brilliant, dealt with divorce, an aspect of marriage barely hinted at in American movies. Macpherson wrote the script. Faye was given a good but unsympathetic role as the betrayed, gun-toting Jessie, and there were a lot of eye-catching incidents and caustic and amusing titles. It was hot stuff for the sweethearts of returning newly worldly wise soldiers.

To Elliott Dexter (playing Charles Murdock) goes the "honor" of appearing in DeMille's first bathroom scene. Trying to shave, he finds his basin full of his sluttish wife's strands of hair. Her dirty combs and messy napkins litter his side of the basin instead of hers. In stumbles Sophie Murdock (Sylvia Ashton), a lazy jellyfish, marvelously gross. Why would a man marry such an unappealing slob? A witty series of flashbacks depicts the dainty-footed slip of a girl he married, played by the pretty Pickford-like new contract girl Wanda Hawley. DeMille's policy of creating new stars was beginning to pay off.

The long shots of her feet introduce something that henceforth will play a delectable part in DeMille's films, like "drawers" in von Stroheim's and "keyholes" in Lubitsch's, if not quite as much as Monument Valley with John Ford. For a time, feet were seen as a DeMille trademark. The reason behind DeMille's ankle shots may have owed a little to Freud, but with the more liberal attitudes and shorter skirts, it was logical he should focus below the knee.

Murdock wants a divorce. On a hunting trip, he meets lovely brunette Juliet Raeburn (the beautiful, sophisticated Florence Vidor), and a platonic but caring relationship grows up between them. When Sophie puts two and two together she turns on him: "You go out and have all the fun you want, but I'll never divorce you—NEVER."

But Charles has eyes only for Juliet, and lovely Florence Vidor, in the second of her two films for DeMille, has all the breeding and elegance to make his infatuation understandable. He tells her that he can't live without her. She replies that he is in no position to talk to her like that. It may be 1918 and she may have shortened her skirt, but she's still a respectable, self-supporting widow. Despondent at this new rejection, Murdock develops a plan to take the two girls out.

There is also a murder: Murdock's business partner Berkeley, shot by his vengeful mistress when caught two-timing. DeMille had become expert at staging murders in suspicious, dimly lit surroundings, and cinematographer Wyckoff excelled at dark tones, subtly lit close-ups, and depth of focus, which contributed much to the handsome appearance of the film. It may be sordid but it's exciting.

Despite the usual contrivances that move the plot forward, DeMille's treatment of his potentially risqué subject holds the attention. His visualization never drags and is full of beautiful imagery. Its outlook was very advanced. In neat cutaway, DeMille makes it obvious that the children side with their father in his quarrel; they too don't like having a slovenly mother. At the crunch, pistol-packing Jessie is also shown sympathetically. If anyone in the story is to be condemned, it is Sophie Murdock and the philanderer Berkeley.

There was so much plot, daringly and expressively handled, that there was bound to be a delicious shock and a frenzy of censorship. When the film was first screened for Zukor and others in the New York office, DeMille remembered, "They were outraged. . . . It was such strong stuff that they were scared by it. Lasky was in a fit and Zukor was in a state."

Head office, whose idea the film had been, now had serious reservations about releasing it. Apparently no one except Lasky had bothered to read the script. Otherwise they might not have been shocked at the film's highly critical view of those bulwarks of America, home, motherhood, marriage, and money. Moreover, the rich were shown on screen as a gluttonous, bawdy lot. The public were used to seeing the rich as powerful, greedy, and dictatorial. Here DeMille was also showing the rich as sanctimonious hypocrites. It was amazing, though, and a sign of DeMille's success, that Zukor, and even Lasky, after all their years in the business, still reacted so strongly to the power of film to turn a critical paragraph in a book into an explosive condemnation on the big screen. "They had just finished this tremendous campaign," recalled DeMille, "half a million dollars it had cost them, for nothing but pure, white as snow, pictures. And though business was dying they were not going to release it. That's when I took it down [from the shelf] and ran it myself in a nearby town to get an audience reaction. It had not been playing long when people began to get up and go out to telephone their friends to hurry down to see it. Husbands particularly telephoned wives to come down: Let supper go, but come down and see *Old Wives for New*. When the screening was finished, there was so much new audience in the theater that the manager had to screen it again. He was still screening it well after midnight. When I reported that to New York, opposition crumbled." *Old Wives for New* went out and quadrupled its cost, another feather in DeMille's cap.

It's important to realize that when DeMille called *Whispering Chorus* a failure, he said it in angry response to criticism of *Old Wives for New*. Although critics thought his plots and his focus on excessive indulgence catered to the masses, he considered his "popular" work to be worth no less than his "serious" work. In a manner worthy of Belasco, he declared, "I stopped making pictures for critics. I make pictures for people." He continued to draw the public's curiosity, and with it the critics' ire. Both went to his films, but for different reasons. In a way, the critical reaction to DeMille's later work was like a paranoid echo of what had originally kept him from succeeding on Broadway. His answer was to insert in his work all those things they were sure to loathe. Since his greatest success was to come as a maker of epics, a form rarely appreciated as having artistic merit, DeMille would deliberately not cite the failure of his first epic. Instead, he elected to deny *Whispering Chorus*, his great critical success.

DeMille set out to establish for himself a personality as large as Pickford, Chaplin, and Fairbanks. Not everything written about him showed him in a kindly light. At first, the jibes were good-natured. He became known as "King of the Bathtub" and "Ruler of all the Plumbers." Then, as his success increased, the remarks became sarcastic. Reports of his demands and outbursts released a flood of mockery. An outcome of his success was that other directors' names were also to go above the title. But, once a director's name became as well-known as that of his stars, his work was open to the same scrutiny. When films failed, fingers were pointed at the director.

At some point, DeMille sat down and figured out the ingredients behind the popularity of *Old Wives for New*. For two years, audiences lived through a war. Except for Sennett-type slapstick, it was assumed that lightness would be in bad taste. The moral fallout from the Victorian era lingered much longer in America than in England, and longer still in Hollywood. Even before Washington had to resort to sending out urgent telegrams to the studios requesting a cessation of war films, DeMille spotted the public's craving for a change. He was a man who read the papers. He was always asking for ideas. Throughout his career, he listened to friends, to family, to his growing children and their friends. His was already showing the latest films up at the house and discussing them. With the American public glutted with patriotism and hatred, DeMille concluded that now was the time to give them something different: sizzling, luxurious, a story with a trip abroad without guns and soldiers in trenches. Something a bit risqué to follow all that noble sacrifice. Such ruminations, together with America's newfound sense of self and wealth, were to lead him to one of the most fascinating human relationships, that between master and servant. That conflict, spelled out in the titles or implied in the looks with which the "have-nots" eyed the "haves," was to become key to many of DeMille's upcoming plots. Other directors would follow his path, and do it with a greater irony.

He realized the commercial value in the issue of "class" and worked that vein before anyone else. In the 1920s, "class" would become one of the major (if unspoken) topics in the American popular conscience. The old and unbending class struggle, the germ at the core of the old world's decline, had been unwittingly carried past the Ellis Island inspectors by the flood of refugees along with their other cultural baggage. As soon as they were established, these attitudes re-emerged in the new land and drove tracks through towns and cities, dividing and classifying people by their spending power, and then by how much longer some had it. Successful first-generation immigrants were considered to be the nouveau riche, but some became industrial barons. Multigenerational wealth made the families like the Vanderbilts and

Astors America's equivalent of British aristocracy, legitimizing their wealth by marrying their sons and daughters to European nobility. DeMille wasn't concerned with how the rich really lived, but rather how a person without money *thought* they lived. Later, into DeMille's shoes would step Erich von Stroheim, Charlie Chaplin, and Ernst Lubitsch to mine this rich field further.

A week after wrapping *Old Wives for New*—at a speed reminiscent of his first year, and made possible by having a team who knew his needs back to front—DeMille was at work on a comedy about love in all the wrong places called *We can't Have Everything*, adapted by William from a popular novel.

The younger sibling liked to give his stories that extra fillip: a mention of water, and he saw the potential for a flood. A man lighting a match might be capable of starting a bigger fire. This time he didn't have to look hard for his big scene, for the author had already written one. The Hollywood film studio in the story was supposed to go up in flames, putting the company out of business. But another bout of studio economy brought orders to cut back. "If I took out all the things they asked me," he moaned to his brother, "there wouldn't be a damn thing in my pictures anybody would want to see." "The most expensive pictures are not always the best," responded William. "Neither are the cheapest," his brother snapped back. From a story standpoint, a blazing studio with lots of people running around and plenty of physical danger is a lot more interesting than the sight of business ledgers full of black ink. The only solution in *We can't Have Everything* was to accept the title and cut the blaze. DeMille had proved long ago that he could do films on a shoestring budget, but he didn't want to do so again. It galled him to cut costs, and the day would come when he simply refused. Then all of a sudden, in the midst of filming, life imitated art. The newly built Lasky studio caught fire.

William rushed out of his office and found the stage and an adjacent building burning like tinder, with the whole studio force trying to get it under control. Knowing what this would mean to DeMille, who was out on location, he quickly commandeered three cameramen and told them to start shooting the blaze from every conceivable angle: "Give me long-shots, close-ups, fade-ins and fade-outs. Get the fire department when it arrives, and feature the man with the hose. One of you get on the roof of the laboratory and get the fire from there." It was all he could do without cast and crew, but he got about three thousand feet of "all that beautiful black smoke and flame which photographed like a million dollars." He was starting to sound like his brother. DeMille had a slightly different version of who did what: "All of the fire department in Los Angeles was there. I said, 'Listen everybody. Get out to the stage. I'm going to write the script as I go. Here's our burning studio that we cut out of the picture. Get the cameras set up!' The firemen were annoyed because they saw what we were doing. . . . They didn't want a building falling on us. . . . After it had stopped burning, I went back and put in flares to get the close-up shots, kindled some more fire around just to finish it. Shots of people cursing, raging and tearing their hair; people rushing to get things out of their dressing rooms. It was wonderful stuff." Damage to the newly built Lasky studio was estimated at $100,000, but DeMille dismissed the loss to Lasky when they next spoke: "We'll get it back with the picture. One thing is destroyed so that something new may be created. We have fared well enough through the crisis."

In its review of *We can't Have Everything*, the *New York Times* singled out the fire: "The scene of a burning moving picture studio, which is said to have been made possible by the opportune fire at the Lasky studio in California—is remarkable, both for the staged confusion of the studio people and the many entertaining scenes concerned with the making of the movie . . . the capable hand and eye of Mr. DeMille are evident throughout the picture."

DeMille then followed with another anti-German subject, *Till I Come Back to You*. For its climax, none other than King Albert of the Belgians intervenes to save our American hero, Captain Jefferson, court-martialed for interfering with the US Army's plan to blow up enemy lines, from the firing squad. He has been too noble to admit he had done so only to save the lives of the beautiful Belgian girl played by Florence Vidor and the sixty-five young war orphans she was looking after. A DeMille hero man did not boast of his good deeds, not even if his life depended on it. The film's title was inspired by the pledge that King Albert had made to his people. In what was considered a startling gimmick, the king was portrayed by an actor. That year Blanche Sweet was in the midst of filming *The Unpardonable Sin* when her producers got a letter from Washington telling them to cut down on the atrocities in this anti-German drama. "We knew then that the war was over," she said. Now war films were to become as unpopular as the defeated Kaiser.

In late 1918, DeMille made his first of two remakes of *The Squaw Man*. This time, Elliott Dexter played the role made famous by Dustin Farnum. Ann Little, a contract player, was Nat-U-Rich, and Julia Faye portrayed Lady Mabel, a rise in station and a temporary break from maids, water rats, and membership in the emotional army of loose women known only by their first name. DeMille made it for a little over $40,000, but it grossed six times that.

CHAPTER FIFTEEN

HOLLYWOOD'S FOUR BIGGEST NAMES, PICKFORD, CHAPLIN, FAIRBANKS, and DeMille, were about to add a fifth to their ranks. Gloria Swanson would, in her first film for DeMille, become overnight a symbol of Hollywood glamour. Glamorous, yes, but by no stretch of the imagination was she a conventional beauty. She was barely five feet tall, her head was large, and she was slightly bow-backed. When Swanson joined Paramount, her dramatic range was average. But she was a good sport, trained by Mack Sennett to take pratfalls and had developed a self-deprecating humor. She possessed a natural flair for comedy like a lot of beautiful women who don't take them themselves too seriously.

But this background did not prepare her to become the idol of millions of women and an object of fantasy for countless men. Kings and queens are not respected for their physical appearance, but for their air of total assurance. Great stars have that air, and Gloria had it more than most, that confidence which carried her over the heads of her peers. After three films with DeMille, she grew tall enough to rival Pickford as a box-office attraction. "I have gone through a long apprenticeship," she said in 1922, two years before Edward Steichen made his masterful portrait of her veiled that celebrated her status as a cinema icon. "I have gone through enough of being nobody. I have decided that when I am a star, I will be every inch and every moment the star! Everybody from the studio gateman to the highest executive will know it." She had an inner glow, and even when she played "poor," it was evident from her conviction that "poor" only existed as a dramatic stepping-stone.

Swanson always portrayed sympathetic characters, and her gowns were sensational. Better than any other of DeMille's stars, she took to the boudoir and the bath with a conviction that made what she did there a matter of breathless concern to fans who couldn't get enough of her clothes, her problems, and her resolution of assorted on-screen marital dilemmas. With the dew of the century still fresh on her brow, she shared her public's dreams, their ambitions, and their taste for make-believe. Swanson was childishly convincing and, long before Elizabeth Taylor, showed a natural flair for publicity. "The public, not I, made Gloria Swanson a star," wrote DeMille.

In tandem with her fame was a sense of reality. Swanson later delighted to tell how she cooled a gushing fan: "And aren't you disappointed to be meeting in the flesh a little runt with horse-teeth like me!"

Swanson, a veteran of eight mediocre dramas at Triangle Film Corporation, came half-formed as an actress to DeMille. She was already the wrong side of twenty. If not exactly Eliza Doolittle, the right Henry Higgins could give her the high gloss and bright sheen necessary to elevate her in the public's mind from a pretty and spirited young actress into a poised, well-groomed star. DeMille and Swanson were perfect collaborators. DeMille wanted to be a star-maker and Swanson wanted to be a star. They were both idealists. Although he was born and raised along the liberal eastern seaboard and she in the conservative Midwest, neither was the type to let the coulter rust.

"Swanson would be satisfied with nothing less than top stardom," said her friend and contemporary Adela Rogers St. Johns. "It was partly an over compensation for her height—she was really very tiny—and I think the unhappiness of her parents' marriage and her own two abortive marital attempts had made her a little bitter and determined that the law of compensation would work for her someway, somehow."

It was an afternoon early in 1918 when she received a call from Oscar Goodstadt, the casting director at Famous Players-Lasky, to go and see DeMille. "Everybody knew where it was," recalled Swanson. "It took up a whole block at Sunset and Vine. It was here Mary Pickford worked. And Douglas Fairbanks. And almighty God himself, Cecil B. DeMille. Any notions I may have had of style or elegance evaporated the moment I was ushered into Mr. DeMille's paneled office. It was vast and somber, with tall stained-glass windows and deep polar-bear rugs. Light from the windows shone on ancient firearms and other weapons on the walls, and the elevated desk and chair resembled nothing so much as a throne. I felt like a peanut poised on teetering high heels."

She was twenty-one. He was imperial. "When he stood up behind the desk, he seemed to tower. Not yet forty, he seemed ageless, magisterial. He wore his baldness like an expensive hat, as if it were out of the question for him to have hair like other men. A sprig of laurel maybe, but not ordinary hair. He was wearing gleaming boots and riding breeches that fit him like a glove. He came over and took my hand, led me to a large sofa and sat down beside me, and proceeded to look clear through me. He said that he had seen me in a little Sennett picture and had never forgotten me, and that at the moment he was preparing a picture in which he wanted to use me."

But Swanson was committed to Triangle and couldn't get free. She felt that "the greatest opportunity of my life had been snatched away unjustly." Before 1918 was out, Triangle would go bust. She was told to be at Famous Players-Lasky "tomorrow morning at seven." "When I drove up to the studio the next morning, one of Mr. DeMille's assistants was waiting to show me to my dressing room. A few minutes later, Pinkerton detectives arrived with

three velvet-lined jewel chests. Everything was real, and I was supposed to
pick what I wanted to go with the dress. Mr. DeMille always had his actresses
pick out the jewelry they wore in his films so that they would act as if they
owned it. . . . A few minutes before ten an assistant director came to lead me
to the set. We stood off to one side as Mr. DeMille entered like Caesar, with
a whole retinue of people in his wake. Everyone stood in rapt silence as Mr.
DeMille's eyes swept over the set. Looking at every detail with absolute con-
centration, he peeled off his field jacket and a Filipino boy behind him caught
it as it left his hand. When he was ready to sit down, the Filipino boy deftly
shoved a director's chair under him."

DeMille's staff increased in number, his unit by now the size of a small
army. Stories about his behavior started to spread. He was well into his role
as Director General, complete with exquisite wardrobe and chairboys with
chairs to catch the royal derriere. The press loved these stories, all seen as
evidence of his monumental ego. But as he explained, "When you direct a
small cast in a drawing-room setting, you don't mind doing things for yourself. But when you have 5,000 people waiting for you to tell them what to
do somewhere out in a hard location, you don't want to have to worry about
where you're going to sit when you need to think. It's all a matter of logis-
tics. I make big films and I don't want distractions." DeMille directed his film
actors much the way he had his stage-trained actors—by giving them as little
direction as possible.

"The actors never used a script," Swanson recalled, echoing Farrar. "Mr.
DeMille told us carefully what the story was about and what each scene
meant, but he never gave specific instructions or directions. One day shortly
after I started work on the film, a young actor asked Mr. DeMille if he would
explain to him how he wanted him to play such and such a scene.

"'Certainly not!' Mr. DeMille bellowed. 'This is not an acting school. I
hired you because I trust you to be professional. When you do something
wrong, that is when I will talk to you!'

"Each day during the lunch hour he watched the previous day's rushes,
and he allowed his actors to watch them too, in order to catch their mistakes,
discover any bad habits they saw themselves developing and eliminate them,
and fill out the characters they were playing. Under Mr. DeMille I began to
see how telling small gestures and expressions could be if an actress knew
how to control them. It was part of his genius to let his actors make up
their own characters, just as he let them pick their own jewelry" Off-screen,
Swanson was befriended by her first DeMille co-star, Elliott Dexter, and his
exquisitely beautiful wife Marie Doro, who introduced her to "the movie industry's glamorous set." The class system was already in good working order.

DeMille had embarked on a series of films depicting marriage with a new
slant, and none too subtly at that. These films were all about one and the
same thing: how men and women acted when they got home and shared the
same bathroom. The husband wasn't going off to war; the wife wasn't being

sold off to slavery to pay debts. They had each other, but their marriage was getting stale, and DeMille's scripts showed how to rekindle past romance.

Don't Change Your Husband was in production as the Armistice was declared and, with a bigger budget to indulge the creation of expensive luxuries, DeMille had the perfect subject for the frivolous new mood the weary country was longing for, even down to the risqué title, an obvious reference to *Old Wives for New*. Macpherson's original story and screenplay told of Leila Denby Porter, who divorces busy, neglectful James, "whose breath reeks of onions," to marry Schulyer von Sutphen, a very stylish chap, only to discover she's landed herself a gambler whose breath "stinks of liquor," snores, and who two-times her with a girl nicknamed Toodles (Julia Faye). She divorces him, puts on a bathing suit, and sets out to win back the mate whose true value, onions and all, she now appreciates.

Paramount's accountants certainly had no cause to complain about the deals DeMille struck with his actors. They were receiving little more in 1918 than they had been paid three years earlier. "They have you sewed up for four years for no money at all," said Swanson's fiancé, Herbert Somborn, the president of Equity Pictures. He apparently failed to notice that the one thing she wouldn't take was orders from a husband after their divorce about her career. More important than money, with *Don't Change Your Husband*, Gloria Swanson became a star. Once again, the costumes and sets were spectacular. "Working for Mr. DeMillle was like playing house in the world's most expensive department store," recalled Swanson. "Going home at night to your own house and furniture was always a bit of a letdown. I finally said to him one day. 'Mr. DeMille, you're giving me terribly expensive tastes.' 'There's nothing wrong with wanting the best,' he said. 'I always do. That's why I want you to be the leading lady again in my next film.' Before I could say anything, he laughed and grabbed my hand and patted it."

One of the highlights audiences had to look forward to in DeMille's films of this period were be his "visions," episodes in which the modern-day lovers were translated to earlier historical periods to replay scenes (with new sets and wardrobe). DeMille introduced this device in *The Devil Stone*, where Farrar imagined herself a Viking queen. Swanson continued the tradition in *Don't Change Your Husband*, erotically gowned, posed on black marble, with glistening Nubians kneeling all around, one acting as a footrest, as she slowly goes through a strongbox flowing with jewels. In another vision, she is a scantily clad nymph with flowers in her hair, chased through the glades by a faun. In a third, Swanson is on a swing by a gigantic pool, surrounded by dozens of half-naked girls—all fantasies Swanson's character Leila imagined to help resolve her domestic mess.

"Seymour bathing suits will be de rigueur this season," puns the anonymous author of "Filmy Phantasmagoria" in *Theatre Magazine* for February 1919, who accurately prophesizes that the film "will attract more public attention than the peace conference . . . More women see DeMille's pictures than read fashion magazines. . . . It is within bounds to say that the taste of the masses has been developed more by Cecil B. DeMille."

Even with tongue in cheek, this was praise indeed, coming from a theater magazine. Worn by Swanson and others, the fashions invented or adapted from the latest European designs by Claire West—and the bizarre coiffures created for Swanson by the studio's hairdresser, a black woman referred to as "the celebrated Hattie"—were photographed and featured everywhere the printed page could reach. West, who ever since *Joan the Woman* had grown supreme in designing costumes for DeMille, was lauded for her work with Swanson in the *Woman's Home Companion* as someone who "lies awake at nights planning how to make Gloria Swanson's lovely back look more lovely, how to express a critical moment in the film drama by a charming bit of lace, or the shape of a fan."

The New York designer Howard Greer, fresh in Hollywood, describes the studio at the time of his arrival. "The Ladies' Wardrobe was situated on the second floor of a concrete mausoleum on the northwest corner of the lot. On the ground floor was the Men's Wardrobe, easily identified by the strong and pungent male odor of well-worn shoes and shirts and uniforms; upstairs was the more refined and ladylike smell of tarnished metal cloth, stale make-up, and scorched material on ironing boards. Several cramped cubicles served as offices, two slightly larger cubicles were used as fitting rooms, a spacious stockroom was piled higher with laces, brocades, and glittering embroideries, an enormous workroom housed the seamstresses, and a yawning cavity of a place held the completed, used, and discarded costumes."

As befitted a new idol, Swanson was kept as busy before the stills cameras as she was behind the film camera. A steady stream of dazzling portraits by Nelson Evans, Edwin Bower Hesser, Witzel, Karl Struss, Edward Steichen, and Donald Biddle Keyes poured out to satisfy an insatiable demand.

But the pressure was telling on DeMille. DeMille to Lasky (February 4, 1919): "Think it very serious mistake to try to make me finish this picture for March release. . . . I promised to get stills underway by tomorrow but to do this would cost nearly three thousand dollars to buy ready-made gowns. My request is that all my productions be moved forward at least one month and even then the dates will be difficult to meet. If you want me to make good pictures I absolutely cannot be rushed in my work. If our policy is to really make good pictures and fewer of them, let's start now. I cannot possibly make more than five pictures in a year and have them of the kind we all want."

DeMille would claim that *For Better, For Worse* had a theme at once timely and daring for a film released only five months after the Armistice and the return of the soldiers. But his tale of a soldier's return was a synthetic and dishonest tearjerker. Written by DeMille's brother William, collaborating with Jeanie Macpherson, the script was little more than a thinly disguised defense of men who, like DeMille, stayed behind as others followed the bugle call, disguised by the addition of Swanson in outrageous millinery.

In one of the most famous scenes in silent films, Gloria Swanson finds herself lavishly gowned and alone with a lion in DeMille's 1919 classic *Male and Female*. Photo: Karl Struss. Courtesy John Kobal Foundation

Elliott Dexter plays Ned, a doctor who declines a commission because he must take charge of a children's hospital in his hometown. Swanson's character, his girlfriend, represents unreasoning prejudice—"A girl never forgives a man who stays home when he is needed over there"—and she marries Richard Burton, played by Tom Forman, Ned's rival, who is about to go overseas.

When Swanson runs down a little girl and can't find a doctor, she appreciates the importance of Ned having remained behind. News quickly follows that Richard has been killed. At the party to announce her engagement to Ned, Richard returns, his right hand gone and one side of his face horribly scarred. Swanson tries but can't accept her husband in his condition. Richard finds another woman and he and Swanson divorce. Swanson married Ned after all.

The best part of this film is its period detail. The script's manipulation is too crass, without the nuance typically found in works by William deMille and Macpherson. Swanson's character is too stubborn; Ned too noble. There is little attempt at characterization until the end when poor Richard returns. Nevertheless, the writers took a successful play and turned it into an even more successful film at the box office.

By now there was gossip about Swanson and "the Chief." In this case, it wasn't Calpurnia but Cleopatra who was the last to know. "A week or so into filming," Swanson claimed, "Mr. DeMille himself came over to me when we finished shooting for the day and said in a playful stage whisper that everyone on the set could hear, 'Leave the key under the mat as usual.' Sam Wood, his assistant, and the cameraman started laughing, but I said I didn't get the joke. 'Haven't you heard?' Mr. DeMille asked. 'You and I are having a torrid love affair. That's what the columnists say.' Now everybody was roaring with laughter, but I was stiff with shock. 'There, there. You'll just have to get used to that sort of thing,' Mr. DeMille said. 'It's what happens when you become famous in Hollywood. Besides, columnists never bother to print the truth if they can think of something more interesting.' . . . I myself was too much in awe of him to fall in love with him, but I could see how it could happen."

When Swanson wrote her autobiography, there was no reason not to mention an affair with DeMille had there had been one. She wrote plenty about the others but, according to some sources, she had actually tried to seduce *him*. Late in his life, while in a mellow mood, DeMille told his granddaughter of the time he sat watching rushes with only Swanson beside him. As the granddaughter remembered, "He said they were sitting, watching the rushes, and they were alone. Slowly she worked her way over to him, and finally she was sitting in his lap, sitting there, curled up like a kitten, and he said, 'I never moved my hands from off the side of the chair. I never put her back in her seat or expressed any feeling. I kept my hands to myself. It was very difficult, but she finally got off me and went back to her seat.'" His reasons for refusing the opportunity were more practical: "I had a star who was in love with me. I could pull more out of her in a day if we remained friends. If we became lovers I would have lost some of my control."

After two films together, Swanson and DeMille were about to make their most celebrated film together. Sam Goldwyn made a big splash with his announcement that his company would specialize in making "great films by great authors." DeMille started to look around for works by "great writers," too.

He asked Lasky to obtain the motion picture rights to a story that intrigued him, J. M. Barrie's hugely successful play *The Admirable Crichton*. In January, Lasky wired DeMille that the deal had been closed. Indeed, Barrie the creator of *Peter Pan* had sold the rights to all his plays and to any plays or novels that he might write in the future to Paramount—"surely a high mark of confidence from an impressive source," recounted an impressed DeMille. Reportedly, Barrie was paid $100,000 plus 50 percent of the profits, the same deal Lasky had made earlier with Belasco. (Another wholesale story buy was the entire output of the Western novelist Zane Grey.)

DeMille feared the public would not be aware that *The Admirable Crichton* referred to the perfect butler, and instead think "admiral" and therefore sea drama (which they got) or a costume drama (which they also got). One hot night, he woke with a cry of *"Male and Female*!" "Oh, go to sleep!" snapped his wife. He came up with a title that no one could confuse (though they kept Barrie's original title in Britain) and used it without consulting with or informing the author.

The New York office was shocked. Sir James Barrie was a distinguished writer—how would he react to such tampering? If Barrie was angry, and talked to the press, it could affect Paramount's relationship with their other authors. Besides Barrie, Paramount had deals in various stages with such British writers as H. G. Wells, Arnold Bennett, and Somerset Maugham. For as long as possible, nothing was said to Sir James, though his contract contained a clause obliging Paramount to show him the film scenarios of his plays before releasing them in Great Britain.

Swanson's role was magnificent. Her character would be ultra-haughty, and she got to take the most famous bath of the day, in a spectacular bathroom. As the steam rose, the camera selected such important details as a bottle, marked "Rose Toilet Water." "Humanity is assuredly growing cleaner," the subtitle wrote, but also less artistic. "Women bathe more often, but not as beautifully as did their Ancient Sisters: for surely a Bath Room should express as much Art and Beauty as our overrated Drawing Rooms—on which we spend much money, and no time." Surrounded by the most luxurious sets shown on screen to date, Swanson complains to her maid Tweeny (played by Lila Lee), "You've been growing careless, of late, about my bath—remember, I don't want it over 70 degrees!"

A DeMille touch worthy of von Stroheim is the audience's first glimpse of Lady Mary, through the eyes of a little twelve-year-old boy bringing her breakfast. Looking cautiously left to right, he bends down to the keyhole. With a smile on his prepubescent lips, he sees Swanson asleep in her bed, one bare hand and wrist dangling out of it. She stirs, she turns, she doesn't waken. "As Lady Mary," remembered Swanson, "I would wear the most exotic array of costumes imaginable. In society I would wear afternoon dresses of the finest Belgian lace, and evening gowns made of satin and moleskin and gold beads. On the desert island I would wear animal skins. I would also have an elaborate bathtub scene wearing nothing at all, and if that weren't enough, Mr. DeMille and Jeanie Macpherson had added a 'vision' set in ancient Babylon in which I would wear a dress of pearls and feathers and be tossed into a den of real lions."

The gowns for this vision of old Babylon were the work of a twenty-year-old newcomer, Mitchell Leisen, an architectural student from Michigan, who began his film career on *Male and Female*. Young, thin, delicate, and fey, Leisen was excited by the commission. "I had been raised on *The Woman God Forgot* and all the DeMille spectacles. . . . I had never designed any costumes in my life, but I thought, 'What the hell.' I went through Ted Shawn's library of art books at the public library, and I made three sketches. I took them to DeMille and he asked me what I wanted for them. Taking a wild flier, I said, '$300 apiece.' He said, 'Well, just wait in the outer office.' He came back and said, 'I'll give you a hundred dollars apiece for these and a year's contract for a hundred dollars a week . . .' So I've been here ever since. . . .

"Claire West was the head of wardrobe at the Lasky studio and she wasn't about to have me making anything in her workroom. She stuck me in a little room about 4 x 6-foot with six seamstresses, and I sweated the whole thing out myself. . . .

"We did Tommy Meighan's costume for the king and one for Bebe Daniels who was the king's mistress. Bebe was a fairly tall girl, but Gloria Swanson is a very small person, very short. I wanted to give her high heels to give her more stature. I couldn't just put French heels on her, which were in style at the time [1919], because it would have been a terrible anachronism. I finally hit upon the idea of making wooden clogs for her that were in the shape of Babylonian bulls standing on their forelegs with wings that came up on the side of Gloria's feet and held them on. . . .

"I finally hit upon the idea of making the train in batik. I painted the pattern on the fabric with plain, ordinary beeswax, then I dyed it, being very careful not to crack the wax, or the pattern would have had a cracked effect. Where there was wax the cloth didn't take any dye. Then I pressed the material, melting the wax and leaving a pattern. We embroidered with pearls for the peacock's eyes [for her headdress]."

According to the French author Raymond Bachollet's[6] book on the designer Paul Iribe, DeMille asked him to create a Swanson costume as a one-off. Realized entirely in white pearls, and weighing a ton, it created a sensation, helped no doubt by Karl Struss's superb portraits that were circulated widely. "Paul Iribe was DeMille's French art director," said Lesisen. "I used to have knock-down-drag-out fights with him and he'd fire me. DeMille didn't fire me so much. At the end of the day, Iribe would suddenly drop everything on my shoulders and go home. I remember one time I worked all night long trying to get a set for a big carnival sort of thing. At 6:00 in the morning, I decided that I would go home and take a bath, and then come back and finish what had to be done. I fell asleep on the bathroom floor and I didn't wake up until 10:00. I tore back to the studio and Iribe was in flames because he had had to go in there and finish this thing up. That was one of the times I got fired; maybe it was the last, I can't remember."

In 1921, Leisen left DeMille and joined production designer Wilfred Buckland to work for Mary Pickford and Douglas Fairbanks. He returned to DeMille in 1925, and remained as his costume and set designer, art and assistant director, and right-hand man until the end of *Sign of the Cross*.

Another future director, Henry Hathaway, also started out his career on *Male and Female*. And one of America's most celebrated artists, Walt Disney, apparently began his illustrious career doing posters and advertising sketches at $12 a week for the studio's advertising department. While this did not

---

6. Raymond Bachollet, *Paul Iribe* (Denoel, 1982)

mark the beginning of DeMille and Disney's lifelong mutual admiration society (Disney pointed out the connection to DeMille forty years later), early on he saw the young cartoonist as an authentically creative American genius.

For *Man and Woman*, there would be at least two weeks on location on the uninhabited island of Santa Cruz off the California coast at Santa Barbara. "While we were there," said Swanson, "we would rough it like the characters in the story." Everyone got seasick on the boat, and Swanson's distress was increased when two Gila monsters, brought for the film, got loose during the storm. But, "like the Almighty himself," acknowledged Swanson, "Mr. DeMille managed to bring order out of chaos, and he didn't have seven days to do it. . . . He let nothing stand in his way, and soon he had infused us all with his spirit. We did things cheerfully on Santa Cruz that we would flatly have refused to do in any other picture or for any other director."

Elliott Dexter had fallen seriously ill, so to portray Crichton, DeMille replaced him with Thomas Meighan. They had worked together four years earlier in *Kindling*. Meighan had wanted to play the part of the perfect butler who becomes "king" when the family is shipwrecked on a deserted island, ruling over those whose servant he had been, ever since he saw the play. He delighted the company and subsequently silent film lip-readers with his off-the-cuff humor. When Swanson has to dig her teeth into his brawny arm, Meighan asked, "Have a little pepper and salt, Gloria?" DeMille was won over, despite the fact that the Irishman was a heavy drinker. "Tommy always gave me his word when we started on a film that he wouldn't touch a drink. . . . He never broke it, no matter how long the film took, . . . but then he would come to me and say, "Am I free? Am I alright?' And when I'd say, that's it, off he went on a nice alcoholic spree." In one sequence, Crichton, on the hunt for game, returns with a dead leopard draped around his shoulders.

For DeMille, a stuffed animal wouldn't do. "He was so beautiful," recalled DeMille, "the most beautiful leopard I've ever seen. . . . He had killed a man the day before and I read that he was going to be destroyed and I called up and said, Well, let me destroy him. I'll buy him—what do you want for him? They said $2.50, and I said, 'You got a deal. Send him over.' I was going to kill him and then hang him on Tommy's shoulder. But when I saw him there and he was so wonderful, a magnificent looking beast, I said, 'You can't kill him. . . . Let's chloroform him.' And they said, 'There's not enough chloroform in the world.' I said, 'Sure there is. Go down to the drugstore and they'll give you some five gallon cans of chloroform.' We covered the cage with a cloth, and I told them to get me about a dozen sponges. Then we poured this on and stuffed the sponges in one at a time. The leopard, of course, didn't enjoy being chloroformed. There was this roar of rage and the cage rocking back and forth and Tommy sitting with his eyes glued on this thing saying, 'My God, my God.' We lifted the leopard and hung him on Tommy's shoulder. The leopard was absolutely out cold—not a motion, but you'd hear this 'R-r-r-umb-r-r-r—.' Tom had a slightly greenish look, due, no doubt, to the mingled odors of leopard and chloroform right under his nose, and he was to play as if they weren't there. This was a hell of a love scene. Tom instantly became Crichton, while the dainty Gloria, who had been holding herself somewhat aloof from these preliminaries, jumped into her part and placed her hand on Minnie's flank as the action started. And Tommy, looking into those soulful eyes of Gloria's was saying, 'My God, Mr. DeMille, he's coming to—he's coming to! When I finally finished—the leopard weighed about 300 pounds—Tommy, who couldn't throw twenty feet in his life, must have tossed him 20 feet. The leopard didn't come to—it was the next day before he revived. That leopard had been a killer, but after that you could go and tweak him by the whiskers and he would look at you with love in his eyes and say, 'Strike me on the other side.' A completely changed animal, and he was all his life, as long as he lived."

Even with all precautions taken, DeMille's actors knew there would come the moment when they would be asked to do something extraordinary. So it was that, when the family yacht crashed on the rocks, Meaghan's life was saved when he was pulled from the sea by a Hawaiian prop man.

If Swanson was cool with her co-starring leopard, she was positively radiant when it came time to film back in Hollywood her big scene with the lions, costumed in her dress of a thousand pearls. DeMille claimed the lion was old and toothless. There was no way to fake these scenes or use a double, though a sharpshooter was on hand in case of emergencies, and DeMille always carried his gun. "She never even asked if there were any safeguards," DeMille would tell friends. "That's what's so wonderful about Gloria." According to her, DeMille said she should play the two sequences "in the manner of a very dignified Christian saint": "In the first I had to descend the steps and approach the entrance to the den. The set for this scene had been constructed in an enormous swimming pool, painted entirely with black lacquer and converted into an arena. Around the edge of the arena were arches and a flight of stairs leading down to it. Heavy wire mesh enclosed the whole set. I was told to remain perfectly calm, for the gate was made of painted wood and therefore easily breakable. If a lion got excited or angry and jumped up against it, he could smash right through it.

"Once I was in costume, Mr. DeMille escorted me into the great-enclosed set. When the lights hit me, I walked across the floor of the throne room toward the steps. . . . At a given moment the trainers cracked their whips and the lions were released. I could see the shape of the animals beyond the gate. I took a few more steps forward, then froze, petrified, as one lion unexpectedly moved to the side of the gate and bounded up out of the den, landing a few feet away from me." But she carried on. On the next take the same thing happened. The lion trainers shouted to her to stay absolutely still. Finally, a trainer stepped in front of her and drove the animal back with his whip and chain. Swanson had never moved and showed no fear.

"That's it!" DeMille yelled. "Cut! Fine!" Although he never doubted that she would be all right, he felt guilty about having put his young star through so much danger and fear. He was even prepared to drop the next lion scene, one in which, as Swanson recalled, "I had to lie on my stomach, and have the lion put his paw on my bare back." But if there is any doubt why DeMille loved her as an actress, and what drew her fans to her, what happened next provides the answer.

Knowing how much this scene, based on the famous painting *The Lion's Bride*, meant to DeMille, Swanson insisted on going on. "This time I had to lie on the floor and remain absolutely still. I would ruin the scene if I couldn't control my breathing. My back was bare to the waist. They put a piece of canvas on my back to keep the lion's claws from making the slightest scratch. I could hear a lion's claws scratching the floor as the trainer led him in on a leash. Then I could hear another trainer whisper to Mr. DeMille, who came and knelt beside me. 'I must ask you something for your own safety,' he whispered. 'You're not menstruating, are you?' 'No,' I replied softly. He stood up and said to the trainer, 'We can proceed. Everything's fine.' Then I could hear the lion breathing near me. The keeper brought the lion up to me and he put his paw on the canvas. Ever so slowly they pulled the canvas aside until I could feel his paw on my skin. Every hair on my head was standing on end. I could hear the camera grinding and then the crack of the trainer's whip. Every cell in my body quivered when the animal roared. His hot breath seemed to go up and down my spine."

The New York photographer Karl Struss began his cinematic career as a special stills photographer on this film. "I shot a lot of stills of Gloria Swanson, those with the lion on top of her as well. . . . I went down into the pit, I had a low camera tripod, you see I had to open the lens to get the composition of her and the lion; and then I had to close the shutter, put the plate holder in, pull the slide, I had to set the shutter and give it an exposure of about one second and half, stop it down to 16, put the slide back in, get the camera out, and the whole time Swanson is lying there with the lion on her back. DeMille was more scared than she was." The whole scene, including stills, had taken only a few minutes. Only now that it was all over did Swanson collapse and cry. "How lovely," DeMille said. "I was beginning to think that you were the perfect machine, that you could do anything. But now I know you're much more than that. You're a real woman." No wonder that he hadn't wanted to ruin their working relationship with an affair. From his personal collection of precious and semiprecious knickknacks, he invited her to choose whatever she desired as a reward for bravery. She recovered selecting a gold-mesh evening bag with an emerald clip. "It was during this film that Mr. DeMille began to call me 'young fellow,'" remembered Swanson, "as if I were one of the boys. In the days and weeks that followed, he never called me anything else."

Only one problem remained. How to break the news of the title to Sir James? The London office, even more in awe of theatrical and literary reputations than the New York office, sat on tenterhooks, convinced of their American employer's crassness. By coincidence, Lasky traveled to London on the boat carrying the first print, and with much care a screening was set up for Sir James in a private projection room.

"Sir James," Lasky stammered, "it wasn't my idea, but you see, sir, the American idiom isn't exactly the King's English, and our director, Cecil De-Mille, is a very determined and sometimes difficult man. And . . . well . . . he decided to call it *Male and Female*." The canny Scotsman pondered the news. "Capital!" he exclaimed. "I wish I'd thought of that myself!"

A quixotic footnote is provided by the British filmmaker Herbert Wilcox from a conversation he had with Barrie during which Barrie deemed "charming," both "Americans and Paramount"—"and very generous they are, too. Why? Well, they pay me a lot of money for my plays, but never use the material. It is all new stuff and ideas—some very original."

"Don't you resent that?" I asked him. "Oh no, not at all. You see they not only change the play—they change the title!"

Male and Female was a colossal hit. It had cost $168,619.28 to make and, aided by the new deals the company had initiated with exhibitors and its own large and growing chain of theaters, it went far above any previous rental to become Paramount's first film to pass the million-dollar mark. It grossed $1,256,226.59, almost $1 million more than any of DeMille's previous films.

CHAPTER SIXTEEN

BECAUSE *DON'T CHANGE YOUR HUSBAND* PROVED SO PROFITABLE, WHEN DeMille filmed another of his brother's stories he used a similar title, *Why Change Your Wife?* The story is a variation on *Old Wives for New*, with Swanson as a formerly fun-loving woman whom marriage turns prim and dowdy. Bebe Daniels, a veteran of films since the age of seven and now on her way to movie stardom, played the second female lead. The eighteen-year-old had made her debut for DeMille in *Male and Female* as a Babylonian courtesan and now she would portray a pleasure-loving flapper. Swanson's husband played by Thomas Meighan takes up with Daniels (a variation on the usual Julia Faye roles), marries her and discovers that marriage has made her a worse drudge than Swanson. When he comes across his first wife again, now changed back into the girl he married, they reconcile. Given the cost of legal fees for divorces, he must be a very rich husband.

"DeMille was noted for his caustic tongue," recalled Daniels, frail but still alert in old age in London, "and for giving people a dressing-down on the set. Perhaps he thought he got the best out of actors that way. Up till now I had escaped the storm, but one day the heavens opened and I got the drenching of a lifetime. I'll never forget it. I was sitting on a desk wearing a fringe dress. I had to stand up and walk over to Tommy Meighan. Every time I did so the fringe of my dress caught in the knob of a desk drawer and gave me a very awkward start to the action. In the middle of the second take, DeMille stopped the camera and said: 'Bebe, you did that as gracefully as an elephant. Maybe I should get someone to teach you how to walk.' I felt as though somebody had given me a blow in the pit of the stomach. I was so hurt I could not come to my own defense, when suddenly a little property boy spoke up (at the risk of losing his job): 'Maybe if you take the drawers out of that desk, Mr. DeMille, she can do the scene.'

"Later she confronted her tormentor in his office. 'I am very sorry, but I have never had anyone speak as crossly as you did to me this afternoon. I don't belong in drama, I belong in comedy and—I had better go back. Will you just please tear up my contract and forget all about it?'

Bebe Daniels (left) and Gloria Swanson play romantic rivals in DeMille's 1920 potboiler *Why Change Your Wife?* Courtesy John Kobal Foundation

"There was a moment's pause before he threw back his head, and laughed, and laughed, and *laughed*. Then he said: 'You mean you'd give up a four-year contract with Paramount just for that. . . . With all have I planned for you?'

"I said yes. Then he explained that he hadn't intended to hurt my feelings, and asked would I feel any better if next morning he apologized to me in front of the whole cast. He was probably pulling my leg, but it helped to heal my wounded pride."

Shot in a month, *Why Change Your Wife?* was DeMille's second film to break the million-dollar barrier, grossing $1,016,245.87 worldwide.

The fifth film in DeMille's lucrative "marriage" cycle was *Something to Think About*. Today these films would all have the same title with a Roman numeral at the end. The film reunited Swanson with Elliott Dexter as co-star. Jeanie Macpherson wrote the rather limp story, which DeMille considered "the first of my modern pictures to embody a religious theme": "it is the faith of Elliott Dexter's housekeeper, played by Claire McDowell, which keeps him from despair, and it is her inspired wisdom and her prayer that win through in the end to reconciliation and deep love." Swanson looked

Between takes on *Why Change Your Wife* (1920), with its typically lavish DeMille set. If you look closely at the top of the stairs, Gloria Swanson stands with an umbrella over her shoulder. Courtesy John Kobal Foundation

magnificent wearing a different dress each time she was on screen. In the fourteen months she had been with DeMille, Swanson had become a strikingly beautiful woman and skilled emotional actress, able to create a mood with something as simple as a knowing glance, and in this film the stars had their work cut out for them and reverted to their own personality whenever characterization got bogged down.

One gathers that Swanson and Mcpherson did not like each other. Apparently, Macpherson behaved as though she had a new rival and made cutting comments at Swanson's expense. Perhaps Macpherson had heard rumors of the attempted seduction in DeMille's screening room. Tension between the two existed for most of the time Swanson worked for the Chief. Mrs. deMille had Gloria for tea, but Macpherson had no such interest in making friends of potential rivals. Swanson was becoming too big a star to care.

Riding the crest of the DeMille-Swanson wave, *Something to Think About* cost $168,330, and grossed $915,848.51. Swanson took some time off to prepare for the birth of her first child.

Although Paramount was growing, Adolph Zukor, ever the pragmatic businessman, remained more cautious than his energetic young partner. DeMille was not easy to manage. He didn't think the studio's policy that films should be tailored to a certain commercial length and brought in on a pre-agreed budget, should apply to him. DeMille expected that Paramount should support him wholeheartedly in all his projects. This would eventually lead to a confrontation between Zukor and DeMille.

The movie industry was not only growing but changing. United Artists was formed in 1919 as a conglomerate of stars and directors producing their own films and keeping most of the revenue. This at first astounded and then shook the other studios as they saw how the independents prospered. The films Pickford, Fairbanks, and Chaplin, and others made in this arrangement were the foundations of celebrated fortunes.

DeMille, as he informed Lasky, was constantly being approached by other studios, offering him the moon: "United Artists came to me with a proposition yesterday guaranteeing to net me not less than three hundred thousand per picture with gross of not less than seven hundred and fifty thousand. I went over their books as I told Garbutt and Connick that I would. Pickford has in three months taken in six hundred and six thousand dollars cash on Pollyanna in this country. A man here named Greenhill offers them two hundred and fifty thousand cash advance against sixty-forty percent for the rest of the world for each picture. If I only make two pictures per year and the United Artists only lasted two years I could make more than under a five year contract as outlined between us.

When Fairbanks and Pickford's pictures were earning far less than my pictures are now earning, the company deemed them worth ten and fifteen thousand per week against a profit of one half of their pictures. The company pays Mary Miles Minter ten thousand per week with her pictures scarcely breaking even." (Swanson, a bigger draw than any other Paramount actress, was only earning $400.)

"I am sure it is not the intention of you, Zukor or the company to penalize me for my desire to remain with you and because of my past loyalty to the company, but it seems to me to resolve itself into one of two things: either the company is rewarding me on our newly proposed basis of five thousand per week for my past services only and not for my present earning power, believing that my pictures are not financially strong, in which case the offer is too large and I should not want to remain, or else they are deliberately paying me on a different basis *from the other stars* [author's italics] because I am regarded as one of the family."

In time, DeMille secured himself a contract with Paramount giving him $6,500 a week "as advance against a gross budget of $290,000 per picture." He must have been satisfied, for on May 8 he renewed with Paramount for another five years. "But it may have become clear why, in the same year of 1920," he wrote in his autobiography, "I judged it wise to form a company of my own. I felt that the day might be coming when an independent company might be a useful entity for me to have around. Cecil B. DeMille Productions was formed in 1920 as a partnership, with Mrs. deMille, Neil McCarthy, and Ella King Adams, Mrs. deMille's youthful and brilliant stepmother who was also my script reader, as my partners. The company was incorporated, under the same name, in 1923."

When Mary Pickford and Douglas Fairbanks went off on a delayed honeymoon traveling around the world, they found it impossible to get away from their fans. There had never been attention like this before, short of a Victory Parade, and it boosted the standing of all stars. Public acclamations would become a regular part of a star's trips away from the security and comfort of the studio.

Radio was now sweeping America at a speed not known since the early nickelodeons, and the nation's fascination with "sound drama" and "radio stars" put enough of a dent in the box office to be of concern. Ironically, Lee DeForset set up his Phonofilm Company in 1922, and as early as 1923, he offered his system both to Adolph Zukor at Paramount and Carl Laemmle at Universal. Both turned him down. There would be no interest until the breakthrough by Vitaphone in 1926.

Hollywood's usual reaction to any threat was to make bigger films. But stars were getting more expensive. The bigger and more cost-conscious the studios grew, the more they wanted money for expansion, and the less they wanted to pay for their players, not to mention their sorely overtaxed, underpaid staff. There wasn't much studio employees could do except form a union. Stars, boosted by publicity and their fan mail, suddenly read about what others were earning. Suddenly, childish gratitude for a contract and the thrill of working with a DeMille was no longer enough to bridge the gap that stretched between their $400 a week paycheck and another star's $10,000. Female stars fought back by claiming illness in the middle of a production. A few years later, Paramount would lose Valentino, the hottest property in the film world. Agreeing to his terms would have been better for the studio than the loss of this golden gander, but the studio refused, and Valentino went off to earn a fortune giving dance exhibitions around the country and producing his own films.

As Director General, DeMille was both more sympathetic and shrewder in these matters than his accountants back east. While his own contracts with his actors were far from generous, he took on fledging actors and, when he saw they were popular enough to go off and star on their own, released them. The secret correspondence concerning Wallace Reid's contract—one of the most popular stars on Paramount's roster—gives an insight into company thinking.

Lasky to DeMille (personal, May 26, 1920): "While we agree with you that Reid is underpaid and that it is undoubtedly proper to increase his compensation again, we must make increases of this kind very difficult to obtain and should only give in an inch at a time. Am sure you realize that no matter how we adjust Reid's contract now, the very fact that he obtains increase in his compensation in spite of his contract, will make him come back again in a few months or another year and attempt to get another raise. If this is inherent condition of the business and if we cannot overcome constant adjustments of compensation in legal and binding contracts, at least we should make it as difficult as possible for our employees to get increased compensation where they have binding contracts, so that they will not get thought that company is easy or that they can increase their compensation any time they feel like kicking up row."

The ongoing campaign to promote DeMille's name as much as any star meant that his name would have to be distinct and separate from that of his brother. Although William's style was quite different from his, DeMille wanted to make the division clear, fearing that a potential confusion in the public's mind might adversely affect the profits on his films. He couldn't ask William, the elder, to change his name but he wanted the public to know of only one DeMille. It may have been unnecessary: Pickford had a brother and sister in the business, and Chaplin had a brother. So did John Ford and Henry King, and their public was not confused. William was a critic's darling, but his box-office receipts were usually tepid. "William deMille's pictures are of such a different type from mine," DeMille wrote to Zukor, "that an audience going to theatre expecting to see a DeMille picture is disappointed. As the matter is very delicate for me to handle I wish you would see if some method of differentiating between the two brands can be worked out."

The critics were able to tell the difference, and many, like *Life* magazine's eccentric Robert Sherwood, took special delight in taking potshots at DeMille's films, even when praising work by William. William was praised for "wisdom and good taste," which was "typical of its intelligent director"—the implication being that DeMille was not. These jibes pleased neither brother. When humorist Robert Benchley described William as "the subtle and intelligent member of the deMille family," William told his daughter, "I wish they would not use me as a hammer with which to whack Cecil." The only thing which ever made her father lose his temper, said Agnes, was criticism against his brother.

It was not uncommon for stars like Pickford and Chaplin to earn lucrative licensing fees promoting projects. DeMille's films had shown that this could be done with inanimate objects as well—the clothes in his films, the carpets, curtains, and plumbing fixtures, had all caught the public's imagination. They did not come from a catalogue. The studio made lucrative deals with stores and suppliers to advertise fixtures used in DeMille films. DeMille told the wardrobe department, "Don't design anything anybody could possibly buy in a store." At least not until after the film came out. Howard Greer, who'd worked with Paul Poiret in Paris and Madame Lucile in New York, believed Hollywood designs were every bit as good as work found in Europe. DeMille

Agnes Ayres starred for DeMille in his 1921 production *Forbidden Fruit*. Courtesy John Kobal
Foundation

felt that if clothing worn in his films was marketable, he wanted a share. Paramount's top brass considered the question. The studio might have paid for
them, but DeMille dreamt them up and made them marketable to the public.

With that matter settled, DeMille went back to work on *Forbidden Fruit*,
another high society fashion show, but this time without Swanson in the
lead role. Agnes Ayres, a protégé of Lasky, starred in the film which was a
jazzed up remake of *The Golden Chance*, directed by DeMille in 1915. Here he
returned to the story of a poor seamstress who suddenly has the chance to

dress up and enjoy a good meal when her employer finds that the beauty she invited to sit next to a young millionaire has the mumps. DeMille described it as "a rather slight story with a Cinderella theme." The lengthy dressing ritual, in a room of Byzantine size and splendor, appealed to fans. Clothes are paraded, feathers and furs enough to have wiped out the inhabitants of a small forest. A suitcase-sized jewel box spills out with necklaces, bracelets, brooches, rings, pins, and pearls. At midnight, the party ends and everything goes back to where it came from, but there are more complications before the seamstress gets her millionaire.

The film is given a lift by its supporting cast. The husband played by Clarence Burton would be at home in a Warhol movie; Julia Faye, demoted here to portraying a maid, looks disgruntled and reveals a bright humor. Theodore Kosloff, the colorful Russian who at that time ran the Paramount dance school, was Giuseppe, "a man who has served not only to the best families in New York but two years in Sing Sing." He was also hired to choreograph the fairy-tale sequence and apparently also oversaw the costumes. In fact, these exquisite Bakst-like creations, which must have absorbed much of the films very large budget, were the work of Natacha Rambova, about to depart the Kosloff menagerie.

The set and costumes for the dream sequence in the ballroom of the castle were the talk of Hollywood. Evelyn Scott, the daughter of a DeMille's screenwriter Beulah Marie Dix, who visited the shooting, recalled: "Agnes Ayres, Cinderella in a huge powered wig and a mass of glittering and partly see-through skirt, had to descend a staircase made of glass. Water flowed beneath the stairs which, between the takes, got covered to protect their shine. Walking down them in glass slippers must have needed as much courage as climbing up the walls of Orleans." Where the glass steps led on to the glass floor of the glass ballroom, two wide shallow pools were constructed. Rising from the surface of these pools were eight octagonal glass pillars, each bearing at its apex a large basket of blown glass fruit. During filming, black swans made these fountains their home. Over all this crystal expanse a canopy to rival a circus tent was hung to emphasize the beauty of the reflections on the crystalline floor. Everyone walked on their own reflection. How Karl Struss and Alvin Wyckoff managed to shoot it without the canvas showing was a miracle. It took two days and the greater part of one night to film this episode. "He put a moral at the end," Evelyn Scott put in a nutshell when she remarked, "but along the way there was idle luxury, preening selfishness, lots of overdress, and some undress."

The assembled film ran to eleven reels. Since DeMille had just agreed not to make films longer than seven, a lot of cutting was required. Despite the dazzling displays of sets and costumes, the film, though profitable, didn't attain the financial returns of DeMille's recent features. It's hard to see why DeMille allowed himself to spend so much time and money on window dressing. He needed a solid property.

DeMille is depicted on the set of *The Affairs of Anatol* with his bevy of leading ladies. From left (rear): Maude Wayne, Bebe Daniels, Wanda Hawley, Polly Moran, Gloria Swanson, Agnes Ayres, Julia Faye; (front): Ruth Miller, Shannon Day. Courtesy John Kobal Foundation

Jesse Lasky suggested adapting *Anatol*, Arthur Schnitzler's twenty-four-year-old Viennese sex-shocker. "I think this would be one of the biggest events in the picture game and the sort of DeMille sensation the public is waiting for and if you undertake picture with cast as I describe above it will top all other DeMille features in gross returns." It was re-titled *The Affairs of Anatol*, and Swanson was cast co-starring top Paramount star Wallace Reid, by this time suffering heavily from his drug addiction. It would be Swanson's last film under DeMille's direction. Swanson had been elevated to the ranks of Paramount stardom on May 10. Even with a new baby, Swanson agreed to make the film, and she also agreed to work under the terms of her old contract, not her new star contract. Once again her name would be printed in smaller type than that of DeMille on the film's advertising and promotion. "I thought it would be like old home week. It turned out instead to be torture. First of all, shooting began before I really felt up to it. I was worried that my figure wasn't quite back to normal. . . . In addition, I insisted on nursing Gloria, which meant that I had to be up at least by six every morning besides getting up at least once during the night. Herbert's resultant concern over my health combined with his irritation that I was making this film at all, strained our marriage almost to the breaking point. . . . Wallace Reid, the male star, was a cause of constant anxiety to me. I heard endless rumors that he was an addict, and although I never saw him take drugs, his behavior never seemed quite right." (He kept making passes at her.)

And there was the constant tension with Macpherson. While they were making *Affairs of Anatol*, a remark of hers became the straw that broke the camel's back: "One day in front of everyone she said with a cutting edge, 'Goodness me, but you do stay on the plump side, don't you, Gloria?'

"'You'd be plump too if you were nursing a baby,' I said and stomped out of the room. I went straight to Mr. DeMille and asked him if the costume looked all right. He said it looked fine. Then I asked him if I looked all right. He said of course. 'Well, Miss Macpherson doesn't seem to think so,' I said, and I could feel my lip trembling. He came over and put his hand on my shoulders. 'That's because you're a star, young fellow, and Miss Macpherson isn't,' he said. 'As a star you have to learn to hear what you want to hear, ignore what you have to ignore. You have to learn to take the cream and leave the milk. Always remember that.' Whatever *The Affairs of Anatol* cost me, that moment more than made up for it."

For *The Affairs of Anatol*, Lasky brought in the innovative French designer Paul Iribe, who had previously designed Swanson's costly pearl gown for *Male and Female*. Although primarily a set designer, Iribe did costumes as well and his humorously suggestive octopus costume for Bebe Daniels, with the suckers on the tentacles represented by pearls, was a sensation. There was nothing in his costumes the censors could object to but much an imaginative audience could feast on. Iribe brought DeMille what he most craved: something new, something no other director had thought of—in this case, Art Nouveau style. DeMille, whose work until now was an American's idea of continental sophistication, now had the real thing. He would describe Iribe as "one of the best art directors I have ever had." The two men became friends, and Iribe worked on most of DeMille's films over the course of the decade.

Somerset Maugham, another of "the celebrated British authors" brought to Hollywood, claimed *The Affairs of Anatol* contained original ideas that he had told to DeMille. Considering that the deal was $10,000 for every story filmed, Maugham was concerned. Lasky alerted DeMille, but listening and lifting was a typical Hollywood ploy, and as long as the man speaking wasn't under contract, studios felt under no obligation to acknowledge other people's original ideas. Maugham was entertained to dinner at the DeMille house and convinced of his error. The author left Hollywood soon thereafter, leaving behind a story, "The Ordeal," for which he was paid and which was filmed the following year.

When Jesse had first gone shopping for famous authors, he spent Paramount's money on the bestsellers, the queens of the bodice-ripper, whose works shocked and captivated a naïve society before the war, and sold millions: Marie Corelli (*The Sorrows of Satan*), Ethel M. Hull (*The Sheik*), Quida (who gave the world *Cigarette*, the famed self-lighter!) and, perhaps the most famous of all, Elinor Glyn, author of *Three Weeks*, who arrived in Hollywood in time to make a perfect fourth at bridge in a DeMille drawing room. Mrs. Glyn was not a disappointment to an expectant Swanson, who may have come from the sticks but wasn't a hick or easily overawed: "Her British dignity was devastating. She was the first woman I'd ever seen wearing false eyelashes, and although she was old enough to be my grandmother, she got away with it. She had small, squinty eyes and took tiny steps when she walked. Her teeth were too even and white to be real, she smelled like a cathedral full of incense, and she talked a blue streak. Her hair was the color of red ink, and she wore it wrapped around her head like an elaborate turban. She was something from another world. 'Egyptian!' she pronounced, pointing at me with a hand covered with rings and bangles, at our first meeting. 'Extraordinary, quite extraordinary. You're such a tiny, dainty little thing. But of course if your proportions are perfect, they can make you any size they want, can't they? But, my dear,' she said, spacing the words exaggeratedly, 'your proportions are Egyptian—anyone can see that when you turn your head. You have lived in another time. Definitely Egyptian, no doubt about it.'"

But Glyn soon she came to feel she and her fellow authors had been lured to Hollywood merely as a publicity stunt: "*The Great Moment* my first scenario was treated with the usual contempt, and a continuity writer felt it was not exiting enough, and in the effort to increase the 'suspense' the whole story was turned into a farce. I was terribly distressed no one wanted our advice, our assistance, nor did they intend to take it. All they required was the use of our names to act as shields against the critics." It was DeMille who rescued her first scenario, *The Great Moment*—starring Swanson as an eighteenth-century French marquise, and directed by DeMille's former first assistant director, Sam Wood—"from utter destruction" when he happened to stroll into the studio one day just as the director was remarking, "Say, boys, I guess you all think you know just what ought to be done, but I certainly can't think how to end this story myself." "My eye caught that of Cecil DeMille, and I felt that he had seen the joke. Greatly encouraged, I ventured to propose that perhaps the author might be able to help a little by suggesting the end!

"Then Cecil DeMille laughed out loud. I have always been grateful to him for that comprehending laugh, for it eased my path very much henceforward, as he was a very influential person in the Lasky studio. With his powerful influence on my side I was in the future accorded wonderfully considerate treatment in comparison with that meted out to the rest."

In the next decade, Glyn would write or adapt her stories for the screen, and became a force to be reckoned with at the studios she graced. On her return to London, she betrayed her amusement at the colony's lack of breeding, which all her efforts at refinement could not change. "Where else in the world," she asked, "will you find a colored cook bursting into a drawing room to say, 'You folks better hustle to dinner if you don't want the stuff to get cold?'"

Lasky and DeMille had known that great care would need to be taken with *The Affairs of Anatol*, since its hero, a bachelor with a lot of affairs behind him who values illusion over truth, was more outrageous than the American censor would allow. So, first of all, he had to end up married. By casting the glorious Gloria as the wife, they also telegraphed a happy outcome. Some reviewers felt that all that was left of the original was the title. "It should be enormously popular," wrote the caustic Robert Sherwood, who thought little of DeMille's pandering to the masses, "especially with those who think Schnitzler is a cheese." But what none of the admirers of the original *Anatol* knew was that DeMille's original version had then to be heavily cut before the studio could risk sending it out. A film that cost $200,000 couldn't afford to have its chances diminished by censors.

Of course, despite all the carping from critics and the sniping from censors, *The Affairs of Anatol* was the smash Lasky had predicted.

CHAPTER SEVENTEEN

RELIEVED IN 1922 OF THE BURDEN OF SUPPORTING A STRUGGLING AIRLINE, DeMille became a banker: "In 1922, I [was] elected a vice-president of the newly organized Federal Trust and Savings Bank of Hollywood. Since the banks were becoming more and more interested in motion pictures, I thought it would be a good idea to have a foot in their camp; and a new bank in Hollywood apparently thought it would be good to have a motion picture man among its officers. Times had changed since we had had to do our banking at Hall's grocery store. Through this new venture began my business association and life-long friendship with the Italian immigrant's son. . . . A. P. Giannini."

Giannini was "the one name that counted" behind countless corporate names, most significantly the Bank of America. DeMille served in various capacities over the years, becoming vice president of the Commercial National Bank of Los Angeles in 1923, and president of the Culver City Commercial and Savings Bank in 1925. He enjoyed telling how he approved a loan of $200,000 to Sam Goldwyn (not realizing at first that Giannini had already turned it down) without submitting the request to headquarters in San Francisco, and then going up there and defending his decision to Giannini and his right-hand man, James A. Bacigalupi. "'You gentlemen made me vice-president of a bank and chairman of the motion picture loan committee. Why? Did you want me for window-dressing? I'm not very good at that. If that is all you want me for, you can have my resignation. If you want me because I know something about motion picture values, that you don't know then I've got to have full authority to pass on motion picture loans. You say Sam Goldwyn has no assets. You're right. He hasn't. He has no assets, except talent, which is the only asset worth anything in the motion picture business. I made that loan on talent and on character, and that is the basis every motion picture loan is going to be made on while I am chairman of the committee of the Commercial National Bank. Now, gentlemen, do I have the authority? Or do I resign?' Mr. Bacigalupi stalked out. When he was out of earshot, A. P. gave me a long look. 'It's all right, C. B.,' he said, 'But don't do it too often.'"

It had been seven years since Zukor's Famous Player's joined with the Lasky Company to become to movies what Ford was to cars, Eastman to film,

Hearst to the press, and Getty to oil. So it must have felt to the shareholders in Paramount, the vital distributing arm that had grown out of these success-ful mergers. Hodkinson had come and gone. Goldwyn had come and gone. Pickford had been and gone. But the studio continued to move from strength to strength. Even with competition from radio, they sold everything they made. They had the stars who people wanted to see, in the sort of light, frivo-lous, escapist fare in which they wanted to see them. Inevitably accountants, bookkeepers, and lawyers had become an influential part of the organiza-tion. The Zukor-Lasky Company had become paramount in the film world. Even if others made films as good or better, they made money from the first turn of the raw film in the cameras to delivering them at the stage door.

Zukor had set the precedent all the other companies would follow. They had opened studios in England, on the continent, and in Bombay. They had a chain of newly built premier cinemas that stretched from Vienna to San Francisco. This ensured an outlet for all of their product even though Euro-peans in general preferred Westerns, serial, and any sort of far-fetched action stuff, and comedies—the more slapstick the better—to all that "Hollywood" sophistication and drawing room nonsense. By 1921, Paramount owned 303 theaters, ensuring first-run exhibition in many areas. Later in the decade, by which time their major rival, First National, had begun to disintegrate, many of the component companies sold out to Paramount. By 1931, they con-trolled nearly one thousand theaters, including a large number of first-run houses. At the time of Lasky's trip to London in 1921, they were well on their way to creating the mighty circuit which fifty years later remained a part of the vast ABC television empire.

With studios and money abroad, it was not uncommon now for Lasky stars and directors to go overseas in search of exciting locations. In 1915, De-Mille had had to make do with the California coastline for a story requiring one of Europe's glamorous watering holes. Now the company could send a cast and crew to the Riviera. Soon Hollywood craftsmen would be able to simulate even this location in their studios, but for the moment it gave a great boost to American audiences who'd only heard about it from books or from their men returning from overseas. The gesture wasn't as extravagant as it sounds, since it was a way to make use of Lasky funds that were locked up overseas.

The Lasky studio by this point covered an expanse of two city blocks con-taining five stages, three closed and two open. The staff of upward of 1,000 people was composed of: "carpenters and helpers—175; laboratory—175; wardrobe—120; publicity—10; scenario—50; camera—34; drapery—3; art—8; casting—3; research—5; property—36; plasterers—9; electrical—38; property construction—11; painting and paperhanging—10; purchasing—6; auditing—16; time-keeping—4; asst. director—10; directors—9; regular stock company of actors—about 34." This was not counting stars, extras, and peo-ple hired when and as needed—the thousands who streamed into the city daily with no more than their dreams in their pockets. Nor did this figure take into consideration the New York operation. Writing to Cecil in October 1921, Jesse could suggest that "it is my personal opinion that if you feel like taking a flyer in our stock, now is the time to do so. I am so strongly of the opinion that our stock is a good buy anywhere from $50 to $55 that my conscience would bother me if I did not convey this information to you."

The year 1921 began well enough for DeMille. He was at work on a film called *Fool's Paradise*. Although it wasn't founded on prescience, the title didn't hurt at the box office. The plot was an old-fashioned drama in contemporary dress that allowed Cecil to range in location from a bordello in a Mexican border oil town to a despot's palace in Siam, and provided plenty of opportunity for Iribe to wield his talent. It featured a new leading man, Conrad Nagel, a matinee idol of the New York stage, who would now become a romantic star of scores of Hollywood films in the 1920s and '30s, as well as a loyal DeMille man in the latter's fight against Actor's Equity.

Nagel: "In those days it took a long time to travel to Hollywood. It took five days by train besides that long ridiculous layover in Chicago. And when I got there, I hated it. You see, we came out of the bitter cold of New York into the terrific warmth of California, and it was all I could do to stay awake. I'd get on the set, and if I could stand still for two minutes, I'd doze off. So after four or five days I went to the railroad office and got a Pullman reservation back to New York to make sure I'd leave the minute the picture was finished. Then Mr. Lasky called me in and offered me a five-year contract with options at the end of every year. And the salary—it was money never heard of in the legitimate theater. And fifty-two straight weeks. I couldn't do a thing except sign it. I went out to make one picture and stayed twenty years!

"I loved working with Cecil B. DeMille and with William deMille. William deMille's approach was entirely psychological. That was very good for a good actor. He picked everything to pieces so that you knew exactly why you were doing what you did. Cecil DeMille was more of a showman, one of those truly great figures of show business. A lot of people claim that he was a phony, a show-off. He was not that; he was just a superb showman."

Nagel had already made a guest appearance in *Forbidden Fruit*, in which he played himself. But some of the exploits dreamed up for him made *Fool's Paradise* sound like the granddaddy of all the Indiana Jones movies. As usual, when DeMille paired animals with actors there were problems. In *Fool's Paradise*, it was the bears, as Jacqueline Logan, one of the female leads, recalled: "During the allegorical part . . . I was supposed to come on in this sled. The bear decided he wanted to get into the sleigh because his feet got cold on the ice, and this enormous bear did. He sat on me. I had an awful time wriggling out and walking off the set. I wasn't all that frightened because we had met each other. I had fed him chocolate before the scene started."

And the crocodiles (Florida alligators were substituted) were another problem. Nagel has to jump into the crocodile pit to retrieve a glove as a test of his love. "And the crocodiles were so tired" recalled Meehan, that "they wouldn't move until old horsemeat was held over them. And after Conrad had beaten the tired animals with his white dinner coat, he took the glove and started to climb up the break-away vines, which shouldn't have broken away, but did, and Nagel fell back into the pit. This time the alligators became active and C. B. leapt after him to keep them away." Smart as DeMille was at spotting new talent, he was generally stronger on women, and he had no eye for and little interest in the new breed of sheiks, lounge lizards, and great lover types that were becoming the rage. It was always the boy next door or the solid family type who would win C. B.'s heroines. Cecil had no eye for male sex appeal. His own name above the title was all the "male" attraction his films needed. So it was that he could sit through an advance showing of *The Sheik* and not notice Valentino. But the nation had found a new sensation, and a new term with which to rate a hot lover: girls became Shebas, and men became Sheiks.

In the course of production, DeMille received his regular reminder from New York of the bills he was running up. Letter from Lasky (May 21, 1921): "At this moment it seems absolutely unwise to invest more than $290,000 in the average DeMille production. I still think that you ought to make one big super production a year and as your contract does not allow you to do so, that might also be arranged while you are in New York." Over the next few years, the wrangling over money between DeMille and the company would accompany almost every new production. But despite front office fears about future earnings in the industry, *Fool's Paradise* made nearly $1,000,000.

It was a crazy time in Hollywood, in America. The Jazz Age had begun. Stars, like everyone else, had begun to revel in their new wealth and fame and the access it gave them to pleasure. "Oh, the parties we used to have!" Gloria Swanson recalled, and put a world of meaning into that sentence: "In those days the pubic wanted us to live like kings and queens. So we did and why not? We were in love with life. We were making more money than we ever dreamed existed and there was no reason to believe it would ever stop."

Swanson put a golden bathtub in her black marble bathroom. Soon her yearly clothing bill, all part of the image given her reputation as a leader of fashion, would amount to: fur coats, $25,000; wraps, $10,000; gowns, $50,000; stockings, $9,000; shoes, $5,000; headdresses, $5,000. (Birds of Paradise did not come cheap.) Perfume alone came to $6,000, but her salary easily covered it; by 1925, she was earning $900,000 a year. The cut in salary she had taken when she first went to work for DeMille had paid off handsomely.

Other stars were spending just as much. Valentino built himself a Spanish-Moorish dream castle on a hilltop and called it Falcon Lair, replete with a black marble, black leather bedroom. Marion Davies had a hundred-room ocean house at Santa Monica with an all-gold saloon, two bars, a private movie theater, and a huge swimming pool spanned by a marble bridge.

Everybody had a fantastic custom-made car: Swanson a leopard-upholstered Lancia; Valentino a custom-built Voisin tourer with a coiled cobra radiator cap. Tom Mix, the cowboy star, so recently just a $5-a-day cowboy, put steer horns on the front of his car. Naturally these cheerful excesses were a gift to the press. Nobody saw where it would lead.

Those who weren't in some way involved in the scandals could claim, truthfully, that they knew nothing about it until they read it in the papers. Of course, they would have been aware of drug-taking and drinking, but so many were doing it that it didn't seem out of the ordinary. But there was a price to be paid for all this joy in living. The disaster was about to start. It involved one of Paramount's biggest assets, Roscoe Arbuckle, one of the most popular comics in the world.

On Friday, September 3, "Fatty" drove to San Francisco to celebrate his new three-year, $3 million contract. But, with girls and booze aplenty, the events in the three adjoining suites at the luxurious Hotel St. Francis were anything but benign. On Labor Day afternoon, a starlet suffering massive internal injuries was rushed to hospital, where she died on September 10, and Arbuckle, a 266-pound, baby-faced mischief-maker, second only to Chaplin in popularity, was accused of her murder.

The ensuring scandal and trial opened Hollywood and its morals to public scrutiny the likes of which it had never known, for which it was not prepared, and which almost immediately took its toll at the box office. In Connecticut, women vigilantes ripped down the screen in a theater showing an Arbuckle comedy. In Wyoming, cowhands shot up the screen of a movie house showing an Arbuckle short. Barrages of bottles and eggs were reported everywhere.

The small town with a great deal of money had developed a gold rush mentality. No one heeded the rumblings that had been going on for three years, when outlets were still roadhouses at the edge of the town. But all of it now exploded in the community's face. Everything the local inhabitants had feared when "the movies" first came to town was now about to become true in a rush. "Hollywood became the most notorious community on the face of the earth," wrote the critic and future playwright Robert Sherwood, amusingly, "being associated in the public mind with such historic boroughs as Nineveh, Tyre, Babylon, Sodom and Gomorrah. It was the subject of many an ardent sermon, and consequently it became a mecca for tourists."

Paramount's executives panicked, tore up Arbuckle's contract, and withdrew his films, writing off millions already spent on them and the profits they would never see. The empire was threatened with ruin from within and without. "The Arbuckle situation has been a frightful blow to our company," Jesse wrote to Cecil on September 19. "It will cause us a very big loss of money and, for the time being, is actually hurting the business in some theaters." By October 4, he was adding that "the company's policy for the next few

Leatrice Joy starred in four DeMille films beginning with *Saturday Night* (1922), followed by *Manslaughter* (1922), *The Ten Commandments* (1923), and *Triumph* (1924). Photo: Evans, L.A. Courtesy John Kobal Foundation

months will be a most concervative [*sic*] one. There will be no expansion of any kind and in fact, wherever possible, investment in theaters, etc. will be gotten rid of, so we can accumulate as much cash as possible."

Saturday Night, on which DeMille began principal photography on September 26, was the film in which he was to launch Leatrice Joy, his new "Swanson," to stardom. In keeping with his promise that this was one of his economy priced productions, DeMille dramatized two parallel romances, each of which dealt with class distinction. Joy played a society heiress who suddenly sees in her chauffeur a white knight when he saves them both from certain death, and marries him, though this means being disinherited, while her one-time fiancé, Conrad Nagel, is drawn to and marries the daughter of a laundress. As her philosophical mother remarks over her washboard, "Isn't it strange,—that those who live in Palaces, want cottages! And those who live in cottages want LIMOUSINES and LINGERIE!" The film concludes with the two rich lovers happily united, leaving the chauffeur free to marry the impish daughter of the laundress.

Joy had a background in two-reel comedies, and in shorts with Oliver Hardy, pre-Laurel. DeMille once called her a true director's star. Like Swanson, she launched all sorts of trends, including a boyish, parted down the middle haircut which she described as a feather's edge and everyone else called "the Bob." Like Swanson, she had a husband who was to be a thorn in DeMille's side: John Gilbert, not yet one of the greatest romantic idols, who already drank, swore, loathed his mother, and didn't knuckle to bosses. DeMille saw her in a Goldwyn film, with her long dark hair, big smile, and easy, outgoing temperament reminiscent of a younger Farrar, and signed her.

Initially actress and director got off to a nearly fatal false start. Joy was different from Gloria: she was bigger, bonnier, earthier, and rounder, and not as flamboyant. After the first few days, he seriously considered replacing her, but once he stopped trying to force her into the Swanson mold, their association became one of the happiest and most enduring. "To me [he] was a gentleman," she said later. "He stood up when I came in. And he was very patient. He would explain things so minutely that I could understand him. We didn't go into tizzies about rehearsing time and time and time again. I had nothing like that. I made him laugh. Maybe I was naïve. Like an old man takes a young girl to Paris, and he sees Paris through her eyes."

To celebrate the completion of *Saturday Night* on January 2, three months and one week after he had begun it, DeMille threw a belated New Year's party for his cast and crew up at Paradise. Julia was the hostess. Joy, accompanied by Gilbert, remembered, "That was the only time I was there. And Brooks, the man from the jewelers, was there with trays, and you could pick anything you wanted. My mother had a gold mesh purse that I admired so much, and she lost it, so there was one on the tray with diamonds and things, and I picked that. A beautiful party."

Saturday Night had some good subtitles, a couple of saucy scenes, the latest in lingerie, and a bang-up Halloween party, all of which moved at a good pace, aided by fine cutting that turned many of Macpherson's homilies into smart wisecracks.

Shortly afterwards, DeMille, accompanied and guided by Paul Irbe and his Japanese valet, made his first trip to Europe, an opportunity to escape from all the news about Fatty Arbuckle, which was getting more sordid with each passing day. Arbuckle had been acquitted on his first trial in November. But because the decision was 10-2 in his favor, a mistrial was declared. The second jury voted 10-2 for his conviction. Another mistrial was declared.

DeMille traveled first to Paris and then to Rome, where he was to have an audience with Pope Benedict XV on January 22, which turned out to be the day the pope died. Then DeMille was taken ill with acute rheumatic fever in Paris at the end of the trip. For a long time, he couldn't move, but an old friend came and watched over him until he could be moved by stretcher, hoisted aboard an Atlantic liner, and at last brought to Hollywood on February 3, where he was eventually able to walk and gradually use his arms and hands again.

He returned to a Hollywood firmly in the grip of scandal. The press, who made Arbuckle the scapegoat in their circulation wars, made a fair trial virtually impossible. At last, on April 12, the third and last trial ended with Arbuckle's acquittal and exoneration by the jury. But his career was in ruins.

The next day, Lasky, whose belief in the fair-mindedness of men exceeds that of all studio chiefs, cabled DeMille: "Suggest you state to newspapers we will release Arbuckle pictures immediately bringing no pressure one way or another on exhibitors leaving reception of pictures up to American public. Arbuckle having been acquitted of any crime it would be grave injustice and unfair to him for us to take any other position. You may state also leading theaters of New York planning to show pictures immediately." This was contrary to Zukor's order to drop all the pictures, but the possibility of regaining losses helped to change minds.

More scandals were to come, all from DeMille's company, and concerning people he knew, had worked with, even was working with at the moment. On the night of February 1, 1922, two days before he got back, his fellow Paramount director William Desmond Taylor was found murdered. That opened a much larger can of worms, since it brought the drug problem out into the open, and by inference ruined the career of Paramount's golden-haired Mary Miles Minter and of the nation's most adored comedienne, Mabel Normand.

In a letter to Jesse, Cecil touches on another potentially fine mess: "Kosloff has received a Black Hand letter instructing him to deposit Ten thousand dollars in a certain spot or he will be killed, giving him until Saturday to pay the money. You will gather from the above that life in Hollywood is not as dull as the Screen Writers' Guild propaganda would indicate."

More farcical than anything else, but potentially more damaging for the box office, was the surprise marriage in Mexico on May 13 of Rudolph Valentino to Natacha Rambova, when it was found out that his first bizarre marriage had not been legally dissolved. Rudy had a passion for falling for, and then marrying, strong, bossy women who did not like to consummate their wedding vows. The threatened disclosure that the "great lover" and Paramount's hottest new property seemed only to be able to find love with women who didn't like men was damaging enough. He also spent a night in prison on a charge of bigamy.

The case blew over. A man willing to go to prison for love is a hero everywhere. None of the spicier ingredients reached the public, though rumors would pursue Rudy to his early grave that he was homosexual.

With so many newshounds all truffling for dirt, it just needed a hint to be fanned into a front-page fire. Now Gloria Swanson chose this time to divorce her husband. Before all hell had broken loose, she would give out such titillating quotes to the fan magazine as: "I not only believe in divorce. I sometimes think I don't believe in marriage at all." Swanson had been practicing what she preached: her husband, Herbert Somborn, had proof of at least one affair, maybe more. Since it also involved another famous director connected to Paramount, the wildly attractive Mickey Neilan—"my once-for-all wild Irish love" Swanson called him—who happened to be married to another big star, Blanche Sweet, clearly there was a lot at stake.

She told Lasky that she wanted a divorce. "'Impossible,' he said. 'Why?' I asked, bristling. Why?' he repeated, in an excited yap. 'Because after Fatty Arbuckle's little escapade last week, we are sitting on a keg of dynamite. We can't afford the slightest whiff of scandal. That's why.'"

In spite of Lasky's warnings—indeed, partly as his bribe to get her to do *Beyond the Rocks* with Valentino—Gloria and Mickey enjoyed an unofficial "honeymoon" in Paris. She was at home again when she received a legal document through the post. "I saw lots of names in capital letters, arranged alphabetically: CECIL DEMILLE, three Paramount executives (known as the KKKs) ROBERT KANE, SAMUEL KATZ and SIDNEY KENT, JESSE LASKY, MARSHALL NEILAN, SAM WOOD, ADOLPH ZUKOR—fourteen names in all, ranging from people I didn't even know to the man I loved. 'Oh, my God,' I gasped when I finally realized that Herbert was suing me for divorce on the grounds of adultery with fourteen men.

"Next I received a call from Mr. DeMille, who asked if I would come to his home that following afternoon. When I arrived, Mr. DeMille led me to his library and closed the door. He unlocked his desk drawer and pulled out a copy of the document. "'I'm sure you know about this,' he said and sat me down. He told me he knew how I must feel, but he said that no matter how angry I might be, we had to keep this out of the papers. The columnists had all been predicting, he said, that Herbert Somborn intended to sue for divorce, and they had hinted broadly that he expected his suit to be bitterly contested.

"'I'm not afraid to fight,' I said, 'and I'm sure I can win. This is irresponsible and mud-slinging. Why, Mr. DeMille, you're on that list yourself. You know it's a pack of lies. And poor little Mr. Zukor, Now, really.'

"'Mickey Neilan is also on the list,' he said quietly."

How seriously this matter was regarded by DeMille and Lasky can be gleaned from a curious telegram sent from Will Hays to DeMille at his home: "Let there be not the shadow of a doubt if this affair becomes known the principal star will be barred from pictures and permanently kept from the screen."

Gloria was the studio's hottest female property and she had a lot to lose, but she was a fighter. She was against paying anything. Paramount's head must have been reeling. But Cecil and Jesse asked Gloria up to the house and showed her the telegram. It shook her to realize how her private life, if things weren't sorted out quietly, could ruin her career. She began to give way.

There followed a month of strenuous, secret negotiations in which all the names were changed, more than one telegram service was used, and everything was labeled "personal and confidential." As many as three telegrams were sent at a time, all on the same subject, each using only every third word to communicate a coded message. Somborn wanted a fortune, based on Swanson's earnings from the time of the contract she signed in 1920, when she was becoming a star, and which Somborn had handled for her. "Situation has not looked good last two days," wrote Jesse on February 27. "Am convinced it is either big blackmail for one hundred and fifty or some big interests are trying to attack us stop."

Eventually the case was settled. Somborn's silence had been bought. But it had been a messy deal. Of course, despite DeMille's personal regard for Gloria, the studio wasn't just helping her out of compassion. For a time, she even felt that they were using the situation to renegotiate her contract down. True or not, she was their hottest property and worth millions, with millions more tied up in films waiting for release. By the deal the studio struck with her lawyers, Swanson agreed to make another film over and above those she was contracted for. The conditions included a morality clause in case of any subsequent "adulterous conduct or immoral relations with men other than her husband, and such charges or any of them are published in the public press," in which case Swanson would be out on her own. Paramount was merely covering their bets. "The studio was putting me on a tight leash," she reflected with resignation. "They were scaring me into being a well-behaved star. Telling me that unless I toed the line, they could cut me off. I was angry and humiliated, but I signed everything." Swanson was nothing if not a realist, but the studio had lost any loyalty she might have felt.

Swanson made her films, even though she had discovered something concerning her situation that made her wiser than her years and cost her a few more illusions. At an industry banquet some time after her divorce was behind her, she met Will Hays. "When I arrived, I was escorted to the dais and, to my horror, given the honored position next to Will Hays. He spoke to me, and I gave him an icy hello. Being as coldly correct as I knew how, I said I didn't think we had anything to say to each other.

"'I don't understand,' he said. 'I am a great fan of yours, and you have given me the cold shoulder all evening. What have I done to deserve it?'

"'Only one thing,' I said. 'You sent that telegram to Mr. DeMille.'

"'What telegram?'

"'The telegram that concerned me and my divorce.'

"'But I never sent any telegram to DeMille about you or your divorce.'

This photo was taken in March 1922 shortly after Will Hays was appointed chairman of the Motion Picture Producers and Distributors of America (MPPDA), where his real job as the movie czar was to enhance Hollywood's reputation after a series of scandals. Photo: International. Courtesy John Kobal Foundation

"'Mr. Hays . . . I saw it. Mr. DeMille showed it to me. You said if I contested my husband's suit for divorce, it would endanger the entire motion picture industry.'

"'Miss Swanson—Gloria—I give you my word,' he said, 'I never sent any such telegram.'

"What shattered me was that Mr. DeMille must have been a party to the scene staged at his home. Mr. DeMille was my idol, on another plane altogether from the rest of Hollywood. Had he known the telegram was a fake? Of course, he must have. Nevertheless, I couldn't bring myself to accuse him or have an ugly scene with him. Mr. Lasky would do for that. I strode from my bungalow to his office in full make-up and costume. . . . In the voice of the concerned diplomat and executive, he said, 'Is anything the matter?'

"'Yes, there is,' I said. 'I talked to Will Hays last night about a certain telegram. I could have you put in jail.' His eyes were popping. . . . Mr. Lasky said he could understand my feelings, but I had to believe that he had done what he felt was right. Mr. DeMille had told him I had plans to fight Somborn in court. That would have meant the ruin of a great career.

"'Stop right there, Mr. Lasky. I just wanted to hear you admit it.'"

Not long after Swanson announced that after completing *Prodigal Daughters*, she would make all of her future films at the Long Island studio in New York. Her reason was creative freedom and convenience: the Long Island studio was twenty minutes by subway from Times Square. Paramount concocted a rash of silly stories about her departure from Hollywood, but Lasky and DeMille knew why Swanson left.

Now Cecil B. DeMille, with a capital "D" to ennoble the family name, and with that name above the titles of all his films in lettering the same size as the title, looked for other girls he could turn into stars.

CHAPTER EIGHTEEN

IF DEMILLE AND LASKY FELT ANY GUILT ABOUT THEIR BEHAVIOR TOWARDS Swanson, there is no indication found in their papers. Besides, DeMille was about to be dragged into another marriage battle, whose wreck would land on Paramount's shores if something wasn't done about it.

This one involved his current star, Leatrice Joy and her daredevil husband, John Gilbert, when their messy divorce threatened to get out of hand. The Joy-Gilbert divorce had come to DeMille's attention the previous year, several weeks after Joy had been signed and begun work in his new film. While potentially less explosive than the Swanson divorce, the case, if it reached court would feature another Paramount star in the news. The studio couldn't afford further tarnish.

In early 1922, Joy and Gilbert, madly in love, had gone to Tijuana and had a ceremony of sorts performed, and they were now living together. They had told no one about it because they didn't want Jack's vindictive soon-to-be ex-wife, Olive Burwell, to find out until his divorce from her was final—which it was by the time Joy signed with DeMille. Had DeMille known about Joy's "marriage," he might not have cast her. Joy recalled DeMille's feeling about Gilbert: "When he heard that I was going to marry Jack, he said. 'I wouldn't use him as a fertilizer on my plants.'" Joy believed that DeMille didn't like Jack personally, and the reason lay in their backgrounds. It was the derogatory way Gilbert spoke of his own mother in front of Louis B. Mayer, which so incensed that bellicose man that he knocked Gilbert out. But DeMille, unlike Mayer, was no prude. A slur on somebody else's mother wasn't a slur on his.

Joy's little white lie was foolish. The former Mrs. Gilbert found out and to get an increase in her alimony, threatened her ex-husband with bigamy. Gilbert defied her to do her worst—the same scenario as Swanson. Joy turned to DeMille before the whole story turned up on his breakfast table. Three weeks into filming was too late for him to do anything to try to help. But, as with Swanson, the price was that Joy's behavior henceforth was to be impeccable.

Like the Swanson-Somborn divorce, it dragged on for more than a year. Lasky wondered if they shouldn't just tell the press and risk the damage.

Ultimately the case was resolved, but it had put such a strain on Joy's marriage that she and Gilbert divorced in August 1924.

Other scandals couldn't be hushed up with money. Early in the New Year, on January 18, came the death of Wallace Reid, one of the studio's most popular male stars. He had looked haggard and beat the previous November when he was shooting *Clarence*. When he collapsed on the set, Lasky had forced him to tell the truth about his drug addiction. As Reid's death hit the front pages, Lasky, against the strong opposition of his fellow board members, let it be known that Reid's addiction was the result of an accident while working on a film. The heavy doses of morphine he was given enabled him to continue working. Lasky's genuine gesture of friendship and respect for the young man's memory turned Reid's tarnished image into that of a hero fighting against terrible odds. The studio's admission even had a benefit, casting Reid as honest men caught in an unfortunate vice.

In the grip of the shower of scandals that took place in 1922, Hollywood had begun to turn in on itself. With fear of retribution at the box office, studio heads gathered and agreed to invite an in-house censor to monitor their community. Enter the former postmaster general of America, now official Hollywood watchdog, Will Hays.

Before Hays arrived, DeMille was back at work, though he still walked with a limp and had to wear a brace on his left arm. *Manslaughter* would include all the currently hot ingredients that caused moral outrage. The budget was increased to $337,000, and when the orgy scene was expanded from a "vision" to an integral part of the story, the final cost soared close to $400,000. But it proved to be sound at the box office when *Manslaughter* became an enormous hit.

Leatrice Joy was not a great actress, but she was right as the pampered Lydia. A society darling, she is responsible for the death of a traffic officer, and through the efforts of the young district attorney (Thomas Meighan) who loves her, she is sentenced to two years in prison. Despite the harrowing stunts, the magnificence of the flashback, and the realism of the prison scenes, it was another go at extending the *Admirable Crichton* theme, though it is the weakest of the three DeMille romances about class distinction. Macpherson adapted it from one of the lesser-known novels by Alice Duer Miller, best remembered for that stirring sentimental eulogy, *The White Cliffs of Dover*.

She went further than ever to get the facts right. "To get the authentic atmosphere," explained DeMille, "Jeanie Macpherson went to Detroit, stole a fur piece by prearrangement from a friend of hers, was arrested with the goods on her, and sent to jail (under the name of Angie Brown). Apart from Jeanie's obliging friend, the only person in Detroit who knew of the circumstances was one police official known to her family and to Famous Players Lasky." After being arrested under her pseudonym, and declining to pay the fine, Jeanie was taken to the jail cells. Her plan was jeopardized when a friendly officer said he would try to have her released since this was only her first offense. Fortunately, it came to nothing.

In handcuffs, Macpherson was taken to a cell on the second tier of the block. Windowless, it measured 6 feet x 6 feet x 5 feet, furnished only with a broken down chair, tin washbasin, pail, and pitcher. Her description of the place helped Joy with her performance and Paul Iribe in his designs. Ironically, Macpherson's first experience there was seeing a film in the prison chapel, a terrible documentary about the Panama Canal. In the midst of this dreary film, a girl yelled out, "My Gawd, can't they give us a love story?" Whether Preston Sturges was told this story by Macpherson when later they both worked at Paramount, or whether he just heard it secondhand, he used it almost verbatim in *Sullivan's Travels*.

Supper on her first night consisted of moldy bread, bitter coffee, and a large dish of prunes. She had trouble falling asleep, with women screaming, yelling, or comforting one another. At last, she managed to drop off, only to wake up again. "I was awakened by a peculiar crawling sensation that meant but one thing—vermin! I prayed for daylight, I wanted to scream and beat my head against the stonewalls of the cell, anything to push them away. I was on the verge of panic." She told friends later that she made an attempt at escape, was caught, and returned to her cell for two more days and nights.

After three days of bad food and sleepless but instructive nights, she had lost twelve pounds and was sick with hunger and loss of sleep. "Fortunately," recalled DeMille, "[her police official friend] was around when Macpherson came to the conclusion that three days in the Detroit lock-up had given her all the ideas for atmosphere she needed." "I have seen women's souls stripped naked," she told the press on her return to Hollywood. "I wouldn't go through that experience again for any amount of money. But I wouldn't sell it for an even greater amount."

Manslaughter became one of the first occasions where DeMille used "matte shots," in which a character is superimposed against another background, using a new laboratory process. He would later overuse the device to the point where it became a cliché. Alvin Wyckoff, nearing the end of his working relationship with DeMille, also made exhausting experiments with experimental lighting. "In the prison scenes (the heroine) is at first bitterly rebellious," he told *Table Talk*, "and then later becomes normal and almost happy. These changes in temperament of the character we emphasized by lighting. Where she was in a bitter mood I resorted to lighting that emphasized the hard shadows and brought out all the bitterness in her face. . . . As she changed in the story, the lighting was altered until at the finish her face was luminous both in action and illumination." The prison scenes are remarkable for that day and age, the mood being carried through from Iribe's design for the prison interiors to the scenes of the inmates' life and behavior.

But before Joy is sent down, there is a lengthy flashback to ancient Rome. There had already been an earlier brief foreshadowing when Meighan, arriving late at a party, walks in on the guests in the middle of the latest craze, an indoor pogo stick race. He turns to Joy and warns her, "We're no different today than Rome at its worst! Why, this dance—with its booze and license—is little better than a Feast of Bacchus!" And we get a glimpse of Roman decadence 450 AD. "The accident that killed the policeman was a spectacular climax to an exciting chase: When you talk about people with nerve, I think of a man named Leo Noemus. Leatrice was driving a car. And she was being pursued by a motorcycle officer. I wanted her to make a quick turn so as to escape him and he couldn't change his speed and he was to hit the car broadside at the hood and be thrown completely over the hood and killed, for which she had to go to prison. Well, we didn't trick it. It was before that kind of trick effect could be done—and Leo Noemus said he would do the stunt. We rehearsed the skids once or twice. We substituted another driver for Leatrice—and started the motorcycle down and timed it so it would come right. And we put mattresses on the other side of the road and covered these with dirt. And then we did it. He hit the thing exactly. He was thrown completely over the hood, the motorcycle was wrecked. He broke his collarbone and that's all. Nobody would believe that story."

Now Lydia is on trial, on a charge of manslaughter, and the trial takes up the rest of the picture. In his emotional summing-up, Meighan, torn between love and duty, draws a parallel between the jazzy decadence of the twenties and the last days of the Roman Empire, ruined by its debauchery. DeMille created a virtual reconstruction of John Martin's painting *Belshazzar's Feast*—as one critic put it, "men and women half-stupid with drink in an orgy of pure self-satisfying pleasure, dancing girls, satyrs springing from the walls to join in the revel, and a rider upon a black charger who was dressed in skin and followed by a swarm of hideous barbarians more like animals than men."

Not since *Joan the Woman* and *The Woman God Forgot* had DeMille had an opportunity to show off his flair for crowd scenes as he did with this Kosloff-staged bacchanalia. America was, however, tiring of tales focusing on Hollywood orgies, with beautiful helpless starlets at the mercy of strong, ruthless men. DeMille had once given the public what they enjoyed: a good old-fashioned story with a strong narrative. He believed that the threat of censure would lead to prudence and moderation in the conduct of his audiences.

In an era of a new sophistication among America's intelligentsia, DeMille's films were starting to be held up to ridicule. DeMille, though, was a great deal more honest than his critics. Future generations, raised on film and more socially permissive society, had no problem recognizing and enjoying a DeMille film for what it was. And as DeMille's critical standing as a director began to decline in the United States, he continued to be admired abroad. In Japan in 1921, a young boy named Akira Kurosawa began to keep a list of the ten best movies he had seen each year. In the first two years *Male and Female* and *Fool's Paradise* were included.

From this point through the 1950s, the Hays Office, with its prudish restrictions, was calling the censorship shots on Hollywood. Do's and Don'ts became the norm. A wit nicknamed Hays the "Czar of all the Rushes." But as long as profits weren't affected and bad news was kept from the public, the studios toed the line. Married couples no longer slept in the same bed. But that same year Ernst Lubitsch arrived, and brought to the screen the gift of true sophistication. Thanks to the impish German and Hays, the American screen grew up.

Lasky got back from Europe to find DeMille in a ferment of excitement over his completed film and bubbling with new projects. DeMille to Lasky (June 30, 1922): "I have in mind three stories and I should like to get your viewpoint on them by wire: One is Kate Jordan's novel, *The Next Corner*. The second is a novel, a detective story entitled *Suspense*. . . . Done as I would do it, in the highest of high society, with the richest of rich surroundings. Where the raise of an eyebrow would take the place of the shot of a gun. . . . The third, and at present my choice, is a flapper story in defense of the flapper. It is an original by Jeanie. There are wonderful parts in it for Theodore Kosloff, Elliott Dexter, and one other strong leading man, and two wonderful women's parts: This story brings in splendidly Jack London's *Before Adam*, the prehistoric tale that we have both wanted to do for so long. It is a new and different type of love story, but with tremendous heart, interest, drama and comedy, as well as the spectacular appeal of the prehistoric period, and it would be atypical DeMille Production.

"How does the title—*Dumb and Bobbed*—strike you?"

He called the film *Adam's Rib*. *Dumb and Boobed* might have been a better title for DeMille's lesson to flappers with a moral set in the Neanderthal age. Comedy was never his forte, nor that of the actors he cast.

The Canadian actress Pauline Garon (his first blonde heroine in years) was given the lead. Before settling on her he had also considered May McAvoy, a diminutive brunette whose career had taken off after *Sentimental Tommy*, another of Paramount's J. M. Barrie properties. While McAvoy was acting in *Only 38*, directed by William, she kept catching a glimpse of DeMille studying her. "He made me very nervous. Then one day, just after I finished a scene, he was introduced to me, and he said smiling, 'I've been watching you, Miss McAvoy.'

"I told him I knew he had.

"'I've made up my mind, I'd like you to play the lead in my next picture.'

"I was naturally very flattered. Then without taking his eyes off me, he said, 'You may not be so pleased, Miss McAvoy, when you hear the two conditions. First, you'll have to cut your hair very short.' That didn't bother me, really. I'd been thinking about having my hair fashionably shingled anyway. He still hadn't taken his eyes off me. 'In this picture,' he said, 'there are flashbacks to the Stone Age. And you'll have to appear in the first part of the picture in very little more than a fig leaf.'

"'I'm afraid, Mr. DeMille, you've got the wrong girl,' I said, as coldly as I could.

"The smile faded from his face and he walked off the set. He never spoke to me again. I had said 'no' to him.

"I was amused when Mr. DeMille gave the girl's role in *Adam's Rib* to one of my good friends, Pauline Garon, and she wasn't half as nude in her tiger skins as most of us were when we went bathing at Santa Monica. But *Adam's Rib* was the worst picture DeMille ever made, and I was glad I had no part in it.

"At first I didn't realize there would be consequences. But then all the roles I had had my heart set on seemed to be going to other actresses, and I sat around for eight months with no films and I believe that this was because I dared to say 'no' to Mr. DeMille."

While it seems a bit far-fetched to believe that DeMille's response to McAvoy's rejection was to ruin her future prospects, there is a negative reference to her in one of his telegrams to Lasky outlining ideas for future stars for the company. (McAvoy later played in *Ben Hur* and *The Jazz Singer*, which ensured her motion picture legacy.)

Since *Joan the Woman*, DeMille had been considering filming in color. Technology was sufficiently advanced that color sequences were announced as a special feature of *Adam's Rib*. Color would be "spotted" through the regular greys, blacks, and whites of the celluloid, and reached through a color register ring system worked out by the head of the studio's color process department. Its use, unexpected and ravishing, occurs at the ball given by the neglected wife of a Chicago broker for the exiled king of Moravia (Theodore Kosloff). A large group of dancers were furnished with Japanese lanterns, and when the main lights in the room were turned out and the lanterns lit, each pair was "spotted" in a different color—red, blue, yellow, purple, a myriad of tints—with the colors reflected on the faces of the bearers.

As DeMille had told Lasky, he intended the story to be a defense of young women. In different hands much of the plot, minus the Jack London flashback, served Howard Hawks for his classic screwball comedy, *Bringing Up Baby*, right down to the prehistoric fossils, work preoccupied paleontologist and "screwball" young heiress who brings it all crashing down. In DeMille's version, the heroine tries to protect her mother from making a foolish mistake by running off with the flirtatious king. As one of Macpherson's titles put it, "The dangerous age for a woman is from 3–70." DeMille saw *Adam's Rib* as a "defense of the flapper," "in which a typical modern teenager, apparently as light in the head as on her toes, shows the courage, intelligence, and devotion needed to save her parents' marriage. The flashback to prehistoric times also enabled her to show that bare legs, short skirts, and feminine resourcefulness were nothing new."

The "prehistoric" scenes, originally to have been shot in California's Redwood forest, ended up being built at the studio. There are no birds in this

sky, no creatures in the forest, no fish in the water, and only five fur-clad humans. Nonetheless, the forest is a miracle of design and studio craftsmanship,
anticipating the fabulous forest in Fritz Lang's *Siegfried* (1924). At 112 x 252
feet, it was the largest set ever built inside a studio, and was said to be one
of the marvels of recent cinema constructions. It covered over 26,000 square
feet, had 200 feet of running stream with a fall of eighteen feet, a pool, a
fallen tree, and a cave. There were fifteen huge trees, twelve over fifty feet in
circumference, 12,000 ferns, and nearly six tons of Oregon moss. It supposedly took 400 carpenters and plasterers to make this forest. "It cost thousands
and thousands, and will return thousands," DeMille claimed. Creating his
own forest rather than shooting the real thing was to enable him to put the
lights where he wanted them.

Convinced he had something special and wanting to record the magnificent sets for posterity, DeMille continued his practice of looking for the best
available photographers. He brought Edward S. Curtis to the studio. Curtis,
who had an important reputation documenting American Indians, was in
need of money to set up a studio in Los Angeles and to pay alimony to his
ex-wife. Curtis shot special art for DeMille of the flashback scenes, and would
do so again for *The Ten Commandments*, where he also received a photographic
credit. Since Curtis didn't take stills, he wasn't restricted to DeMille's lighting set ups and dramatic staging, and was free to shoot in his own style. In
their majestic stillness, his photographs for *Adam's Rib* promise more than the
movie delivers.

The critics were united in deploring this flapper story. "Astoundingly Silly
and Tedious Film at the Rivoli," ran the headline in the *New York American*.

During the making of *Adam's Rib*, DeMille and his wife, as leaders of Hollywood's top social echelon, played hosts to the year's most famous couple who
had married in the summer of 1922, Lord Louis and Lady Edwina Mountbatten. She was rich and famously unpleasant. He was weak but overwhelming
ambitious. But they came from England and had titles. As the summit of
their American Grand Tour, they came to Hollywood to meet all the stars.
Film producers flattered the dashing Mountbatten by telling him that he was
good-looking enough to be a star in Hollywood. His lady was on the prowl
and made an unsuccessful pass at Chaplin, or so the British-born comedian
claimed in his autobiography. During their last days in Hollywood, DeMille
invited them to the studio and then up into the hills where he was shooting
a scene. The director's cameraman instructed "Dickie" on how to make the
best use of his new 35-millimeter movie camera.

The intense curiosity about the movie capital naturally inspired a number
of filmed exposés, including *Souls for Sale* (about the frightful risks that movie stars must take for the sake of their art), *Mary of the Movies, Merton of the
Movies, Hazel from Hollywood, Night Life in Hollywood,* and the best of the lot,
Hollywood. Lasky, fresh from his triumph with *The Covered Wagon*, produced
this classic burlesque of the standard Hollywood story, small-town girl goes

to Hollywood, gets a job, and becomes a star. *Hollywood*'s (1923) star was an actress named Hope Drown, but this seems to be her only film credit.

For *Hollywood*, Lasky's friends, including DeMille surrounded by his production team, and a host of Hollywood luminaries, appeared as themselves. Fatty Arbuckle is seen standing in a line of extras at the Christie Comedy Studios looking for work. After Hope Drown has been refused, he steps up, but the window is slammed down bearing a large "CLOSED" sign. Fiction was imitating life; the public didn't want any more of Fatty Arbuckle.

Something else happened in 1922, but the full story has only surfaced now. No one would have guessed the truth. From DeMille's account in his autobiography, written forty years after the fact, "Mrs. deMille opened our home to two others who appealed to her and me infinitely more than all the celebrities and all the dear friends who have enjoyed Mrs. deMille's hospitality for longer or shorter periods. These two came to stay. One was a dark and beautiful little girl, a Canadian war orphan. The other was a baby boy, who was found in Neil McCarthy's car; and it seemed to Mrs. deMille and me providential that if Cecilia was to have a sister, John should have a brother, and so our two children became four. The little girl, Katherine, has carried the name deMille on for another generation in motion pictures as a talented actress. The baby boy, Richard, is following in my father's and my brother's footsteps as a scholar." The operative words are "my brother." Few readers outside his lawyer and his family would care exactly when Katherine and Richard were adopted, unless there was a story behind it. DeMille continued to keep it secret from certain members of his own family to the end of his life. The secret had nothing to do with Katherine, who was brought into the home two years earlier, when she was nine years old; it was how Richard (who was not formally adopted until 1940) came to join the family.

Unlike John and Katherine, who had been introduced to the family by Constance, Richard was brought home by DeMille. Because Richard was a real deMille. He was not Cecil's son, but rather William was his father. His mother was the writer Lorna Moon, who'd worked for both brothers. One thing more the two brothers had in common were their affairs with scriptwriters. "In 1920, Lorna wrote a saucy letter to Cecil B. DeMille," explains Richard himself, "telling him all the things that were wrong with his movie *Male and Female,* and he invited her to come to Hollywood to see if she could do better. . . . While working on *The Affairs of Anatol,* she met and fell in love with William. They didn't collaborate on scripts. They simply made beautiful music together and produced another writer. Lorna Moon is a pen name. She told many false stories about her life, which journalists and would be historians have believed."

Like Macpherson, Lorna Moon was a Scot, a redhead, and a writer. She had credits on *The Affairs of Anatol* and two other Swanson films, *Don't Tell Everything* and *Her Husband's Trademark.* At times, these early titles seem to telegraph the private lives of those concerned. Lorna adapted *Her Husband's*

Trademark from a story by Clara Beranger, who would become William's wife (Lorna got the baby, but Clara won the ring.).

William, of course, was kind, sophisticated, literate, amusing—and a complete coward when it came to breaking bad news to his wife. Besides which they already had two young daughters. There was no way he could confess to Anna. To complicate matters further, Lorna found out that she was pregnant and simultaneously that she had tuberculosis. She had her baby away from the film colony in a tuberculosis sanatorium in suburban Monrovia on February 12, 1922.

After nine months of carrying on as a single parent, the strain of her illness and the call of her career led Moon to give her son up. She had done this before, having (according to her son) left her two previous children with their fathers in Canada. With little Richard she was confident that he would be taken care of. Anna deMille and her daughters never knew the truth about Richard, and had she known the truth it is unlikely she would have accepted the innocent offspring of her husband's philandering. (Richard's half-sister Agnes only found out the truth of his paternity while I was doing the research for this book.) William's divorce five years later, to marry Clara Beranger, had a traumatic effect on Anna.

But there was no question of a deMille going to an orphanage, and especially the only son born to either brother. DeMille confided the truth to Constance and they agreed to take the child. When Neil McCarthy announced to the press one chilly morning in November that he had found the baby on his back doorstep, it was even reported that the child was suffering from rickets. He turned naturally to Constance, he claimed, because of her association with orphanages. DeMille's wife was above suspicion. Perhaps DeMille, Constance, and William understood how life in the DeMille household suddenly bore a farcical similarity to half a dozen plots the brothers had or were in the process of writing and/or directing.

William deMille made only two mentions of his second wife, and one of Lorna Moon, in his book. Except for telling his daughter, Cecilia, and swearing her to secrecy, DeMille told none of the others. Richard learned who his parents were at the age of thirty-three, when DeMille told him after William died. By then, of course, he had guessed.

Katherine's adoption covered no skeletons. Evelyn Scott recalls that Katherine Lester, for this was her name, "was an orphan with a thrillingly romantic history (thrilling to me, that is perhaps not to her)," and Lenore Coffee, another family friend and DeMille chronicler, adds that Katherine was the "child of an Italian mother and a Canadian father who had been killed in the war. DeMille had the father's life and career traced and found that he had a very honorable record and a decoration; all this was put together for Katherine, and when he gave this to her he said, 'This is for you to keep, Katherine, so that you will always remember that you had a fine father who was a brave man.'"

DeMille aboard his 100-foot, twin-masted yacht that he named *Seaward* (circa 1935). Courtesy
John Kobal Foundation

What happened next was tragic, but more typical than one might suppose
during those struggling years. According to Katherine, her mother, knowing
she was dying of tuberculosis, set out to take her fatherless little girl all the
way from Canada across the length and breadth of the United States in a
broken-down car to California, where her husband's parents lived. They had
disowned their son, but she had no one else to turn to, and wanted to see her
Katherine safe before she died. On the long journey, never knowing if she
would survive from one day to the next, before they went to sleep she took
the precaution of pinning a note on her daughter's nightgown explaining

who she was and where they were going, and praying that the kind person who read it would help get her child to her grandparents. In the daytime, the note was attached to Katherine's little red coat. They made it to California, but they didn't find the relatives. Her mother died, and Katherine ended up in an orphanage, where everybody who saw her was struck by the brown-eyed, intensely silent little girl. "So this was all a fairy-tale to me, to have been in an orphanage," recalled Katherine, "and I met this lady, this white-haired charming lady—and just because somebody had bought me a little dress and I showed it to her and she was impressed, and she wanted me to come to dinner. I don't think I had in all my life outside the orphanage, sat down at a table with more than two or three people.

"And that's why I was told later that they thought for a long time whether or not they should adopt me—because I didn't say anything. I wasn't scared, but I had so much to listen to, so much to see. . . .

"I considered DeMille a father. He was the central, focal point. He was the one you looked forward to, to come home; he was head of the dinner table; he was all of that. And I think that's what we thought a father was for. But he was a good listener. He would listen as if what you had to say was very important. And he felt that we were the audience, and that's who he made his films for, his audience."

The children attended the Hollywood School for Girls. One of their class-mates, soon to become a regular visitor to the DeMille household and later to appear in several of DeMille's films, was young Joel McCrea: "I went to school with Cecilia. . . . I liked her, she was a nice girl. And L. B. Mayer's two daughters were there, Irene and Edith. And both Irene and Edith, and the cousins of Cecilia, Margaret, and Agnes, the choreographer, we were all friends." Edith Head, prior to starting her career as dress designer, taught there. McCrea continued: "It was a most unusual school. Every student had some connection with the motion picture industry. My pupils included Agnes, Cecilia, and Katherine deMille. Every time DeMille was shooting a big scene at the studio, school closed down and we went over to Paramount to watch. Then someone else's father or uncle would start a picture and we'd go to join the fun. That's the kind of school it was; we gave everyone good grades and flunked no one."

Around that time, DeMille acquired one of the status symbols of the tru-ly well-to-do, a 120-foot-long ocean going yacht, the *Seaward*. On it he in-dulged himself and his closest friends (with either Jeanie Macpherson or Julia Faye in tow) as often as he could between films. Being smart as well as rich, he also hired the yacht out when he needed it for a film. The next year, he added a splendid racing launch, the *Cecilia*, built to his specifications in the Lasky studio workshops: twenty-three feet long, made of mahogany, driven by a BMW motor with 300 horsepower and good enough to be entered in the Gar Wood speedboat races in 1923 . . . except that before then it blew up and almost killed him.

Having finished *Adam's Rib*, and with a new child at home, DeMille made plans for a vacation on board his yacht; in January, he set off on a six-week cruise to Tiburón, a barren island off the coast of Mexico in the Gulf of California. His guests included the big game hunter Carmen Runyon, John H. Fisher, Paul Iribe, Dr. Frank Watson, the wireless operator Joseph Kane, and Captain William Bethel of San Francisco.

Just before the voyage was to begin, on January 2, DeMille entered the Los Angeles Yacht Club motorboat race in his boat *Cecilia*. He started out confidently with his mechanic on board. Suddenly the carburetor backfired and the gasoline tank blew up, hurling both men into the water. His mechanic blacked out, and DeMille had to hold his head above water to prevent him from drowning. When the referee's schooner picked them up, the mechanic was still unconscious, his face black and scalded, and DeMille's eyebrow and eyelashes had been singed off. The *Cecilia* was no more. But it didn't spoil his love of the sea.

Five days later, the party set sail on the *Seaward*. At first they enjoyed perfect weather. Iribe kept the log, DeMille kept a diary. They harpooned blanket rays weighing 70 pounds, caught a pair of hammerhead sharks, which they tied to the rear of the motorboat, and encountered a school of whales. Finally, on their way to Tiburón, crossing the Infernal Channel, a tremendous storm blew up. DeMille cabled Gladys: "Northwest gale has made it impossible to reach Tiburón. Hours of drenching rain and we have been blown clear across the Gulf. *Seaward* is behaving splendidly but this wind and sea would stop anything." Before turning back, they rescued another launch that had capsized while full of businessmen.

Back in Hollywood, he learned that Wallace Reid had died. But Reid's death broke the curse. Though the good life continued to roll, with Will Hays's help the media was kept under control. Hays had been a member of President Harding's cabinet; he was a Presbyterian elder, a member of the Masons, the Knights of Pythias, the Kiwanians, Rotarians, Moose, Elks, and now the $100,000-a-year Czar of Hollywood. He had the look of a man people could trust. And all over Hollywood studios were busy changing the image of Hollywood as the home of the long race to hell. Publicity departments now commissioned picture spreads of the stars at home doing everyday tasks, working in the kitchen, playing the piano, or, like Cosmopolitan star Marion Davies, mistress of the publisher W. R. Hearst, doing her own house cleaning!

CHAPTER NINETEEN

EGYPT AND THE BIBLE HAD FASCINATED DEMILLE SINCE CHILDHOOD. NOW, as if by a miracle, ancient Egypt had leapt out of the Bible and onto the front pages of newspapers. On November 4, 1922, news of the discovery of the antechamber of the tomb of Tutankhamen by a team of British Egyptologists unleashed a wave of curiosity for all things to do with this previously little known Lord of the Three Kingdoms. Tutankhamen was responsible for re-awakening DeMille's interest in the Bible's version of God's selection of the tribes of Israelites as his "chosen people."

With new discoveries being made daily in the sands of Egypt, over the next six months, as DeMille was in pre-production on his film, *The Ten Commandments*, "Egypt fever" built up and captured the public: makeup, hairstyles, wardrobes, and accessories all reflected this growing fascination. Thousands of years of Egyptian civilization were telescoped into a craze for trinkets. Drugstore sirens wore their hair in Cleopatra bangs, men flaunted slave bracelets on wrists and ankles. Graffiti became fashionable hieroglyphics. Ancient superstitions became enthralling speculations. Crystal balls and tarot cards were once again popular pastimes.

Before DeMille set out on his project, Ernst Lubitsch had made two films on an Egyptian theme, neither with the sort of budget DeMille required, and they had had only limited distribution in America. The best that Hollywood had come up with so far were gauche sheiks and contrived bella donnas, scented and burnoosed, but Egyptian in name only. All this was to change with *The Ten Commandments*.

The idea for letting the public "appear" to pick his next project had been a brilliant stratagem. It came to DeMille while he was shooting *Adam's Rib*. On Sunday morning, October 3, 1922, the front page of the *Los Angeles Times* announced: "THOUSAND DOLLARS FOR AN IDEA; GOT ONE! Cecil DeMille Offers Fat Prize for Real Notion for His Next Film Play." The contest lasted twenty-seven days. The first item on the budget for this new project was the hiring and organizing of a staff for the reading and sorting of the letters. "I was struck by the number that suggested a religious theme," wrote DeMille, "and there was one that . . . kept coming back again and again to my mind. It was not from a professional writer. It was from a manufacturer of lubricating oil in Lansing, Michigan. His name was F. C. Nelson, and this is the beginning of the one page he wrote: 'You cannot break the Ten Commandments—they will break you.'"

By November, the genuine excitement over the discovery of Tutankhamen's tomb now also included the announcement from Hollywood that eight people, out of the more than 34,000 who had replied, would each receive the $1,000 prize for suggesting *The Ten Commandments* as the winning subject.

Six of the eight winners of the contest, including the oil man with the "title" touch, were still alive at the time of the remake thirty-three years later and invited to that premiere. "The oil geologist was particularly interesting," said Kiesling, "because he was a very profane man who interlarded his entire conversation with wild western profanity. When the gentleman was asked why he had suggested *The Ten Commandments* as an idea he said, 'Any person who doesn't believe in or live by the Ten Commandments is just a plain God damn fool.'"

Famous Players-Lasky now found themselves launched on a costly project by what appeared to be "popular choice." DeMille's trick for getting around the company's admonitions to economize could not have been lost on its leaders. So far all they had was a title and a spiraling budget that began with the first postbag. From the start, it was clear that this film would cost more than any previous DeMille feature.

Having settled on the story of Moses, DeMille and his team of writers began to develop a story. He intended to shoot the film as ten stories, with ten writers each responsible for one commandment, but after ten months this proved impossible. In the end, Macpherson wrote the script and received sole writing credit. Her script showed Moses receiving the ten commandments in the first half of the film, and the second half showed how they were applied in modern life—and what happens when you break them.

When it came to casting the well-known biblical protagonists DeMille decided on actors who looked as if they had stepped out of old master paintings, with impressive bearings and physiques. Moses and his brother Aaron were played by Theodore Roberts and his old friend James Neill; virile French-born Charles de Roche was Pharaoh. Julia Faye played Pharaoh's wife. The only new face in this group of DeMille regulars was Estelle Taylor, an attractive relative newcomer making a name in pictures as a vamp, who was selected to play Miriam, the good Hebrew girl who went inexplicably bad around the golden calf. No name in his cast rivaled that of DeMille.

DeMille's casting of these roles shows how he saw the people in the Bible. Younger and more impressionable than his brother when their father died, DeMille took his image of Moses, Abraham, and the Christ not from his mother's people, the Belascos and Frohmans, or from the flood of Orthodox Jews swarming in the streets of New York, but from the religious images passed up to the present from icons through the Renaissance, and grounded in those muscularized, Christianized works by nineteenth-century artists like Ford Madox Brown, James Tissot, and Gustave Dore. Moses was a massive figure who differed from Pharaoh mainly by having a beard that had been trimmed by Michelangelo's barber. When it came time to the New Testament, DeMille's Pharisees went to their local Vidal Sassoon. His concept of Jesus came down to him from the brushstroke of Donatello, not the blood of David.

DeMille reserved the use of rising young favorites for the modern section. Obviously a Swanson would have been ideal for the female lead, but not only was she too expensive for the budget, she now worked out of New York. Regrettably, DeMille failed to use the glorious Mary Astor, one of the most attractive and talented actresses in movies. Instead, the part went to Leatrice Joy. It was as much a matter of personal pride for DeMille. This one had to be good.

Out of the Famous Players pool of rising stars, he selected Richard Dix, a furrow-browed cross between Thomas Meighan and Wallace Reid, for John the good brother who lives and works by strict adherence to the laws of Moses. Instead of the gorgeous but expensive Betty Blythe, or the exotic and even more expensive Alla Nazimova, DeMille selected Paramount's own Nita Naldi, a Follies beauty with the look and personality of a somewhat drowsy anaconda, as the venomous vamp who seduces the younger of the two brothers played by Rod La Roque.

The voluptuous Naldi, proud of her body and quick to show it in all its naked glory, came to films from the Ziegfeld stage. She slunk for DeMille in yards of black crepe as the leprous Eurasian Sally Lung. In the least of her roles, she would find her claim to movie immortality. This was in part attributable to Howard Greer's wardrobe and for the stills of her posing in the archetypal manner of the 1920s vamp as recreated in later musical spoofs of the era like *Singin' in the Rain*. In fact, Naldi's type—a run-off of Theda Bara, with more kohl on her eyes than the whole of Wales—was already out of date; the new trend was towards Pola Negri's woman of the world. DeMille wanted a woman out of another world, like those found in Burne-Jones's paintings.

Rod La Rocque, her victim, had the disarming self-deprecating smile women like. His rise after *The Ten Commandments* on was rapid; his salary was amended the following year to $1,250 a week.

The first problem had been to find a site large and remote enough to serve for the biblical prologue showing the bondage of the tribes of Israel and their great Exodus into the wilderness. Several barren miles outside the town of Guadalupe, California, 200 miles north of Hollywood, was a neglected waste of sand, winds, and dunes. It was land worthless for all purposes except one: DeMille's.

Besides the colossal sets he also needed a place to house his cast and workmen. This was a huge undertaking. In six short weeks, his team constructed a flourishing town with a population of 2,500 souls. There were old men and old women, rich and poor, artists, artisans, craftsmen, laborers, all sorts and classes. And, as Rod La Rocque and Leatrice Joy remembered, everybody, even those not needed for this sequence, wanted to be part of it. Five hundred and fifty tents, arranged roughly along a system of paths and roadways in the sand, were erected. A special pumping station with capacity of 36,000 gallons of water a day was constructed. Electricity and telephone connections were established with the town four miles away. There were plumbers, electricians, painters, sculptors, and carpenters. Busiest of all were the cooks at the camp mess hall; over 7,500 meals were served every day at fifty cents a person.

Roy Burns's career with DeMille began in the deserts of Guadalupe when he was a waiter assigned to DeMille's table. It didn't take more than a day to convince DeMille that he was capable of bigger jobs. He brought Burns back to Hollywood as a property man, and he stayed with DeMille until health forced him to retire after completing work on *The Greatest Show on Earth*. For those thirty years, Burns served as DeMille's purchasing agent. Stocky, humorless, and irascible, he was reckoned one of the toughest traders in the movie mart. A co-worker recalled that "Burns moved in mysterious ways, never revealing the nature of the outcome of one of his trading missions except in whispers to the boss. He was always going back and forth, and said little to anyone else, except to C. B., mouth to ear, and as if he was about to tell him of the discovery of ten more commandments."

With his sets for the temples and the palaces of the pharaohs in the Valley of the Kings, DeMille intended to eclipse the memory of the fabled Babylonian set for *Intolerance* and the Nottingham Castle created by Wilfred Buckland for *Robin Hood*. For spectacle DeMille would brook no rival. Instead of the giant elephants toppling the walls of Griffith's Babylon, DeMille went better with the awesome splendors of biblical Egypt: the pyramids, twenty-four sphinxes, thousands of Hebrews in bondage; Pharaoh in his glory riding past the huge seated colossi, some thirty-five feet high, of his predecessors outside the gates of the city of Karnak; the golden calf, as well as the more conventional divine wonders described in the Bible: the wall of fire; the parting of the Red Sea; the giving of the laws. Much of this would be filmed in the latest miracle of film technology: color.

Although the budget had already reached $800,000 before any shooting had begun, relations between DeMille and Zukor remained cordial. More costs were added, not all of which were DeMille's fault. He couldn't help it that a hoof-and-mouth disease epidemic had broken out on the coast that April. Since the Exodus required a lot of horses, oxen, and other livestock, this was a problem. The Exodus was held up until healthy animals could be located.

And who would have expected problems from his own staff? But there was Kosloff going all moody in the middle of choreographing the orgy around the golden calf. "During the seven years we have worked together," he wrote to DeMille, "I have been fed only upon hopes without fulfillment, while many of those around me have received the things that were promised them; this insincere attitude towards me has at last brought me to the conclusion that, for my own honesty, and on account of my deep personal regard for you, I must decline the continuation of our work together in the future. Your sincere friend, Theodore Kosloff."

Kosloff's reasons were valid, but his timing was bad. It was one month before principal photography was to begin. It sounded like Buckland and *Joan the Woman* all over again. The rift must have sorted itself out since Kosloff was back with DeMille as actor in his next film, but he did not complete the choreography nor appear in *The Ten Commandments*.

With Wyckoff out of the picture, DeMille was looking for a new cameraman. Arthur C. Miller was renowned for the ravishing work he had done with director George Fitzmaurice. Miller signed a one-year contract, starting with *The Ten Commandments*, only then to discover Fitzmaurice was counting on him to shoot the first film to be made in Rome, *The Eternal City*. "My remorse was so strong that I returned to Mr. DeMille's office and told him how I felt. He opened the drawer of his desk, took out the six signed copies of the contract, gently tore them in pieces, and dropped them into the wastepaper basket. Then he looked me straight in the eye and said, 'I can appreciate your feelings.'" A new, young cameraman took over, J. Peverell Marley, who would work with DeMille for years, including on the remake of *The Ten Commandments*. The color photography would be shot by Ray Rennahan.

The unit went on location in May, recalled Kiesling: "We had 2,500 people and 3,000 animals in this camp on the sand dunes. The largest location ever made in motion pictures at that time. They were there something over ten days and it cost per day about $40,000. All cars were parked at the foot of the sand dunes and from that point to the top of the sand dunes where the camp was laid out, transportation was entirely primitive. One could walk with difficulty over the deep sand. Great dray horses, oxen, and western ponies, needed for the film were also used to carry properties, extras, etc. over sand dunes in sand sleds. It was a sight in the early morning to see scores of these sand sleds streaming out over the dunes."

The camp wasn't close to anything. A road had to be built across the miles of peat bogs to the nearby town, and another path, two miles in length, led to the highest dune on which stood the City of Ramses, the largest exterior ever constructed. A special street department was organized and detailed to keep these rough highways in moderate repair while work was going on. Their task was to transport the materials for the building of the ancient city.

The set built to represent the famous Egyptian citadel measured 750 feet in width and 109 feet in height. On the walls on either side was a seventy-foot bas-relief of two archers, including their chariots and horses. There were pyramids and outbuildings, pillars, pediments, plinths, walls, and gates. It included everything that could be achieved with 550,000 feet of lumber—enough to build fifty ordinary five-room bungalows, 300 tons of plaster, 25,000 pounds of nails, and seventy-five miles of cables and bracing wire to keep the winds from blowing it all away. The four giant thirty-five-foot statues of the seated Ramses II flanking the gates of the city weighed about 39 tons, and were copied form the originals at Abu Simbel. The front of the city covered nearly three times the area occupied by the castle set in Douglas Fairbanks's film *Robin Hood*.

It was approached by an avenue lined with twenty-four sphinxes, each of which weighed over four tons. Transporting them by truck from the studio workshops in Hollywood to the desert locations had its own unforeseen problems. What a sight it must have been for the locals to see these colossal alabaster statues in stately procession on the back of trucks setting out of the gates of the Famous Player-Lasky on their way up the coast, only to have to stop and their heads carefully removed when they reached a bridge too low to pass under. Once on location, with majesty and mystery restored, the sphinxes lined a processional route that extended out from the gates of the city.

People identified DeMille with his sets as much as his stories. An ironic sort of tribute came to light fifty years later in a book written by a man in prison—a young student of architecture who had been the official architect of Hitler's Germany. "I took no pleasure in Cecil B. DeMille's bombastic pomp," writes Albert Speer in his autobiography *Inside the Third Reich*, "never suspecting that ten years later I myself would be going his movie architecture one better. As a student I thought his films examples of 'American tastelessness.' . . . In my design for the façade of his [Hitler's] palace, there was no opening except for the great steel entrance gate and a door to a balcony from which Hitler could show himself to the crowd. But this balcony was now suspended five stories high above the street. This frowning façade still seems to me to communicate an accurate image of the remote Leader who had in the meantime moved into realms of self-idolatry. During my imprisonment, this design, with its red mosaics, its pillars, its bronze lions and gilded silhouettes, had assumed in my memory a bright, almost pleasant character. But when I once again saw the color photographs of the model, after a lapse of more than twenty-one years, I was struck by the resemblance to a Cecil B. DeMille set. Along with its fantastic quality I also became aware of the cruel element in this architecture. It had been the very expression of a tyranny."

Clare West, in charge of wardrobe, assisted by Howard Greer and Ethel Chaffin, used 333,000 yards of cloth, nearly sixteen miles of material, to make over 3,000 costumes, which, with labor, came at a cost of $84,673.75. For facial makeup, two tons of talcum powder and 500 gallons of glycerin were used. A wig-making establishment gave up all other business for the duration to get the thousands of wigs and beards required for Israelites and Egyptians ready in time. Footwear was another key item.

Salvatore Ferragamo, the famous "shoemaker of dreams," was brought in to work on the film. "It was my first commission for a shoe wardrobe of a spectacle film of such immensity, and it staggered me. I had never designed shoes for the Babylonian-Egyptian-Hebraic period, and my knowledge of the times was nil. On an inspiration I sat down and designed a high-fronted shoe with a mask reaching halfway up the shinbone, and on the masks I placed the heads of beasts—lions and leopards and strange mythological creatures. For the Egyptians I designed an open half-shoe with sandal effect. When the girl I now employed to turn my rough pencil sketches into detailed instructions had completed her work I took the results to DeMille. I knew him already as a man with an immense capacity for detail. Therefore I wondered how my inspiration would look in the eyes of his mastery of period.

"He was delighted and enthusiastic. He had no corrections to make, but I had—or thought I had. To satisfy my curiosity I went to the local library and scanned every book I could find which might give me a clue to the closeness of my imagined ideas to the actual footwear of the real Mosaic period. I found virtually nothing. It remains a fact—still true today—that the footwear of the ancients has never been adequately described or catalogued. . . . I was thus unable to confirm my inspiration from the records, yet my designs harmonized perfectly with the costumes of the Mosaic period—because, I believe, I had remembered them." (Besides his sole'ing of feet, DeMille shared Ferragamo's "belief in the reincarnation of Man.")

Paul Iribe had charge of the production design, but given the size of the project, he had many assistants. Los Angeles sculptor Henry Lyon was part of the team as was designer Frank McComas, who was in charge of the building of the canyon at the foot of Mount Sinai.

It was inevitable that all this work and excitement surrounding it would attract the attention of the press. For once, DeMille's publicity director had no need to dream up good stories. Everybody wanted to know about it. DeMille entertained local and foreign dignitaries. Upon their arrival, they found themselves amid sand dunes, some 100 feet high, stretching twenty miles north along the ocean to Pismo Beach, the largest expanse of dunes in the state. They found among the rolling sands of Guadalupe the royal city of Karnak, four millenniums and 10,000 miles from the ancient original, resurrected on two acres of restless, shifting, oil-bearing dunes. After being wined and dined on the best a Paramount location had to offer, the visitors returned to their homes carrying excited stories with them.

When the cast wasn't needed, some like old-timer Theodore Roberts wiled away the hot days fishing. There was a stream right around the edge of the sand dunes, which ran out into the ocean, and Moses could be found there catching fresh trout for DeMille and others.

On location DeMille was struck by inspiration. As he gazed about at the thousands of extras gathered together in preparation for his Exodus, it struck him that what this crowd lacked were some "authentic" Orthodox Jews. The start of shooting was delayed a bit longer while he sent to Los Angeles for several hundred, believing "rightly that, both in appearance in their deep emotional response to the significance of the Exodus, they would give the best possible performance as the Children of Israel." This "inspiration" created an additional problem which could have been circumvented had he had an Orthodox Jew on his team. "On that first fateful day the dinner provided by our commissary department consisted of ham. I was sent posthaste to Los Angeles for people competent to set up a strictly kosher kitchen to take care of our Orthodox extra players from then on." In a film recreating one of the great chapters in Hebrew history, someone should have thought of this early on.

To Zukor, "kosher" was just another bill. Soon, hearing the voices from the finance office in New York, he began to fear that expenses were spiraling out of control. Pharaoh and his men had been blinded by the Khamsin, that sandstorm God sent to obscure the sun and put fear in their hearts. Zukor's Khamsin was a blinding swirl of red on ledgers. Out in the desert of Guadalupe stood DeMille, his chair to hand, his megaphone at the ready as he galvanized his great flock, feeling capable of anything. Lasky and sales chief Sid Kent went to see him to convince him to curb expenses.

The army of actors were in the charge of his assistant director Cullen Tate and thirty-five aides. All the players were organized in strict army fashion. Each assistant was in charge of a unit, which marched to and from meals and the set with military discipline and precision. "It became a family affair," said Rod La Rocque. "The 'modern' cast went up to the desert as assistants and extras in biblical mob scenes. When we did the modern segments, players who had been in the biblical part joined in our scenes. It was integrated, undivided, one story—which, at that time, was a remarkable thing."

One who visited the set was the British filmmaker Herbert Wilcox, best remembered today for making Anna Neagle's *Queen Victoria*. "Dressed in his proverbial breeches and top boots, [DeMille] was directing, through an enormous megaphone, an open-air scene of a vast procession of biblical humans and animals. Never had I witnessed such production value. His organization was superb. Whilst the procession was in progress his publicity chief whispered in his ear, and DeMille, as if by magic stopped everything and in a stentorian voice announced through his megaphone that a great British film producer had arrived on the set. He eulogized my immortal contribution to motion pictures and pointed his index finger at me. Charming of him, since prior to that moment I doubt if he even knew my name. The thousands of extras applauded me as DeMille shook me by the hand and then, horror of horrors, the great brass band in the procession struck up 'Tipperary' and, as though taking up their cue, the elephants, started off again and the gargantuan procession followed. It was certainly a long way to Tipperary!"

The future director Edward Dmytryk, then working at the studio as "a teen-aged projectionist in army khakis," recalled Theodore Roberts, was "standing on a rocky eminence built on one of the stage floors and shrouded in tarpaulin, receiving God's Commandments while lightning, created by electricians wielding scissor arcs, crashed around him."

Another future director, Mervyn LeRoy, was hired on as one of the children of Israel: "I was just one of a crowd that would number . . . some 3,500 people. Almost all my friends were in the mob scene, too, so it was pleasant work. . . . We were awakened at dawn by a bugle-blowing reveille. We lined up for breakfast at the mess tents. Then we were divided into groups, which were called by military names—platoons and companies—with assistant directors in charge. They had military titles, too. Lieutenants were in command of platoons, captains in command of companies. These officers gave us our instructions. They, in turn, had gotten their instructions from colonels and generals. At the pinnacle of this mountain of military officialdom was the commanding general, DeMille himself. It was off limits for any but a select few to approach him directly. The picture dragged on. We struggled through the sand in temperatures well over 100 degrees. I gobbled salt tablets and drank water, but I still lost weight."

DeMille "had such discipline on the set," said yet another future director, Henry Hathaway. "We . . . had a scene down and out in the ocean. He was looking for a shot, and he looked through his finder, and he walked into the water to find a good angle for the Exodus, and Anne, and Hezi Tate, his assistant, and Mitchell Leisen and all of his staff, there, were about eight of them, they all followed him into it, up to their waist, and he's still looking. They had not a damn thing to do with finding his angle for him. They just followed him in, in case he needed something."

But there is also another classic anecdote from the filming which shows a rather different DeMille, as Leatrice Joy tells: "On one of those big scenes he wanted silence, this girl kept talking—and he waited, and she kept talking and talking, until finally he said, 'Young lady, will you come up here.' And he asked her what was so interesting. He said, 'When I say silence, that means you, it means me, it means everybody.' And she looked at him, a spunky little kid. And he said, 'What were you talking about that was so interesting?' She said, 'I don't wish to tell you.' He said, 'Why not? Go ahead.' She said, 'I said, "When will that son of a bitch call lunch?"'—that's what I said.' And he laughed, he laughed more than anyone. And he called lunch."

It was a story which would resurface on numerous sets over the years. Finally, DeMille even used it himself in the trailer for a film.

The presence of so many photographers and their assistants on the film gave rise to a classic Hollywood anecdote about DeMille. The thousands of (poorly paid) Hebrews had left Pharaoh's great city on cue. The scene had been full of those little touches that brought DeMille's masses to life: a baby goat stopping in its tracks to suckle; a little girl seen between the legs of adults and passing livestock; a wooden doll in one hand, the thumb of her other hand in her mouth, clearly lost in the crowd, even as the horde moves on all around. The whole thing had gone without a hitch. A feeling of exultation hung in the air. It would be hard and costly to do it again or better. Now DeMille went from cameraman to cameraman asking, almost redundantly, "Did you get it? Did you get it all?"

But Peverell Marley, Ray Rennahan, J. F. Westerburg, Archie Stout—each man he approached had a downcast look. The camera had jammed; the film had buckled up; another cameraman's assistant had forgotten to take off the lens cap; the fourth man had had a hair in the gate. At last, he came to the cameraman who had been furthest from the action, but who had been positioned on a rock to get a truly spectacular shot of the Israelites walking toward the Red Sea—and now yelled the immortal phrase: "Ready when you are, C. B."

Child star Diana Serra Cary's father, Jack Montgomery, was among the posse of cowboy extras and stuntmen. "DeMille needed crack riders, and at least six hundred of them, to bring to life his version of the pursuit of the Israelites to Pharaoh's armies. But Hollywood at that time did not yet have even a hundred men to put into the field, so DeMille hired every cowboy available, and then picked up another two hundred riders from the San Jose area. Through his military contacts he was able to obtain three hundred field artillerymen from a San Francisco army post, plus two troops of Eleventh State Cavalry and a battery of field artillery from the presidio at Monterey. Besides their totally divergent approaches to similar situations, it was common knowledge that ever since before the West was won, the wild, unfettered frontiersmen and the strict, order-bound troops had gotten along about as cordially as a bull and a bear. They went at riding, fighting and even living from completely antipathetic points of view."

Apparently DeMille was aware of this deep-seated antagonism, and planned to turn it to his advantage by casting the army on the side of Pharaoh and the cowboys as Israelites. Rumors were rife that in consequence the battle scenes would be enhanced by elements of real animosity. In his account, DeMille refers to the extras as "timid cowpunchers" and, given his time at P.M.C., it made sense that he looked up to the military and down on the cowboys. But he admits that, though he'd been warned, he didn't fully realize the strength of the antagonism until the scene was being shot. By then it was too late. Diana Cary picks up the story: "The following week the company moved from Santa Maria to Muroc Dry Lake in the middle of the Mojave Desert, for the long waited Egyptian-Israelite battle scenes. By that time the climate was ripe for a confrontation between the cowboys and cannoneer. One hundred Hollywood riders and the San Jose band gathered on the hard–packed white sands under the rays of a rising sun that felt like molten lead. Their bodies had been painted from head to heel with brown body makeup. They stood in their chariots or sat on their restless mounts waiting for DeMille to give the signal for the charge.

"But instead, he pointed out the steep bluff down which he wanted the cowboys to race their teams and chariots, as they fled before the Egyptian host. The cowboys sized up the job and objected. DeMille listened . . . and then (as he himself told the story over the years) he decided to shame the cowboys into carrying out his plan. Calling to his eleven-year-old daughter Cecilia, who was riding her pony on the same hill, he ordered her to gallop down the slope at full speed. Complying delightedly, she made the descent at breakneck speed and without injury. Turning to the cowboys with a disdainful smile, DeMille said, 'Well, if a little girl like Ciddy can do it, why can't you?'

"Jack Padjan then went on to inform DeMille that not only was the situation itself dangerous, but the artillerymen intended to use the occasion to make good their claim to superior horsemanship by riding over every cowboy in their path. 'When I finished talking,' Jack recalled, 'he looked right through me and said, "I must confess, my sympathies are with the artillerymen."' Furious, the cowboy delegation went back to their companions, climbed into their chariots and saddles and waited stoically for the order to charge."

With the aid of slow motion, rewind, and top-frame technology one can see the excitement of the action more clearly. To slow down the descending hordes of Pharaoh's soldiers, a wall of flames rises up from the sand. The casts have the same look of amazement as the audience. Seconds after hundreds of horses and chariots take off in pursuit the screen is filled with a golden cloud, made up in part of dust and sand and the bright reflection of the harsh sun on the burnished helmets of Pharaoh's soldiers, and on the wheels of their racing chariots and the spearheads. The view, as far as the eye can see, is a furious sea of white sand lashed up into a storm by pounding hoofs that threatens to obliterate the chariots from sight. Only when it cuts to another angle are the horses and chariots closest to the first camera seen clearly.

Meanwhile, reaching the high dunes, the fleeing Hebrew horses and carriages make their descent in snake formation. Almost immediately horses are seen buried up to their knees and chariots to their axles. Some lose their balance. Others come rushing over the bluff, not knowing what has happened to the vanguard, are themselves tripped by the sand, sending horses and riders tumbling, overturning even as other carriages thunder up from behind and alongside. Considering we are only seeing what DeMille wants us to see, and that he was conscious (given his track record) of critics looking for casualties, even with quick cutting to confuse the senses, he kept enough of the footage to convince one that there must have been a great deal more than he actually shows.

The whole chase is over far too quickly on the screen, but it must have seemed like an eternity to the participants. Men flipped like puppets out of carriages that have suddenly ground to a standstill or overturned. That no one was killed, or even seriously hurt, seems a miracle greater than the parting of the Red Sea. Clearly, shaming these riders into risking their lives and limbs for what is after all only a movie constitutes an excess of arrogance on C. B.'s part.

DeMille took precautions. He loved animals, but the film always came first. If he looked, behaved, and felt like a commanding officer sending his troops off to fight, it was because he wanted this struggle between the Egyptians and the Israelites to look as much like the real thing as possible. God would intervene when He had to, but DeMille's Israelites had to do their bit. And the cowboys had become the chosen people, whether they liked it or not.

DeMille wanted to film the parting of the Red Sea based on drawings by Gustav Dore. "I hope it is not irreverent to say that the waters of the Red Sea had been parted only once before in history," he wrote later, "and when I gave Roy Pomeroy the assignment of doing it again, I was almost literally asking for a miracle. But it was done."

The parting of the Red Sea was regarded for years as one of the screen marvels of the decade—real men and horses clearly seen underwater in close-up floating about in the avalanche of water that hit the Egyptian charioteers as the sea closed over them. How was it done? DeMille refused to expand. So everyone else has. "Roy Pomeroy was really fantastic," said Rod LaRocque. "You wouldn't believe how he did the Red Sea scene. Two blocks of Jell-O, carved with waves, were set on a huge table, which was split in the center. These two blocks were held together with water rushing over them. On cue, things like winches turned the blocks and separated them as water came over the edge. With the screen Jell-O shimmering and going away, they ran the thing forward, and it closed. When it was reversed, it opened."

Edward Dmytryk also claimed to remember that Roy Pomeroy, "create[d] the parting of the Red Sea in a little spillway built on a workbench no larger than a snooker table. The shot must have cost a few hundred dollars. A few decades later, for the remake, C. B. spent several million dollars to create an effect that looked not one dime better."

In his autobiography, DeMille didn't enlarge on the works of man but he had a tale of divine intervention. "The crossing of the Red Sea did require the construction of certain posts and wires along the seashore at Guadalupe, to serve as guidelines for the Israelites so that their line of march would not stray outside the area which the special effects department needed to have circumscribed for its later work. In order that these fences would not cast shadows where they would be seen on the film, the scene had to be shot precisely at high noon.

"At 11:45, I was on an elevated platform with one of the cameras, the Children of Israel where massed and expectant at their starting point, the Orthodox Jews among them in an exalted state of fervent emotion, the musicians were tuned and ready to being the 'Largo' from the New World Symphony for mood music to accompany the surge of liberated humanity into the hands of God. Everyone was keyed to the highest pitch. It was one of those moments that gives a director his greatest thrill of creative power and achievement—and his greatest anxiety lest one slip on his part, one second of inattention or indecision, cause him to lose his grip on the whole situation and weaken the invisible bond that exists between his will and every single one of the thousands of individuals in the scene."

Then DeMille noticed that the sand over which his casts were to march looked nothing like sand that had just been at the bottom of the sea. The sun was rising. "I called out an offer of a reward, I forget whether it was $100 or $500, to anyone who would come up with an idea of how to save the scene; but in the agonizing silence no one spoke.

"Then looking out at the ocean, only a few hundred feet away, I saw a bed of kelp floating near the shore. That was it! Calling out for everyone to follow me, I was off the platform and wading into the surf, coming back with armfuls of kelp to strew between the lines of posts, whose shadows were growing shorter and shorter.

"From Theodore Roberts to the latest and lowliest of the production crew, there was a wild rush into the ocean by everyone on the location. Stars, cameramen, musicians, the thousands of extras, everyone plunged in to bring back and spread the kelp. In less than ten minutes the long path between the fences looked as it should, as the bottom of the sea would look if the water were suddenly lifted up in walls on either side. Back on the platform I blew the whistle that signaled 'Action!' The musicians began those first three familiar, haunting notes of Dvorak's 'Largo.' The first of the Children of Israel moved forward, their faces lifted, tears streaming down their cheeks. I looked at my watch and at the sun. It was exactly noon." After hearing this tale of Divine assistance, DeMille's friend, the humorist Will Rogers, quipped, "I prefer the bit God did better." At any rate, Pomeroy's parting looked a lot cleaner and more realistic than the more elaborate and costlier special effects version in the Technicolor remake, where a blue outline clearly defined where the red sea left off and the animation began.

They were out on location for six weeks: four weeks to set things up, two weeks to shoot, and a few additional days to break, dismantle, and bury the set so it couldn't be used by anyone else. "Three hard-working drivers were on the road on a twenty-four-hour schedule," explained assistant director Barrett Kiesling, "taking footage back and forth between the laboratories and Guadalupe. Mr. DeMille saw his rushes almost every night, however these rushes were black and white. Technicolor in those days took about three weeks to process."

The first six reels, the part for which this film is still remembered, deal with the events in the Book of Exodus that concern Moses leading the Children of Israel out of bondage from Egypt and through the Red Sea into the Promised Land. Large sections of these biblical events were filmed in an early two color Technicolor process with exciting results. From black and white, the audience were transported into a sea of hues, shimmering greens and reds and golds, yellow ochres, burnt umbers, and raw siennas. The effect was fantastical. The second, modern-day part would be in black and while.

Even as DeMille was being the Moses of Guadalupe, Zukor was making like Pharaoh seeing a plague on the house of Paramount in every new item of expense. Before one frame of film was in the can, he had seen the bills

for the scenario amount to $50,000.25; the cost for the thousands of ex-
tras came to $156,718.67; architects, $33,631.02; carpenters, $132,456.58;
prop expenses amounted to $56.515.36, and the location expenses, which
including dressing locations, auto, horse and boat hire, company traveling
time, transportation, hotels and meals (lunch alone would come to 7,500
sandwiches, 2,500 apples and oranges and 400 gallons of coffee), came to a
staggering $410,4236.63. All of *Manslaughter* cost $20,000 less. By the time
it was completed, the Egyptian prologue, half the film's running time, cost
more than two-thirds of the final budget, and there was still the modern
story to be filmed.

Before Moses had as yet received his tablets amid the costly light and
storm effects, and the necessary orgy even begun, Lasky, pulled between
loyalty to the company and friendship to DeMille, was reporting to Zukor:
"Have had to ride Cecil pretty hard last few weeks account of *The Ten Commandments* going so far over his estimate. Finally today he came from meeting of his bank and advised me he believes he is in position to take picture
off our hands, reimburse us for our investment and finance completion of
picture, in which event he would make arrangements with us to distribute it
for small percentage of profits after parties financing picture have recouped
its cost."

DeMille, stressed and pressured, had proposed buying the film for the
$1,000,000 that Famous Players had already spent. In secret negotiations,
Neil McCarthy had raised the money from a consortium made up of Joseph
M. Schenk, Jules Brulatour, the head of Kodak, and A. P. Giannini of the
Bank of America. Giannini had asked McCarthy for a financial statement of
Cecil B. DeMille Productions and time to consider; McCarthy told him there
was no time: DeMille needed half a million to close the deal and he needed
it now. Giannini had one other question: "Is it a good picture?" McCarthy
said it was. DeMille got the loan. In the end, he wouldn't need it, but the
occasion had introduced him to a man after his own heart. Meanwhile, his
ability to raise such a vast amount of money so quickly on the strength of
his name and his past record, provided an exhilarating boost to DeMille's
self-confidence at a time when his colleagues in the company he had helped
to build showed serious doubts about his ability to come up with the goods.
Most directors in a situation similar to DeMille's succumbed and followed the
studio line. DeMille met the challenge head on.

Peace was made. But it put a further dent in the relationship between
Zukor and DeMille, who had called Zukor's bluff. Famous Players-Lasky had
caved in, not DeMille. As far as Zukor was concerned, though DeMille had
won the round, in his defiance he had betrayed the studio. In retrospect,
DeMille acknowledged that "such a strain had been placed upon a business
relationship that it would not stand the next major crisis."

When principal photography was completed on August 26, DeMille was
still with Famous Players-Lasky. Four days later, DeMille, off on his boat

before starting on the editing, heard from Lasky, who was concerned and anxious to repair what damage may have been done. Lasky to DeMille (August 30, 1923): "I never saw such hustle and energy, and such enthusiasm back of a picture as is being displayed in the preparation for *The Ten Commandments*. On Broadway from 43rd to 44th Street, [we] are building the largest electric sign ever to be displayed in New York. The sign will show a dash of chariots across the entire front of the (Putnam) building. As the chariots disappear on the side of the building on 44th Street, a huge electric sign will flash 'Cecil DeMille's *THE TEN COMMANDMENTS*.' This one advertisement alone is priceless . . . the picture is going to have the greatest handling of any picture brought into New York."

Meanwhile, there was a sad event. DeMille's mother died at age seventy. Beatrice had remained nothing if not independent. DeMille had bought her a house on 2026 Argyle Avenue in Hollywood. She liked it, but soon after she rented an apartment in Long Beach where she could hide away and write. She was as independent as her sons. Her illness was known only to very few and she only told DeMille when it was too late for him to do anything. "Up until the very end, almost, we played our little money game. It was our little game that told me mother was dying. She came to me one day and asked for a few hundred dollars for what she described rather vaguely as medical expenses. I thought it was the game again, and made the answering gambit. Mother did not play up as usual. Tears came into her eyes. She had to tell me then. She was not playing our game. She had learned that she had cancer. . . . My mother was one of the strongest and most wise and understanding women I have ever known. Until she died, I consulted her always about my work, about my most personal affairs; and she never failed to understand." All the while, he was out in the desert shooting the Exodus of her race, this redoubtable woman was dying. This was the film "inspired" by all those evenings when his father read aloud to the family. And now, as DeMille was about to achieve his greatest success, on October 8, two months before the film would premiere in Los Angeles, Beatrice Samuel deMille, play-broker, playwright, widow, and mother, died.

For forty-one years, his mother had bossed him, cajoled him, flattered him, embarrassed him, praised him, warned him, encouraged him, employed him, badgered him, made him feel guilty, and showered him with pride. She had lived to see him make the dreams she shared, but never realized with his father, come true. She saw her son become bigger than Belasco. With her death a door closed in DeMille's life.

The Ten Commandments opened at Grauman's Egyptian Theatre in Hollywood on December 4, 1923. DeMille had commissioned a special musical score from Hugo Riesenfeld. Each performance would to be accompanied by an orchestra and the theater's magnificent Wurlitzer organ. The organ, designed by Hope Jones, was akin to a complete orchestra in one instrument. It could do almost anything, create a sob or a din like you never heard in all your life. It had only one flaw, it almost brought the newly completed house down. "Those great Wurlitzers had what was called a thunder stop," explains Gaylord Carter, the star cinema organist of the silent era. "A thunder stop consisted of a huge pipe thirty-two feet long, maybe five feet square at the top, with a big reed at the bottom. The vibration it gave off was so powerful you can only compare it to an earthquake. A friend of mine was the organist when *The Ten Commandments* opened at the Egyptian in 1923. He used the thunder stop for the scene when Moses received the tablets from God. The theater literally shook and rumbled. The sound almost cracked the pillars. Hundreds, maybe thousands, of people might have been killed. Sid Grauman, who owned the theater, was so afraid of the thunder stop that he had it disconnected. In building the theater, the architect hadn't allowed for the thunderstop."

After the opening a flood of congratulatory letters and telegrams poured in: "Am still in a whirl of amazement over your colossal achievement which marks a decade of advance. It has out DeMilled DeMille and leaves your contemporaries still at the post, Thos. H. Ince." "It is a magnificent picture. Kindest regards, Ernst Lubitsch." Despite its orgy, Will Hays sent "praise and more praise. *The Ten Commandments* is more than a picture. It is an institution. It is magnificent."

There was one accolade arriving on Christmas Eve, which touched De-Mille more deeply than any other: "I congratulate you, dear Cecil, on your wonderful achievement in *The Ten Commandments.* I'm proud of the little boy I used to bring candy to at Echo Lake, whose father was one of the most brilliant men that ever lived and the sweetness of whose mother I shall never forget. The DeMille family are all tucked away in my heart. A Merry Christmas to you and your dear ones. David Belasco."

This Hollywood hyperbole was echoed by the popular press. *Photoplay* editorialized that *The Ten Commandments* was "the best photoplay ever made . . . it will last as long as the film on which it is recorded. It wipes the slate clean of charges of an immoral influence against the screen."

At the end of the film's first Los Angeles run, Sid Grauman wrote to say, "Thank you for giving Grauman's Egyptian Theatre the greatest picture the world has ever seen. I greatly admire you for the uplift to the industry in this gift to the people. We close the final week with a gross of twenty-nine thousand seven hundred seventy dollars and seventy five cents, Paramount's rental twelve thousand dollars for final week." At the Cohen cinema, it ran for thirty weeks, averaging $14,000 a week. It played for over a year on Broadway. After the film finished its long-run engagements, and in early 1925 was about to go out on national release, there were requests by Paramount for it to be shortened to allow for more screenings and increased, quicker profits.

Inevitably, all sorts of people now came out of the woodwork claiming the idea or the story had been theirs. It happened to DeMille with increasing regularity, and not always without cause. He would have to fight plagiarism claims on *Feet of Clay*, made the following year, on *The King of Kings*, and on a story of teenage lynch mobs, *This Day and Age*, in 1933. Now, after the film had been in theaters for some time, a woman in Atlanta went to court claiming that she had mailed a copy of her story in 1918 to the Famous Players-Lasky Corporation, and that it had never been returned. Two years later, when the case came to court, Macpherson, as the writer, was the chief witness. "Another angle of the plagiarism trial is interesting because it involves Hallett Abend, managing editor of the *Los Angeles Times*. Mr. Abend at the time of the preview was quite angry with Mr. DeMille, because the picture was not shown to him in a projection room but he was taken by me with great secrecy to a small theater in Alhambra. This theater was not even partially lighted but was pitch dark, so Mr. Abend could not make notes. Therefore [in] his review he referred to the departure of the Israelites on their flight from Egypt, exactly opposite as it was shown in the picture. If the titles said that they left in the middle of the night, Mr. Abend said they left the next morning or vice versa. When the woman in Atlanta claimed Mr. DeMille had stolen her story she made Mr. Abend's errors, and later it was proved that she had bought a program of *The Ten Commandments* at a showing of the picture in Atlanta. The synopsis that appeared in that program was not the official synopsis of the picture but was Abend's review word for word, so therefore because she repeated Abend's errors it was direct proof that she had copied from the program."

There is a curious footnote to this legendary production. In the years since DeMille made *The Ten Commandments*, attitudes toward movies and Hollywood's cultural contribution have lured new generations to investigate its past. In the fall of 1984, newspapers in California were suddenly full of whimsical articles about a curious find made by a thirty-two-year-old local filmmaker and writer Peter Brosnan. Brosnan had been alerted by another film buff, Bruce Cardozo, to two paragraphs in DeMille's autobiography: "If 1,000 years from now archeologists happen to dig beneath the sands of the Guadalupe, I hope they will not rush into print with the amazing news that Egyptian civilization, far from being confined to the Valley of the Nile, extended all the way to the Pacific coast of North America.

"The sphinxes they will find were buried there when we had finished with them, and dismantled our huge net of the gates of Pharaoh's city." DeMille had destroyed what he could and buried the rest for a simple practical reason: he wasn't going to leave an elaborate, expensive, and unique set standing for any fly-by-night company to rush in and turn out a quick *Daughter of the Pharaoh* or *Sins of the Nile*.

These enthusiastic local historians now set out for the desert. Sand is a fabled preservative. Long-surviving locals of this Latino-Italian-Swiss-Filipino-Chinese colony 170 miles north of Los Angeles recalled DeMille, dressing up as Egyptians and Hebrews, and being told to make a run for it for $5 a day

and food. With his friends and a whiskbroom, Brosnan uncovered that huge
head of a plaster horse beneath a sandy shroud. The head came from one of
the two bas-relief chariot horses on the walls of DeMille's fabled city. What
they found, reported the *Los Angeles Times*, "shows not-so-ancient Egypt as a
deep layer of junk. Six decades of wind, rain, salt, sun, horses, boondockers
and dune buggies have trashed once identifiable shapes into shards." The
staff writer who trudged out to look over their find saw, "large pieces of
plaster, lots of pieces of statuary sticking out of the sand, an awful lot of
wood and concrete." But the young zealots saw history in "the lines of the
set, [which] confirm it was 800 feet wide, where the walls had been . . . and
pieces of black plaster from what we suspect were the bottom halves of the
Ramses statues."

Brosnan, on the other hand, claimed that "what is all over Guadalupe
Dunes has passed from local junk to international artifacts of great cultural
and social significance. And recovering them, learning what has been forgotten and discovering what we never knew, is what archaeology is all about."
Then he set about trying to raise the money for his dig. His budget was a
mere half million.

It still continues. Nothing about DeMille is cheap. He would have enjoyed
the fuss made over his old sets and the confused theories they provoked for
their burial. He had been that sort of wildly curious boy himself. He was a
man who saw ahead, who had a sense of humor, and was obsessive about
historical accuracy. The last laugh may yet turn out to be his own. Meanwhile, there is a desert full of nuts and bolts for any collector who wants
them.

CHAPTER TWENTY

I BELIEVE that furnishing amusement and recreation to people is one
of the highest forms of human service.
I BELIEVE that to have a part in this work is a God-given privilege.
I BELIEVE that PARAMOUNT pictures are the largest single factor in
freeing people from the humdrums of everyday life.
I BELIEVE IN OUR LEADERS.
I BELIEVE that in helping to develop PARAMOUNT I am developing
all that is best in my life.
AMEN.

Whether this memo was intended as a joke or not, it was over the interpretation of the line before the "AMEN" that DeMille and Adolph Zukor found themselves at odds.

Following *The Ten Commandments*, DeMille in short order made three films. By the completion of the third, his future at Famous Players-Lasky was in jeopardy. In 1928, several years later, he gave an interview to *Hollywood Magazine*, headlined "Youthful Poverty had Bearing on DeM Career." "Because I have always shown something of wealth in my pictures," he is quoted as saying, "I seem to have drawn myself into a controversy which has to take a personal tinge. Some say I know nothing but rich people, that I couldn't do a simple human drama of poverty. Others say I totally misrepresent the wealthy, that no rich people in the world ever acted like my millionaires. Let me tell you something. Wealth, as the wealthy know it, is not at all interesting to the poverty-stricken. It is too much a matter of course. It is too comfortably placid. Your poor person wants to see wealth, colorful, interesting, exotic. He has an ideal of it, many more times brightly colored than reality. How do I know because, when doing twenty weeks solid of one-night stands without a bath, or when broke and discouraged at the three to six month lay-off, my dreams of wealth were nothing like they seem. No, indeed, I saw color, lights, fun, things striking and unusual."

The first of these three studies in imagined luxury, *Triumph*, starred Rod La Roque and DeMille's Hungarian find, Victor Varconi (who had come to his attention when he screened the Austrian epic *Sodom and Gomorrah*) as two half-brothers, both unwitting rivals for the same girl, Leatrice Joy, who, at four months pregnant, played a modern young woman, a factory worker with ambitions of becoming an opera star. La Roque is a rich wastrel to whom their dying father leaves everything, including the factory which made the family fortune. His father's will contains a secret proviso: if, in two years, La Roque hasn't ceased his playboy ways, then the estate passes to Varconi, the factory foreman. Joy places her singing ambitions before either man. Her singing of an aria from Berlioz's opera *Romeo and Juliet* allows La Roque and Varconi to imagine each as Romeo to her Juliet. And it is conveniently overheard by an impresario played by DeMille regular Theodore Kosloff, visiting the flat below.

This is as close as DeMille ever got to filming Shakespeare. He had wanted to film the tragedy with Joy as Juliet, Rudolph Valentino as Romeo, and Wallace Reid as Mercutio, but Lasky had wired that he "would jump on a train and come across the continent and try and lock you up rather than let you make such a terrible mistake." "Outside of *The Three Musketeers* and one or two other very big productions, costume plays are no more in vogue than they ever were."

Sets, including the factory interior, were designed by Paul Iribe, and were as realistic as those created for *Manslaughter*. But there are ingredients here one wouldn't have expected from DeMille. He had been much moved by the lot of the downtrodden masses in Russia. "I tell you it's all wrong," exclaims Joy in an impassioned moment. "If the rich would only divide their money, half the trouble in the world would be wiped out."

Of course, this was Christian philosophy as much as communist rhetoric. DeMille was swayed by the message he preached in *The Ten Commandments*. But by the mid-twenties, the initial fear of the new communist Russia was waning. Even men like Theodore Kosloff, who claimed to have known Kerensky, met Tsar Nicholas, and worked with Chekhov on his production of *The Cherry Orchard* and Tchaikovsky on *Pique Dame*, now spoke full of optimism: "It was only the other day at the Lasky studio in Hollywood that I received word from my sister that the Moscow Bolsheviks had returned $50,000 worth of jewels stolen from my safety deposit box in 1914. Such an action in Russia presages the return of all Europe to normalcy. . . .

"Whatever errors the Bolsheviks may have made, they must be given credit for a definite effort to awaken 128,000,000 people who for generations had been able to neither read nor write, whose ignorance made them live in squalor." It was a mistaken belief shared by many sympathetic to the Russian regime.

Triumph opened on April 20, 1924, promoted as a social satire, and audiences in Russia and Germany staggering under postwar inflation would have applauded the moral that inherited wealth corrupts. In the end, all three of the protagonists have chosen the correct path. La Roque gets Joy, and Varconi a girl who had long been making hapless eyes at him—a small part played by ZaSu Pitts, who was about to gain screen immortality later the same year in von Stroheim's version of *Greed*.

After DeMille criticized the inadequate promotion of his films, especially those with small budgets, Lasky brought back the notorious Harry Reichenbach to run Paramount's publicity department. Since leaving the Lasky Company back in 1914, the publicist had become legendary for campaigns using monkeys and lions. His gimmicks for *Triumph* could have done with an orangutan or two. "I arranged for a puzzle ad in seven newspapers, four morning and three evening, and in each paper listed the names of the other six. Each ad carried one letter of the picture's title spelled out as a word. The reader who could put together the seven letters first and deliver the solved puzzle to the Paramount office would receive a $100 prize. The next two hundred and fifty solvers would get free tickets to the picture. The ad ran like this:

TEA ARE EYE YOU EM PEA AITCH
T   R   I   U   M   P   H

"It was a triumph in every respect. I was paid $1,500 for it. Thousands of solutions were received at the Paramount office." The film had cost a quarter of a million to make and did fair business.

No longer Director General, DeMille nevertheless continued to have a far greater stake in the company than any other producer or director. His unit was a small studio within the larger parent company. What DeMille saved on salaries went to production costs. Of course, there were areas which created resentment among other producers on the lot. Once such instance, noted Lasky, had occurred just prior to work on *Triumph*: "During your absence . . . Jeanie made the unfortunate mistake of trying to engage our designer, Howard Greer. Greer is one of our regular employees and is under a year's verbal agreement not to ask for an increase of salary until the year has expired. Jeanie importuning him hasn't had any too good an effect, and you put yourself in the same position as I would if I tried to engage Paul Iribe or John Fisher without first asking if you could spare either of them . . ."

In May, Adolph Zukor was a guest on DeMille's yacht. Zukor had recently turned fifty (he was seven years older than Jesse and eight years older than Cecil). Though a ruthless fighter, he was also quiet and reserved, moderate in eating and drinking, far too busy for any dissipation. He had known DeMille for ten years, but nothing had broken down the professional distance. Not even visits to Paradise or cruises on the *Seaward* could turn these two into "Adolph" and "Cecil."

Feet of Clay followed *Triumph*. It was in production for three months and has been a lost film ever since its release. Even DeMille, who had a copy of every other one of his films, somehow didn't have a print of *Triumph* in his vault. The project was begun, as all his films were, full of hope that it would be the biggest and the best of its kind.

DeMille signed Estelle Taylor to replace Joy as his principal female featured player while the latter was on maternity leave. *Feet of Clay* required Taylor to be in a scene in the water. She was terrified of water and, while making the film, almost drowned. When DeMille subsequently arranged for an extra to be thrown in the water to complete the scene, Taylor told DeMille off in front of the whole cast. It was a scene worthy of one of his films, but it lost her the role. The outburst didn't destroy Estelle's career but it didn't help it much either. She continued to play vamps, a breed who shunned water that wasn't bottled. She was replaced by Vera Reynolds, whom he plucked from slapstick comedy. "When I first saw her I saw only her feet! A scene was being made where the upper parts of the players were hidden by a screen door. But this little girl was acting accurately, impressively, clearly to her toes. I said then: 'There's a real actress.'"

He had previously spotted Florence Vidor's potential "because he felt she was aristocratic and because she had pretty ankles. He believes that feet tell as important a story as the hands." Leatrice Joy went as far as to say that she "knew DeMille was a foot fetishist. One heard these things through the grapevine. One time for a scene he had me put my foot outside of a bed. I said, 'It looks very awkward to me. I mean, you wouldn't hang your leg out like that.' But he said, 'All right, all right. I just thought it would be nice to see.' That's why he liked Julia. The most perfect legs you ever saw."

This new film even had "feet" in the title. Rod La Roque shared the male lead with another up-and-coming romantic type, Ricardo Cortez, who, with the advent of sound, played hundreds of suave and sleazy heavies who no longer killed only with their eyes. Since no one has seen the film since its release, one falls back on La Roque for his memories of the film: "Vera Reynolds was in that with us. We're despondent and make an attempt at suicide. We turn on the gas in our cramped two-bit apartment. There's all this mist and all of us lost souls are going beyond to the other world, one guy with the noose still on his neck. He had been hanged. We're walking, mystified, hand in hand. Victor Varconi is the judge, maybe St. Peter, who knows? One person must go this way, another that way, depending upon the judgment that Varconi makes. When one of us starts asking for mercy from him, the hangman says, 'I only turn the pages. The writing is your own.' He turns a piece of cellophane. It's crystal clear."

Though the sets, both ultra-modern and profoundly spiritual, were credited to Paul Iribe, he was assisted by Norman Bel Geddes, the current Broadway sensation. Bel Geddes was the creator of the spectacular sets for the American production of Max Reinhardt's play *The Miracle*, worthy in size and spectacle of DeMille. He went to design several productions for him. "Never have I seen a man with so preeminent a position splash so fondly about in mediocrity, and, like a child building a sand castle, so serenely convinced that he was producing works of art. Despite this, I found I could get along with him without strong argument or flare-up, maybe because I learned quickly that there was no point in arguing. He would have his way. We got on so well, in fact, that DeMille eventually offered me a two-year contract as his art director. I think he was quite annoyed when I refused."

Bel Geddes added to the DeMille myth more by hearsay than by witness. Two years after departing DeMille, Geddes was brought back to Paramount to design and direct the climactic fight between the forces of heaven and hell in D. W. Griffith's *The Sorrows of Satan*, on a giant staircase leading to the gates of heaven. The occasion gave Bel Geddes the chance to study and compare the two directors. "C. B. and D. W. were pioneers in what has become an extremely vital and influential force in contemporary life. Between them, for better or for worse, they put Hollywood on the map and drew up the plans for its destiny. C. B. stretched its horizons to the breaking point, and sometimes beyond. D. W., in his quiet way, wet its standards, and they endure, some of them, to this day. If I prefer D. W.'s strength and control, it does not mean that I have lost sight of the value, even of the necessity, of a Cecil B. DeMille. He committed many artistic sins, but their very flamboyance lent them a grace that the sins of his imitators have never had. Finally, if I prefer D. W. to C. B., it is probably because I preferred the man D. W. to the man C. B. Which is only to say that D. W. was more nearly my idea of what director should be, sensitive, artistically inclined—exactly what I would have hoped to be had I become a motion-picture director myself. Thus do we all seek our own images."

Even with Geddes's imaginative designs and the story's aim to focus on modern youth, *Feet of Clay* was not one of DeMille's great hits with the critics. "The film was a flow of fleeting scenes," pronounced the *New York Times*, "like a nightmare one might have experienced following an afternoon at Long Beach, a lobster dinner, and cramming into the same evening a flamboyant cabaret show and that inspiring play *Outward Bound*." That last hit must have stung the hardest. When the playwright's London agent saw *Feet of Clay*, he felt that his author had been plagiarized without financial reward and took DeMille and Paramount to court. It would prove to be a lengthy case that wasn't settled until 1927. The *New York Post* critic was also unkind: "Nothing you could say in less than double this space could begin to describe the horrors of this film. Its story with its society and heavenly background should be preserved for posterity as an example of what shouldn't be done in the movies. The acting hasn't even the saving grace of being bad, and the title sounds as if having been written while the author was under the influence of a quarter in the slot gas meter. *Feet of Clay* is just one of those movie monstrosities that make you suspect that its producers have heads made of the same material." *Feet of Clay*'s negative reviews hurt it at the box office, and being restrained by a court order from being shown in the United Kingdom and Europe lost further revenue.

For *The Golden Bed*, DeMille created the candy ball, one of the most outlandish sequences he filmed. Here is Julia Faye (right) being offered an oversized candy cane by a woman in a costume made of candy canes. Courtesy John Kobal Foundation

A couple of months later, after completing *Feet of Clay*, DeMille took Sidney Kent on a cruise. The company's exhausted manager of sales had been ill, and DeMille invited him to come out and spend a month fishing, resting, and regaining his strength. When he was ready to return to his post, Kent, overcome with gratitude, asked, "C. B., I wish there was some way I could repay you for the wonderful time you have given me, but what can anyone do for you? You have everything. But is there anything in the world I can do for you?" DeMille asked for a bag of roasted chestnuts, the kind you only got in New York, the ones that kept your hands warm in the winter while you ate them.

DeMille's last film for the studio under his old contract, *The Golden Bed*, began shooting on October 16, 1924. His team was with him: Paul Iribe, Mitchell Leisen, Peverell Marley, Jeanie Macpherson on the script, and Julia Faye on hand as the social rival to the star for the title of "hostess with the mostest." Howard Greer dressed the stars.

DeMille in a portrait taken circa 1929 by New York photographer Irving Chidnoff. Courtesy John Kobal Foundation

Photographer Karl Struss made this iconic portrait of Gloria Swanson in costume for DeMille's *Male and Female* (1919). Courtesy John Kobal Foundation

Swanson's costumes became more elaborate as her stardom increased, but even in a bathing suit her glamour radiates, as seen in this portrait taken during the production of *Why Change Your Wife?* (1920). Estate of John Kobal

James Abbé made this portrait in the mid-1920s of DeMille in his Hancock Park home surrounded by his trophies from hunting, fishing, and filmmaking. Estate of John Kobal

A Roman orgy was featured in the contemporary drama *Manslaughter* (1922) as a morality tale, but also as an opportunity to add the exoticism DeMIlle's public craved. Courtesy John Kobal Foundation

For *Manslaughter* (1922), DeMille adorned his cast in his usual extravagant costumes, and once again surrounded his female star, here Leatrice Joy, with wild animals. Estate of John Kobal

Jacqueline Logan portrayed Mary Magdalene in *The King of Kings* (1927). Courtesy John Kobal Foundation

Mitchell Leisen, who would later go on to be a top Hollywood director, designed the magnificent sets for *The King of Kings* (1927). Estate of John Kobal

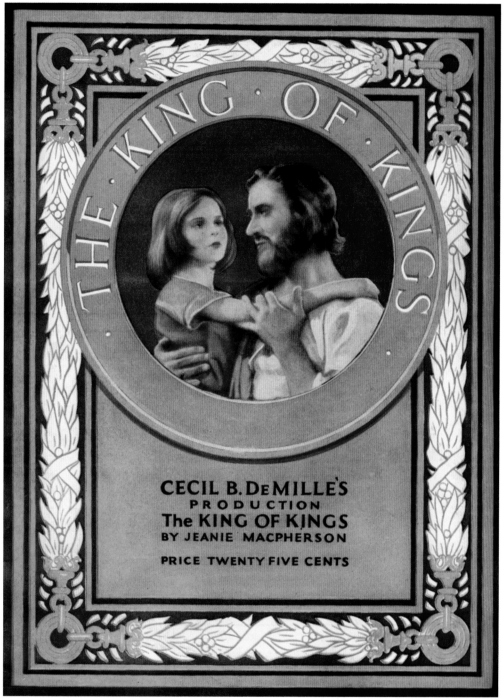

Souvenir programs were created for prestigious and expensive productions such as *The King of Kings* (1927) and were eagerly purchased by fans. Courtesy John Kobal Foundation

The song *Live and Love Today* was sung by the star of *Madam Satan* (1930), Kay Johnson. Sheet music was popular in the 1920s and 1930s and fans avidly purchased the latest songs. Courtesy John Kobal Foundation

A visual centerpiece of *Madam Satan* (1930) was the Ballet Mécanique, set in the interior of a zeppelin. Russian dancer Theodore Kosloff plays "Electricity," top center, with sparks seen to be flying out of his head. Courtesy John Kobal Foundation

Hedy Lamarr, playing Delilah wears the spectacular peacock dress for *Samson and Delilah* (1949). Estate of Cecil B. DeMille

George Sanders portraying the Saran of Gaza co-starred with Hedy Lamarr and Victor Mature in *Samson and Delilah* (1949). Estate of Cecil B. DeMille

Charlton Heston plays Moses in DeMille's final film, *The Ten Commandments* (1956). Estate of Cecil B. DeMille

Edward S. Curtis worked for DeMille during the filming of *The Ten Commandments* (1923), on which he served as a still photographer. He printed many of his photographs in cyanotype, which produces a luxurious blue tone. Courtesy John Kobal Foundation

Jimmy Stewart had one of his most surprising roles playing the clown, Buttons, in *The Greatest Show on Earth* (1952). Courtesy John Kobal Foundation

A lot of thought had been given to find the right lead actress. DeMille was convinced it would make her a major star, for the role was large and substantial and glamorous—a Swanson part for a new Swanson. DeMille to Lasky (September 30, 1924): "Must have brilliant vivacious and extremely beautiful woman capable of real great acting. . . . The whole picture hangs on this part and I must get someone with great beauty and personality for it. It is almost biggest feminine role of any DeMille picture. Leatrice is too wholesome for it. Ralston is a little too cold and dignified and unmoved for part. Need someone with the beauty and looks of Mildred Harris and the soul of Pola Negri."

Plenty of people tell of DeMille's arrogance. Whether or not he was aware of it, DeMille's thoughtless responses to Lasky efforts on his behalf convey an unattractive side of his personality. Every time Lasky suggested a play or story that would make a good film, DeMille shot it down. For *The Golden Bed*, Lasky was promoting the young Esther Ralston. Knowing that Lasky had a more than professional interest in the young actress, DeMille dismissed her as a possibility. Eventually he settled on Lillian Rich.

Now came the time for the reading of the script. There are few surviving records of these readings except for *The Golden Bed*. Sitting comfortably in chairs arranged in a circle around his desk, the cast listened to DeMille reading, assisted by some member of his secretarial staff for the smaller parts. With the room in semi-darkness, and DeMille in his big chair behind his big desk with the cathedral-like windows and soft spot beamed down on him to give him a Caesarian look, he began. His rich, resonant theatrical delivery can be imagined by anyone who saw him in *Sunset Blvd*. The effect was spellbinding. He would make little jokes and fill in missing details with reminiscences from his days of struggle in show business.

Now and then inspiration would strike him during these readings for bits of dialogue, which Macpherson would then fit in. Or he'd have an idea a particular dress, something that looked like $10,000 or so, which Howard Greer would have to design. Or a detail for the set, like a white bear rug for the seduction scene by the blazing fire where the husband would catch his wife in the arms of another. Gladys Rosson would keep track of all these additions and changes, and make notes to give them to the cast after the reading was over. No matter how the film might turn out on the screen, on these occasions DeMille made his cast feel that the production would be something special for all of them.

Originally, *The Golden Bed*, a "gift to the House of Peake by a grateful Louis XV," was meant to be shot in Paramount's New York studios, but because of the scale of the production it was decided to film in Hollywood and use Washington state for the Alpine exteriors.

When the story opens, the Peakes are decaying Southern gentility—"bred to spend money but too finely bred to earn it"—down to a golden bed, with two daughters through whom Colonel Peake (Henry B. Walthall, the Little

Colonel of Griffith's *The Birth of a Nation*, himself fallen on hard times) hopes to regain their wealth. The younger, Margaret (Vera Reynolds), is willing to go to work since she wouldn't marry for anything but love. Her older sister, Flora Lee (Lillian Rich), wouldn't recognize love if it didn't come attached to a safety deposit key. She marries the rich marquis de San Pilar (Theodore Kosloff), who discovers, during a mountain climbing holiday, that his beautiful wife has a string of admirers, including his best friend, who happens to be sharing his climber's rope with him. In a touch that could be out of von Stroheim, the marquis had seen his wife *in flagrante delicto* on a white bear rug by the fire, just as a cuckoo pops out of the clock. Now, three thousand feet up the Jungfrau, a fight breaks out between the two men. Flora watches both men plunge down the icy chasm. A marvelous dreamlike effect is created, as the two twirling falling figures, growing smaller in size, appear to float like astronauts in space before turning into lost specks.

While filming these scenes at Mount Rainier, Washington, DeMille's new star had a near-fatal accident. "Film Star Rescued" was the headline from the *Portland Telegram* on Tuesday evening, October 28, "Guide saves Lillian Rich from Death." The article recounted: "Narrow escapes in a blizzard sweeping down from the summit of Mount Rainier and the loss of $22,000 in film equipment were suffered by a party headed by Cecil B. DeMille that was engaged in filming Alpine scenes on the mountain Sunday afternoon. The party was on Nisqually Glacier when the blizzard suddenly broke. Three guides immediately divided the party into three sections and abandoning all property, conducted them from the glacier. Miss Lillian Rich, and two other women in the party, were carried with difficulty by the men who were rendered numb by the icy winds. Two guides who went to the scene yesterday brought back word that the property had been blown away or covered with snow and debris. Eight men were left by DeMille to salvage the valuable cameras and other equipment, and they will work with the eight forest rangers and three guides on duty at the mountain."

Sincere Vera Reynolds watches helplessly as her sister takes husband number two, Rod La Roque, the boss of a candy factory, and proceeds to bankrupt him with her demands for dresses. The film's *piece de resistance* is the extravagant "candy ball" she goads him into sponsoring, with twelve children "coming out of a gigantic box of chocolate drops and a fountain that pours grape-juice." It sent DeMille's budget for a film with no huge star salaries soaring over $400,000.

The lavish wardrobe for the heroine of *The Golden Bed* was designed by Howard Greer. One of his assistants was a young art teacher called Edith Head, who would become the doyenne of Hollywood dress designers. In her memoirs, she recalled the sticky mess she got into in her first film job: "I drew girls dressed as lollypops, peppermint sticks, chocolate drops. Howard asked me if I knew how the designs could be executed and I assured him they were simple. So he took the rather amusing sketches to Mr. DeMille, who prompt-ly okayed them.

"Came the day of shooting and, shortly after, came a blast from Mr. DeMi-lle who was never a patient man. The peppermint sticks had started cracking during the dance routines. Using real candy proved to be a mess. I'd put can-dy on their heads, on their shoulders: whenever they got within a half a foot of each other, the candy would stick. From that day on, I've never drawn anything I couldn't make."

"The main difficulty in filming the scene," noted the *Los Angeles Sunday Times*, reporting along the way that the extras grew high on grapefruit juice spiked with gin, "was to make candy look like candy. On the screen the ready-made substitutes made of satin and wood look much more like sweets than the candy itself. Consequently, the only way in which the candy idea could be put over was for guests to go about nibbling from the various plants and flowers. 'Have a rosebud on me,' says one extra to another, and presto, realism is accomplished." Besides "rosebuds," men also munched on wom-en's bras and panties.

Begun too late to be ready for Christmas, *The Golden Bed* hit a serious cold spell on its January release. Now that DeMille no longer had Paramount to cover for him, even *Photoplay* condemned it as "Cecil B. DeMille's last and perhaps worst picture under his contract with this producing company. A lavishly stupid spectacle. A pearl onion in a platinum setting."

In fact, all three films—*Triumph*, *Feet of Clay*, and *The Golden Bed*—made the studio a handsome profit but it was not enough. According to Lasky, DeMille's lavish expenditures meant, "rental terms had to be jacked up to meet the strain, and the conservative elements on Zukor's staff didn't favor risking such sums on a single picture. I was informed that Cecil was going to get the ax unless he allowed his contract to be altered to give the company more control over his pictures."

Lasky was telescoping a number of factors to make a point about the prob-lem between DeMille and Zukor. Whether the handling of publicity for his films, or fussing about stars, or a hundred other grievances, real or imagined, raised by DeMille, all came down to more power and money for himself. He had been laying the groundwork all year to strengthen his position when the time came to renew his contract at the end of 1924. Events were moving to a climax.

CHAPTER TWENTY-ONE

SINCE *THE TEN COMMANDMENTS* IT WAS BECOMING CLEAR THAT THE DAY of reckoning between DeMille and Zukor was on the horizon. Zukor, operating from New York, had been quietly marginalizing DeMille and giving increasing decision-making influence to the company's new treasurer, Sidney Kent. Lasky remained, as vice president, part of Zukor's inner circle. This must have been hard on Lasky because of his history with and loyalty to DeMille. Zukor spelled out the company's idea of a "fair" deal with a difficult colleague. Adolph Zukor to Jesse Lasky (December 2, 1924): "Dear Mr. Lasky, . . . I have come to the conclusion that we ought to suggest a new proposition to Cecil . . . Cecil to draw $3500 a week while he is shooting a picture, this amount to be added to cost of negative whether big or small picture; Cost of production to be mutually agreed upon in advance."

Zukor wanted a product that came in on time and wouldn't rock the schedule. This left little room for directors like von Stroheim or Griffith, or increasingly DeMille, artists who were impossible to control even though their films brought great prestige and sometimes great profits. It's a surprise that so much good work came out of what was just becoming a factory. Zukor continued, "Profit on Cecil's pictures to be split between us 50/50. While I consider this a very liberal proposition owing to the fact that we do all the financing I nevertheless feel that owing to Cecil's *long association* and the fact that he is a member of our organization I will not have any trouble putting it over." "Long association" seems a mild description of one of the three original founders of the parent company. But it is this sort of reasoning that cost Zukor some of his biggest earners, like Pickford, Swanson, and later Valentino. No matter how difficult, they still made enormous profits and gave the studio its preeminent standing. Furthermore, Zukor went on, "the suggested arrangement must carry with it also the condition that Cecil will not retain under contract a number of people for whom he has only occasional use and whose continuous employment makes cost of negatives prohibitive. Ways and means must be found for a plan which will enable Cecil to work economically at the studio and the minute he stops shooting all overhead expense must cease." The gist is that DeMille's power needed to be curtailed.

His unit must be disbanded. "His" staff must be "our" staff, people who are responsible primarily to Famous Player-Lasky. This paragraph, as Zukor must have foreseen, was the one to incense DeMille the most. "If after reading this letter," Zukor concluded, "you feel that you can suggest some arrangement which you feel would be better I will be very glad indeed to know it. However, after studying conditions for months I fail to find a solution better than the one I proposed. I am most anxious that the changes and new arrangement be made before Cecil leaves California in order to dispose of this enormous burden without unnecessary delay, and also we must come to a fairly definite arrangement before he starts his next production."

For DeMille to have submitted would have reduced him to merely an employee of the company. Given his pride and success, and the fact that he was a founder and partner, there was no way he would submit to such terms, any more than would have Mary Pickford. Zukor forced Lasky to tell DeMille—our way or out.

Sensing the inevitable, DeMille had given his lawyer the go-ahead to write to Joseph M. Schenck, the president of the United Artists Corporation, a man Lasky had highly endorsed to DeMille when it seemed he would go into the company earlier that year. Neil S. McCarthy to Joseph Schenk (December 11, 1924): "My thought concerning DeMille is that he should now develop his own organization directing two pictures a year and producing several others with other directors under his supervision, similar to methods followed by Ince. DeMille really great executive and could deliver great product in this manner in addition to his own personally directed pictures."

Joseph M. Schenck to Neil McCarthy (December 13, 1924): "Your proposition regarding DeMille appeals to me. Wire me details particularly how many pictures per year he wants to supervise also what terms you want. We will finance the pictures. Sailing on Majestic Wednesday, so work fast." It is clear from these secret negotiations that McCarthy did not expect DeMille to stay until he met with Zukor.

As tension was mounting DeMille wrote to his friend Sidney Kent on December 15, 1924: "My feeling is that working in my own studio would possibly for all time end the constant misunderstanding there seems to be between us. Mr. Zukor's proposition to me . . . suggesting that I draw thirty-five hundred weekly while shooting is to my mind so far removed from my requirements that I am sending this wire to you instead of to him in the hope that in presenting it to him, you can without prejudicing the interests of Paramount *which I know mean more to you than anything else*, bring about an understanding between us, but time is terribly short."

Meanwhile, the deal with Joseph Schenck fell through. Three days after receiving DeMille's cable, Kent wired back with Zukor's ultimatum: "It is not your advance we object to as much as the added expense caused by your separate unit from which we feel you get no return commensurate with the expense it costs us. Mr. Zukor feels that this must be taken off our backs . . .

Zukor's letter must be the general basis upon which we meet." The same day, DeMille's lawyer, Neil McCarthy, cabled one of his old business partners, John C. Flinn: "DeMille contemplating purchase of Thomas Ince Studios and of making on that lot his own personally directed pictures. If he closes deal would you care to contract with him for pictures similar to those Ince was producing for you. . . . With you in charge of distribution and my client directing two pictures a year and supervising another group and as executive head of all production a new company can be developed in the industry along the lines of Paramount with every probability of assured success."

Flinn to McCarthy: "Intensely interested your telegram and would be interested not only in supervised series but also personally directed series if terms could be worked out."

In his version of the events, DeMille says that he had secretly proposed buying the Ince studios to Lasky as soon as he heard of the shocking death of Ince, and that Lasky passed the information on to his colleagues in New York, but Famous Players-Lasky vetoed the idea, thus leaving the studio available. The exchange with Lasky sounds as if DeMille was suggesting that Lasky might come with him and start a new company. Lasky, referring the matter to Famous Players, was signaling DeMille that he was planning to stay put.

The fateful lunch meeting with Zukor, Lasky, and Kent took place early in January, in Zukor's office in the thirty-nine story Paramount Building towering over Times Square in New York. The bitterness of the meeting caught DeMille off guard.

It had been a little more than ten years since Zukor and DeMille first met on that dramatic night in September 1915, outside the Famous Players studio on Twenty-sixth Street, just after Zukor's studio had burned down, with Zukor surveying the hot ashes, calm as steel. It was a formidable first impression of a man who would go on to build one of America's greatest companies out of those ashes. DeMille's contacts with Zukor over the intervening years had been infrequent, always polite, but strictly business. They were partners, not friends.

Zukor probably sat quietly. It would have been up to Kent to report on the profits and losses of DeMille's films, and their cost to the company. Then Lasky would make his case for the company, and for his friend, trying to find words that might bridge the chasm between DeMille and Zukor. Zukor would have listened to DeMille—mercurial, confident, equally full of what he believed he had done to build the company from a barn into its present eminence. When DeMille finished, it was Zukor's turn. As he spoke, recalled DeMille, this normally soft-spoken little man who rarely lost his temper put his two clenched fists together and, slowly separating them, said, "Cecil, I can break you like that."

This was not a meeting between David and Goliath, but Saul and David. This lunch was never described in any detail by any of them: it was too bitter. It only surfaced in little asides planted in strange places throughout their books. Zukor had more to say, as DeMille's recounts in his autobiography: "There is no doubt in my mind that those three gentlemen believed they were acting in fairness to the company and to me, as firmly as I believed that the only way I could make good pictures was the way I had been making them. But my long life has had few bitterer moments than when one of those gentlemen said to me, and the other two heard it in un-protesting silence: 'Cecil, you have never been one of us.'"

DeMille dwelled on Zukor's words at this "gentlemen's'" meeting in his private recollections to Art Arthur: "He did one of the most terrible things one man ever did to another—'You're not one of us and you never have been one of us.' To the guy who had built the whole damned structure of pictures for him!"

Of course, Zukor was looking after his own. Famous Players-Lasky came before DeMille and, as Lasky would yet find out, it also came before Lasky. But it wasn't so much in the deed as in the telling that DeMille was hurt. There was something that went much deeper and more personal which surfaced in Zukor's phrase which made it impossible for DeMille to ever forget it. The phrase would come to haunt him: the oath of expulsion. *You're not one of us.* Zukor's angry rejection went to the heart of DeMille's lifestyle, and his failure to resolve it, and Zukor brought it out into the open.

And Lasky, after a decade of mediation, said nothing to soften the blow. "Not lifting a finger," DeMille would recall of his best friend in his autobiography.

It hit DeMille hard, as if Moses had cast him out. Zukor had hit DeMille in his Achilles' heel. It was a tribal matter. Zukor could never have told Lasky that he was not one of them. This "us," this invisible binding clay, had made it possible for Goldwyn to go for help to Sigmund "Pop" Lubin back in 1914, even though Lubin was their sworn enemy. DeMille had wondered what it was Goldwyn could have said to get that wily old man to help, but it had been blood talking: the blood of the heroes of the Bible from which his father used to read to him when he was a boy.

Agnes deMille said that DeMille's denial of his Jewishness was because "he was a snob." Zukor, who came from the loins of DeMille's mother's race, told her son that he wasn't one of them. DeMille's inability to accept the decisions of the Famous Players-Lasky board headed by Zukor meant that he was not one of them. But, it was something deeper than a boardroom struggle that DeMille lost. Zukor's rejection—and Kent's and Lasky's silent acquiescence—yanked at his roots.

Like some sleeping curse awakened, rumors of DeMille's anti-Semitism collected into stories and fanned out to flourish in the postwar 1940s, when a new generation saw him only as an unyielding old-timer. They would surface when he was making *The King of Kings* during his conflict with Mankiewicz at the Screen Directors Guild. And when he worked on his autobiography all the bitterness surfaced. One can hear it in his conversation with Art Arthur in 1955, and again two years later, refusing to accept that the eighty-four-year-old Zukor could have forgotten what was said, as Zukor claimed.

DeMille's contract with Famous Players-Lasky was terminated on January 9, 1925. His European trip, which was supposed to start the next day, was canceled. He stayed in New York to set up his own studio.

Tom Ince's tragic unsolved death aboard William Randolph Hearst's yacht the previous November couldn't have been more advantageous for DeMille. He bought the Ince studios from Mrs. Ince for $500,000 with the financial backing and immensely patient and loyal support of Jeremiah Milbank, a millionaire banker and rail tycoon with a strong religious streak. Milbank had recently formed a new film distributing company, the Producers Distributing Corporation or PDC (later to be absorbed into the Keith-Orpheum circuit with the launch of RKO). Milbank was especially attracted to DeMille's idea for a film on the life of Christ. On February 4, he turned over the Ince studios to PDC in return for common stock and $6,000 a week.

On his return to Hollywood, DeMille asked his secretary Gladys Rosson how things had been going. "Everything very well," she said. "Except for one thing that came in, that I don't understand."

"What was that?"

"This," she said, handing him a piece of paper. "This bill that came to you, for chestnuts." Sidney R. Kent's lack of noblesse was not oblique.

CHAPTER TWENTY-TWO

DEMILLE'S TRANSITION TO STUDIO MOGUL STARTED WITH HIGH HOPES AND much promise. Beulah Marie Dix's daughter, a teenager who spent a lot of her time with DeMille's children, recalled the atmosphere: "Uncle Cecil went to Culver City. He took over the old Ince premises, round the bend from Metro-Goldwyn-Mayer, and set up a studio entirely his own. . . . All directors and writers were on [the second] floor except Uncle Cecil, who had a suite on the third floor, with a white bearskin rug. The reading and research department was up there, too, run by Aunt Constance's stepmother [Ella King Adams]." Cecil B. DeMille Studio opened for business with grand ceremony on February 27, 1925. DeMille was the boss. He ran the whole show—like Goldwyn; like Mayer. And, like them, he named the studio after himself. He transferred his ostentatious baronial office from Famous Players to the Ince studios, which was built along the lines of George Washington's residence at Mount Vernon. Most of DeMille's old unit, a full-scale retinue large enough to stock a new film company, joined him. John Flinn was vice president and looked after the running of the studio, playing a role in the new company similar to Lasky's in the old. Barrett Kiesling was head of publicity. His brother William came over: "It was something of a wrench for me to leave the Lasky studio where, for twelve years, I had watched the company grow from its first crude beginnings to be the most powerful picture organization in the world. But times were changing: we were pioneers no longer. Those gay, adventurous days were gone forever. Company politics and industry reorganization, with the vast sums of money involved in production, had darkened the atmosphere. Our little frontier outpost had been overwhelmed by the city which had grown up around it. Our small advance guard had been broken up by promotion and each member of it was now leading a regiment of his own."

Up at the house, DeMille's personal affairs continued to be run by his pretorian guard headed by Gladys Rosson, who made sure that any newcomer couldn't break into the charmed inner circle. She kept the letters that were to be burned, along with the requests for handouts, the telegrams, the poems, and mash notes sent to him by women, the bills for purchases to be given as gifts and thousands of other items that filled his days. She was in love with her boss, but with Jeanie Macpherson and Julia Faye around, not to mention his wife, she kept her feelings secret, only letting her loyalty show.

But, as DeMille would explain years later to the young elite at Harvard, there was more to setting up a studio then just a good team at the top. You needed good people at every level: "All in all some forty different departments, and frequently as many as 117 professions or arts, must each provide something (to the running of a studio) for a director to work into his production. . . . A [studio head] director, therefore, must know intimately all of the forty departments."

The new company announced a grand total of forty films for its first year, three to be directed by DeMille (in reality, he only made two), and the rest by directors like William K. Howard, Rupert Julian, Paul Sloane, and Paul Stein. DeMille's art director, Paul Iribe, his longtime assistant director Frank Urson, and the actors Donald Crisp and Alan Hale all tried their hand at directing. William deMille, too, directed for the new studio. Except for William Howard and William deMille, this was a pedestrian lot. Their films filled out the schedule, but only Howard's *White Gold* made it into the black.

Looking for talent, DeMille missed some great opportunities. "Von Stroheim asks that we consider him," DeMille wrote to John Flinn in April. "He has left Metro. Are you interested?" Von Stroheim had made *Greed*, and his latest film, *The Merry Widow*, was an enormous hit, but his reputation for excess had preceded him. Flinn, whose concern was to make money and not art, was cool on the idea. DeMille should have known better.

One of the most important priorities was the studio's lineup of box-office stars. As part of DeMille's settlement, Paramount had agreed to let him take any DeMille player he held under contract, as long as that player had not become established as a Paramount star. DeMille and Lasky remained cordial, continuing to share news. Lasky to DeMille (March 26, 1925): "Just before you arrived in New York I negotiated with Bebe Daniels for a new contract. However we could not agree on terms and when she told me she could get more money and better conditions from other producers than I was offering her I advised her frankly that she was a free agent and she could go and negotiate elsewhere without any hard feeling on my part. This was situation when you asked me if we had closed with Bebe and I remember telling you that you were free to negotiate with her." After extensive negotiations and many changes of mind, Daniels resigned with Paramount.

Some things couldn't be spelled out in telegrams for fear others would get wind of it, so Gloria Swanson (for she was) was referred to as "the star." DeMille to John Flinn, Blackstone Hotel, Chicago: "Just finished long conference with star's attorney. He states that if I will direct one or more of star's pictures each year and Neilan one or more, and if we will meet legitimate offer made by star's present company he will and does commit himself that star will sign with us. He talked basis of three-year contract and intimated

Wallace Reid was a popular leading man who worked often for DeMille before his untimely death in 1923, when he was only thirty-one. Courtesy John Kobal Foundation

star wanted one picture annually made in Europe. I told him that he could then consider matter virtually closed as I would agree to meet any bonafide offer made by star's present company." But the star never signed. Swanson went to United Artists.

At the DeMille studio, the star lineup included Rod LaRocque, Jetta Goudal, a talented French-born import who had just made a big hit in a couple of films at Paramount, Julia Faye, Theodore Kosloff, William Boyd (the future Hopalong Cassidy), as well as Jacqueline Logan (George Melford's girl), Vera Reynolds, and those lively former Sennett girls, Marie Prevost and Phyllis Haver in whom DeMille thought he saw future dramatic leading ladies. Phyllis would play Roxie Hart in *Chicago*, but none of these DeMille "baby stars" ever rose much beyond *Getting Gertie's Garter*.

As stars go, this was not an impressive roster, and DeMille knew it. They would need a lot of selling to get the public's attention. DeMille ordered publicist Barrett Kiesling to get behind their stars the same way Paramount's exploitation and sales force had, and told him to promote their stable by reminding the public of such earlier "great" DeMille discoveries as Wallace Reid, Thomas Meighan, Sessue Hayakawa, Gloria Swanson, and Bebe Daniels. Bill Boyd was to be sold as a new Wally Reid and Thomas Meighan type; Rod La Roque as another Elliott Dexter; Victor Varconi as a Jack Gilbert; Jetta Goudal was to be an exotic woman of mystery; Marie Prevost was humor and sex; Vera Reynolds, youth and charm; Phyllis Haver, sex and fascination. Julia Faye had been prominent in forty-eight films, but never had the makings of stardom.

Having access to neither a Bebe Daniels nor a Gloria Swanson, DeMille hoped to promote Leatrice Joy as his studio's number one female star. Her career was definitely on the rise, but she was happy at Paramount. Now her loyalty to DeMille for making her a star was on the line. DeMille told his staff to tell Joy that there would be a great future for her; that she would be their featured female star; that she would get lots of great publicity; and that he was buying special books and plays for her. DeMille guaranteed Joy a fabulous weekly salary, far more than she was getting at Paramount. She signed with him, only to find a puzzled Lasky phoning to say, "DeMille tells me you want to leave us and go with him, aren't you happy here?"

DeMille had promised her the moon, but it quickly became evident that he didn't even have a properly functioning publicity department. A rift formed between Joy and her new studio that would rankle her for the rest of her life. She felt that her career suffered from this move and that she had been tricked by DeMille, playing on her loyalty, into coming over to his studio. Moreover, Joy felt DeMille had implied that Paramount didn't want her, and that she had been used as a pawn in a private quarrel. "Before I left Paramount I was at a turning point in my career. I was on the very crest of stardom. 'I'll make you a real star!' he promised. But you don't have a big studio behind you anymore. You don't have a proper distribution. I'm not so young any more Mr. DeMille. The next three years are crucial with me. And DeMille said, 'We're just growing.' And I said, I don't want to grow, Mr. DeMille. I want to go on. Let me go.

"And I begged him. And he wouldn't do it. He never directed me after that."

DeMille was grieved by this lack of faith from an actress he had made a star. Another sore spot was the influence of her brother, Billy Joy, who had first brought her to DeMille's attention. His brotherly advice often went against the studio's plans.

The strain in their personal relationship was exacerbated when Joy decided to cut her hair. She started seeing her ex-husband John Gilbert hoping to reconcile. One day when Gilbert left for a barber's appointment, Leatrice decided, "Good, I'll get my hair cut too." And had it cut as short as his. Joy was proud of the impact of her decision. "It started a trend. Joan Crawford cut her long hair after she saw mine. It wasn't a 'shingle,' it was a 'feather edge'" Other fashionable celebrities like the dancer Irene Castle and the soigne Lilyan Tashman had already done their bit to make the boyish cut fashionable. But after Joy, because she was in the movies, it became a craze. Girls became boyish—narrow hips, flat chests, and short hair became the rage.

DeMille was furious when he first saw her. He liked his women to look feminine, and the roles selected for her now had to be adapted to her new appearance. Of course, the studio could have made her wear a wig, but, except in costume roles, wigs didn't look natural. And anyway, it wasn't the length of the hair, but the attitude underneath it.

DeMille eventually resigned himself to the change, and did his best to turn Joy into a cinema flapper. In *Vanity*, there was a wedding sequence where she married the boyish-looking Charles Ray. "Good God, Leatrice!" said Gilbert Adrian the costume designer. "I'm going to have to design a special headdress for you. If you stand up with Charles Ray at the altar looking the way you do, it's going to look like two boys getting married."

The time was approaching for DeMille to start on his first production. It had to be a big success—another *Squaw Man*, in effect. He knew all Hollywood, and especially his former colleagues at Paramount, were waiting to see him fail. What he served up was *The Road to Yesterday*, based on a play about reincarnation.

Reincarnation and spiritualism (the theme of *Feet of Clay*) were then in vogue. No American home was complete without its Ouija board for after-dinner communications with departed spirits. Reincarnation had fascinated DeMille long before he heard about Lord Carnarvon and the mummies' tombs along the Nile. *The Road to Yesterday* begins with the searching question, "Is the past responsible for the present?" Given his situation one wonders what DeMille had in mind. The sins of the past had been a recurring theme in many of his films, but usually these were just elaborate inserts into the modern plot. *The Road to Yesterday* was to be his last word on these topics, and past and present were to have equal importance.

The film was budgeted at close to half a million dollars, which in 1925 was an expensive production. Most of it went into the most spectacular train wreck filmed thus far in Hollywood, and into the recreation of an Elizabethan castle. But with "an ego that was beyond the Rocky Mountains," said Joy, DeMille would do an expensive film without the help of a single established star.

Previous DeMille players Vera Reynolds and Bill Boyd were given the second leads, those of a merry flapper and a God-fearing, Boy Scout-leading man preacher, respectively. For his male lead, DeMille chose one of his studio's new stars a young stage actor, the Viennese-born Joseph Schildkraut, son of the celebrated classical actor Rudolph Schildkraut. Good-looking, slim,

Jetta Goudal starred for DeMille in *The Road to Yesterday* (1925) and two other films he produced, but was unhappy about her compensation and successfully sued his company. This success came at a price and soon she found herself unable to get acting work. Courtesy John Kobal Foundation

of middle height, and glistening dark hair, young Schildkraut had the profile of John Barrymore. But when he sneered, and he did so often, it suggested a bad odor for which the leading lady was responsible.

Opposite Schildkraut was Dutch-born Jetta Goudal; they became instant rivals. When both leads felt the same side of his or her face photographed the best, it became somewhat awkward to shoot romantic scenes with both lovers always looking in the same direction. Rumors of Goudal's temperament began soon after she arrived at the studio. Jeanie Macpherson and Gladys Rosson both took an instant dislike to her. Visiting the set, the New York journalist Mordaunt Hall recalled seeing Goudal on set: "She looked sad and nervous. Mr. DeMille had called her and she was not ready. She was even mumbling to herself, as Mr. DeMille had continued directing the scene, apparently having forgotten that he had issued a call for Miss Goudal. But Miss Goudal did not look as if she would forget in a month."

Miss Goudal was eighty-four and wheelchair-bound when I met her, a delightfully vain old lady with eyes like great smudged saucers who declared, "When I joined DeMille, he found out there was nothing I could not do." She paid tribute to her "dearest, nicest, most wonderful, most brilliant papa DeMille." The regard was mutual, and even after her lawsuit in 1929 against the studio over money, they remained in contact on a social level.

The Road to Yesterday was Goudal's second film for the company. DeMille, always on the search for special effects that would add to the drama on the screen, boasted, "We have been to the Grand Canyon to take the special exteriors for *The Road to Yesterday*, always on the search for special effects that would add to the drama. We never hesitate to go anywhere to obtain the results we want." To this end, he was also experimenting with an early 3-D process.

In the film's climax, the heroine runs away from the inn where she and her new husband have come on their honeymoon, and gets on a train. The entire cast seemed to be on it as well—how they all got there, including her husband, or why, was never made clear. DeMille and Macpherson may have thought no one in the audience would be bothered by the incongruity. The train hurtles into the dark. Another train is racing towards it.

The train wreck was partly based on one of DeMille's own near-fatal experiences when he was touring with Constance. He wanted this scene to be a faithful recreation of the real thing. In the film, the crash happens quickly, and all of it was shot from one same angle, with no slow motion, no stop frame, and no close-ups to build tension. It was filmed in one take and it could only be shot once. Word was out that this would be Hollywood's most spectacular train wreck.

According to biographer Charles Higham, "For the train crash scene, DeMille had an exact replica of his favorite K-4 locomotive engine, eighty feet long, like the one that pulled the old Broadway Limited between New York and Chicago." The scene of the crash was shot at night in the Union Pacific freight yards in downtown Los Angeles. . . . The camera was fixed up at the end of a Pullman and the front of the great engine was seen crashing toward the camera, twisting the steel frame and crushing the seats. DeMille built a special device, which swung the entire carriage around in a circle, hurling the passengers from their seats to the roof of the compartments and finally depositing them on top of a shattered window. He also arranged to build one of the Pullmans in lead instead of steel, so that it would crumple effectively and melt under the force of the fire that swept through the carriage. DeMille told the stars that since nothing could be faked, they would be in the gravest danger during the scene. He told Jetta Goudal: 'When I give a signal, you are simply to fall on the cowcatcher on the front of the engine. If you are a moment late or early you will not only kill yourself, you will endanger the lives of everyone else.'"

Of course, despite all the stories and memories of near casualties, the advance planning that went into setting up this scene virtually guaranteed that no one would be hurt. DeMille couldn't afford to endanger any member of his cast. But it seemed real for those who were on the set that day, as Schildraut commented: "My parents were among the guests who had been invited to watch this spectacular scene. But not until days later was I told about Mother's reaction. When the locomotive started to move, Mother suddenly picked up a heavy stick of wood and hid it behind her back. Father looked at her stupefied. "What are you doing?' he asked her. 'If something happens to Pepi in this scene,' she said quietly, without raising her voice, 'I'll kill that guy.' And she pointed at DeMille.

"I had all the bits and pieces wired so that when I pushed a button, it would all fall apart," remembered Mitchell Leisen, who filmed the scene. "Jetta Goudal was supposed to jump across the wreck, and every time we tried to shoot it, she'd chicken out and not do it, and we'd have to spend the rest of the day piecing it back together again. This went on for I don't know how long until she finally did it."

"It was not a pleasant feeling to sit there and wait for that crash, hoping the engineer would stop in time," Schildkraut remembered. "He did stop at the prearranged spot, but we had not thought of the hot steam escaping from the engine. It scorched my face and hands. In spite of my pain, I did not move, according to the script presumably dead, until DeMille whistled the all clear signal and I could climb out of the car. A physician and nurses rushed to my aid. Fortunately, I had not been hurt badly."

As the train engine smashed into their compartment, sending wood and steel and debris flying in all directions, Jetta, still on the snout of the train, is hit by a falling beam. Everybody passes out—and wakes up in Elizabethan England.

Upstairs in her office in Culver City, screenwriter Beulah Marie Dix sat smoothing out the scenes in which the ruined honeymoon was explained. The story moves to Elizabethan England, where Jetta Goudal is a gypsy in love with Schildkraut, a decadent lord who needs to make a rich marriage to save his stately home. Goudal is the runaway heiress he forces to marry him. Crazed with thwarted love, Goudal's arrival at the wedding feast leads the villagers to believe she is a witch. She is to be burned at the stake.

For the wedding feast, DeMille supplied two whole oxen, seven roast suckling pigs, and twenty-six giant hogsheads of liquor. The 100-foot high castle itself was a stunning piece of work with towering walls, a magnificent winding stairs and a courtyard large enough to contain hundreds of revelers.

To light the set for one hour, it was rumored that more electricity was consumed than what was needed for the streetlights of Los Angeles.

The days leading up to this scene were tense. "For close-ups, Goudal herself was lashed to the stake," recalled Elizabeth Scott, "and a fire lit a little distance off so the smoke would blow across her lovely, anguished face. Just as the close-ups ended, the wind shifted, and the smoke and flame blew, not across, but at the stake. It was several moments of acute discomfort for the star before anybody realized she was still lashed tight."

The reaction of DeMille's friends at a private screening of the film was encouraging. "Ran *The Road to Yesterday* last night before Sam Goldwyn, John and Lionel Barrymore, Harold Lloyd and wife, W. R. Hearst, Elinor Glyn and several others," DeMille wrote to John Flinn. "They pronounced it best picture since *The Ten Commandments* and all wildly enthusiastic over Schildkraut and entire cast." But despite its scenic marvels and spectacular effects, the film was a flop. As its producer as well as the head of the studio, no one could shield DeMille from the public's reaction, which was far more damning than his critics. It had cost nearly half a million to produce, and DeMille barely made it back.

The film's failure did not affect the careers of the two stars. They were re-teamed in *The Forbidden Woman*, Goudal's last film for the company. Over the next two-and-a-half years that she was under contract, if Goudal came to DeMille with her problems once she came to him a hundred times. Meanwhile, DeMille had been investigating other outlets for his work. Paul Iribe, who had moved back to Paris, was looking into the European film scene and reporting on the possibilities of DeMille Productions making a picture a piece in France, England, and Germany during the coming year. In New York, John Flinn sought advice from William Vogel and Nathan Burkan. But Vogel quoted Jean Sapene, head of Pathé in Paris, as saying, "Your sending a company over here to make a French picture would be the same as my organization attempting to send a unit to Los Angeles to make a Western." Iribe's reports were not exciting either, and nothing came of these feelers, though DeMille did not give up hopes of a European production.

The responsibility for success rested on DeMille's shoulders and he realized that he wasn't cut out to both run a studio *and* make his own films. And Macpherson wasn't always there to hold his hand and soothe his creative angst. DeMille had more problems arising from the sharing of profits due from Famous Players-Lasky for *The Ten Commandments*. DeMille to Neil McCarthy (October 1, 1925): "Unquestionably if there is any method of avoiding the payment of this debt Famous will resort to it. There is at present approximately one hundred thousand dollars due us."

The new studio was already in trouble. In his letter of October 9, Flinn was concerned, "put right down on paper, clearly and distinctly, a sound commercial scheme to embrace all of our production, our exploitation and our selling. . . . A director's program is impossible. It has been proved so

by experience that the public is not able to distinguish, with the exception
of yourself and one or two others, perhaps, any general characteristics of a
picture by reason of its direction." Flinn's solution for next year's program
was to fall back on traditional American stories, and to "wrap it up with the
American Flag to a very large extent and give it a distinctive national flavor."
Adding, almost as an afterthought, "keeping in mind at all times the proper
protection for the foreign market."

Before his first year was up, DeMille had offered the presidency of Cecil B.
DeMille Productions to Jesse Lasky. But Lasky preferred staying where he
was, and DeMille had to retain the chief executive position in the hope of
building his company to a point where it could independently finance and
produce its own pictures. He was too far extended to back out. It wasn't a
matter of merely supervising: it was all the time spent on originating projects,
buying properties, dealing with a myriad of details, looking to cut costs, and
finding outside sources of money—a thousand and one things in which he
wasn't really interested. All he really wanted was to make his own films.

For his next film, *The Volga Boatman*, DeMille chose a California location,
even though the story was set in Russia. After the box-office disappointment
of *The Road to Yesterday*, this surprising choice for his next epic was a piece of
romantic tosh played out against the Russian Revolution during the ten days
that shook the world. Sergei Eisenstein, who had dealt with this momentous
change in world events with *Potemkin* the year before, in a film that had a
profound impact on all who saw it, including DeMille, had created a masterpiece of rhythmic, orchestrated urgency. DeMille should have borrowed
more imaginatively, as all he took from *Potemkin* was the water, the lovely
sunsets, and the fine lighting effects, and none of the dynamic editing that
made the Russian director's work an outstanding advance in film technique.
DeMille borrowed even less of the underlying politics. As a staunch capi-
talist all too aware of the threat communism had posed in his country, he
decided not to dwell on current events. Instead, it was a story developed as
a means of bringing two people from opposite backgrounds together—happy
ending, fadeout. Eisenstein's inspiration had been the suffering he had seen
all around him. DeMille's, so he claimed, had been a cut-out sign for a Mazda
lamp he'd seen in a New York window: "It was a picture of a group of people
all with their heads bowed except one, whose face was lifted towards the
light. It reminded me of mankind's long struggle for freedom, led by the few
who dared to raise their heads out of the shadows of oppression . . . the title
of the film came, of course, from the urging Russian song made popular in
those days by the magnificent voice of Chaliapin."

With Macpherson busy on other projects, DeMille had brought in a new
writer, Lenore Coffee. "DeMille then gave me a few sheets of paper and I
said, more overcome than I liked to reveal, 'Let me go back to my office and
read these right now. I read very quickly.' When I went back, it was to say,
'You were quite right—this is only a skeleton, but I have an idea for one

scene which is a must, one which will show that the Bolsheviks and the aristocrats can behave equally badly, once in the saddle. When the Bolsheviks are victorious capturing a palace filled with women in beautiful evening gowns and wearing superb jewels, and the men in court dress with decorations, the Volga boatmen harness these proud people into the ropes which pull the barge, while they watch in triumph from the boat.' Mr. DeMille's eyes gleamed. 'That's all I need to know that you're the person to do this script and develop a story.'"

Coffee also described his unusual working style: "Nobody in the US motion picture business has ever done this before or since. Contrary to what often happens, when the end is being shot first and the beginning last, DeMille shot a film precisely in continuity. This meant that every set had to remain standing until every scene in that set had been filmed and approved. So four or five sets could be standing at the same time. But it was a very good method, for it kept the story fluid; you could go back and redo a scene, or add something to a scene, for the set was always ready. His method of writing was even stranger. He would not start with a finished script. He wanted to keep the script as fluid as the production. You were seldom more than five or six days ahead of him, if that, and you had to be tremendously flexible to work this way. In other words, you'd be writing one sequence watching another being shot, seeing the rushes of another, and discussing still another. It was a little exhausting at the start."

Coffee's memories categorically discount the rumors of the DeMille "casting couch." "Quantities of girls were interviewed and I was often present. First of all the girl's face would fall when she saw that Mr. DeMille was not alone. But despite my presence they made a direct play for him. The more this sort of thing went on, the colder and colder Mr. DeMille became." Julia Faye, never far away, and not one to miss potential rivals for the affections of her boss, also cited instances of DeMille's cool disdain of ambitious actresses willing to trade favors for parts. Success and power had long since replaced the need for casual sex to give him reassurance. When everybody wants you, you are less likely to need what they have to offer.

Prior to casting *The Volga Boatman*, DeMille hired Dan Sayre Groesbeck, who would become one of the key figures in the swelling company. Groesbeck was an itinerant "artist and war correspondent," injured by shrapnel in the Russian Revolution, who had painted a mural that stretched to 6,400 square feet, said to be the world's largest, in the Santa Barbara County Courthouse. DeMille, who had long admired and collected his work, briefly brought him onto the payroll during the making of *The Ten Commandments*. For *The Volga Boatman*, Groesbeck drew sketches of all the main characters, and DeMille selected his cast to match the sketches.

From that point until Groesbeck's death, DeMille would pass his sketches around to other members of staff; he used them to raise financing, and liked to hire actors who looked like the figures in the drawings. It was like having his own Gustave Dore on call, a staff artist who could visualize his dreams. In Groesbeck's sketches, plots came to life; a convoy of chained prisoners heaved a barge up the Volga River; a half-naked girl flashed defiance with her body and surrender with her eyes.

In addition to Groesbeck, someone, possibly the actor and writer Ivan Lebedeff, a former officer in the Czar's army, was hired as a technical expert on *The Volga Boatman*. It was his disillusioning discovery that in movies, when the truth clashed with the look, the truth had to go: "They wanted to put it in the present day and make it a Bolshevist film. But I told them that Volga boatmen haven't existed for over fifty years. They got all the details and all the costumes wrong. And because I really tried to get things right and tried to insist they paid me my money and turned me out." Even so, no one in America had yet made a film about the events leading up to the Russian Revolution, and the next would be more than fifty years later, when Warren Beatty co-wrote, directed, and starred in *Reds*.

For DeMille, the struggle that led to the fall of the Russian Empire was merely a sweeping backdrop for the eternal struggle between man and woman, in this case actress Elinor Fair cast as Vera, an aristocrat, and sturdy Billy Boyd as Feodor, the Volga boatman. The two cross paths while she is out for a drive with her fiancé, Prince Dimitri (played by Victor Varconi). When the revolution is in full swing, Feodor is elected leader of a ragged band of revolutionaries who storm Vera's estate, and she offers her life in trade of her father's. Lenore Coffee's dialogue for Feodor and Vera is sharp and sassy. Feodor points to the watch, which reads five to nine, "Say your prayers, at nine you die." She moves the hands up. "I'm not used to waiting!" He returns her brave challenge: "We have waited five hundred years for liberty, you can wait five minutes for *death*."

With thirty seconds remaining, Vera renews her taunt by tearing her dress and using her lipstick to mark an "X" on her bare shoulder. Thoughts of the class struggle vanish, and he takes her in his arms. The lovers escape pursued by a hail of bullets.

They find refuge in a Red Army inn, but then a battalion of the White Army bursts in. DeMille's handling of the sequence was compared to Lubitsch. Standing on top of a long trestle surrounded by the drunken jeering officers, we never see Vera, not even her feet, as her clothes are taken from her, from her headscarf down to her underpinnings. But the sense of her shame and despair is vividly conveyed in the leering expression on the men's faces as they pass items of her clothing among them, laughing and sniffing them. "That scene caused a little difficulty with some censors," reflected DeMille. "You must not, they said, show the undressing of the princess. But in fact we had not shown it. . . . The scene is focused on the faces of the officers: the princess is not seen at all. But the acting and, if I may modestly say so, the direction must have been so good that some censors apparently thought they had witnessed an actual disrobing."

That evening, safe in a palace, a great ball is in progress, the old nobility dance on the edge of the Red volcano. Feodor is chained on the railings above the Volga. Red Army boats are churning up the river. A cannonball shatters the revels. Chandeliers crash on the revelers. The wounded rush in all directions, their finery torn, their tiaras askew. Vera stays to help build the new Russia with Feodor. Dimitri goes into exile.

With Iribe in Paris, Mitchell Leisen was promoted to art director: "The scene where the mob storms the palace and the roof caves in was very dangerous to stage. I rehearsed the extras all morning, but just to be on the safe side, I decided to put on a Cossack uniform and get right into the scene so I could direct them in case anything unexpected happened. You could talk as much as you wanted during a take of a silent film, and I felt that being right in the scene would give me the best possible vantage point. So C. B. yelled, 'Roll it'; the roof caved in; and all the extras ran around just as they'd been told and nobody got hurt—except me. One of the balsa wood columns fell right on my head and knocked me out cold!"

Locations for *The Volga Boatman* were shot in the Sacramento Valley during a particularly cold and rainy period in early November. Every day for more than two weeks, DeMille's cables to Gladys Rosson consisted of moans about the weather, which delayed shooting, froze his cast of poorly clothed boatmen, and added $7,000 to the budget.

But it was worth it. Cameraman Arthur C. Miller's outdoor locations gave the film an epic feel. Miller was already considered one of Hollywood's top cameramen, and DeMille previously had tried to get him for *The Ten Commandments*. He would go on to win Oscars for his work on films like *How Green Was My Valley* and *The Song of Bernadette*. Working with DeMille, Miller found himself in the middle of creative differences that made him wish he'd never signed on: "Some of the cameramen were using panchromatic film on exteriors, particularly when shooting night shots in the daytime. I, too, had made several tests and had decided to use this film on the night scenes that were to be shot in the daytime. This had the advantage of allowing one to shoot a blue sky with a proper filter and end up with a dark sky, thereby simulating night. To photograph the close-ups with panchromatic required alterations in makeup, so whenever the sky area of the picture could be eliminated or blocked out with brush or trees, it was advisable to use the old orthochromatic film. . . .

"The whole procedure was covered thoroughly with Mr. DeMille before we left the Culver City studio. However, when we started shooting on location, either altering the makeup or reloading the camera with ortho film seemed to annoy him considerably . . . the old man looked down and said, 'I don't understand this; first you want this film, then you want another film. Just what do you want?'

"I looked up at him and I said, 'All I want right now, for Christ's sake, is for you to let me alone so I can get the boat going up the river before the sun drops down into the picture!' Well, nobody ever talked to Mr. DeMille like that, I'm sure.

"After we returned to the studio . . . everybody had more to say about photographing the picture than the person whose job it was. About ten days before the picture was finished, I asked Mr. DeMille to cancel our contract. He then repeated the words, 'I told you there would be no getting out of this contract.' I insisted on being replaced, and in a few days another cameraman took over, my punishment being that the photographic credit for *The Volga Boatman* was split with the man who had replaced me on *The Ten Commandments*, J. Peverell Marley."

There were other problems as well. DeMille had begun to fear that he had another potential flop so he looked to others to blame. "Annie Bauchens had been cutting the film all along," Lenore Coffee recalled, "and then came the fateful night when we were to see the first cut. When I say 'we' I mean only DeMille, Annie, and myself. It was at Mr. DeMille's house, and we sat in complete silence. Only the hum of the projection machine could be heard, and when the film ended neither Annie nor I spoke. Nor did DeMille, for a moment. He got up, and, jingling the gold pieces always in his pocket, he walked up and down the room and then stopped in front of us. 'I don't know what I've got here. I know what I *haven't* got, and that is a road show.'"

In the midst of shooting, DeMille received a nostalgic wire from Lasky which moved him deeply: "They are celebrating the twelfth anniversary of the founding of the Lasky Company tonight and have dedicated the evening to me. I don't feel very good about being put in the limelight and taking a lot of credit that properly belongs to you. You may be sure if I get a chance to talk that I won't forget you and will do my best to pay you the tribute you deserve. I don't know why I am wiring this except that when an occasion of this kind arises I miss your presence more than I can tell you. Best regards always. Jesse."

In April 1926, DeMille attended the glamorous star studded premiere of *The Volga Boatman*. From New York, he wrote Julia Faye about her marvelous notices, "Congratulation to my new baby star. Reception given to your performance from beginning to end of picture would have warmed cockles of your heart. Many pronounced you the best thing in the show. All agreed it was your first big chance and that you took every advantage of it. The feeling of the tremendously professional audience was that a new comedienne had come into the film firmament."

According to a biographer of Paul Robeson, Martin Duberman, the man who had given a Native American actress the first starring role in a major movie was, early in the spring of 1926, contemplating an all-black cast film: "The DeMille motion picture office approached [Robeson] with an offer: 'DeMille wants to do a Negro picture' and wanted him for the lead. Negotiations went forward rapidly, and on April 21 Robeson signed a contract to make a picture for DeMille that summer in California. A week later the deal fell through. DeMille decided he had to shoot the film in New York rather than Hollywood, which meant delaying until that fall—and thereby created an unresolvable conflict with Paul's prior scheduling commitments."

A rather odder communication came to DeMille on the very first day of 1926—from Alice Burwell the wife of his friend Harvey Burwell,

Cecil,

This is a bum New Year's Day for me with Harvey away, but I am making a good resolution. You are supposed to have great understanding. I think this may be true enough to chance telling you how I feel without you making more trouble for me by letting Harvey know that I have written to you. H is far too generous—and much too devoted to you or his own good or for my happiness. The most beautiful things we have found he wants to give to you. If you really know women you may imagine how this makes me jump with joy. He worries more about your business than he does for his own or Danes or mine. This doesn't greatly add to my ecstasy. His only object in living seems to be to find some cure for some damn fault of organization at the studio.

Harvey Burwell was among DeMille's closest friends. He was the young cavalry officer DeMille met in 1917 and taught how to fly a plane. In 1922, during DeMille's visit to Paris, when he thought he would die from "an acute rheumatic fever" attack, it had been Harvey, stationed in Germany, who had flown to him and, "took charge of me like a combination of a mother and a commanding general. . . . When I protested at Harvey's insistence on doing personal service for me that it was bad enough to have let trained nurses do, he said, 'C. B., I'd rather do these things for you than shake hands with a lot of people I know!'"

Harvey's devotion to his boss and friend had repercussions in his home life, which his wife told DeMille about in no uncertain if highly emotional terms. It says something about DeMille's friendship that she would write to him about it. Alice Burwell's letter demonstrates the powerful hold DeMille exercised over his friends and to the extent that they sometimes neglected their families for him. DeMille was sympathetic, but ultimately he left this matter for Harvey and Alice to sort out for themselves,

January 11, 1926:

My dear Alice,

Your rather remarkable epistle, dated January first and mailed on January eighth, has been received. I do not care to be drawn into a controversy of bickering and recrimination; and, as the time that I can devote myself and those who are dear to me is so little that I choose to spend it in ways that are beneficial and helpful to my loved ones, and

friends, and not in the childish wrangles of little minds, I shall endeav-
or to comply with your request and send Harvey back to you without
hurting his feelings.

It was Harvey, however, who provided one of the more profound analyses
of DeMille's character, which put the finger right on the most important
problem facing the new studio proprietor, "With the freedom of the good
friend he was, [he] had written out what he called a 'personnel rating' of me,
analyzing some forty qualities on the basis of percentage points. He gave me
100 percent. Only in 'singleness of purpose,' 'magnetism,' 'mental capacity,'
and emotional intellect,' whatever they may be, but some of his remaining
estimates were as follows; administrative ability, 50 per cent; decision, 40 per
cent; tact, 25 per cent; organization zeal, 0 per cent; analysis of routine, 0 per
cent. Harvey took a rather roundabout mathematical way of saying that I
belonged behind a camera, not an executive desk."

Apparently this exchange neither damaged what DeMille describes in his
book as their "life-long friendship," nor, for whatever reason, did he throw
this "curious epistle" away. Harvey enabled DeMille to reflect and unburden
himself without feeling exposed. It was clearly a caring friendship, one man
talking to another. DeMille needn't feel guilty about his success and revealed
that behind the bluster and the showman, the commander and the prosely-
tizer, there was still the boy who had been a dreamer. And who had found
in Harvey someone with whom to share this feeling, just as he had before
with Lasky.

CHAPTER TWENTY-THREE

IN HIS MEMOIRS, DEMILLE SUMMED UP THE EVENTS THAT WOULD PUT AN end to his short-lived career as a head of studio: "Expansion was the order of the day. I can see now that it was overexpansion; . . . but I was responsible for the Culver City studio. We merged with some other independent studios, under the general management of William Sistrom. We put up new buildings at the DeMille studio. We even put in a radio station so that I could keep in touch with the studio when I was sailing the coastal waters in the SEAWARD: and we also bought two clipper ships, the Bohemia and the Indiana, which were undoubtedly seaworthy when they were launched in 1875, but were probably not very reliable assets after they served their purpose for us in a picture."

These were sensitive times for DeMille, full of secret negotiations for raising money while inflated public statements trumpeted grand plans to impress potential backers. Continuing rumors that his studio was in jeopardy were encouraged by Paramount; at their sales conference in Hollywood, Paramount included in a promotional film a joke at his expense. An outraged DeMille was concerned with the effects this joke would have on perspective investors. Thus, when he heard about it the next day, he blew up and demanded a retraction. A public retraction was made, but not forgotten. Everybody loves a laugh, especially one at the expense of the mighty,

Before settling on the New Testament for his next project, DeMille had been planning another Old Testament project about Noah and the flood called *The Deluge*. But work on it had to be scrapped, and the $24,000 already spent on script and research written off, because Warner Bros. had beaten DeMille to the flood with their announcement that they had a production of *Noah's Ark* in the works.

Back to the New Testament. As he had so successfully done with *The Ten Commandments*, DeMille had Barrett Kiesling organize a nationwide contest at a cost of $4,729.80 to find a popular title for his subject. Macpherson was back at his side to write it.

In an article for a woman's magazine, DeMille talked about Macpherson and her importance to him in his work. He generously gave her credit for

75 percent of all his films. Hopelessly in love, she continued to hope and continued to give her all to him. While the papers were full of his Hollywood activities, dealing with banks and building sets, she knew the real man, and that all he really wanted to do was to go fishing. Her personal ambitions had long since been sacrificed for his. He was her Chief. She was his "skamp." The big idea for his next film was the all-pervading topic on their minds.

At this stage, the "big idea" was centered on Judas Iscariot and Mary Magdalene and adapted from the novel *Thirty Pieces of Silver*. With the lengthy lawsuit over *The Ten Commandments* fresh in all their minds, DeMille had put his legal beagles to work to clear any outstanding rights. The Bible may have been in public domain, but others had written about Judas and the Magdalene. Close to twenty books on the subject were bought, including novels, poems, and plays about Judas and/or Magdalene, including such works as Upton Sinclair's *They Call me Carpenter* and Edward Sheldon's *Christ Came to Chicago*. Eventually DeMille settled on a story of the last days of Jesus, and the title *King of Kings*.

H. B. Warner was cast to play Jesus. At fifty, he was two decades older than the man he portrayed. Born in London in 1876, Warner had been in American films since 1914. He had a long and active career, both before and after *The King of Kings*, though he never again played a role of that size or importance. In fact, though the list of his films is impressive, his later roles were nearly all supporting ones. Warner was nominated for an Oscar for Best Supporting Actor in *Lost Horizon*. Like DeMille, he played himself in *Sunset Blvd.*, and had his last role in *The Ten Commandments* two years before his death in 1958. DeMille thought Warner was the perfect combination of virility and sensitivity, authority and restraint, compassion and strength. What he didn't expect but got was a fifty-year-old man who smoked, drank, and was partial to women. During the film, Warner had to retire to his dressing room whenever he was not needed. He was not supposed to smoke, but to merely wait in a reverential state until his next scene was shot. His agony on the cross may not all have been religiously induced.

Among those considered for the Magdalene was Goldwyn's new discovery, the blonde Hungarian sensation Vilma Banky. Britain's Gertrude Lawrence, the rage of New York in *Oh, Kay!*, was also considered for the part. Seena Owen, the Princess Beloved in *Intolerance*, was personally recommended to DeMille by publisher William Randolph Hearst. He also considered Raquel Meller, the fiery Latin star. But as early as 1925, before DeMille claimed that with this subject he didn't need a star, Gloria Swanson had been approached to play the Magdalene in the original Judas story. He tried again. But Swanson chose playing Sadie Thompson in W. Somerset Maugham's *Rain*, one of her greatest triumphs.

Ultimately, DeMille reduced the list from more than thirty to five, and eventually the part went to Jacqueline Logan, who had had a small role in *Fool's Paradise*. She told DeMille that she didn't want to play Mary Magdalene

DeMille insisted that only H. B. Warner could play Christ in *The King of Kings* (1927). Here Warner appears with the apostles at the Last Supper. Photo: William Mortensen. Courtesy John Kobal Foundation

as a bad woman but as a woman who didn't know the difference between right and wrong, and he accepted this interpretation.

There was no shortage of young women who applied at DeMille's gate. DeMille told Art Arthur how two parts were cast with girls who had continuously pestered him: "The chauffeur found a woman named Viola Louie, who used to pursue me all over the place. She was the woman taken in adultery in. . . . I remember once I picked her up halfway between here and Culver City in one of those drenching rains—the lights of my car picked her up. . . . She had timed this thing and waited in this storm."

Then there was, "a very nice girl—she was very poor and everything, she told me. She intimated that it would be very nice to have a trip somewhere and she'd heard of a big ranch called Paradise, and I said, 'I'll take you there some time . . .' And she said, 'I haven't a thing to wear. I'd need clothes.' So I gave her, I think, $150 or $200 to buy some clothes. That weekend I sailed off in the yacht. I anchored not far from another yacht—Somebody came over and said, 'C. B., we've got a crazy woman over here—when she saw your boat she jumped overboard.' I said, 'What?' He said, 'I don't know, some girl somebody picked up and made a date with to take her on the yacht.'" What must the old hypocrite have thought a young man like Arthur, or anyone else hearing this tale, would make of his "selfless" generosity to a young girl?

In a lecture DeMille gave to the Harvard Business School not long after he finished the film, he spoke on the importance of casting: "The theory of casting a picture is a very important and very subtle one. You have got to make a combination that the public wants to see and that will give you the highest point in artistry for the amount of money expended. The director has to fit his cast accordingly. He has to consider the general frame of the picture, and by frame I mean the atmosphere." DeMille personally selected every individual to be used in the picture. Whether stars or extras, all were handpicked. Even the mob scenes were to be peopled by faces appropriate to the Old Testament. He would stalk down the ranks of extras who reported at noon, and he would say, "You are a foot soldier, you, over there, are a soldier on horseback." And his assistant would note down their telephone numbers.

At the time DeMille was casting *The King of Kings*, the trade press noted an event in the film world which would have far reaching consequences: the premiere of *Don Juan* with the synchronize Vitaphone sound process. The end of an era was near even as DeMille made one of the silent classics. Headlines appeared in the papers: "Talkies . . . talkies are coming." But DeMille, usually so quick to latch onto new ideas to keep his films abreast of the times, did not think to include a sound sequence in any part of *King of Kings*.

In the *Los Angeles Times*, Peverell Marley discussed some of the various problems on shooting this film. Marley was encouraged by DeMille to study hundreds of religious paintings. Speaking to the Harvard Business School, DeMille pointed to "one of the most dangerous pitfalls into which those of us who make motion pictures are apt to fall," "the tendency to think too much of the pictorial angle of our work. In my production . . . it would be very easy to overemphasize the purely pictorial at the expense of drama. The world of art is full of remarkable works of great masters, depicting every phase of the life of Jesus. It would be fascinating to reproduce, in screen life, a series of these famous biblical paintings. But if I did that the appeal would be to the eye alone, not to the heart and mind."

Attesting to the importance of King of Kings in his career, DeMille's kept twenty-one scrapbooks. Stills alone cost an average of $40. Originally budgeted around $4,000, the final cost for prints and photographers was almost $10,000. Four cameramen were employed for the Technicolor sequences, which were shot in eleven days and came to $19,767, not including salaries. Food for the scene depicting the Last Supper, a light meal for thirteen people, came in on budget at a modest $3,450. Paul Iribe, who had designed the massive sets for *The Ten Commandments*, returned from France at $1,000 a week.

Housing, feeding, transporting, as well as tending and insuring the animals, came at a great expense. There were ten animal attendants besides Olga, the Leopard Lady. Peverell Marley claimed that more than 1,500,000 feet of negative was exposed. "More than 300 miles of negative which would reach from Los Angeles to San Diego and back."

Makeup was in the hands of the legendary Westmore family, whose combined salary for the eighteen-and-a-half weeks on *The King of Kings* came to nearly $8,000. George Westmore founded the first movie makeup department in 1917, and at one time or another, a Westmore headed up the makeup departments at Paramount, Universal, Warner Brothers, RKO, 20th Century Fox, Selznick, Eagle-Lion, First National, and a dozen other movie lots.

Adrian designed the clothes for the key characters, and hired two newcomers, Gwen Wakeling and Earl Luick, to assist him with the wardrobe for the thousands of extras: the 100 Roman officers, the various Arabs, Jews, Pharisees, Roman Senators, Roman musicians, Egyptian slaves, the forty Assyrians who filled the screen. The studio also rented hundreds of costumes left over from MGM's *Ben Hur*.

Earl Luick, who was to make his name designing the clothes for 1930s films like *Little Caesar*, *The Public Enemy*, and *Svengali*, soon found that he and Gwen Wakeling were more like glorified dhobis, low-caste Indian washer men, than designers. "We had all the dirty work . . . they would send me shopping for fabrics that looked like they might have been hand woven 2,000 years back. I was told never to bring anything inexpensive because CB wouldn't have ok'ed it. . . . Even at that time it was 20 or 30 dollars a yard, which was a hell of a lot of money. Then we would make these robes out for these people and after that they would dump them in a vat of mud, wash them, got them as clean as they could, and then Gwen and I would sit in the back of the wardrobe, with a couple of big stones, and we would rub them: the hands, the sleeves and the elbows, to wear them out: 30 dollars a yard fabric."

Shooting began with all the Hollywood hoopla only monarchs and dictators could muster. To get the right mood from the outset, prayers were said at the opening day ceremony by Rabbi Magnum; Father Lord, representing the Catholic Church; a Greek Orthodox priest; and a Buddhist monk. Also on hand Mohammedans, Christian Science readers, Episcopalians, and members of the Salvation Army. All of them gave the set their blessings. DeMille wanted to insure that not only the public but God too was on his side.

No single item of the production spawned as many stories as the high moral tone DeMille imposed on the behavior, both on screen and off, of his cast. Actors had not merely to play the parts but behave in a manner worthy of their role models. No drinking, no smoking, and no hint of fornication. "Cast of DeMille Film Sign Unusual Contracts," the press reported. "Cecil B. DeMille is now assured that those interpreting sacred characters in *The King of Kings* shall not appear subsequently in portrayals tending to lessen the strength of their biblical characterizations. H. B. Warner, Dorothy Cumming and several other members of DeMille's cast for this screen story of Jesus have signed agreements to accept no screen roles for the next five years without first obtaining DeMille's consent. This consent will not be granted if he believes the characterization differs from the portrayal in *The King of Kings* sufficiently to shock or offend anyone to whom the biblical character is particularly sacred."

A press release stated that "the studio has orders that anyone guilty of any levity or irreverence concerning the film while on location against the greatest character is to be discharged forthwith. A tone of seriousness is being maintained throughout the organization, and the making of this picture is carried on with the attitude of serious propaganda for religion." From the first day the set was kept in a state of reverence. Given that the film took almost five months to shoot there were bound to be lapses, and the worst offender was H. B. Warner, playing Jesus. DeMille couldn't criticize Christ when he arrived late on the set with a fag in his mouth. Katherine deMille, remembered going to an afternoon swimming party and finding "H. B. Warner was there, and I remember coming home and saying to father, and this sounds terrible, that the Lord was little tipsy this afternoon." Lenore Coffee recalled that, "it was very odd to see Harry Warner garbed as Christ walking towards the set with the morning paper under his arm and sometimes smoking. One day I went out to the set to speak with him, but they had left early for lunch and I was startled to see, on the empty cross, a bicycle seat! Now my common sense should have told me that Harry Warner couldn't hang there suspended by his hands and arms, but a bicycle seat attached to the cross had a strangely obscene look."

There is a story, never proven, but still whispered piecemeal. Lenore Coffee was out on Catalina Island, where they were shooting the scenes of the Sea of Galilee. Suddenly they saw, "an elegant yacht nosing its way into the Sea of Galilee! In one moment, all that wonderful sense of the past was shattered. They all made frantic signals, and one man was sent to row out and ask what they were doing in this harbor, which the island had guaranteed would be kept private for the *King of Kings* company . . . When the man returned he was very embarrassed. 'The yacht is for Mr. Warner, sir.' Mr. DeMille asked where did he think he was going? 'Well, he's not actually going anywhere, just to the yacht. It's to be here every night so that Mr. Warner can sleep on board.'"

Coffee and her husband noticed that H. B. Warner, in full regalia, regularly got into a row boat, manned by a man with a camera, who rowed him over to the yacht. Lenore's husband speculated that Warner had a girl on board and that the reason he went back in costume and makeup was, he thought, that she had a fetish to do it with "the Lord." And they concluded that the man rowing Warner had photographed him, and then contacted DeMille's lawyer to blackmail him. If so, with a $2 million production at stake, Hollywood, six years after almost being wrecked by the Arbuckle scandals, now had the know-how and the clout to effect a cover-up.

A widely circulated picture of D. W. Griffith on the set with DeMille and Jeanie Macpherson came about because Griffith had been conferring about working at the studio. With his idol on the set, DeMille asked him to helm the megaphone for one of the scenes. A few hundred feet of film were shot under Griffith's direction.

The biggest scene in *The King of Kings*, the costliest and most elaborate to set up, was of course the earthquake recorded in the twenty-seventh the chapter of Matthew that took place after Christ died on the Cross. This was to be the "big event," which would rival the chariot race in *Ben Hur* or the opening of the Red Sea. Even before it was shot, Kiesling sent out press reports claiming that it was to equal anything ever seen on the screen. Assisting was DeMille's former designer and teacher Wilfred Buckland: "This reproduction of Golgotha or Calvary is said to be the largest exterior ever photographed within a studio, occupying over 50,000 square feet." "The building of this huge temple required 250 carpenters working three shifts for over a month," reported the *Hollywood News*. "An indication of the size . . . was that in excess of 400,000 board feet of lumber were used in building the frame or 50,000 sq. yds. of lath and a corresponding surplus of tar paper and plaster were used in finishing the reconstruction . . . 10,000 pounds of spikes and 180 kegs of smaller nails held together the set."

The temple sequence was budgeted at $54,050, of which the extras' salaries, excluding lunch, came to $24,003. The gate for this set was later rented out for *King Kong* (1933) for the scene on Skull Island, and when Selznick burned Atlanta for *Gone with the Wind* in 1939, the old temple went up in flames. DeMille announced that even the temple would be dwarfed by the judgment hall of Pontius Pilate, which was still under construction.

Tensions were high. While ever bigger sets were being constructed, not only was DeMille in charge of a staggering budget (at least $50 million by current standards), but the studio was in serious financial difficulties. Earlier that year, DeMille and Pathé had merged and announced a grand slate of over forty films, almost as many as Paramount. This overly ambitious program was way beyond the studio's capabilities or means.

To stave off the inevitable, DeMille even suggested a deal with his old company to take the film over. These were delicate negotiations. DeMille to Neil S. McCarthy (November 8): "Suggest you discuss with Lasky deal whereby they take over and complete *King of Kings* reimbursing present backers for much of their investment and giving me some percentage. Picture will cost something less than one million eight hundred thousand and is certain for minimum of six million gross.

Then, in the midst of the production, DeMille and Iribe had a falling out. The difference between what Iribe conceived and what DeMille wanted was not apparent at first. But, according to Charles Higham, "DeMille grew daily more dissatisfied with his sets, finding them too plain, too severe, too dull. . . . They quarreled again when Iribe proposed shooting the crucifixion scene on a mountain. 'How the hell do you get a storm on cue?' DeMille yelled. The final rift came over the scourging scene. Iribe decided on a set made of rough-hewn stone, and DeMille tossed the designs on the floor. 'Is this your final design?' he snarled. 'Yes,' Iribe replied. 'You're God-damn right it's your final design!' DeMille shouted."

Iribe packed his bag and set sail for Paris. Mitchell Leisen took over the art direction. Of course, Leisen was a filmmaker and Iribe was an artist. Thus, Leisen (at $200 a week to Iribe's $1,000) would go on to become a top director, which Iribe never managed. Leisen saw these things from a filmmaker's point of view.

"The crucifixion was coming up," recalled Leisen, "Iribe had made no plans for that at all . . . I sat down on the floor of the office to see what he left me and there was nothing. So I said, 'I will take over this picture, Mr. DeMille, but if you ever mention Paul Iribe's name again, I'll walk right out.' From that day on, I had the reins. . . "

According to Charles Higham, who does not give his source, "Iribe's cyclorama of a ragged sky with drifting cumulus clouds was not to DeMille's liking, but he did not dare to scrap it; instead, Leisen had instructions to do his very best with it. Leisen arranged ten sixty-inch arcs revolving on wheels, giving an impression, through the shadows cast on the cyclorama, that the clouds were moving. He told DeMille it would cost seventy thousand dollars to build steel rafters to support the lights. DeMille became speechless with rage and sank into a chair. But he finally saw the wisdom of Leisen's choice."

"The worst problem was how we were going to keep Christ on the Cross," added Leisen. "I practically went up the wall for two weeks trying to figure out how to do this. We tried a bicycle seat, and he couldn't stand the pressure, and besides, when he died, he couldn't sag and really collapse. I was about to throw in the sponge. Then, I was having dinner one night and my wife's earring came off. It was one of those screw earrings. I said, 'Oh my God, of course!' I made casts of H. B. Warner's hands, and I molded the blood running down in steel. It had a leather pad at the back of the hand and a nail screwed into the steel and pressed into his palm. When he died, he just collapsed, taking the full weight onto his hands. . . .

"In the final shot on the screen a fissure two miles long opens. 180,000 lbs. of rock and sand and 900,000 feet of lumber, sufficient for a town of 90 five-room houses were the physical requirements for the titanic set in which hundreds of players interpret The Crucifixion; 35,000 amperes of electricity, enough to light a city of 10,000 people, were required to cover the area. It is said to exceed by two to one the largest electrical load ever carried by a film studio. Hundreds of huge spotlights, sunlight area arcs and another illuminants were required 'overhead,' a staff of over 200 men high above the setting on rafters and girders."

Evelyn Scott, who worked as an extra in the earthquake sequence, remembered the crucifixion scene vividly: "A tremendous stage at DeMille studio was transformed into the Place of the Skull. . . . For the final moments of the crucifixion, there would only be one take. This was a breakaway set, when the thunder and lightning rent the sky above Golgotha, rifts were to open in the earth, and stunt men would be swallowed in their depths. Though injuries in stunt work were not common now, there was always risk. Since it would be very hard to put Golgotha back together again after the breakaway, and no one wanted to take extra chances with the stunt men, the action would get shot just once. We gripped the balcony railing edge as the signal came, the sky (a cyclorama under lights) turned dark, the earth heaved, and the actors fell to their knees, cried to heaven or were catapulted into clefts. . . . *Lo, I am with you always (Matthew 28:20)* were the comforting Bible words across a city skyline at the end of the picture when it was released. But they were not there at the shooting of the breakaway, and it seemed to us that we were staring into endless chaos."

Katherine deMille remembered the filming of the crucifixion scene, shot late on Christmas day, in another way: "They shot so late, and everybody wanted to get home and get their Christmas. . . . But it was such a huge set, and he [father] picked up the mike and said to them: 'I wish you'd all stop for a moment, but I want to speak to you briefly. I want you to take five minutes to think about what you have seen here tonight. And I want you to think about your family and whom you're going home to. I'll ask the man on the organ to play something, and you can stay quietly and then go home.' And the hush that came over that huge stage, and people began to weep, people got on their knees, walked up toward the Cross—I remember crying. It was just so beautiful, and then after about five minutes he said: 'Go home now, love your family and enjoy your time together.' And they went off and nobody spoke. And there must have been several hundred. There was a strange feeling on that set . . . it was really powerful and they released these doves, and they circled three times and went straight to the crosses."

All the while the millwheels of publicity never ceased turning, making elaborate arrangements for the costly film's release across the land. The composer Hugo Riesenfeld was hired to prepare a music score. A new man was brought in to handle the publicity in the key cities. Deals were made with Grosset & Dunlap to publish a novelization of the film. John Wenger, who made the special front curtains for *Old Ironsides*, *Sorrows of Satan*, and *Beau Geste*, was commissioned to design a "scenic overture" for the New York presentation: "The wonder curtains which achieve the appearance of beautiful tapestries and suggest the story to follow have created comment in the three picture houses they have been shown."

Before the final cut was made, there were important advance screenings, preceded by a special prologue by DeMille: "You are the first in the world to see this pictorial story of the Christ. It is still in rough form, unfinished. We are placing it in your hands, feeling that you will guide us in making any changes or alterations to increase its value and power when finally offered to the public at large. . . . Yours truly, Cecil B. DeMille." The world, apparently, was full of filmmakers. Everyone had an opinion. The overall reaction was that it was too long. Everyone loved the earthquake, but felt there was too much of Jesus and the little children and lambs. Four Gospels in two and half hours was some going.

At the premiere, Griffith acted as master of ceremonies. It was one of the most elaborate affairs of the decade. Tickets for the opening night were $11 each. Crowds estimated at 100,000 were gathered to watch the stars arrive, slowing their entrance to a crawl. By the time Hugo Riesenfeld raised his baton, most of the audience had been seated for more than an hour.

The overture was followed by speeches from Griffith, DeMille, Will Hays, and Mary Pickford. This was followed by a lavish prologue. After all the heat and struggle to get in, the audience (many of whom had to be on a set early in the morning) went from restless to tired before the film even began at 10:20. According to the less than reverential Hearst columnist Dorothy Herzog, a lot of coughing went on. When the intermission came around midnight, about 98 percent of the audience of producers and players who went out in the foyer looked as if they'd been woken up from their sleep.

DeMille was in agony. He had always preferred an early start while the audience was still fresh and bright-eyed. When the film finally finished, it was after one o'clock in the morning. By then, most of the audience staggered out in total silence, interpreted by the kindly as reverential awe, but, according to Miss Herzog, "it was because they were dead asleep and they were so stunned and tired they could hardly wait to stumble home!"

It was one of the unhappiest nights of DeMille's life.

But the film got very good reviews, and when people saw it on subsequent performances, there was usually a lot of applause at the end. Griffith, who never made public comments on other people's films, cabled DeMille, "I want to congratulate you on your marvelous achievement in producing *The King of King*s. It not only is an exquisitely beautiful production but its value to the motion picture industry as the whole is so enormous that I think it is impossible to calculate." *The King of Kings* ran over six months at Grauman's Chinese Theater, where it was seen by over 600,000 people.

For its New York engagement, ticket prices went up to $2.20. The film was 14,200 feet long, or fourteen reels, and ran two hours and thirty-five minutes. It was one of the longest pictures ever released. But after opening, DeMille's was shocked when he learned the cinema owners lopped off virtually all of the opening episode, which highlighted the affair between Mary Magdalene and Judas. Subsequently in the film neither the character of the Magdalene nor Judas made much sense. As DeMille recounted, a man would betray a king for "a lousy thirty pieces of silver. There must have been a dame in the background."

In the 1930s, when a ninety-minute version with sound was released for use by churches and missionaries around the world, and by which time Bill Boyd had become famous as Hopalong Cassidy, the scene in which Boyd, as Simone of Cyrene, helped Christ carry the Cross, had to be cut, as young members of the audience kept shouting "Hoppy, Hoppy" when he appeared.

Another more fundamental cut came earlier and was on more serious grounds. It involved the image of the Jews. DeMille's hero was a Christian, the first Christian. The villains were the Jews. For a people who don't believe Jesus was the Son of God and resent being blamed for the death of the carpenter's son, it was a 2,000-year-old thorn in the side. Yet DeMille had carefully cast the two key men responsible for Christ's death with two of the best actors he had. Rudolph Schildkraut played Caiaphas, and his son, Joseph, was Judas. In 1957, Ann del Valle reminded Art Arthur, "Schildkraut said that he had not heard one criticism of them taking the roles until after the picture was released. . . . I asked him how he had analyzed the character of Judas. He said that Judas did not betray Christ for the thirty pieces of silver, but that he was a political realist; he believed that when Jesus talked about a kingdom and a king that this was literal. When Judas realized that it was not, he felt betrayed by a dreamer. Unfortunately, by that time, however, it was too late for him to back out because he was a pawn in the hands of the high priests." Such a theory was advanced thinking at the time Schildkraut conceived his role. To the world at large, Judas was a bad Jew who betrayed Christ for petty cash.

To calm a high-powered protest from Jewish religious leaders, when the film came out DeMille made a change in titles to lay the complete blame for Jesus's crucifixion on one person, Caiaphas the High Priest. During the earthquake, the tormented man cries out, "Lord God Jehovah! Visit not Thy wrath on Thy people Israel I alone am guilty." But this act of contrition from one high priest did not soothe the many rabbis across the land. "A rabbi on the West Coast gave a lecture in the synagogue violently attacking the picture as anti-Jewish," DeMille confided to Art Arthur thirty years later. "Others who attacked it tried to close it. They said they would go to every Jewish owner of a theater, which played it. We went through a great deal with this picture. We were crucified over and over for it." It was even suggested that the film could start a pogrom.

In his memoirs, DeMille still sounds sad and still perplexed by the reaction. "It was easy enough to ignore the vociferousness of some tiny but militant atheist societies. What was harder to comprehend and cope with was the organized opposition of certain Jewish groups to this filmed history of the greatest Jew who ever lived." DeMille might have done well to reflect on how his maternal grandparents might have felt if they had lived to see his film. For a practicing Christian, it was noble and respectful. For nonbelievers, it was epic history. But if you were a Jew, you saw yourself and your people accused, as always, of standing by and allowing the Christian God to be killed. DeMille was not prejudiced, but even in his seventies he was still astonishingly naïve. There was no way an Orthodox Jew could approve of this film.

Of course, the irony is not just that DeMille was half-Jewish, but that virtually the whole Hollywood hierarchy who attended the premiere, all the producers, Marcus Loew, Louis B. Mayer, Aldolph Zukor, Harry Cohn, the Warner Brothers, and Carl Laemmle, were Jews. What the outcry did was to raise the shadows of anti-Semitism always lurking under America's skirts.

Amazingly, DeMille was then sued for plagiarizing the idea for the story. His accuser was early screen vamp Valeska Surtt, an actress not completely unknown to him from their early Lasky days. "If ever material was safe from predatory attack," wrote his brother William, "we fondly imagined this to be. But we were mistaken. This lady, it seemed during those intervals when she was not displaying her many charms to eager audiences in the Music Hall, had become deeply interested in the New Testament; so much so, indeed, that she had made her own arrangement of its contents. By some strange co-incidence, her arrangement was exactly the same as that of *The King of Kings*, and the injured arranger brought suit for heavy damages; not, however, until two and one half million dollars had been invested in the film. The suit was not successful, but it did prove the point that even material two thousand years old does not deter the much wronged, unknown author from crying 'Stop thief.'" In his defense of his brother, William was far from fair to the vamp-turned-novelist. As DeMille told his lawyer, Surratt had sent him her version, and had gone to court for her rights before the two million had been spent.

When Surratt's million-dollar suit came to court DeMille, an old hand at defending his claims, cited the Four Apostles as his sole source. Eyes looked to heaven. DeMille hadn't made this film for personal gain. Surratt lost out to the four gospels and to Jeanie Macpherson.

How widely Hollywood's market had spread is illustrated by one scene in *The King of Kings*. At the place where Jesus stoops and writes in the sand with His finger, the words could not be replaced with a single translated title. DeMille had this scene photographed twenty-eight times so that H. B. Warner could write it in twenty-eight different languages, including French, Italian, and German, as well as Arabic and Chinese.

A film made with such care naturally produced souvenirs. DeMille continued to stock his house and ranch with some of the beautiful items from his film sets. The gates of Paradise are the actual iron gates used in Pilate's house.

CHAPTER TWENTY-FOUR

QUIETLY, AND WITHOUT ANY OF THE FUSS TYPICAL OF A DEMILLE PRODUC-tion, the first talking picture, *The Jazz Singer*, was being made. Upon its re-lease in 1927, it stole Hollywood's thunder. Movie miracles defeated religious miracles. The silent era was on its way out.

"In the spring of 1928, I realized that there was possibly going to be some drastic change in the DeMille set-up," said Lenore Coffee. "He was growing much more concerned about the coming of sound than the average producer because of his habit of shooting in strict continuity, and with soundstages this could be expensive, for he would have to decide how many sets he could af-ford to keep standing. And I think the complication of sound made him less interested in being the head of a studio; coping with sound for himself was going to be enough of a problem. It was not long after that that I learned that DeMille was closing down the studio and had made a deal to have his own producing unit at, of all places, MGM, and I was to move over with him!"

Other changes of far-reaching importance were happening in the industry, changes in which DeMille was involved from the outset. While he was in New York for the opening of *King of Kings*, he received a telegram from Doug-las Fairbanks: "You are no doubt familiar with the new organization we are forming called the Academy of Motion Picture Arts and Sciences to include all five branches of production. We are now preparing for a big organization dinner and would appreciate it immensely if you will authorize the use of your name as one of the sponsors." DeMille replied that he was pleased to be included.

That July DeMille's problems did not stop at Gethsemane. The Pathé Stu-dios had a severe fire that caused about a quarter of a million dollars' worth of damage. Rod La Rocque and William K. Howard sued to break their con-tracts for not getting enough billing for the films they made. And Jetta Gou-dal was fussing about her contract too.

DeMille stepped in to salvage *Chicago*, based on a satirical play by Maureen Watkins with a script by Lenore Coffee, which he hoped would make Phyllis Haver one of the studio's top attractions. He shot more than a week's work of scenes featuring his blonde discovery as Roxie Hart, an amoral, wisecracking, gum-chewing Chicago woman who shot her husband and got away with it. It was remade in 1941 with Ginger Rogers, and later served as one of the brightest Broadway musicals of the 1970s. DeMille thought enough of it to keep a record of it in his files, but he left directing credit to Frank Urson.

Even with "talkies" on everyone's lips, DeMille next film was another silent, *The Godless Girl*. Before filming began, a copy of Jennie Macpherson's script about a girl who rejected God was sent to the Hays Office for approval. Controversy would surround this exposé of the brutal, state-condoned treatment of young offenders in reform schools.

Research for the film was extensive. Macpherson had spent time visiting a prison when she worked on scenes for *Manslaughter*, but in that film grim realism had to compete visually with ancient Roman extravagance. Hundreds of photos of underage inmates and their grim circumstances were used by Mitchell Leisen to create the realistic sets. DeMille's files were bulging with articles on penal conditions and sworn statements from former inmates that made for sad reading. "Many forms of punishment abandoned by the military organization in civilized countries years ago [are still] in use in several reformatories," wrote an outraged Barrett Kiesling. "Everything shown in this production is taken from an actual case." To give the film some much-needed romance, the plot provided a boys' reform school nearby.

More than a hundred young actors were needed to fill DeMille's prison. An epic search across the forty-eight states was undertaken to find the perfect girl to star as *The Godless Girl*. Lina Basquette, DeMille's choice, recalled her first meeting with him: "Artie Jacobson, who had become a good friend of mine, said, 'Lina, don't make the mistake of a lot of the actresses who have gone all dressed up . . . it's a sixteen-year-old high school girl, so dress down, no makeup, let DeMille see your schoolgirl complexion. And, very important don't let him think that you're afraid of him!' So I took his advice and I went to DeMille in a little navy blue skirt and a white blouse, and dressed up my hair loose and very little makeup, and of course I was then about twenty-one but looked about sixteen."

Lina jumped on one of the large oriental throw rugs scattered across the floor and propelled herself along the slippery floor . . . DeMille asked her, "Young woman, I suppose you never pass a banister without sliding down it?"

"'That's right, Mr. DeMille. How' ja guess it?' I was kind of fresh. I was kind of impudent and fresh with him which he was not accustomed to and which amused him, I think, and besides that's what he wanted in this girl. . . . And then he wanted to see whether I had a separation, he had a thing about women's thighs and a separation. Of course, I had magnificent legs, when I was with Ziegfeld they were the world's most beautiful dancing legs. So, obviously DeMille wanted me to pull my skirt all the way up to see if I had a separation and looked at him and I said, 'Mr. DeMille, I can get an affidavit from Mr. Ziegfeld that I have beautiful legs and no separation of the thighs.' There was a change of lights evidently worked from push buttons at his side.

I stood with arms and legs slightly akimbo. . . . This is ridiculous. . . . I hadn't been lighted by experts on the Broadway stage without knowing what those lights were accomplishing. This DeMille contrivance was arranged to back-light a figure, making it possible to see through a skirt as when one stands against strong sunlight." Ultimately, Basquette was signed and became *The Godless Girl*.

At one time, the great Pavlova encouraged her to become a ballerina. At sixteen, she was a featured dancer in the Follies. In 1925, she met and married the first of her six husbands, the much older but devoted Sam Warner. Warner saved his family's ailing film studio by investing in Vitagraph, the revolutionary sound on disk, but died before he could see the financial rewards with *The Jazz Singer*. Before he died, Warner had made his wife heir to his share in a large family trust. With the success of *The Jazz Singer*, Lina's share was worth a fortune. Warner's family loathed this devil-may-care interloper. When he died, Basquette was in the middle of a film. The press reported that the widow was "back on the set the next day dancing because she felt her husband would be happy to know production hadn't been held up." (Because they didn't explain that the scene required her to dance, they made her sound callous and carefree, but it was in the mood of the roaring twenties.) A lawsuit instigated by Basquette's in-laws over her shares ended with her losing custody of her daughter. *The Godless Girl* was the most important film role in her career, but even before it was finished she found that, due to the surviving Warner brothers influence, she had been blacklisted in Hollywood.

DeMille's daughter and her former swain, the young Joel McCrea, also had small roles. Cecilia was attractive and had a normal interest in horses and men but, although she had appeared in several of her father's films, she apparently showed no desire for a movie career, perhaps because she was raised to be her father's heir. McCrea's chance with DeMille was coming soon.

A *New York Sun* reporter visiting the set elaborately designed by Leisen noted that "the sets were startlingly, grimly realistic: a high, electrically wired fence separated the boys' from the girls' quarters, a guard stood at attention in a tower, holding a rifle, even when not required in a shot, and a 'mud horse' was operated for several days. This was a handbarrow, which the boys in the prison filled with rocks, then refilled every time the rocks were dumped. DeMille showed that stocks were still being used in America, that children were fastened together in squads with iron rings, and locked to their beds at night."

As usual, Peverell Marley worked with great ingenuity. To give the film a documentary feel, he shot it entirely with one camera. "Peverell Marley . . . has accomplished some trick photography which is causing much comment," the *Sun* reporter wrote. "The first represents a riot in a four story building in which the participants battle up and down a staircase. In order to obviate the necessity of a dozen cameras to film, various parts of the riot in close action, medium distance and long shot, Marley arranged for a movable camera carriage, able to be elevated to the top floor or lowered to the first, or to be moved forward or backward at any moment. Marley is credited with an even more interesting shot in this same sequence in which the camera drops from the fourth floor to the first with terrific speed, giving the sensation of a sickening fall. Marley was strapped in a swing seat with the camera in his lap with DeMille in another narrow seat above him. The camera was then started and the swing dropped through the well of a staircase." The effect was original and dizzying.

A group of women specialists in penal reform arrived during shooting to be greeted by the extraordinary sight of DeMille, immaculate in gray, directing Lina Basquette in a scene in which she was cleaning out an extremely filthy trough surrounded by forty squealing pigs. Asked by a reporter from Boston what she was playing, Basquette, dripping ordure from her blue homespun, pulled a battered black felt hat over her eyes to protect them from the sun and said, "I am the Joan of Arc of atheism."

Meanwhile, a romance between Basquette and cameraman Pev Marley was quickly progressing, and caused a confrontation when DeMille threatened to transfer Marley to another project. Constance deMille, who was also present at the time, was on the side of the lovers and eventually changed her husband's mind.

Still, there were ways DeMille could exact a little revenge. Lina Basquette: "That afternoon a scene was shot where Jason and Judy are trapped in a corner by the flames. The fire was chemically treated and its volume controlled by a special, experienced crew. Our clothes, hair, and exposed flesh were smeared with an asbestos coating that fireproofed us against actual burning (so 'twas claimed) but, in any event the heat was unbearable. Photographing the scene through a telephoto lens, DeMille, the cameras and crew were well out of range from the high intensity of the heat. Bellowing through his megaphone, C. B. ordered more flames.

"George Duryea had already fled the scene and then I heard DeMille shout, 'Stay where you are, Judy!' I kept cowering in the corner, improvising new action now that my hero had left me to a fate worse than DeMille's ire. The cameras kept rolling on and on. A leaping flame struck out at my face. Hot damn! I screamed but stayed glued to my acting post. 'Good girl! Great! My Judy! Shoot another gust of fire at her! Yell, Judy! Throw your arms up over your head. Great scene! More flames! That's what I call a *trouper*! What a girl! My Judy! She has *guts*!'

"'Okay! *Okay*! Take away the fire! Cut! *Cut*!'

"I staggered to my feet, took one step and collapsed as a prop man threw a wet blanket over my steaming body. On closer examination, it was discovered that my eyebrows and eyelashes had been singed and blisters had popped up on my forearms."

The Los Angeles premiere was a 1929 Hollywood highlight. To drum up business, an advertisement was placed during the film's second week quoting a letter from the Devil's Angels Branch of the American Association for the Advancement of Atheism, asking if DeMille should question the rights of others to believe or not to believe as they wished.

Another protest came from the members of the Sections of the Juvenile and Adult Protective and Correctional Agencies of the Welfare Council of the City of New York, protesting that the film's portrayal of their institutions "is contrary to the present methods in the reformatories and training schools in this country, and tends to inflame the citizenry against such public institutions and ridicule the officials of such institutions in the eyes of the public."

But the film only did modest business. During that first official year of sound, few "silent" films did well. Ironically, the film turned out to be a huge hit in Russia, though DeMille was only to discover that when he traveled there in 1931.

To DeMille's consternation, throughout the production of his last two films, the lowly Pathé had been gaining more and more influence. From the date of Pathé's merger with the Keith Circuit, on March 10, 1927, everything began to fall apart between DeMille and his studio.

In New York, McCarthy had desperately tried to ameliorate the situation on DeMille's behalf, but now DeMille's worst fears were confirmed. "When banks came into pictures, trouble came in with them," DeMille claimed later. "When we operated on picture money, there was joy in the industry; when we operated on Wall Street money, there was grief in the industry." And he was in the hands of the bankers.

Only the enormous prestige of *King of Kings* had postponed the inevitable, and when Joseph P. Kennedy (who, DeMille felt, despite all their official and unofficial bonhomie, was not in harmony with him) took over as head of the merged studio that was now called RKO, DeMille decided he had to get out.

Although the "amicable" split did not occur for several more months, there was another press item less than a month later which appeared while DeMille was shooting the reformatory fire stating that he had signed with MGM and sold his interest in Pathé. Contract artists were loaned out and various agreements canceled. DeMille was also concerned that some press reports appeared to lay the blame at his door.

DeMille calculated that he was owed $203,000 and offered to settle the remainder of the contract for a further $250,000. As he had threatened to do with *The Ten Commandments* and on *King of Kings*, he again offered to buy back his rights to his film: "If the Company is not able to pay to me the amount which we agree upon in cash, I would be willing to take *The Godless Girl* at its cost price and pay to them the difference." DeMille was no longer running a studio. In his memoirs, he closed the door on this aborted phase in his career: "My chosen work, directing, was suffering both from restrictive outside control and from the mass of administrative detail involved in my being head of a studio. When Joseph P. Kennedy brought his strength to the Pathé organization, I decided ultimately that it would be better for DeMille Productions to sell its Pathé stock, at a very handsome profit, and for me to form another connection free at least from the uncongenial burden of studio administration."

That August, DeMille and his staff were on the move again. MGM not only gave him lavish space, but they paid for Leisen to design the interior of a spacious and attractive bungalow for the DeMille unit.

Following DeMille's departure, Murdock and the bosses at Pathé (now RKO) decided that talkie sequences should be incorporated into *The Godless Girl* to help it at the box office. DeMille was not available, so these were directed by the actor Fritz Feld, best known from talkies for his amusing character roles and for the popping sound of a champagne cork, which he made by bouncing the flat of his hand off his mouth.

CHAPTER TWENTY-FIVE

IN AUGUST 1928, DEMILLE SIGNED AN AGREEMENT WITH HIS OIL BUSINESS associate Louis B. Mayer to make three films at MGM. In the four short years since Metro Pictures bought out Sam Goldwyn (and added Mayer's studio and name), MGM had grown to become the largest, starriest, and most successful of all the studios, first rivaling and then eclipsing Paramount. MGM had stature, money, and glamor. It was perfect for DeMille. It also had high-powered executives whom he did not know, nor had to consider.

Of course, DeMille took most of his personal staff with him, including Jeanie Macpherson (although their intimate relationship was waning), Julia Faye, who worked as a researcher when she was not acting, and Gladys Rosson. On the creative side, there were Mitchell Leisen and Adrian, who would stay behind at MGM when DeMille moved on. DeMille brought the people without whom he could not manage, and who couldn't be laid off between films the way his cameramen or designers could. It was while at MGM that he needed additional secretarial assistance and Florence Cole joined his studio office staff.

DeMille claimed that the idea for *Dynamite* came from a news item, "telling of a prisoner under sentence of death, who was married a few days before his execution." DeMille was exaggerating a bit when he said this, since the items that had given him the idea for a film were about a twenty-year-old girl who married her sweetheart a few minutes before he began to serve a ten-year prison term for robbery, and another about a soprano, Madame Povlaska, who agreed to pay $45 weekly alimony to the wife of the man she was going to marry.

For this film, DeMille could not ignore sound any longer: "I started looking round at what the talkies were doing, then making photographs of stage plays. They were a novelty, but they weren't movies. So I decided I would go back to my old movie formula. I would make a DeM movie and add dialogue to it. That's what *Dynamite* will be, I hope. It has action, and suspense, and glamor and bathtubs. Incidentally, it has sound." It is ironic in view of all that was to happen later between DeMille and the unions that one of the writers for his first talkie, John Howard Lawson, would later emerge as one

Preparing for his first sound film, *Dynamite* (1929), DeMille is shown with dress designer Adrian (right) and French couturier Paul Poiret at center. Photo: Clarence Sinclair Bull. Courtesy John Kobal Foundation

of the key figures of the Hollywood Ten. DeMille had seen *Processional,* Lawson's stage play of 1925, and wanted the writer to model the character of the miner in *Dynamite* on Dynamite Jim, the leading character in the earlier play. Still, Macpherson was given story credit for *Dynamite,* which so infuriated Lawson that he protested to and received an apology but only minor satisfaction of a dialogue credit.

DeMille had become famous for his bathtubs; the tub featured in *Dynamite* was his sixth. So striking had been his previous use of indoor plumbing that by 1929 a character in one of his films couldn't turn a tap on without unleashing a flood of press comment.

In *Dynamite,* a spoiled young woman is in love with her "best" friend's husband. In an audacious scene, the two women barter over him. The heiress offers $50,000, but the wife wants $200,000. They settle for $150,000, one third down and the rest on delivery! At a time when divorce was frowned upon, this attitude was remarkable. The problem: the heiress won't come into her money until she's either married or has reached her twenty-third birthday, and the wife won't grant the divorce until she's shown the money. Ill-disposed to wait, the heiress reads about a man on death row. In return for marrying her, she offers him $10,000.

In a neighboring cell, another inmate with a guitar sings the film's popular title tune. Prison governors across the country were questioned to find one who might corroborate the "facts" presented. All agreed that a prisoner on death row would not be permitted to have a musical instrument of any kind. But the need for a song on the sound-track overrode veracity. The mournful ballad, "How Are We to Know?," sung by the pop idol Russ Colombo in his film debut, featured lyrics by Dorothy Parker.

Charles Bickford, cast as the prisoner, was a curly haired, no-nonsense Irishman and a new face on the screen. He would have a long career in movies. Although he and DeMille fought a lot, he appeared in many DeMille films over the next decade. Bickford wrote about this somewhat stormy relationship in his autobiography *Bulls, Balls, Bicycles and Actors*. "After an exchange of amenities, he invited me to an open house Christmas party which was in progress at his office on the MGM lot. . . . The party . . . was merry, but decorous. . . . a sturdily built, sun-bronzed man came toward me with his hand extended in greeting and although I had never met DeMille, nor seen a picture of him, I knew that this must be he. The pongee sports shirt, well-tailored riding breeches, leather puttees and Napoleonic stride seemed to proclaim the fact that here was the director to end all directors. 'My God.' I thought. 'It's an American Benito Mussolini.'" But if Bickford thought the town was dull, he quickly found that they had ways to enliven things as he returned to his hotel with the "one drunk" at the party, an angel-faced blonde "possessed of a gutter vocabulary that would be taboo in any well-regulated whorehouse." Apparently she was the girlfriend of MGM producer Irving Thalberg.

Bickford also gives a slightly scurrilous account of a New Year's visit to Paradise in honor of his birthday. DeMille asked his preference in women. Bickford was nonplussed. He detected a masculine challenge to prove that he wasn't another Hollywood "fairy." DeMille, as per Bickford's joking request, provided three girls, one blonde, one brunette and one redhead, all wearing a small blue ribbon on which was emblazoned in gold the letters, C. B. After a bit of jostling for supremacy, during which Bickford deliberately acted like a Queen of the May to DeMille's growing discomfort and the girls' puzzlement, Bickford revealed himself as an all-American male by asking who DeMille had lined up for him the next night. "I think that if we had really been kindred spirits, this moment would have given birth to a life-long friendship. His relief at finding me normal opened him up like a flower, and for the rest of the trip he treated me like a long lost son. He subsequently told me that up to the time I tipped the gag, he had been planning ways and means to cancel my contract."

For the female lead the polished, caring, elegant Kay Johnson was a bit too ladylike to play the spoiled and flighty heiress. "For the first time a DeMille heroine wears her elaborate costumes unobtrusively," wrote the columnist Myrtle Gebhard after visiting the set. "It takes a personality not to be dwarfed by his sumptuous ensembles." The object of her affections was a DeMille old-timer, Conrad Nagel, an expert at playing the dull sort of social smoothie who rich women (in movies) were supposed to find attractive. Because of his fine diction, Nagel was incredibly busy in the first years of sound. As soon as the mechanical problems had been solved, however, his starring career was over. The cheerfully calculating wife was played by Julia Faye, who looked more than ever like a little brown wren fallen among peacocks.

Originally the role that went to Faye had been intended for Russ Co-lombo's girlfriend, a promising twenty-year-old blonde appearing in Sennett films, Carole Lombard. She was signed at $150 a week, to rise to $200 on start of filming, but was replaced after DeMille had conducted a screening test and decided she wouldn't do. Seven years later, when DeMille wanted her for Calamity Jane in the *Plainsman*, Lombard, now one of Hollywood's most popular players, was unavailable.

Joel McCrea, a school friend of Cecilia, got his break and fifth billing as Marco the "Sheik": "I'd heard DeMille . . . was going to make his first talkie, so I went to his office. . . . So 12:00 came and he comes striding out. . . . He said, 'When did I first meet you?' I said, 'When I first delivered papers, before I knew Cecilia. When it rained, I'd throw your paper up on the porch. And at Christmas you gave me a silver dollar.' He said, 'Have you still got it?' I said, 'Yes.' He said, 'Come on in.'"

DeMille's explanation of the plot of *Dynamite* was elliptical at best: "She [the girl in story] had made all the arrangements—she would come into the money—marry this guy six months later, the man she was in love with. And Bickford is a widower with this kid, but she wants to marry Conrad Nagel who is her class. . . . Then you have a brawl in a Night Club and a guy gets killed and he confesses to the murder this fellow's up for and he's dying and Bickford is set free. So he comes down; the first place he goes is down to see this girl to tell her he'll give her a divorce. And he arrives while a big party is on. . . . And he comes into this place and she reacts first in amazement that he's out. Then she thinks he's come to blackmail her, and he sees this, and finally he throws everybody out, when he realizes this, and he takes the girl by the hand and takes her upstairs. Then he leaves her and there's a wonderful scene afterwards. She comes in saying, 'You God damned such and such, son of a bitch . . .' and he says, 'Don't worry. You won't see me anymore. I don't want anything from you. You're not even good enough for that.'"

Bickford was taken aback to discover that DeMille intended to read the whole script. "The story began to emerge as a mishmash of contrived situations, peopled with unreal characters and weighted down with dialogue so naïve as to be ridiculous." He claims he fell asleep and was woken by DeMille and the assistant director. At the end of the reading three hours later—"the script may not have been a good one but no one could say it wasn't a thick one"—the assembled company was invited to contribute suggestions. Bickford offered criticism of the dialogue, saying, "I dismissed the incident as of little account, but distorted versions of the story soon began to reverberate from the Hollywood hills. Charlie Bickford had said 'no' to Cecil B. DeMille. A myth was spawned."

Elizabeth "Bessie" McGaffey, who started as one of DeMille's secretaries but was quickly promoted to chief researcher, had to come up with a prison in Pennsylvania close enough to the heroine's home for the purpose of plot. "Could we change the locale to New York?" she mused, since there the prisons were in the heart of the city. But where were the coal mines to be? McGaffey's office by now was crowded with books on every subject, to be consulted in answer to her boss's endless and often intemperate questions. "What do you mean women aren't allowed to marry in prison? Find one where they can!" At Sing Sing prison, she found a warden who allowed it. "In fact, in one instance here, a woman married a condemned prisoner within five minutes prior to his death, thereby becoming wife and a widow in a very short period of time." She made more discoveries,

Dear Jeanie, Bumped into a most peculiar and important question yesterday. *When a criminal is sentenced to the penitentiary he loses his civil rights and cannot make a contract.* In this state he could not legally marry. I went to Neil McCarthy and put the question to him and he thinks that a man *condemned to death* does not lose his civil rights, as he would if condemned to imprisonment. Mr. McCarthy is looking it up for the State of Pennsylvania and if their law is against our story, he will look up the statues [*sic*] of the other coal states—Colorado, Illinois, etc. You see that if our hero could not legally marry our whole major premise falls flat.

Imagine the "widow's" surprise the next day to discover she's still a bride. Her husband-of-convenience has not merely been reprieved but released by the Governor. To prove her their marriage was legal, the heiress has to follow her husband to the dreary little coalmine town where he works as a mining engineer. In the climax she goes down the mine with her lover, only to find them all trapped and narrowly rescued from disaster for a happy ending.

Mitchell Leisen, who'd designed DeMille's glamorous and modern office on the MGM lot, was busy researching the disaster. "Miners at work. Runaway coal car bumps into something breaking electric wires whose sparks cause explosion of coal dust and cave in. Leading characters cut off and in danger from deadly gas. Hero has no fuse so explode dynamite with sledge hammer and breaks through a bulkhead or a stopping into cross entry where air is pure thus saving lives of girl and lover."

DeMille clearly enjoyed making *Dynamite*, even though he was working under the pressure of producing a hit. The mood of the film is set in the first scene, a risky but fun aero wheel sequence. Inside huge wheels, girls rode across the spacious lawn.

DeMille is pictured with the stars of *Dynamite* (1929), Kay Johnson and Julia Faye, seen here in "aero wheels," the rolling contraptions featured in the film. Courtesy John Kobal Foundation

There were all kinds of unexpected problems during the shooting. Two versions were shot, one silent and one sound. Kay Johnson, absolutely at ease in the sound version, became terrified in the silent version, hated to play dumb, and in a kitchen scene dropped a whole box of eggs on the floor. Later, she was stricken with appendicitis and had to be rushed to a hospital, slowing up production for days. She also wrenched a knee during an automobile race scene and for much of the rest of the shooting DeMille had to "borrow" Faye's legs for Johnson's close-ups. DeMille, showing Johnson how to attack Bickford with a perfume bottle, inadvertently hit him over the head with a prop bottle and knocked him out. DeMille gave Bickford and Johnson twenty-dollar gold pieces from his pocket, saying impressively, "Those are DeMille medals. They are only awarded for what I consider magnificent performances."

DeMille's use of sound, above and beyond such devices as songs in unlikely places, is continuously inventive. Daringly (if unpardonably) he added a guitar accompaniment, and the sound of the hammering of the gallows being erected nearby, using two soundtracks in defiance of soundmen's instructions. But after first fearing the new medium, he had become excited by the possibilities of the soundtrack, and became one of the first directors to break free from the dictates of sound experts.

Conrad Nagel later recalled shooting the noisy mine disaster in *Dynamite*: "The climactic scene was a huge explosion in a mine in which Charlie Bickford, Kay Johnson, and I are trapped. There's only one way to get out. . . . We find some dynamite, and we've got air for just so many hours. The dynamite has no caps to set it off; we have a big sledge hammer instead. Now which one of us is going to swing the sledge? It winds up that I do the deed. But there were a lot of technical problems. How to simulate the proper sound effects of the explosion rumbling and roaring. Cecil DeMille, from his old stage days, remembered that when you wanted a roar of great thunder, you had a big trough built back stage and you rolled cannonballs down it. So they built one, and it was perfect. We got the roar of the mine exploding."

"Working with that crude sound equipment was murder," remembered Mitchell Leisen. "There was no way you could dub in any sounds later; all the sound effects had to be recorded during the take. The cave-in the coal mine was tremendously difficult to rig up. Nothing could touch the mikes or they'd go out and we wouldn't have any sound. I set it all up so that the mikes were concealed and papier-mache rocks would fall, and sound effects men banged things next to the mikes to make more noise. I made vents and put big pieces of cardboard covered with coal dust behind them and on a cue, the prop man was supposed to turn a fan onto the dust and blow it in so it would look like the dust was rising from the impact of the boulders on the ground. I gave the cue and the rocks crashed, but when I cued the prop man, he turned his fan in the wrong direction and he blew the dust right into DeMille's face instead of onto the set."

Before the sound system was improved, one of the big problems was in re-dubbing the noisy crowd scenes. When the foreground action was photographed, the masses in the background were so noisy that the dialogue in the foreground was inaudible. DeMille spent between ten days and two weeks in on the dubbing stage.

Dynamite had lots of potential for exploitation: sound, a hit song, coal miner's grime, art deco bathtubs, and dynamite! In fact, everything but Bessie Love and Karl Dane chewing tobacco. The reviews were incredulous but positive, as this one by Dan Thomas: "Cecil DeMille should throw any scripts he has for future religious films into the waste basket, and devote his time to directing pictures depicting present day life . . . it brings DeMille back to the type of film to which he is best suited, modern, contemporary, jazzy."

It was a huge hit everywhere, but it ran into problems in England, not for its length but for its content. The British distributor, sounding more like a small-town censor, took a high moral tone: "The idea of a girl bargaining to pay a large sum of money to a young married woman so that the latter shall divorce her husband, so that the former may marry him, is so opposed to the accepted standard of morality in this country as to be, in our opinion, prohibitive, while the accompanying dialogue is most unacceptable. We therefore think that this film, as presented, is unsuitable for exhibition in this country. . . . Meanwhile, we cannot show the picture at the Empire [Leicester Square] or sell it for general release."

While DeMille was in the midst of shooting his mining disaster, Jetta Goudal's long pending case against Pathé-DeMille came to trial. DeMille's lawyers tried to make out that the problem had been "her temperament." Goudal's claim was for money she was owed on her contract; she was due for a raise which DeMille, because Pathé had by then been running into financial difficulties, wanted to withhold. When Goudal got her first check under the new agreement, it was without the increase. Tenaciously defending her rights, she now found that she had a reputation as a temperamental actress who had cost the studio money. Goudal, as DeMille should have known, was a fighter. And the newly arrived Actors' Union was on her side.

The trial was held in DeMille's bungalow so he wouldn't have far to get back to the set. DeMille implied that Goudal herself was responsible for delays and additional expenditure on costumes resulting in her films running over budget. She demanded to see the books. "So, Mr. DeMille said, 'Well, I don't have those books anymore.' And the judge said he must have them there by 9 the next morning. But DeMille couldn't get them there before 12. And I wish to God someone could have a picture of Mr. Gilbert looking at those books. He looked up at me and said, 'Did you know this?' I said, 'Did I know what?' He said, 'Did you know this last picture they're talking about ran *below* estimate?' So then the books went to the judge. And the judge said, 'Mr. DeMille, I'll give you one minute to withdraw what you said yesterday due to your age and your white hair.' And Mr. DeMille said, 'Well, I guess I'd better withdraw it.'"

After Goudal had won, a new rule was passed which became known as "the Goudal law." Not surprisingly, she now found it virtually impossible to get work. As her counsel had told her before they began the case, though he was 95 percent sure of winning: "Don't forget, if you win you lose." "I said, 'What kind of English is that?' He said, 'Yes, if you win, all the producers will keep hands off. You won't get another company. You can sue a producer, but because the producer thinks he's so much stronger you can't win. Because if you win, they will say, so she won nobody will use you.' And I didn't get any work for a long time."

Goudal's personal relationship with DeMille's family remained unaffected. The following February, she and her husband were among the few "film" guests at the house for Cecilia's marriage to Frank Calvin.

Late in 1929, as the president of the Producers Association, DeMille was due to address the Academy of Motion Picture Arts and Sciences. He planned this important speech, "What is Motion Picture Direction?," carefully.

It was a masterful speech, widely quoted for years thereafter. DeMille touched on everything a director must know and what he must do just when, where, and "how to insert various artistic values into that mosaic which is a completed motion picture. And, last but far from least, the director must be a very practical businessman." He spoke of the current problems dominating the thoughts of the industry: "When the talkie came it brought an immediate problem of adjustment. Should this new thing cleave to its father, the screen, or its mother, the stage? The first impulse was in favor of the mother. For a period we had nothing but photographed stage plays; stage plays reproduced on the screen exactly as they had been done in the theater. These were not right, of course, for they lost the great asset of motion pictures: the asset of fluidity and swiftness of motion. . . . Now we are coming to a period of more exact adjustment. A technique is developing which joins the fluidity of the screen to the laws which rule dialogue. And now we are beginning to have 'talking motion pictures,' as opposed to photographed stage plays."

He spoke of the vital importance of the photographer, the director's most important collaborator. He talked about casting, and saw his role in terms of a conductor, who controls but does not teach his musicians, the actors, how to play their instruments. And he concluded, "In the last analysis, whether we are discussing silent or talking pictures, we must keep it clearly in mind that the major function of a director is that of a storyteller. He must be a master of all the crafts, which underlay this art, and he must be familiar with all the arts, which unite in the making of a motion picture. . . . He may not have conceived the story first, but he has to make it a part of himself before he can put it on the screen; he may not have written it, but it is he who tells it; and upon the force, the clearness, and the art of his telling depends on the value of the work." It was a complete statement of how he worked, and applies equally well today.

CHAPTER TWENTY-SIX

IN SEPTEMBER 1929, THE PRESIDENT OF HOLLYWOOD'S CENTRAL CASTING Bureau and senior vice president of the Association of Motion Picture Producers (AMPP), Fred Beetson, received an unsigned letter from a highly placed undercover agent, telling him in so many words to "hire me or get off the pot."

Dear Mr. B.,

The Producers are going to be sorry if they let this opportunity slip by. If the present program outlined in enclosed report goes through it is going to cost the Producers more than a million dollars, even if they never have a strike, in extra money that they are going to be compelled to pay.

I am sure that Buzzell can be blocked and that I can do it if allowed to attend the National Convention and finish the work that I have started. . . . Without someone there to work against him Buzz Zell will get everything he wants, as he is a slick politician and a clever labor leader. . . .

I have actually stopped two strikes and one boycott. I started to work ten years ago right in the middle of a strike and had the unions all fighting each other over jurisdiction within three weeks and had charge of all the union funds used for strike purposes. I put over a motion which almost doubled the strike benefits which made me strong with the rank and file and at the same time depleted their treasury so they had to call the strike off.

The president rushed this letter to DeMille, then on his second term as the president of the Motion Picture Academy. What had DeMille to do with this? Why would he give the order to hire such a person? In DeMille's autobiography, there was no reference to these events. Instead, this anodyne summing up his time with MGM: "My three years at MGM were not particularly happy ones, except for the persistent loyalty of those who went there with me or who joined me there and were ready to go with me wherever the next move might lead."

By implication, he meant that two out of the three films he made for the studio had been flops, that the Depression had made a great dent in his personal fortune, that the new addition to his staff of loyal Valkyries was devoted secretary Florence Cole, and that on the termination of his contract he had no future prospects. What he does not mention in this brief chapter, even in passing, is anything relating to the severe disruptions created by labors' drive to unionize Los Angeles, and Equity's struggle to gain recognition from the Hollywood studios, or to his own, significant, never before revealed role in the forthcoming battle.

Yet these events, quite separate from his work as a filmmaker, were to take up a significant part of his time and mind while at MGM. From what DeMille's "secret files" revealed, it's apparent that his preoccupation with them, oft-suspected but never proven, may have contributed to his loss of nearly a million dollars on the stock market, and to his leaving MGM virtually washed up after the failure of his films there.

But, although it was tucked away where no one was ever likely to look for it, the story this "secret file" reveals is one the employers in Hollywood all preferred to sweep under the carpet and ignore when they wrote their memoires. Perhaps this is because writing about labor strife can all too easily open up a Pandora's box. Certainly, had any of DeMille's covert participation leaked out at the time, it would have destroyed his reputation, and possibly imperiled the life of the agent whose hiring he personally sanctioned.

Dynamite of a decade of reckless economic upswing. It was an apogee of prohibition and laughing disregard. It was also the year of the St. Valentine's Day massacre. Black Friday, the day the stock market crashed, was still some way off.

In the late spring of 1929, Equity prepared its third onslaught on Hollywood. Like other unions, such as Transport and the Cameramen, but with less success, Equity had long tried to get a foothold in the industry. California was one of the last states to be fully unionized. Los Angeles was the citadel of the open shop, and Hollywood was not only one of the state's most important industries, with many employees, but it had a very high profile. Thus, money-motivated Hollywood would become the Trojan horse by which organized labor was to penetrate anti-union Los Angeles.

In *Stars and Strikes* (1941), Murray Ross explains how "the American Federation of Labor made a valiant attempt to invade filmland in 1916. . . . Successful to some extent, the drive awakened motion picture producers to the existence of a labor problem which required handling by a single agency representing all producers. To deal effectively with labor troubles and other industrial matters, [in 1924] they formed the Motion Picture Producers Association, an open-shop organization of seventeen Hollywood studios. . . . The formation of this trade association marked the beginning of a unified labor policy among Hollywood's major film producers." When movies first began to make a dent on the entertainment industry, the two most powerful unions in the amusement field had been the International Alliance of Theatrical Stage Employees (IATSE) and the American Federation of Musicians, who organized the projectionists and musicians in movie houses. Unlike vaudeville and the legitimate stage, production and exhibition were separate in the movie industry. Thus, after their successful entry into the theaters, the unions turned their attention to film production.

Soon after solving its problems with the theater managers on Broadway, Equity started to watch the Hollywood situation carefully, seizing every opportunity to lay its case before the motion picture producers. The A.F. of L. had granted union control over screen actors to Equity, although initially the screen actors were not so eager to be recruited, for, as Murray Ross found, "the abuses which had impelled the dramatic actors to unionize" (and with which C. B. had been all too familiar during his years on the road) were not prevalent in the motion picture industry. Many screen players, especially the stars, had come directly to the films with little or no stage experience and had little interest in the traditions or history of the theater. They were quite content with their liberal rewards.

Now, more and more were ready to listen. In 1924, Frank Gillmore, Equity's executive secretary had tried to persuade Will Hays to agree to a standard contract, but Hays protested that he did not wish to dictate to the newly formed Producing Managers' Association which he headed and which after all, was paying him his handsome salary.

At that time, Joseph Schenck, a man in good standing with gangsters, producers as well as labor figures, was the president of the AMPP. The repeated accusations by labor that producers were bribing union officials were proved true a few years later when Schenck, now chairman of 20th Century Fox, was shown to have been making payoffs of $50,000 a year, which had been covered up by the studio accounting departments. It was largely through undercover agents that union racketeers Willie Bioff and George Browne of IATSE were exposed and convicted. Schenck himself cooperated with the US government, though he loyally never named the names of the other studio heads involved, and in 1941 was sentenced to a year's imprisonment for this and the usual income tax irregularities.

With Hays's rejection, Equity launched a more aggressive and determined campaign by publicizing the alleged abuses of certain Hollywood studios, especially the powerful Lasky (Paramount) studio. Three-time Oscar-winning cameraman Arthur C. Miller, who was at Paramount for some of this, had known and worked for DeMille, and was later the vice president of the board of governors of the militant American Society of Cinematographers, spoke to the film historian Leonard Maltin shortly before his death. "The period from 1925 to 1929 is considered by most cinematographers to be the murderous years. I don't believe there ever was or ever will be a time when the employer in the motion picture business showed less consideration for those he employed than in this period. A company, under some pretense or another of an emergency, would be called back after dinner. The 'emergency' might be to have an actor finish his part or to kill a set. No matter what the excuse, the company worked until eleven o'clock at night. Nothing was ever said about extra compensation for the extra hours worked. The so-called emergencies grew more frequent throughout the industry until some companies were including Wednesday nights until eleven in the shooting schedule of their pictures. Then Saturday nights were added, and that usually meant working until daybreak after a full day. The bargaining sessions (between employers and cameramen) that followed finally concluded in a contract agreement between us. The agreement stipulated a minimum wage but, more important, also the working hours and conditions. The Producers held out for a paragraph that included the words 'in case of an emergency,' which meant that they could call anything they chose an emergency, especially money. As expected, quite a few producers attempted to make their entire picture under this emergency clause." Without specifically mentioning his former boss, Miller added that the positive changes, when they came, were only possible because "some of the adamant old guard producers had disappeared from the scene."

Other such abuses had included a "salary list" that was kept on file at the AMPP with a view to preventing actors from raising their salaries between pictures when freelancing. Actors were also given layoffs without salary. Studios sometimes requested the actors to share the studios' railroad fares, sleepers, and hotel bills when going away on location. Sometimes, while being laid off during a production because the script was being changed or new sets had to be built, an actor would be shunted into another film then in the works to play a small part at no extra salary. These practices and others like them were reported by Equity to its members.

For a time, things improved. In November 1926, ten years after the first campaign to unionize the industry, the Producers affixed their signatures to their first union agreement, commonly known in the industry as the Studio Basic Agreement, under which the five major unions, known as the Internationals' Committee (and soon to be castigated by other Labor Leaders as little more than "Producers' men"), came to regularly meet and negotiate with the Producers. "What we are trying to do is to maintain an open shop," claimed producer Joe Kennedy (who then ran Pathé Films), "without prejudice to union labor." To show their good faith, the Producers even launched the Central Casting Corporation, financed and controlled by them. Soon this body would also be seen to be as corrupt as the discredited Service Bureau for Extras which it had been set up to replace.

Of course, although in theory Equity's plan for a closed shop to look after all those who appeared on the screen affected the highest as well as the lowest (i.e., stars as well as bit part actors), in practice it was only the small fry who were concerned. While all performers in a film may have been obliged to pay union dues and in theory come out on strike if so required, in fact this was a business built on stars. Who, whether union or employer, would dare order a Swanson or a Garbo to do anything she didn't want to do?

Thus, Equity was prepared to sign up people who could not be considered professional actors, but had congregated in Los Angeles, drawn by the climate and the dazzling glamor of the movies. That most of the more attractive or enterprising among them ended up as waitresses, prostitutes, or pimps deterred none. To boast that you worked in the movies—even just a few days a year—made starvation worthwhile.

Those casting calls were like a cattle market, attracting stranded circus performers and professional athletes as well as musicians, stunt performers, midgets, freaks, and models fallen on hard times. At a typical casting call, whether for a party scene or a historical romp, they could find themselves competing with a former state supreme court judge, a New York policeman, an ex-clergyman, and dozens of one-time lawyers, physicians, and society ladies, all for the privilege of $5.50 a day. There were exotic entrants such as a British brigadier general, over a hundred Mexican revolutionists, two Russian generals, an Italian flying ace, a former Chinese provincial governor, a sardine fisherman from Finland, and a man whose sole claim was that he had the longest and whitest beard in the business.

What would such a motley lot care about union membership when it was clearly their individuality, or their inability to fit into regular society, that had brought them together? The answer was the abuses they all suffered, which were flagrant. Everyone connected with the industry, from Will Hays to Frank Gillmore, knew something had to be done. But there were a lot of them, and while nothing could move a star if the star didn't want to be moved, 10,000 unionized extras would be a force to be reckoned with.

But Equity failed to receive the support of the rank and file for a standard contract. Having gotten some of what they wanted, these actors and stars only wanted to get on with their work. The Producers therefore balked at the proposal for an Equity shop, and instead in May 1927, established the Academy of Motion Picture Arts and Sciences. Destined to become another subject of heated controversy, and best known for its annual Oscar awards, it was to be an organization in which all the producing factors in motion pictures might have an equal voice. This sort of glamorous smoke screen dazzled the eyes and clouded the judgment of actors dreaming of stardom. Of course, the real power lay with the AMPP, and its first president was DeMille's brother William—hardly your typical "studio man."

Whatever Equity felt about the Producers' ploy, the actors were enthusiastic. But then, in an economy drive that summer, the Producers' association unanimously decided on an industry-wide salary reduction of ten percent for all non-union labor. (High salaried producers and executives magnanimously declared that they too would accept salary reductions from 10 to 25 percent; on their salaries, hardly a hardship.)

The Academy gave the Producers a way out, and they undertook instead to look for other means to economize, and though by 1929 there had already been three strikes by studio craftsmen and cameramen, and the IATSE had launched a movement to form one big union of all studio crafts, the unions' quarreling among themselves meant they could not threaten the industry with a general strike.

But something revolutionary was happening in the industry that was to change the whole ball-game.

Sound.

The talkies had galvanized the industry. Hollywood scoured Broadway for "voices." Contrary to Hollywood's boast that one could find all the trained voices one needed in Los Angeles, the studios canvassed the legitimate and musical comedy stages for them. This brought many Equity members to the screen.

Ironically, if it hadn't been for Warner Brothers' desperate gamble on the Vitaphone to rescue their flailing operations, the unions might never have had the chance this technical advancement provided. The actors came in droves, and they were all unionized. Thus, in March 1929, while the studios, traumatized by the enormous new costs of the installation of sound equipment in their studios and in the conversion of their theaters, had taken their eye off the ball, Equity seized its opportunity.

Even now, rather than look to its own narrow-minded restrictive trade practices, Hollywood chose to see communists under the bed, when in reality the cause was the reckless greed and callous disregard of the employers, men who ironically had just recently pulled themselves up by their bootstraps from the same swamp as the people they were trying to keep down.

And so it happened that while DeMille was in the last stages of work on his first talkie, he slid into the murky world of espionage and subterfuge. But why DeMille, and not Louis B. Mayer, or Carl Laemmle, or Warner, or any of the other anti-union studio heads?

Over the years, DeMille protested to little avail that he had nothing against unions, that he himself was a member of several. But as a Paramount executive would relate to an FBI agent in 1953, "DeMille is inclined to be intolerant of labor, and the foundation's [the DeMille Foundation for Political Freedoms] objectives are to oppose organized labor and change labor contract policies." DeMille's suspiciousness of the union's involvement whenever anything went wrong on one of his sets was to last for the rest of his life. When a light blew on his set, it was due to the unions; if an elephant dropped a brick during a take, that was the unions, too.

Like a growing number of Americans in his position, DeMille believed that unions and communism were linked, and that the atheists who had protested against *The Godless Girl* were communist inspired. This was simplistic, but easier to swallow than the harsh truth that a silent film made in

1928 failed because, as he should have known, the public preferred any sort of "talkie."

The problem posed by the unions in the spring of 1929 saw DeMille's fears realized, and in the battle ahead he saw himself on the side of the moguls. As a result, that was how his peers began to see and judge him and his work. It could be argued that it was his closed mind on closed shops that caused his reputation to suffer, and his work from now on to be treated on a par with that of a Barnum and Bailey. His tastes were mocked, his execution dismissed. Even now, when the pendulum might be said to have swung back, critics still begin their reappraisal of films like *The Ten Commandments* with a note of surprise that his films hold up as well as they do. But in another turn of the wheel, it would be he, not sentimental Capra or tough Ford, who became the symbol of what new generations, and thus history, perceived to be "Hollywood."

The generally held view of DeMille as a crony of the employers was not undeserved. The clues came to be hidden in a shabby old box buried among his household files. The contents, covering June 1929 to February 1931, had the smell of old gunpowder, dusty and acrid, like half-finished cigarettes. Below a sheet headed "Top Secret" almost every report had the same heading. They reveal that DeMille had been in touch with, and by implication encouraging, an agent to subvert, disrupt, and report on the most secret plotting of the leaders of the A.F. of L. and the various communist agencies in Los Angeles.

Much has been written about this union assault on Hollywood, but usually based on readily available facts. But DeMille's scribbled, barely decipherable notes, the urgent memos rushed from Thalberg's secretary in the executive building to DeMille's secretary in his private bungalow, copies of the employer's battle plans, labor's strategies, communist manifestos for nationwide unrest, and so much more, read like the bits of a mighty jigsaw slowly taking form.

It's in the light of their revelations that something DeMille told Art Arthur now makes startling sense. Arthur had queried him in a general way about "commies who worked for C. B." (he cited DeMille's early employment of such indicted Hollywood Ten writers as Albert Maltz, John Howard Lawson, and the actor Howard da Silva). In their conversation, DeMille spoke of his participation in some primitive undercover work back when America entered World War I, (and the unions made their first foray into Hollywood), when the patriotic DeMille organized the Lasky Home Guard. The name he dangled before Arthur was none other than J. Edgar Hoover, though it should be said that in the fifties, Hoover, the now discredited head of the FBI, was still highly regarded by many in the film industry. "There was a meeting down there with J. Edgar Hoover. In the First World War, you see, we had something called the U.S. Intelligence. . . . This was a secret organization, like the FBI that went all through the First World War, but it was not terribly well handled. Those who were good were very good, but they picked a lot of people who weren't very good. Now on the second [World War II] when I talked, to Dick Hood. 'There'll be no card, no badge, no anything. Nothing but a headache—that's all we can give you. But we need people. But you don't belong to the FBI: you're on your own; if you get into trouble, that's it, as far as you're concerned.' There were several of us that accepted it on that basis."

In 1948, DeMille, aged sixty-seven, was transferred to the honorary reserve. Why would a busy film director be appointed to a military post in late middle age? It suggests strong circumstantial evidence that DeMille was an active member of the intelligence community.

It is natural to assume that DeMille would have retained certain friendships made back in 1917. He was not attracted to the underhand. He was never an informer. But, as with his brief exposure to military schooling, this early brush with Hoover consolidated certain of his values. This was DeMille the artichoke slayer, the young Lochinvar, always ready to fight for grand and glorious causes like Cuba and Mexico. This was "C. B. DeMille, Special Agent."

To Arthur's further suggestion that DeMille must qualify as "the earliest and certainly the No. 1 target in the town for the Hollywood branch of the [Communist] party," DeMille admitted (with just a hint of pride): "I would think so, because that's what led to a good many of the unhappy traditions about me." The seeds of these traditions lay buried in the box which Gladys had marked "Secret File."

Now DeMille was in charge of the AMPP strategy.

By June, Frank Gillmore had secured a mandate from Equity's Hollywood members for contracts backed by an Equity shop in sound pictures. Their terms included demands for a forty-eight-hour week, payment for overtime, a clearer definition of starting dates, and a compulsory arbitration of all difficulties. Furthermore, contracts should specify that Equity members were not to play with non-union actors. Unless the Producers accepted these requirements, Equity threatened to paralyze the studios.

Certain of support, Equity issued this order on June 4: "From this date no member of Equity may set foot on any stage, set, or location in any capacity of any kind until the present crisis is over. This should be particularly noted by all those members who received, or expected to receive, offers of extra or atmosphere work."

It amounted to the first official salvo in the war.

Naturally Gillmore's conditions struck at the heart of the employers' authority and were unacceptable. The Producers felt confident of once again defeating Equity.

On June 10, while negotiations with Gillmore were still above board, DeMille received a letter from Don Wilkie, a private investigator, apparently in response to a phone call, advocating that the Producers plant an undercover agent in Equity. The letter recommended "a general investigation of the attitude of leading Equity members. . . . [and] to tie up to someone who could, from day to day, give us the verbal picture of Frank Gillmore's and Charley Miller's [Equity's man in Los Angeles] reaction to the situation as it developed. . . . Beetson agreed fully with this and was also enthusiastic, I judged, over the idea that if a rift could be created in the ranks of Equity it would also be advisable. . . . I already have gathered absolute proof that this fight is a very serious one, and that it will not be won by either side until there has been a real battle. . . .

"I believe this fight boiled down is a definite move upon the part of American Federation of Labor to do in Southern California what they have heretofore been unable to: namely, put Unionized labor on its feet. I feel that the Equity fight is merely a technical maneuver and that the battle which will follow will spread on all grounds, including Unionized labor in the East."

The letter makes clear that he has known DeMille from previous times, probably from their days as undercover agents in 1917. But DeMille, on behalf of the Producers Association, did not wish to be recorded as giving personal approval: "I think you have anticipated maters to some extent. Certain associates of mine had suggested they might have need of a service such as you conduct. . . . I very strongly recommended your integrity and ability, but I believe as yet no decision has been reached."

These "associates," whose contributions funded the Producers' aims and offices, included the financial controllers on the East Coast, more used to dealing with unions and not all of them united on the urgency for such a drastic course of action.

DeMille's last official act before leaving for his holidays was to issue a statement on the Equity situation. "I am going away for my summer vacation, which will be a short one, and then I am coming back soon to begin my new picture. I shall be able to cast it without difficulty. There are plenty of actors, Equity and non-Equity available. The producers do not need any sympathy. We are able to cast and produce all the pictures we want to produce. We could perhaps cast and produce more pictures than all the studios combined plan to produce." This assertion of supreme confidence came as a shock to Equity, who had expected to find no more than two hundred players under contract. Instead, there were enough important actors, not counting non-Equity members, to enable the studios to continue to turn out films. Equity was also disappointed to find that its allied unions in the A.F. of L. did not intend to participate in their battle at this point.

On July 14, Equity was officially accepted as a member of the Central Labor Council of Los Angeles. The A.F. of L. in Washington now seconded Equity's efforts to organize sound and talking pictures. Even more than moral support, they agreed to give financial aid when needed. Such a move, giving Equity serious financial clout, had to be taken seriously by the Producers. Meetings between the two sides were arranged.

On August 5, at a meeting with DeMille and Louis B. Mayer present, Gillmore presented new proposals involving a rather complicated formula built around 80 percent representation in all casts. These were the same conditions they had obtained in the legitimate field in 1924. After retiring for about fifteen minutes to think this over, the Producers returned and rejected any fixed percentage as unacceptable. Their only concession was an offer to negotiate with Equity for all Equity members.

By August 8, it must have appeared to all parties that negotiations were getting them nowhere.

There was further disarray within Equity as actors, fearing for their future, accepted the contract the studio offered. Once again internal dissension threatened the success of the entire undertaking. Lionel Barrymore, Louise Dresser, Marie Dressler, and John Gilbert, all of whom worked at MGM and other prominent Hollywood members of Equity maintained that they had never encountered the abuses which Equity had cited. They could not see why Equity injected itself into a situation where it could do no good and was not wanted.

The dispute between Equity and the studios had become a situation in which men whose work derived from the film industry had to think about whose side they were on. But if the Producers felt like rubbing their hands, it was still early days. And DeMille knew it.

DeMille issued a statement on August 20 in acknowledgment of Gillmore's, made prior to the Equity president's departure for chastisement in New York, in which Gillmore had effectively conceded (temporary) defeat: "We are glad that Frank Gillmore, president of the Actors' Equity Association of New York, has officially notified members of his association to accept work when it is offered in the motion picture studios. There was no occasion for the attempted invasion of the motion picture industry by the stage Actors' Equity Association of New York. There was no reason for the turmoil and unrest initiated by Mr. Gillmore's unexpected ultimatum of June 4th. . . . It is a striking commentary upon the whole situation to reflect that during the more than ten weeks since the delivery of Mr. Gillmore's ultimatum and the consequent endeavor to prevent production, not a single picture was disbanded, postponed or canceled. During this same period also production in Hollywood was at its highest peak. To those who refused to accept dictation from the New York group, we express our appreciation. To those who felt required to support Mr. Gillmore, we say that the controversy is ended."

Equity had momentarily withdrawn from Hollywood, but only to marshal its forces and return under new leadership less gentlemanly than Gillmore. The first round may have been won, but the battle was far from over.

The Producers decided to go ahead with the Academy. On September 19, DeMille's rough draft outlined the new course he thought they should take: "No matter what the Union labor situation is, the industry should have one institution representing all its branches. . . . If it were well established, it would certainly be a potent factor in molding public opinion, and acting as arbiter in the event of trouble between any of its branches—whether Unionized or not. . . .

"To Sum Up: We should foster the new organization of the actors here, keeping them as free as possible of Union entanglements."

His proposal was derided by the A.F. of L. leadership in an article headed "PICTURE PRODUCERS FORM COMPANY UNION." "Hollywood motion picture producers have formed a 'company union' of film players in an attempt to ward off another organization campaign by the Actors' Equity Association, the bona fide Labor Union affiliated with the A.F. of L., according to word received at the Equity office here. The movie bosses concede some of the demands made by Equity last summer and in return compel the 'company union' to agree 'to refuse to support or countenance a strike or other radical action by any group of actors that might be injurious to the motion picture industry so long as the letter and spirit of the agreement is observed.'

"'Just another "company union" plan,' said President Frank Gillmore of Equity. 'It is not likely to bring happiness and content to the artists who accept it. Equity is willing to admit it lost the first battle to Unionize Hollywood, but it will not abandon the campaign.'"

Now the A.F. of L. would use Equity as a stalking horse to make their bid for the control of Southern California, and the new leaders of the Equity campaign were about to play hardball. On one of his undated memos DeMille had written:

"Get man who agent suggests to join I.A.T.A.C."

The murky part was about to commence.

CHAPTER TWENTY-SEVEN

IN RESPONSE TO THE LETTER RECEIVED BY FRED BEETSON, DEMILLE MADE the decision to "tie up [that] someone" who, as Wilkie had written, "could, from day to day, give us the verbal picture of Frank Gillmore's and Charley Miller's reaction to the situation as it developed."

Besides Beetson, Garbutt, and DeMille, the only other people to know about this were Louis B. Mayer, Irving Thalberg, and Gladys Rosson. From now on, there would be regular weekly reports, the first of which, marked "STRICTLY CONFIDENTIAL," was dated September 29.

The reports made exciting reading. The agent eventually revealed himself as a senior figure in the union movement. Though his reports were unidentified, his name was Jackson. This only emerged after he'd been reporting for almost a year when suddenly out of the blue, he signed his name.

Jackson, it also turned out, had been reporting to the Justice Department in Washington on Union activities for many years. In his capacity as an informer, Jackson, gave evidence (in camera) to the 1930 Congressional Committee on Communism.

The agent got himself onto several committees; he was a delegate to the convention of the California State Federation of Labor at Long Beach and, as he told Beetson, was due to attend the National Convention of the American Federation of Labor (A.F. of L.) being held in Canada.

The agent's first report contained early references to another key player in the unfolding drama, J. W. Buzzell, the secretary/treasurer of the Central Labor Council of Los Angeles, who replaced Gillmore as the Producers' principal adversary, and was said to be in cahoots with Equity officials Gillmore and Dullzell in New York and Charley Miller in Los Angeles. The threat of communist agitators, always a sure bait to get the employers jumping, was also raised. Reporting on the rise of communism was, as it turned out, probably the agent's key job for his bosses in the Secret Service of the Justice Department, or whoever it was that pulled his string: "When Buzzell is able to get the left wing element of all the studio unions together they can do a lot of plotting and it is a sure thing that they will keep the workers discontent and unhappy all the time."

The agent also had access to internal mail among union officials, copies of which he supplied whenever he could as proof of his close links to the top people. The agent claimed he personally stopped two big Eastern leaders from attending a mass meeting by pretending that his car had broken down, then circulated the rumor that they were out on a drunk. He claims he got unions to fight amongst themselves and stopped a national boycott. If he accomplished even half of the things he claimed, he was clearly of enormous value to the Producers.

His double-spaced report filling eight pages was forwarded to Louis B. Mayer. The next report, dated the twelfth, was sent from the Toronto Convention, where he had been elected to the Boycotts Committee. He told them that he had surreptitiously tried to blacken Buzzell's name and stop the granting of a charter: "If given enough power Buzzell would probably swing the entire Los Angeles movement over to the revolutionist. . . . Frank Gillmore is busy holding conferences but does not seem to be getting anywhere. He and Buzzell are very thick and if their program had gone over they would have been able to pull a general strike in the Movie Industry."

The next report, dated October 23, upon the agent's return from Toronto, reports on the upcoming arrival of union hired gangsters in Los Angeles. The "STRICTLY CONFIDENTIAL" seven-page report typed on October 23 gave forewarning that the Painters Union had agreed to "force the Producers to establish closed shop conditions on all building construction work in all Motion Picture Studios in Los Angeles and vicinity. . . . One of the most important actions that Agent was let in on was a secret meeting held just before he left [Toronto]. . . . It was decided to unionize L.A. to establish the five-day week and ten dollars per day minimum in all building trades and to unionize the movie industry by hijack and gangster methods."

In blood-curdling language Buzzell told the agent that "it's going to be hard with such men as Conrade [sic] Nagel and a few other traitors, and such crooks as Fred Beetson . . . will be taken care of. Following this gang are bomb makers. Six hundred have been used in Chicago so far this year to make reluctant merchants and employers come to terms. A perfect machine has been organized to handle a national boycott should this become necessary."

The agent followed this with reports on union action to be taken against some of the studios for health violations on the overcrowded, overheated soundstages; for the dismissal from the union of several men on the MGM lot for not paying their dues; for the use of non-union labor on the Lasky lot, etc. Warner Bros. was also due for trouble because of their restrictive work practices.

Three days later, not quite without warning as is usually claimed, another major event intruded on DeMille's peace of mind: the stock market crashed. He had been expecting something along these lines, ever since Julia Faye, at a dinner up at San Simeon, heard Hearst's right-hand man, Arthur Brisbane, warn of an imminent crash like none they had ever known before. Faye rushed to warn DeMille. But his instructions to Gladys Rosson were not specific enough: "She had dutifully called the brokers as soon as she received my instructions. She gave them the order which we always gave when we were selling, to offer the stocks at a half-point above the market. But the desperately tumbling market had never climbed that half-point. There were no takers at our price."

Gladys's fidelity to their customary rule cost him approximately $1,000,000. DeMille, who did blow up over small things, was magnanimous when it came to this huge and costly misunderstanding. He took the blame for not having spelled out to her that "when I said 'sell' *that* time, I meant sell that minute at any price." What this mistake suggests is the enormous pressure under which they were all working at this time.

June 11, 1929, brought the "CONFIDENTIAL" report that "several high powered labor leaders are already in Los Angeles lining up and uniting all the groups and factions into one solid organization.

On the eighth, with a cover note from Mayer's secretary addressed to Gladys indicating that Mayer had seen it, came a letter to DeMille from Conrad Nagel of the Academy, with a two-page summary of the Academy's suggested proposals for a new standard contract to be raised with the Producers. The most important point was a forty-eight-hour week for actors.

By January 1930, with DeMille in the last stages of pre-production for *Madame Satan*, "J" was reporting that unionization was growing: they were even trying to get the police and firemen to start unions, and promising that the following week he would provide "the names of those who are active and are working against the producers . . . all the disloyal employees in the studios from the stars and cameramen down to the common laborers."

With the A.F. of L. support, Equity was assured that when one union went on strike, the others would follow. Help came from many sources, not all union and not all expected. From this time on, syndicated crime took a serious interest in films, drawn, as everyone else was, by the glamor. The ominous news came: "The Boom Boom boys are leaving Chicago for the Pacific coast."

Every side played every angle to keep the pot stirred. Buzzell, Dullzell, Miller, and Blix raised their boogies, and Beetson, Garbutt, DeMille, and their crowd did their best to raise fears of union domination. It was the two sides' way of negotiating the size of the slice of the pie the one would have to give and the other would accept. Ultimately the only one to pay would be the public, with increased ticket prices.

"J" kept DeMille up to date on the mobster situation, providing the names of the leaders and their fields of activity. He reported that Cantrell had a conference with Frank Smeede, who had arrived in Los Angeles from Chicago to organize the Street Car Platform men. Smeede and Cantrell turned out to be old pals, both being prominent in the racketeering among the unions in

Chicago about two years ago. The agent "knows Smeede pretty well and has invited Smeede and Cantrell to dinner at one of the clubs this week . . . to get some inside information."

"J" also provided the labor leaders who were known to him to be racketeers. They included S. Reckles, from Chicago, who claimed to have made $50,000 in one month in Chicago; W. J Hoffman, who was working out a plan to organize the clerks in the large down town stores; Sam Curnough, who was working with the reds and stirring up the Rubber Workers at the Goodyear Plant; M. D. Kolack, who was working with the packing house employees; Dick Dungey, formerly a machinist in Chicago, now organizing the auto mechanics; and Tom Corcoran, who, DeMille was told, claimed to represent the building trades and who threatened to raise a "lot of hell" with scab contactors before the summer was over.

Whatever danger or convictions for his dangerous work "J" might face, he was earning a regular salary, more than could be said for a lot of people in America both in and outside the unions and the studios at the time. Hollywood was slowly becoming conscious of the effects of the Depression. Clara Bow's career was in a shambles and her studio did nothing to help her. John Gilbert's career was a fiasco. Most of the former silent stars now worked for little money in quickly produced films for Poverty Row studios. Overnight, the public forgot stars like Evelyn Brent, Colleen Moore, Lillian Gish, Lars Hanson, Antonio Moreno, Blanche Sweet, Mae McAvoy, Leatrice Joy, Jetta Goudal, and dozens of others, who either retired, fell into support, returned to try their luck in their own countries, or continued on in foreign-language versions of the sort of films they had once starred in.

But "J" and the Producers weren't concerned with the rise or fall of stars. There would always be more where those came from, and already a whole string of new faces were dazzling eye and ear: Maurice Chevalier, Marlene Dietrich, Joan Crawford, Norma Shearer, Jeanette MacDonald, Janet Gaynor, James Cagney, and Gary Cooper had already helped to wipe the memories of Norma Talmadge, Thomas Meighan, Corinne Griffith, and others from the public's mind. The Hollywood trade press reported that "in defense against the growth of baseball, mini-golf and the Depression, a 10 cent policy was introduced by Eastern Film House chains; double feature policies are also set for circuits."

As DeMille gathered his cast together for a reading of the final script for *Madame Satan*, he received "J's" report of increased control within the unions on February 17, 1930: "Buzzell told officers . . . they should get busy and get all non-card men out of the studios by hook or crook as all is fair in a situation of this kind. . . . Buzzell told Blix that unless the unions put the screws under the non-union men who are still hanging on that it is going to hurt the entire movement. Union men will feel that they should not pay dues when the scabs are getting all the benefits without paying them, and a non-union person in any group is like a rotten apple in a basket it spoils the others."

CHAPTER TWENTY-EIGHT

IS IT ANY WONDER THAT IN 1930, BESET WITH SO MANY WORRIES AND distractions, not to mention his sidelines which now included an Epsom Salts mine, a stock brokerage, an herb tea firm, an airline, a chain of grocery stores, various apartment houses and restaurants, investments in banks, and some of the most lucrative real estate holdings in Los Angeles, DeMille set out to make the most lavish musical ever seen on the screen?

Madam Satan was his first musical venture since he had sung light opera and wrote a one-act revue for Jesse Lasky. For this art deco musical fantasy with a huge budget and outrageous sets and costumes, the only thing old was the story since it was virtually the same as Johann Strauss's *Die Fledermaus*. By the time he finished it, less than six months later, musicals were dying at the box office. And when, after much desperate cutting and changing, the film was ready for release, they were dead.

Events were moving at a ferocious pace. Headlines from *Film Daily* give a taste:

FEBRUARY 11: "70 color features are set for 1930." Color was still primitive and used mostly in musicals. DeMille decided to shoot several sequences of his film in early two-tone Technicolor.

MARCH 17: A survey showed that "78% of film fans prefer only Talkies." That must have been reassuring, since hardly anyone in Hollywood was making any other sort of film, except Chaplin, whose *City Lights*, a silent comedy with music and sound effects, was one of the year's hits. Most of the remaining silent pictures in America were the films made specifically for black audiences.

MAY 29: "A clamor for Westerns was the latest thing. 10,000 exhibitors say the customers love outdoor films." Paramount revived their Zane Grey series. Westerns were a phenomenon because the public found them to be "original" and not, "like 9 out of every 15 other films, rehashes of never very good plays," like *The Flirting Widow*, *The Office Wife*, or *Virtuous Husband*, where everyone talked but nothing moved, except the public banging their seats on the way out.

AUGUST 17: "58 Westerns were announced on 1930–31 schedule."
Among these was DeMille's third remake of *The Squaw Man*.

By the year's end, "19,900 of World's 62,365 houses had been wired for
sound." Few corners of the paying globe were left mute. The American accent and "Yankee" slang traveled far and wide. With all the money spent on
rewiring, there was little left over for widescreen or color or anything else
that would cost more.

With Peverell Marley unavailable as cameraman for *Madam Satan*, Gladys
Rosson's distinguished brother, Harold, took over. Hal Rosson, a nice chap
with a soft voice and military bearing, worked on two films with DeMille
before helping to establish MGM's great visual style and glorify their fabled
beauties, most notably the star who would become his wife, Jean Harlow.

Like most of the Rosson clan, Harold adored DeMille. Long after they
worked together he made a point of boasting of their friendship, which
couldn't have endeared him to a lot of his fellow cameramen. As he told
Leonard Maltin, "I went to MGM studio at the request of Mr. DeMille." Besides the technically tricky *Madame Satan*, Rosson photographed DeMille's
remake of *The Squaw Man*.

On the strength of *Dynamite*'s success and with the Depression not yet
effecting the box office, the original budget was high: $1.3 million. Lacking
a big star, DeMille cast ladylike Kay Johnson, who had just completed a role
in King Vidor's widescreen version of *Billy the Kid*. With her Garboesque con-
tralto Johnson sounded splendid.

Madam Satan was the story of an oppressively respectable wife who goes
to a masked ball disguised as an alluring siren to flirt with her two-timing
husband, played by Reginald Denny because, as he admits, he has been wandering "far from my own fireside in search of—fire!" The "fire" was provided
by voluptuous brunette Broadway belter Lillian Roth. The wife, disguised as
Madam Satan, shows that she can out vamp any rival, if that is what it takes
to keep her husband.

The idea for this story had come via writer Gladys Unger, who had suggested Johann Strauss's *Die Fledermaus* when DeMille was still wondering what
he might do next. His adaptation of the classic operetta kept the mask and
ball, but the rest, now that he wasn't going to use the glorious music, was so
changed and mangled that he could get away without crediting Strauss for
the story. Besides, Strauss hadn't invented the central conflict of wife and
mistress fighting over a philandering hero, he had merely champagned it.
So Jeanie Macpherson, for her version of the old triangle, replaced Strauss's
champagne with some old beer by amalgamating the best bits. *Die Fledermaus*
ended up as just another springboard for Jennie Macpherson's favorite story
of two starkly contrasting women fighting over the same virile man.

From once having been the sole author of most of DeMille's scripts, and
at one time even acknowledged publicly by him for contributing 75 percent

Star of *Madam Satan* (1930), Kay Johnson is seen wearing one of Adrian's brilliant costumes for the film. Photo: James Manatt. Courtesy John Kobal Foundation

of the success to all his films, Macpherson was now but one writer among three. Their once romantically charged relationship was drawing to a close, and it now also appeared that their working relationship was no longer happy. *Madam Satan* was to be Macpherson's last major screen credit until DeMille hired her again five years later.

For years, Macpherson's financial affairs had been handled for her by DeMille's office. Gladys Rosson was probably Jeanie's closet friend and confidant. But Macpherson never realized, until too late, that Rosson was also in love with the boss. With a mortgage, a mother, and other relatives to support, Macpherson's weekly salary of $1,000 plus occasional royalties from the book versions of her scripts never seemed enough. She had been one of the most highly paid screenwriters in the business only a few years before, but the Depression took its toll on her as well.

"Did she leave?" Art Arthur asked DeMille. "Yes. . . . It was when I was at MGM that that happened. . . . Until I met her [again] when she was very hard up, she didn't find it very easy. I was very fond of her. I loved her spirit and brilliance and courage and Scotch determination, so I got her to come back, writing for me, supervising for me. . . .

DeMille is shown with the cast of *Madam Satan* (1930) on the set of the Zeppelin ballroom that is featured in the film's climax. Photo: James Manatt. Courtesy John Kobal Foundation

"She came in here one day and lay down on the sofa and said, 'Cecil, I'm really sick.' And I said, 'I know you are, Jeanie.' She said, 'I need the salary but I'm afraid I can't do the work.' I said, 'Your salary will continue as long as you want it.' A week later Frank Freeman came to me and said, 'I know Jeanie's charged to your production, but what is she doing now?' I said, 'Frank, I don't think it'll be very much longer that she'll be on the payroll.' He looked at me and said, 'Oh. All right.' We paid her until she died [1946]. She died of cancer."

Four of the original eight songs for *Madam Satan* were written by Jack King, who had sprung to fame when he wrote "How am I to Know" for *Dynamite*. Working earlier with Dorothy Parker, now he wrote with his vaudeville partner Elsie Janis supplying the anodyne lyrics. The other songs were the work of MGM's resident composer Herbert Stothart, who had co-written the music for Rudolf Frimml's stage hit *Rose Marie*, as well as writing for such previous MGM musicals as *The Roque Song* and *Call of the Flesh*.

On February 10, DeMille gathered his cast together for a reading of the finished script. Surrounded by his serviceable but far from exciting cast—besides Johnson, there was Reginald Denny, Lillian Roth, Roland Young, and

Elsa Peterson—DeMille regaled them with it, playing all of their parts, generally acting it the way he wanted it played. The rest would be up to them.

Two weeks later, rehearsals for *Madam Satan* began. Mitchell Leisen had designed a magnificent and outdone the glass-domed "palaces" springing up in the nation's big cities. DeMille could walk all over it and think to himself, "Mine, all mine."

The idea for the spectacular finale came to DeMille as a result of his daily study of the news for examples of funny and outrageous behavior by America's youth. His attention had been caught by a rash of headlines in the last frantic days of the Jazz Age about people hiring Zeppelins for parties, as when a party of forty-four Americans charted the Graf Zeppelin for an eight-hour celebration, and ended their revels with some of them hired to leap out of the airships for a stunt.

As he had done with the human hoop-race across the lawns in *Dynamite*, so now, if it was outlandish and eye-catching enough, he needed only one such item to stir his imagination. Instead of forty-four people, DeMille had four hundred. Instead of a couple bailing out, he had them all leaping and screaming. To ensure that his public wouldn't try to follow the entertaining leaps his imagination took, he ended the stunt on a gag that had his characters land in all manner of strange places: Kay Johnson lands in the rumble seat of a petter's auto; Roland Young is snagged on a tree in a lion's den; a girl dressed as Shiva descends into a crap game; a fat boy lands on a tramp in a park; and Lillian Roth crashes through the skylight of a Turkish bath. He wasn't trying to be subtle.

In an interview, DeMille elaborated on the need for such spectacle: "Every time I attempt one of these big effects I realize that I am taking a terrible risk. Trying to put 'spectacle' into plays or photoplays has caused more premature eclipses for directors than any other single element.

"Spectacle should be abandoned without compunction the minute a director finds he cannot work it definitely into his plot structure. It cannot be a separate and unrelated thing, to the power of our story to hold public audience is doomed."

Lillian Roth was one of those jumping from the Zeppelin, as she recalled in her autobiography: "The plot of *Madam Satan* called for me to steal Reginald Denny from Kay Johnson, who played his wife. We were supposed to be attending a masquerade ball on a Zeppelin. At the height of the festivities, the Zeppelin cracks up and begins to sink. . . .

"[Adrian] had prepared a startling costume. I was to come to the ball as a pheasant—iridescent golden bra, iridescent golden shorts, and stemming out behind, tremendous pheasant feathers. . . . After DeMille obtained an interior shot of me in the zeppelin, he said, 'Tomorrow you're going to jump. The zeppelin will be breaking up. You'll jump from there.'

"I followed his pointing finger, and stared, open-mouthed. More than 200 feet above our heads was a narrow ledge. Far below it was a net. Me, jump from up there?' I gasped, 'Into that net? In high heels and feathers? Oh, Mr. DeMille, I couldn't possibly!'

"Nine o'clock next morning, Mr. DeMille said, 'All right, Lillian, here's where you jump.'"

Madam Satan marked the screen debut of DeMille's daughter, Katherine, in what he described as a "decorative but non-speaking role." The proud papa did not want his actions to seem tainted by standard practices: "One might almost say that I bent backward when I gave her her role at the masquerade party in the picture, I cast her as one of the wives of King Henry VIII, surely a horrid fate for anyone's daughter." Katherine was another early leaper: "The Zeppelin gets struck by lightning, and there's big effects and music and everybody was to jump. It was a big jump. Like in the circus. About 40 feet. But none of the women wanted to jump. And I heard him say, 'Katie, will you please jump?' He hated that sort of thing, because he was a gutsy guy, he really was. That's why he didn't respect an awful lot of actors very much. . . . Well, I knew that it would be all right. So I just told myself it's like jumping into the water."

After watching others do it, Roth, though she trembled, leapt: "I jumped, thinking of things to say to Paramount if I survived. DeMille had a way of saying 'jump' and you jumped. Not once, but five times before he was satisfied."

But there was more to come. "Almost as appalling was the scene that followed," wrote Roth. "I was to rebound out of the net and crash through the glass skylight of a men's Turkish bath. Perched on a narrow ledge, where I was held by a stage hand so I couldn't tumble, I was to plunge through a large sheet of candy glass, which photographed like the real thing, but supposedly was far safer."

Before costs spiraled, DeMille planned the finale to end in Hell, full of fire and ice and a lot of naked girls, for which Wilfred Buckland was brought back. But costs and other pressures were taking their toll, and Hell was scrapped. As Mitchell Leisen told David Chierichetti, "*Madam Satan* was hell. Metro didn't have enough soundstages for all the pictures they were shooting, so each stage had three companies who worked eight-hour shifts. The first company worked from eight in the morning to four in the afternoon, then they left and another company came in until midnight, and then the last bunch worked from midnight until eight in the morning. This meant that we had to dismantle the entire set every night before we left, and then reassemble it as quickly as possible the next day so we could start working without losing much time. To make matters worse, the party on the Graf Zeppelin was all in two-color Technicolor, which required an enormous amount of light and was so limited in its range, it was harder to design than it would be in black and white. The strain was so great I had a nervous breakdown and had to quit entirely for a while. But it was a long picture, and they were still shooting when the doctors let me come back and work an hour a day."

DeMille explained to Louis B. Mayer the technical problem created by the use of color for the already overburdened Zeppelin sequence. "On account of inter-cutting with the storm miniature of the Zep being tossed through the air and the people jumping off in the air, it is impossible to use Technicolor on the miniature. Black and white hand color will have to be used and each release print will have to have from eighteen to twenty splices on the Zep sequence. Technicolor cannot be used for these miniature shots, which have to be cranked at eight times the normal speed which Technicolor cannot make."

There had been other novel ideas to test his excited cameraman's heart, such as a glass floor on the airship through which to photograph New York's illuminated skyline. After much work to solve that technical problem, it had to be discarded. But the film, according to Rosson, was still a "cameraman's dream project."

While DeMille was making *Madam Satan*, the Depression began gnawing away at the very fiber of the nation, and studios were ruthlessly cutting costs and laying off employees between pictures. On April 2, a week after *Film Daily* had reported an impressive total of 421 features set for 1930–31, Universal Studios announced the reduction of their features for the year to a mere twenty. The cuts forced on the studios by the Depression and disintegrating economy gave them the excuse for further cost-cutting which was bound to affect their response to union demands. On June 4, the trade press reported "that Unions are asked to lower wage scales to keep cinemas open." To aid an industry in crisis, what else could the union leaders do but sacrifice many of their recent gains when negotiating for jobs? People just weren't going to the movies in the numbers they used to, and those studios who were heavily in hock to the banks were facing threats of receivership. Only MGM was thriving.

On May 2, principal production on *Madam Satan* was finished. Now DeMille had other things to worry about. The alarming news wasn't that he had encountered union sabotage on his teeming set (though there was quite a bit of that going on), but that musicals were dying at the box office.

DeMille had placed his faith in what he read in the papers. In 1929, *Broadway Melody*, MGM's first musical won the first and only Oscar for best picture that musicals would receive for the next twenty-two years. In the months before the stock market crash, every studio had music in its films, even their silent ones, and several hundred all-musical films were in production for 1930 release. Hollywood confidently continued to make everybody sing, whether gangsters or cowboys or nobles in the court of the Louis. They sang about sunrises and sunsets and downpours in-between. They sang on horseback and rooftop. Even people on the breadlines sang.

Madam Satan was to be the biggest and the best—ultra-moderne, "tres jazz hot," as the French would have said—and looking at the advance stills, it must have seemed worth waiting for. But by the time of the film's release, all the stops that DeMille and his team of writers had pulled out to make it the biggest musical of them all now assured its burial. Its failure wasn't a lapse in taste. It wasn't even a matter of whether DeMille was the right director for a musical, since that consideration has never troubled the studios. It was all a matter of timing.

Six months earlier, *Madam Satan* would have broken all records. Two years later, after musicals returned to favor with *42nd Street*, it would have done OK. But in the fall of 1930, it was doomed. *Dynamite* had had one song, and it became a hit. *Madam Satan* had eight songs, and audiences protested that they made the film drag.

When publicist Barrett Kiesling sent DeMille his breakdown of the public's reaction at the first sneak preview, he focused not on the success of the songs, but on the status of *Madam Satan* as a genuine laugh picture: "I sat in a nest of sheiks and flappers of high school age. They got all the comedy gags but sagged a bit on some of the songs. . . . They were restless during the 'Going Nowhere' and 'Catwalk' numbers. They were very restless during 'This is love.' Flapper next to me said, 'OH—another song!' The whole reaction seemed to be that they had been worked up to a high pitch of farce in the first half and that the long spell of song at the fore part of the second half let them down. They accepted the songs, to my mind, in a sort of 'let's get the next laugh' spirit."

More blunt than Kiesling was Pete Smith, then in charge of the MGM's publicity department and concerned with the cost of promotion.

Pete Smith to DeMille (July 30): "There are several points when you feel the story is over and something else happens. The point where Young goes out singing could be a good finish to the story.

"Some of the close-ups following the Zep breakup of people hanging to parachutes struck me as very 'Mack Sennety' but I understand the public howled at these shots last night and after all, that's the answer.

"Summing up I should say keep all the drama, the love and the laughs in the picture and cut down on singing, dancing and you will have a box office picture that moves right along and an attraction that will more than please the popular price type of audience."

While it wasn't unusual for a major production to go through a number of cuts and changes as a result of negative reactions at early previews, and while MGM producer Irving Thalberg was even known to scrap a completed film and start over rather than spoil the studio's image with a bad film, absorbing its loss in their total budget, *Madam Satan* was a special case, because of DeMille's deal with the studio, and had he scrapped it, he would personally have to come up with the cost. There is a note of caution in the reports his staff were relaying from the previews.

Fifty years later, a new generation raised on incense and grass found the film a howling success at the New York Film Festival. They proclaimed it a classic. But not in 1930. Even his staff, who seemed to be spending a lot of their time attending previews, couldn't give him better news.

With so many opinions stacked against him, DeMille could only tell Anne Bauchens to keep cutting, even though he knew it would ruin his picture. And he was right. On the first preview after the cuts, Kiesling reported "a storm of laughs, 239 of these outburst or eighteen more than at the San Bernardino screening." Louis B. Mayer told Kiesling to tell DeMille that "several hundred feet should still come out."

The goal of making it a "howling" success kept Kiesling busy creating ornate black and silver art deco posters and title cards for the lobbies. Cross-country tours were set up featuring Adrian's spectacular costumes including the magnificent floor-length red velvet cape as the piece de resistance. Fifty years later, I found this cape, with its swaths of silver and jet-black bugle beads, sparkling mischievously inside a see-through dry cleaning bag at the back of a closet in one of DeMille's guest rooms.

As if things weren't unfair enough, *Vanity Fair*, which had profiled DeMille so handsomely three years earlier, now changed their opinion and put him at the top of their "We Nominate for Oblivion" column. In words echoing a communist manifesto but personalizing Hollywood's ills and hanging them around DeMille it dismissed him as, "a Hollywood Producer whose deluxe spectacles have been largely responsible for the incredibly distorted values of love, high life and wealth which have been formulated in the minds of the American film goers: because he is the acknowledged messiah of sunken bathtubs, ermine tailed boudoir gowns, plush footmen and tiger skin rugs; and finally because with every resource at his command so many fine plots and talented actors and actresses have been just so much grist to DeMille of the false gods of Hollywood."

Despite (or perhaps because of) all the cuts, and without a song worth singing, *Madam Satan* was not a success. It cost a little less than a million dollars, but took in only three-quarters of that. DeMille was notified by MGM that his contract would probably not be renewed beyond the three films agreed. He had one left to go.

A year shy of his fiftieth birthday, DeMille was to be taught an important lesson. With age and increasing security, a man's work is in danger of becoming more reflective of what he owns than of what he feels. The acquisition of assets tends to make a man cautious for his future. This change in his thinking, and the change in role from creator to craftsman, steals up on him gradually. His peers even admire his later work for its polish and execution. But filmmakers fall into the category of having to think like bankers. The overriding need for revenue, for hits to finance more work, is why movies are dictated by business needs first, artistic ones second, if there is room and time.

Now, once again, DeMille found himself in this dilemma. Ever since he left Paramount seven years earlier, the producer in him had struggled with the filmmaker. When he was a young filmmaker he had created trends. Now he had fallen into the trap of following others. Technically his MGM films were as good as any other being made. But both were accounted flops. DeMille's problem as a filmmaker was that he had lost faith in his own judgment. With one more picture left on his contract, he was desperately looking for a sure-fire project with which to regain a firm footing.

CHAPTER TWENTY-NINE

AS ONE PROJECT ENDED, THERE WAS ALWAYS A GREAT SCOURING FOR ideas for DeMille's next film. Early in the year, while he was still completing work on *Madam Satan*, DeMille's mother-in-law, Ella K. Adams, was fully occupied reading hundreds of plays, books, and short stories. She regularly reported to her son-in-law on new scriptwriters who might be useful to him, and wrote synopses on anything she thought might make a good project. For *Dynamite*, DeMille had found his story in the papers. *Madam Satan* was no more than Gladys Unger's idea for modernizing the classic Johann Strauss operetta *Die Fledermaus*. But now he was desperate. Nothing showed this more clearly than the enormous flood of memos from Adams exceeding anything in his files before. Among the hundreds of notes were suggestions for a life of Robert Burns; Dickens's *The Pickwick Papers*; Lewis Carroll's *Alice in Wonderland*; Erich Maria Remarque's sensational bestseller *All Quiet in the Western Front*; and *Scarface* by Armitage Trail. DeMille passed up the chance to make *Scarface*, which, directed by Howard Hawks, would become the gangster classic that raised the genre to new heights. At last, in desperation, with time for a decision drawing to a close, and after consulting with Mayer, DeMille decided that his third film would be nothing less than his third remake of the film with which he began in the business, *The Squaw Man*. He hoped, perhaps, to cash in on the sudden craze sweeping the country for Westerns.

Since he was going to update the story, Bessie McGaffey was back on research. She found that "the old west" was still alive and shooting, with cattle rustling still prevalent in the state of Wyoming, watering rights still hotly fought over in the streets and courts of Nevada, and bandits still robbing banks with six shooters in Kansas City. *The Squaw Man* had all of these timeless ingredients and more. "I love this story so much that as long as I live I will make it every ten years," DeMille said. He was still planning to remake it in more liberal times shortly before his death. Had he lived to do so he would again have been in the forefront of those who would now see Native Americans in a sympathetic light. But in 1931, he couldn't have felt as confident of his third version as he sounded since there was only one, rather thin, scrapbook on the film.

At this time, "J's" weekly reports never ceased to add to DeMille's concerns. He also received disturbing information about the spread of labor unrest from Garbutt: "There is serious talk of a strike in the Movies soon, unless the studio officials decide to sign up a new agreement with the unions. They are making a special drive to get as many into the union as possible before they make their demands." Furthermore, there were rumors of communist infiltration in Hollywood: "Communists are slowly getting control of the Labor Unions of the Country and other organizations, and of the order issued very recently urging the young communists to enlist in the U.S. Army and Navy so that they will be in a position to kill the officers when the time comes for the revolution." Shades of *Potemkin* on the Potomac. With such fears stirring the mind, is it any wonder that Hollywood—bastion of the simple soul, erroneously credited with the few genuine works of art that inevitably slipped through the six hundred commercial films produced per year—would suspect the worst when the time came?

Fighting supposed communist infiltration in their studios, seeing shades of communist subversion in Ginger Rogers's hanging blinds with the help of her co-workers in *Tender Comrades*, would become one of the industry's and especially DeMille's major obsessions in the years ahead. In the months leading up to the start of filming, DeMille had worked with Leisen and Buckland seeking suitable locations, and with his writers on updating the story for a less romantic age. In London, Leisen was doing research, seeing shows, and keeping his eye out for an actress who could play Lady Diana:

> Letter to DeMille from Leisen (August 27, 1930): The general information here is that Kay [Johnson] is perfect for the English girl . . . and is certainly much better than anyone they feel we could get here. She is rated as our best Actress and immensely popular. Have been to a play every night but so far seen no one that we would be interested in for this picture.

In fact, the "ideal" actress for the role was already rising to the top, lovely Madeleine Carroll, whom DeMille would try unsuccessfully to obtain when he made *The Crusades*, and with whom he finally worked with when he made *North West Mounted Police*.

The usual exhaustive research went into finding the best US location: From DeMille to Buckland (September 9): "You and party will proceed from Los Angeles to Salt Lake City, Utah; thence by rail to Rock Springs, Wyoming, to Ft. Washakie on the edge of the Shoshone Reservation, known as the Wind River Reservation. You will get what data and information of types, customs, habits, costumes, etc. in the towns around this reservation, including Thermopolis, Hudson, Arapahoe, Kirby, and any other towns that seems [*sic*] picturesque or interesting to you in this locality. At Hudson there are coal mines, and I am informed that the local color is very brilliant."

Buckland did numerous sketches of Indians and their habitat. In the thirty years since the play had been written, the Indians' living conditions had deteriorated even further. But this film was not to be an exploration of white man's guilt. Colonel Tim McCoy, the Western star and expert on Indian ways, was an old friend who would be waiting to guide Buckland when he arrived in Blackfoot country.

DeMille, even in the midst of his growing concerns, never lost his passion for research: "To clarify in your mind the purpose of this expedition, it is not to secure a location for the photographing of this picture, but to advise me of the conditions of 'frontier life,' as it is in the cattle towns of today, such as drinking, gathering places, whether in trading posts, stores, or old saloons. Whether stuff is served openly or under cover of soft drink; how much loose gambling you see. Whether the men wear their guns into town, and on the range; how you find cowboys and Indians dressed, both on their reservations and in town. What the main causes of quarrels are between ranchmen, how much cattle rustling there seems to be and how it seems to be done; any possible quarrels over water or water holes, or fence lines. Inter-marriage between whites and Indians."

All the while, money (and work) was in short supply. In the course of all these swirling external events, the genuinely considerate part of DeMille's nature survived. Pev Marley's vaudeville tour, as well as his three-year marriage, was nearly over, and he informed DeMille of his availability. But ultimately Marley, whose last credit had been on some MGM films in early 1930, was not to work again at his craft until DeMille hired him for *This Day and Age* in 1933.

Problems in the country caused by the Depression were galloping from bad to worse. On September 16, *The Trade Press* reported, "Movie houses preferred using girl ushers to cut expenses—usherettes are favored because of lower pay asked." Leisen, who had done all the production designs on *Dynamite* and *Madam Satan*, but who had had to share his credit with MGM's department head, Cedric Gibbons, was elevated to assistant director on *Squaw Man* for his years of loyal work. Leisen: "Art directors often have a lot of say about how a scene will be lit and set up in terms of the movements of the actors and camera. I had been setting the cameras for DeMille for a long time because he wanted to get as much as he could out of my sets. DeMille's natural inclination was to always shoot the master take straight on, so that when we started breaking it down for close-ups and over-the-shoulder shots, you'd have to reverse the angle and there'd be no set behind them. No matter how big my sets were, he'd get stuck, and I'd be summoned from wherever I was to bail him out."

While preparations for the start of shooting were being made, DeMille continued to assemble his cast from whoever he saw and liked. It made for good publicity. A favorite item over the years concerned DeMille's loyalty in casting small parts with old actors fallen on hard times. This time there were

For his third filming of *The Squaw Man* (1931), DeMille cast Lupe Velez as Naturich, the tragic Native American heroine. Courtesy John Kobal Foundation

small parts for Raymond Hatton, an early DeMille regular and now in cowboy pictures as the hero's side kick, and for Julia Faye and the "original Lady Diana," Winifred Kingstone, as British party girls. Always looking to enhance his reputation as a spotter of future stars, he kept his eyes out for new faces.

The film also brought Warner Baxter back to DeMille. Since working for him as the suave lounge lizard in *The Golden Bed*, Baxter had gained a mustache, a voice, and an Oscar for his portrayal of the Cisco Kid in *In Old Arizona*. Baxter, best remembered now for his role as the Broadway producer in *42nd Street*, was a serviceable, all-around actor who worked in everything from drama to comedy, low budget detective series to big-budget musicals.

Although DeMille had enjoyed looking at the usual number of girls for the role of the Squaw, and at one point had almost settled for Lillian Bond, a British brunette, he chose the hit of the "Wampas Baby" dinner, Le Roy Prinz's Mexican discovery, the volatile and beautiful Lupe Velez "on account of [her] tremendous popularity abroad we could probably make a silent version of the picture from the sound version for release in European countries. Therefore, we have cast Lupe Velez for the part of the squaw."

After Leisen's failure to come up with a "British" actress who could play the Squaw Man's sweetheart, DeMille found his perfect cool lady when he went to see his editor's work on *The Great Meadow*: Eleanor Boardman, a wonderful actress in silent films often directed by her former husband King Vidor. Not long after completing *The Squaw Man*, Boardman moved to Europe with her new husband, director Henry D'Arrast. She should not have retired so soon. Her place in Hollywood was taken by actresses like Irene Dunne, who arrived about that time to make her first film, and who made her reputation playing very much Boardman's sort of role: women who could be understated, polite, caring, and intelligent, without being boring or dull. According to Boardman, "DeMille was very pompous by this time. He was very tough, and he was very nasty with people. . . . In my presence he yelled at people, and swore at them. . . . He wasn't nice with a lot of the people on the set. He would humiliate them, and bawl them out on the set in front of other people."

DeMille's current problems were no excuse for this behavior since it remained consistent over the years, but he was showing more than the usual signs of doubt. One such sign could be gathered from his having no less than four writers, including Gladys Unger, Lenore Coffee, Josephine Lovett, and Lucien Hubbard, responsible for the continuity, and Elsie Janis on tap for dialogue, on a script that had served him twice already. Lenore Coffee, who would also work for him on *Four Frightened People*, was, like so many, having professional problems—only four minor films since leaving DeMille. Coffee: "My husband ran into DeMille at MGM, who asked what I was doing, for he would like to have me on *The Squaw Man*. . . . I had a meeting that very afternoon with both DeMille and Elsie, who had some really good ideas, and *The Squaw Man* was still a good story. That night we opened a bottle of champagne for we thought everything was going to be splendid from now on. And so it would have been if Mr. DeMille had not had an emergency appendix operation only a few weeks later. That changed everything. He was rushed to the Cedars of Lebanon Hospital and made a fairly good recovery, but would have to rest for quite a long time. . . . By the time he was ready to leave the hospital, he also knew he would be leaving MGM."

During DeMille's lengthy convalescence, he read a lot, not least of which was Agent Jackson's reports. These, including his eighty-six-page report to Congressman Hamilton Fish, make for fascinating reading for those interested in the American government's deep concern over suspected communist penetration of American institutions.

On June 10, 1930, he reported, "Agent is the only person who is a member of the underground section of this revolutionary movement who has so far submitted a report. Agent is going to present this and testify at a secret hearing so that he will not be uncovered. At this hearing Agent is going to be able to show that certain high union officials are being influenced by the Communists. . . . [He] is sure that there will be a house cleaning here as labor leaders are very much afraid of the radical movement in the unions." By way of a summary of the position, he declares, "Of course there is always going to be trouble in the industry as long as there are union agreements."

Even with his intestines on fire this was hardly DeMille's cup of tea. But now he also had a condensed version of Jackson's report to Congressman Fish, marked "CONFIDENTIAL" and headed "Communist Activities." It described a three-year plan, "to be designated as 'Our answer to the U.S. investigation of Communist Propaganda,'" and described a form of "pyramid" recruiting. "There are about two million persons in this country now who are friendly to the movement; who are members of some of the expressions of the Party. Each one of this is to be instructed to bring in two others by January First 1932, which will make a total of six million sympathizers and members; the second year each of these must get two more members making eighteen million by January First 1933 and so on the next year for a total of fifty-four million. Any member who does not secure two members in one year will not be considered worthy of the title of Comrade and will be dismissed from the Party."

In reading these reports, one is constantly aware of the frequent derogatory racial and religious references to various minorities; in one part of the report, there are references to "Abe Shaw, whose real name is Abe Shapiro." In another part, Jackson describes a "mixed dance" at which "Party members were ordered to dance with the Negroes which they did."

Mind you, even men like Irving Thalberg were not averse to making pejorative remarks about tourists from Iowa. What emerges in the latrine of life is that the average worker, whatever the high principals expressed by his union, is just as intolerant as the next man. As DeMille recovered, grapes, flowers, and telegrams bombarded his room. He heard from Anne Bauchens, who had been editing two MGM Westerns while waiting to start on his film. These had been started when the widescreen process seemed to be one of the ways ahead.

Bauchens experience stopped DeMille from adding that expense to his budget. October 16, 1930: "I'm not sure whether you would be interested in Grandeur film or not. If you did as they are on *Great Meadow* and shot everything on the 2 films you might find it interesting. The technique is entirely different, in that you have no real close shots or individual shots. The exterior scenes are marvelous though, and you can take in such a wide territory at one time." By February, DeMille had fully recovered, so it was time to make movies. At 9:45 a.m., Thursday, February 5, 1931, Warner Baxter, and the rest of the cast gathered in his bungalow for the reading. Since this was listed as a reading for "the English cast" there may have been a foreign-language version planned.

For four months, there had been no word from Jackson. Finally, the last of his reports to be stored in Gladys's secret file arrived. With it he had enclosed a copy of a letter from Paul Dullzell in New York to Charley Miller in Hollywood confirming that Gillmore was now out of the picture, and uttering warnings about the leaky nature of the union's communications, which seemed to be with Beetson an hour after they had been typed out.

The character and identify of "Jackson" remain fascinating subjects for speculation. Jackson spent many years working as an undercover agent of the US government, most likely the Justice Department or perhaps the Treasury Department. Money was important to him, and he speaks readily of others who either flaunt their dollars or try to obtain bribes. He seems to have held a selection of union posts, but he was always anxious to solicit work and all invoices were presented most punctually. What did he do with all that money? Did he store it away or did it finance some expensive, secret vice? And there is the question of risk. He speaks quite frequently of the dangers of detection and they were clearly very real at a time when the unions were engaged in open warfare with Los Angeles. He remains a fascinating enigma. Incredibly, no one had ever sussed the identity of the informant. Did his wife have a nervous breakdown? Did his marriage crack-up under the strain? Was there a movie in this? Or were there many?

Hollywood's producers knew all about shady dealings first hand but historians chose to see them as vulgar simpletons or crass exploits of female flesh or, occasionally, as heroes in the fight of intellectuals against the view of the public as children. Even Buzzell, from what Jackson reports in one of his last missives, was not above being a film critic. With his final words, Jackson is lost to history, or at any rate to DeMille's files: "Agent is on the trail of several things which he will report later if successful." But he never did. It appears that the AMPP's economy cuts had even struck at the Secret Service. "J" had nothing more to offer them. But, as he had previously forecast, problems with both forces would dog the studios for years to come, until Old Hollywood was only a shadow of its former self. Hollywood's battle with the unions and communism in the industry continued in different forms, climaxing in the McCarthy hearings and the notorious blacklist that dominated the last decade of the studio system. The old moguls fought against TV for survival, but did so without the richer blood that had made their previous work so vital.

Shooting on *The Squaw Man* started on February 9. The film was to be a romantic vision of the west, subtle and reticent, nostalgic for a world that was fast disappearing. As before, the story opens in England, but now the time is 1923. A party is being given in the grounds of the duplicitous Lord Kerhill's lavish estate with an elaborate fundraising Gymkhana for the benefit of the regimental orphanage. The occasion provided DeMille with an excuse to stage the sort of eye-catching spectacle he loved. (Maybe that was why, having gotten it out of his system in films, he never threw a single memorable bash in his home.) Here, watched by hundreds of villagers and their wives and children, were Mounted Musical Chairs; Slicing the Apple (troops trying to slice apples and lemons in half at the gallop); Tent Pegging; and a Gretna Green Race where officers rode up to their female guests, dismounted, got the girls on to the saddle, got "married," remounted, and finished the course. Other events included a Balaclava Melee with Lord Kerhill (Paul Cavanagh) leading one team and Wyngate (Warner Baxter) the other. Lady Diana (Eleanor Boardman) is one of the judges. During the earlier scenes of the hunt, a problem with animals occurred. The dogs broke loose and created pandemonium with DeMille yelling to everyone to help round them up.

Prinz: "All the dogs broke loose, and they were supposed to be going across the camera for a long shot. And DeMille screamed, 'L. P., get out there and help them get those dogs together.' I said, 'Mr. DeMille, my contract says Dance Director!' He had a temper. [Once] I didn't hear him, and he yelled, 'LeRoy Prinz!' and hit me [hard on the head with a microphone]. And I said, 'You sonofabitch!' And he said, 'Calm down, calm down.' Very unusual, [but] DeMille was God. . . . With me he took everything. He was very proud of the fact that he had been a pilot once upon a time. And I was an ace. Yeah. He was always proud of saying, 'He's a madman, but he had one hell of a war record.' Listen, DeMille was a hidden genius. He'd pick your brains to death, yet he'd know better than you what you could give him."

The festivities end scandalously when it is discovered that the funds have been stolen. Blame is attached to Wyngate, after which he goes off to the wilds of Arizona, where he marries his squaw and bumps into Lady Diana again. Contrary to the beginning of his career, this time DeMille decided to shoot most of *The Squaw Man* in Arizona's supposedly inhospitable climate, sending his camera and crew to a location a stone's throw from Flagstaff. Meanwhile, the real-life Lady Diana (Constance deMille) was also on the scene, visiting her husband on his location while his "squaw" (Julia Faye) was back in Los Angeles. But in the age of the telephone there was no safety in mere distance.

Boardman: "I remember we were up in Arizona, on location, and Mrs. deMille came along . . . and Julia Faye called him, and he was asked to take the phone in a private booth in a drugstore. We were in a little town out in nowhere, and Mrs. deMille walked into the store when he was talking to Julia Faye. And that was when she found out that there was really something going on between the two. That was a big drama. It had been going on for years but it was just that night, while we were on location, that she discovered it."

The film, without other complications, was finished on schedule on March 26, forty days and six hours after shooting started. While DeMille had brought the film in almost $200,000 under its original budget of $742,398.52, it still lost more than $200,000 at the box office.

DeMille: "It was a good picture. But in the economic conditions of the time it was a predestined failure. . . . I do not enjoy failure. Almost the only time I feel physically weary and without energy, if my health is otherwise good, is when I am doing something which is not succeeding. If I am doing something that holds any promise of achievement, I can keep at it until I drop. I may fall asleep at the dinner table; but after three or four hours' rest I am ready to do my deep breathing and push-ups the next morning, and start another day. After *The Squaw Man*, though, I do not know whether MGM or I was more relieved that my contract had come to an end."

In addition to being out of work and professionally wounded, the last two years had been sad in other respects for DeMille. An article titled "The Death Films of Hollywood" reported that many of DeMille's friends and co-workers on *King of Kings* had died: "Members of the company who have passed on included (his old friend) James Neill, who played the Apostle James; Robert Edeson, who played the part of Matthew; Rudolph Schidkraut, who portrayed the High Priest Calaphas, and George Siegmann, who was Barabbas; Frank Urson, assistant director on the picture, dove into shallow water in a Chicago pool two years ago [circa 1929] and was instantly killed, William Crowthers, casting director for the picture, died a year or so ago, London, and Lou Goodstadt, business manager for the company, passed away shortly before. Even Roy Burns, property man throughout the production, hovered near death several times during a six months' period of illness."

Back in February, at the beginning of shooting *The Squaw Man*, DeMille knew his time at MGM was up, so he was busy making alternate plans. He gathered top directors at his house: Frank Borzage, Lewis Milestone, and King Vidor. There they formulated a plan for their creative futures outside the established system. Their idea anticipated a similar plan by a later generation of directors, including Francis Ford Coppola, William Friedkin, and Peter Bogdanovich, to pool their talents for total creative freedom. Like the earlier attempt, it eventually foundered for lack of backing. Back then it had been DeMille's idea to put together a group of men who seemed to him to be the real creative minds in the business, as distinct from producers seeking a buck. Of course, they had the talent but they needed to find capital to finance them. DeMille: "Should we have been surprised that the financiers and bookkeepers did not share our enthusiasm? In May of 1931, I had to write to my three associates that progress in obtaining financing and distribution for our Directors' Guild had been 'difficult and slow,' which was an understatement, because 'the heads of the large producing and distributing organizations fear that . . . the revolutionary idea of the director selecting and making his own productions . . . might lead to a general revision of the present system' and that 'the chaotic condition in which all the industry is at the present time . . .

has resulted in a state of panic in the mind of the producer which tends to make him fear any departure from the beaten path." This guild "petered out in a desert of indifference."

Of course, 1931 was not an ideal time in which to raise financing. Ultimately only Borzage made any films under this scheme. Both films—*Man's Castle*, dealing with the effects of the Depression on good but simple souls, and *No Greater Glory*, about children caught up in the Depression—were excellent but neither made any money. After that he too returned to hiring out his services to the studios. DeMille's contract with MGM was over. His term as the president of the AMPP was also over. The new president was Louis B. Mayer, his vice president, Jack L. Warner. In a short while, DeMille had gone from being a peer of the most senior studio executives to one amongst many jobbing directors. Now he wasn't even listed among the membership of the AMPP. Putting the best face on it he could manage, he announced that he and Mrs. deMille were going on a long postponed holiday to Europe. In fact, the "holiday" was to Russia, and in fact it was largely a fishing expedition to scout for work. Although his public image was still intact, he was on the verge of being washed up in Hollywood.

The films DeMille made in the remaining twenty-seven years of his life are the ones he is best remembered for by the public, and by and large the least admired by the critics. In these years, the reputation that grew up around him is the one that has endured making his name synonymous with everything that is "Hollywood."

CHAPTER THIRTY

IN FEBRUARY 1931, THE UNBELIEVABLE HAPPENED. CECIL BLOUNT DEMILLE was out of work. The great prince and captain of the movie industry, whose name had for so long been synonymous with glamor, spectacle, and above all success, found himself unemployed and apparently unemployable.

Even so, as he planned a trip that would take him far from the scene of disaster, seeds were being sown for the film he would make on his return. In his memoirs, DeMille credits Ben Schulberg for bringing him back to Paramount, but leading up to it had been Jesse Lasky, who had been in correspondence regarding what would become *The Sign of the Cross*. Unfortunately for DeMille, major programming decisions now had to be put before a board. The board did not care for DeMille's proposition, and Lasky's position was no longer secure enough to override them.

His trip grew into an extended vacation with Constance, a world tour that would include Europe, Russia, and the Middle East. He had long wanted to go to Russia, and by combining business with pleasure, the costs could all be written off. In March, after receiving Lasky's news and with no certainty of a job when he returned, the DeMilles took off for New York.

DeMille was going to do this expedition first class all the way, especially having heard about living and travel conditions in Russia. He wanted to make sure there would be deluxe suites in the finest hotels, the choicest meals, a private automobile and chauffeur constantly at his disposal, and, most importantly of all, a special English-speaking guide/interpreter familiar with the moving picture industry in Russia. Gladys Unger dealt with everything. During this long and exciting trip, he never ceased to plan for the movie that would put him back on the map.

En route the couple made nostalgic visits to the Pennsylvania Military College, where DeMille had left before graduating and was awarded an honorary degree, and to his old home on Pompton Lake. They sailed June 24, on the luxurious *Ile de France*, after DeMille had started negotiations to purchase the rights to Wilson Barrett's play *The Sign of the Cross*.

Why *The Sign of the Cross* instead of *Quo Vadis*, which was virtually the same story? Both had the same blonde Christian heroine, and the same handsome

Roman tribune who converted out of love for her; in both cases, a debauched empress fancied the Tribune, and both featured lions galore. But when Barrett wrote his play, adaptations bordering on plagiarism were the norm in the theater. An "original" idea for a play often consisted of seeing a play before someone else did, and changing the names of its characters.

The film rights belonged to Mary Pickford, who had bought it in 1924 as a possible project for herself, but first DeMille had to straighten out unexpected difficulties with the author's daughter, Dorothea. Dollars did the trick, thousands upon thousands of them. Pickford, a notoriously hard bargainer, raised her price from $30,000 to $50,000.

The DeMilles' first stop was London, where they "did" the West End and spotted Charles Laughton, whom DeMille would cast as Nero. In Berlin, they were joined by Theodore Kosloff. DeMille had found a new excitement. He was delirious with travel. In long letters, he regaled his readers with fascinating reports on everything that came into his acquisitive and teeming mind, from the state of the European film industry to the quality of his food in Russia. He was a workaholic, but fortunately he knew how to enjoy life.

In Russia, DeMille found himself burdened with an official guide, Madame Levina; in the end he palmed her off on Constance. On September 4, he cabled his lawyer urgently requesting equipment. He explained what was going on in an excitable letter to Gladys Unger: "The Mejrabpom-Film, which is the government, owned International Film Co. of Russia asked me to sit in conference with them on the subject of my doing a picture in Russia. 'I wish I could tell you the amazing experiences in this city,' he went on. There is nothing like it in the world unless it was Rome after its fall or Paris after the revolution. We have been to the theatre every night. The finest production of Grand Opera I have ever seen, in the most beautiful opera house in the world with a packed audience.

"I have had perfect freedom, have been everywhere from the top to the bottom. Almost nothing that you have heard about it is true—America and the rest of the world have little conception of what the facts here are. There is more drama in one block on a street of Moscow than I have ever seen in an entire city anywhere else." While his political leanings might have made one think of this as something diametrically opposed to everything he stood for—Russia, after all, was the home of the communism he so feared—they had an important film industry.

The Russians idolized him. He was the big director from the West. They were still showing his old silent films (though there was no reference to his *Volga Boatman*), and there was particular admiration for *The Godless Girl*. In their memoirs, both William and DeMille expressed amused surprise at why this film was so popular there. "The film was practically out of date by the time it was released," wrote William. "Except in Russia . . . he found himself hailed as a leader of New Thought. . . . He had made the picture to show how necessary is a belief in God, but the crafty Russians by a few deft changes in the film had made him a brilliant Apostle of Atheism." "It was not until the end of my trip that someone enlightened me," added DeMille. "The Russians simply did not screen the last redeeming reel, but played the rest of the picture as a document of American police brutality and the glorious spreading of atheism among American youth."

He was now offered what the Russians must have considered a very handsome proposition, given their economic conditions. For DeMille's services as director, they offered him five times the salary their own top directors were earning. But there were snags, particularly with regard to the exchange rate of the ruble.

DeMille's enthusiasm was genuine, but he was unwilling to sacrifice one cent to art. Many years later in his autobiography, he stressed freedom rather than economics as the reason for his disenchantment with the idea of working in the USSR. He was appalled to discover that a representative of every class of film worker took part in decision making: "A film director in the Soviet Union did not have the individual freedom we had in the United Sates, even with all our harassment by the financiers. Not for nothing were the studios in Russia called 'film factories.'"

Their demanding schedule now saw them travel 2,300 miles down the Volga by boat to Stalingrad, then across the Steppes by train to Georgia, and from there by car to Batum, where they would sail on a French boat across the Black Sea to Istanbul. Here an important friendship was formed. The State Department official assigned to interview DeMille and discover what he had learned in Russia was Joseph Grew, a right-wing diplomat, with whom DeMille later co-operated in connection with the Crusade for Freedom and Radio Free Europe.

DeMille and Constance soon slipped back into more comfortable Western ways: "Only someone who has spent time in Russia can fully understand what a beautiful sight the French steward in his clean white collar was, when we went in to dinner and he showed us to a table with a clean cloth and napkins; we sat down and breathed the air of freedom."

There was no more talk of India, which would doubtless have unsettled them in other ways, and after visits to Egypt and the Holy Land they returned to New York on the *Augustus* on November 24, five months after they first set sail.

A letter from John Flinn awaited him with some good news: "A proposition to purchase the silent rights for $30,000 and the dialogue rights at a cost from the English owners plus the expense of the negotiation for the dialogue rights. This would close the entire matter somewhere around $38,000."

Meanwhile, DeMille's non-movie business interests were holding up well even as the Depression was raging. Rentals from his properties alone were making him almost $50,000, before tax and upkeep. Even with a decrease of nearly half a million in market value of his various holdings, Gladys Unger could still report a handsome surplus by year's end of over $1.5 million. This while other people, including many of his employees, were selling off or mortgaging their properties to make ends meet. DeMille was rumored to be one of the richest men in Hollywood.

At last the deal for *The Sign of the Cross* was clinched, at less than half of what Pickford had originally asked. It came at an opportune moment. By February 1932, even DeMille's own finances were beginning to be affected by the Depression. His lawyer had been forced to mortgage even the Laughlin Park property (ironically recently renamed 2000 DeMille Drive), and the income tax authorities were claiming over $1.5 million in back payments. In the house on the hill, 1932 started in considerable gloom.

But DeMille still hadn't made a deal with a studio. Now he took the matter into his own hands. He went to see Ben Schulberg, who was then head of Paramount with rights to *The Sign of the Cross*. "He was just on the way out as head of Paramount. Manny Cohen was going to come in. . . . He said, 'This is a great subject and you're the one man who can do it.' So we started a deal, and in the middle of the deal Manny Cohen comes in, is put in charge, and we finished the deal together, the three of us. Manny Cohen would probably never have taken it except, with Schulberg, the deal was made. And then Jesse was on the way out."

At last, things were on the move.

CHAPTER THIRTY-ONE

THE DEPRESSION HAD CAUGHT PARAMOUNT IN THE MIDST OF LARGE OUT-
lays on new sound films; on their extensive foreign-language productions;
on costly new soundstages for their studios in France and England, as well as
on their East Coast studios at Astoria and Long Island; and on the ill-timed
purchase of additional chains of glittering movie palaces in which to show
their product.

But the films weren't doing so well. Paramount's slogan, "If it's a Paramount picture, it's the best show in town," wasn't convincing the public.
In 1930, *Morocco* starring Marlene Dietrich tided them over. In 1932, Mae
West's films and DeMille's *Sign of the Cross* were all they had to keep from
going under. While ticket prices were being slashed to ten cents and double
features were being instituted to pull in the customers, no one really knew
what the public wanted. Public surveys first reported that they wanted melo-
dramas; then it was comedies; then there was a clamor for Westerns, so Paramount launched its Zane Grey series. Musicals were enormously popular,
then suddenly nobody was going to musicals anymore. Studios jumped from
one bandwagon to the next.

Paramount was already in disarray when Manny Cohen, serving as his
personal assistant, insinuated his way into Jesse Lasky's confidence. When
the board convened to deal with the latest crisis, it was Lasky who had to explain why the studio wasn't right more often in the choice of the films they
offered. Accusations flew from all sides. To prove his point, Lasky naturally
expected the tireless Cohen to come up with the relevant figures. Instead,
Cohen remained silent, and when he did speak, he led the attack against his
boss. The meeting ended with Lasky's sacking, and his assistant was appointed to fill his place. Adolph Zukor, who might have been expected to stand up
for his partner in the company they had founded, did nothing. The reward
for his treachery from Cohen was the loss of his high office and exile to a
humble company outpost in South America. In their respective memoirs,
none of the key figures in Cohen's rise had a good word to say about him.

DeMille returned to the studio to find Zukor a beaten-down old man.
Years later DeMille told his granddaughter, "When I walked into his office,

Zukor was drinking. I walked over and I took the bottle, put it in the drawer and closed the drawer. And then I sat down, and I told him what he was. I told him what a great man he'd been; what an industry he'd helped found. I left Zukor believing in himself, with tears in his eyes."

Lasky was ousted in the spring of 1932. One of Lasky's last favors to DeMille, in the face of much opposition, was to sign Charles Laughton, whom DeMille had seen in London and wanted for the role of Nero in *The Sign of the Cross*. "Cecil B. DeMille visualized Nero as the 'menace' in the film," wrote his long-suffering wife, the actress Elsa Lanchester, in her memoir *Charles Laughton and I*, "whereas Charles thought him merely funny. DeMille was shocked by the idea, but after a long argument Charles got his own way and was allowed to give Nero a preciousness which he felt would make the orgies more evil. Charles always felt that in a film of this sort there was no option but to make the villain, Nero in this case, a laughing stock to the audience. The film script too seemed to offer every encouragement to make this creature a figure of fun. Charles enjoyed mouthing the words 'delicious debauchery,' but Cecil B. DeMille never did see his own epic from this angle. After the preview he rang Charles up and said that the audience had laughed at him, but this had been Charles's intention all the time."

DeMille selected the Austrian-born British actress Elissa Landi as the saintly Mercia over 500 others because "she conveys mysticism with sense. She combines the pure with the wholesome. She has the depths of the age in her eyes. She has today in her body and tomorrow in her spirit." Nevertheless, he had first thought of this peerless virgin for the part of Poppaea!

Then DeMille spotted Claudette Colbert crossing the lot and asked, "How would you like to play the wickedest woman in the world?" Colbert, whose career as a sweet innocent was going nowhere, jumped at the offer. She came away a star. At the launch, DeMille described her as "like a beautiful, poisonous cobra."

The conditions DeMille now had to accept from the company he had once helped to build were odious. He was only allowed to bring Mitchell Leisen and Roy Burns onto the payroll (though he contrived to reinstate both his secretary Florence Cole and his editor Anne Bauchens in short order). He had to work under close supervision, with Emmanuel Cohen breathing down his neck to keep him to an extremely tight budget, a paltry $650,000 for an epic recreating ancient Rome. "His greeting to me," recalled DeMille, "was: 'Remember, Cecil, you are on trial with this picture.' Manny was my greatest trial."

"Do I remember *The Sign of the Cross*?" asked choreographer LeRoy Prinz when I interviewed him years later. "Sure, we did that on the back lot. . . . You don't suppose that DeMille staged it, do you? You don't suppose that those extras at $75 a day didn't have to be coached? DeMille just came on the set when I was good and ready. . . . Do you remember when Moses brought that tribe down and the girls did that big rain dance in the middle

Elissa Landi portrayed Mercia, the Christian maid who, in a dramatic scene from *The Sign of the Cross* (1932), is sent to her death in the Roman Colosseum. Photo by Otto Dyar. Courtesy John Kobal Foundation

of the floor? That was staged and shot the same day. I said, 'Mr. DeMille, set your cameras. We may get it the first time.'"

Karl Struss would be the cameraman, and Mitchell Leisen, who had also left MGM after *The Squaw Man*, the art director. The tight budget proved a challenge for Leisen: "I used every trick I could think of. The arena was a miniature. We built several flights of stairs with ramps at each level so the people walked in, and that was all. As the crowd entered the arena, we panned straight up because there was nothing on either side. We had a tiny segment of the arena, and when you see close-ups of the spectators, we used a prism lens which turned it over and doubled the size of the crowd." Many costumes were rented or reused from *King of Kings*.

Claudette Colbert as Empress Poppaea in *The Sign of the Cross* (1932) takes a bath in pool filled with asses' milk. Photo by Otto Dyar. Courtesy John Kobal Foundation

"Audiences were very much moved," enthused William Everson, "or perhaps stimulated would be a better word, by the sight of Colbert's Poppaea taking a bath in asses' milk while a brace of cats lap contentedly from the side of the pool!" But the asses' milk was actually Klim (milk spelt backwards): powdered milk. "The Klim was so warm my bangs came uncurled," recalled Colbert in 1984. "When the electricians forgot to turn off all the hot lights for an hour while we were at lunch it congealed and the Klim turned to cream cheese. They removed my bellybutton," she added with a sideswipe at the Hays Office. "Did you ever see a tummy without a navel? It's very weird."

Leisen also remembered Colbert's bath of asses' milk: "DeMille wanted the milk to just barely cover her nipples, so the day before, I had Claudette stand in the pool and I measured her to get the level just right. We had compressed air blowing up from the bottom to make it foamy, and Claudette said, 'Ooh, it tickles!' . . . We finished up and got her out of it. She got cleaned up and went to dinner. Without the air, the surface of the clabber became very smooth. While we were eating, one of the New York executives was taking a tour around the set. He thought the white stuff was a marble floor, so he stepped right on it and slowly began to sink! He was the most awful mess you ever saw."

Despite its cost and its tightly constructed sets, *The Sign of the Cross* was hailed, at least by Paramount, as the "First Talking Motion Picture Spectacle." According to the publicity, DeMille used almost 7,500 extras for the crowd scenes. Charles Higham says that DeMille hired dwarfs and giantesses from circuses to fight one another, while the gladiators were trained by General van Konifkoff and Captain Clifford McClagen. In 1954, DeMille told Art Arthur about the problems created by the use of so many animals: "I got these elephants from the circus, you know, and they were supposed to be in the arena removing the dead, scooping them up and pulling them to one side to clean the arena out between the acts and get rid of the bodies. We rehearsed the scene fine, everything was fine. I said, 'Camera,' and everybody started to shout and applaud and everything else, and all the elephants stood on their heads! They thought, 'This is the act.' They all stood on their heads with their feet in the air! It was one of the funniest things . . . we had about 26 lions and 5 experts on. The lions were getting $25 a day apiece or something like that, and these fellows figured they could stay there forever. We wasted a full day trying to get these lions to go up stairs. . . . After two days, and these lions wouldn't go up the stairs, I said to one of these trainers, 'Listen, this is costing a frightful amount of money. When are those lions going to go up those stairs?' And this man came to me and said, 'Well, lions don't go up stairs.' And the second day when they came to me with that, I said, 'Well, by God, these lions are going up stairs.' And I took a wooden chair and I started to wham around. . . . And up the stairs they went and that's the shot you see. They jumped over each other getting up, scrambled and fought, all to get away from me!"

And then there were the crocodiles. The last time he'd worked with these reptiles had been in *Fool's Paradise*. Serving as stuntman was Joe Bonomo: "DeMille sent for me one day. 'Joe, I've got to do something, my regular stuntmen are backing away from. They just say, "Get Bonomo. He'll try anything."' I was to play a Christian martyr, be thrown into a pit of hungry crocodiles and be devoured before the eyes of the Roman spectators. Before I could answer yes or no, he said, 'Figure it out, Joe, and make it good,' gave me a pat on the back and was gone, leaving me standing there. It happened I knew about crocodiles. The crocodile has a double-hinged jaw—that is, both the upper and the lower jaw can move, either together or independently. In addition, it is smaller, much faster and far more vicious than the cumbersome, more complacent alligator. . . . I had an idea to substitute the crocodiles with alligators. One reason for choosing alligators was that he lacks the double-hinged jaw the crocodile possesses. Only his lower jaw moves, and that hinges down. If you can catch his lower jaw when it is open, you can hold it open, unless he twists away."

DeMille agreed to the substitution, as most people didn't know the difference. "The next day, I was thrown into the pit, with six alligators. I had taken the precaution earlier to station five men just out of camera range with long

poles with big cloth wads on the ends of them to watch the other five, and
shove the wads into their mouths if they started to move. As I hit the mud,
I grabbed him by a front leg—the one away from the side where the cameras were going to shoot the death scene. We wrestled for a moment, and he
opened his big lower jaw. I grabbed it with my left hand, held it open and half
put my head in his mouth, but from the side away from the cameras.

"I quickly pulled him down on top of me, kicking my legs in the air so it
looked as though the gator had me down. As the cameras stopped shooting,
I got the hell out.

"DeMille used to carry a few twenty-dollar gold pieces with him in those
days, and when he was particularly thrilled by a performance, he would give
one to the actor or actress. To possess a DeMille gold piece was a mark of
distinction much like an Academy 'Oscar' is today. I got one for that alligator
sequence. Everyone said it was great footage. As a matter of fact, it was too
great. At the preview women fainted. It was too macabre for public viewing.
So, one of the greatest alligator-gobbles-man scenes in the history of motion
pictures wound up on the cutting-room floor."

On October 6, the last day of shooting, DeMille's assistant Roy Burns
rushed up to him in the middle of a take and announced, "We've just used
up the budget." DeMille picked up his megaphone and yelled "Cut!" Anne
Bauchens had to deal with the missing bits of the story using all her considerable ingenuity.

The Sign of the Cross completed a trinity of pictures: *The Ten Commandments*
was the giving of the law, *The King of Kings* the interpretation of the law, and
The Sign of the Cross was the preservation of the law. (*The Crusades*, three years
later, must have been the trampling of the law.)

After its first official screening, DeMille was under pressure to cut some
of the tougher scenes: lesbians, gorillas, nude girls, lions, alligators, pygmies,
Amazons, asses' milk baths, and some saucy dialogue. Letter from DeMille to
Mr. Verne Wickham, motion picture editor, *Press-Telegram and Morning Sun*,
Long Beach, California (November 12): "I am following your suggestion in
the toning down and elimination of some of the arena horrors, such as, the
gorilla and the girl, and eliminating some of the crocodile shots. While it is
my purpose to give the audience all it can stand of the realism of a Roman
Holiday for the purpose, as of course you observed, of making the final love
scene and the scene of the Christians ascending the stairs to the arena the
more powerful, it is my opinion that the reason the audience is so held by
the last two reels is that they have seen from the arena floor that it is no
theatrical entertainment up there, and that these people are really going to a
terrible, though glorious, death."

As seen now over the credits, Rome burns and Nero plucks his harp and
hams to the smoke and scrams coming from below, while his court is gathered up and down the steps leading to his throne as if watching a dinner
show. It's the third day of Rome's conflagration. Nero, gloating, his superb

Holding props for his latest film, *The Sign of the Cross* (1932), DeMille publicizes his latest directing effort. The helmet worn by Fredric March rests on the desk. Courtesy John Kobal Foundation

velvet robes by Leisen, looks like an old beauty resentful of young faces: he
primps and poses, slipping about on his marble throne as if it were a water-
bed. Images succeed one another deplete with sybaritic luxury and sensual
decadence. Delicately beaten armor shimmers alluringly in the rays of the
sun, with chains around every ankle and covered with jeweled belts and
golden buckles. By the well, in the heart of the square, a Roman lash strikes
exposed Christian skin. A smile cracks across the soldier's face. The prefect of
Rome, Marcus Superbus (Fredric March) arrives in time to stop the stoning
by Romans of two bearded Christians and is attracted by the beauty and spirit
of the blonde with them (Elissa Landi). Christianity is represented by a series
of wholesome, healthy, but drab-looking faces.

Photoplay's editor, who saw himself as a moral judge for his readers, had
mixed feelings: "I left the theater with the feeling that I had not been emo-
tionally or spiritually satisfied. . . . Whether such spectacles are bad taste or
good entertainment is, of course, for the individuals that make up picture
audiences to determine for themselves."

The *London Times* also reviewed the film in somewhat grudging terms:
"Though not a good film, and at times perilously near to becoming a dull

one, Mr. Cecil B. DeMille's elaborate version of the *Sign of the Cross* will probably command popularity. It has something of most things: sport, voluptuous-
ness, splendour and cruelty, even religion. The acting is, with two exceptions,
indifferent, and the spectacle, lavish as it may be, is wholly unselective."

But DeMille had an unexpected supporter in John Grierson, father of the
British documentary: "Cecil. B. DeMille is out of fashion among the critics.
But, as is my custom, I have seen *The Sign of the Cross* twice over, and am still
an unrepentant admirer. There is no director to touch him in command of
the medium: certainly none who strikes such awe into my professional mind.
There is another measure of DeMille. He is the only Jewish director who is
not afraid of being his Jewish self; and the thin and squeamish Western mind
may not therefore be fit judge of his Oriental opulence. *The Sign of the Cross*,
by a curious irony, is the best of them all, better even than *The Ten Commandments*. It takes a Jew possibly to appreciate the Christian story. . . . it is at heart
a Jewish story; it is a story of a humility which no other race knows anything
about; and the oppression which is the other half of it can properly be understood only by a people who, back of everything they say, do or pretend,
have the most vivid sense and knowledge of oppression in the world. . . . It
is gloriously horrifying, as by one who understands both the delight of Nero
and the delight of the Christians. Only a Jew, I believe, could understand
both points of view."

Grierson's fulsome appreciation of the special perception brought to a subject by a Jewish director was certainly remarkable. It is doubtful if this was in
any way to the great Episcopalian's taste—indeed, if DeMille saw the review
he must have been horrified. But this issue would continue to surface in his
life in different forms.

Given the mixed critical reaction to *The Sign of the Cross*, this might be
an opportune moment to discuss another criticism often leveled at DeMille:
hypocrisy. No one ever accused directors like Capra and Ford of sentimentality—not because they were better at their craft, but because at the time their
homespun and appealing emotionalism was more fashionable at the time.
As Infante, the great Cuban writer and hopeless film aficionado, observed,
"Great directors are dictators with a keen eye and a film sense. Like John
Ford. . . . Some directors are magicians and ventriloquists. Orson Welles is
this kind of prestidigitator. Some are one-take wonders, like Buñuel. Some,
like William Wyler, are just the opposite. Most directors are a pain in the
director's chair seat."

DeMille certainly belonged to the latter group, but he also had a great
director's eye. Instead of "creating," he wanted to recreate for history the
great images that had influenced his childhood. But he was far more than
a copyist. If he hadn't done it, no one else in Hollywood would have. His
choice was much like that a writer makes about the kind of writer he wishes to be. Even though our regard for the novelist is higher, it doesn't make
the biographer or historian a lesser artist. Sadly, however, that was not how

Hollywood tended to perceive DeMille's contribution. The press book gives some interesting insights into how he hoped the film would be appreciated: "Students of world affairs will find one of the most startling parallels to modern times. For life in ancient Rome is singularly similar in many of its aspects to life in modern America. The story of the luxury and extravagance of Rome finds a striking reflection in our easy life prior to the fateful autumn of 1929."

The Sign of the Cross cost $750,000, and earned $2,000,000 at a time when films were lucky if they made their costs back. As before, and would be the case again a few years later, with his back against the wall he had turned up trumps! DeMille was once again a force to be reckoned with, and after a year in the wilderness suddenly everybody wanted him. Paramount gave him a permanent office and greater freedom in production decisions, but not before he had been in touch to sound out Sidney Kent at Fox . . .

CHAPTER THIRTY-TWO

NEXT CAME TWO PICTURES WHICH WERE A FAR CRY FROM DEMILLE'S HIS-torical spectaculars. The first drew on one of his early experiences. According to an interview DeMille gave at that time to a less-than-knowledgeable British journalist, the story had its origins in gang violence witnessed by the young DeMille while acting in Chicago.

This Day and Age—the original title was to be *Money*, and other working titles included *Pay Day* and *Battle Cry*—was a story of civic-minded youth who took the law into their own hands when the police and the judicial system became unable to cope with the criminal element in their town. The intention was to show how the youth of a nation steps in to clean up graft, financial crookedness, political chicanery, and gangster slaughter. In its way, *This Day and Age* is not dissimilar to 1970s-era films like *Death Wish*, and other vigilante-type movies in which a group of people find that the world is corrupt and decide to take the law into their own hands.

The story was credited to Bartlett Cormack, who had previously written *Racket*, another film with a gangster theme. DeMille's principal photographer was Peverell Marley, back with DeMille after divorcing Lina Basquette. The art director was Hans Dreier, who was in charge of Paramount's teeming art department, assisted by Roland Anderson.

DeMille hoped to cast either Jack LaRue or George Raft, both specialists in gangster roles, in the role of Louis Garrett, the lead crook. Instead, DeMille turned to Charles Bickford, despite a previous falling out that neither man explained in his memoirs. Bickford had also appeared in *The Squaw Man*.

The film's leading lady was a heralded new discovery, Judith Allen. DeMille first saw her on the Paramount lot when he was looking for a naïve young girl to play the hero's high school sweetheart. He announced that the girl cast must not only be truly naïve and young, but she must also be a virgin.

After this film, Allen appeared in a few others for Paramount, but her reputation was spoiled when it was discovered that she was not a virginal young discovery but an experienced actress named Mari Coleman, a girl from New England. Worse followed when the papers revealed that Judith Allen was an unhappily married lady and that her husband, Gus Sonnenberg, had been a wrestler. Their divorce wasn't final when she got her Hollywood chance.

When Gus saw her pictures in the papers with Gary Cooper, he became jealous and went to the press with his story. The discovery of her past life could not have endeared her to the old man in what must have seemed to him like a replay of his earlier problems with Leatrice Joy and John Gilbert.

Steve Smith (Richard Cromwell) and Morry Dover (Ben Alexander) are rivals for the affections of Gay Merrick (Judith Allen). Steve, who plans to become a lawyer, is spending the week working in the DA's office.

A black sedan drives up outside the shop of the local Jewish tailor, and Max (Fuzzy Knight), a lisping henchman to the head of the gang, throws a bomb into the shop because Herman the tailor hasn't paid any protection money. The store is a wreck. But Herman is a patriotic American who will not be intimidated even though the police tell him there is not much they can do for him. Max's boss Louis Garrett (Charles Bickford) is furious with him for not having done a better job and disappears to finish it off.

Steve has already discovered that the police are helpless, and that the courts of law are virtually useless since they are in the pockets of the gangsters. To show Steve just how difficult it is to beat the gangsters, the DA brings him to court, and the accused before the bench is none other than Garrett. The testimony of a witness is questioned—the shop was dark—and the judge dismisses the case for lack of evidence.

Steve is totally disillusioned, but some of the other students who knew and liked Herman decide to play detective and look for other evidence with which to incriminate Garrett. They find one of Louis's cufflinks proving he was at the crime scene.

While the boys are rifling through Garrett's belongings in his apartment, he arrives and knocks one down and shoots the other, who falls down the ladder while trying to escape. Garrett calls the police and accuses the boy still in his apartment of robbery and murder. Before he dies, he gives the third member of their little group the cufflink they found in Garrett's apartment.

The death of his school friend prompts Steve to send out a call to all the other schools in town and tells them they are going to go rat catching. They capture Garrett, tie him up, and take him to a deserted barn. There, the hobbled Garrett walks like an ape to much laughter of the hundreds of students gathered. It is the first really powerful moment in the movie and is, of course, taken from the climatic trial sequence of Fritz Lang's *M*. (Later, in Hollywood, Lang would deal with "lynch law" mentality again in his classic film *Fury*).

They stand Garrett on top of some planks and force him to swear on the Bible. Garrett is still not taking the boys seriously, and so they tie him by a rope and remove the planks, below which is a dark pit. Garrett discovers that the pit is crawling with rats. They keep lowering him until at last in terror he screams out his confession, and tells them it wasn't his fault—it was "the little man." The "little man" turns out to be a group of civic leaders who had been using Garrett to do their dirty work. The police arrive at the barn in time to nab Garrett's mob. This time the law has evidence, and the chief of police turns all of the students into "deputy sheriffs" to legalize their illegal actions. The hundreds of students, with a cowering Garrett lifted high above their heads, march through the town singing patriotic songs like "Yankee Doodle Dandy" and "Oh! Susanna."

DeMille's epic of modern youth was heavily promoted by the studio as "the first great spectacle of modern times." In reality, the film was a modest thing, taking place mostly in the high school, a few streets, and a nightclub. Not until the last third, when eleven of the students gang-up to take justice, do we have what amounts to a DeMillean crowd. The posters exaggerated the spectacle, showing DeMille towering with megaphone and looking out over a cast of thousands and trumpeting, "Five thousand new faces. Five thousand new stars. Among them Hollywood's second generation. Sons of famous players." (As part of the crowd, the cast included the sons and daughters of a lot of former Hollywood stars like Wallace Reid Jr. and Erich von Stroheim Jr. None had a significant role—it was all for show and publicity.)

Since the talents involved in this project included people like cinematographer Pev Marley, there were bound to be some effective moments. The film is well lit, the sets are well built, and the camerawork is flawless. (The funeral address is shot from inside the grave—a sort of coffin's-eye view of things.) Nevertheless, the film is blatantly crude, slipshod in continuity, absurdly exaggerated to make its points, faulty in reproduction of character (the high school students all looked old enough to be college graduates, while the leading lady looked like a married woman, which she was), and ultimately funny because of its insult to the intelligence. If it had been made by high school students its ineptitude could have been justified—its "fascist" subtext might have served as a warning of what was wrong with the school system. Made by a director of DeMille's stature for a major studio as popular entertainment, it simply boggles the mind. Amazingly, perhaps aided by the high moral mood of the time, the reviews were fairly good.

After *This Day and Age* was released, Lang and his producers took DeMille to court over its blatant plagiarism. (There is a good deal of correspondence relating to charges of plagiarism of at least two other works.) More than one critic had noticed the similarity between the two films. What could DeMille have been thinking? Was it just Hollywood provincialism on DeMille's part to think that anything made abroad didn't have any rights in the United States? Or that it wouldn't have been seen?

Initially, DeMille had planned to move on from *This Day and Age* to *End of the World*, but when it was discovered that another studio was about to start work on *The Deluge*, he scrapped the idea and went on immediately to *Four Frightened People*.

Four Frightened People was DeMille's sixth all-talking picture. Apparently, DeMille got the idea from reading E. Arnot Robertson's original novel, an action story of survivors from a plague ship who escape into the Malayan jungle. As reworked by DeMille, it became a Hawaiian remake of *Male and*

Female, minus the butler. In her autobiography, Lenore Coffee, who co-scripted *Four Frightened People* (with Bartlett Cormack again), makes no mention of it. Unusually for DeMille, who liked a long pre-production time, he stopped work on *This Day and Age* at 9:27 on a Friday evening, and shot the first tests on the jungle film at 9:28.

Everything one reads or hears about the film bears out one's feeling that it was shot while DeMille was on vacation. The film has that look, as if the small cast and the crew they needed was all they took. While they were on location in Hawaii, everyone except DeMille came down with dysentery, fever, or severe headaches brought on by the humidity. According to Charles Higham, he rejoiced in the ordeal: "Wakened in the mornings by an army bugle, he would walk naked from his bed and out into the jungle, defying a snake or a poisonous reptile to sting him to death. Then he would dive into an available stream and swim as far as he could." To prove to the company that they should not worry about sharks, DeMille is said by Higham to have stripped and swum in the waters himself. "Now who's afraid of sharks?" he demanded.

Filming started on September 16, 1933, and finished on November 3. The art director was Roland Anderson, the photographer Karl Struss. The film is visually ravishing, and although it was filmed in black and white, there is a strong sense of primitive, majestic wilderness, suggesting that DeMille and Anderson had been looking at the paintings of Henri Rousseau. While one has to admit that the plot is fundamentally silly, it's still a lot of fun, and actually quite feminist, as the women come on a great deal more strongly than the men.

Herbert Marshall made his Hollywood debut in this film, having been originally scheduled to play in *The White Woman* with Dorothea Wieck. He plays a humble and unassuming chemist who in this fearsome crisis takes over leadership of the group. On returning to civilization he asserts himself and, defying his wife and mother-in-law, runs off with Claudette Colbert, who played Judy. On June 3, DeMille wrote ruefully to Manny Cohen that in suggesting Marshall, who would need to wear native costume, he had forgotten that the actor had a wooden leg.

Just before shooting began Claudette Colbert went down with appendicitis, and for a time it seemed that she would have to be replaced, so rumor had it, by Gloria Swanson. That, no doubt, was sufficient to convince Colbert that she would recuperate on the voyage to Hawaii. The incident inspired a remarkable letter from Manny Cohen: This sudden illness of Miss Colbert's was, of course, unfortunate, and I am beginning to wonder who is responsible for these illnesses of the various artists, particularly female artists. Just as a matter of check-up, I am wondering whether you may be guilty, and if so, tell me what the trick is. Maybe you also know the trick of keeping them well, especially when they are about to go into a production or during the course of production. I understand that you sent word that you were very well pleased with the locations, and I am, therefore, more hopeful of a great picture right off nature's griddle, but for heaven's sake, don't you start getting sick with malaria or typhoid, or any of the maladies that are common down there. Now I am praying for your health, as well as for your success.

Notwithstanding this friendly overture, DeMille held Manny Cohen partly responsible for the failure of *Four Frightened People*. It was unfortunate that when it came to the final cutting of the picture, DeMille was called away to Washington to fight his tax case. Cohen took it upon himself to make the final cut, with disastrous results. "He cut more than the picture," reflected DeMille. "My throat went along with it."

But Cohen and Arthur couldn't take the blame for everything. Mitchell Leisen criticized DeMille for shooting through a two-inch lens, which, in his view, diminished the background scenes. And there was trouble with the censor,

> Night letter to New York (January 17, 1934): Censor elimination requested in following words—"All views where Judy's naked body is distinctly shown under waterfall"—footage was eliminated to confirm with above. However, censors should realize it is anybody's guess as to the word "distinctly," and in present cut version, we sincerely feel there are no full body naked views "distinctly shown" and we wish to protest the further cutting at this point. E. Cohen.

The film was released on January 25, 1934, and, with or without Judy's naked body, it flopped, though the critics, noting the departure from DeMille's normal style, enjoyed its humor. "The fifth frightened person was the audience," quipped Claudette Colbert.

CHAPTER THIRTY-THREE

PROBABLY WITH SOME RELIEF, DEMILLE FELL BACK ON A FORMULA ZUKOR had always approved of, "an epic with sex." *Cleopatra*, first filmed in 1918 with Theda Bara, was announced, with shooting to commence in March 1934.

The original suggestion was that Fredric March would play Mark Antony and Charles Laughton, Julius Caesar. John Barrymore was offered the role of Mark Antony when March turned it down, but his fee proved too stiff. A newcomer from the London stage, Henry Wilcoxon, who would become a close friend, took the role, while Warren William was chosen over Laughton as Caesar. But always it was Claudette Colbert for Cleopatra.

Interviewed in 1978, upon her return to the stage at the age of seventy-three in *The Kingfisher*, Colbert was asked which of her films she'd most liked to own, "Well, the obvious ones of course. *It Happened One Night*, which won me my Oscar; *Arise My Love*, which I made in 1940 with Ray Milland; *Cleopatra* and *The Sign of the Cross*, both directed by Cecil B. DeMille and both of which I'd like to own, just for laughs."

Directors found Colbert demanding. For one thing, she had a reputation for getting sick. For another, she wanted only her left profile to be photographed, the lights had to be just right, and she was said to be bossy, stubborn, and fickle about her clothes. One man alone pleased her: "I always wore clothes by Travis Banton: he was a great designer." Originally, Mitchell Leisen was to do the costumes for *Cleopatra*, but he left to become a director, and temporarily confusion reigned. "DeMille said to me, 'I have to have Travis,'" recalled Natalie Taylor (Visart), a friend of the DeMille family who had originally joined the production to work with Leisen, "because there was no one she [Claudette Colbert] had any confidence in. . . . Well, he was Travis, and she felt secure."

Banton, head of Paramount's costume department, was recognized from the moment he arrived at the studio in 1924 as one of the great designers. From Clara Bow to Mae West, they adored him and demanded him. His clothes were as influential in molding public tastes as Adrian's at MGM. Regardless of the period, Banton could mesh historical fidelity with timeless

Claudette Colbert portrayed the Egyptian queen in DeMille's *Cleopatra* (1934). Photo by Ray Jones. Courtesy John Kobal Foundation

chic. Whether designing for a Cleopatra, a Park Avenue hostess, an upwardly mobile career girl, or something only Mae West could wear, he came up with creations that made the stars who wore them seem to do so with the flair that comes from natural selection.

Travis was like a God to them, and God help any who tried to take him away, or, what was increasingly more likely, fire him. For Travis had a problem. He drank. His bouts with the bottle resulted in absence from the lot for days on end, a fact which had to be kept secret from the money troubled, economy-minded business heads. For years, however, stars of the caliber of Carole Lombard, Marlene Dietrich, and Claudette Colbert refused to work with anyone else. Not until Lombard and Dietrich had left the studio, after which Colbert switched her allegiance to Edith Head, was it possible to drop him.

DeMille had inquired if his niece, Agnes, would be available to do a dance in *Cleopatra*, and initially all went swimmingly; a memo from him records that she would do two numbers, the dance of the bull and the fire dance. "At story conference we had decided it would be on the theme of Europa and the Bull," says Ralph Jester, who had taken over the costume design for a while between Leisen's departure and Banton's hiring. "I don't know where the idea came from. Cleopatra was a pure blooded Greek, you know, she wasn't Egyptian. So we were justified in thinking up something out of Greek mythology."

But there were difficulties between Agnes and DeMille, which led finally to Leroy Prinz taking over the choreography. "Agnes showed him what she proposed to do," recalled Jester, "and it had a great deal of Martha Graham in it, as every modern dance did in those days. There was a long silence, and DeMille looked at her with that piercing gaze he liked to affect, and he said, 'The audience will laugh themselves right out of their seats.' DeMille fired her. The next day I went to him and begged him. I said I realized there were elements that the American public wasn't ready for yet, but to let me work with Agnes—she's a dear friend of mine, we get along beautifully, and she knows I'm a friend of Martha Graham and respect her choreography greatly and we could modify these movements, but he wouldn't hear of it. He said, 'I'll get LeRoy to do it.'"

There had been no love lost between Prinz and Agnes, two people similar in their need to control, and diametrically opposed in their notions of what was and what was not "good." "He had Agnes, who didn't know what the hell she was doing, either," said Prinz, "riding on the back of the bull and across the stage. In the meantime, I had girls dressed as mermaids with no water on them until I got ready to pull them out. Then Agnes was supposed to come on. I said to DeMille, 'What is she supposed to come on? "What is she supposed to do? Stand on her head?'

"He said: 'What do you want?'"

"I said: 'I want somebody with some brains.'"

"He said: 'Change her.'"

"I said: 'Agnes, goodbye.'"

"I'm an angry little bastard, but I can't help it. Because the minute you kiss one ass around here, you kiss forty."

Although DeMille came to grief with his niece, he was rather more successful in organizing publicity for *Cleopatra* by way of fashion tie-ups:

Memo to Robert Gillham, Al Wilkie, and Bill Pine (copy to Cecil B. De-Mille) from Tom Baily (March 2, 1934): Bill Thomas announced a tie-up with a shoe manufacturer who is going to put on the market a Cleopatra sandal based on designs for those Claudette Colbert will wear in her role in the picture. No jewelry tie-ups are feasible, but it was agreed that if gowns, shoes and hats go over, everything else will naturally follow. Gretchen Messer has a tie-up with a hat designer who will make the first Cleopatra hat. . . . Cooper has a convention tie-up coming up in May at which the hairdressers and cosmetologists of eleven Western States will introduce new hairstyles. They have agreed to introduce a Cleopatra hair dress as the highlight of the convention.

An on-set view of the magnificent barge DeMille had created for *Cleopatra*. Estate of John Kobal

As filming progressed, problems of censorship once more loomed. DeMille dealt with them in his most sanctimonious manner,

Letter to Samuel D. Schwartz, chairman, Pennsylvania State Board of Censors (April 20, 1934): In the case of *Cleopatra*, which I am now producing as authentically and historically correct as I know how, I wanted to assure you that there will be no 'shock' displays of the sort you mention. . . . Certainly I do not believe that any opprobrium can be attached to the picture on the basis of what is referred to in your letter as "the disgusting display of bosoms." I am extremely anxious to become familiar with your point of view in this matter, as in all matters connected with the proper presentation of a picture to the public, and want personally to assure you of my deep respect and regard for your findings.

Liberty magazine reported that 600 ostrich feathers went into the arch over Cleopatra's couch, and that the bathtub, measuring 100 x 150 feet, was the largest DeMille had ever used, a replica of an ancient Roman bath. Twelve researchers had worked nine months before a camera crank turned. Four tons of amour was cast in the studio foundries, 185 pounds of clothing were worn by Antony in the love scene (110 pounds of armor, 75 pounds of gowns), Cleopatra's barge was duplicated exactly from history. DeMille had no need to draw upon his imagination; the scene had all been written down in exquisite, incredible detail by eyewitnesses. The entire picture was filmed in two months.

The sea battle in *Cleopatra* would have cost about a million dollars to stage realistically. This was obviously out of the question, so the effect was created by montage. "The miniatures of the sea fight, like those of the royal barge, were built by Art Smith and photographed by J. D. Jennings," wrote Gordon Jennings of Paramount's special effects department in the December 1934 edition of *American Cinematographer*: "It is interesting to note that though on the screen a fleet of 35 or more galleys appear to be engaged, in reality but two miniature galleys were used . . . They were multiplied into two opposing fleets by split screen double exposures. The closer shots of the battle were made by using these two miniatures with often a number of less finished miniatures in the background as cut-outs, and sometime some of these shots were combined for optical printing. . . .

"The land battles were filmed using more conventional methods, using small groups of actors. Some of these scenes were intercut with, or super-imposed on stock shots of chariots and horsemen made 14 years ago for Mr. DeMille's *Ten Commandments*."

For one of the film's most celebrated sequences, the seduction on the barge, it was an Alma Tadema painting come to life. DeMille recreated the painting of the rose petals, which now rained from the ceiling, conjuring up the image of debauched Romans being exquisitely crushed to death by a shower of them. Claudette Colbert, meanwhile, recalled the famous scene where Cleopatra is delivered to Caesar packaged in an oriental rug. "It was quite difficult to be rolled into a rug and breathe and come out looking pleased with yourself. [But] we only had to do that scene once."

Ralph Jester had some interesting things to say about DeMille's attitude to film titles: "He had this idea that the audience got its mind set right from the very first titles, and they should be resplendent and impressive. In those days the main title was a lettered card, but DeMille had me dream up and create the main title for *Cleopatra*. This was the first damn picture I had ever done. I don't know why he had this confidence in me. But I sat in my office, and I used parts of sets we had used, and I shot and directed the titles. I had live people, and instead of a card I had one of our sphinxes or monuments in pink granite, and I had the names of the cast as though they were incised. And you moved around this with a moving camera."

Cleopatra was released in July 1934 to positive reviews. It was common-place by then for critics to review DeMille with a tongue-in-cheek tone, or to make some show of not indulging too wholeheartedly in the DeMille fantasy, but it was clear that even they couldn't avoid succumbing to the pictorial ravishment of this particular film. It may perhaps be DeMille's finest, most successfully satisfying picture, because it's neither Shakespeare nor Shaw, but rather a child's idea of "other" times, when everything was more splendid, more spectacular, more romantic, more colorful. It had been expected to be a runaway triumph, but it was at best only moderately successful.

One way or another, most reviewers didn't seem to like Claudette Colbert. They didn't really think she was Queen of Egypt, or a queen of anything else for that matter. "Miss Colbert's best moment is the death of Cleo," said the *Variety* critic. "The rest of the evening she's a cross between a lady of the evening and a rough soubrette in a country melodrama."

And the critic in the *New Yorker* began: "I am inclined to consider the dialogue in *Cleopatra* the worst I have ever heard in the Talkies. It is definite backyard liveliness, like gossip over the clothesline. Nor is it helped by an occasional Shakespearian overtone."

Certainly the dialogue had its lapses, but critics who focused on that to the exclusion of the whole largely missed the point that DeMille's most significant critic, the public, did not. "What you have to do is to appeal to the American audience in terms of what the American audience thinks is great and heroic," explains Ralph Jester, adding, "A lot of my costume designs were intentionally unauthentic. . . . The least authentic picture as far as costumes are concerned was *Cleopatra*. No designer in those days paid any attention to authenticity. Nothing was authentic about it."

Other critically acclaimed directors at one time or another succumbed and made a spectacle, but none equaled DeMille's success in the genre.

One wonders how Joseph L. Mankiewicz felt—not least due to his antipathy towards DeMille—about the unflattering comparison of his *Cleopatra* (1963) with DeMille's by Herman G. Weinberg, not normally noted as a De-Mille fan: "Any movie on this subject is made as catnip for the mob, so be it. But if you're going to do it, *some* mystery, *some* witchery has to be there. There is not a moment of these qualities in the Mankiewicz version, but there is even more than a suggestion of it in passages in the DeMille version (with Claudette Colbert), especially in the sequence where Cleopatra entertains Marc Antony on her barge floating down the moonlit Nile. . . .

"Which makes the Mankiewicz barge scene look like it was staged by the drama coach of Wellesley College for the annual senior prom. You have to hand it to DeMille. He may not have been the cinema genius he thought he was, but he always knew what he was doing, even when it was absurd. In the movies, absurdity doesn't matter—it's natural to the medium which is, basically, one of fantasy and the flight of the imagination through clever tricks of the camera, natural suspension of belief, etc. (Besides, where are there so many good-looking people except in the wonderful never-never land of the movies?)"

Flights of imagination and good-looking people did not save the film in Rome, however, where its premiere was greeted by riots, catcalls, and derisive laughter, though the responsibility for this was pinned afterwards on the city's students. The Roman critics called the film a travesty, and a burlesque garbed in ridiculous pomp.

Meanwhile, DeMille's family was growing. In May 1934, Cecilia Calvin gave birth to a son, and in September John was married to Louise Antoinette Denker. Katherine was a bridesmaid at the wedding, and her career subsequently flourished when she appeared opposite Mae West in *Belle of the Nineties*, directed by Leo McCarey in 1934. Every week at Laughlin Park, the "Family Forum," consisting of DeMille, Constance, Katherine, John, and Richard, would gather at dinner, and often bring up ideas for future DeMille films. On one such occasion, it was John who suggested *The Crusades*.

CHAPTER THIRTY-FOUR

FROM THE MOMENT IT WAS KNOWN THAT DEMILLE WAS ABOUT TO BEGIN work on a film about *The Crusades*, letters began to flood into his office, such as the following,

> Dear Mr. DeMille,
>
> Knowing your plans for a magnificent picture in *The Crusades*, I send you an account of an artistic composition that may interest you. The Saracens, as you know, sold Christian women when captured, like cattle, nude . . . they were bound with their own veils in long lines . . . chained neck to neck with heavy collars. One could have views of such a string from behind—even close-ups to the waist. . . . It is surprising how many people like to see slave market scenes and girls in chains, especially manacles.

DeMille had been drawn to the subject years before, inspired by books like *The Talisman* and by a painting by Dan Sayre Groesbeck that hung in his living room. The painting depicted peasants being blessed before setting off for the Holy Land.

"I shall say that the Crusaders were far from being Christians" wrote Rousseau. "They were soldiers of the priests. They were citizens of the Church; they were fighting for its spiritual homeland, which it had in some strange way made temporal. Strictly speaking, this comes under the heading of paganism; for since the Gospel never sets up any national religion, holy war is impossible among Christians." Impossible or not, 600,000 people met their death with the song of God on their lips. DeMille's reason for now making a story about this tortured phase in Christianity's bloody battles to free the Holy Sepulcher was, "Part of the cycle, which began with *The Ten Commandments* and continued through *The King of Kings, The Sign of the Cross*. And besides, a couple of paintings in the library, paintings I've passed daily for the past fifty years of the Crusades. . . . It's the BIGGEST thing I've ever attempted."

The Crusades take us back to that dark era in Western civilization when religious wars first became fashionable, when Christians were busy killing Moslems and Moslems Christians, all in the name of God and Allah. What a difference a name makes when it becomes an excuse for conducting a war. The constantly warring rulers of Christendom, desperate for a way out of their own domestic problems, undertook the noble cause of liberating the Holy Land to distract attention from their economic disarray and give their lands a chance to recover. It proved an inspired way of getting rid of the hotheaded nobles who were making a nuisance of themselves in the "civilized" kingdoms of Europe. Redeeming Jerusalem, thousands of miles from their borders, was seen as a just war, a holy war, and when has God not been a good excuse to go out and kill? There were the additional attractions of fabled riches, a special Papal dispensation of all sins. Everyone, Philip of France, Duke Frederick of Germany, Leopold of Austria, William of Sicily, and Richard of England, got into the act.

Of course, some care had to be taken that the film did not offend the citizens of one country or another to the detriment of the box office. The problem was solved by creating a devious, scheming minor noble, Conrad, marquis of Montferrat, played by a cheerfully sneering Joseph Schildkrault from a country far too small for Paramount to worry about the feelings of its inhabitants.

One thing was clear to DeMille: Since those interminable Crusades lasting three centuries had produced no other hero as well known to English speaking audiences as the Lionhearted Richard, King Richard I of England, who had joined the Crusades as a way of avoiding having to marry Alys, the sister of King Philip of France. Once committed, though it would cost England dear, Richard was determined that his part in the Crusades should be glorious and dazzling, outshining all other monarchs, and worthy of a ruler who had the resources of Europe's most stable kingdom to back him. DeMille's writers would have to telescope the highlights of three centuries of warfare into 12,000 feet of film and focus on one of Richards's failed attempts to recapture the Holy Sepulcher.

Unfortunately, unlike the blameless noble hero he was made out to be by Sir Walter Scott and the Robin Hood stories, England's blonde warrior king, the John F. Kennedy of his day, was also notoriously irresponsible and hot-tempered, cold and cruel: he allowed 2,600 prisoners, mostly innocent women and children, to be massacred at Acre.

Of course, DeMille couldn't resolve in one movie what the Crusades hadn't resolved in three centuries, and, while it might be all right to alter history's hemlines to appeal to the public, he couldn't give Richard what a God had denied him. Though Richard conquered Acre, Arsuf, and Joppa, he never regained Jerusalem from Saladin, and that, after all, was the whole point of the Crusades.

In addition, there was no way any American-made movie could be made without an attractive female protagonist, even though DeMille's hero historically had never shown any interest in women. Richards's queen, Berengaria, was strictly a business arrangement, while his sexual preferences were so scandalous that even in those licentious days he was required by the pope to do penance for sodomy.

Nevertheless, despite all these snags, DeMille refused to consider any other hero for his story. Scott and Kingsley had done their work too well—and so Richard remains an enigma posing as a man, instead of the other way round.

To get the audience to relate to such a man requires a star with charismatic qualities. Gary Cooper could do it, and he later became the movies' embodiment of the Hemingway hero. Spencer Tracy and Bing Crosby, in their different ways, both played men of the cloth without losing their charisma, and won Oscars for their efforts. But Henry Wilcoxon, fresh from having played Marc Antony, was not of that caliber. He was good when he took his helmet off, less when he spoke. Wilcoxon never becomes an exciting hero and thus a worthy adversary of the great Saladin.

On the other hand, DeMille clearly admired the Arabs, and wanted them shown as "more intelligent and cultured than the Christians, and their great leader as perfect and gentle a knight as any in Christendom." Ian Keith, a fine and handsome character who appeared in numerous DeMille films, from *The Sign of the Cross* to *The Ten Commandments*, had what he considered the best role of his career as Saladin, and played him with enormous dignity and style. Saladin being the attractive character that he is, the temptation is to go over to his side.

One is left with a film whose visual look is heroic, with much of the detailed and fascinating treatment of events almost documentary in flavor, but with the men and women in it merely players. Only a few of the fifty-seven characters come to life.

When DeMille's writers were beginning preliminary work on licking these problems into shape, *Cleopatra* had just been released. The whiff of profit made the air around Paramount smell sweet. DeMille felt such confidence in *The Crusades'* box-office appeal that he decided to spare only unnecessary costs in recreating a world for which, unlike *Cleopatra*, there were neither standing sets nor existing costumes from other films to help defray costs.

Sheets of instructions and queries were sent to every head of department. DeMille wanted to know what type of siege engines were used, so his librarian had to get *Larousse Illustre*, a French encyclopedia, from the New York Public Library. His Texas-born right-hand man, the New York-educated and "would be New York intellectual" Ralph Jester, who was in charge of wardrobe, was told to "use a lot of metal and leather." Sheaves of instructions directed Jester to take note of the straight swords and the armor on the backs of the hands and not the palms. DeMille wanted him to make heavy rubber maces on chains with rubber spikes and knots.

Ann Sheridan, who would go on to become Hollywood's Oomph Girl, and later a film star, was an uncredited extra in *The Crusades* (1936). Estate of John Kobal

Nothing escaped his eagle eye. Jester was told to "see Mr. [Harold] Lamb's negative photos of two seals of Richard, and note: the top one shows the legging of chain armor comes below the knee, almost like mesh armor boots. It also shows chain link armor. The bottom one is apparently studded armor which suggests to me the possibility of making leather jackets and then studding them with steel heads very closely. It would perhaps make a much easier costume to move in than all chain armor. In the lower one, also, note the Lion on the helmet, and some lines that apparently represent plumes." He had to find out what the fragment of the Cross would be carried in. "DeMille studied every single sketch," Jester noted. "He loved to look at sketches."

With Harold Lamb sailing on the *Seaward* in July, DeMille went over an early script, emphasizing not just the broad outlines, but bits of business for the big scenes like the battle of Acre. For instance: "A woman dying who throws herself in the moat to help fill it up; makes some speech to a Muslim to the effect that she is throwing herself in so the Christians may cross over to the cross."

Armed with Groesbeck's powerful artwork of the Saracens entering the captured city (based on the picture of Mohammed the Third entering

Jerusalem), its inhabitants cowering under lash and sword, and with his persuasive oratorical skills, DeMille sold Paramount's executives on the project even though money was tight. No objections regarding costs were raised during one of the last conferences, held January 7 in Emmanuel Cohen's office, prior to the start of shooting three weeks later. At the meeting, held in the presence of Cohen (who was ousted a month later), bookkeepers, accountants, and sales people waxed enthusiastic about the script's "great spiritual power" and its "great religious quality," all working themselves up to such a pitch that the box-office returns were in before the film was even started. The budget was okayed and it wasn't considered necessary to insure such an expensive project at the box office with anything other than DeMille's name, although an "all-star" cast was duly and dutifully proclaimed.

But a DeMille picture didn't need stars. A DeMille picture was a star! Adolph Zukor, hanging on as president in name if not in power, sent DeMille an enthusiastic telegram: "Of opinion *Crusades* will be such obviously important box-office picture anyway, [Claudette] Colbert not needed to strengthen cast from box-office standpoint and suggest she be transferred to another picture in order to provide additional strong box-office release for spring."

Colbert had been DeMille's choice for Berengaria, but now she was one of Hollywood's hottest stars and didn't see herself playing the bride to a broadsword, especially not when it was wielded by Henry Wilcoxon playing Richard. The writers spent seven months wrestling to bring Berengaria to life, praying that the right actress just might pull it off. The search was on for the perfect Mrs. Lionheart.

Doubts were expressed in Cohen's office, a soft-spoken Barney Glazer rising to ask, "Will we get in trouble with England and English colonies for your suggestion that Berengaria, Queen or near Queen, was desired of and spent some time in the tent of Saladin? It is a daring invention."

"I would think not," responded DeMille. "Even in England they thought Berengaria was a steamship until we started the picture."

To allay further doubts, Harold Lamb, responsible for the book that was the basis for much of the film, explained that "as a matter of fact we know nothing about her except where she came from, where she was crowned, and where she was married to Richard, and that she appeared to the pope in Rome, but everything else in her history is a blank."

DeMille considered enchanting newcomer Margaret Sullavan, and invited her up to his house to test her, but concluded that her "type" wouldn't put up with being kicked around so much. Another serious contender was exotic Merle Oberon, who had been in one American film, *Folies Bergère*. As the new girl in town, and with Samuel Goldwyn about to sign her, Oberon was mentioned in every column and suggested for every film at the time.

DeMille had an actress in mind, the beautiful, blonde, British-born Madeleine Carroll, who would eventually star in DeMille's first Technicolor picture,

North West Mounted Police. But word came back that Gaumont-British refused to release her. Her American film debut directed by John Ford, had been a flop, and her British bosses were discreetly helping her out, since she didn't want her second attempt at stardom to be as a camp follower in *Crusades*.

A shooting date was set, and still no Berengaria. Luckily, DeMille was able to get Loretta Young, a rising star in Hollywood's firmament, who would have been the perfect choice in the first place. Only now, since it was clear to her bosses at 20th Century that getting her was a matter of urgency, Paramount had to pay a lot more for her. At $25,000 for ten weeks, and then $1,923 a week, she was receiving more than double what any other actor received.

At twenty-one, Loretta Young was a star with a promising future although she did not yet wield the power of Colbert. What Young could and would do, once she was told that she had to, was look after her image on the screen. "I always had input on everything I put on my head, my body and my face. . . . I read the script and I knew the outline of the costume was long-waisted, and those marvelous chiffon things that went around like this, and so I decided I wanted a long blonde wig. I think I was thinking of Rapunzel, who let down her golden hair!

"So months later they called me and asked me if I'd mind coming to the studio as the wig had arrived . . . these two gorgeous golden long hair wigs, below my knees. And I got them on and they were so heavy I couldn't lift my head. I thought, 'God. They are going to kill me! What am I going to do? I can't cut it off!' They had been months going all over the world finding the right hair and dyeing it just the right color and then making the wigs. . . . I had the same hairdresser who had been with me for ten years by that time, and she went and got some scissors. And she parted the hair and cut some off, so I had bangs, you see? I put on the dress, the costume, and Lucille got hold of the hair and pinned it to the dress, then she did the same with the other side.

"So, in *The Crusades* . . . I had my hair pinned to my dress! I don't know why I didn't break my neck! The bangs helped, and then we would braid it, braid the sides, and then put veils over it . . . anything to keep it from showing. Well, that was the beginning of the 'page boy' . . . Well, that marvelous look came because I wanted to look like Rapunzel!"

Now they needed a score. When the current mode was to arrange snippets of popular melodies, DeMille insisted on original scores for his films, arguing that the soundtracks played an important part in their overall effectiveness. While he had been very happy with Rudolph Kopp's scores for *The Sign of the Cross* and *Cleopatra*, DeMille was always on the lookout for new talents, and toyed with the idea of hiring Leopold Stokowski, the prematurely white-haired wunderkind of the podium. However, the conductor, who found immortality with Mickey Mouse in *Fantasia*, wasn't as eager as DeMille might have expected, "his time is so completely taken up between now and January that he could not do preparation work on *The Crusades* music."

Fortunately, DeMille convinced Koop to return and compose a terrific score—one that could be stirring when Christian souls were called on to take up arms; martial when the Crusaders marched; romantic when Berengaria appeared; and exotic when she was Saladin's prisoner in his luxurious silken tent. It always sounded authentic and when pilgrims and crusaders had to sing, they had a Te Deum with suitable lyrics by Harold Lamb.

With a cast of thousands to dress, the film required a lot of assistants. Five different people designed shoes; others designed only hoods and helmets. So many people were working on the costumes, though only Travis Banton and Ralph Jester received screen credits, that forty years later it was impossible for Jester, who was "responsible for everyone who went before the camera," to remember any but the most familiar faces. But the results, beautifully drawn and painted down to the last detail, were gorgeous, with men defiant in bright cloaks and golden armor, chaps grinning in Lincoln green caps and glowering in turbans, and women of all kinds, camp followers, street walkers, slave girls, nuns, and Sultan's favorites, all dressed in a style to be popularized by *Esquire* in the following years. Travis Banton's ambitious personal assistant, Edith Head, was on hand to carry out any small alterations in Banton's design, as well as to help fit the minor women in the cast. She ended up as the most celebrated designer in Hollywood's history and eventually took over Banton's job at Paramount.

DeMille saw to it that Wilcoxon was provided with a medieval king's menagerie, several fierce-looking hounds at his heels, and instructions to "start carrying the falcon around. Pick out the best bird we have and have him start carrying him around until the bird knows him."

Besides sending to Norway for Loretta's hair, the studio's researchers went everywhere the crusaders had come from for authentic costumes and props, so DeMille would be sure to get all the details right, or know why he didn't. Nothing went from the drawing board to the workroom without his approval.

It was also a way of saving money since things in Europe were cheaper. The Paramount representative in Berlin was asked to contact the famed Theatrekunst Herman Kaufman, who had done the costumes for the silent *Ben Hur*, to make the string mesh armor: "We might be able to buy theses outfits in Germany and bring them into this country under the heading of theatrical costumes, bond them, and then send them back." And while he was doing that, he was also told to get a replica of the famous bent crown of Hungary. DeMille had a reason of his own for that.

DeMille loved to insert intentional anachronisms into his films, like the Roman soldiers shooting dice in *Cleopatra*, or Joan of Arc using a fourteenth-century safety pin, or a bra for his Philistine temptress in *Samson and*

Delilah. As he'd hoped, he received indignant letters drawing his attention to "that old second hand crown with the bent cross."

But the errors DeMille allowed to "slip in" were historically verifiable. Each fact had to be checked; for example, on the way to Jerusalem, the crusaders usually carried the Cross on their shoulders, but on their return it was carried over the heart. The Muslims used liquid fire and flame-throwing weapons in battle as far back as the 1180s.

The courage of the movie's stuntmen was also real, even if the cumbersome armor they wore wasn't always. "I wanted to do arms and armor of the period," Ralph Jester explained, "which, strictly speaking, you really cannot do. One reason is that in the twelfth century, besides all of the chain mail they wore bucket helmets, and obviously you cannot have an actor speaking with a bucket over his head. And if you raise it up like that, you're two or three centuries later. So I made a thing that slid up."

Memos in the early stages of production track DeMille's dependence on Groesbeck's visualizations: "You wanted to get Dan Groesbeck in and talk money to him . . . and how many sketches he could get out in a week or make a deal on accepted sketches." Groesbeck's sketches were heroic and sensuous, a cross between Dore and Dulac for a deluxe edition of the *Arabian Nights.* DeMille shot these as drawn.

With Windsor Castle, Sherwood Forest, and Acre as locations, by far the largest expenses were the sets. Whenever it was possible—as with interiors of tents and castles—they used existing sets. DeMille went back to his own production of *The Road to Yesterday* for the mattes and miniatures originally designed by Anton Grot. The money Paramount would have to pay to Cecil B. DeMille Productions for the use of these items would offset his storage costs. (It wasn't anybody's business that the storage was actually in his house and his offices on the Paramount lot). But the bulk of the sets were new, and here too, as with the armor, fresh talents were needed and found.

The very first drawing I saw on opening the package on *The Crusades* in DeMille's basement was a vividly detailed sketch for the assault on "The Gates of Acre." The perspective was from a mobile wooden battlement crowded with crusaders as it moved toward the walls of the city's parapets lined with defending Saracens. A battering ram stood ready, and to the right there were crusaders scaling a ladder leaning against a turret. The energetic detail was a delight. It was signed by the film's designer Roland Anderson, but his assistant, responsible for the sketch, was a newcomer. His name was there in smaller script, Nozaki. Al Nozaki, a Japanese American, went on to a long and distinguished film career in his own right. But he started with DeMille, on *The Crusades*, with this drawing.

Somebody else who remembered the Battle at Acre was William Walling Jr., a Paramount portrait photographer. Normally, as a gallery man, Walling wouldn't be shooting scene stills, but because of long-standing and recurring differences between the studios and the photographer's union, most of the publicity and unit photographers at the studios were once again on strike. Retired photographers were being brought back; freelance photographers were being hired by the picture, but with six hundred films being produced, there were too few men to go around, and so the portrait photographers, because they were not part of the union, were made to do double duty. One result of this was that John Engstead, who was employed in Paramount's publicity department as a stylist, got his start taking portraits, while Walling, who had previous experience shooting stills, was put back on the sets.

Bill Walling was a feisty redheaded Irishman and not a man to be ordered about by anyone. And DeMille gave a lot of harsh commands during the production. A clash was inevitable. "The first day I showed up on the set things were not ready to shoot," remembered Walling, "so I went over and started looking at this newspaper. And out of the corner of my eye I saw DeMille looking at me. I thought, 'Oh, hell, now I'm in trouble, I know it.' . . . Anyway, when Saladin and his horde were coming through an archway and they had shot the master scene, I had my camera up on the tripod with the moving picture cameras. His way of getting people to pay attention was by abusing somebody. . . . He turned to me: 'What are you set up so high for?' I said, 'If I go any lower shooting through that arch, we'll see the RKO water tower!' And he says to me with his microphone for a mouth, 'Your father was a fine actor . . . but you're a lousy stills man.'"

Unlike Walling, DeMille's longtime second-unit director, Art Rosson, let DeMille's tirades roll off him like water off a duck's back: "I don't remember a single time when he approved immediately any scene I ever shot, and of course he would jump up and down on what he felt were wasted dollars. I remember one time we were watching some test footage and he jumped up and yelled, 'That stuff is terrible, just terrible! Whoever shot it' (making a point not to look at me). 'It has to go.' So I said, 'Well you shot it.' Without reacting he said, 'Well, it still has to go.'"

For the siege of Acre, no realism was spared. Seventeen people were injured, including DeMille, who stuck his head out from behind his screen and got a blunt arrow on his chin. DeMille, who had stood in a swamp full of crocodiles to show Conrad Nagel how it was done in *Fool's Paradise*, and who thought nothing of tussling with lions and leopards to get them into an arena or convince a cowardly star to emulate him, took this blow in his stride.

The cadaverous John Carradine, painter, actor, and poet, who got started on his long career in movies with DeMille as a crowd extra in *The Sign of the Cross*, had graduated to playing a martyr in the Crusades: "I saw him do an extraordinary thing. He had a scene with men in Gothic armor under which was a suit of chain mail, all of which together weighed about 115 pounds. The men had to leap from a fighting tower which was truncated, wider at the bottom than it was at the top. And when the bottom was against the castle wall, the top was about twelve feet away. He wanted his stuntmen in their

Gothic armor to leap from the top of the fighting tower to the castle wall . . . and no one would try it. So DeMille put on the armor and did it himself. And he was then over fifty years of age. I saw him do it."

DeMille expected his cast to follow his example. Loretta Young recalled a scene "where an arrow passes right in front of my face. DeMille had an archery specialist there, but he said, 'No, I'll do this. I don't want anything to happen to her, and I am absolute tops in archery.' It was nighttime and late, and the press was on the set, and I thought, 'Well, he said he can do it, he's the director.' I let him do it three times . . . and he just missed my face every time."

Her independent mind stood Loretta Young in good stead when it came to animating the listless Berengaria, whom history and the script had given little animation, but though the virile Henry Wilcoxon, young, good-looking, and British, seemed born to play Richard, and subsequently became a fine character actor (earning him DeMille's friendship and eventually the position of associate producer), for Young his Richard had a lot of take but little give: "Either he was terribly uninterested in me . . . and I couldn't understand why, because at least all the other men found me very attractive . . . or he was embarrassed or something. But he was very wooden. If I leaned on him, he was stiff. There was one scene I was doing with him and he said his line of dialogue. I was so busy looking at him and being in love with him that I didn't respond with my line right away. And Henry said, 'Forgot your dialogue, huh?' And I looked at him . . . I was so surprised . . . and I said, 'No. I was acting.' And he said, 'Oh.'"

The point of casting an established personality like Loretta Young was her proven rapport with the audience. But if DeMille's main consideration was to match his actors to a drawing by Groesbeck—fine for small parts like the assembled European kings who had the look of stone statues—he was more likely to find himself with a cast of thigh-slapping Vikings or old bores. With Young's Berengaria, the audience warmed to her beauty, her vulnerable charm, her spirited response—until at last one concluded that the only reason she stuck with Richard was out of duty, especially after she was captured by Saladin (Ian Keith), who showered her with gifts, treated her like a queen, and behaved like a lover worth having. There had been a lot of discussion between DeMille and his writers about Berengaria's motive for sacrificing herself for Richard, and no one could come up with a suitable reason why she should love this man enough to be willing to die for him. As Paramount's Benjamin Glazer pointed out, "This girl is first attracted then repelled and insulted on her wedding day. She is socked into the ship and then he rather clumsily tries to get in bed with her. . . . She's no Joan of Arc. You haven't told us she would want to die for the Crusades. She's a piece of luggage."

Yet it is through Berengaria that the story derives its great spiritual significance, brotherhood and peace, the spirit of Christianity. Under the guidance of a sympathetic director like Frank Capra or Frank Borzage, Young was an actress of extraordinary eloquence. With DeMille, she had to rely on herself: "DeMille wasn't interested in individual performances, he was interested in the overall effect. He said to me, 'My dear young lady, I direct thousands of people, not two people. That's why I hire stars to play the leads in my pictures. Whatever you do will be better than anything I tell you.'"

Young, a tuning fork to emotion, brings a human element that was lacking elsewhere. Inevitably she outshines Richard. Her character as written had been simpering, coy, petulant, and confused. Young was none of these. Had the role been kept subordinate, like that of the Virgin Mary or the Magdalene in *The King of Kings*, the audience's sympathies wouldn't have been so easily distracted.

One of the other fifty-six speaking parts was cast with DeMille's daughter, Katherine, who had made her film debut as a dress extra in *Madam Satan*. She had been pretty enough to play one of the six wives of Henry VIII in the costume ball aboard the Zeppelin. Now she was a beauty, and much in demand, so nobody could accuse DeMille of nepotism in casting Katherine as Alys of France, Berengaria's jealous rival. Working for her father gave her no special privileges; once you worked for him, you were just another person he hired.

But there was a lot of tension building up. Groesbeck stormed off after a row, not to return for several years. Ralph Jester had no doubts about the lack of opportunity to reason with DeMille or appeal to his sense of fair play: "I never felt there was a sense of regret in him. You couldn't sit down with a guy like that and say, 'Look, C. B., aren't you ashamed of the way you behaved?' He'd throw you out; wouldn't listen to you. I'm sure he always thought he was right."

What Ralph failed to remember was that the wardrobe department at Paramount was in disarray at the time because of the uncertainty among the studio's top echelon. Even so, there came a point when he would hand in his notice and then DeMille would have to get him back.

Bill Walling grew angry recalling the day he finally had enough: "I lasted at the most four days on the production. And after lunch that day I got off the lot, got in my car, drove home, and then went to Canada."

Walling's replacement was Earl "Wimpey" Crowley. To Earl, a guy with a drinking problem and a penchant for practical jokes who was used to working on the quick and easy Westerns which Paramount turned out for the bottom half of their bills, all men were buddies. "So Crowley walks on the set," explains Walling, "puts his camera down, walks up to DeMille, slaps him on the back, and says, 'C. B., this sure beats working on Westerns.' C. B. didn't know what to do. He could never deal with a drunk, and his ammunition of sarcasm would have been wasted on Crowley. Crowley worked for two days, but there were never any proofs, because whatever he shot didn't turn out.

Finally, he was fired, and they got a stills photographer to take care of the pictures."

DeMille wasn't amused by Crowley, but he enjoyed a joke as much as anyone. These jokes were usually of his own devising, staged for reporters and visitors on the set, but not everyone working for him knew this, and so they were often handed down as wild examples of his megalomania. One in particular surfaced time and again, told by different actors on the sets of different movies. Leatrice Joy remembered it from *The Ten Commandments*. This was Loretta Young's version, from when she'd been sitting by the open door of her dressing room on the edge of the set: "It was almost lunchtime, and there were two girls sitting outside. They were just talking. The parapet, where he was directing, must have been 100 yards away, all the way on the other side of the set. One girl said to the other, 'I'm starving. I wonder when the old bald-headed sonofabitch is going to call lunch.'

"From the other side of the stage this voice came, 'Young lady, would you mind repeating what you just said?'

"Of course, they went right on talking, because they didn't think he meant them. He said, 'The two young ladies still beside Miss Young's dressing room . . . would you mind standing up please?'

"So there was this dead silence, and they kind of looked at each other. He went on, 'Young lady, you on the left, would you mind repeating what you just said?'

"Finally, she sort of whispered it, but he said, 'No, out loud.' So she'd just had it and said, 'I said, "I wonder when that old bald-headed sonofabitch is going to call lunch."'

"Well, he says, 'OK. Lunch. Back in an hour.'"

The incident Young recalled, and another like it, had been staged for the promotional trailer for the film. One was for a short entitled *Hollywood Extra Girl*, the story of one of the hundreds of Sadie Glutzes and Elmer Joneses who came to Hollywood to try to make it in the movies. In the script, she was Susanne Emery, age nineteen, height five foot four. The camera followed her from her meager shared bedroom to the studio. Along the way, hungry fans preparing for their own onslaught on the gates of the golden kingdom found out what it was "really" like to be an extra on one of DeMille's sets.

These trailers, full of fancy cuts and tricky montages, served up forthcoming slices of Hollywood hokum as if they were *The Plow that Broke the Plains*. But DeMille's trailers, showing him in all stages of production, bending over the scripts, appearing to decide what scenes to be included, discussing armor with Ralph Jester, script changes with Harold Lamb, and angles with his cameraman Victor Milner, conveyed a thrill about the process more genuine and spontaneous than he sometimes got into the actual film. In these shorts, he was not bogged down by the demands of running time to rush the viewer's eye past all that fascinating detail.

These shorts, in brief, often give a truer idea of the spectacular richness the studio had at its command. Here one could see laid out the bundles of valuable skins and costly fabrics; the armorers at work; the helmets shaped, the shoes fitted; the costumes debated; the sets being constructed; DeMille approving a drawing for a wig; explaining, to a seriously nodding Ralph Jester, why there could be only authentic props in his movies instead of the perfectly good copy of a sword Ralph had brought him for approval, and making his point by taking it and splintering it as if it had been a match, before leaving a stunned Jester to return to his set where thousands of extras awaited instructions from their master. DeMille was the head of the octopus; his assistants were his arms.

On the set his assistant directors, like so many lieutenants and sergeant majors, prepared the way, moving here and there, marshaling the mobs for the battle. One sees the great DeMille, master of millions, in his customary breeches and high-laced puttees, calm, in control, riding the giant camera crane like Ahab on the back of his whale. Of course, DeMille is wonderfully entertaining: the trailers allowed him to act again, playing up the image of himself as the man dedicated to giving the best. Other directors also featured themselves in such promotional shorts, but only DeMille starred in them. It was a shrewd move, and had the effect of making him one of the few directors whose face and wardrobe were as familiar to the public as any of the stars. Not everyone realized there was a difference between his on- and off-screen selves, and his critics only saw this as further proof that DeMille was confusing himself with the God of his movies. Until Alfred Hitchcock's TV appearances in the 1950s, DeMille's was the *only* name above the title that could pack them into the cinemas.

During the months the film was in production, the facts that grab people's attention during a depression—money and the things it can buy—made the papers. The Metropolitan Museum's armor expert Julien Arrchea was offered $150 per month and transportation both ways to consult on the armor. The sets came to $150,000; the costumes amounted to a further $112,000, or one tenth of the final budget. *Time* magazine reported that 10,000 people drew paychecks of one sort or another, and that 300,000 feet of film was shot. One set, a pier and boat in Marseilles, covered four acres on the Paramount lot, built for a scene that appeared on only 100 feet of the film. The siege tower was five stories high, weighed 35 tons, and at the time was the biggest prop ever used in the cinema. The catapult at Acre shot real fireballs. For three months, 220 horses were boarded on the lot. The picture used 500 shields, 1,000 swords, 750 yards of chain mail made out of silver lacquered wool, 50 gallons of red collodion for blood, and 2,500 pounds of crepe hair for beards.

Exaggeration was nothing new: Universal had done it when von Stroheim needed a set of Monte Carlo for *Foolish Wives*, which it billed as the first "million-dollar set"—later fueling accusations that von Stroheim was an irresponsible spendthrift. DeMille was too shrewd to let himself be caught like that, having never forgotten his own debacle over expense on *The Ten Commandments*. He never spent foolishly, which is to say, everything could be accounted for. At the same time, his films reaped the benefits from the promise of opulent imagery in his prospective public's mind. Gladys Unger kept the real figures.

At last, the end was in sight. From start to finish, including some additional shooting, filming had taken nine months. And all this time, the fanfare never ceased. "We feel *The Crusades* is the biggest picture we have ever undertaken," the press department thundered, "and should do a much bigger world business than *The Sign of the Cross*, *Cleopatra*, and even *The Ten Commandments*."

It was a hope shared by all at Paramount, from Adolph Zukor, whose position relied on DeMille's success, down to the gateman, for the economic chill of the Depression had Paramount by the throat and threatened every job. Studio heads were in turmoil as one executive followed another out the door, from Cohen to Ernst Lubitsch to B. P. Schulberg. DeMille kept as far away from divisive internal politics as he could. Secretly, perhaps, he enjoyed the fantasy of his former enemies coming to him, caps in hand, to offer him the crown. But after his failure running his own studio, he wasn't tempted. His present position had all of the benefits and none of the drawbacks.

The Crusades was only his eighth all-talking picture, but it was his sixtieth film in twenty years. The public was promised the greatest movie of its kind ever made, and that wasn't such an exaggeration. There hadn't been many other films about the Crusades except for Fairbanks's silent *Robin Hood*, much of it set during the time of the Crusades.

DeMille's film certainly was one of the costliest. Including the final process work, the film came in at $1,424,872.24, or $300,000 over the original budget. In 1935, $300,000 was the budget for an average film. The reasons were to become a major source of dispute when it became evident that the film wouldn't recoup its cost for years, whereas the studio was moving rapidly to the brink of dissolution.

And expenses on *The Crusades* were still mounting even after DeMille handed it in, because his contract stipulated a lavish promotional campaign in all the major capitals of the world. This was as important to him as his obsession with exploitable production values.

For decades, gimmicks had paved the way for new movies, and sometimes they even managed to work. Although nobody thought *The Crusades* needed such tricks, for the Paris premiere the cinema was turned into a medieval castle and the ticket-takers and ushers were dressed as knights and pageboys. There was a similar setup at the Carlton Cinema in the Haymarket. In New York, they staged a battle, but one fellow got a splinter in his finger.

In Europe (including Montferrat!), and as far away as India, the public loved *The Crusades*, perhaps because it was dubbed in France, Germany, and Italy. The cinematographer Nestor Almendros recalled his enthusiasm as a little boy when the film opened in Madrid and his teacher, who was violently opposed to movies, told the class that here was a film he could recommend with pride.

The United Kingdom was different. Wilcoxon thought it only failed there because of timing. *The Crusades* opened at the same time King George V died. George V and Queen Mary had been popular and the Empire was in mourning for a month. All theaters were closed out of respect. All the money spent on publicity and promotion was for naught.

Europe might account for up to 40 percent of a film's gross, but America was a film's key market, and here the reaction was less satisfactory. The problem in the States wasn't a dead king. The new age that dawned with Shirley Temple rejected the film as being religious without being spiritual. And it failed to satisfy dramatically—the public was confused by the conflicting motives. Was Saladin the good guy or the bad guy? Was Richard in the war for his own glory or for God's? Who was Berengaria, and why had they never heard of her before? And in the end, Richard was, as he had been, still a failure. The public of 1935 wasn't yet prepared for films in which the story ends without the hero getting what he went out to get. Richard claimed to have had a divine vision, but nothing about him in this film suggested he had truly seen the light. Audiences looking for an escape instead got DeMille's most deeply felt sermon since *The King of Kings*. What they really wanted was the sort of film the critics would have slaughtered with glee.

Dramatic defects and historical inconsistencies aside, measured by its production values and DeMille's powerful staging, *The Crusades* is worthy of mention in the same breath as Fritz Lang's *Nibelungen*, and two superb films that show its influence, Eisenstein's *Alexander Nevsky* (1938) and Alessandro Blasetti's swashbuckling epic *Il Corono di Ferro*. Visually, much of *The Crusades* is stunning, although it would have benefited enormously from being shot on location rather than in studio sets, which would have given it a sense of space without which many of the crowd scenes seem merely crowded. The stills don't capture that feeling either. Fortunately, the artwork more than compensates.

DeMille's critics treated the film and its maker with scant regard. The review in *Time* magazine was typical: "As a picture, it is historically worthless, didactically treacherous, artistically absurd. . . . Yet the film is rich in entertainment. It is a million dollar sideshow which has at least three features which distinguish it from the previous line of DeMille extravaganzas. It is the noisiest, it is the biggest, and it contains no baths."

The London critic John Marks went further: "An impressive object-lesson in the art of unprincipled and profitable waste . . . the dialogue was futile, its low water mark being reached in a conversation between villains playing chess, in which every move was a check, every remark a melodramatic innuendo."

Besides these two reviews, there were none better that weren't paid for. Although DeMille always maintained that he didn't bother with reviews unless they were written on a banker's check, those who knew him said that these snipings could send him into reflections of such bitterness that a deep caution was bred in all who surrounded him in the days that followed. The bad reviews in the smart press wouldn't have bothered Paramount if the film had made money. As the disappointing box-office returns dashed any hopes for a miracle, the film's cost became one of the key issues in the studio's ruinous internecine fighting. The rot had been going on for almost five years, with one head replacing another, each one worse or more inadequate than the last. Paramount's affairs were so confused while DeMille was in production that in April, in the last weeks of shooting and months after Cohen had been asked to resign, DeMille's fellow director Ernst Lubitsch was put in charge of production.

As it seemed that *The Crusades* losses would approach $700,000, Adolph Zukor, who had counted on DeMille to re-establish the credibility of the old-timers, cried, "The king is dead." He was a bit premature, unless he was referring to himself, since by the time the dust cleared, Zukor would resign the presidency to Barney Balaban. Paramount never had it so bad.

CHAPTER THIRTY-FIVE

LUX RADIO THEATRE WAS LAUNCHED IN THE SUMMER OF 1936, THE FRUIT of a deal that DeMille had negotiated with Lever Brothers, the powerful soap manufacturers. Lever Brothers acquired the King of the Bathtub, a perfect front for their product, while DeMille acquired a weekly radio audience and the means to become a national public figure. His contract, the first of its kind with a film director, would pay him $100,000 a year, eventually rising to $125,000.

The old Music Box Theatre on Hollywood Boulevard was used for these shows. It seated one thousand, and hundreds more had to be turned away each week. DeMille missed neither rehearsal nor performance, and when he was ill, was taken to the theater on a stretcher, even though all he did was to open and close the show and run through it with the cast before the performance. A junior producer worked on it during the week.

DeMille kept tabs on the Lux Radio Theatre. It had to bear his mark. Presiding over the program was a role he loved, his very own Roosevelt-type fireside chat with the American public, and indeed Roosevelt used the Lux show figures for comparison with his own radio broadcasts. By the time he was forced to quit the show on January 22, 1945, DeMille was a household name, and a radio fixture, like Jack Benny, Fred Allen, and Amos and Andy. To the great American public, he had truly become Mr. Hollywood, the man who opened each show with the memorable words "Greetings from Hollywood, ladies and gentlemen." DeMille took his role seriously. He had been an actor, and in a certain sort of way this made him a star.

F. Scott Fitzgerald's last mistress, the columnist Sheilah Graham, reported on the early shows: "On Monday evening, 1 June 1936, I was backstage at the Music Box Theater on Hollywood Boulevard for the first show. Clark Gable and Marlene Dietrich were starred in *The Legionnaire and the Lady* and were delighted to be reading from a script, instead of having to memorize their lines. The following Monday, William Powell and Myrna Loy were repeating their roles in a condensed version of *The Thin Man*. Asta was also at hand, or rather heel, to bark at the right moments."

In a scene straight out of one of her lover's stories, Graham provides her own view of the by now rumor-fabled Paradise: "I had been a guest on the DeMille show, and perhaps that gave him the idea of inviting me to his ranch in the country for a weekend. I was warned about the peacocks that screamed through the night sounding like a woman being murdered. But I was not prepared for the Big Production that was a regular feature of the weekends. On arrival, the male guests were given a choice: they could hunt for tame mountain lions in the hills, or they could clean out the swimming pool. The ladies were supposed to rest in their rooms. I don't know what C. B. was doing, but there wasn't a man in sight until the late afternoon, when we would all change for the evening festivities. No drinks were allowed until eight o'clock, when Mr. DeMille would appear in a sort of white cowboy regalia, with large white leather gloves with which he embraced a cocktail shaker adorned with bells, which chimed melodiously as he shook the contents. Until eight o'clock, the ladies had to wait on the men, carrying drinks to them, lighting their cigarettes, bringing chairs for them to sit on. But when dinner was announced the situation was reversed. The men would wait on the ladies. They led us to our seats at the table, where there was a present for each of us. I was glad when the weekend ended on Sunday after a buffet lunch and we were all driven back to Hollywood."

As we shall see, the Lux project ended somewhat unhappily for DeMille, though in the severance of his relationship with the program, he gained the inspiration for a new project, the Freedom Foundation, which gave him a huge amount of satisfaction. Meanwhile, in the nine years of his association with the Lux Radio Theatre, he supervised the production of no fewer than 288 plays, which not only gave listening pleasure to millions, but also provided employment for a large number of actors, technicians, and Lever Brothers employees.

Meanwhile, with film production costs having to be curtailed and historical epics once again out of fashion, DeMille returned to the genre he had elevated into the major leagues back in 1914. Three years before John Ford would make his seminal *Stagecoach*, DeMille made a film that lifted the Western above the small-budget horse operas into which it had drifted, and launched it as an adult genre.

The Plainsman wasn't DeMille's first Western—not by a mile. His last film at MGM had been a Western. A lot of films and a lot of other genres had floated under the bridge since then, but it was a fortuitous move, just as *The Sign of the Cross* had been when he released it at the height of the Depression. Westerns had always retained their popularity with the Saturday morning crowd, but their standing had sorely slipped. They were little more than the second half of a double bill, popular in rural communities but derided by the big cities and their critics. No major director was interesting in helming a Western. DeMille decided to take the Western by the scruff and yank it back

DeMille watches *The Plainsman* (1934) starring Gary Cooper and Jean Arthur in his home theater.
Courtesy John Kobal Foundation

to the top. What was more, with *The Plainsman* he elevated a minor lawman,
Wild Bill Hickok, to the front ranks of Western heroes.

The subject, strong men taming the West and opening it up for civilization, was an interesting but unsurprising choice. It appealed to DeMille
for a number of reasons, one being a return to the films which first made
his name. It brought him together with Gary Cooper, his star in four films.
Though originally the film was to be about the well-known Indian fighter
and master showman Buffalo Bill, as the story was developed the emphasis
changed on DeMille's insistence to the less known gunslinger of Dodge City,

Wild Bill Hickok, played by Cooper. Subtly, DeMille slyly chose to identify not with the world famous Buffalo Bill, who ended his life as a master showman, touring his Wild West extravaganzas across America and Europe well into the twentieth century, but rather with the taciturn Hickok. Thus, a minor character in Western mythology entered the front ranks of American Western heroes, where he has remained ever since. A sweet little triumph for DeMille, who not only put himself back on the map but also showed the power of the medium for conferring mythic status on the hero of his choice. DeMille visualized Hickok as a representative of that dogged, individualistic spirit which built democracy in America. He had a phrase, "I will not be put upon." That was Hickok's phrase. It was about the same as the fathers on the American Revolution. They, too, would not be put upon. So, when their tea was taxed, they decided they would not be put upon, and that's exactly what Bill Hickok did. He decided to shoot.

Iron Eyes Cody was to spend a great deal of time on *The Plainsman*, and not just as an actor. In his autobiography, subtitled *My Life as a Hollywood Indian*, he relates how he began as a technical advisor under contract to Paramount in 1925 at the age of eighteen. He claimed, incidentally, that in 1922 Lasky had tried to get DeMille to direct *The Covered Wagon*, the first Western epic, and mentioned that DeMille had a name for the "overweight white guys we used to dress up as Indians . . . Red Beer Bellies."

The plot of *The Plainsman* wasn't exactly authentic, as Cody (or perhaps his ghostwriter, Collin Perry) makes plain: "It should be mentioned here that if you always suspected *The Plainsman* was complete nonsense from a historical standpoint, you're right. The real Calamity Jane was a vulgar, tobacco-chewing, raw-boned kid who resembled nothing more alluring than an oversized Huckleberry Finn, minus the charm of innocence. She was a great shot and horsewoman, but Wild Bill Hickok certainly did no romancing with her. Hickok was also shown in the Battle of Arickaree, which he never set eyes on. There's no historical hint of him ever attempting to warn anyone of the impending Custer battle."

The Plainsman marked the arrival in the DeMille family of twenty-one-year-old Mexican American Anthony Quinn, who had entered films the previous year and who would marry Katherine deMille. In his autobiography, he recalls that while "waiting for a job in Ensenada, Mexico, on one of the fishing ships that occasionally pulled into port, I picked up a discarded Los Angeles paper. I read an article that said C. B. DeMille was having difficulty casting a picture called *The Plainsman*. He couldn't find enough authentic Indians to play some important parts called for by the script.

"That night, Bert and I thumbed our way north to the American border. . . . I changed my shirt and hurried to Paramount Studios, where the casting office was full of people looking for jobs.

"'Will you please tell Mr. Joe Egley that I am here?' I told the receptionist.

"'Who are you?' she asked.

"'Tell him Anthony Quinn is here,' I said. I gave her some clippings that I always carried with me, reviews of the plays that I had done. 'Tell him that Mr. Cecil B. DeMille wants to see me,' I added. 'I understand you're looking for a young Indian. I'm an Indian and I came to apply for the job.'

"DeMille said to bring me right over. As we walked out of the office, the casting director said, 'Listen, don't tell the old man that you know English. Pretend you can't speak it at all. I promised to find him a real Cheyenne.'"

Maintaining his deception, Quinn landed the part. He memorized four to five pages of Cheyenne, under the impression that his character was that of a young Indian warrior making an impassioned speech against the white man and inciting the Indian nation to go to war. He even learned to ride a horse.

But Chico Day, brother of the actor Gilbert Roland, then starting out his career as a young assistant director, explained to Quinn that he would not be addressing 10,000 Indians, but simply talking to Gary Cooper. Everything he had planned was for nothing. He even discovered that he had to sing a song. The cat was out of the bag when, after Quinn made a wrong move and DeMille started screaming at him, he accidentally replied in English. But in standing up to DeMille he won approval: "A hundred and fifty people . . . held their breath as DeMille and I stared at each other for what seemed an awfully long time. He suddenly turned around and said, 'The boy's right. We'll change the set-up.' And there was a sigh of relief from everybody. I did the scene my way. It had been such a horrible day for everybody that when I had finished my four-page speech in one take everybody broke out in applause. DeMille came over and shook my hand. He was very sweet. 'Thank you, and I am sorry about all the confusion. People shouldn't have lied to me. Even if I had known you weren't Cheyenne, I would have hired you, because you were right for the part. We wouldn't have had to go through all this. I think it is one of the most auspicious beginnings for an actor I've ever seen in my life.'"

The composer on *The Plainsman* was the left-wing George Antheil, whose best-known work was originally composed to accompany the experimental Fernand Leger film *Ballet Mechanique*. As he recounted in his autobiography, *Bad Boy of Music,* he was responsible for an even more unlikely encounter between DeMille and Salvador Dali, "At the Paramount Studios I was writing a type of music not at all unsympathetic to me, music describing the saga of Wild Bill Hickok of the West's great romantic period. . . . When, for the first time, I met Salvador Dali at his own request, I said to him, 'Look here, Dali, you and I are two of a kind. The only thing is, I'm a little older, and at this exact moment of my destiny I'm endeavoring to make a good impression over at Paramount. C. B. DeMille thinks I'm crazy and is watching me like a hawk.'

"'Ah! C. B. DeMille! He is the greatest surrealist in all the world!' Dali said ecstatically.

"'Too true,' I murmured, 'but will you behave yourself if I take you over to see him? He is also my boss.'

"'But I only wish to kiss his hands,' Dali said reprovingly.

"So I took Dali over to Paramount, where he kissed C. B. DeMille's hands. Most fortunately DeMille saw nothing whatsoever amiss in this. Dali immediately started cooing: 'Ah, Cecil B. DeMille! I have met you at last, *you*, the *greatest surrealist* on earth!'

"DeMille looked first charmed, then puzzled. He turned around, but none of his henchmen were present to interpret. 'What is a surrealist?' he asked.

"I explained. 'It's a new European art movement, Mr. DeMille, a kind of realism but more real than realism—"super-realism," so to speak.'

"'Oh,' said DeMille, getting it, 'a kind of super-colossal realism?'

"'To put it lightly,' I said, 'yes.'

"'Very interesting,' said DeMille. 'I should like to know more about it.'

"'Ah,' interrupted Dali, 'but you do know all about it, C. B. DeMille. You are the veritable *king of the surrealists.*'"

DeMille accepted this label in silence. He was now the king of the surrealists, and Dali said so in the next morning's papers. Incredulous reporters interviewed DeMille and asked him if this was so. DeMille said it was. The item was read by everybody in Paramount.

In addition to a few backhanded compliments, one of the most flattering reviews of *The Plainsman* was penned by Graham Greene: "There has always been a touch of genius as well as absurdity in this warm-hearted sentimental Salvationist. *The Crusades*, *The Ten Commandments* were comic and naïve, but no director since Griffith handled crowds so convincingly. Now startlingly Mr. DeMille seems to have grown up. *The Plainsman* is certainly the finest Western since *The Virginian*; perhaps it is the finest Western in the history of film."

The review continued with compliments being handed out all round, and DeMille was lauded as the architect of what might well turn out to be a new art form. Admittedly, Greene seemed hardly able to believe that he had been watching a DeMille picture, but all in all DeMille had much to be pleased about. From his copy of his voting form for the 1938 Academy Awards, one can see that he voted *The Plainsman* first place for direction (followed by *The Good Earth*, *Captains Courageous*, *The Awful Truth*, and *Stage Door*).

On the heels of this success, DeMille started work on another slice of American history, *The Buccaneer*, a film about Jean Lafitte, the privateer who had helped America to win the Battle of New Orleans. An article entitled "It Must Be Love," by William Herbert, "Cecil B. DeMille's favorite publicity man," in *Jones Mag* of September 1937, described preparations: "It is fascinating to watch the DeMille staff grow, and spread and blossom with an idea. Jeanie Macpherson was assigned to research. She built herself an igloo of books and dove into it, not to emerge for weeks. Frank Calvin was enlisted to start looking up data on arms, events and expressions of the period. Any time you met one of the staff, including the secretaries, you were liable to be greeted with, 'Did you know that the expression "son of a gun" came from the fact that women giving birth to children aboard ship were usually lashed to a gun?'"

By mid-July, the second unit was ready. Led by William H. Pine, recently promoted to associate producer, and Arthur Rosson, Hollywood's ace action director for big productions, they braved red bugs, crocodiles, and mosquitos, to film events in the life of Lafitte right where they occurred, in the Delta country. By the time the picture went into production on DeMille's fifty-sixth birthday, August 12, the unit had swelled to a technical force of almost 200, most of them veterans of many a DeMille campaign.

On *The Buccaneer,* Dan Sayre Groesbeck came back into DeMille's life. Much had happened to him in the intervening years, including a little matter of an uncertified check and a spell in a French jail. DeMille got him out. As ever, his input proved vital.

On June 1, 1937, the *Los Angeles Evening Herald* published an interview with Groesbeck referring to his work as a muralist and the wide distribution of his paintings in galleries and museums in Europe and America. Groesbeck took the opportunity to explain some of his theories, and in particular his view of the artist/designer's role in movies. "I am convinced," he said, "that every shot you see on the screen there should be as many square inches of dark as light, and that the light should be focused in the proper places. Otherwise the eyes of the audience tire easily. A picture properly composed throughout of dark values, can be sat through for hours without strain on the eyes."

Cameramen and electricians agreed with him and adopted his suggestions. Another thing Groesbeck insisted on was that caricature is essential in designing for the movies. "The artist is needed for emphasizing where emphasis is required. For example, we must costume hundreds of pirates for *The Buccaneer*. A belt, a buckle, a kerchief round the head, is scaled to those actually worn by the pirates to look as if the studio were trying to economize on material. That is the effect of the camera . . . to minimize. The artist, therefore, scales certain details of costumes and sets to counteract this effect. It's good drama, and though the players sometimes look overdressed on the set, that look vanishes when they appear on the screen."

In May 1934, before Paramount canceled the original *The Buccaneer* project, it was announced that George Bancroft, the star of several Josef von Sternberg films, might return to Paramount to star in the title role, but the part eventually went to Fredric March, though at one point DeMille had hoped to get Gary Cooper. DeMille initially cast Henry Wilcoxon, fresh from *Cleopatra,* but when it came time to make the movie his role went to someone else.

Simultaneous with DeMille's announcement of *The Buccaneer*, Sam Goldwyn announced a film to be called *The Pirate's Lady*, starring Gary Cooper (though Cooper ended up starring in *Marco Polo* instead). Paramount was furious with Goldwyn for having lured away Cooper, one of the top box-office attractions, and instituted a $5 million suit against Goldwyn, charging him with star theft, but it seems that all was fair in love and movies.

To the cast of *The Buccaneer* was added Franciska Gaal, one of the most popular cabaret and stage performers in Central Europe between the wars. She had also played lighthearted heroines in Hungarian, Austrian, and German romantic films of the early thirties. As always, DeMille tried to find parts for his old actors, so he duly slotted in silent serial star Buddy Roosevelt and Mae Busch, who was working in Laurel and Hardy films. Things did not work out so well with Charles Bickford, who walked out on his part when he discovered it consisted of only one scene. And for the first time in ten years DeMille signed a new artist, beautiful blonde Evelyn Keyes from Atlanta, to a seven-year contract. In her autobiography, she would coin a remarkable metaphor: "Director is God's perfect occupation. On a movie set, his is the Word, make no mistake." Continuing with this analogy she characterized DeMille as leaning towards "the wrathful, no-other-Gods-before-me style."

Reviewers seemed to like *The Buccaneer*, commenting particularly on its professionalism and its agreeable mix of doctored history and dazzling spectacle. *Weekly Variety* (January 12, 1938) put it thus: "DeMille, in again re-coursing to American history, obviously recognized the necessity for adulterating fact with palatable celluloid fiction, and his scriveners have seen to it that both are well blended. In typical DeMille manner he broadly sweeps the spectacular on the screen, including not a little of the American flagstuff, which is stirringly fitting for the occasion, and yet at the same time the British sensitivities have been well preserved." It was important to consider these sensibilities if the film was to be a success in England, and DeMille larded the rout of British infantry with substantial helpings of good old British pluck.

While DeMille was taking *The Buccaneer* film on its promotional tour, his much-loved daughter Cecilia got married. Her marriage to Frank Calvin had ended in divorce, and on January 21, 1938, she wed Joseph Harper. (Calvin later married Harper's sister.) Shortly after the wedding, it is said that DeMille inadvertently introduced his new son-in-law as "Frank Calvin," but Harper merely smiled and responded, "Thank you very much, Mr. Goldwyn." Their daughter, Citzie, had been born before the divorce finalized. She wrote: "Since Mother always lived next door to Grandfather, I divided myself between the two and lived where I wanted to," They both liked the arrangement and so did I. . . . Mother was Grandfather's most important ally throughout his life since his mother died. She became what his mother was. She never was more than down the hill from him at any time in her life, and totally devoted her entire life to him. The first husband didn't fit the category, the second did. She had dinner with him almost every night. We *never* dined at home, never . . . we always dined at the big house with Grandfather. Nobody in the world can say enough marvelous things about Joe Harper, including Grandfather, who adored him. It was the one real man friend, male friend, I think I ever saw Grandfather confide in. And he did confide in him, to where Joe would listen to Grandfather and not tell mother. It was a good relationship."

DeMille's family was growing all the time. In October 1937, Katherine got married. Anthony Quinn related the story in his autobiography: "Mr. DeMille and I had had an excellent relationship. I had developed a great respect for him, even a secret admiration. He had seemed to have a sincere respect for my work. Often during the shooting of the two pictures I had done with him he'd spoken to me with great encouragement.

"Now, when he saw me in his house as a potential son-in-law, I sensed a change. I was no longer the actor but some kind of a threat, an interloper into his close family circle. No doubt he thought his adopted daughter could do much better than marrying a struggling young actor whose future was still a big question mark.

"The rest of the family sitting around at dinner gave me very little thought. Katie had brought other young men to dinner who had eventually disappeared. They wondered how many dinners I would survive.

"After dessert the butler went around the table setting the demi-tasse service for coffee. I had ignored the small cube of sugar, since I didn't know how to extricate them without using my fingers. In front of the small coffee cup I saw a small receptacle containing what I thought was sugar. There was a tiny spoon at the side. I reached over and spooned it into my cup of coffee. I saw Katie looking at me. I didn't catch the warning. I smiled back and drank the brew. I had poured salt into the coffee. Apparently, other members of the family had witnessed my *faux pas*. Nobody said a word. I drank the coffee and smiled desperately, hoping I wouldn't vomit all over the doilies and the highly polished table. Katie later admitted that after the incident she definitely decided I might be worthy marrying."

Quinn married Katherine deMille on October 2, 1937, and DeMille gave her away. But he did little to advance his son-in-law's career. Quinn's part in the forthcoming *Union Pacific* was so small, he said in 1968, "I found it embarrassing." When he was no longer married and was asked about his relations with his father-in-law, Quinn told a reporter, "I would rather not comment on my relationship with Cecil B. DeMille, either socially or professionally, except to say that I am glad to have met him and am grateful that he was foresighted enough to adopt my former wife." However, by the time Quinn gave an interview to the BBC for a program on DeMille, his attitude had softened: "I didn't [regard him as a father] then. I do now. Interestingly enough, this has only happened in the last 10–15 years. I think as I've watched my sons grow up and defy me, I think that I realize that I went through a very natural process perhaps erroneously, maybe it's easier because now of course I can romanticize him, I don't have him there . . . in front of me to defy, and for the past 10 years I've become very fond of that father figure, and I'm sorry we didn't share it when he was alive."

With *The Buccaneer* behind him, DeMille toyed briefly with a story about the Hudson's Bay Company, but on finding that 20th Century Fox was working on a similar subject and was close to production, he decided instead to make a film about the building of the first transcontinental railroad.

For this project, he enlisted the help of William M. Jeffers, the president of Union Pacific, thus beginning a friendship that led to many things. Jeffers put all the resources of the railroad, including its archives, at DeMille's disposal, and lent him his fastest track-laying crew to re-enact the famous race between his own company and its great rival Central Pacific.

All this time DeMille was putting together the technical information on which a period piece like this depended.

Letter to DeMille from Joe de Yong (March 23, 1938): If you recall the detailed construction drawings I made for the Levee Cart in *The Plainsman*, it will serve as an example of the same accurate information which I have on *all* forms of Western Transportation, except trains. This transportation detail includes costumes, types, and customs of Packers Bull Whackers & Jerkline outfits.

The leading male role went to Joel McCrea, though DeMille had originally wanted Gary Cooper for the part. McCrea left behind reams of correspondence on the complicated contractual maneuvers and trade-offs required to change studios for the coveted role. Also cast with McCrea was Robert Preston. When asked what he thought of DeMille professionally, Preston replied: "He was no director. For over two weeks of shooting, Stanwyck and I were alone in a boxcar, and because there were no crowd scenes, no special effects, just two people acting, you'd never have known the old man was on the set. He didn't know what to do with it, except just roll and print. He didn't know what to tell us. Also, he was not a nice person, politically or any other way. I think the only man DeMille ever envied was Hitler."

Then, taking a pause to see if he's said quite what he intended to, Preston adds, "It's no secret how I felt about him. Eventually, by turning things down, I'd insulted him, and so we had no relationship at all in his last years."

McCrea didn't care for Preston's contention that working for DeMille was like working for Hitler: "I can't understand that, and I really disagree 100 percent. On *Union Pacific*, and I had never heard of Preston until then, he was treated just as well as Stanwyck and I. He was never bawled out; the boy did well. And DeMille was very friendly and boosted him. During *Union Pacific*, DeMille was quite sick: he wouldn't change the first day's shooting, but he'd had a prostate operation. I think that's what it was, because he couldn't move around much, but he got on the boom. They brought him in on a stretcher. He was a showman; he dressed it and he acted it, but I never felt he was so cold that he would let anyone suffer."

DeMille hoped that Claudette Colbert would play the female lead, where she would be courted by McCrea and the villainous Brian Donlevy, but his hopes came to naught. The leading female role went to Barbara Stanwyck, an actress whose professionalism and lack of temperament impressed DeMille hugely. He wrote of Stanwyck that he had never worked with an actress who was "more co-operative, less temperamental, and better workman"—in his lexicon, the latter being the highest compliment.

Natalie Visart was recalled to the fold to do her bit on the costumes. It was all post-Civil War, though Barbara Stanwyck's clothes were nondescript—in skirts, jackets, and blouses—since she was portraying a postmistress.

Because DeMille was recovering from a prostate operation, according to Charles Higham, he permitted some scenes to be directed by other hands, including Arthur Rossen and James Hogan. There was nothing nondescript about what Stanwyck was called upon to do on location, as Iron Eyes Cody explains: "Rossen had our leading lady, Barbara Stanwyck, jumping from railroad cars and allowing real arrows (shot by me), as well as bullets, to blast a canister of molasses over her head, which she then allowed to pour all over her. Despite what some say, though, she never let herself be chased by a buffalo. That was accomplished by a process shot. . . .

"The final scene in *Union Pacific* showed the driving of the golden spike which joined the track-laying teams and completed the transcontinental railroad. It was a beaut, a fine example of what the epic master did best. Shot in Canoga Park, near Hollywood, the scene had C. B. himself at the helm. The golden spike used was the real thing: the actual one from the 1869 ceremony, spirited down from a special vault in the Wells Fargo Bank in San Francisco [the one actually driven with hammers in the film, of course, was a copy]. The two trains again, perfect replicas in every detail, touched cowcatchers, and a full brass band struck up. Officials and businessmen stood about radiating an air of self-congratulation, the Chinese and Irish laborers flung their hats to the wind and cheered to the tune of the locomotives' whistles."

For one reason or another, perhaps the multiplicity of directors, the film ran far too long, and occasioned a flood of anxious telegrams in the spring of 1939, although complaints about length were on the whole mitigated by generally approving noises as to content. *Weekly Variety* had no doubts: "Paramount and DeMille have a box-office winner in *Union Pacific*. It's a socko spec, surefire for big grosses right down the line. On its size and scope, the DeMille production is undeniable film fare." That would certainly have cheered DeMille, and he must have loved a letter he received later in the month from that fine "workman," his leading lady,

Letter to DeMille from Barbara Stanwyck (May 28, 1939): Thanks for my beautiful nickels. If they bring me as much luck as the others—everything will be all right! I am still counting the time until I work for you again and always I shall be grateful to you for your kindness.

Devotedly,

Barbara

Their correspondence continued later in the year. Stanwyck's remark in October that "I knew you were not feeling well and I did not want to bother you" reminds us that he was still in the wars. She was putting it mildly. The prostate operation had been carried out pretty brutally, in DeMille's opinion, and for several years afterwards his health was a major worry. He told Art Arthur that in 1940 his doctor informed him that as a result of the operation he had an incurable infection and would be dead in two years. During this period, he grew steadily worse and "made plans accordingly." Then, quite miraculously, streptomycin appeared on the scene, and after a handful of injections, he was cured.

However ill he may have felt, DeMille kept hard at work. He directed one film with which he is not normally credited, *Land of Liberty*, a compilation of newsreel shots and stock material from classic films which record the progress of American history in suitably patriotic manner. It appeared at the Golden Gate Exposition and the New York World's Fair, was highly successful, and went on general release in January 1941. During the war, it was periodically updated, reduced to 16mm size for use in schools, and such funds as it raised were earmarked for war charities. DeMille justifiably prided himself on the contribution this film made to Hollywood's reputation and to the country's civilian morale.

Ill as DeMille may have felt in the aftermath of his surgery, one thing must have cheered him considerably. On June 9, 1939, encouraged by the success of *Union Pacific*, Paramount signed DeMille to a further four-year contract. Henceforth, DeMille's master works would be filmed in the full majesty and richness of glorious Technicolor . . .

CHAPTER THIRTY-SIX

AS DEMILLE PUT IT IN HIS MEMOIRS, THE ONLY WAR THAT CONCERNED HIM closely in 1939 was the Riel Rebellion—in fact, two rebellions during the late nineteenth century by the Metis people (Canadian mestizos) that had taken place in the Canadian provinces of Manitoba and Saskatchewan. He had been searching for material for his next film that would be a variation on his normal themes but still provide plenty of spectacle and manly adventure. *North West Mounted Police* fit the bill perfectly. It reworked and distorted a smallish incident in Canadian frontier history in splendidly confident style.

If not a masterpiece of historical interpretation, the film was a landmark for being the first feature film that DeMille made exclusively in color. It was also a color first for Gary Cooper, who had until then only appeared in isolated color sequences. On November 7, 1940, Bosley Crowther, a critic who was far from being an unmitigated fan of DeMille's, described his reaction to the film in the *New York Times*: "All along we knew that Cecil B. DeMille and Technicolor were fated to meet; all along we expected that the result would be something to see. But barely did we anticipate anything quite so colossal to emerge from that historic conjunction as *North West Mounted Police*."

Pierre Berton, in his book *Hollywood's Canada*, researched the pre-production activities of DeMille's assistants in considerable detail, mainly to prove his thesis that Hollywood distorted Canadian history and national identity to the point of caricature. While *North West Mounted Police* was hailed by international critics, including Canadians, as the most authentic picture ever made about the Mounties, as Berton showed in fascinating detail, DeMille both turned history topsy-turvy *and* managed to give the impression that the Mounties themselves had okayed the film.

As Berton points out, the studio's assumption that the Mounted Police were hungry for publicity and would jump at the chance to see themselves on the screen may have been a widely held notion in Hollywood, where everybody thrived on publicity, good or bad, but the Mounted Police's attitude was actually the antithesis of Hollywood's. In Ottawa, Commissioner Samuel Taylor Wood, who had taken over as Canada's top mounted policeman in 1938, had no intention of buckling under the kind of Hollywood pressure

DeMille is shown between takes of *North West Mounted Police* (1940) with his stars Gary Cooper and Madeleine Carroll. Photo by G. E. Richardson. Courtesy John Kobal Foundation

that had embarrassed the Mounted Police for some two decades. His response to Paramount's request was guarded: he didn't object to helping in a minor way, but only if the force was granted total script control! William Pine, DeMille's associate producer, and Frank Calvin, Paramount's research chief, went to Canada in July, but were unable to win him over.

Letter from Commissioner Wood to William Pine: I trust you will forgive my frankness if I explain further that the type of picture you have in mind appears to be one more attempt of the melodramatic type, and I cannot refrain from feeling some disappointment, as I had imagined you had an opportunity of making a better picture, showing the spirit, and history of the Force, than has heretofore been produced, but this does not seem to be what is intended.

Pine responded with hasty reassurances that "any motion picture Cecil B. DeMille produces will be true in detail and based on fact. He never garbles facts or distorts history." But at Wood's insistence the picture was renamed from *Royal Canadian Mounted Police*.

The RCMP had every reason to hate the Mountie movies. Hollywood routinely got everything wrong, including the uniform. And the Mounties were not the only ones to suffer. Berton concedes that the Metis had previously been depicted in more than sixty Hollywood movies as villains of the deepest dye: sneaky, untrustworthy degenerates who coveted defenseless white women, sold bad whisky to the Indians, and let others take the rap for their crimes. They served the same purpose as the mulatto villain in Griffith's *The Birth of a Nation* (and with much less public uproar), or as half-castes in a score of exotic films about Asia. According to Berton, "The historical and anthropological truth about the Metis is almost the exact opposite of the impression conveyed by the movies. To present them as a lawless breed, constantly pursued by the mounted police, is to fly directly in the face of established fact. They did *not* sell whisky to the Indian; that crime must be laid at the feet of the white men, first the great fur-trading companies, and later the American renegades who built the notorious whisky forts in what is now southern Alberta. It was the Metis and not the white men who first brought the law to the untrammeled north-west . . . unable to wait for the Canadian government to bring the law to the prairie country, [they] set up laws of their own, organizing a local government and a real estate code . . . and all this took place before the arrival of the North West Mounted Police. It was not Metis lawlessness that brought the police; it was the depredations of white invaders from south of the border, [who] murdered Indians, poisoned wolves, exchanged rotgut whisky for furs, and were a law unto themselves. Before the police came, the Metis communities acted as the only brake against widespread mayhem instigated by white predators."

DeMille went in person to Duck Lake, Saskatchewan, the scene of the so-called Duck Lake Massacre, which led to the North West Rebellion of 1885. Louis Riel, known as "the father of Manitoba," had responded to the Metis's pleas to present their grievances to the Canadian government when, as the result of a misunderstanding and certainly of a blunder by the mounted police, shots were fired, and a fracas followed in which three mounted policemen and nine volunteers were killed, eleven were wounded, and the Metis suffered five casualties. Frank Calvin began to compile a file on the rebellion, and by September (just as the war in Europe broke out) four writers were at work on a script. Press releases blithely reported that "full co-operation in the making of the picture had been promised DeMille by officials of Canada's famous mounted police."

Once a script was ready, DeMille sent Pine to Ottawa by air to deliver it personally. So far, so good. Commander Wood went so far as to lend the production a training instructor from Regina, Sergeant Major G. F. Griffin, to put the actors through their paces. By this time, DeMille had been forced by budget considerations to abandon any idea of location shooting in Canada; the film was to be shot on the studio's back lot (although it was supposedly set entirely in Saskatchewan, DeMille could not resist showing the Rockies behind his main title). For his first film in color, the Mounties were an apt subject; he saw in his mind's eye a moving procession of red-coated riders brilliant against the stark white of the Canadian snow, doubtless stained with Technicolor blood!

The publicity mills began to grind as soon as the cameras did. A series of ideas were being mooted behind the scenes, several of which were put to Bruce Carruthers, a former mounted policeman who had set himself up as a freelance technical director in the movie capital. One was a plan to hold the world premiere of the film in Canada, with the RCMP and Prime Minister in attendance. Carruthers advised that he couldn't see anyone from the Canadian government enthusing over a picture "which portrayed the police as deserters and nincompoops." He was convinced that the original script had been changed, and that it now contained elements that had either been kept from Commissioner Wood or inserted later. In a letter to Wood, he warned, "As it is customary to figure on 12% of the production cost for exploitation, DeMille will move Heaven and Earth with $240,000 to get publicity in any and every way possible."

Clark Gable had been touted for the leading role in *North West Mounted Police*, but when he wasn't available, Joel McCrea was next in line. Following their success in *Union Pacific*, DeMille wanted to work with him and Barbara Stanwyck again because, as he told McCrea, they were so easy to work with and did their job so well. He sent McCrea the script for the role of Dusty Rivers, and McCrea read it and thought he would like to play it. Then DeMille called him into his office some time later and there was Gary Cooper. Apparently, Cooper had a deal that had fallen through, so he was available, and as far as DeMille was concerned, here was a chance to have a big star and, according McCrea, "the only guy that he never failed to tell me how much he liked."

"So DeMille said, "Here, you have a choice. One of you can play Dusty and the other can play the other part.'

"I said to DeMille, 'Well, you showed me the part of Dusty, and obviously it's good for Coop, but I don't know whether I want to play the other role,' and he said, 'We'll toss a coin, and one will do Dusty and the other will do the other.'

"I said, 'Well, I don't think I want to be in this film, I really don't want to be in it.' And we shook hands and that was fine.

"But later on, outside, Cooper said, 'Look, if you want the part, tell me, and I'll tell him I'm not available.'

"And I said, 'No, Coop, because every time the old man is going to look through his viewfinder, looking at a scene or a crowd, and seeing just me

DeMille confers with his male leads for *North West Mounted Police* (1940), Gary Cooper and Robert Preston. Photo by G. E. Richardson. Courtesy John Kobal Foundation

when he could have seen you—or the both of us—I just don't want that. It isn't worth it.'

"That's why I wasn't in *North West Mounted Police*, because the other part simply wasn't good enough. It wasn't what I wanted to do. And I don't know what happened to Stanwyck, but she wasn't in it either."

A foreign actress was sought to play the part of Louvette, a half-breed slave. Iron Eyes Cody tells a story about the eventual casting of Paulette Goddard in the role: "DeMille's only difficulty was coming up with an actress for the role of Louvette, a half-breed slave, which he envisioned as having 'fiery sexuality, tempered by a soft heart.' He despaired, thinking that a woman of that nature didn't exist anymore. Then, an extremely beautiful woman I had met years earlier when she was married to Charlie Chaplin, stormed into his office one afternoon dressed up as a gypsy. . . .

"'So-o-o-o!' she said, throwing herself down in one of his leather-uphol-stered chairs and hoisting a leg baring a naked foot upon on his desk. "You theenk you're one beeg shot director, eh? Well, I am Louvette!" C. B. took one look at Paulette Goddard's perfectly shaped arch and, gasping, signed her up immediately."

The part of April Logan, who is courted by Texas Ranger Rivers (Cooper) and police sergeant Brett (Preston Foster) went to Madeleine Carroll, the cool English beauty who had been a hat model before her stage debut in 1927 and later starred in Alfred Hitchcock's *Secret Agent* and *The 39 Steps*. Though perhaps a less meaty part than that played by Goddard, it was very much a starring role, and not a man in the audience but gulped when Cooper manfully yielded her to Sergeant Brett.

Natalie Visart recalled the challenges of working in color: "In black and white, we had a little glass that we wore around our neck on a black cord, and we could hold it up and see what value it was going to look like in black and white. And that was extremely useful, but that didn't work with Technicolor. . . . It depended on the lighting. . . . You see, in black and white, all you had to do was figure what the contrast would be in grey and black and white. But the first thing we did in color, we had the Technicolor people breathing down our necks, saying, 'You can't do this,' and 'You can't do that.' 'You have to dip it in No. 1 or No. 3,' and, 'It's got to be brought down.' But then we got so we didn't pay any attention to them."

In *Hollywood's Canada*, Berton recounts in detail the events surrounding the North West Rebellion of 1885 to show "what it was that Cecil B. DeMille was doing to Canadian history. . . . DeMille did more than twist these historical facts to suit his purpose. He turned them inside out." He contradicts the introduction to the film, voiced by DeMille himself, almost line by line, and continues, "It is unnecessary to follow the rest of the picture in detail. Its polished production and big names only partially obscured the fact that Hollywood's most publicized director had employed the same clichés that had been standard in Mountie movies since the early days."

For *North West Mounted Police*, Hollywood invented fur hats of its own design. These hats, which bore little relation to the real fur hats the RCMP uses in cold weather, were so successful that the Paramount costume department subsequently rented them out to other production companies, so that moviegoers became used to seeing Mounties galloping about even in the sweltering heat of the summer with their heads encased in fur!

With the picture nearing completion, Paramount stepped up its campaign to hold the premiere in Canada—if not in Ottawa, then in Regina, headquarters of the Mounted Police, where they were promised the co-operation of the local Board of Trade. Wood warned the commanding officer at Regina that "the claims for the picture are extravagant" and that he shouldn't provide escorts "or anything of that nature," but, however reluctantly, the Mounted Police found themselves sucked in. They could hardly refuse the Board of Trade's invitation to lead the parade on horseback, and they were needed at the premiere to help hold back the crowds. In short, they were totally outsmarted. "DeMille managed to achieve all his objectives and get what he demanded when he first set out to make a movie about the mounted police," Berton continues, "especially the undeniable visual evidence that convinced the average moviegoer that this was an official motion picture, blessed by the top officer of the force."

The film had its world premiere in Regina, Saskatchewan, on October 21, 1940 (Trafalgar Day). It was an unhappy time for Madeleine Carroll. Shortly before leaving for the premiere she learned that her sister had been killed in an air raid in London during the Blitz, and an additional worry was the knowledge that her parents were still in England and refused to leave. DeMille was hugely impressed by the courage and professionalism that she showed in continuing with the promotion. Being the Anglophile that he was, he must have derived a quiet satisfaction from her behavior.

Reviewers liked the film and praised its lofty ideals, while welcoming DeMille's conversion to the full-length color feature. The picture received a total of five Academy Award nominations, and Anne Bauchens deservedly won an Oscar for her editing. Years later, DeMille recalled the picture as one that gave "American audiences a warm and true conception of the valor of the British Commonwealth and its peoples." If he had been unlucky in his timing with the Crusades, this time Adolph gave him a perfect launch.

Berton concludes: "The question of historical accuracy was not seriously debated." Only Charles Jefferys, the Canadian historian and artist, seemed to have realized the lengths to which DeMille had gone to change history. "Only a genius could have evolved from historic facts such a masterpiece of misinformation," he wrote in the *Canadian Historical Review*. That kind of comment, of course, did not bother the great director. When somebody asked him why he had switched sides and given the Gatling gun to the Metis—whereas it was actually being tested in battle for the first time by an American cavalryman and Indian fighter, Lieutenant Arthur Howard, on the side of the militia dispatched by the Canadian government to help put down the rebellion, the impression that a handful of red coated police managed to contain the rebellion, and not an overpowering military force, was continued throughout the picture—"he brushed the question aside. He had to do it, he explained, in order to increase the odds against the North West Mounted Police and make them look like greater heroes."

In March 1941, while the DeMille machine was spooling up for its next project, a film, which DeMille hoped, would rival *Gone With The Wind*, fate struck him a terrible blow. His grandson, Christopher Quinn, drowned. "In March, 1941, little Christopher Quinn, not yet three," DeMille wrote later, "with a big and wonderful world to explore, somehow escaped our watchfulness for a few minutes, trudged across the street from our home, was drawn by the magic shimmer of a pond on the property of my neighbor, W. C. Fields, slipped or in his eagerness leaned over it too far, and was drowned. He would be in college now, perhaps beginning to think of a life work, perhaps of marriage. But he left us when the world was still big and wonderful and unexplored; when his world was untouched by anything but innocence and love; and of such is the kingdom of heaven."

Katherine recalled, "I think one of the most tender times I've ever seen in my father was when my son was drowned." She said subsequently: "I've never forgotten it. He came to the house and I had been called from the rehearsal, and I was in shock. Just his tender sweetness. He still couldn't say it to me, because what can you say at a moment like that? . . . He was deeply disturbed by it. He had a great heart, but it was hard for him to show it." W. C. Fields had his cement-bottomed lily pond drained after this incident.

Ray Milland, born Reginald Truscott-Jones, had only made a handful of films in his native Great Britain when, in 1929, he was approached by MGM vice president J. Robert Rubin, with the age-old words, "How would you like to go to Hollywood?"

He was cast to play the lead in *Reap the Wild Wind*, DeMille's antebellum saga of wreckers and salvage masters in the Florida Keys. The *pièce de résistance* in this picture was to be a sequence in which Milland, searching a wreck for evidence that would incriminate his rival John Wayne, does battle with a giant squid. Milland recalled a tragicomical interlude during the making: "It [the battle] was staged in what is known as the Big Tank at Paramount Studios. The tank was almost the size of a football field and about twenty-five feet deep at the deepest part. Down there they had built a marine wonderland: the hull of a wrecked ship, strange and jagged rocks. A slowly moving aqueous forest. And caves, dark and frightening. . . .

"Right in the middle of this sequence I was told that I had to attend a party . . . I was tired, but there was no way out, I had to go to this brawl. To make matters worse, they served only champagne, of which I am not particularly fond. It gives me terrible heartburn and an even worse hangover, but as a protective device I drank it anyway. . . .

"Finally, at four a.m. the party was finished, and so was I. Stoned. I got home about five, parked my car on the lawn (I couldn't find the garage), and stumbled into the house. I knocked on my butler's door, told him to awaken me at five-thirty and get me to the studio by 6:15 a.m.

"I came out of the coma about an hour and half later as they were putting me into a suit of long underwear that I wore under the diving suit. I was still stoned, but now had a terrible headache. . . . I begged the prop men and the diving technicians to put me in the diving suit and lower me to the bottom of the tank before DeMille came on the set. Besides, I wanted that mixture of air and oxygen they pumped down to me. They did it and thereby saved my life. In about half an hour the lack of body weight and that heavenly mixture began to have their effect. . . .

"Somehow, I remained alive until lunchtime, whereupon my cronies quickly hustled me to my dressing room and started feeding me their pet cures for a hangover. Lynne Overman gave me three little black pills which he swore were the source of life. I swallowed them with a little tomato juice.

Then John Wayne came in and gave me two monstrous green capsules, which he insisted I wash down with a little gin. Finally, just before I was to be carted back to the tank, Bob Benchley came in. He said the only *real* cure was a wineglass full of Worcestershire sauce with a raw egg in it, which he just happened to have with him. By this time, I was beyond caring, so I swallowed that too.

"The rest of the afternoon was a nightmare and best forgotten. But De-Mille never tumbled. About five o'clock they called it a day, and when they hauled me up I was horrified to see that DeMille had not left the set and was waiting for me. . . . In front of everyone, DeMille stated that in all his years in Hollywood and in the theater he had never seen a finer or more perceptive day's acting than he had that day. Then he dramatically presented me with his personal Academy Award, a Virginia Dare half-dollar. After a handshake full of sincerity, he and his entourage left the set in columns of threes. I felt like a louse letting him appear a fool in front of all those people who were in the know."

The Paramount giant squid cost about $12,000 and provided excellent value. Most of the underwater scenes were filmed off the island of Santa Catalina or in the tank, and there was eight weeks of location filming in Florida and South Carolina. At the end of all this effort, it is good to record that the special effects unit very deservedly won an Oscar.

Apart from his stars and the ubiquitous Hedda Hopper as Aunt Henrietta Beresford, DeMille sentimentally found room for a number of former stars in a ballroom scene, including Mildred Harris (Chaplin's first wife), Claire McDowell, Dorothy Sebastian, Monte Blue, William Cabanne, Maurice Costello, Billy Elmer, Elmo Lincoln, and the director George Melford. And as always there were members of his repertory company of technical staff in attendance.

Reap the Wild Wind was released on March 19, 1942, and DeMille's old sparring partner Bosley Crowther was somewhat delphic in the *New York Times*, "After thirty years of making motion pictures, Cecil B DeMille has pretty well learned the trade . . . thus it is not surprising that *Reap the Wild Wind*, his anniversary film, is the essence of all his experience, the apogee of his art and as jam-full a motion picture as has ever played two hours upon a screen."

In the *New York Post*, Arthur Winsten wrapped nothing up: "*Reap the Wild Wind* is a massive and colorful tapestry in which technical proficiency deserves the top honors. . . . Distinguished performances are not possible in a DeMille pageant. But among those who are adequate and more than adequate in looks are Paulette Goddard, Susan Hayward, Ray Milland and John Wayne.

Interestingly, when the film was re-released in 1954, Wayne and Hayward were billed above Milland and Goddard, whose fame by then was in decline.

At about this time, DeMille revived his idea for a sequel to *The King of Kings*, to be called *The Queen of Queens*. He hired his brother William to research and work on the script, and brought back his old friend from *The King of Kings*, Father Lord.

After reading William's scenario, which was based on the play *Family Portrait*, Father Lord sent both the brothers a seven-page criticism as to why it should not be made. He had been told by Jeanie Macpherson long before to say "no" whenever the situation called for it. She recalled, "I had said 'no' whenever I thought a scene in *The King of Kings* simply would not do for the story of Christ. Now I was saying 'no' to an entire subject. [After that] Mr. DeMille regarded me a little sorrowfully and reminded me that I had blocked the production of *The Queen of Queens*. Personally, I think that was Mr. DeMille's good luck."

There had been other problems, such as the title. "In the British territories, chiefly Great Britain and Australia," DeMille was advised, "a fairy or pansy is referred to as a queen, and the Paramount men in London feared a ribald element might make a play on the title."

While *The Queen of Queens* was running the gauntlet with Lord, DeMille was considering the possibility of a film version of Hemingway's classic *For Whom the Bell Tolls*. Back in October 1940, while the two men were aboard a train going to Chicago for the opening of *North West Mounted Police*, he had obtained Gary Cooper's agreement to play the leading role. Jeanie Macpherson was assigned to the project, and had spent six months on the screenplay when DeMille relinquished his interest in the picture to Paramount. In his autobiography, he says that this was because he had been asked to make a Latin American picture, presumably to improve America's relations with her neighbors, but there seem to have been other reasons, including nervousness about the Church's attitude to such a topic. One way or other, the project foundered. Of course, in 1943 the film, which under Sam Wood's direction paired Ingrid Bergman with Gary Cooper, became a huge success for Paramount and soon assumed classic status.

As for the Latin American film, *Rurales*, this also became a non-runner. In an inter-office communication to Frank Freeman, DeMille expressed disquiet about it, fearing it could be used by political schemers to drive a wedge between Mexico and the United States. So *Rurales* also bit the dust.

In the end, DeMille got the idea for his next film from President Roosevelt himself, as he related to Art Arthur: "The idea came from a speech of the President's. . . . It was 1942. . . . Right after Pearl Harbor and everything had happened. Things were dark as they could be, and the President needed to talk to the people and he needed to cheer them up, so he told them three stories of great heroism. The first story that he told was the story of Dr. Wassell and these sixteen wounded men left on Java, all alone, with the Japs pouring in, taking possession, and how he got them out."

The wounded men were United States Marines who were badly hurt at the Battle of Macassar. Wassell, a navy doctor, was told to leave them to the mercies of the Japanese, whose attitude to Allied prisoners was, after the fall of Hong Kong on Christmas Day 1941, known all too well. "I was listening here [to Roosevelt's speech], Frank [Freeman] was listening in the Beverly Hills Hotel. . . . When he was half way through I said to Sidney [Biddell], 'This is our next picture. The minute he stops talking, let's get first Freeman and get him quickly, and then get the White House, and we'll seal it tonight, because tomorrow everybody in the world will want him. . . .

"Wassell was sent for, ordered in, told he was to fly to America on orders of secretary of navy. . . . He was told he was being taken to Los Angeles and he said, 'What are they taking me there for?' And they said, 'I don't know.' He was taken there and he walked into my office here not knowing what on earth he was here for. Right from Java. He looked at me and said, 'Well, can you tell me what I'm doing here?' And I said, 'Yes I'll tell you. You're here because I'm going to make a story of your life.' He said, 'Movies? Me? Let me get out of here!' I said, 'Wait a minute. You're under orders. This is for navy relief.' He said, 'Oh, if it's for navy relief, I'll do anything for the navy—but I wouldn't do anything for movies—nothing!'

"Wassell and I went around with the picture from city to city and talked on the radio. Wassell kept saying, 'This is 99 percent fact. Everything you see in that picture is 99 percent fact.'"

This was a film very much to DeMille's liking, and Gary Cooper, who played Corydon Wassell, the hillbilly doctor from Arkansas, was perfect for the part. The screenplay was worked up by James Hilton from interviews with Wassell and the survivors who could be traced. It contains a goodly load of war film clichés, but audiences loved it.

Seeing it now, one is constantly struck by the lack of gore, guts, or grime. For much of the film, the war zone seems only vaguely hazardous, and, given the dire circumstances in which they find themselves, no one seems particularly uncomfortable or out of humor. One cannot help remembering that the director was a man who, despite his military rank and love of adventure, had never seen a bullet fired in anger. Was it ignorance or a desire to sanitize that led him to purge his action films of any clue to the sordid realities of combat?

DeMille went to Washington for the opening of *The Story of Dr. Wassell*, and was received by the president along with the hero of the film and his wife. He records that the critics universally lambasted the film accusing it of departing from the facts. Nothing new about that. James Agee's review in the *Nation* (June 10, 1944) gives a sense of the critical reaction: "I do not feel I need to have been there to know that his story is one of the great ones of this war; also, that it could be much better told through moving pictures than by any other means; also that on both counts Cecil DeMille's screen version of it is to be regretted beyond qualification. It whips the story, in every foot, into a nacreous foam of lies whose speciousness is only the more painful because Mr. DeMille is so obviously free from any desire to alter the truth except for what he considers to be its own advantage. All the more touching, and terrifying, is the fact that Dr. Wassell himself thinks that the picture, with a few trifling exceptions, is true and good."

But the public thoroughly enjoyed DeMille's confection, however far it may have strayed from reality, and the good, long-suffering doctor survived all this to become a rear admiral. One man, Dennis O'Keefe (Hoppy), particularly distinguished himself in *The Story of Dr. Wassell*, and on the strength of his portrayal of the marine Hopkins who kept on firing until the ammo ran out went on to a successful movie career. As a role it was perhaps even more attractive to DeMille than that of the heroic navy medic.

Lloyd Anderson was construction co coordinator on *The Story of Dr. Wassell*, and he has some interesting things to say about DeMille. In particular, he resists the idea that DeMille's tirades were unjustified, or that there was permanent acrimony between him and the unions. "I never found anybody who had a real hatred for DeMille. From my point of view, he was King at Paramount. And what he wanted, we were all ready and willing to supply. He created jobs, he did great things for the business. I never heard anybody say that they felt that he was undermining them or that he was against the unions or that he was against any of us. He was Dad, he was head of the family, for Christ's sake. He represented everything in the industry. He was the old man. I admired and respected DeMille and I liked him."

Lloyd Anderson gave this final assessment of the old man himself: "You'd break your ass to work for DeMille. Because he was the whole can of peas, he was motion pictures. A DeMille picture was an epic. It was a milestone in motion picture making. A DeMille picture was the ultimate in motion picture making. . . . I think he was just a dedicated, hard-working son of a bitch."

CHAPTER THIRTY-SEVEN

ON AUGUST 16, 1944, DEMILLE RECEIVED A LETTER THAT WAS TO DETER-mine perhaps the main thrust and inspiration of the remaining fifteen years of his life. It was sent by the local branch of AFRA, the American Federation of Radio Artists, a labor union to which he perforce belonged. The letter enclosed a notice of assessment requesting him to pay the sum of one dollar into a campaign fund, to be used by AFRA in its forthcoming battle against Proposition Twelve.

DeMille had never heard of Proposition Twelve, but he quickly discovered that it was something of which he greatly disapproved. It was a proposed amendment to the constitution of California that would outlaw the closed shop, a procedure whereby unions effectively prevented employers from giv-ing work to non-union personnel. The offending letter, arriving four days after his sixty-third birthday, so outraged DeMille that it hugely rejuvenated the sexagenarian director, providing him with a whole regiment of windmills at which to tilt until his dying day.

As recounted earlier, since 1936 DeMille had been producing the Lux Ra-dio Hour for an audience that had risen to perhaps forty million people. For this and his other radio activities, he received an annual income close to $125,000. But his right to work on radio depended upon his membership in AFRA, and by refusing to pay the one-dollar assessment he put his income at risk. The Lux program meant a great deal to DeMille. He saw it as more than hosting a popular show built around his name, but as a way of reaching out to poor and rich alike by bringing high-grade entertainment to every corner of the land. It was a romantic notion, and there is some irony in the fact that the very love of democracy which attracted DeMille to radio as a medium was instrumental in forcing it from his grasp.

During World War II, Lux Radio Hour played much the same role in the national consciousness as did *ITMA* in Britain. (*ITMA—It's That Man Again—*was a BBC weekly review that spawned a myriad of popular catchphrases and boosted national morale at some of the worst moments of the war.) But for all its prestige, and despite the enormous pleasure he derived from pro-ducing radio theater, DeMille was prepared to jettison everything for the sake of principle. Whatever one might think about his reaction and its costly outcome, there is no denying that the man truly believed in what he stood for.

DeMille sought advice from his attorney, Neil McCarthy, and was told if he refused to pay the one-dollar assessment that the union would probably suspend him and prevent him from working on the air. With classic lawyerly caution, McCarthy predicated that if he went to court to attempt to prevent this suspension as being unconstitutional, the outcome would not be easy to predict. Constitutional law was not an exact science, opined McCarthy, and the decisions of the courts in constitutional questions were a matter of psychology and social viewpoint. As the spirit of the time was pro-labor, it would probably not be possible to find a court that would take a robust position in support of DeMille. DeMille's reaction, McCarthy recalled, was uncompromising: "That is wrong in principle. If this action of the union is upheld by the courts it means because a man belongs to a union the union could compel him to contribute his money, whether it be a dime or a dollar, for a political principle to which he may be opposed."

DeMille then asked McCarthy what the cost of such a lawsuit would be. McCarthy replied: "This will take us three or four years to run through the courts. We will probably lose, and you will be giving up $125,000 a year." McCarthy went on to explain that he would donate his own legal services in view of the principle at stake.

In due course, meetings were arranged with local representatives of the union. They told DeMille and McCarthy that since DeMille was a member of AFRA, his contract with the union permitted it to invade his constitutional rights. McCarthy retorted that no contract was binding upon a man which invaded his inalienable, constitutional rights: that the Declaration of Independence had recited that it was a fundamental principle of American law that man was endowed with certain inalienable rights, that the right of free speech was property, and that it was the policy of the government that such an inalienable right could not be canceled by contract.

All these discussions with union representatives seem to have taken place in a friendly atmosphere and without rancor on DeMille's part. The union men contended that it was only a small matter, while he explained that in his view it was "a large and vital matter," since it involved the invasion of the basic rights of an American citizen, and it was the surrendering of these basic rights little by little that would eventually lose for Americans all that their forefathers had won for them.

In stating his case, DeMille became increasingly lyrical and histrionic. He said he owed an obligation "to himself as a citizen, and to his children, and to his ancestors who had helped to lay the foundations of liberty in this country." He called attention to the fact that one of the first Dutch mayors of New York was an ancestor, and another had signed the Declaration of Independence, and that he could not betray the principles for which they had fought just so that he could make money on a radio program. The union people offered to let someone else pay the assessment, but DeMille would not budge, and eventually the matter came to trial.

The Supreme Court of California ruled that as a union member DeMille was bound by his contract, and that the union had every right to make the assessment of one dollar. Justice Shank avoided the basic principle at issue—namely, that no contract should be binding which invades the inalienable constitutional rights of the citizen. McCarthy petitioned the Supreme Court of the United States, but that court refused to hear the case again on the basis that it had already been dealt with (presumably satisfactorily) by the Supreme Court of California.

DeMille remained adamant. He declared that it was highly un-American for any institution to require you to pay tribute before you could be allowed to work. He made speeches, and appeared on a friendly radio station in Omaha to advance his case. Large numbers of sympathetic listeners sent him money to continue the fight, and he paid these funds into an account at the Bank of America pending some means of putting their money to good use.

The heartland of America was behind him. But there was plenty of opposition orchestrated by the communist press. Several years later, Louis Budenz (a communist defector) told DeMille that the Communist Party had marked him down, along with Fulton Lewis Jr., as one of two people who must be silenced.

William M. Jeffers, the president of Union Pacific and a friend since the making of DeMille's railroad saga, now urged him to set up an organization to educate the public on the rights they were at risk of losing. DeMille acted quickly, and in September 1945, he set up the DeMille Foundation for Political Freedom, a trust whose foremost objective was an assault on the closed shop. DeMille, McCarthy, and Sidney Biddell (associate producer on *The Story of Dr. Wassell*) were trustees, and Jeffers was the first chairman of the board.

DeMille had introduced his last radio play on January 22, 1945, and, since the American Federation of Radio Artists was to become the American Federation of Television and Radio Artists, he would soon be banned from performing on television as well. He could appear to promote one of his films, but not to work. But there was a positive side to this affair, for though he had lost $125,000 dollars a year, plus a job that he loved, he had now gained a cause, and to a man of DeMille's age, income, politics, and general disposition, that wasn't such a bad exchange.

The foundation got off to a good start by attracting the interest of many influential people. It concentrated on lobbying and educating, helped by many donations, and by the bank account which DeMille had developed from the gifts of his well-wishers and admirers. One of these was a young man, Gordon Mounts, then working in the army air corps, who read about DeMille's confrontation in the papers and, as he put it, went cold turkey to Bill Jeffers, who put him in contact with DeMille's office. DeMille was so taken with the enthusiasm of the young man that he took him on to specialize in the lobbying and fundraising work of the foundation. According to Mounts, DeMille did not see himself fighting the unions so much as fighting "government of, by, and especially for the Hoffas, the Becks, the Bridges, and the Reuthers"—i.e., the overweening leaders and not the rank and file.

Eventually, Mounts was dispatched all over the US to drum up support and establish a war chest. Clearly, the prominence of DeMille's name eased the path of the young executive director as he made his rounds raising money and establishing contacts. As Mounts put it, "If you said Cecil B. DeMille then you were talking about the first cousin of God. Every home in America knew him. Every theatergoer knew him. Every young person. Every old person, your dog Ruff would know him."

An early success was DeMille's appearance before the drafting committees that were working on the Taft-Hartley bill on labor relations. (President Taft's nephew, the publisher Hulbert Taft, was to become a great supporter of the DeMille foundation.) In Mount's opinion, it was only the intervention of DeMille that secured the inclusion in that bill of a clause prohibiting the closed shop in interstate commercial relations.

DeMille was prepared to go anywhere if the occasion demanded it, and he was certainly most happy to use the glamor of Hollywood if that would help. If some dignitary from the Middle West wanted a tour of the studio, Gordon Mounts had carte blanche to arrange it, and lunch with a famous star or director if that too was required. In the service of "the cause," DeMille cheerfully traveled to Ohio to address a joint session of the state legislature, or to New York to address the chamber of commerce.

Donald Hayne, a former Dominican friar, was recruited to the foundation's ranks to write DeMille's political speeches. For a time, this somewhat louche individual reputedly got closer to DeMille than almost anyone, according to Mounts—closer even than DeMille's family. Hayne took over the role that Father Daniel Lord had enjoyed in DeMille's life until the two men fell out over *The Queen of Queens* (the Virgin Mary project). Mounts, who knew Hayne well, gave this picture of the man: "He was a Dominican friar who left the Church, then returned to it and left it again, married, sired children, and was very clearly bisexual. . . . He was also an extraordinarily intelligent man, a good speechwriter, a good speaker, a witty acerbic man, much in the style of George Sanders, but whose laugh was high-pitched and very feminine."

Mounts took the view that given Hayne's contacts in the higher reaches of the Catholic Church, he probably had some watching brief over DeMille, and was charged with "bending a major force to take a position that would be compatible with the Church's [political] position."

Given the Church's fierce opposition to the spread of atheistic communism, DeMille's very public espousal of anti-union attitudes must have made him an attractive plum for churchmen to pick. Mounts likened Hayne to

Father Joseph, Cardinal Richelieu's private chaplain and confessor. While he said kind things about Hayne, he plainly felt that Hayne exercised a great deal of intellectual influence over DeMille.

At this point in his life, DeMille was quite ready for someone like Donald Hayne, the son that neither of his two adopted boys turned out to be, who could be spiritual counselor, political adviser, and friend, with an intellect that considerably excited him. What Hayne liked about DeMille was his strength, his mastery, how he punched through anything in front of him, right or wrong, and his kind of virility, a basic masculinity that must have struck a strong chord in the complicated, changeable Hayne. And he must surely have been delighted to find in DeMille a spokesman for his own beliefs, a powerful figure who, when he spoke, would be listened to, whereas he, a renegade, bisexual friar, could never command such an audience.

At some point, this troubled cleric rendered his patron a signal disservice, however. DeMille was sixty-six, set in his opinions, and highly receptive to attitudes that supported his, particularly if they encompassed conspiracy theories, and "Donald Hayne saw Reds everywhere," said Mounts. "Everything seems to tie in together in that kind of person in his own feverish imagination." It was Hayne, according to Mounts, who put DeMille in touch with Senator Joseph McCarthy.

One must remember that by the late 1940s, communism was advancing everywhere: Eastern Europe had fallen, Indo-China and Malaya were threatened, and Chiang Kai-shek was near defeat. Even before Korea and the Rosenbergs, there was every reason for a patriot to feel apprehensive. Hayne, with good connections in the Church, would certainly have been able to put McCarthy and DeMille in contact, and whatever reservations he may have had about the alcoholic senator from Wisconsin, it seems likely that in a Jesuitical way DeMille could have satisfied himself that the end justified the means.

Fortunately, the flirtation did not last, though Henry Noerdlinger reported that DeMille made speeches in support of McCarthy. In 1950, the foundation certainly attracted unfavorable publicity, when it was alleged that under the leadership of Tom Gerbich, a strike-busting former head of Republic Steel, it had been passing the names of left-wing directors and writers to the California State Un-American Activities Committee, which in turn was forwarding them to Washington. But it wasn't long before DeMille saw that Joe McCarthy was not for him. Nevertheless, the relationship gave him moments of quiet shame, and it was something he regretted for the rest of his life.

During the mid-1950s, the momentum of the foundation began to waver, and eventually it was only the rock solid determination of its founder that kept the thing going. As Gordon Mounts eloquently put it, "He was in it, his heart was in it, his energies were in it until the day he died. I don't care what he was in or what real estate thing, or what motion picture script he was working on, who he was going to cast, this was always on his mind . . . he never, never let defeat get in the way of the principle."

Mounts left in 1952 to pursue a career in business, but Hayne remained at DeMille's side until the end. For much of that time he was engaged on the autobiography. Members of the family came to think that the friar's excessive devotion to DeMille's image accounted for the book's cautious and uncontroversial tone. Mounts blamed Hayne for castrating the authentic voice of DeMille, maybe out of the best possible motives, but it is also likely that he couldn't see what he was doing, perhaps because he had written a lot for DeMille, and was used to DeMille bringing things alive with his oratorical skills, things that were bland on paper but that DeMille could color with his voice, with his latent, hammy theatrical skills. Without DeMille's voice the book lacks bite.

DeMille, when he came to a certain passage, would have slowed his speech, would have raised his eyes, paused, and, for example, made the whole passage on the right to work, which was the DeMille Foundation, and therefore the last major thing in his life, come alive on the page. Yet Hayne gave it very little space because he feared that here was another area in which DeMille might not look quite right. That was a pity, because, properly written, such a passage might have blown away much of the fog which clouded DeMille's political reputation.

The foundation remained on DeMille's mind until the very end of his life, and no doubt many of his peers thought it a strange obsession. The foundation was shut down within a short time after his death, but in its heyday it achieved much and gave its founder ample opportunity to say his piece about life, liberty, and all things that he held dear.

Through persistent lobbying and the assiduous cultivation of influential politicians, by the time of DeMille's death nineteen states were persuaded to legislate internally against the closed shop. It would be nice to think that DeMille could look down from whichever part of the ether it is that he inhabits to see his position finally vindicated in June 1961, when the Supreme Court ruled in a Georgia case that a labor union may not use a member's dues for any cause against the expressed wishes of that member.

Success in his battles against the closed shop was achieved by DeMille's fierce will. Without commitment nothing is achieved, but a thin line divides commitment from obsession. As we shall see, DeMille seemed to cross that line in the autumn of 1950, when with similar zeal he fought to impose his will on fellow members of the Screen Directors Guild. But that, as they say, is another story.

CHAPTER THIRTY-EIGHT

UNCONQUERED WAS DEMILLE'S FIRST FEATURE IN THREE YEARS. IT WAS A saga of American frontier days made at a time when men like DeMille felt that the old values, the American frontier spirit, needed to be re-established. It brought together Gary Cooper and Paulette Goddard again from *North West Mounted Police* and, as Bosley Crowther put it in the *New York Times* on October 19, 1947, "it tells a tempestuous story of a doughty frontiersman's escapades among the British redcoats and the redskins in the pre-Revolutionary wilds." Crowther went on to point out that the film was "as viciously anti-redskin as *The Birth of a Nation* was anti-Negro long years back."

Wilfred Buckland had been doing some research work for DeMille a year before shooting began, and two of his letters, presumably written at a time when the script was still underway, concern suggestions for an "Escape from Indians": "The prototype of this idea is found at Niagara Falls, where behind the falls there is a recess or cave known as 'The Cave of the Winds'; which has been made accessible to visitors, and where they are hidden by the curtain of water in front of them. A similar device might be used to vanish the Fugitives. Their Hunter guide naturally would not attempt their rescue without a definite plan which is to hide them in a recess he knows of, behind the Falls of the nearby stream."

This idea seems to have been taken up and elaborated, as suggested in the following undated press release: "Mothers who insist they are going to get their daughter into pictures if it kills them should have been alongside Cecil B. DeMille at Paramount the other day when he was applying his impersonal, epic touch in a scene involving Paulette Goddard and Gary Cooper.

Imagine your daughter clinging to an overhead branch some twenty feet from the ground, and being swung through thousands of gallons of water pouring down on her from a fifty-foot height. That was the little feat DeMille called upon Paulette Goddard and Gary [*sic*] to perform for him in the climactic scene in *Unconquered*, an episode in which the two successfully elude Indians after a long and hazardous flight in a canoe."

Unconquered being a story featuring Indians, Iron Eyes Cody strode into the picture once again: "It was 1947, and *Unconquered* was another massive

DeMille epic, this one about indentured servants in the American colonies. Paulette had a pretty tough role to play, requiring her to be tortured by yours truly, whipped, chased in a canoe over a waterfall, sold as an indentured servant on an auction block, and to scrub a tavern floor while scruffy men made lurid advances. I chased Coop and her throughout half the picture in the canoe over the rapids. I shot a flaming arrow into her skirt, and threw fireballs at her during the siege of Fort Pitt. . . . DeMille constantly tried to shame her into submitting to these dangers, but she held fast to her own safety measures, and to her cognac. I love Paulette, but her performance was less than professional in this one. She was never to work on a DeMille picture again."

Unconquered was released on September 24, 1947, giving rise to some enjoyable banter among the reviewers. Here is James Agee in *Time* (October 27, 1947), giving a very full "appreciation" of the film and its eminent producer: "*Unconquered* (Paramount) is Cecil Blount DeMille's florid, $5,000,000, Technicolor celebration of Gary Cooper's virility, Paulette Goddard's femininity and the American frontier spirit. The movie is getting such stentorian ballyhoo that a lot of cinemagoers are likely to think less of it than it deserves. It is, to be sure, a huge, high-colored chunk of hokum; but the most old-fashioned thing about it is its exuberance, a quality which 66 year old Director DeMille preserves almost single-handed from the old days when even the people who laughed at movies couldn't help liking them."

When everything is said and done, it was a positive review, and a fair depiction of DeMille and what he was all about. The *New York Times* as we have seen was rather less charitable. It was left to the *Los Angeles Times* to utter unstinting praise: "Spectacularly, stirringly and with full panoply of gaudy color, Cecil B. DeMille again screen-vitalizes a chapter out of American history." This was exactly what the Champion of Democracy wished to hear.

But in 1947, DeMille was more concerned with the communist threat, and he renewed his old association with J. Edgar Hoover. One member of the cast of *Unconquered* had particularly disturbed DeMille. As the scholarly Henry Noerdlinger, another recent acquisition to DeMille's research staff recalls, DeMille was very close to J. Edgar Hoover, and he was visited regularly by an agent of the FBI—certainly at least once a month, and sometimes more often: "The reason I know this is because the guy always went into my office and sat down, and he never learned my name, he always called me Mr. Norden. So in the files somewhere I am Mr. Norden."

In the back of Noerdlinger's mind during the telling of this anecdote was the actor Howard da Silva, who received third billing in the film. Why DeMille cast this New York theater actor remains a mystery. He was a fine actor and worked for Paramount for six years between 1945 and 1951, but his film career suffered a major setback when he refused to testify before the House Un-American Activities Committee. By then, it was already well known that da Silva was a communist. According to Noerdlinger, it had not been a secret

Stand-ins for Victor Mature and Hedy Lamarr were used for this dramatic scene from *Samson and Delilah* (1949). Courtesy John Kobal Foundation

when he first met da Silva on *Unconquered* either. It was Noerdlinger's theory "that DeMille hired him so that he could be better observed."

Conscientious patriot that he was, it seems hard to believe that DeMille would hire someone to play a major role—the second male lead in a $5 million production—unless they were also thoroughly suitable for the part. As DeMille, who would have seen da Silva in *The Lost Weekend* and other Paramount films, recalled for Art Arthur on the subject of communist sympathizers who worked for him: "I liked Howard very much. At that time it was not known he was Red. I liked the way he worked. I had a talk with him. He came into my office one day and I said, 'I heard some pretty strong things about you—I'd like to hear it from you.' And I mentioned what I had heard. He turned into a coiled rattlesnake right on the couch—everything fell away from him and he was another human being. I was put in my place by trying to suggest he reform. That was the last time I saw him."

The man who would later defy HUAC was not going to let himself be intimidated by DeMille. Work continued, but it couldn't have been pleasant. Da Silva, a former steel worker, gave an excellent performance as the heavy.

It is doubtful those FBI visitors Noerdinger remembers were there because of DaSilva alone. What does seem probable is that the Freedom Foundation, in the course of its work, came across the names of certain left-wingers working in the movies. According to Kenneth L. Geist, the foundation complied "dossiers on all Screen Directors' leftist affiliations. These dossiers acquired spurious legitimacy when leaked to legislative committees like California State Senator Jack Tenney's, which would, in turn, feed them to the House Un-American Activities Committee."

If *Samson and Delilah* proved anything, it was to contradict the generally held and constantly reaffirmed theory about DeMille: while he was a master of mass movement, he was insecure when it came to handling emotional, intimate relationships.

DeMille himself agreed with this assessment, yet *Samson and Delilah* proves it false. It is seen and judged to be an epic because it is biblical in its settings. But in fact it is anything but epic, consisting of a fight between two little provinces, the Philistines and the Danites, at a time when kingdoms were still little more than cabbage patches. Of course, it contains elements of heroism, but the religious difference between two warring neighbors was not an upheaval on a world scale. The Philistines were a small, though sophisticated, part of the Babylonian empire, whereas the Danites were one of the seven tribes of Israel.

Rather, the whole film is a domestic tragedy, about a man who, like Romeo, went outside his own race for love. Except for the spectacular destruction of the temple of Dagon, the film was almost totally an intimate drama about two people, filmed mostly in two shots. If it hadn't been for the costumes, which we automatically associate with history and therefore epics, what DeMille made was actually a very small, very personal romantic tragedy, with God thrown in to lift it from the everyday.

Of course, what does give the film an epic quality is its pictorial influence, which is primarily that of late eighteenth- and early nineteenth-century French art. Time and again, the powerful images on screen echo historical paintings. But the finest moment is the most intimate, when Delilah, after discovering that Samson has been blinded, wakes from her sleep tormented by what she has seen and the tragedy she has brought upon the man she loves. Alone in her bed, dressed in a white night gown, her bountiful hair dramatically disarrayed and her face ravaged by grief, this composition brings old art to life.

DeMille had originally intended to make *Samson and Delilah* back in 1935, with Henry Wilcoxon playing Samson (Wilcoxon did play in the 1949 film, but not as Samson, and by then he had acquired something of an American accent), Harold Lamb had been engaged on a treatment back then which formed the basis of the eventual script. Conferences had taken place to discuss the treatment, and these gave rise to questions that had been forwarded to Ella Adams to research. Ralph Jester had also been caught up in the scripting process, for which he would be rewarded fifteen years later with a screen credit.

Back in 1935, an anonymous letter from Atlanta addressed simply to "Mr. Cecil DeMille, Hollywood, California," was certain: "Put Evelyn Brent as 'Delilah' in your Samson and Delilah picture. You can't go wrong in this, as you did not go wrong when you used C. Colbert. Brent is not only pretty, but has that cold calculating personality so necessary to depict 'Delilah.'"

By 1948, the list of possibilities had grown:

> Memo (March 11, 1948): The following I have reason to presume are available for the part of Delilah: Alida Valli; Gene Tierney; Maureen O'Hara; Hedy Lamar [*sic*]; Greer Garson; Lizabeth Scott; Jean Simmons
>   For the part of Samson: Errol Flynn; Robert Taylor; Victor Mature; Burt Lancaster Saran; Michael Redgrave
>   My thought is an unknown Samson rather than a known, such as John Bromfield, William Hoper, teamed with Jean Simmons.

The lists grew and grew, including, it would appear, almost anyone still living who had ever set foot or face before a camera. After much cogitation, the two main parts went to Victor Mature and Hedy Lamarr who, as DeMille said rather coyly in his autobiography, embodied "the essence of maleness and attractive femininity." Other parts went to George Sanders, who made a formidable Saran of Gaza; Angela Lansbury, golden-haired and athletic as Semadar, the sister of Delilah; Henry Wilcoxon, as the rough, tough Philistine Ahtur, who made sure that he and not Samson got Semadar; and an assortment of old friends and lovers, including Julia Faye, Victor Varconi, and Pedro de Cordoba.

At the same time, incidental music was being sought. DeMille had clearly set his sights high, and was soliciting music (unsuccessfully) from the composers Saint-Saens and Khachaturian. Saint-Saens's publisher refused to grant permission, and legal counsel Russell Holman advised, "The Russian government is probably still angry at Hollywood because the music of Khachaturian and two other important Russian composers was used, illegally by the Russian interpretation, in the anti-Communist Fox picture *The Iron Curtain*. Frankly, I suggest that DeMille does not pursue this idea."

In the end, the musical score was written by the longtime Paramount composer-arranger Victor Young, who had worked for DeMille on *Reap the Wild Wind*, and would do so again on *The Greatest Show on Earth*.

Meanwhile, the production team had been rounded up and was hard at work. Ralph Jester went to North Africa in search of locations and props, and kept DeMille informed of his progress. His report provides a fascinating insight into the work of a movie scout engaged in a major overseas reconnaissance. Indeed, his own activities might have provided excellent material for a film, "The consensus of opinion seems to indicate that the Oasis of Bou-Saada will offer us the best possibilities. It is along the caravan route running

Hedy Lamarr and Victor Mature, the two glamourous stars of *Samson and Delilah* (1949). Courtesy John Kobal Foundation

east and west along the Sahara at the northern edge. We have been warned of the heat, but I imagine it will be no worse than, say, Yuma at this time. . . .

"Later I am contacting a local merchant recommended to me by my friends at the National Geographic in Washington, a Mr. Zagha, who knows where things in Algeria can be bought or made. I have already spotted two beautiful brass pieces here in our hotel, which is owned by a local architect who is a great art collector. Zagha may know of similar ones. They are called 'bru-el-parfums' and are used by the sheriffs to burn perfumed incense in their palaces. . . . "Yesterday I overheard a Frenchman having difficulties about a taxi and offered him a lift. He proved to be Balmain, one of the top Paris dress designers, down here for a charity benefit with his models. An idea occurred to me. . . . We could ask the six or seven best dressmakers in Paris to give us their idea of what Delilah looked like in her most seductive moments. The sketches need never be used, or we might buy them, but it might be good for a story in one of the big national magazines."

A few days later, Jester wrote to DeMille giving a further appreciation of the pros and cons of filming in French North Africa. From his combination of military exactness, technical know-how, and artistic sensitivity, one gets a flavor of the many qualities required of senior staff sent abroad to scout for a DeMille epic: "Bou-Saada (Algeria) offers a rather wide variety of terrain, with flora quite characteristic of the classic type of oasis lots of palm trees and a variety of lavender oleander (called 'lauriers roses') in abundance near water. I am told this will stay in bloom thru most of July. Plenty of wild, rocky ground reddish in color, where rock is exposed as well as sand dunes on the Sahara side. To give you a choice, both types of terrain could be shot. . . .

"After seeing oases here, I feel that Tyler's sketch of the pool and tent is too "open-aired." An oasis is characterized by deep, cool, mysterious and inviting shade in its more romantic corners. Waters flow thru with a running commentary of restfulness. More dense shade in our set might cut down on the cost of architectural elements.

"In Morocco, the nature of the landscape is only slightly different as far as the feasible locations investigated are concerned. The mountains just south of Taza rise to six thousand feet and are covered with chenes de liege (cork oak). To my disappointment, Taza looked better to the eye than in the camera, perhaps because of its high spaciousness, which is difficult to seize in a lens. Around Fez and westward the soil and the buildings made of it are a dull adobe color, which gives no contrast between houses and background.

"The exception to this is in the low mountains northwest of Meknes. Here, around Moulay-Idriss and Volubilis, the terrain had good character is spotted with olive groves and is without palms. Our trip to the south of Marrakesh may alter this opinion, but there are points in favor of staying within the above range."

While Jester was sweating it out in North Africa, DeMille set about arranging a contract with his leading lady. In her autobiography, Hedy Lamarr wrote of her "feud" with DeMille, though the term is barely substantiated. The account starts at a lunch date with an agent she calls Sidney, who told her that DeMille had been asking if Betty Hutton was available for the part of Delilah. Her own agent promptly phoned DeMille and received an invitation to coffee in his office the next day, although he wondered whether or not the whole idea had been planted in the first place through Sidney so that he would call DeMille. "That night I opened my Bible for the first time in months," writes Lamarr, "and the more I read, the more fascinated I became. Next day, by appointment, I was asked into the great man's office. . . . I hadn't realized he had an accent. And when I spoke he smiled and said, 'We might have a difficult time understanding each other.' It wasn't just a joke. I could hardly make out what he was saying. . . .

"When all the pleasantries were dispensed with, suddenly we were look-ing at beautiful sketches of scenes from the forthcoming *Samson and Delilah*. The moment I heard it would be in Technicolor, I wanted to do it. I had never done a movie in color, and my vanity succumbed under the very possibility.

"DeMille then said, 'Hedy, I have followed your career. You have become an important personality. You will be bigger. How would you like to play Delilah in *Samson and Delilah*?' He held up his hand. 'Don't say anything. I will call you tomorrow.'" DeMille didn't call the next day, which made Hedy nervous. "I was furious with him and myself. I decided I wouldn't do his sex-and-scripture spectacle even if he begged me on his knees." Two days later, the call came, this time an invitation to tea, and an offer of the coveted role.

Lamarr's agent had warned her that DeMille was an egomaniac but bril-liant. He anticipated that the two of them would be fighting every inch of the way, and advised her not to win individual battles only to lose the war. She promised to respect her director's genius: "Though the picture was to be one of the huge money-earners of all time and my reviews fabulous, we had lots of trouble. The very first day Edith Head, the famous fashion expert at Para-mount, came down on the set with the gown I was to wear in the first scene. I said, 'It's beautiful but it does not fit the mood I have. This is too drab. I'm supposed to excite Samson.'

"Mr. DeMille came over to referee. He looked at the dress on me and said, 'I see nothing wrong with it.'

"I said, 'I want a gown that says something positive, not one that just has nothing wrong with it.'

"Mr. DeMille scowled. However, he ordered a camera test and I looked at it on screen. 'It's *not* right,' he told Edith Head. 'Let's try the same thing in red.' In red it was exciting and I wore that. Round one."

Edith Head recalled working with DeMille and Lamarr: "For the ending of *Samson and Delilah*, the temple scene, I sketched Hedy Lamarr in peacock blues and greens with a long flowing cape to suggest the bird.

"'Why not use real peacock feathers?' asked Mr. DeMille. 'Make a whole dress of peacock feathers.'

"'They're almost impossible to get,' I said.

"'No peacock feathers?'

"'I tried not long ago to get some for a Lamour turban,' I said. 'But even if we could get feathers, I think it would be almost impossible to make a dress of them.'

"My mistake. It was like waving a red flag before a very active bull.

"'I'll supply the feathers,' he said.

"A few days later, a station wagon filled with plumage arrived, Mr. De-Mille at the wheel. 'I have a ranch,' he explained. 'We raise peacocks. I just spent the week-end picking up fallen feathers.'

"So, I designed and we made a magnificent dress that transformed Hedy into the most exotic of birds. Mr. DeMille was so proud of it he took it home when the picture ended. (I might also add that the picture brought me an

Academy Award, toward which the peacock dress probably contributed no little.)"

So after all the research, adventure, and effort, spanning the best part of fifteen years, how did it all turn out? The film was released on Trafalgar Day, October 21, 1949, and among the usual sniping (the *New Yorker* called it "preposterous" and "essentially worthless"), DeMille received some gratifying bouquets: "A fantastic picture for this era in its size, in its lavishness, in the corniness of its storytelling and in its old-fashioned technique. But it adds up to first-class entertainment, whether laughing at it or with it, neither the hipsters nor the squares will find any of its two hours and eight minutes dull or un-enjoyable . . . as for the kids, Samson is the greatest invention since Superman," said *Weekly Variety*, October 26, 1949. "If DeMille can outdo DeMille, this time it has been done. For in *Samson and Delilah* he has come up with a king-size attraction which showmen everywhere will long have cause to remember," wrote Red Kann in the *Motion Picture Herald*, October 22, 1949. And Bosley Crowther in the *New York Times* of December 22, 1949, spoke kindly of *Samson and Delilah*: "The first thing to be said about it, before the echoes have even died, is that, if ever there was a movie for DeMillions, here it is . . . There are more flowing garments in this picture, more chariots, more temples, more peacock plumes, more animals, more pillows, more spear-carriers, more beads and more sex than ever before."

With his two most recent films doing well at the box office, and the foundation making progress, as America entered the second half of the twentieth century DeMille had good reason to be pleased with life. But there was to be gilt on the lily, for the veteran director was about to score a late-blooming success in his old profession. In 1950, DeMille was given a part in Billy Wilder's marvelous cynical and wildly romantic tale of old Hollywood, *Sunset Blvd*. It reunited DeMille with the "young fella" of his early days, Gloria Swanson, now playing the demented silent star, Norma Desmond. At the time, DeMille and Billy Wilder spoke to the film critic and movie columnist Ezra Goodman: "DeMille was such an eminent Hollywood figure that he was cast in the role of DeMille in *Sunset Blvd.*, a movie about the movies. In 1949, Billy Wilder directed DeMille in a scene in which the director was depicted shooting a scene for his own movie, *Samson and Delilah*. . . . Billy Wilder said that, 'It's easy to direct DeMille. He understands the camera moves and what is needed. Of course, he had to overcome a certain, shall we say, shyness at first, but he was fine after that. He takes to direction like a fish to water.' When it was all over, DeMille stepped into a portable dressing room to recover from the ordeal of portraying Cecil B. DeMille on the screen. 'It's harder to play a director than to be a real one,' he said. 'Sometimes it's hard to do either.' He added, 'I am thinking of retaliating by casting Wilder in my next picture.'"

A glow must have warmed DeMille after this escapade and the receipt of so much well-deserved praise from his peers. The disappointment of the

DeMille took an important featured role in Billy Wilder's *Sunset Blvd.* (1950). He is shown here with old friend and the film's star, Gloria Swanson. Courtesy John Kobal Foundation

Lux affair was long behind him, and with numerous projects afoot, he now seemed to be entering into a golden autumn.

All too soon this pleasant atmosphere was shattered. DeMille was not usually a man to indulge in hubris—he had been through far too much to take anything for granted—but as 1950 wore on his behavior veered dangerously close to the hubristic, and in October, he engineered a confrontation that brought him the worst publicity and the most crushing defeat of his long public life.

CHAPTER THIRTY-NINE

IN COMING TO TERMS WITH DEMILLE'S EXTRAORDINARY BEHAVIOR DURING his notorious attempt to unseat Joseph Mankiewicz from the presidency of the Screen Directors Guild, behavior which with the benefit of hindsight seems almost to verge on insanity, one must not forget his personal obsession with democracy, or the political climate of 1950.

The late 1940s had seen spy scandals, the Berlin Airlift, the Hollywood Ten, and finally the outbreak of the Korean War. We have seen that long before the fall of the Iron Curtain, DeMille had been fighting his own private war for democracy, but now his most fevered suspicions seemed to be coming true.

In September 1949, the Russians announced that they had the atom bomb. In January 1950, Harry Gold (Raymond) confessed that he had obtained nuclear secrets from Klaus Fuchs (the British scientist employed at Los Alamos) and passed them to Soviet agents in "the crime of the century," according to J. Edgar Hoover. On May 2, 1950, Gold revealed the existence of a second spy at Los Alamos, Donald Greenglass, who said he had been recruited by his brother-in-law, Julius Rosenberg.

It may well be that the arrest of Rosenberg on July 17, 1950, and of his wife, Ethel, a month later, triggered something in DeMille's overheated imagination, for there is really no other way to describe his outrageous behavior during the next few weeks. With Mankiewicz abroad DeMille decided, largely on his own authority, that there must be a purge of the Screen Directors Guild. His objective was to flush out any subversive who might be lurking in the guild, but his methods were unpleasantly similar to those of the totalitarian regimes he despised. Inevitably one suspects that the fearsome Jesuitical logic of ex-Friar Hayne might have influenced his thinking.

But to be fair, DeMille was a man of his generation, and before Vietnam changed everything, it was typical for Americans to equate freedom with the flag. For most of his life, dating back to World War I, DeMille had been a dedicated patriot. In one of his last public utterances on the subject, to the Los Angeles Rotary Club on September 19, 1958, though speaking in favor of the right to work, he referred to "the cause of individual freedom, for which

I speak with all the strength I have." Foreign ideologies, and those who supported them, were anathema to a man born in 1881, especially one whose patriotism had not been tested in the heat of battle. However, even if DeMille had been briefly drawn to Senator McCarthy and spoke in his support, it was the Screen Directors affair that brought him true notoriety.

Other directors, an intelligent lot, were also aware of what was going on, but none of them had fought the battle for as long as he. Besides, they were filmmakers, not politicians, and they expected the government to look after these things. Not so DeMille, the great individualist, who believed that it was every citizen's duty to uphold the constitution. This had been his Holy Grail throughout his long life, and in its pursuit he involved himself in a series of underhanded actions for which he was to be greatly reviled.

The meeting of the Screen Directors Guild in the Crystal Room of the Beverly Hills Hotel, on the night of Sunday, October 22, 1950, is remembered for different reasons by different sources, none of them favorable to either DeMille's staunchly right-wing position or to his conduct that night. None of it, though, was as simple as it seemed. Everyone points out that DeMille tried to get Mankiewicz removed from his post. Yet, few writing about this "night of the long knives" in the Crystal Room mention that only six months earlier, it had been DeMille who had touted Mankiewicz for the job.

What did DeMille think about Mankiewicz that would alter so radically that he suddenly wanted him dethroned? Repeated attempts to get Mankiewicz to explain either this, or the subsequent shift in DeMille's attitude, have come to nothing. Everyone knows why they fell out. But why did DeMille ever raise and support Mankiewicz's candidacy for the job? Maybe he felt a sympathetic bond with the younger man; both men were second sons whose adored fathers died when they were still young, and who grew up in the shadow of brilliant older brothers. Although Mankiewicz was raised in a Jewish household, he was not known as a practicing Jew. Both men married outside their faith and carried on numerous affairs outside their marriage. They both established their towering and highly individual personalities through movies as writers, directors, and ultimately as their own producers.

Mankiewicz began his career in Hollywood with Paramount in 1929 while DeMille was at MGM, and he was still there when DeMille returned. He became one of the studio's producers in 1935, and left the following year to become a full-fledged producer at MGM, where he made his reputation with a succession of successful Joan Crawford vehicles.

But in his five years at Paramount there had been plenty of time for the older man to have noticed the younger. Mankiewicz was notoriously aloof from the Hollywood pack, but to DeMille he must have seemed like kin. Apparently, according to the recollection of DeMille's granddaughter, the younger man had been up to the house prior to his election to the presidency, one which DeMille actively promoted. These bare facts suggest that there may have been more to their relationship prior to 1950 than would be immediately apparent. The young man DeMille liked had now become a forty-one-year-old, two-time Oscar winner who had very little in common with the older man. While not overtly political, Mankiewicz was not prepared to be pushed around.

The given reason for the falling out between the kingmaker and the president was Mankiewicz's opposition to DeMille's plan to have all guild members take a membership loyalty oath similar to that required of union officers by the Taft-Hartley Act, an act which Mankiewicz himself had signed. The objective, of course, was to expose and purge communists and other dissidents. Mankiewicz's biographer, Kenneth L. Geist, writes, "On August 18th, the day after Mankiewicz had sailed from Le Havre, when telephone communication was impracticable, DeMille convened a special emergency meeting of the board of SDG to draft a by-law making a non-communist oath compulsory for its present membership and those seeking admission to the SDG. To create a show of endorsement for their action and to expose any dissidents, the board 'courteously' mailed out numbered open ballots with boxes to be checked 'Yes' or 'No' underneath the (proposed) oath. The results (547 'Yes' and 14 'No' on the 618 ballots mailed) might have seemed to indicate widespread support for the oath, were it not for the unpublicized fact that the balloting was open."

When Mankiewicz, who had been on holiday in Europe after completing *All About Eve*, arrived in New York on August 23, he was assailed by reporters wanting to hear his opinion on the oath, which had become the talk of the industry.

He explained he knew nothing of either the oath or the emergency which prompted it. Clearly, he wasn't too concerned, because he didn't return to Hollywood until two weeks later, on September 5, whereupon he convened a meeting of the board of guild. It was then that he was blandly informed that all the guilds and unions in Hollywood were expected to adopt a mandatory oath, and that the board wanted their guild to be first. Said Mankiewicz to Elia Kazan, who went to question him forty years later, "The meeting got savage . . . after a while I'd made up my mind, and I went ahead and ordered our secretary to call a general meeting of our members for the very next Sunday night. Whereupon DeMille walked out of the place, slamming the door behind him. . . . Well, the next day I got a request, would I come over to DeMille's office at Paramount from where the whole thing was being run, and when I got there, they were waiting for me, most of the national board. DeMille said they were willing to resubmit the loyalty oath on a closed ballot for another vote. 'But,' he said, 'of course we'd want a statement from you, Joe, before we did that.'

"'What kind of a statement?' I said.

"Now these are DeMille's exact words: 'You might call it an act of contrition,' he said.

"Then I cursed them all and left."

On September 14, Mankiewicz returned to New York to accept a B'Nai Brith award as "the one who did the most in the field of art during the preceding year to further the American democratic ideal." At the ceremony, he gave a passionate indictment of the witch-hunt climate, which had already caused so much suffering in the industry. From this point on, Mankiewicz set his face against the loyalty oath, and questioned its legality: "According to the Taft-Hartley Act, we have not the right to deny a man the right to work because he won't sign an affidavit."

The board, led by DeMille, refused to acknowledge this objection, though their legal adviser supported Mankiewicz. It is a neat piece of irony that DeMille's Foundation for Political Freedom, sometimes referred to by those who were involved with it as the Foundation for Americanism, had by its determined lobbying been instrumental in amending the Taft-Hartley Act so as to exclude "closed shop" provisions in connection with inter-state trade.

Mankiewicz's wife, the actress Rose Stradner, a refugee from Nazi Austria, was passionately concerned with American historical precedent and while her marriage may not have been happy, she certainly had the influence to urge her wandering husband to stay firm in the matter.

Mankiewicz and his board were now at loggerheads, and the DeMille faction wanted him out. One can only assume that DeMille must have felt betrayed by the man he had personally selected. The ferocity of DeMille's attack on the liberal wing, as represented in his eyes by Mankiewicz, is simply not explicable by any other means. He must already have suspected that Mankiewicz would not play ball with him in imposing the loyalty oath, or else he would have waited another five days until Mankiewicz had come back.

The problem that ensued was not the oath, but the handling of the vote. DeMille behaved throughout in the most offensive and autocratic manner, as if he were on the set with a particularly uninspiring group of underlings. This time, however, the "underlings" got his number.

DeMille's supporters now called a secret meeting of the board and other sympathetic members for 6 p.m. on October 11. Known Mankiewicz partisans were deliberately excluded, often by underhanded means. For instance, the telegram inviting board member and former guild president George Stevens did not arrive at his Paramount office, a short distance from DeMille's, until 6:30 p.m.

The outcome of this meeting was a decision to recall (i.e., depose) Mankiewicz as president of the guild, by means of a ballot on anonymous stationery. The entire text was as follows: "This is a ballot to recall Joe Mankiewicz. Sign here . . . Yes." No reasons were given. As Mankiewicz subsequently pointed out, "the recall 'ballot' is a refinement over the open ballot which the membership was forced to use in voting on the non-Communist oath. That ballot permitted members to vote either 'Yes' or 'No.' The recall ballot permits the choice of either voting 'Yes' or 'Not at all.'"

DeMille, assisted by board secretary Vernon Keays, now had to deliver the ballot secretly so that no loyalist could tip off Mankiewicz as to what was intended against him. By now, the recall committee seems to have gone totally off the rails. It is hard to discern what exactly DeMille was after. Did he think another president—whether a Republican, Democrat, or left-wing liberal—would allow him to ride roughshod over the membership and impose his will? We must leave the events to unravel themselves.

To sack the president, 60 percent of the guild's membership was needed. Fifty-five names were scratched from the list of potential addresses and, in a move reminiscent of the sequence from Capra's *Meet John Doe* (1941), in which the corrupt reactionary played by Edward Arnold sends out a uniformed cyclist to stave off the ideological threat of Gary Cooper, motorcycle messengers were dispatched into the night to hand-deliver ballots. (Ironically, Capra was among the members of the recall committee.) Recall committee members now set about ringing up directors of their acquaintance to persuade them to vote in favor of the ballot. Some had convinced themselves that the expulsion of Mankiewicz was their patriotic duty.

But the Mankiewicz supporters learned about the plot. They met in a back room of Chasen's Restaurant to draft a response. It was a distinguished gathering, including the four Oscar winners for best director before Mankiewicz: Billy Wilder (who had just finished directing DeMille in the acerbic *Sunset Blvd.*), William Wyler, Elia Kazan, and John Huston. Martin Gang, Mankiewicz's attorney, advocated a two-fold measure to counter the recall, consisting of a legal injunction to halt the circulation of ballots and a petition for a general meeting of the membership.

The problem was that the petition required twenty-five signatures. This was in itself quite difficult at that hour of the evening, and the act of petitioning was most definitely going to risk DeMille's wrath. One of the petitioners, Richard Brooks, another emerging Young Turk in the postwar industry, remembers that agents were advising their clients of the danger of signing, especially immigrants whose final citizenship had not come through, and one or two petitioners suddenly dropped out. It was a time of great fear. The Hollywood Ten had not been convicted that long ago, and many formerly successful writers and directors now found themselves made unemployable by rumor. While no one has ever suggested that DeMille kept any man out of a job, nevertheless his perceived position was closely identified with the attitudes that Senator McCarthy was to fan into a blaze.

The following morning, when a delegation went to file the petition at the guild offices, they found them closed, although they were normally open on Saturdays. Various other devices were employed to obstruct the petitioners, including the sudden absence of the secretary, Keays, whose wife contended he had left town before breakfast. It later transpired he had been making furtive trips to the guild at odd hours all through the weekend. In any case, the petition was duly served early on Monday morning.

The Austro-German screenwriter Walter Reisch described the emergency meeting on Sunday, October 22 at 7:30 as "the most tumultuous meeting in Hollywood," and Mankiewicz called it "the most dramatic evening in my life." Over the seven and half hours that ensued, passionate speeches, heady insults, and outraged self-righteousness contended with each other for attention. According to Geist, Mankiewicz's opening speech was drafted by H. C. Potter and John Huston (no mention of Kazan). It was very clever in that it never used the first person until the very end. Only when Mankiewicz referred to the "Politburo" quality of the recall committee's instigation as "so foreign to everything I've ever known or learned as an American" did his emotion show through. He won over his audience immediately with this report, and nonplussed the recall faction led by DeMille.

With almost every director in Hollywood present at that meeting, Kazan kept out of the hall, fearing that DeMille or one of his stooges might spot him and, knowing Kazan to be a friend of Mankiewicz's, raise the bogey of Kazan's former membership of the Communist Party as part of their attack against Mankiewicz. In his autobiography, Kazan said it was he who helped draft Mankiewicz's speech, making no mention of H. C. Potter. He wrote passionately about the events of that night: "All hell broke loose . . . Cecil B. DeMille was going for throats, including mine. He'd gathered the most conservative directors onto the guild's national board to work with him to uncover and discredit left-wingers in the membership and make their continuing to work as directors impossible. He would do this by drawing up a list of those who refused to sign a loyalty oath, then delivering this list of undesirables, inside a guild-franked envelope, to the head of every studio in town."

From time to time during the evening, DeMille lost his customary self-possession, and made several highly disingenuous remarks that were later lampooned by those speaking in opposition to him. "No one has accused Mr. Mankiewicz of being a communist," he said at one point. "When I nominated him for president of this guild, I thought he was a good American, and I still think he is a good American." So what was the problem?

Before the evening was out DeMille played many sentimental tunes, including some which seemed to dramatize, even romanticize, the current war: "There is nothing I want from the guild . . . my race is nearing its end . . . you all read this morning about the American boys who were prisoners who were taken out, promised food, and then were machine-gunned with their hands tied behind their backs." All this to get his guild to be the first to sign in Hollywood?

Having missed firsthand combat in both wars, DeMille's passion was in no way dented, but his position was hopelessly flawed. The most rabid of his enemies were those who had seen action and knew of the truly sordid nature of war. In their revulsion against flag-waving sentimentality, they perhaps unfairly saw DeMille as an armchair warrior.

On being taunted with this accusation from the floor, DeMille made a serious blunder. He read off a list of the Red Front organizations with which some of the twenty-five petitioners had been affiliated. The list had been drawn, he contended, from the reports of the 1947–49 Un-American Activities Committee of the California Legislature. This reference to one of the most painful incidents in Hollywood's muddled political history, to a roomful of people with friends who had suffered its effects, unleashed a full cargo of pent-up resentment. Kazan quotes Mankiewicz:[7] "They booed him until he sat down. I didn't say anything. I didn't have to. When DeMille heard those boos, he knew the meeting had turned against him. He was beat."

Joseph L. Mankiewicz, thirty-seven years and four Oscars on his mantelpiece later, had no need to muddy the events of the evening. He had every right to remain bitter about what DeMille tried to do to him.

The venerable John Cromwell, a long-standing liberal who would give up films and return to Broadway for most of the next decade, rose to launch the counterattack. He pointed out DeMille's hypocrisy in pleading for unity in the guild while making "acrimonious" and "unfounded accusations" about its members. "I resent paper patriots who stand up and holler, 'I am an American' and contend that no one else is," said the Paramount writer and director Don Hartman, one of the petitioners. "I think there is no possibility of honesty," he went on, referring to the open ballot, "when you ask people to vote and tell them they are likely to lose their jobs unless they vote the way you want them to vote." Herbert Leeds, a former investigator of communists for the Office of Strategic Services, pointed out that "probably everyone, or almost everyone, who has any prominence at all, by giving $5 to a worthy charity has had his name on a communist-front organization. In the State of California, there are three hundred Jewish communist front organizations, so it is almost impossible for anyone to stay off one."

The episode of the shutting of the guild offices cued the evening's coup de grace. George Stevens, the eminent director, still shocked with the memories of battle and the corpses he had seen in Belsen, rose to describe the story of the machinations behind the recall ballot's preparation at the guild. He detailed all the damaging facts, the locking-up of membership lists, the list of possible Mankiewicz supporters, and the false cover stories given to members of the guild's staff. "It was rigged, and it was organized, and it was supposed to work . . . if the integrity of the membership of this guild . . . hadn't frustrated that recall, Mr. Mankiewicz would have been out . . . he would just have been smeared and out . . . brother, if they [the communists] can do it better, they are pretty good." As soon as he had finished his report, he announced, he intended to resign from the board.

DeMille rose to protest against the charge of conspiracy, and Stevens rebutted by pointing to the recent resignations of Clarence Brown and Frank

---

7.Elia Kazan, *A Life*, 1988.

Capra from the committee after they had learned of the tactics of DeMille and Keays.

Vernon Keays got up to apologize for his actions. He confessed that he had only taken the job out of penury, and claimed he had given in to the demands of the committee because it represented a quorum of the board of directors.

Don Hartman now went in for the kill. "Mr. DeMille, I have charges against you and I would like to put them before the meeting. You now go further. You say if anyone speaks in his defense it is proof of his guilt. When you speak in your defense that is not proof of your guilt. . . . I accuse you of misconduct in the guild, and I ask you for your resignation." This was received with tumultuous applause. DeMille was now wounded mortally, but he showed no emotion. The motion was seconded by John Cromwell and Ralph Seiden, a former second-unit director for DeMille who had long nurtured his grievances against the tyrant infamous for his abuse of subordinates.

"This has been going on for years," roared William Wyler, furious over DeMille's smears. "I am sick and tired of having people question my loyalty to my country. And the next time I hear somebody do it, I am going to kick hell out of them. I don't care how old he is, or how big."

Now a very well-known director rose to his feet. "I am a director of Westerns," said John Ford. "I am one of the founders of this guild, and I would like to state that I have been on Mr. Mankiewicz's side of the fight all through it. . . . I don't think we should put ourselves in the position of putting out derogatory information about a director, whether he is a communist, beats his mother-in-law, or beats dogs. I don't agree with C. B. DeMille. I admire him—I don't like him, but I admire him. If DeMille is recalled, your guild is busted up."

"Everybody has apologized," he concluded. "Everybody has had their say, and Joe had been vindicated. What we need is a motion to adjourn."

Everyone now realized that things had gone too far. There were few who really wanted DeMille to be completely humiliated. Mankiewicz therefore asked Ralph Seiden if he would withdraw his second if Don Hartman would withdraw his motion asking for DeMille's resignation, but Seiden refused.

In the midst of the discussion, Ford rose with a breathtaking proposal. "I believe there is only one alternative and that is for the board of directors to resign and to elect a new board of directors." The effect of this proposal was to save DeMille's face, albeit in a limited way. Each of the board members now rose in turn to offer his resignation. The sight of DeMille regally descending from the podium to the floor and retreating to the back of the hall past rows of heads averted from his defiant gaze, "bald head held high," as the former DeMille child actor Robert Parrish put it, is an indelible memory for many of the evening's chief participants, who could not help but mourn the titan's fall as deeply as they despised his tactics.

The room emptied quickly, leaving only DeMille and Mankiewicz behind with their various supporters. It was a scene that Mankiewicz incorporated in his Capraesque film *People will Talk*, where the wretched, defeated Elwell trudged through the university's corridor as the exonerated Dr. Praetorius conducts a triumphant overture. The difference was that DeMille did not give anyone the satisfaction of looking defeated. When he got home early that morning, he brought none of his defeat back with him, and he makes no mention whatsoever of the affair in his autobiography. But the next day at the studio over lunch, looking gloomily down at his plate, he said, "If you don't think our country is in danger, you should have been at last night's meeting." As far as he was concerned, like the British Field Marshal Montgomery, he was right and all the rest were wrong.

Ultimately, the fireworks ended in a damp squib. In an open letter to the guild on Friday, October 27, Mankiewicz asked the membership of the guild to get on and sign the loyalty oath as voluntary act in affirmation of their confidence in the guild, setting aside all reservations regarding the oath.

DeMille's thinking had been muddled, for even as he opposed compulsory union memberships with all his might, he wished to impose a compulsory repudiation of communism as a condition of belonging to the Screen Directors Guild. On a later occasion, he asked, "Does the right to work belong to the worker or the union?" In October 1950, he might have had some difficulty answering this.

DeMille's worst moment in this sad business had been when he proposed to the board that all directors, on completing a film, should submit to the guild a report on whatever they had been able to find out about the political convictions of everyone connected with the film, particularly writers and actors. This information would then be on file at the guild so that directors could check on the loyalty of those who wanted jobs. The loathsome suggestion was soundly defeated, but it has a particularly sinister ring when one bears in mind the activities of the DeMille Foundation, which allegedly complied dossiers on screen directors' political affiliations.

It is sad to note that in attempting to achieve what he saw as the greater good, DeMille descended to the methods of those he despised. It is a policy that over the years has discredited and demoralized many institutions, from the Society of Jesus to the CIA. As we know, DeMille had had a long love affair with intelligence work that probably started back in 1917 with the American Protective League. There is no doubt that he knew J. Edgar Hoover, and one hopes that this monstrous scheme to spy on writers and actors was an unfortunate aberration following a heavy night with the director of the FBI.

It must have saddened DeMille that so many of the directors whose work he most admired were now against him. Through Mankiewicz, he may even have hoped to become part of a new generation, in a way that he had never quite been part of his own, but he had learned the hard way that there was no true sympathy between them. The enigma remains: was Mankiewicz a favorite son, a scapegoat, a decoy, or just a great deal less amenable than DeMille had expected? Had DeMille's super-patriotism unhinged him, or did the unexpected outbreak of war in Korea in some way force his hand?

It is important not to dismiss DeMille's side of this unfortunate affair out of hand just because of his unscrupulous behavior. He did have reason to suspect some writers and directors of subversive and underhand behavior. Many years later, Edward Dmytryk recalled how communists in the Writers' Guild delayed all important votes until late in the evening when less fanatical members had gone home to bed. And Adrian Scott, one of the Hollywood Ten, had on one occasion replaced a right-wing writer with John Wexley, a notable left-winger, by telling his producer that the former's writing was unsatisfactory without even having read it.

While DeMille did not get far with his Hollywood surveillance project, he found other ways of contributing to the battle for democracy. Foremost among his contacts was Joseph Grew, the right-wing diplomat who had de-briefed him in Istanbul when he came out of Russia in 1932. The two men had kept in touch, and Grew involved DeMille in both the Crusade for Free-dom and Radio Free Europe. It would take many volumes and much re-search to do justice to every aspect of DeMille's intensely full and active life: suffice to say, if he believed in something, he devoted himself to it totally.

There were repercussions from that night, mostly to the detriment of De-Mille's reputation. Not only was he seen as a right-wing super-patriot with extreme reactionary attitudes, he was also now characterized as completely out of touch with reality and cut off from the very men he most admired. Worst of all, as a result of many Jewish left-wing intellectuals having felt threatened by his attitude, the story began to circulate that he was an an-ti-Semite.[8] His image was not so WASPY that no one remembered his own antecedents: he was perceived as being anti-Semitic because a great pro-portion of his critics were Jewish intellectuals only recently arrived in Hol-lywood. Goldwyn, Lasky, and many of his friends being Jewish carried no weight, and that he was neither anti-Semitic nor anti-foreigner, and worked with both throughout his long career, was conveniently forgotten.

What could be said of DeMille was that he believed very firmly in the su-periority of his country and its values and that anyone who disagreed with him on such matters was at best foolish and most probably suspect. Richard deMille put the case for his father very fairly: "DeMille's mother, whom he adored, was foreign-born; it is hard to believe he could count foreign birth against anyone. Foreign ideas he might count against them, alien ideology, loyalty to the Soviet experiment rather than to the Constitution. Conceivably

8. At the time of Kobal's 1991 writing, the official SDG Minutes had not been publicly published. It is recorded in the SDG Minutes that DeMille never mentioned nor used anti-Semitic words in his speech. His main concern was the infiltration of communism in the movie industry.

he suspected Mankiewicz of all these things and wanted him to swear they were not true; Mankiewicz was willing to swear, but only at DeMille. De-Mille suspected Mankiewicz of being an enemy of the people. The suspicion was mutual. Mankiewicz prevailed at the meeting but, if memory serves, the guild soon voted to support the loyalty oath, so maybe it was just DeMille they didn't like."

In the interest of ending the account of this affair on a cheerful note, we might note that during the marathon seven-and-a-half-hour meeting DeMille alone among all the directors did not excuse himself for a visit to the loo. Hence the immortal remark of Tom Pryor, bureau chief of the *New York Times*: "There's no doubt about it. DeMille has the greatest courage in town and the strongest kidney!"

CHAPTER FORTY

INVETERATE OLD-STAGER THAT HE WAS, DEMILLE ALWAYS ENJOYED RE-
counting the incident or adventure that first inspired his choice of subject
matter. With *The Greatest Show on Earth* it was "an inconspicuous item in the
Hollywood Reporter. It said that Ringling Bros. and Barnum and Bailey were
interested in the possibility that a motion picture might be made about their
circus. Within five minutes I was closeted with Henry Ginsberg, the head
of production at Paramount, closing the deal for my next picture." It was
natural that such a project would appeal to DeMille. All that was wild and
romantic in his nature responded to the glamorous, vagabond character of
circus people.

In his autobiography, DeMille described his wish to make a picture that
would be about the circus itself, rather than one which merely had a circus
background. He prepared himself well, traveling with a circus on its trek
through several states of the Middle West, picking up slang, spotting bits of
business, and dictating reams of notes to the unflagging Gladys Rosson, who
accompanied him. With his love of what could perhaps best be described as
"active service," DeMille, saw the circus almost as a huge and exclusive com-
mando unit: "It is an army. It is a family. It is a city, always on the move. It is
an agile giant. It is sweat and fatigue and danger endured to send a rippling
wave of thrills and laughter across a continent. All the nations of the world
are represented in it, but those who are 'with it' form a tight clan set apart
from everyone else in the world."

Dorothy Lamour recalled the casting: "Betty Hutton was the first to be
signed after her zealous campaign to get the role of Holly, the trapeze artist."
Henry Wilcoxon remembered that Hutton had some stiff international competition for the role and had some interesting things to say about the casting
for Holly: "I'll tell you the one who was up for the part, and would have been
given it if the person who had her under contract had said yes, and that man
was Howard Hughes—Gina Lollobridgida. Yep, I thought she'd be very good
too. Because there are a lot of Spanish-type girls in the circus. Although I
think God was on our side when Hughes said no, because then our second
choice was Betty Huttton. And Betty Hutton has that circussy quality. I was

Betty Hutton soaring as a trapeze artist in *The Greatest Show on Earth* (1952). Courtesy John Kobal Foundation

all for her, I'll tell you that. I felt she had that brassy, circus quality, she had sawdust in her veins, as Chuck Heston had to say."

One way or another, DeMille had the satisfaction of being wooed by squadrons of ambitious young and not so young ladies who "adorned [his office] with floral tributes . . . until it looked like an exotic garden or a funeral parlor."

"Dottie" Lamour, being seven years older than Hutton and a mother, was not in the running for high-wire adventures, and moreover had just had a hysterectomy, but she captured the part of Phyllis, "the Girl with the Iron

Playing the circus manager in *The Greatest Show on Earth* (1952) launched Charlton Heston to movie stardom. Courtesy John Kobal Foundation

Jaw." She asked her doctor if he approved of such a role. "Yes Dorothy," he said, "I think it would be right as long as it isn't too strenuous. What kind of role is it?"

"I looked at him. 'I have to hang by my teeth.'"

Lucille Ball was then signed to play Angel the Elephant Girl (a role that Paulette Goddard had tried her darnedest to snare), but had to withdraw because of impending motherhood. Replacing Lucy was Gloria Grahame. Charlton Heston, fresh from his film debut in *Dark City*, was cast as the circus manager. And Cornel Wilde and Lyle Better were assigned top roles. Wilde, who was an Olympic standard fencer, played the part of Sebastian the glamorous aerialist, a trapeze act for which another sword-wielding actor, Stewart Granger, was also considered.

In her book, Lamour also quoted James Stewart, who played Buttons the Clown, a character with a past that catches up with him, who was coached by the classic clown, Emmett Kelly: "I had always loved the circus, and when I heard that DeMille was making a circus film, I sent a wire and asked if I could be in it and play a clown. You see, everyone wanted to do this picture. We all had our dreams about running away and joining the circus. . . . We actually did performances in front of live audiences to get the feel of it. It didn't take long before we all felt that we were a part of the circus family. There's something about circus life: you get engulfed in it."

"We all worked very hard on this film," wrote Lamour, "going into the circus version of 'basic training' for weeks before shooting actually started. Paramount sent me to a dentist who took an impression of my teeth and made upper and lower plates, into which my own teeth fitted perfectly. Then both plates were tightly attached to a wide leather strip. Get the picture? At the end of the strap was a swivel device that hooked onto the rope that would lift me 40 feet into the air. . . .

"Without a net!. . . .

"Slowly, they pulled me up as I froze into a ballet pose. When I reached the top, I had to spread my arms and legs and turn, then twirl like crazy. I've always had a terrific fear of heights, but this didn't bother me too much. All I could see was the top of the tent, and I was pretty close to it. Mr. DeMille wanted complete authenticity, so we planned to go to Sarasota, Florida, Ringling Brothers' winter training grounds, and then go out on the road with the circus, shooting scenes in different cities."

Filming began at the circus's winter quarters in Sarasota, where DeMille let it be known that he would film the great circus parade and the 50,000 or so people who would crowd the streets to see it go by. This innocent-sounding scene led to an outraged protest in the *New Age*, a Masonic journal which took strong exception to the spectacle of a Catholic priest, Father Elslander, blessing the circus train. DeMille, himself a Freemason, retaliated with a staunch and indignant defense of the shot, and to his satisfaction received many letters of support from fellow Masons who read and approved his published reply.

After a month of shooting in Florida and a spell in Hollywood, where studio work took place, DeMille rejoined the circus. From now on, much of the film was made under "active service" conditions, with the stars taking part in actual performances in Washington and Philadelphia. This presented the cameramen with a colossal challenge, especially with regard to lighting, but the trio of Barnes, Marley, and Kelley defeated all obstacles.

Quite apart from his troubles with the Freemasons, DeMille had to contend with Father Thomas F. Little of the Legion of Decency. This reverent and intrusive gentleman disapproved of certain costumes; furthermore, he objected to the film's sympathetic treatment of Buttons, the James Stewart character, a mercy-killing doctor who sought anonymity in the role of a circus clown. DeMille repudiated the tiresome cleric's views on both counts, and took particular pleasure in a letter of approval which he received from a convent whose nuns had screened the picture for the children in their charge.

The reviewers were generally kind, though as usual a few snipers could not resist their chance. Even so, the worst that could be said was that DeMille introduced unnecessary love interests and "a rambling crisscross of implications." The *Saturday Review* of January 12, 1952, hit the nail pretty squarely on the head: "He [DeMille] is obviously enraptured by all the tinseled glamor, awed by the feats of daring, impressed by the sense of danger that lurks everywhere in circus life. And all of this he has captured with his unrivaled sense of what will make a good movie. Here, he doesn't have to pretend an historical accuracy or assume a religious sententiousness. Here, against the background of a circus, all the faults that caused such critical mutterings about *Samson and Delilah* are converted into positive virtues. Here it's right for DeMille to be vulgar, obvious, gaudy. For what else is a circus? In this film any other approach would produce the same pretentiousness that vitiated his earlier epics."

Looking at the picture now, one is struck by a certain naiveté in the dialogue, which must have seemed fairly laughable even in 1952. Here is Sebastian (Wilde) thanking Brad (Heston), who has provoked him into flexing his damaged hand, thus proving that he is not a cripple: "You crazy, wonderful fool! You realized with my wings clipped I'd never marry Holly, now you've raised me into the air again. You are Circus!"

There are, of course, plenty of DeMillean precedents for such squirm-making exchanges. One thinks of Madeleine Carroll casting adoring eyes at Gary Cooper in *North West Mounted Police*: "Dusty, you're an angel in leather."

Such infelicities apart, and there are quite a few in *The Greatest Show on Earth*, there are also some wonderful little cameos. Glum-looking children watch the circus while their parents chortle with delight: Hope and Crosby among the audience observe a Lamour act in deadpan silence; an older woman who is knitting sees everything without missing a stitch; a couple smile at each other intimately during the waltz music. These were the little bits of business that DeMille was always good at, providing he didn't let cliché intrude, and they remind one that in his day he had been a marvelous director of silent films.

Now at seventy, with all the fun and adventure of the circus movie behind him, DeMille turned his attention to a remake of the film, which perhaps more than any other, was most associated with his name. As DeMille approached his eighth decade, he thought much about the past twenty years. During that period, he had passed from middle to old age, and massive

human tragedies had succeeded one another in an unbroken chain. There
had been fascism, the Depression, Spain and Abyssinia, World War II, the
Iron Curtain, colonial wars, and finally Korea, and throughout all this period
the virulent spread of totalitarianism. As he remarked in his autobiography,
"the world required a reminder of the Law of God," and that "the law of God
is the essential bedrock of human freedom."

First he considered a modern vehicle for this theme. His hero would be
a public official in some American city who would stand up for "the right"
against corruption and immorality. There were shades here of *This Day and
Age*, with a plot that would clearly demonstrate the consequence of breaking
the Ten Commandments. According to DeMille, he then began to think of
the Bible itself as providing a more "timeless" illustration of the values which
he so admired. One cannot fault his logic, but it was probably no more than
a rationalization of his wish to film a spectacle that would outdo anything
in the history of cinema. A spectacular remake of his 1923 film, that story of
slavery and liberation, would sound the trumpet for all who suffered under
totalitarian governments, and would be a glorious end to his career if by
some misfortune it should be the last picture that he would make. One cannot help feeling that by now he was considering that possibility.

Paramount, with the full approval of Zukor and Balaban, took the bait, approving *The Ten Commandments* enthusiastically, but so colossal was the project and so considerable Paramount's exposure that DeMille offered to accept
a much smaller percentage return than usual. The final production costs of
the film would be $13,282,712.35, and it ran over three hours, but by August
12, 1959, it had grossed $83,600,000 worldwide, and set records at the box
office to become the second most commercially successful film after *Gone
With The Wind*. This time Paramount got it right.

Having established the subject matter, theme, and cost of his new project,
and with a four-man team of scriptwriters in action (Jesse Lasky Jr., Frederic
Frank, Aeneas MacKenzie, and Jack Gariss), DeMille turned his attention to
the casting.

First there was Moses. DeMille had been very pleased with Charlton Heston in *The Greatest Show on Earth*, and now arranged for him to be sketched
with a white beard. Putting this sketch next to a photograph of Michelangelo's bust of Moses, DeMille decided that there was a substantial likeness, and
that Heston was perfect for the role.

Next there was Moses's brother, Dathan, to consider. That part went to
someone across whose reputation McCarthyism had cast a shadow. DeMille's humanity toward Edward G. Robinson, whose political views were the
antithesis of his own, does him enduring credit. "It was obvious," said Robinson subsequently, "that while I was forgiven my premature anti-fascism, I
was doomed, both by age and former political leanings, to a slow graveyard.
The top directors and producers wouldn't have me and, while I'm grateful
to those who did in the period and bow low to them for their guts, what I

needed was recognition again by a top figure in the industry. I've already mentioned the name of that top figure—Cecil B. DeMille. . . . Cecil B. DeMille returned me to films. Cecil B. DeMille restored my self-respect."

There were to be two pharaohs in the picture, Sethi and Rameses the Second. DeMille was on a visit to New York with Gladys Rosson, Cecilia, and Donald Hayne when Rosson persuaded him, rather against his will, to see *The King and I*. According to DeMille himself, he was much taken with Yul Brynner's performance, went backstage during the interval, and talked him into playing the part of Rameses the Second. It was to be the beginning of a unique friendship, for Brynner had the sort of confident, manly presence that appealed to DeMille.

Alone among actors, Brynner would be allowed to attend the 8 a.m. viewing of the previous day's rushes. DeMille wouldn't see them in the evening in case exhaustion led him to make mistakes. One can judge how much DeMille respected Brynner, who before this had himself been a distinguished TV director, from the fact that he not only allowed the actor to make comments on the rushes, but also listened to them.

It was Brynner's doctor who came to DeMille's rescue when he had a heart attack in November of that year, but there had been a time when DeMille rendered invaluable medical aid to Brynner himself. The actor had been appearing in *The King and I* at a Los Angeles theater when his nose was almost ripped off in an accident. In desperation Brynner called DeMille, rousing the great man from his bed. DeMille fixed everything: he sent Henry Wilcoxon to the theater with a pair of squad cars, and arranged for plastic surgeons to be provided with a plaster cast of Brynner's head. The nose, which according to Brynner was at one time hanging by its nostrils, made a complete recovery, and featured importantly in the Rameses role.

Other important parts were played by Yvonne De Carlo (Sephora, the wife of Moses), Anne Baxter (Nefertiti), John Derek (Joshua), and Debra Paget (Lilia). As usual, DeMille found parts for his old retainers. H. B. Warner played Amminidab, Julia Faye played Elisheba, and, after bumping into John Carradine in the street, the ex-sculptor played Aaron, in his first DeMille film since 1935.

Henry Wilcoxon, who was a strong right arm to DeMille, described how he became less of an actor and more of an assistant. From time to time, it seems, says Wilcoxon, DeMille found visualization difficult: "Sometimes if there was difficulty with a scene, I'd write my version of it and leave it on his desk. And then with sketches and drawings we'd sit at this long able we called the Last Supper table. DeMille in the center, and Berenice Mosk his secretary on one side and me on the other, then the various members of the staff all the way along. There'd be a discussion about things, and while we were talking I'd have a little pad and sketch out my ideas and very quietly slip it over to De-Mille, and he'd look at it and hold it up and say, 'Yeah, that's what I mean.' I thought very much the way DeMille thought in terms of story."

The Ten Commandments (1956) was filmed on location in Egypt. Here DeMille, with his typical flourish, directs Charlton Heston as Moses. Estate of John Kobal

Wilcoxon went on to describe how he weeded out items that might attract DeMille's disapproval, for certain scenes demanded a spirit of reverence. One remembers DeMille's strictures during *The King of Kings*, when swearing and unsuitable behavior were banned from the set.

With the production well under way, momentous events were taking place in Egypt. After a coup by junior army officers, the portly, girl-chasing King Farouk went into exile and in due course abdicated. There was a short regency in favor of his son, and then in June 1953 the monarchy was abolished and a republic proclaimed. DeMille, ever the pragmatist, made it his business to get on with the new president, General Neguib, and after initialing a friendly correspondence felt able to dispatch his production manager, Donald Robb, to the republic. Robb's varied tasks included the construction of enormous props such as the gates of Per Rameses, and the organization of food and housing for the hordes of Egyptian villagers who, together with their cattle and domestic fowls, would re-enact the Exodus.

It was a stupendous logistical challenge, and few moviemakers would have attempted it in a Middle Eastern country that had just been through a revolution. But that wasn't all. Now DeMille announced that he would be going to Egypt himself.

If one is looking for evidence that DeMille was in his own time a truly world-famous figure, a household name, one need look no further than the way in which he was received in the young Republic. It certainly did not hurt him that the prime minister, Colonel Gamal Abdel Nasser, and General Amer, his minister of war, were both fans of American movies, or that Nasser's fellow officers had once nicknamed him "Henry Wilcoxon." The Egyptian press was kind to DeMille, though somewhat concerned at the screen portrayal of Moses, a prophet who was important to Muslims. DeMille responded by saying that the Muslim prime minister of Pakistan had welcomed the making of this film as a means of welding together all enemies of atheistic communism.

DeMille was in Egypt for two months. In October 1954, he went filming on Mount Sinai, living in tented accommodation on a high plateau accessible only by foot or camel. It was a typical desert climate, hot in the day and cold at night, and despite all precautions, the crew went down regularly with "gippy tummy." As DeMille put it delicately in his memoirs, "We all lost weight, almost visibly from day to day." Recalling this time, Brynner said he thought DeMille's chronic diarrhea might have brought on the heart attack that was to strike him down.

Late in November, DeMille was directing a special effects sequence at Beni Youssef when, as he put it, his "chest filled with pain." A high-powered team of doctors examined him and advised that he must retire forthwith to an oxygen tent, and must remain in bed, with or without oxygen, for several weeks. Little did they understand their patient. DeMille, in the middle of a mega-production dear to his heart, was like Eisenhower on the eve of D-Day. He was not about to become an invalid.

Happily, help was at hand. Physician Max Jacobsen, Yul Brynner's doctor, was on a visit to Egypt. He looked over DeMille and told him that if he was sensible and took things easily he could get up almost immediately. DeMille had had enough experience of ill health to know about doctors. With Jacobsen hovering, he got up, acted sensibly, and was soon on the road to recovery. On December 3, 1954, DeMille handed over the producing baton to Henry Wilcoxon, said goodbye to his crew, and flew back to Hollywood. From now on it was to be studio work. His long career as a location director was finally over.

There are many entertaining anecdotes about the making of this picture, not a few of them told ruefully by those who experienced DeMille's displeasure. Here is Henry Wilcoxon: "A very important scene: where the baby Moses is placed into the ark into the Nile. An important thing for us was where his mother Yochabel takes a little piece of Levi cloth and covers the baby up for warmth. It was a messy day, and it was on the tank on the back lot. We'd put the bulrushes in, and DeMille had to be taken out to the camera platform on a boat. Martha Scott as the mother (and the baby was Charlton Heston's son) had it all ready, and he says, 'All ready? Ready. Action.' And she gently opens the lid, and Miriam hands her the baby, and she lays the baby in the ark and covers him with the Levi cloth. And then the Levi cloth rucks a little and she puts it back, out of the frame of the picture, and everybody was delighted. And he says, 'OK. Cut. Print.'

"And I stepped forward and said, 'You can't use that take.'

"He says, 'Oh? Why not, pray?'

"I said, 'Because I was standing right by the side of the camera, and when she lifted the Levi cloth and smoothed it out, I saw a modern safety pin.'

"And he asked if anybody else had seen it and they all said no. . . .

"Well, I said nothing more about it. The picture came out, but every time one of about 150 letters that came in saying, 'We saw a modern safety pin.' I put them on his desk every time! With a great big arrow!"

There was also an incident where a piece of Kleenex was left inadvertently on the sweaty head of Jannes (Douglas Dumbrille) by a distracted makeup man. It ruined a large and important scene, but according to Brynner, De-Mille took the disaster in his stride, instructing his underlings to find the delinquent and chuck him into the nearest pond.

Anne Baxter recalled another amusing scene: "The first day we shot together, Charlton Heston and I had a passionate love scene. I knelt by the right side of his bared chest as he reclined on an Egyptian version of a Recamier couch. The camera shot across his pectorals at my adoring, upturned face. He had an admirable amount of chest hair, I noted. We rehearsed for about half an hour. Mr. DeMille helped me up off my cramped knees and Heston mysteriously disappeared. An hour later he returned to the hush of the set without chest hair. Nothing whatever was said. I learned later all you could see was my nose peeking over the curly mass, like the moon coming over the mountain."

Edith Head is among five names credited for costumes, "DeMille is master of the super production, a perfectionist on the encyclopedic detail demanded by his plunges into history. When you do the headdress for Nefertiti, you'd better be prepared to quote volume and page to verify that this will match the replica found in the Egyptian queen's very tomb. . . . DeMille wants color sketches always; he has a color print made of the sketch and blows it up giant-size, to compare with the finished costume when you finally show it. If the original sketch had seven pearls on the shoulder strap, if the drape revealed the leg to half-way between knee and thigh, be quite certain the finished costume is identical."

Ralph Jester is also among those credited for costumes. Like a mischievous schoolboy, he was always in and out of trouble with DeMille, finding it quite impossible not to bait and tease the great man, and being regularly sacked and reinstated: "He [DeMille] had rather poor powers of visualization. He wanted everything sketched or drawn out for him in the colors they were going to be. I developed a little trick with him. If I had a costume that I wanted to get into work quickly to meet the deadline, I would present half a dozen sketches, but I would not let him see the one I wanted to do first, because

I wanted him to be able to throw out three or four. Sure enough, it would almost always work that way."

Jester spoke of DeMille's single-mindedness, which led to a certain pettiness when he felt that members of his staff were failing to live and breathe a picture, the picture that he was creating in a cauldron of artistic stress and suffering: "He excluded Edith Head and me from that foundation grant, because he said we were too independent. I think he meant independent-minded, not financially." The grant referred to here was a sort of "end-of-career" present from DeMille to a number of his favorite long-term crew. The money came from his personal profits on the film.

In his autobiography, DeMille casts some light on why he demanded total immersion on a picture. He gives two examples of how difficult problems were solved by people who were thinking and breathing the picture out of office hours, and on the whole one sympathizes with him. He had Red Seas to part, burning bushes to ignite, and Angels of Death to strike the first-born. Not surprisingly, he had kind words for those who helped him, especially when they weren't on duty at the time. Jester may not have always been popular with DeMille, but he came up with the goods when he had to.

In the early months of 1955, while DeMille was busy at the studios and no doubt driving his doctors to distraction, his brother William was entering the final stages of his battle with cancer. He died on March 5 at the age of seventy-six. DeMille and he had their differences, plenty of them, a fact which had been noted by the FBI when DeMille was being investigated for an important government post (head of the International Information Administration). There had been difficulties over Agnes, and professional jealousies resulting from DeMille's massive success compared to that of his older brother, but perhaps the real cause of difficulty lay in DeMille's suspicion that William had really been his mother's favorite. Nevertheless, blood is blood, and family meant a lot to DeMille. No doubt he was grateful that he could return from the funeral to lose himself in a massive quantity of studio work.

DeMille finished *The Ten Commandments* in the studio on August 13, 1955, the day after his seventy-fourth birthday. After that came months of editing, dubbing, musical-tracking, and so forth, until the picture was ready for its preview. This took place in Salt Lake City, far enough from Hollywood to get a useful audience reaction, but suitable in that it was a center of the serious-minded and devout. DeMille, a man of eclectic religious interests, had a particular regard for the president of the Mormon Church, David O. McKay, and he doubtless enjoyed this opportunity to renew an old friendship.

The Ten Commandments was finally released on October 5, 1956, and as usual the reviews were mixed. *Newsweek* (November 5, 1956) warned viewers that they might find "a DeMille production a trying experience now and then, but a very educational one. They are bound to be, as their parents and grandparents were, impressed." *Time* (November 12, 1956) was less kind: "And the result of all these stupendous efforts? Something roughly comparable to an eight-foot chorus girl pretty well put together, but much too big and much too flashy. . . . With insuperable piety. Cinemogul DeMille claims that he has tried 'to translate the Bible back to its original form,' the form in which it was lived. Yet what he has really done is to throw sex and sand into the movie-goers' eyes for almost twice as long as anybody else has ever dared to."

The film did not open in Europe until the autumn of 1957, and Paramount, keen to get it off to a good start, dispatched DeMille in an ambassadorial role. He was received more like a visiting monarch. He was blessed by Pope Pius XII and decorated by the president of Italy, after which he collected a Legion of Honor in Paris and a Royal Film Performance in London. But for DeMille there was no question as to what marked the supreme moment of his tour. It came when Winston Churchill invited him to his home in Hyde Park Gate for a private half-hour of conversation.

Although *The Ten Commandments* was to be DeMille's last work as a producer/director, he did have one final contribution to make on the screen. In 1958, Anthony Quinn directed a remake of *The Buccaneer*. It was produced by Henry Wilcoxon, and DeMille was brought in in "an advisory capacity," but there were huge differences between the two men regarding the way they felt the Lafitte story should be told. Quinn wanted it to be a parable of the vicious, osmotic relationship between big business and organized crime. He wrote a new, socially conscious script with Abby Mann (who went on to win an Academy Award for *Judgment at Nuremburg*), but DeMille would have none of it. Quinn, after much internal struggle, decided that "as a son figure" he would prefer not to disappoint the old man. Nevertheless, it was a huge sacrifice, and something about which he had extremely mixed feelings: "It was really whether I [should] choose to walk. And if I had walked out of it I felt that I would have disappointed him as a son figure. Suddenly that became more important, that I fulfill that role and the role of director, and I gave in. I was so hurt by the outcome of that picture, because Mr. DeMille went and re-cut the picture to his measure and his idea of what the picture was about. . . . But the interesting thing was that [it] was much more important for me to fulfill the father/son relationship than the director/producer relationship."

Anthony Quinn movingly summarized his feelings about his former father-in-law: "His weakness was possibly the fact that he was terrified of people seeing his vulnerability. That's what I noticed that last time when I saw him. That's what I found out about him. He was deeply touched by his vulnerability. . . . Well, no man is God, no man is that sure of himself. We're all vulnerable, and I think that we all hide vulnerability. I hide it constantly from my children, so I mean he was terrified of you seeing him as a human being. Absolutely."

Quinn went on to voice very similar thoughts to those expressed by Yul Brynner, who said that DeMille was a man who felt so much alone "because most people lived in fear of him." "Let me say that the last man I would want to be is Cecil B. DeMille, because I'm sure he was a very lonely man, in spite of all the show . . . eventually it must have been terribly exhausting. Even politically, the man was of such power that he felt that he had to be in control of everything. I mean all that wasted energy. . . . He could have done something so wonderful, humane, with that talent and that energy. One wonders if the bits of celluloid one leaves behind . . . is that enough to justify that suffering?"

"Wasted energy." Quinn said this perhaps without thinking about, or perhaps even knowing about, all of DeMille's political initiatives, but it is surprising that he, who after all had known DeMille since the 1930s, did not read more significance into such things as the DeMille Foundation and the battle at the Screen Directors Guild.

These ventures absorbed massive amounts of DeMille's energy, and they most certainly had a humane dimension, for DeMille saw freedom as something which all people required if they were to achieve fulfilment and moral stature. He equated freedom with all that was best in the United States, a country and an idea which he venerated with almost religious zeal. It was to this ideal, a free and truly democratic America, that he sacrificed the $125,000 per year that went down the drain with Lux radio, and the dirt which stuck after that night at the Screen Directors Guild.

When one looks back through DeMille's life, the films upon which his fame and fortune depended, those "bits of celluloid," were by no stretch of the imagination all that there was to him. One remembers the Lasky Home Guard, Mercury Aviation, Lux Radio Theatre, Radio Free Europe, the Crusade for Freedom, the DeMille Foundation, the stars that he made or helped to make, and the countless directors, designers, cameramen and soundmen, scriptwriters and stuntmen who owed their start and, in some cases when they were down on their luck, their survival to DeMille's essentially generous nature.

Toward the time of DeMille's death, a film of the life of Baden-Powell was being planned. Jesse Lasky Jr., Henry Wilcoxon, and the British filmmaker Sidney Box were working on a script suitably entitled *On My Honor*. "He wanted to do the life of Baden-Powell," recalled John Carradine, "and he wanted to do the life of Churchill. Two years after *The Ten Commandments*—when I was working on *Around the World in Eighty Days*—I went to call on him. I took my late wife with me, and he was most gracious and charming, and showed me all the things he was doing to get ready for the Baden-Powell project. He was a nice man, a good man."

Both give an insight into DeMille's character. Baden-Powell and Churchill were two men who displayed qualities that he admired in abundance. "B-P," the heroic savior of Ladysmith, was a man of action and practical, Christian virtues. Churchill, not quite such a Christian, had been the savior of the free world, but he had also ridden with the Lancers at Omdurman. It was this

A portrait from the late 1950s of DeMille and his wife, Constance. Photo: Bill Avery. Estate of John Kobal

cocktail of knightly virtues that appealed so strongly to all that was romantic in DeMille's nature.

Churchill, in particular, may have attracted DeMille for other, perhaps subconscious reasons. The two men had much in common. Workaholics with elephantine egos, penners of charming and kindly notes, actors in the public domain who were deeply insecure and perhaps for that reason given to cruelty, both men were physically brave, superb in command, patchy as husbands. But Churchill, who had hoped that he might lead and perhaps be killed at the Rhine Crossing, was a depressive whose life had been plagued by his "black dog," while DeMille, whatever his former son-in-law might say, was probably at bottom a happy man.

As it turned out, nature continued to favor him, for DeMille, with so many plans still in prospect, was blessed with a quick and comparatively early death, while his hero, ill and mentally confused, sank into a lengthy, miserable twilight.

In those last months of his life, DeMille was engaged on his autobiography. Henry Wilcoxon explains (maybe not entirely accurately) why there are comparatively so few reminiscences of DeMille's childhood and parents in it: "I must say he did talk about his father more than he did his mother. I don't think that's because he didn't love her. I think she was a very powerful lady: she had her own school and she was an agent. She may have given William a little more attention professionally than she gave Cecil—I get the feeling that the elder son was more the apple of his mother's eye. But I don't think he ever thought that his mother was ever anything else but wonderful to him, and I think he had great respect and love for her."

In talking about DeMille's spirituality, Wilcoxon casts light upon what might have motivated that grandson of the Church into making one vast religious picture after another: "He was a very religious man. I even prefer the word devout. He really did believe in a divine mind. This I know. And he did believe in our power in using a piece of divine mind that had been entrusted to each one of us. . . . that we are given a power of good or evil in this world, and he devoutly believed that we [should] follow the main leadings of the piece of divinity that has been entrusted to us. The Logos theory."

An eclectic thinker before the days of TM and Hindu swamis, DeMille was genuinely open-minded about religion. He was not a regular churchgoer, and he had friends from every creed and denomination. In essence, he believed that the divine mind makes itself known to us through many forms of worship, and that when it speaks to us, we ignore it at our peril.

Katherine deMille had her reservations about the autobiography: "I didn't enjoy the book, but I did like some of the things he told about his childhood. He and Mother would entertain us for hours at the table about their days of one-night stands, getting off these old trains in the middle of the night, carrying their luggage and walking up dirt roads. . . . But the early chapters of his book are very tender, the warmest and most real part of the whole book. And if I were to say anything about C. B., it would be that he was an honorable man."

Constance was unwell at the end of DeMille's life, for some years a victim of Alzheimer's disease, though she would outlive her husband by a year (Julia Faye, the only other surviving member of his harem, died in 1966, still a cheerful funny woman): "Family was very important to him. She wasn't very well then, you know. I would often go up to the house to keep her a little company. Father was so happy about that, and it meant an awful lot to him.

Because she was quite sick in the latter years. I imagine he had some pretty honest talks with Constance. He had a great respect and affection for her. And I know when she became so ill in the end and became so childish, he was so tender about it. It was one of the most beautiful things I've ever seen."

The last weeks and months of DeMille's life were very much in character. Three and half years after the incident at Beni Youssef, he had another heart attack. It struck him down on June 18, 1958, just after a visit to Washington, where he had been testifying before a House subcommittee on the right to work. This was a far more serious attack than the one in North Africa, but he continued to go into the studio, and nothing would deter him from campaigning for the right to work amendment in the forthcoming November ballot.

The Buccaneer was due to be premiered in December, and DeMille had promised that he would attend the openings. It was not in the DeMille code to let down his friends and, quite against the advice of his family, he appeared at both the New Orleans and New York openings.

It was not long before his doctors got the upper hand. DeMille struggled into the studio a few more times, but left it for the last time on January 9. Now, finally accepting medical advice, and to the huge relief of his family, he agreed to work at home. He died there in his own bed, in his sleep, of a heart attack at 5 a.m. on January 21, 1959.

CHAPTER FORTY-ONE

THAT PART OF HOLLYWOOD WHERE DEMILLE BUILT HIS HOUSE, THE PALACE from which he ruled his huge empire, is now just another bit of modern Hollywood. Many of the "old houses" with film history attached to them are highly sought by newcomers who are willing to pay the going rate for nostalgia.

The "old barn" has been moved again since DeMille was there. Now it stands not far from his home, just off Vine Street before it turns into the Hollywood freeway. It is a minor tourist sight for out-of-towners in search of Hollywood history. The walls of the old barn have been whitewashed and covered with blowups of black and white photographs, fuzzy memorials of the "good old days."

There are half-hearted civic efforts to restore Hollywood Boulevard to some of its former glory. But it's a hard task, short of exporting all the massage parlors, run-down hotels, clip joints, trinket shops, and fast food emporia. Had DeMille been alive today, the man who saw stories everywhere would surely have found one here. But one is glad he is not alive, that death protected him, that he went to his grave still certain of his country's mission and the values of those who lead it.

So what was his contribution? He didn't invent the biblical epic—Griffith did that with *Judith of Bethulia* in 1913—but DeMille brought it to new heights. He did invent something which is a part of twentieth-century world culture: the "Hollywood" of unsophisticated, unstinting, unsubtle, outrageous, exuberant, and thoroughly joyful excess.

Quite early in his film career, DeMille realized that epic characters need to be treated like superstars. Forget about anachronism and suspect dialogue; what he was after was empathy, a relationship between his characters and the audience. He achieved this by the use of spectacle, and by the flagrant display of every form of human weakness, liberally spiced with sentimentality and sadism. By these means, the likes of Samson, Moses, and Joan of Arc became vulnerable and interesting human creatures with whom we can experience some fellow feeling. It was here that DeMille broke new ground, providing an ever-enthusiastic public with a unique concoction of education,

411

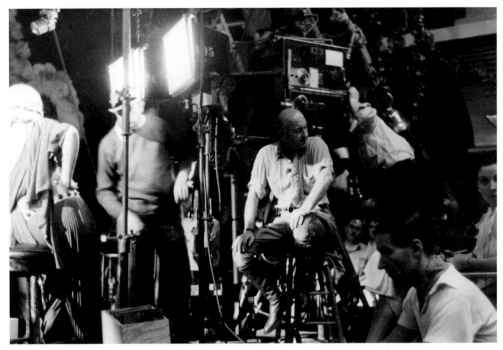

This is the way DeMille wished to be remembered, at work, in the midst of directing another great picture. Estate of John Kobal

spectacle, and high-minded comment. DeMille is rightly remembered for these epics. They were enjoyable, and they distracted and entertained us in tragic times.

But why is he also remembered with a sort of affectionate indulgence that puts him into quite a different category from other film producers? Perhaps because, however one chooses to see him—as showman, educator, or master of hokum—he stands for something which has gone from America but was always attractive to its friends: a sort of naïve, generous, big-thinking self-confidence which believed that all things were possible and all things were certainly for the best in this best of all possible worlds.

On the sixth of July, I had a dream.

I was up at the house. I had almost finished the book, but I was there to look around. Suddenly, an old but very distinguished-looking man wearing a black Armani suit with a smart white silk scarf around his neck came down the stairs on his way to a limousine, which had drawn up outside. There were other, somewhat younger men with him—companions? Friends? Employees?

Suddenly I realized that this elegant old man was DeMille! I was filled with amazement. With wonder. With confusion. He was *alive*. He looked frail but incredibly elegant and fit. I knew he must be old, over a hundred, older even than Adolph Zukor, who died at age 103. But I had thought he was dead—when all this time I had been up at the house researching his life, he had been there!

Things were moving as in a dream, which is to say differently than you want them to. One abrupt move, and things change or vanish. Somehow I knew to be careful. No fast moves. Yet I had to speak to him before he left the house.

"Mr. DeMille," I said.

He looked and smiled.

"I've been writing a book about you. Your life. In two volumes."[9]

He smiled and said, "That seems rather large."

I said, "So were you."

His associates drew close. He obviously had an important dinner to attend, and they wanted him to get there.

But, overcome by the moment as I was, I had to ask him something. Even in a dream I had to make sure he was fully compos mentis. I followed him down the stone steps leading from the front door to his limousine. DeMille was now inside the car, the window rolled down.

"Do you remember Ruth Rogers?"

There was a small, bemused smile on his face. "Sure," he said. "She ended up modeling furs."

Oh God! How wonderful! He had remembered. It was something no one else had ever known, but I had found it and he remembered.

"I must see you, Mr. DeMille. I must talk to you. There is so much I want to ask you about . . ."

He didn't say yes, and he didn't say no, but he smiled at me as the car drove away.

I knew I wasn't going to give up now. God, he remembered it all! I could hardly wait. I turned to Citzie, who had suddenly appeared, and said, "But he's been living here all this time!"—but I was too awed and overcome to be angry with her for having kept this information from me.

And there I woke up, my heart pounding in my chest.

Later that morning, I looked at the chapter I had written four years ago and not looked at since, in which I raise Ruth Rogers, and she *had* gone into modeling after her stage career had failed, before she went on to make a career for herself as a journalist. I had had a sense of the past.

---

9. The original manuscript was conceived in two volumes.

ACKNOWLEDGMENTS

A NUMBER OF PEOPLE GAVE TO ME GENEROUSLY OF TIME, INFORMATION, and confidence to bring John's manuscript to publication. John was selective in his writing projects, as he once told me that when he committed to a project he had to believe in it, as it consumed him. DeMille was just the man who stirred up John's passion and commitment to writing about the man and his time. The research into DeMille's life and the very beginnings of the movies was over a ten-year period.

After languishing for twenty-four years, I asked for John's manuscript back from Knopf. When I arrived at the office in New York in 2015, with a backpack, I was overwhelmed to a see a box with 1,832 pages, plus photographs. Undaunted I carried the pages to Macy's for a suitcase and brought them back to Canada to begin my task to bring John's final work to the public.

There were many people who were of enormous help to John during his ten years of work on the DeMille manuscript. He surrounded himself with great, loyal and gifted friends.

I am personally indebted to Robert Dance (New York), who steered me to the University Press of Mississippi, and was instrumental in bringing this work to its publication. He read and reread the manuscript in every stage. He gave generously of his time and worked tirelessly in selecting photographs, writing captions and liaising with Craig Gill of the University Press of Mississippi.

I have had the good fortune for the support, time, and encouragement of these key people. Many thanks to:

• Simon Crocker (UK), chairman of the Kobal Foundation, has been supportive with his time and advice since John's death. He gave freely of his advice and negotiated all contracts. Through his enormous publication contacts he secured the structural editor Graham Coster.
• Graham Coster, (UK) editor and publisher of Safe Haven Books, for taking on the formidable structural task and bringing the two-volume, 1,100-page work to one volume.

• Louise Stein Plaschkes (USA) read the manuscript in its earliest stages for Knopf, when it was more than twice its present length. Her skillful editing reduced the manuscript of 1,832 pages to a manageable 1,100.
• Craig Gill, (USA) director of the University Press of Mississippi, and his board members for recognizing this historical writing, and including it in their Hollywood Legends series.
• John Russell Taylor, (UK) for invaluable advice and guidance and encouragement throughout these past twenty-eight-plus years.
• Cecilia DeMille Presley, (USA) DeMille's granddaughter, whom I wrote to in 1999 to tell her that Knopf was going to publish and then didn't hear from me until I reclaimed the manuscript in 2015. She read the manuscript and encouraged me to bring it to the public.

Many thanks to the friends, and in particular Linda Schwebke, who read the chapters as I typed them, and gave me their support and encouragement to continue towards the book's publication. My brother, Peter P. Kobal, and sons, David P. Ferguson, and Philip J. Ferguson, who never lost faith that the book would be published.

As two volumes needed to be reduced to one, some of John's writing about DeMille's early years had to be eliminated. In the end, my time and effort over the past twenty-eight years was to ensure John's "opus magnum" was published.

With love from his little sister,
Monika Kobal
2019

INDEX

ABOUT THE AUTHOR

Photo by Peggo Cromer

John Kobal (1940–91) was a preeminent film historian and collector of Hollywood film photography. The author of over thirty books on film and film photography, he is credited with essentially rediscovering the great Hollywood studio photographers—including George Hurrell, Laszlo Willinger, Clarence Sinclair Bull, and Ted Allan—who were employed by the movie studios to create the glamorous, iconic portraits of the most famous and intriguing stars of the day that now epitomize Hollywood. In 1990, he formed the John Kobal Foundation as a charity to which he donated the photographic negatives and fine art photographs that he had collected over the years.